The Works of Ibn Wāḍiḥ al-Yaʿqūbī

Volume 2

Islamic History and Civilization

STUDIES AND TEXTS

VOLUME 152/2

The titles published in this series are listed at *brill.com/ihc*

The Works of Ibn Wāḍiḥ al-Yaʿqūbī

An English Translation

VOLUME 2

Edited by

Matthew S. Gordon
Chase F. Robinson
Everett K. Rowson
Michael Fishbein

BRILL

LEIDEN | BOSTON

Cover illustration: Tulunid gold dinar, Egypt, 266/879-880. The David Collection (Copenhagen), No. C 119. Photo by Pernille Klemp.

The Library of Congress Cataloging-in-Publication Data is available online at http://catalog.loc.gov

Typeface for the Latin, Greek, and Cyrillic scripts: “Brill”. See and download: brill.com/brill-typeface.

ISSN 0929-2403
ISBN 978-90-04-35619-1 (hardback, vol. 1)
ISBN 978-90-04-35620-7 (hardback, vol. 2)
ISBN 978-90-04-35621-4 (hardback, vol. 3)
ISBN 978-90-04-36414-1 (e-book, vol. 1)
ISBN 978-90-04-36415-8 (e-book, vol. 2)
ISBN 978-90-04-36416-5 (e-book, vol. 3)

This book is printed on acid-free paper and produced in a sustainable manner.

Contents

VOLUME 1

Acknowledgements VII
List of Contributors IX

Introduction 1
Matthew S. Gordon

Ibn Wāḍiḥ al-Yaʿqūbī: A Biographical Sketch 9
Sean Anthony and Matthew S. Gordon

Manuscripts, Printed Editions, and Translations of al-Yaʿqūbī's Works 23
Everett K. Rowson

The Book of the Adaptation of Men to Their Time and Their Dominant Characteristics in Every Age (Mushākalat al-nās li-zamānihim wa-mā yaglibu ʿalayhim fī kull ʿaṣr) 29

The Geography (Kitāb al-Buldān) 61

Fragments 201

A Fragments from the Lost Part of the Geography 203
B Fragments from Other Works 208
C New Fragments 218
D Passages Attributed to al-Yaʿqūbī in Ibn al-Dāya, *Kitāb al-Mukāfaʾa wa-Ḥusn al-ʿUqbā* 225

General Bibliography 235

VOLUME 2

The History (Taʾrīkh)
Adam to Pre-Islamic Arabia 259

VOLUME 3

The History (Taʾrīkh)
Adam to Pre-Islamic Arabia

In the Name of God, the Merciful, the Compassionate

... against Adam. Nothing of what God created complied with him[1] except the snake.[2] When Adam saw the delight to be found in the Garden[3] he said, "Would that there were a way to dwell here forever!" When Iblīs heard this from him, he set his hopes on him and began to weep. Adam and Eve looked at him weeping, and said to him, "What is making you weep?" He said: "Because the two of you will be leaving all of this. *Your Lord has only prohibited you from this tree lest you become angels, or lest you become immortals." And he swore to them, "Truly, I am for you a sincere adviser."*[4]

The clothing of Adam and Eve was garments of light. When they tasted of the tree, their private parts became apparent to them. The People of the Book[5] maintain that Adam's stay on the earth, before entering the garden, was for three hours, and for three hours he and Eve lived in happiness and dignity, before they ate of the tree and their private parts became apparent to them.[6] When his private parts became apparent to Adam, he took a leaf from the tree and put it on himself. Then he cried out, "Here I am, O Lord, naked, having eaten from the tree which You forbade me." God said: "Return to the earth from which you were created. I will subject to you and to your offspring the birds of the heavens and the fish of the seas."

God expelled Adam and Eve from where they had been, according to the People | of the Book, at the ninth hour on Friday. They fell down to the earth, 1:3
sad and weeping. Their fall was onto the nearest of the earth's mountains to the Garden. It was in the land of India. Some people, however, say it was onto Abū

1 That is, complied with Iblīs, the devil, in his scheme to cause Adam to disobey God.

2 Reading 'snake' with M. The refusal of the animals, except the snake, to cooperate with the devil is a detail that can be found in al-Ṭabarī, *Taʾrīkh*, 1:105.

3 Arabic, *mā fī l-jannati min al-naʿīm*, echoes an expression that occurs eleven times in the Qurʾān—eight times in the plural as *jannāt al-naʿīm* ("gardens of delight" in Rodwell's translation, "Gardens of Bliss" in Arberry's) and three times in the singular.

4 Qurʾān 7:20–21 (trans. Arberry). Unless otherwise indicated, Qurʾānic verses will be given in the 1955 translation by A. J. Arberry.

5 Arabic, *Ahl al-Kitāb*; that is, the Jews and Christians.

6 These details in al-Yaʿqūbī, like many details of antediluvian history, echo those in a Christian source that has come down to us in a Syriac version entitled *Mʿarrat Gazzē* (The Cave of Treasures) and in an early Arabic translation. Attributed in the manuscripts to St. Efrem the Syrian (c. 306–373 CE), the authorship of the work is now thought to be by a later member of his school. The work can be consulted in the edition by Carl Bezold, *Die Schatzhöhle*, which contains the Syriac and Arabic texts, as well as a German translation. There is an English translation by E. A. Wallis Budge, *The Book of the Cave of Treasures*.

Qubays, a mountain in Mecca. Adam settled in a cave in that mountain, which he named the Cave of the Treasure,[7] and he prayed to God to sanctify it.

Some report that when Adam fell, his weeping became great and his sadness over leaving the Garden persisted. Thereupon, God inspired him to say: "There is no God except You. Glory and praise to You! I have done evil and have wronged myself. Forgive me, for You are the All-forgiving, the All-compassionate."[8] *Then Adam received words from his Lord, and He turned toward him*[9] and *chose him*.[10] He sent down to him the Black Stone from the Garden in which it was, and He commanded him to convey it to Mecca and build a house for it.[11] So he went to Mecca and built the house, and he circumambulated it. Next, God ordered him to sacrifice to Him, then to pray to Him and glorify Him. Gabriel went out with him, until he stood at ʿArafāt.[12] Gabriel said to him, "At this place your Lord has commanded you to stand for Him." Then he went on with him to Mecca. When Iblīs blocked his way, Gabriel said, "Pelt him." So Adam pelted him with stones.[13] Then he reached the valley of Mecca, and the angels received him and said to him: "O Adam, your pilgrimage went well! We have made the pilgrimage to this house before you for two thousand years."

Then God sent down wheat to Adam and commanded him to eat of his toil. So he plowed and planted. Then he harvested, threshed, ground, kneaded, and baked. When he finished, his brow was bathed in sweat. Then he ate. When he was full, what was in his belly weighed heavily. So Gabriel came down to him and spread his legs. When what was in his belly came out, Adam sensed an odor that was disgusting. "What is this?" he asked. Gabriel said to him, "The odor of the wheat."

1:4 Adam had intercourse with Eve; she conceived and gave birth to | a boy and a girl. He named the boy Cain and the girl Lūbidhā. Then she conceived again and gave birth to a boy and a girl. He named the boy Abel and the girl Iqlīmā.[14] When

7 Cf. *Schatzhöhle*, ed. Bezold, 7–8, 32–33; trans. Budge, 69.

8 The language echoes Qurʾān 28:16, though in the Qurʾān the speaker is Moses.

9 Qurʾān 2:37.

10 Qurʾān 20:22.

11 Another possible translation, "… and build a house for Him." The Kaʿba is often called "God's House," *Bayt Allāh*. The Black Stone is the stone that is built into its eastern corner.

12 ʿArafāt (or in the singular form, ʿArafa) is a plain about 21 km (13 miles) east of Mecca. It is the site of the central ceremonies of the pilgrimage. The assembly of pilgrims there is called "a standing" (*wuqūf*), and al-Yaʿqūbī alludes to this terminology here.

13 This throwing of stones became part of the Islamic pilgrimage. It is done by the pilgrims returning from ʿArafāt to Mecca, at Minā, where there is a construction called al-Jamra, which symbolizes the devil.

14 These names occur in *Schatzhöhle*, 8, 34–35 (trans. Budge, 69) as Labūdā (Syriac and Ara-

his children grew up and reached marriage age, Adam said to Eve, "Command Cain to marry Iqlīmā, who was born with Abel, and command Abel to marry Lūbidhā, who was born with Cain." Then Cain became envious of him (that is, Abel), because he was marrying his sister, who had been born with him.[15]

Some have reported that God sent down a Houri[16] from Paradise to Abel and married him to her, and He brought out a female Jinn to Cain and married him to her. So Cain was jealous of his brother on account of the Houri. Adam then told both of them to make an offering. Abel offered some figs from his crop; Cain offered God the best ram among his sheep. God accepted Abel's offering, but He did not accept Cain's offering, and so he grew more ill-willed and jealous. Satan made the murder of his brother appear attractive to him, so he crushed him to death with stones. God therefore became angry with Cain and cursed him. He sent him down off the Holy Mountain to a land called Nod.[17]

Adam and Eve remained in mourning for Abel for a very long time, until it was said that a veritable river emerged from their tears. After he had become one hundred and thirty years old, Adam had intercourse with Eve and she conceived and gave birth to a boy. He named him Seth, and of Adam's sons he was the one who most closely resembled Adam. Then Adam married Seth off, and a boy was born to him when he was a hundred and sixty-five years old; he named him Enosh. Then a boy was born to Enosh, and he named him Kenan. Then a boy was born to Kenan and he named him Mahalalel. These were born during Adam's life and in his time.

When it came time for Adam's demise, his son Seth, together with his son | 1:5
and his son's son, came to him, and he prayed over them and asked a blessing for them. He entrusted his last will and testament to Seth, and he commanded him to preserve his body and put it, when he died, in the Cave of the Treasure. Furthermore, he (that is, Seth) should give charge to his sons and sons' sons, and each one should pass it on at his own demise: that when they came down from their mountain, they should take his body and put it in the middle of

bic) and as Qlīmat (Syriac), Iqlīmyā (Arabic)—the vocalization in each case is uncertain. The same names in variant form can be found in al-Ṭabarī, *Taʾrīkh*, 1:144, 146.

15 *Schatzhöhle*, ibid., adds that Labūdā, Cain's twin sister, was beautiful, presumably more beautiful than Abel's twin, so that Cain wanted to marry his own twin sister, which scandalized Adam. Cf. al-Ṭabarī, *Taʾrīkh*, 1:138.

16 Arabic, *ḥawrāʾ* "a woman fair of complexion, with intense whiteness of the 'white' of the eye," more commonly used in its plural form *ḥūr* to designate the women promised by the Qurʾān to believers in Paradise. See the article by A. J. Wensinck and Ch. Pellat in *EI*², s.v. Ḥūr.

17 As corrected by the Leiden editor from MSS Anūr.

the earth.[18] He commanded his son Seth to take charge after him among their progeny, command them to fear God and worship Him aright, and forbid them to mingle with the accursed Cain and his offspring. Then he prayed over those sons of his and their wives and children. He died on the sixth of Nīsān, a Friday, at the very hour when he was created. He was, as it is agreed, nine hundred and thirty years old.

Seth, the Son of Adam

After the death of Adam, his son Seth arose. He used to bid his people to fear God and to do good works. They, along with their wives and children, used to praise God and to hallow Him. There was no enmity among them, nor any envy, hatred, recrimination, lying, or breaking of promises. When one of them wanted to swear, he said, "No, by the blood of Abel."[19]

When Seth's death was imminent, his sons and the sons of his sons came to him. They were at that time: Enosh, Kenan, Mahalalel, Jared, and Enoch, with their wives and their sons. He prayed over them and invoked a blessing upon them. He ordered them and made them swear by the blood of Abel that none of them would go down from the holy mountain, that they would not allow any of their children to go down from it, and that they would not mingle with the children of the accursed Cain. He gave his testament to his son Enosh and commanded him to take custody of the body of Adam, fear God, and command his people to fear God and to worship aright. Then he died on Tuesday, the twenty-seventh of Āb, at the third hour of the day. He was nine hundred and twelve years old.

1:6 Enosh, the Son of Seth

After the death of his father, Enosh, the son of Seth, undertook to keep the testament of his father and grandfather. He worshipped God aright, and commanded his people to worship aright. In his days the accursed Cain was killed.

18 In the *Schatzhöhle*, this is given a Christian interpretation. The middle or center of the world is identified as Jerusalem, and Adam asks that his body be buried there, "for in that place shall redemption be effected for me and for all my children." (*Schatzhöhle*, 9, 40–41; trans. Budge, 72). Although these specifically Christian details may have been known to al-Yaʿqūbī, he omits them from his account.

19 A similar formula is found in *Schatzhöhle*, 10, 44–45; trans. Budge, 75.

The blind Lamech threw a stone at him and crushed his head, and so he died. After Enosh was ninety years old, Kenan was born to him. When the death of Enosh was imminent, his sons and his sons' sons gathered around him: Kenan, Mahalalel, Jared, Enoch, and Methuselah, along with their wives and their sons. He prayed over them and invoked a blessing upon them. He forbade them to go down from their holy mountain, or to let any of their sons mingle with the offspring of the accursed Cain. He put Kenan in charge of the body of Adam. He ordered them to pray in his presence and to hallow God frequently. He died on the third of Tishrīn I, at sunset. He was nine hundred and sixty-five years old.

Kenan, the Son of Enosh

Kenan, the son of Enosh, arose. He was a gentle, god-fearing, and holy man. He undertook among his people to obey God, worship aright, and follow the testament of Adam and Seth. Mahalalel had been born to him after he was seventy years old. When his death drew near, his sons and the sons of his sons, Mahalalel, Jared, Methuselah, Lamech, and their wives and children, assembled around him. He prayed over them and invoked a blessing upon them. He made them swear by the blood of Abel that none of them would go down from their holy mountain to the offspring of the accursed Cain. He made his testament to Mahalalel and commanded him to take charge of the body of Adam. Kenan died; he was nine hundred and twenty years old.

Mahalalel, the Son of Kenan 1:7

After the death of Kenan, Mahalalel, the son of Kenan, arose. He undertook among his people to obey God and follow the testament of his father. Jared was born to him when he was sixty-five years old. When Mahalalel's death drew near, he made his testament to his son Jared and gave him charge of the body of Adam. Mahalalel died on Sunday, the second of Nīsān, at the third hour of the day. He was eight hundred and ninety-five years old.

Jared, the Son of Mahalalel

After the death of Mahalalel, Jared arose. He was a believing man, perfect in his works and worship of God, praying frequently by night and by day, and therefore God increased his lifespan. Enoch was born to him when he was sixty-two years old. In Jared's fortieth year, the first millennium was completed.[20]

When five hundred years of Jared's life had passed, the sons of Seth broke the covenant and pacts that had existed among them, and they started going down to the land where the sons of Cain were.[21] Their going down began when Satan took to himself two devils from among mankind—one was named Jubal, the other Tubal-cain—and taught them the arts of singing and playing instruments. Jubal fashioned flutes, lutes, guitars, and horns; Tubal-cain fashioned drums, tambourines, and cymbals. The sons of Cain had no work to occupy them, and they made no remembrance except before Satan. They used to do forbidden and sinful things and would come together for depravity. Their old
1:8 men and women were even keener for it than the youths. They would | gather to play flutes, drums, tambourines, guitars, and cymbals, shouting and laughing, until the people of the mountain, the sons of Seth, heard their voices. A hundred of their men decided to go down to the sons of Cain, to see what these sounds were. When Jared received word of this, he went to them and implored them by God. He reminded them of the testament of their fathers, and swore against them by the blood of Abel. Enoch, the son of Jared, rose up among them and said, "Know that if any of you disobeys our father Jared, breaks the covenants of our fathers, and goes down from our mountain, we will never let him come up again." But they insisted on going down; and when they went down, they commingled with the daughters of Cain, having first engaged in depravities.

When the death of Jared drew near, his sons and the sons of his sons, Enoch, Methuselah, Lamech, and Noah, gathered around him. He prayed over them and invoked a blessing upon them. He forbade them to go down from the holy mountain, and he said: "Inevitably you will go down to the lowland. Whoever of you is the last to go down, let him take with him the body of our father Adam and let him put it in the midst of the earth as he ordered us." He commanded his son Enoch not to cease praying in the Cave of Treasure. Then he died on Friday, the first of Adhār, at sunset. He was nine hundred and sixty-two years old.

---

20 In the biblical section of his history, al-Yaʿqūbī follows a chronology of millennia similar to that in the *Schatzhöhle*. In the latter work the schema is more functional, as the coming of Christ occurs precisely at the middle of the fifth millennium, as prophesied. Al-Yaʿqūbī drops the schema after mentioning the end of the fourth millennium.

21 Parallel: *Schatzhöhle*, 14–16, 58–69; trans. Budge, 84–90. Cf. al-Ṭabarī, *Taʾrīkh*, 1:168–170.

Enoch, the Son of Jared

Then Enoch, the son of Jared, arose after Jared and carried on the worship of God. When he was sixty-five years old, Methuselah was born to him. The sons of Seth, their wives, and their children, started to go down. In dismay, Enoch summoned his progeny—Methuselah, Lamech, and Noah—and said to them, "I know that God will punish this community with a heavy punishment in which there is no mercy." Enoch was the first to write | with the pen. He was 1:9
the prophet Idrīs.[22] He commanded his offspring to worship God with sincerity and to apply themselves to truth and certainty. Then God lifted him up when he was three hundred years old.

Methuselah, the Son of Enoch

Then Methuselah, the son of Enoch, carried on the worship of God and obedience to Him. When he was one hundred and eighty-seven years old, Lamech was born to him. It was in this era that God sent a revelation to Noah and informed him that He would send the deluge upon the people, and He ordered him to build a wooden ship. When Noah completed three hundred and forty-four years, the second millennium was completed. Methuselah died on the twenty-first of Aylūl, a Thursday. He was nine hundred and sixty years old.

Lamech, the Son of Methusaleh

After his father, Lamech carried on the worship of God and obedience to Him. A son had been born to him when he was one hundred and eighty-two years old. In his era the giants became numerous—that was because when the sons of Seth had intercourse with the daughters of Cain, the latter bore them the giants.

When Lamech's death approached, he summoned Noah, Shem, Ham, and Japheth, and their wives. None of the sons of Seth were left on the mountain

22 Idrīs is a prophet mentioned twice in the Qur'ān (19:56–57, 21:85–86). On the basis of Qur'ān 19:57 ("We raised him up to a high place"), he was identified with the biblical Enoch, who, in Rabbinical and later legend, on the basis of the enigmatic language in Genesis 5:24 ("Enoch walked with God; then he was no more because God took him"), was said to have been raised to heaven (hence his relatively short lifespan—only 300 years in al-Yaʿqūbī, 365 years in Genesis 5:23). See the article by G. Vajda in *EI*^{2}, s.v. Idrīs.

who had not gone down to the sons of Cain except them—eight persons, and before the deluge they had no children. Lamech prayed over them and invoked a blessing upon them. Then he wept and said to them: "No one remains of our race except these eight persons. I ask God, who created Adam and Eve alone and multiplied their offspring, to save you from this wrath that He has prepared
1:10 for the evil community, multiply your offspring until | they fill the earth, grant you the blessing of our father Adam, and give rule to your offspring. I am going to die, and none of the people of wrath will escape, except you, Noah. When I die, take me and put me in the Cave of Treasure. When God wills for you to board the boat, take the body of our father Adam, bring it down with you, and put it in the middle of the upper deck of the boat. You and your sons stay on the east side of the boat; let your wife and your daughters-in-law stay on the west side of it, and let the body of Adam be between you. Do not cross over to your wives, and let not your wives cross over to you. Do not eat or drink with them or approach them until you disembark from the boat. When the deluge goes away and you disembark from the boat, pray[23] by the body of Adam. Then command your eldest son Shem to take the body of Adam and put it in the middle of the earth, and let him set one of his children with it to take charge of it. Let the man be a person dedicated during his lifetime to God's service.[24] Let him not marry a woman, or build a house, or shed blood, or offer an animal or bird offering. God will send one of the angels with him to guide him to the middle of the earth and to keep him company."

Lamech died on Sunday, the seventeenth of Adhār, at the ninth hour of the day. He was seven hundred and seventy-seven years old.

Noah

God, may He be glorified and exalted, sent a revelation to Noah in the days of his grandfather Enoch, who was the prophet Idrīs, before God lifted up Idrīs; He commanded Noah to warn his people, forbid them from the sins they had been committing, and caution them about the punishment. He continued to worship God and to pray for his people. He devoted himself entirely to the

23 The imperative is in the masculine singular, indicating that it is addressed to Noah alone. This is emphasized by the inclusion of the masculine singular pronoun *anta* after the imperative.

24 The Arabic uses the word *ḥabr*, which usually refers to Jewish scholars. The Syriac text of *Schatzhöhle*, 84–85, has *nzīrā*, a Nazarite, a loanword from Hebrew *nāzīr*, translated in the Arabic by *nāsik taqī*, "a pious ascetic."

worship of God | and to prayer for his people, not marrying women for five 1:11
hundred years. Then God sent him a revelation to marry Haykal, the daughter of Nāmūsā, the son of Enoch.[25] He informed him that He was going to send the deluge over the earth. He commanded him to make the boat in which God saved him and his family, and to make it with three decks, a lower, a middle, and an upper one. He commanded him to make its length three hundred cubits by the cubit of Noah, its width fifty cubits, and its depth thirty cubits, and to make its compartments out of wooden planks. The bottom deck would be for the animals—tame, wild, and predators—the middle one for the birds, and the upper one for Noah and the people of his household. Containers of water and a place for food were to be put on the upper one. Children were born to Noah after he was five hundred years old.

When Noah finished working on the boat—when the offspring of Cain and those of the offspring of Seth who had commingled with them saw him working on the ark, they ridiculed him—when he finished, he invited them to board it. He informed them that God was going to send the deluge over the whole earth, to cleanse it of disobedient people, but not one of them responded to him. So he and his offspring went up to the Cave of Treasure. They carried down the body of Adam and put it in the middle of the upper deck of the boat on Friday, the seventeenth of Ādhār. He brought the birds into the middle deck, and he brought the domestic and wild animals into the lower deck. He closed it up when the sun went down.

God sent water from the heavens and broke open the springs of the earth, *and the waters met for a matter decreed.*[26] The whole earth, including the mountains, was covered, and the world was darkened. The light of the sun and the moon went out, so that night and day were the same. According to what the astrologers say, Cancer was in the ascendant at the time God sent the water. The
sun, the moon, Saturn, Mercury, | and the ascending node[27] were all together in 1:12

25 The form of this name is evidence that al-Yaʿqūbī worked from the Arabic translation of the *Schatzhöhle*, not from the Syriac. The Syriac (*Schatzhöhle*, 82–85) gives the name of Noah's wife as Haykal, the daughter of Nāmūs (Nāmūsā in some manuscripts), the *daughter* of Enoch. In the Arabic translation this becomes Haykal, the daughter of Nāmūsā, the *son* of Enoch, as in al-Yaʿqūbī.

26 Cf. Qurʾān 54:11–12: "Then We opened the gates of heaven unto water torrential, and made the earth to gush with fountains, and the waters met for a matter decreed."

27 In astronomy and astrology, a node is a point where the plane of the orbit of some celestial body (here the moon) crosses the plane of the ecliptic (the path traced by the sun in its apparent annual circuit against the background of the fixed stars). At the ascending node, the body's path (here the moon) crosses the ecliptic from south to north; at the descending

the last minute of Pisces. The water continued from heaven and earth for forty days, until it rose fifteen cubits above every mountain. Then it stopped, after no spot of the earth remained without water covering it and overwhelming it. The boat circled the whole earth until it came to Mecca, and it went around the House for a week.[28] Then the water receded after five months, beginning on the seventeenth of Ayyār, until the thirteenth of Tishrīn I.

Some have reported that Noah boarded the boat on the first day of Rajab and that *it came to rest on al-Jūdī*[29] in Muḥarram, which came to be numbered as the first of the months—but the People of the Book disagree on this point.

When *it came to rest on al-Jūdī*, which is a mountain in the vicinity of Mosul, God, exalted be He, commanded the water of the heavens to return whence it had come, and commanded the earth to it swallow up its water. Noah waited for four months after the boat halted. Then he sent out the raven,[30] to find out how things stood with the water. It found corpses floating on the water, settled upon them, and did not return. Then he sent out the dove. It brought back an olive leaf, so he knew that the water had gone. He came out on the twenty-seventh of Ayyār. A full year and ten days elapsed between his embarking on the boat and his emergence from it. When he and his family came back to the earth, they built a city and named it Thamānīn.[31] When Noah emerged from the boat and saw people's bones glimmering, it grieved him and saddened him. God revealed to him, "I will not send the deluge onto the earth ever again after this."

---

node, it crosses from north to south. The location of the moon's ascending and descending nodes is of interest to astronomers and astrologers because a lunar or solar eclipse can occur only when the moon is at or near a node.

28 The detail of the boat's circling the Kaʿba also appears in al-Ṭabarī, *Taʾrīkh*, 1:193, 197.

29 Qurʾān 11:44.

30 Arabic *ghurāb* (cognate to Hebrew *ʿōrēb*, the word used in Genesis 8:7) designates both the crow and the raven; however, given the raven's ability to soar, its intelligence, and its fondness for carrion, given also the Jewish and Christian exegetical tradition, it is best translated as raven.

31 The name means Eighty in Arabic. Indeed, al-Ṭabarī, *Taʾrīkh*, 1:194–197, says "he called it Thamānīn because he had built a house there for each of the men who were with him; they were eighty." However, he also reports other traditions that place the number of individuals on the boat with Noah as eight (al-Yaʿqūbī's tradition), seven, or ten. The form Thamānīn (the oblique case of Thamānūn) may be a folk etymology for a name not originally Arabic. *Schatzhöhle*, 102–103, has Tmānōn (Syriac) and Thamānūn (Arabic), but with the note in both the Syriac and Arabic, "named because of the *eight* souls who had come out with him." In Syriac, Tmānōn would not mean eighty (*tmānīn* in Syriac), but would be a form from the base of *tmānē* (eight) + the diminutive suffix *-ōn*.

When Noah emerged from the boat, he locked it with a lock and handed the key to his son Shem. Then Noah tilled and planted a vineyard, and he cultivated the earth. One day while Noah was sleeping, his garment became uncovered, and his son Ham saw his private parts and laughed. His brothers Shem and Japheth were told, and the two of them took a garment, | brought it to him with 1:13
their faces turned away from him, and put the garment over him. When Noah awoke from his sleep and learned of the affair, he cursed Canaan, the son of Ham, but he did not curse Ham—the Copts, the Ethiopians, and the Indians are the offspring of the latter.

Canaan was the first of the offspring of Noah to return to the works of the sons of Cain. He devoted himself to musical instruments, singing, flutes, drums, guitars, and cymbals. He obeyed Satan in amusement and idleness.

Noah divided the earth among his offspring.[32] To Shem he allotted the middle of the earth: the sacred area and its surroundings,[33] Yemen and Ḥaḍramawt, extending to Oman, to al-Baḥrayn, to ʿĀlij and Yabrīn, and Wabār, al-Daww and al-Dahnāʾ. To Ham he allotted the land of the west and the coastal areas.[34] He begot Cush son of Ham, Canaan son of Ham, the Nubians, the Zanj, and the Ethiopians. Noah's son Japheth settled in the region between the east and the west. Born to him were Gomer, Tubal,[35] Māsh,[36] Meshech, and Magog. Gomer begat the Slavs; Tubal begat Burjān;[37] Māsh begot the Turks and the Khazars;[38] Meshech begot al-Ashbān;[39] Magog begot Yagog and Magog. These were in the eastern part of the earth, by the Turks. The homes of the Slavs and the Burjān were in the land of the Romans, before the Romans existed. These were the offspring of Japheth.

After disembarking from the boat, Noah lived three hundred and sixty years. When the death of Noah was imminent, his three sons, Shem, Ham, and

32 Parallel traditions about the descendents of Noah may be found in al-Ṭabarī, *Taʾrīkh*, 1:211 ff.

33 Arabic, *al-Ḥaram*, referring to Mecca.

34 To an Arabic reader, *arḍ al-maghrib wa-l-sawāḥil*, would suggest North Africa (the Maghreb) along with the east coast of Africa. *Sawāḥil* (coasts) is the source of the name of the language Swahili (Arabic *sawāḥilī*) spoken along the coast of East Africa familiar to Arab traders.

35 Ed. Leiden, M: Shūbal (twice).

36 Sic Ed. Leiden, M; perhaps to be identified with Madai of Genesis 10:2.

37 Cf. al-Ṭabarī, *Taʾrīkh*, 1:218. The translator, William M. Brinner (*The History of al-Ṭabarī*, II, 17n) sees a possible reference to the Bulgars.

38 Sic ed. Leiden (*al-Khazar*); M *al-juzur* (the islands).

39 Cf. al-Ṭabarī, *Taʾrīkh*, 1:218. The translator, William M. Brinner (ibid., 16n) notes that the name (possibly to be read Ishbān) may conceal a reference to the city of Iṣbahān or to Spain.

Japheth, and their sons, gathered around him. He gave them his testament and commanded them to worship God. He commanded that when he died,
1:14 Shem should enter the boat unbeknownst to anyone and remove Adam's body; | Melchizedek, the son of Lamech son of Shem, was to go with him, for God had chosen him to be with Adam's body in the middle of the earth in the holy place. He said to him: "Shem, when you and Melchizedek set out, God will send an angel with you to guide you on the way and to show you the middle of the earth. Tell no one what you are doing. This command is Adam's testament, with which he charged his sons, and they passed on the charge one to another, until it has come to you. When you arrive at the place which the angel will show you, put Adam's body in it. Then command Melchizedek not to depart from it and to have no work except the worship of God. Command him not to marry any woman, or build any building, or shed any blood, or dress in any garment except the skins of wild animals, or cut his hair or nails. Let him sit alone and constantly praise God." Then Noah died in Ayyār, on a Wednesday. He lived for nine hundred and fifty years, just as God, exalted be He, has related: *a thousand years, less fifty*.[40]

Shem, the Son of Noah

After his father, Shem, the son of Noah, carried on the worship of God and obedience to Him. Arpachshad had been born to him when he was one hundred and two years old. Seth then set out; he opened the boat, took Adam's body, and brought it down, keeping it a secret from his brothers and his family. Summoning his brothers Japheth and Ham, he said to them: "My father gave me a charge and commanded me to go to the sea, examine the earth, and then return. Do not move on until I come back to you, and take good care of my wife and son." His brothers said to him, "Go in God's keeping; for you know that the earth is
1:15 devastated, and we fear that predatory animals may harm you." Shem said, | "God will send an angel, and so, God willing, I will fear nothing." Shem summoned his son Lamech and said to him and to his wife Yozedek,[41] "Send your son Melchizedek with me, to keep me company on the way." The two of them said to him, "Go, rightly guided." To his two brothers, his wife, and his son, Shem said: "You know that our father Noah charged me and commanded me to seal

---

40 Qur'ān 29:14.

41 The text in the MSS (*yā wazdaq*) is meaningless. The easiest solution is to change one letter (omit the *alif*), which yields the name of Lamech's wife Yōzadaq (= Yozedek) given in *Schatzhöhle*, 116–117.

the boat, and that neither I nor any other person should enter it. Therefore, let none of you come near the boat."

Then Shem set out, and his son with him. The angel appeared to them and was with them continually, until he brought them to the place where they were commanded to put the body of Adam. It is said to be in the mosque of Minā, by the minaret; however, the People of the Book say it is in Syria, in the Holy Land. The ground opened up and they put the body in it; then it closed over it. Shem said to Melchizedek, the son of Lamech son of Shem: "Remain here and worship God aright. God will send you an angel every day to keep you company." Then he said goodbye to him and left. When he came to his family, and his son Lamech asked him about Melchizedek, he said, "He died on the way and I buried him." So his father and his mother grieved for him.

When death drew near for Shem, he gave his testament to his son Arpachshad. Shem died on Thursday, the seventh of Aylūl. He was six hundred years old.

Arpachshad, the Son of Shem

Then Arpachshad, the son of Shem, carried on the worship of God and obedience to Him. After he was one hundred and eighty-five years old, Shelah had been born to him. The offspring of Noah had scattered throughout the lands, and the giants and the violent among them had grown numerous. | Canaan, the 1:16
son of Ham, corrupted the offspring of Noah, and they committed sins openly.

When death was imminent for Arpachshad, he gathered his offspring and family to him and gave them his testament, that they should worship God and avoid sins. He said to his son Shelah, "Accept my testament, and carry on in your family after me, acting in obedience to God." He died on Sunday, the twenty-third of Nīsān. He was four hundred and sixty-five years old.

Shelah, the Son of Arpachshad

Then Shelah, the son of Arpachshad, arose among his people, commanding them to obey God, forbidding them to sin against Him, and warning them of the wrath and punishment that had befallen the sinful people. Eber had been born to him when he was one hundred and thirty years old. When his death was imminent, he gave his testament to his son Eber son of Shelah. He commanded him to avoid the deeds of the sons of Cain, the accursed. He died on Monday, the thirteenth of Ādhār. He was four hundred and thirty years old.

Eber, the Son of Shelah

Then Eber, the son of Shelah, arose, summoning his people to obey God and warning the sons of Shem son of Noah against commingling with the progeny of Canaan son of Ham, who had altered the religion of his fathers and had committed sins. When Eber was one hundred and thirty-four years old, Peleg had been born to him. When Eber's death was imminent, he gave his testament to his son Peleg. He said to him: "My son, when the offspring of the accursed Cain committed many sins against God and the offspring of Seth joined with them, God sent wrath upon them. Therefore, do not enter, you or your family, into the community[42] of the sons of Canaan."

1:17 Eber died on Thursday the twenty-third of Tishrīn I. | He was three hundred and forty years old; others say one hundred and sixty-four.

Peleg, the Son of Eber

After Eber, his son Peleg arose, calling people to obey God. In his time, Noah's progeny gathered in Babylon. This was because Māsh, the son of Aram son of Shem son of Noah, came to the land of Babylon. He begot Nimrod the Mighty[43] and Nabīṭ,[44] who was the father of the Nabataeans[45] and the first who dug canals, planted trees, and cultivated the land. The language of all of

---

42 Arabic, *milla*. The word primarily means a religion or sect and occurs in the Qurʾān referring both to heathen religions (as here) and to the "religion of Abraham (*millat Ibrāhīm*)," that is, true monotheism. See the article by F. Buhl in EI^{2}, s.v. Milla.

43 Arabic: *Namrūd al-jabbār*. The primary meaning in Arabic of *jabbār* (a loan from Hebrew or Aramaic) is "one who magnifies himself, or behaves proudly or haughtily or insolently …: imperious, or domineering, by absolute force and power; overbearing; tyrannical; a tyrant" (Lane, *Lexicon*, s.v.). The word also became a synonym for "giant." In Genesis 10:8–9, Nimrod is called first *gibbōr* (RSV "a mighty warrior") and then *gibbōr ṣayid* (RSV "a mighty hunter"). Although Nimrod is not mentioned by name in the Qurʾān, he is alluded to. On the development of the story in Islamic sources, see the article by B. Heller in EI^{2}, s.v. Namrūd.

44 M: *Yanbiṭ*.

45 Arabic, *al-nabaṭ*. The Arabic term designated two distinct groups: the Nabataeans of Syria (*nabaṭ al-shām*), a people probably of Arab origin who controlled a kingdom centered on the city of Petra in late Hellenistic and Roman times, and the Nabataeans of Iraq (*nabaṭ al-ʿirāq*), a term that eventually extended to include all of the Aramaic-speaking population of Mesopotamia. See the article by T. Fahd in EI^{2}, s.v. Nabaṭ.

them was Syriac,[46] which had been the language of Adam. When they were gathered in Babylon, they said to each other, "Let us build a building whose foundation is the earth and whose summit the sky." When they started building, they said, "We will use it as a stronghold to preserve us from the deluge." But God destroyed their stronghold and divided their languages into seventy-two languages, and they divided into seventy-two groups from that place of theirs. There were nineteen languages among the progeny of Shem, sixteen among the progeny of Ham, and thirty-seven among the progeny of Japheth. When they saw the state they were in, they came together to Peleg son of Eber. He said to them, "No single land can hold you, given the division of your languages." They said, "Divide the land among us." So he divided it for them. The progeny of Japheth son of Noah received China, India, Sind, the lands of the Turks, those of the Khazars, Tibet, the lands of the Bulgars, Daylam, and the territory adjoining Khurāsān. The king of the sons of Japheth at that time was Jamshādh.[47] The progeny of Ham received the land of the west and the territory beyond the Euphrates to the setting of the sun. The progeny of Shem received the Hijāz, Yemen, and the rest of the earth.

When Peleg was thirty years old, Reu had been born to him. When the death of Peleg was imminent, he gave his testament to his son Reu. Peleg died on
Friday, the twelfth | of Aylūl. He was two hundred and thirty-nine years old. 1:18

Reu, the Son of Peleg

Reu, the son of Peleg, arose after his father, after the languages had divided into seventy-two divisions. Nineteen of them belonged to the sons of Shem, sixteen to the offspring of Ham, and thirty-seven to the offspring of Japheth. Nimrod the Mighty lived in his time. His home was in Babylon, and he was the one who began to build the citadel and the first to make a crown. He reigned for sixty-

---

46 Arabic uses *suryānī* (Syriac) to designate the Aramaic language generally, not only its later Christian literary form known as Syriac. Since Qur'ān 2:31 states that God "taught Adam the names, all of them," the language used by Adam became a subject of interest to Islamic writers. One tradition, followed here by al-Yaʿqūbī, identified the language as Syriac, that is, Aramaic. Other traditions identified it as Arabic. See the article by R. Tottoli in EI^{3}, s.v. Adam.

47 Jam Shād (written as two words in ed. Leiden and M) is the Iranian hero better known by the form of his name in Ferdousi's *Shahnameh*: Jamshīd. The name derives ultimately from Avestan *Yima Khshaēta* (Yima the Brilliant). See the article by Cl. Huart and H. Massé in EI^{2}, s.v. Dj̲amshīd.

seven years. When Reu was thirty-two years old, Serug had been born to him. When Reu was seventy-four years old, the third millennium was completed. When Reu's death was imminent, he gave his testament to his son Serug. Reu died on Wednesday, the fourteenth of Nīsān. He was two hundred years old.

Serug, the Son of Reu

Serug, the son of Reu, arose among the offspring of Shem after the death of his father. The giants[48] had grown numerous and had done violence in the land. Idols were worshipped for the first time in the time of Serug. The beginning of idolatry was that when a person dear to someone died, such as a father, a brother, or a child, he would make an idol in the likeness of the dead person and call it by the person's name. When the next generation came along after them, they thought—Satan proposed it to them—that these had been made to be worshipped, and therefore they worshipped them. Then God divided their religion. Some of them worshipped idols; some of them worshipped the sun; some of them worshipped the moon; some of them worshipped birds; some of them worshipped stones; some of them worshipped trees; some of them
1:19 worshipped water; some of them worshipped the wind. | Satan seduced them, led them astray, and made them rebellious.

When Serug was one hundred and thirty years old, Nahor had been born to him. When Serug's death was imminent, he gave his testament to his son Nahor, commanding him to worship God. Serug died on Sunday, the twenty-seventh of Āb. He was two hundred and thirty years old.

Nahor, the Son of Serug

Nahor succeeded his father. In his time the worship of idols increased. God commanded the earth and it shook mankind with a strong earthquake, so that those idols fell; but they paid no attention to this and put other idols in their place. Also in his time, sorcery, divination, and augury appeared, and people sacrificed their children to the satans. Weights and measures were established. Nahor lived for one hundred and forty-eight years.

48 Arabic, *jabābira*, pl. of *jabbār*, used previously as the epithet of Nimrod; perhaps simply "mighty men."

The giants of that age were [the offspring of] ʿĀd, son of Uz,[49] son of Aram, son of Shem, son of Noah. They spread through the land, and their habitations were from the highlands of Ḥaḍramawt as far as the valleys of Najrān. When they wrought havoc and did violence, God sent Hūd, son of [ʿAbdallāh, son of Ribāḥ, son of] al-Khalūd,[50] son of ʿĀd, son of Uz, son of Aram, son of Shem, son of Noah. He called them to worship God, obey Him and avoid forbidden things, but they called him a liar. God therefore cut off the rain from them for three years. So they sent a delegation to the Holy House to pray for rain. They kept circumambulating the house and praying energetically[51] for forty mornings. Then they caught sight of two clouds: one was white and contained rain and mercy, the other [was black] and contained punishment and retribution. They heard a voice calling to them, "Choose which of them you want." They said, "We choose the black one." It passed over their heads; and when it approached their country, Hūd said to them, | "In this cloud there is a punishment that has 1:20
over-shadowed you." "No," they said, "it is a cloud that will bring us rain." But it brought a black wind that burnt up everything over which it passed, and none of them escaped except Hūd. It is said that Luqmān, son of ʿĀd, escaped, too, and lived as long as the lifetime granted to seven vultures.[52]

When ʿĀd passed away, the sons of Thamūd, son of Jāzar, son of Thamūd,[53] son of Aram, son of Shem, son of Noah, moved into their territories; their kings used to live in al-Ḥijr.[54] When they did violence, God sent Ṣāliḥ, son of Tāliḥ, son of Ṣādūq, son of Hūd,[55] to them as a prophet. They asked him to give them a sign. So God brought out of the earth for them a she-camel along with its foal. Ṣāliḥ said to them: "One day is for this camel to come to the water; one day is for you to do so. Take care not to turn her away from the water." But they called him

49 Arabic *ʿŪṣ* (as in Hebrew, RSV Uz).

50 M: *al-Jalūd*: corrected in ed. Leiden on the basis of al-Ṭabarī, *Taʾrīkh*, 1:231. For a summary of the Arabic traditions about this prophet mentioned in the Qurʾān, but not in the Bible, see the article by A. J. Wensinck and Ch. Pellat in *EI*², s.v. Hūd.

51 Arabic, *yasʿawna*, which has a number of senses: exert oneself energetically, go at a fast pace. In the latter sense it became a technical term for the running between the hills of Ṣafā and Marwa that forms part of the Islamic pilgrimage. The text may imply that this rite existed even in the time of the prophet Hūd.

52 For the legend of Luqmān, who became proverbial for his wisdom and longevity, see the article by B. Heller and N. A. Stillman in *EI*², s.v. Luḳmān.

53 For "Thamūd, son of Jāzar, son of Thamūd, son of Aram" al-Ṭabarī, *Taʾrīkh*, 1:244, has only "Thamūd, son of Jāthir, son of Aram." (Jāthir is apparently Gether of Genesis 10:23).

54 Al-Ḥijr is the site known now as Madāʾin Ṣāliḥ in northwestern Saudi Arabia. See the article by F. S. Vidal in *EI*², s.v. al-Ḥidjr.

55 MSS Thamūd; corrected by Houtsma on the basis of cod. Schefer.

a liar, and one of their men, someone called Qudār, arose and hamstrung her—he struck her hamstring with a sword. Her foal went up to high place; there it brayed, and God sent a punishment upon them. None of them escaped except a woman called al-Dharīʿa. The Arabs made Qudār proverbial.[56]

Terah, the Son of Nahor

Nahor's son Terah, the father of 'God's friend' Abraham,[57] lived in the age of Nimrod the Mighty. Nimrod was the first to worship fire and bow down to it. That was because a fire once emerged from the earth; he approached it and bowed down to it, and a satan addressed him from within it, so he built a building over it and appointed attendants for it.

In that age, people applied themselves to the science of astronomy. They calculated the eclipses of the sun and moon, and the movements of the planets
1:21 and the fixed stars. They discoursed | about the celestial sphere and the signs of the zodiac. The one who taught this to Nimrod was a man called Yonṭon.[58] Terah—he is Āzar,[59] the father of Abraham—was a contemporary of Nimrod the Mighty. The astronomers made calculations for Nimrod. They told him that someone would be born in his kingdom who would find fault with his religion, rebuke him, destroy his idols, and disunite his community. Nimrod therefore decreed that the belly of anyone born in his kingdom should be rent open; and this was done, until Abraham was born and his parents concealed him. They kept him secret and put him in a cave where no one could know of him. His birthplace was at Kūthā Rabbā.[60] Abraham was born when Terah was one hundred and seventy years old. Terah, his father, lived for two hundred and five years.

56 That is, proverbial for ill fortune and bad luck; see al-Thaʿālibī, *Thimār al-qulūb*, 30.

57 Arabic, *khalīl Allāh*, based on Qurʾān 4:125.

58 Correcting the apparent reading of M (Yanṭiq) on the basis of *Schatzhöhle*, 138 (trans. Budge, 143), where this Yonṭon is identified as a son of Noah with whom Nimrod studied for three years. Cf. Sidney H. Griffith, *The Bible in Arabic*, 190.

59 Qurʾān 6:74.

60 A city in Mesopotamia, biblical Cuthah (2 Kings 17:24), known in Islamic tradition as the place where Abraham was thrown into the fire by Nimrod. Cf. Griffith, *The Bible in Arabic*, 191; Guy Le Strange, *The Lands of the Eastern Caliphate*, 68.

Abraham

Abraham grew up in the time of Nimrod the Mighty. When he left the cave where he had been, he turned his gaze to the heavens, looked at Venus, saw a shining star, and said, "This is my Lord; He has height and elevation."[61] Then the star disappeared. He said, "My Lord would not disappear." Then he saw the moon when it rose. He said, "This is my Lord." But it was not long before the moon disappeared. *He said, "If my Lord does not guide me I shall surely be of the people gone astray."*[62] When daytime came, the sun rose. He said, "This is my Lord; this one is the most luminous, the brightest." When the sun disappeared he said, "It disappeared; my Lord would not disappear." Thus has God related his story and his affair.

When Abraham became older, he marveled when he saw his people worshipping idols. He would say, *"Do you worship what you carve?"*[63] And they would say, "Your father has taught you this."[64] | He would say, "My father is 1:22
certainly among those going astray." What he said became known among his people and the people talked about it.

God sent him as a prophet. He dispatched Gabriel to him, and he taught him his religion. He began to say to his people, *"I am quit of what you associate (with God)."*[65] A report about him reached Nimrod, and he sent a messenger to him forbidding him from this. Then Abraham began to smash their idols.[66] He would say to one, "Defend yourself!" Nimrod kindled a fire and put him into a catapult and shot him into it. So God sent an inspiration to the fire, *"Be coolness and safety for Abraham."*[67] He sat in the midst of the fire, unharmed by it. Nimrod said, "Whoever adopts a god, let him adopt one like the god of Abraham!" Lot believed along with him. Lot was the son of his brother, Haran son of Terah.

God commanded Abraham to leave the country of Nimrod for Syria,[68] the Holy Land. Abraham, his wife Sarah—she was the daughter of Haran, the son

---

61 The narrative is based on Qur'ān 6:74–79. Two versions of it appear in al-Ṭabarī, *Taʾrīkh*, 1:255, 258.

62 Qur'ān 6:77.

63 Qur'ān 37:95.

64 Sic MSS, including M. Houtsma unnecessarily corrects this in ed. Leiden to "has taught *us*."

65 Qur'ān 6:78.

66 The story of Abraham's smashing the idols is based on Qur'ān 21:51–70. Cf. al-Ṭabarī, *Taʾrīkh*, 1:259–260.

67 Qur'ān 21:69.

68 Arabic, *al-Shaʾm* (or *al-Shām*), designates the countries of the Levant northwest of the

of his paternal uncle Nahor—and Lot the son of Haran[69] left to emigrate to where God commanded them. They settled in the land of Palestine. His wealth and the wealth of Lot increased. Abraham said to Lot: "God has increased our wealth and livestock for us. Therefore, go apart from us, and settle in the cities of Sodom and Gomorrah"—near the place where Abraham was. When Lot came to the city[70] of Sodom and Gomorrah and settled there, the king of that region came upon him, fought with him, and took his wealth. Abraham went and rescued his wealth.[71]

God enriched Abraham with much wealth. He said, "Lord, what am I to do with wealth, when I have no offspring?" God sent a revelation, "I will multiply your offspring until they become as numerous as the stars."

Sarah had a slave-girl named Hagar, and she gave her to Abraham. He had intercourse with Hagar, and she conceived and bore Ishmael. Abraham was
1:23 then eighty-six years old. God said, "I will multiply your offspring | and set lasting dominion among them forever, so that no one shall know their number."

When Hagar bore a child, Sarah became jealous. She said, "Take her and her child away from me." He took her away, along with Ishmael, and brought them to Mecca. He settled them at the Sacred House and left them. Hagar said to him, "In whose care are you leaving us?" He said, "In the care of the Lord of this building." And he said, "O God, *I have made* my son *to dwell in a valley where is no sown land by Thy Holy House*."[72]

The water that Hagar had with her ran out, and Ishmael became very thirsty. Hagar set out to search for water. She climbed onto al-Ṣafā and saw a bird standing near it.[73] She came back, and the bird had scratched the earth with its feet, and water came out. She collected it so that it would not run off. This is the well of Zamzam.[74]

Arabian peninsula generally, and is not restricted to modern Syria. On its designation as "the Holy Land," see Griffith, *The Bible in Arabic*, 192, note 74.

69 Confusingly, both Abraham's brother and his cousin are named Haran. The Arabic distinguishes them: Abraham's brother is called *Hārān* b. Tārakh; his cousin is called *Khārān* b. Nāḥūr. However, the scribe himself seems to have become confused and wrote Khārān b. Tārakh once, correcting it to Hārān. Cf. al-Ṭabarī, *Taʾrīkh*, 1:266.

70 Sic.

71 Cf. Genesis 14, especially v. 12–16.

72 Cf. Qurʾān 14:37.

73 Possibly, "near him," i.e., near Ishmael. The masculine pronoun is ambiguous, as the name of the hill al-Ṣafā can be either masculine or feminine.

74 The stories about the origins of this well located beside the sacred mosque in Mecca are summarized in the article by Jacqueline Chabbi in *EI*^{2}, s.v. Zamzam.

Lot's people committed sins. They used to approach male beings[75]—that was because Iblīs once appeared to them in the form of a beardless youth and commanded them to have intercourse with him. They came to have such an appetite for it that they abandoned having intercourse with women and took to having intercourse with males. Lot forbade them to do it, but they did not stop. They committed such outrages in their judgments that they became proverbial for outrage and people said, "More unjust than a judgment of Sodom!" If a man among them did something loathsome to someone, and the latter hit him or flogged him, he would say to him, "Give me a wage for what I did to you." They had two judges, named Shaqrī and Shaqrūnī, who judged unjustly, wrongfully, and outrageously.[76]

When the actions and injustice of Lot's people increased, God sent angels to destroy them. They stayed with Abraham, who used to receive visitors and extend hospitality. When they stopped with him, he offered them a roasted calf. When he saw them not eating, he became suspicious, and so they made themselves known to him.[77] They said, "We are messengers of your Lord, come for the destruction of this town." They meant the town of Sodom, where the people of Lot were. *Abraham said to them, | "Lot is there." They said, "We know* 1:24
well who is there; we will certainly save him and his family, except for his wife."[78] Sarah, Abraham's wife, was standing there, and she marveled at what they said; and so they gave her the good news of Isaac. She said, *"Shall I give birth, being an old woman, and this my husband is an old man?"*[79] Abraham was a hundred years old, and she was ninety.

When the angels came to Lot and his wife saw them, she sent out smoke to her people.[80] So they approached Lot and said, "Hand us your guests." He said, "Do not dishonor me regarding my guests."[81] When they persisted, Gabriel turned them away and blinded them. Then (the angels) said to Lot, "We will kill

---

75 The language echoes Qur'ān 26:165 and 54:33–39.

76 The names reflect Jewish tradition (from Hebrew *sheqer*, falsehood). See Ginzberg, *Legends of the Jews*, 1:246–247; discussed by Griffith, *The Bible in Arabic*, 193, note 80.

77 The language echoes Qur'ān 11:70.

78 Qur'ān 29:32.

79 Qur'ān 11:72.

80 Arabic, *dakhkhanat li-qawmihā*, is ambiguous. One tradition sees her as being an unbeliever who intentionally signaled the Sodomites about the arrival of the guests; another sees her as unintentionally alerting them to the arrival of guests because of the smoke of her cooking fire.

81 Echoing Qur'ān 15:68.

them." "When?" he asked. "In the morning," they said. He said, "Will you give them time until morning?" Gabriel said to him, *"Is not the morning near?"*[82] When it was dawn, Gabriel said to him, "Leave!" and then he overturned the city on them. It is also said that a fire descended upon them. None of them was saved. Lot's wife was among them, and she was turned to salt. None of them remained to tell of it.

God gave Abraham Isaac the son of Sarah, and people marveled at it. They said, "An old man of a hundred years and an old woman of ninety years!" Isaac turned out to resemble Abraham very closely.

Abraham used to visit Ishmael and his mother all the time.[83] When Ishmael grew up and became a man, he married a woman from the tribe of Jurhum.[84] Once Abraham came to visit him and did not find him. Ishmael's mother had died, so Abraham spoke with his wife, but her attitude did not please him. He asked her about Ishmael, and she said that he was out in the pasture. He said, "When he comes back, tell him: Change the threshold of your door."[85] When Ishmael came back from his pasture, his wife said to him, "An old man came here asking for you." Ishmael said, "What did he say to you?" She said, "He said to me, 'Tell him: Change the threshold of your door.'" "You are loosed," he said; and he divorced her and married al-Ḥayfāʾ, the daughter of Muḍāḍ, of the tribe of Jurhum. Abraham came back to them a year later. He stopped at the house of Ishmael and did not find him, but he found his wife. "How are you?" he asked.
1:25 "Well," she said. "May it be so!" he said; | "Where is your husband?" She said, "He is not here. Stay a while." He said, "I cannot." She said, "Give me your head, that I may kiss it." He did so, and said, "When your husband comes back, greet him, and say to him: Hold fast to the threshold of your door." When Ishmael came back, his wife gave him the report about Abraham. He bent down to the imprint of his foot, to kiss it.

Then God ordered Abraham to build the Kaʿba, raise its foundations, issue the call to the pilgrimage among the people, and show them its rituals.[86] Abraham and Ishmael built up the foundations, until they reached the place of the stone. At that point Mount Abū Qubays called out to Abraham, "I have something in trust for you"—and it gave him the stone, and he put it in its place.

---

82 Qurʾān 11:81.

83 Two versions of the following story can be found in al-Ṭabarī, *Taʾrīkh*, 1:281–285.

84 An ancient Arab tribe said to have controlled the Kaʿba before the advent of the Quraysh. See the article by W. Montgomery Watt in *EI*², s.v. Djurhum.

85 The term *ʿataba* (threshold) is used metonymically of a wife. See Lane, *Lexicon*, s.v.

86 Parallel, al-Ṭabarī, *Taʾrīkh*, 1:274–277.

Abraham issued the call to the pilgrimage among the people.[87] When the Day of Tarwiya[88] came, Gabriel said to him, "Provide yourself with water!"—and so it was named *Tarwiya*. Then he came to Minā, and Gabriel said to him, "Spend the night here!" Then he came to ʿArafāt, and there he built a mosque of white stones, where he prayed the noon and afternoon prayers. Then Gabriel directed him to ʿArafāt and said to him, "This is ʿArafāt; recognize it!"[89]—and so it was given the name ʿArafāt. Then he rushed him away[90] from ʿArafāt, and when he came opposite the two narrow places, he said to him, "Advance!"—and so it was named al-Muzdalifa.[91] He said to him, "Join together the two prayers!"—and so it was named Jamʿ.[92] When he reached the Waymark,[93] he slept there, and God commanded him to sacrifice his son.[94] Accounts differ about whether it was Ishmael or Isaac. Some say it was Ishmael, because it was he who had established his house and home there, whereas Isaac was in Syria. Others say it was Isaac, because Abraham had sent Ishmael away and had sent his mother away with him; also, Isaac at that time was a boy, while Ishmael was a man who

87 Other accounts of Abraham's institution of the rites of the pilgrimage may be found in al-Ṭabarī, *Taʾrīkh*, 1:286–289.

88 Arabic, *Yawm al-Tarwiya*, the eighth day of Dhū l-Ḥijja, the day when the pilgrims provided themselves with water for the journey to ʿArafāt, here explained as derived from the phrase, *Tarawwi min al-māʾ* (Provide yourself with water). Other explanations were also given. See Lane, *Lexicon*, s.v.

89 The Arabic, *hādhihi ʿArafāt fa-ʿrifhā*, explains the name as derived from the verb *ʿarafa* (know, recognize).

90 Arabic, *afāḍa bihī*, which gives the technical term (*ifāḍa*) for the return of the pilgrims from ʿArafāt.

91 Another etymologizing explanation: He said to him *izdalif*, and so it was named *al-Muzdalifa*.

92 Another etymologizing explanation: He said to him *ijmaʿ* the two prayers, and so it was named *Jamʿ*.

93 Arabic, *al-Mashʿar*, which occurs in Qurʾān 2:198, "But when you press on from Arafat, then remember God at the Holy Waymark." The word can mean, "guidepost," or "place of religious rites." The commentators disagree about whether it means Muzdalifa, Jamʿ, or Mecca itself. See al-Ṭabarī, *Jāmiʿ al-bayān* (ed. Boulaq) 2:167–169.

94 Ed. Leiden puts a section mark between, "… he slept there" and "God commanded him to sacrifice his son." M has no such indication, and it is more natural to read the two statements, connected as they are by the conjunction *fa-* ("and so," or "and therefore") as linked, since some traditions imply that the command was imparted to Abraham in a dream. In fact, the narrative in al-Yaʿqūbī continues "in the morning," suggesting that the command indeed was given while Abraham slept. Cf. al-Ṭabarī, *Taʾrīkh*, 1:295. The placing of Abraham's sacrifice of his son in the context of the pilgrimage has been identified as a specifically Shiʿite element; cf. Reuven Firestone, *Journeys in Holy Lands*, 120–121.

had already fathered a child. The accounts have multiplied concerning this one or that one, and people differ about them.[95]

In the morning, Abraham came to Minā and said to the boy, "Take me to visit the House." Then he said to his son, "God has commanded me to sacrifice you." He said, *"My father, do as you are commanded."*[96] So he took a knife, made him
1:26 lie down at Jamrat al-ʿAqaba,[97] and threw | a donkey's saddle-cloth under him. He put the blade to his throat, and he turned his face away from him. Gabriel turned the blade away. Abraham looked, and behold the blade had been turned away. He did that three times. Then a cry was heard: *"O Abraham, you have confirmed the vision."*[98] Gabriel took the boy, and, when a ram came down from the summit of Mount Thabīr, he put it in his place and sacrificed it. The People of the Book say that it was Isaac and that he did this to him in the desert of the Amorites in Syria.[99]

When Abraham finished his pilgrimage and was about to depart, he gave his testament to his son Ishmael, to stay by the Holy House and conduct the pilgrimage and its rites for the people. He told him that God would multiply his numbers, make his progeny fruitful, and establish blessings and prosperity among his children.

Sarah died when they reached Syria, and Abraham married Keturah, who bore him many children. They were Zimran, Jokshan, Medan, Midian, Ishbak, and Shuah.[100] Abraham died; the day of his death was Tuesday, the tenth of Āb. He was one hundred and ninety-five years old.

Isaac, the Son of Abraham

When Abraham died in Syria, Isaac arose after him. He married Rebekah, the daughter of Bethuel. She became pregnant, and her pregnancy became heavy. God revealed to Isaac, "I will bring from her womb two peoples and two nations, and will make the younger greater than the elder." Rebekah bore the twins Esau and Jacob. Esau emerged first, and Jacob emerged after him, his heel with Esau's

---

95 See, for example, al-Ṭabarī, *Taʾrīkh*, 1:290–301.

96 Qurʾān 37:102.

97 On the pilgrimage route between Mecca and ʿArafāt, there are three halting places in the Valley of Minā where pilgrims throw stones at a pillar said to represent Satan. Each is called a *jamra* (pebble). Jamrat al-ʿAqaba is the *jamra* closest to Mecca.

98 Qurʾān 37:104–105.

99 For this location, cf. *Schatzhöhle*, 146 (trans. Budge, 149).

100 Cf. Genesis 25:1–2, and al-Ṭabarī, *Taʾrīkh*, 1:345.

heel; so he was named Jacob.[101] On the day that a son was born to him, Isaac
was | sixty years old. 1:27

Isaac loved Esau, and Rebekah loved Jacob. Isaac dwelt in the valley of Gerar. He had lost his eyesight, so he said to his son Esau, "Take your sword and your bow and go out and hunt some game for me, that I may eat and bless you before I die." Rebekah his mother heard this and said to Jacob, "Make food for your father: Go to the flock, take two kids, make food, and bring it to your father, so that the blessing may settle on you." He said, "I am afraid that he will curse me." She said, "If he curses you, may your curse be upon me." So Jacob went and took two kids. He slaughtered them, cooked them, and brought them to Isaac.

Esau had hairy arms. Jacob therefore took the skins of the two kids and put them on his forearms. When he set the food before his father, the latter said, "The voice is Jacob's voice, but the touch is Esau's touch." Then he blessed him, prayed for him, and said to him, "Be head over your brothers."

When Esau came with his game, Isaac said to him, "Who set the food before me, and I blessed him?—and blessed he shall be!" Esau said, "My brother Jacob has cheated me." Isaac said to him, "I have made him head over you and over his brothers." Then he prayed for him and said, "You shall settle on the heights of the land."[102]

Isaac commanded Jacob to travel to Ḥarrān, to be with Laban,[103] the son of [Bethuel, the son of Nahor,] the brother of Abraham. Isaac feared for him from Esau. He ordered him not to marry any of the women of the Canaanites. So Jacob went to Ḥarrān, to his maternal uncle Laban. Isaac's lifespan was one hundred and eighty-five years.

---

101 The derivation of Jacob's name (Arabic *Yaʿqūb*, Hebrew *Yaʿaqōḇ*) from the word for heel (Arabic *ʿaqib*, Hebrew *ʿāqēḇ*) works equally well in both languages. Cf. Genesis 25:26.

102 The text of al-Yaʿqūbī, which is meant to reflect Genesis 27:39, is problematic. The MSS, including M, read, *ʿalā sumrati l-arḍi tanzilu*, which means, "On the duskiness of the land you shall settle." Houtsma emended this to, *ʿalā samiyyati l-arḍi tanzilu*, which is what I have translated. I suspect that the original reading was *ʿalā samīnati l-arḍi tanzilu*, "On the fattest of the land you shall settle." (The phrase is attested in Arabic; see Lane, *Lexicon*, s.v. *samīn*.) This would exactly render the Hebrew, *mishmannē hā-ʾāreṣ yihyeh mōshāḇeḵā*, "The fatnesses of the land shall be your dwelling," as well as the Syriac (Peshitta) understanding of it, *b-shumānah d-arʿā nehwe mawtḇāk*. The translation, "Away from the fatness of the earth …" (RSV) is based on an exegetical tradition (as old as the Septuagint) that sees the initial *mīm* of *mishmannē* as a shortening of the preposition *min*, from. Neither the Syriac nor al-Yaʿqūbī follows this tradition.

103 Reading as emended by Houtsma. The text of the MSS is corrupt at this point. It reads, "to Ḥarrān, to be with his child Laban, the son of Abraham, the brother of Isaac."

Jacob, the Son of Isaac

1:28 Then Isaac said to Jacob: "God has made you a prophet and has made your offspring prophets. He has conferred wealth and blessing on you." He ordered him to travel to Paddān, which is in a place in Syria. So he traveled to Paddān; and when he entered it, he saw a woman with a flock of sheep at a well, wanting to water her sheep, but on the wellhead there was a stone which could be lifted only by several men. He asked her who she was, and she said, "I am the daughter of Laban." Now Laban was Jacob's maternal uncle. So he removed the stone and drew water for her. He went to his uncle, and the latter gave her[104] to him in marriage. Jacob said, "Rachel, her sister, is the one who was designated for me." He said: "This one is the elder. I will give you Rachel to marry, too." So he married both of them together.[105]

He went in to Leah first, and with her he fathered Reuben, Simeon, Levi, Judah, Issachar, and Zebulun, as well as a girl named Dinah. Then his uncle gave him his other daughter, Rachel, in marriage. Children were slow in coming for her, so that she was distressed. Then God granted her Joseph and Benjamin. Jacob had intercourse with Zilpah, a servant girl of Leah, and by him she bore Gad, Asher, and Naphtali. Then he had intercourse with Rachel's slave, and she bore Dan.

Some say that Jacob married Rachel before Leah. The People of the Book say that he married both of them at the same time. Rachel died, but Leah survived.

Joseph was the most beloved of Jacob's children to Jacob, because he was the most beautiful of them in countenance, and his mother was the most beloved of his wives to him. His brothers envied him for this. They took him out with them, and the events that God has recounted in His mighty book took place, until Joseph was sold and enslaved.[106] He was away from his father for forty years. Then God returned him to him. Joseph brought them all together in Egypt, according to what God recounted in His book.

1:29 A number of children were born to Joseph in Egypt. | Jacob stayed in Egypt seventeen years. When it was time for him to die, he charged his son Joseph that

104 Sic MSS. One is tempted to correct *iyyāhā*, "her," to *Liyā*, "Leah," which would make better sense: "He went to his uncle, but the latter gave Leah to him in marriage." This would refer to Laban's trick of substituting Leah for Rachel on the wedding night (Genesis 29:23). However, al-Yaʿqūbī's method of condensation and summarization leaves the matter unclear.

105 This is forbidden by Qurʾān 4:23, which, however, seems to make an exception for this case: "Forbidden to you are … and that you should take to you two sisters together, unless it be a thing of the past."

106 The greater part of Sura 12 of the Qurʾān is devoted to the story of Joseph.

his offspring should not bury him in Egypt. He died when he was one hundred and forty years old.

The Offspring of Jacob

Jacob had twelve sons:[107] Reuben, Simeon, Levi, Judah, Issachar, Zebulun, Joseph, Benjamin, Gad, Asher, Dan, and Naphtali. These are the sons of Jacob; they are the sons of Israel,[108] and they are the tribes.[109] Reuben's sons were Hanoch, Pallu, Hezron, and Carmi. Simeon's sons were Jemuel, Jamin, and Shaul. Levi's sons were Gershon, Kohath, and Merari. Judah's sons were Er, Onan, Shelah, Perez, and Zerah. Issachar's sons were Tola, Puvah, Iob, and Shimron. Asher's sons were Imnah, Ishvah, Ishvi, Beriah, and Serah.[110] The sons of Zebulun were Sered, Elon, and Jahleel. The sons of Joseph in the land of Egypt were Ephraim and Manasseh. Benjamin's sons were Bela, Becher, Ashbel, Naaman, Ehi, Muppim, Huppim, and Ard. Gad's sons were Ziphion, Shuni, Ezbon, Eri, Arodi, and Areli. Naphtali's sons were Jahzeel, Guni, Jezer, and Shillem. These were the children of Jacob, and his childrens' children, who were assembled with Joseph in Egypt, along with the offspring of Joseph who were
born in Egypt. | He gave them land and said, "Plant, and a fifth of what comes 1:30
up belongs to Pharaoh."

When Jacob's time to die came, he gathered his children and his children's children. He blessed them, prayed for them, and made a pronouncement to each of them.[111] He gave Joseph his sword and his bow. Joseph brought his sons Manasseh and Ephraim to him, putting Manasseh on his right and Ephraim on his left, because Manasseh was the eldest; but Jacob put his right hand over

107 Cf. Genesis 46:8–27, which al-Yaʿqūbī follows exactly, making allowance for copyists' errors in the spelling of these non-Arabic names.

108 The MSS have *Isrāʾīl Allāh*. This puzzling expression may be (1) a copyist's error (as the Leiden editor implies), (2) a longer version of Israel-Jacob's name (Isrāʾīl-Allāh, on the pattern of ʿAbd-Allāh), or (3) a qualification, "God's Israel," in the sense that God favored Israel with a series of prophets in his progeny.

109 Arabic, *asbāṭ*, a word that occurs five times in the Qurʾān, always referring to the tribes of Israel. Arabic exegetes gave various explanations of it, but it is probably borrowed from Hebrew *shēḇeṭ* (tribe). See the article by Ella Landau-Tasseron in *Encyclopaedia of the Qurʾān*, s.v. Tribes and Clans.

110 Genesis 46:17 identifies Serah as a daughter of Asher. She will appear below in al-Yaʿqūbī's narrative as the woman who showed Moses where the coffin of Joseph was hidden.

111 Cf. Genesis 49, the testament of Jacob addressed to each of his sons in turn.

onto Ephraim. He charged Joseph to carry him away and to bury him beside the tomb of Abraham and Isaac.

When Jacob died they continued to weep for him for seventy days. Then Joseph carried him away, taking with him some young servants of the people of Egypt. He brought him to the land of Palestine and buried him beside the grave of Abraham and Isaac. When they had finished burying Jacob, Joseph said to his brothers, "Return with me to the land of Egypt." But they, fearing him, said to him, "Your father Jacob charged you to forgive us our sin." He said, "Do not fear me, for I fear God." So their hearts were soothed, and they returned to the land of Egypt and stayed there.

Joseph lived a long time in Egypt. When it came time for him to die, he gathered the children of Israel and said: "After a time you will leave the land of Egypt, when God sends a man called Moses son of Amram, of the offspring of Levi son of Jacob. God will remember you and raise you up. Take my body out of this land, and bury me by the graves of my fathers." Joseph died at the age of one hundred and ten. He was put into a coffin of stone, and was put into the Nile.[112]

The prophet Job lived in that era. He was the son of Amos, son of Zerah, son of Reuel, son of Esau, son of Isaac, son of Abraham. He was very wealthy. God put him to the test because of a sin that he had committed, but he gave thanks to God and endured patiently. Then God lifted the trial from him and returned his wealth to him and doubled it.

Moses, the Son of Amram

1:31 Moses, the son of Amram, the son of Kohath, the son of Levi, the son of Jacob, was born in Egypt in the time of Pharaoh the Mighty, who was al-Walīd ibn Muṣʿab—some say that his name was Ẓalmī.[113] The children of Israel were in Egypt at that time, having lived since the time of Joseph in slavery and servitude.

112 Cf. al-Ṭabarī, *Taʾrīkh*, 1:413. For a summary of the Jewish sources for this story, including the story of how Moses miraculously was able to find the coffin and thus fulfill the promise to bury Joseph by his fathers, narrated by al-Yaʿqūbī below, see Ginzberg, *The Legends of the Jews*, 2:181–184; 3:122. Cf. al-Ṭabarī, *Taʾrīkh*, 1:482–483, 486.

113 The assigning of an Arabic name to the Pharaoh of the time of Moses occurs in many Arabic historians. Cf. al-Ṭabarī, *Taʾrīkh*, 1:378, 412, and 444, where this al-Walīd b. Muṣʿab, an infidel, is said to have succeeded his brother Qābūs b. Muṣʿab, who had believed in the religion of Joseph.

Pharaoh's sorcerers and priests had said to him: "At this time a child will be born of the children of Israel who will despoil you of your rule, and your destruction will be because of him." Pharaoh had ruled Egypt for a long time, enjoying such security that he said, *"I am your Lord, the Most High!"*[114] He gave orders for a guard to be set over every pregnant woman of the children of Israel, so that whenever one of their woman gave birth to a boy, her child was killed. When Moses' mother went into labor, the midwife said to her, "I will conceal it for you." So when she gave birth, the midwife said to the guard, "Only blood came out of her."

God sent an inspiration to the mother of Moses: "Make a chest and put him in it. Bring it out at night and put it into Egypt's Nile." She did this. The wind pushed it and drove it to the shore, and Pharaoh's wife, seeing it, came close enough to pick it up. When she opened the chest and saw Moses, she was seized with love for him. She said to Pharaoh, "Let us adopt him as a son." She sought someone to nurse him, but he took nothing from the wet nurses until his mother came; from her he took milk. He grew to be a handsome youth and matured more quickly than other boys mature.

Joseph had said to the sons of Israel, "You will not cease to be in torment until a curly-haired boy comes of the offspring of Levi son of Jacob, one called Moses son of Amram." When the children of Israel had been in this state for a long time, they cried out and came to one of their elders. He said to them, "It is as if he were already with you!" While they were talking, Moses stood by them. | 1:32
When the elder saw him, he recognized him by the description. "What is your name?" he asked. "Moses," he said. "Whose son are you?" he asked. "The son of Amram," he said. So he and the people stood up; they kissed his hands and his feet, and he took them as followers.[115]

One day Moses entered one of the cities of Egypt, and behold one of his followers was fighting with a man of Pharaoh's family. So Moses struck the man and killed him. Pharaoh and Pharaoh's family got word of it, and they planned to kill him. When he learned of this, he set out on his own alone, wandering until he came to Midian. He hired himself out to the prophet Shuʿayb, the son of Nūnab, the son of ʿAnqā, the son of Midian, the son of Abraham, on condition that he give him one of his two daughters in marriage.[116]

114 Qur'ān 79:24.

115 Arabic, "He took them as a *shīʿa*." The word has overtones of a party or sect, as in the phrase, *shīʿat ʿAlī*, the partisans of ʿAlī.

116 The identification of the biblical Jethro, Moses' father-in-law, with the Qur'ānic prophet Shuʿayb is based on the connection of both to Midian. No such connection is implied in the Qur'ān. In al-Ṭabarī, *Ta'rīkh*, 1:365, Jethro is said to have been Shuʿayb, while at 1:462,

Having fulfilled his term of employment, Moses set out with his wife for the Holy House, according to the report about him that God has related in His mighty book.[117] While Moses was traveling on his way, he saw a fire and headed toward it, leaving his household behind. When he came near, there was a bush blazing with fire from its bottom to its top. When he drew near, his soul held back; he was apprehensive, and his fear grew great. Then God, may He be glorified and exalted, called out to him, *"Moses, do not fear, for surely you are safe."*[118] So his fear subsided. God commanded him to throw down his staff; he threw it down, and it became a snake as big as the trunk of a palm tree. Then God commanded him to pick it up, and it became a staff.

God sent him to Pharaoh and commanded him to go to him and summon him to worship God. The command distressed Moses to his very heart. So God said: "I command you to go to one of my slaves who has disregarded my grace, does not fear my devising, and maintains that he does not know me. I swear by my strength: were it not for justice and the agreement which I have put between me and my creation, I would strike him the blow of a mighty One at whose wrath heaven and earth grow angry." Moses said: "O God, strengthen my arm by means of my brother Aaron. *I have killed a soul among them, and I fear they*
1:33 *will kill me.*"[119] | God said to him: "I have done it. Go, you and your brother, with my signs, and bring out the children of Israel. This is the time for me to bring them out of slavery and servitude." So Moses returned his wife to her father. He and his brother Aaron went to Pharaoh and told him what God had sent him to say. He informed the Israelites, and their happiness was great; they knew that Joseph had told them the truth.

Then they traveled to Pharaoh's gate. Moses was wearing a tunic of wool; around his waist was a rope of fiber, and in his hand was a staff. He was forbidden entry. So he struck the gate with the staff, and the doors opened. He

---

Jethro is said to have been the nephew of Shuʿayb. The names in the genealogy of Shuʿayb are uncertain. M has Shuʿayb b. Nūnab b. ʿAyā (ed. Leiden corrects to ʿAnqā, on the basis of al-Masʿūdī, *Murūj*, 1:54 [§86]) b. Madān (for Madyan?) b. Ibrāhīm.

117 The narrative that follows is based on Qurʾān 28:29 ff. Lacking in the Qurʾānic account is any mention of the Holy House (*Bayt al-Maqdis*, the normal designation for Jerusalem) as a destination. However, in al-Ṭabarī, *Taʾrīkh*, 1:447, there is a report that Pharaoh dreamt that "a fire came from Bayt al-Maqdis until it overcame the houses of Egypt; the Egyptians were burned, while the Israelites were left." (Trans. W. M. Brinner.) Moses' return to Egypt via Palestine would demonstrate that Pharaoh's dream was fulfilled.

118 Qurʾān 28:31.

119 Qurʾān 28:33, 35.

entered and said to Pharaoh:[120] "I am the messenger of the Lord of the worlds. He has sent me to you so that you should believe in Him and send the children of Israel with me." Pharaoh, deeming this to be an affair of great magnitude, said to him, "Produce a sign by which we may know your truthfulness." So Moses threw down his staff, and it became an enormous snake with its mouth open. It bent toward Pharaoh, who asked Moses to ward it off from him. Then Moses put his hand into the front of his tunic and brought it out white, without the bane of leprosy.

Pharaoh wanted to believe in him, but Haman[121] said to him, "O king, are there none among your servants who can do the like of this?" He brought sorcerers from the whole country, and they were informed about Moses. They spent time making hollow ropes and hollow staffs out of cow skins, embellishing them and putting mercury into them. They heated the places onto which they intended to throw down the ropes and staffs. Then Pharaoh took his seat and had Moses brought in, and the sorcerers threw down their ropes and staffs. When the mercury was heated, it moved, and the ropes and staffs "walked." Then Moses threw his staff down, and it devoured everything until nothing remained. The sorcerers recoiled. Pharaoh had some of them killed.

God sent Moses to Pharaoh with signs: the staff, the hand that came out | 1:34
of his bosom white, locusts, lice, frogs, blood, and the death of the first-born. When this kept happening to them, Pharaoh said to him, "If you remove the wrath from us, we will believe and send the children of Israel out with you." So God removed it from them, but they did not believe.

God commanded Moses to bring the sons of Israel out. When they were about to leave, he looked for the body of Joseph son of Jacob, to take it with him, as Joseph had commanded the children of Israel. Serah, the daughter of Asher son of Jacob, came to him and said, "Will you guarantee my survival[122] so that I will guide you to it?" He gave her the guarantee, and she brought him

120 The narrative echoes Qurʾān 7:103 ff.

121 The Qurʾān makes Haman, who appears in the Bible as the evil counselor of King Ahasuerus in the book of Esther, into an archetype of evil counsel at the court of Pharaoh in Egypt. See Qurʾān 28:6, 8, 38; 40:24, 36. In 29:39, Haman, Korah, and Pharaoh are linked as rejecters of Moses' signs.

122 The Arabic (*taḍmanu lī al-baqāʾ*) is somewhat enigmatic. Al-Ṭabarī's version provides two rather different interpretations. In the first version, the woman wants to be guaranteed a room in paradise with Moses. In that case, *baqāʾ* would be a virtual synonym of *khulūd*, immortality. In his second version, the woman wants to be assured that Moses will not leave her behind; she merely wants to *survive* (the more general meaning of *baqāʾ*). See al-Ṭabarī, *Taʾrīkh*, 1:482–483, 486.

to a place by the Nile and said to him, "It is here!" Moses took four plates of gold. On one he drew the figure of an eagle, on another the figure of a lion, on another the figure of a man, and on another the figure of a bull.[123] On each plate he wrote the Greatest Name of God.[124] He threw them into the water, and the stone casket containing Joseph's body floated up. One plate, on which was the figure of a bull, remained in Moses' possession. He gave it to Serah, the daughter of Asher, and he took away the casket.

Moses set out with the children of Israel. They were six hundred thousand mature men. Pharaoh and his army pursued him, but God drowned them all—they were a million horsemen. Gabriel is said to have come down while Pharaoh and his men were trying to enter in pursuit of them. When Gabriel descended, not a single horse of Pharaoh's cavalry had yet crossed. Gabriel was on a filly, and Pharaoh was on a horse with a long tail. Gabriel entered the sea. Pharaoh's horse caught sight of Gabriel's filly and plunged into the sea after her; Pharaoh's men followed him and all of them—Pharaoh and all his men—drowned.[125] The sea closed over them, and Moses went into the desert.

1:35 The children of Israel began to urge him to enter into the Holy Land quickly, | but God revealed to Moses that it was forbidden to them for forty years, so they stayed in the desert. When their thirst became very great, God revealed to Moses that he should strike the rock with his staff. Moses stood up angrily and struck the rock. Twelve springs gushed forth, a spring for each tribe to drink from. But God revealed to Moses: "You struck the rock before hallowing me and did not mention my name; therefore you, too, will not leave the desert." He commanded him to build the tent of meeting[126] there, to put the sanctuary[127]

---

123 The four figures are mentioned in the versions of the story in Ginzberg, *The Legends of the Jews*, 2:181–184, and 3:122, where the lion, the man, the eagle, and the bull are identified as "the beings represented on the Celestial Throne." The ultimate source for these figures is the Prophet Ezekiel's vision of four living creatures that draw the divine chariot in Ezekiel 1. They also appear in Revelation 4:6–8.

124 Arabic, *ism Allāh al-aʿẓam*. This detail is not in the material recorded by Ginzberg or in al-Ṭabarī. In this context, the Greatest Name of God would be the Tetragrammaton, YHWH, to which magical powers are often attributed.

125 Cf. al-Ṭabarī, *Taʾrīkh*, 1:487–488.

126 Arabic, *qubbat al-zamān*, "the dome-tent of time." It appears to be a literal translation of Hebrew *ōhel mōʿēd*, rendered in the RSV by "tent of meeting." Hebrew *mōʿēd*, like its Arabic cognate *mawʿid*, can mean both the time of a meeting and the meeting itself. The Targums and the Syriac Peshitta both render the phrase as "the tabernacle of time" (Syriac *mashkan zabnā*), and this seems to be the source of the phrase in al-Yaʿqūbī.

127 Arabic, *al-haykal*.

in it, and to put the ark of the presence[128] in the sanctuary. Aaron was to be the priest of that sanctuary, which no one but he was to enter. He[129] collected the yarn of the women of the children of Israel and it was woven into cloth, and he collected all their jewelry. He made a tent one hundred cubits long; in its high place was the sanctuary, and in the high place of the sanctuary was the ark of the presence. This work of his took place in the second year of his exodus from Egypt. In it he put a table of gold. He made golden bells for the tabernacle and crowned the tabernacle with jewels. In it he put a golden censer for the incense. In it he put a golden lamp stand crowned with jewels. Aaron alone used to enter the tabernacle to sanctify God, while Moses was by the curtain and the rest of the children of Israel were in the tent. A cloud used to hover over the tabernacle, and it would not leave it. God commanded them to offer their offerings. He said to Moses:[130] "Say to the children of Israel that they shall offer an offering free of blemishes, of cattle and sheep. They shall put the fat of the offering on the altar and sprinkle the blood over it also. Any part of the offering is lawful for the sons of Aaron exclusively; it is forbidden for anyone else. Anyone who commits a sin, let him offer an offering to God at the altar according to what he can afford: from the cattle or the herd, or two turtle-doves, or two young pigeons."

God revealed to Moses that he should to write the Ten Verses[131] on two 1:36
tablets of emerald, and he wrote them as God commanded him. These are the Ten Verses:

> God said: I am the Lord, who brought you out of the land of the house of slavery and servitude. You shall have no other god but me.
>
> You shall not take for yourself a likeness or an image resembling me from above the heavens or under the earth. You shall not bow down to them or worship them; for I am the Lord, the omnipotent king, exacting the debts of the fathers from the sons: my vengeance is threefold and

128 Arabic, *tābūt al-sakīna*, literally, "the ark of the Sakīna." Arabic *sakīna* is borrowed from Hebrew *shəḵīna*. The Hebrew word itself is post-Biblical, but was a way of referring to the "glory of the Lord" that filled the tabernacle after its erection and consecration (Exodus 40:34). See the article by T. Fahd in *EI*², s.v. Sakīna.

129 That is, Moses.

130 Cf. Leviticus 5:7.

131 Arabic, *al-ʿashr al-āyāt*, the ten signs or ten verses. Perhaps this is an echo of the Hebrew as rendered by the Syriac. In Exodus 20:1–17, the commandments are introduced by the formula, "God spoke all these words (*dəḇārīm*)." The Peshitta renders *dəbārīm* by *petḡāmē*, which means both "words" and "verses," and this explains the use of *āyāt*.

fourfold for whoever hates me, but I work my benefits for whoever loves me and keeps my commandment to the thousands of thousands, for those who love me, who keep my commandments.

Third: you shall not swear by the name of the Lord falsely, because God will not acquit anyone who swears by His name falsely.

Remember the sabbath day, to keep it pure. Work for six days and strive in all your works, but the seventh day is the sabbath of the Lord your God; you shall not do any work on it—you, [your son,] your daughter, your slave, your maidservant, your cattle, your beasts, or anyone living in your towns. For in six days God created heaven and earth, the stars, and all that is eminent in the heavens.[132] Therefore God blessed the seventh day and made it pure.

Honor your father and your mother, that your days may be long in the land that the Lord your God has given you.

You shall not kill.

You shall not commit adultery.

You shall not steal.

You shall not bear false witness against your companion.

You shall not covet your companion's house, his wife, his slave, his maidservant, his ox, his ass, or any of your companion's wealth.

1:37 Moses ascended Mount Sinai. He stayed forty days and wrote | the Torah. Finding him slow to return, the children of Israel said to Aaron, "Moses has gone away, and we do not think he will return."[133] Then they took their wives' jewels, and out of them they made a hollow calf into which the wind would enter and make a mooing sound inside. God said to Moses: "The children of Israel have taken a calf and have worshipped it instead of me. Let me destroy them." Moses

132 Arabic, *wa-jamīʿa mā faraʿa fī l-samāʾ*. The sense might also be, "and all that ascends into the heavens." It is unclear why al-Yaʿqūbī, whose version of the Ten Commandments is very close to the original, suddenly introduces a phrase that is not in the original, and, to compound the mystery, leaves out the words "but rested on the seventh day." The notion that God "rested" is explicitly rejected by Qurʾān 50:38: "We created the heavens and the earth, and what between them is, in six days, and no weariness touched Us." Yet al-Yaʿqūbī usually does not change Jewish and Christian accounts that do not accord with the Qurʾān. For example, he relates the Christian accounts of the crucifixion faithfully; only afterward does he note that the Qurʾān, which he deems the true account, says that Jesus was not really crucified. So the reason for the omission here is not clear.

133 Cf. Exodus 32.

prayed for them and said, "Lord, be mindful for their sake of Abraham, Isaac, and Jacob, and let the people of Egypt not rejoice at their misfortune."

Moses came down from the mountain after forty days. When he saw the calf and saw them cleaving to it, his anger became intense, and he threw down the tablets and broke them. He put the blame on the head of his brother Aaron. He looked at the calf mooing, and he broke it up and crushed it until he made it like dust and scattered it on the water. He said to the sons of Levi, "Unsheathe your swords, and kill whomever you can of those who worshipped the calf." So the sons of Levi unsheathed their swords, and in one hour they killed a great number of people. God said to them, "Exterminate anyone who took a god other than me."

God commanded Moses to count the sons of Israel and to appoint over each tribe a good and virtuous man.[134] The number of those who had reached twenty years and upward, until sixty, those who could bear arms, was six hundred and three thousand, five hundred and fifty men. His counting of them took place two years after their exodus from Egypt. The head of the sons of Judah was Nahshon son of Amminadab, and the number of those with him of his tribe was seventy-four thousand, six hundred men. The head of the sons of Issachar was Nethanel son of Zuar, and the number of those with him was fifty-four thousand, four hundred men. The head of the tribe of Zebulun was Eliab son
of | Helon, and the number of those with him was fifty-seven thousand, four 1:38
hundred men. The head of the tribe of the sons of Reuben was Elizur son of Shedeur, and the number of those with him was forty-seven[135] thousand, five hundred men. The head of the sons of Simeon was Shelumiel son of Zurishaddai, and the number of those with him was fifty-nine[136] thousand, three hundred men. The head of the sons of Gad was Eliasaph son of Deuel, and the number of those with him was forty-five thousand, six hundred and fifty men. The head of the sons of Ephraim was Elishama son of Ammihud, and the number of those with him was forty thousand, five hundred men. The head of the sons of Manasseh was Gamaliel son of Pedahzur, and the number of those with him was thirty-two thousand, two hundred men. The head of the sons of Benjamin was Abidan son of Gideoni, and the number of those with him was sixty-five[137] thousand, four hundred men. The head of the sons of Dan was

134 Cf. Numbers 1.

135 Probably a copyist's error for forty-six, as in Numbers 1:20.

136 The copyist, reversing the digits, has written ninety-five. Ed. Leiden corrects on the basis of Numbers 1:23.

137 Probably a copyist's error for thirty-five, as in Numbers 1:37.

Ahiezer son of Ammishaddai, and the number of those with him was thirty-two[138] thousand, seven hundred men. The head of the sons of Asher was Pagiel son of Ochran, and the number of those with him was forty-one thousand, five hundred men. The head of the tribe of Naphtali was Ahira son of Enan, and the number of those with him was fifty-three thousand, four hundred men. The sons of Levi were the servants and guards of the tent of meeting, so they were not added with them. They were held in special honor and holiness for the service and cleansing of the tent of meeting. This is the number of the children of Israel, the name of the head of each of their tribes, and how many of the tribe he had with him, according to what is in the fourth book of the Torah.

1:39 God commanded Moses to tell the heads of the tribes of the sons of Israel that every leader among should make an offering.[139] The offering of each of them was to be a silver plate of one hundred thirty shekels,[140] a silver strainer[141] of seventy shekels, a plate full of white flour mixed with oil, a golden flask of ten shekels full of perfume, a bull, a ram, a yearling lamb, and a female yearling goat. The perfect sacrifice was two bulls, five rams, five kids, and five yearling lambs.

God commanded Moses to say to the children of Israel that they should sacrifice a yellow cow, a flawless one with no blemish on it.[142] He was to take its blood and sprinkle it onto the ropes of the tent of meeting. Then he was to burn it and its hide. Another man was to come and gather up the ashes and move them to a certain place. When anyone wanted to be purified, he was to put some of the ashes into water, and he would become pure.

Moses and the children of Israel stayed in the desert a long time. Their food was manna, and the manna was like coriander seed which they would grind with hand mills and make into loaves, so that their food was delicious, more delicious than anything else.[143] It used to come down to them at night, and they would collect it in the daytime. But they raised a clamor, wept, and

---

138 Probably a copyist's error for sixty-two, as in Numbers 1:39.

139 Cf. Numbers 7.

140 That is, weighing 130 shekels. Al-Yaʿqūbī uses the Arabic cognate *mithqāl.*

141 Arabic *miṣfāh.* The Hebrew has *mizrāq,* RSV "basin." The Syriac translates this as *shāḥlā,* meaning both "dish, plate" and "strainer," cf. Michael Sokoloff, *Syriac Lexicon,* 1543. This is another instance of al-Yaʿqūbī's reliance on Syriac mediation of the biblical text.

142 Cf. Numbers 19, where the sacrifice of a red heifer and the use of the ashes are described. Al-Yaʿqūbī's characterization of its color as *ṣafrā',* yellow, rather than red, was influenced by Qur'ān 2:69, which calls the animal *baqara ṣafrā'.*

143 Cf. the description of the manna in Exodus 16:4–36; Numbers 11:7–9.

began to say:[144] "Who will give us meat to eat? Do you not remember what we used to eat in Egypt: fish, cucumbers, melons, leeks, onions, and garlic?" Moses became increasingly distressed at this. They began saying, "Give us meat to eat." Moses said, "O God, I have no strength to deal with the children of Israel." God therefore revealed to him, "I am going to give you meat to eat"—and he sent them quail. God told them that he would to bring them out into Syria. Moses therefore sent Joshua son of Nun [and others][145] to Syria, to the land of the sons of Canaan, to bring him information about it. The children of Israel said, "We have no power | to fight giants." 1:40

God gave Moses permission to take vengeance on the people of Midian.[146] So he dispatched twelve thousand men of the children of Israel. They killed all the people of Midian and killed their kings. There were five kings: Evi, Rekem, Zur, Hur, and Reba. Balaam son of Beor was killed in the fighting—he was a prophet and had advised the king of Midian to send women against the army of the children of Israel to corrupt them, and so Moses had become enraged. God commanded Moses to divide the spoils among the children of Israel and to take from them one item of every fifty and set it aside for God, to give it to the children of Aaron. Then God commanded him to dispatch the children of Israel to Syria to fight the people who were there. So he dispatched a large army. They began traveling little by little, encamping and saying, "We are afraid of the giants"—and they stayed in the mountains of Seir. So God said to Moses: "The children of Israel have disobeyed my command. Let them therefore buy food at a price, and let them now be subject to those who used to be subject to them." This took place after Moses had killed Sihon, the king of the Amorites, and had declared his land lawful booty.[147]

In the fortieth year of their stay in the wilderness, which is the desert of Sinai, God revealed to Moses: "I am going to take Aaron to myself. Bring him up the mountain so that my angels can come to take his spirit."[148] So Moses took his brother Aaron by the hand, and when he brought him up the mountain—no one was with him except Aaron's son Eleazar—and arrived atop the mountain, there was a bed there with some garments on it. Moses said to him, "My brother, put on these clean garments, which God has prepared for you to meet him
in." So Aaron put them on. | Then he stretched out on the bed and died, and 1:41
Moses prayed over him. When the children of Israel did not see Aaron, they

144 Cf. Numbers 11:4–35.

145 Added by the Leiden editor. The sending of the spies is based on Numbers 13.

146 Cf. Numbers 31.

147 Cf. Numbers 21:21–32.

148 Cf. Numbers 20:23–29; 33:38–39.

raised a clamor and said, "Where is Aaron?" Moses said to them, "God took him to himself." They were disquieted. Aaron had been beloved among them and gentle toward them. God therefore raised him up for them on the bed, so that they saw his face and they knew that he had died.[149] At that time Aaron was one hundred twenty-three years old. He had four children: Nadab, Abihu, Eleazar, and Ithamar. Nadab and Abihu passed away while he was still alive, and Eleazar and Ithamar remained. Eleazar took the place of Aaron, officiating in the tent of meeting.

Moses summoned Joshua son of Nun and said to him before the children of Israel: "Go, and make strong your heart, for you shall bring the children of Israel into the land of the descendants of Canaan, which God has bequeathed to them. Give this Torah to the priests of the sons of Levi, who have been caring for the ark of the presence. Revere God's dwelling, and keep His commandments, which He has set out clearly for you in the Torah." He enjoined them to follow what is in it, and he blessed them.

Part of what God commanded the children of Israel by the tongue of Moses was the following:

> Remember the day when you stood before God, when God said to me, "Assemble this people before me, that I may make them to hear my word, so that they will fear me all the days of their lives."[150] You stood at the foot of the mountain, and the mountain was burning with fire to the heart of the heavens. God spoke to me from the midst of the fire; you heard the voice, but you did not see the likeness. God commanded you to learn the Ten Verses.[151] He commanded me to teach you the statutes and the ordinance for you to observe in the land to which you are going. Keep watch over yourselves, and make no idols, the likeness of male or female,
> 1:42 of anything | that creeps on the ground, or of anything in the sea. Do not raise your heads to the heavens to worship the stars.
>
> God has sworn that I shall not enter the good land. I shall die in this land and not cross the Jordan, but you will cross over and come into the good land that God has given to you as an inheritance. Do not stray from

149 Cf. Ginzberg, *Legends of the Jews*, 3:320–327, for the Jewish legends about the death of Aaron. According to one of these, when the Israelites refused to believe that Aaron was dead—they suspected that Moses or Eleazar had murdered him—God commanded the angels to raise Aaron's bier in the air so that all might see how peacefully he had died. The same detail is incorporated into an Islamic account in al-Ṭabarī, *Taʾrīkh*, 1:501–503.

150 Cf. Deuteronomy 4:10 ff.

151 See note 131 above.

the covenant of God your Lord, which He made with you, by making idols. Do not do evil deeds before your God, if you have come into the good land; for, if you disobey, you will soon perish and be dispersed among the peoples. If you serve what human hands make of wood and stone, they will not see; you will pray, and your prayer will not be heard. But God, who is compassionate to you, will hear your voices.

It is not fitting for anyone who has heard from God the like of what you have heard, or who has seen the like of what you have seen, to disobey God. You have seen what God did to the people of Egypt while you watched. God is the Lord; there is no other than He, who made you to see His fire and to hear His voice. He loved your forefathers and chose their descendants. He destroyed for you a people who were greater and mightier than you. God will bring you into the good land and will give it to you as an inheritance. So keep His statutes that He has commanded you and enjoined upon you, that He may do good to you and to your descendants after you and that your days in the land may be many.

Obey God's commandment that He has commanded you; do not turn from it to the right or to the left. Travel every path that your Lord has commanded you, that He may do good to you. Love God with all your hearts, with your determination and your mind.[152] Tell your children of these things, and perform them. Recite them in your houses, put them as a sign between your eyes, and write them in your dwellings. God will give you | large towns that you did not build, houses full of goods that 1:43
you did not fill up, stone-lined wells that you did not dig, and vineyards and olive trees that you did not plant. So do not forget God; fear Him, serve Him, swear by His name, and do not follow any other god. Beware of God's anger, which will destroy you from the face of the earth, and do not betray God: obey His commandment, and do what is good and true.

Remember when you were slaves of Pharaoh, but God brought you out with a strong hand and with wondrous great signs that drove Pharaoh and his men to destruction before your eyes. God says to you: "I will give you the good land and power over the peoples who are before you. I will grant you victory over the Hittites, the Girgashites, the Amorites, the Canaanites, the Perezzites, the Hivites, and the Jebusites[153]—these seven nations who are more numerous and stronger than you." And when God

152 Reading with M, *bālikum*, for ed. Leiden, *mālikum* (your wealth).

153 The transmission of these names is quite uncertain in the MSS. M reads: "the Giants (*al-Jabbārīn*), the Khurāsānians, the Jordanians, the Canaanites, the ʿIrāzians, the Ḥarrānians, and the Nablusīs." Ed. Leiden corrects on the basis of Deuteronomy 7:1.

grants you victory over them, strike them and stone them; show them no mercy, and grant them no covenant. Do not marry your daughters to them, lest they become a stumbling block for you and turn your children away from me, so that they serve a god other than me, and my anger grows strong against you, so that I quickly destroy you. But break up their idols, cut down their altars, destroy their offerings and set them on fire. If you heed my commandment and keep my judgments, I will preserve your blessings for you and the covenant that I made with your fathers. I will multiply you, and I will make your seed and your livestock fruitful.

Make over to God a share in your wealth. Assist the orphan from it, the widow, the poor, the weak, and the one living with you who has no farmland.

When you judge between two, act justly. Do not accept bribes, for a
1:44 bribe | blinds the eyes of the arbitrators.[154] You shall not plant a tree by an altar. You shall not sacrifice an offering of a bull or ram on which there is a blemish.[155] Kill anyone who makes idols to be worshipped instead of God. If it is reported to you that someone is worshipping the sun, the moon, the stars, or any of the luminaries, make inquiry about him. If you learn that it is true, stone him to death with rocks.

In cases involving the death penalty, do not accept the testimony of one person, but[156] the testimony of two or three witnesses. When the witnesses testify against someone subject to the death penalty, let the witnesses appear and let them stretch out their hands toward the one who is to be killed. Whenever the judgment is too difficult for you, refer to the learned and the priests.

Whoever kills a man accidentally without intending it, let him flee from the avenger of blood, so he cannot reach him and so that you do not shed the blood of an innocent man.[157] Any man who kills an innocent man intentionally shall be put to death, but you shall not put anyone to death until testimony against him is furnished before the learned man or the judge.[158] If the judge discovers that someone has given false testimony, it shall be done to the witness as he intended to do to the one against

154 Cf. Deuteronomy 16:19.

155 Cf. Deuteronomy 17:1 ff.

156 Emending MSS *wa-lā* (and not, nor) to *wa-lākin* (but) as suggested by ed. Leiden. Cf. Deuteronomy 17:6.

157 Cf. Deuteronomy 19:1–7.

158 Reading *aw* (or) with M; ed. Leiden *wa-* (and).

whom the testimony was given: life for life, eye for eye, hand for hand, and foot for foot.[159]

When you go to war against a people and come to their town, first call them to peace.[160] If they accept your offer, levy a tribute on them. If they do not surrender, you shall kill everyone who carries a weapon, but you shall not destroy the town's trees.

God said to Moses:[161] When you go out to fight your enemy, and God allows you to prevail over them, and you see among the captives a woman whom you desire to take for yourself, bring her into your house: uncover her head, cut her nails, remove from her the clothes in which she was captured, and lodge her in your house for three months to weep | for her 1:45
father and her mother; then regard her as lawfully yours. If you dislike her after you have cohabited with her, send her away. You shall not sell her, nor shall you accept a price for her after you have lain with her.

Any son who rebels against his father,[162] does not obey him, and does not accept his command, let his father bring him out to the elders of his people,[163] and let them stone him, that the evil and the abomination[164] may depart from you and that his likes among the children of Israel may beware.

If anyone of you finds a stray, a ewe or a bull or a donkey that has strayed from its owner, let him return it to its owner; and if he does not find him, let him pen it up at his own house until its owner arrives.[165]

You shall not wear garments woven of cotton and wool together. Put fringes on the ends of your garments.[166]

Any man who casts aspersions at his wife and accuses her of immorality, and it is not true of her, let him pay a fine of a hundred dirhams,[167] and she shall be his wife forever. But if his accusation against her is true, let her be stoned.

---

159 Cf. Deuteronomy 19:16–21.

160 Cf. Deuteronomy 20:10 ff.

161 Cf. Deuteronomy 21:10 ff.

162 Cf. Deuteronomy 21:18 ff.

163 Reading with M, *shaʿbihi* (of his people); ed. Leiden has *sabʿa* (seven).

164 Sic ed. Leiden (*faẓīʿa*); M reads *qaṭīʿa*, severance (of kinship ties).

165 Cf. Deuteronomy 22:1–3.

166 Cf. Deuteronomy 22:11–12.

167 Deuteronomy 22:19 specifies a fine of 100 shekels. Al-Yaʿqūbī has substituted the corresponding Islamic coin.

Any man who is found committing adultery with a woman who has a husband, let them both be killed.[168] But any man who overpowers a woman against her will, let the man be killed. Any man who lies with a girl who is under the guardianship of her father, and he deflowers her, and he loves her, let him give her father fifty silver shekels, and she shall be his wife forever; he shall not send her away.

It is not permitted for a man to touch a woman whom his father has touched, neither shall he look upon her nakedness. A man in a state of uncleanness shall not enter one of God's mosques. Do not charge usury for silver or for gold. When you make a vow, do not postpone its fulfillment. Keep a promise, when you have made a covenant to someone, and do not break the promise, for God loves him who keeps his promise.

Avoid anyone who has leprosy, and stay far from him.[169] You shall not withhold the wage of a hired man.[170] You shall not punish a father for the
1:46 sin of his son, or a son for the sin | of his father. Pay the alms[171] from your wealth and your harvests to the religious official as an offering to God, and give to the poor, the widows, the orphans, the destitute, and the travelers.

When you enter the good land, make an altar for the sanctuary of smooth stones. And let the religious authorities of the children of Israel say: "Cursed be anyone who leads a blind man astray from the way. Cursed be anyone who gives an unjust judgment against the poor, the orphan, or the widow. Cursed be anyone who lies with his father's wife. Cursed be anyone who lies with an animal. Cursed be anyone who lies with his sister or his mother. Cursed be anyone who lies with his wife's mother. Cursed be anyone who slanders[172] his brother in secret. Cursed be anyone who takes a bribe to kill an innocent soul wrongfully. Cursed be anyone who does not keep God's commandment."

---

168 Cf. Deuteronomy 22:22 ff.

169 Cf. Deuteronomy 24:8–9.

170 Cf. Deuteronomy 24:14 ff.

171 *Zakāh*, the word used here, is used regularly for the alms that Muslims are obliged to give to the community for the upkeep of the poor. The word translated as "religious official" is *ḥabr*, which can be applied to any religious scholar, but in later Christian usage applies to high authorities such as a bishop; one might think of a "chief priest." However, in the next paragraph, the word in its plural form, *aḥbār*, corresponds to "the Levites" in Deuteronomy 27:14; and this may be the intended meaning here.

172 Literally, "who eats the flesh of his brother."

> Then Moses said to them, "I have transmitted to you God's ordinances and acquainted you with His commandment; so follow it and do it.[173] I am one hundred twenty years old, and my death is approaching. Here is Joshua the son of Nun, who shall be in charge among you after me. Listen to him and obey his command, for he will judge rightfully among you. Cursed be anyone who opposes him and disobeys him."

There were seven months between Aaron's death and the coming of death to Moses. Then Moses ascended Mt. Nebo. He looked toward Syria, and God said to him, "This is the land that I guaranteed to Abraham, Isaac, and Jacob that I would give to their descendants. I have let you see it with your own eyes, but you shall not enter it." Moses died in that place; Joshua son of Nun buried him, but no one knows where his grave is.[174]

The Prophets and Kings of the Israelites after Moses[175]

It came to pass that when Moses' death was imminent, God, may He be glorified and exalted, commanded him to bring Joshua son of Nun—Joshua son of Nun was of the tribe of Joseph son of Jacob—into the tent of meeting, sanctify him, and lay his hand on his body, | that his blessing might pass into him, and 1:47
commission him to take his place after him among the children of Israel. Moses did this; and so, when Moses died, Joshua arose among the children of Israel. He came out of the wilderness one day after the death of Moses—some of the People of the Book say it was thirty days—and went into Syria. The giants were there, the offspring of Amalek son of Lud son of Shem son of Noah.[176] The first of them to reign as king was al-Samayda' son of Hawbar.[177] He came from the land of Tihāma[178] into Syria intending to raid the children of Israel, but Joshua

173 Cf. Deuteronomy 31.

174 Cf. Deuteronomy 34.

175 This section and the sections following, until the section on "The Messiah, Jesus son of Mary" (ed. Leiden, 1:46–73), have been translated and annotated by R. Y. Ebied and L. R. Wickham as, "Al-Yaʿḳūbī's Account of the Israelite Prophets and Kings."

176 The Amalekites are mentioned in Numbers 13:28–29.

177 Cf. al-Yaʿqūbī, 1:253, where al-Samaydaʿ is said to have gone to Syria after a failed attempt to wrest control of Mecca and the Kaʿba from the tribe of Jurhum. The story is also told in al-Masʿūdī, *Murūj*, 1:56 (§ 91), 2:165 (§ 945–946), and 2:263 (§ 1147).

178 Tihāma is the Red Sea coast of the Arabian peninsula, loosely including Mecca.

son of Nun dispatched someone against him who killed him. A group of his father's sons arose after him, but Joshua killed them.

Joshua traveled until he reached al-Balqāʾ, where he encountered a man called Balak, after whom al-Balqāʾ was named.[179] They began to go out to do battle with him, but Joshua could not kill a single one of their men. He asked about this and was told that in Balak's city there was a woman astrologer who would turn her pudendum toward the sun and make calculations. When she was finished, the devices would be shown to her,[180] and no one whose time was up would go out on that day. So Joshua made two prostrations[181] and prayed that God would set the sun back one hour, and it was set back one hour for him. Her calculation therefore became confused for her, and she said to Balak, "Consider what they are asking of you, and give it to them, for my calculation has become confused for me." He said, "Examine your instruments carefully, and get something out of them, for there will be no truce without a fight." So she examined the devices without knowing what she was doing, due to the confusion of the matter for her, and they were slaughtered as no people had ever been slaughtered. They asked Joshua for a truce, but he refused it to them until they would hand the woman over to him. Balak said, "I will not hand her over." She said, "Hand me over to him." So he handed her over to him, and he offered a truce. She said to him, "Do you find anything in what was sent down to your master about the killing of women?" He said, "No." She said, "Then I hereby enter your religion." He said, "Go to live in another city." And he settled
1:48 her in another | city.

After Joshua son of Nun conquered al-Balqāʾ, the children of Israel engaged in much whoring and wine drinking. They lay with the women, and fornication

---

179 Al-Balqāʾ was one of the Arabic names for what is now called Jordan. Al-Yaʿqūbī has amalgamated into one narrative the Moabite king Balak (Bālaq in Arabic) from Numbers 22–24, the woman astrologer (an echo of the prostitute Rahab who plays a part in the capture of Jericho) from Joshua 6, and the miraculous stopping of the sun at the battle against the Amorites at Gibeon from Joshua 10.

180 Sic ed. Leiden, but there is a textual problem. M reads, *ʿuriḍat ʿalayhā l-khayl*, "the *horsemen* would be shown to her." But there is no subsequent mention of horsemen, and no soldier, horse or foot, was being killed. Ed. Leiden, following C, which clearly indicates that the first letter of the last word is *ḥ*, not *kh*, reads *al-ḥiyal* (the devices), which accords with her subsequently being brought "her instruments" (*āla*). The "devices" presumably are astronomical instruments, although it is just possible that the sense is that the *strategies* (another sense of *ḥiyal*) were submitted to her for approval.

181 The term used for a prostration, *rakʿa*, is the standard Islamic liturgical terminology.

increased among them. This was grievous to Joshua son of Nun. He told them to fear God and warned them of His chastisement, but they did not take the warning. So God sent a revelation to Joshua son of Nun: "If you wish, I will give their enemy power over them; or, if you wish, I will destroy them by means of droughts; or, if you wish, by means of a quick, speedy death." He said: "They are the children of Israel. I would not have You give their enemy power over them, or that they should perish by means of droughts, but rather by means of a quick death." So the plague fell upon them, and seventy thousand died at one time.[182] Joshua's days among the children of Israel after the death of Moses son of Amram were twenty-seven years.

After Joshua son of Nun, Cushan the Infidel[183] was over the children of Israel; he remained among them for eight years. After Cushan came Othniel son of Kenaz, Caleb's brother, of the tribe of Judah son of Jacob, for [forty] years. When the wrongdoing and insolence of the children of Israel had increased, God gave Cushan,[184] the Mighty One of Moab, power over them. When Othniel became ruler, he killed Cushan and ruled for forty years.

Then the children of Israel reverted to unbelief, and God therefore gave Eglon king of Moab power over them for fifteen years. When they repented, God sent to them a man named Ehud[185] son of Gera of the tribe of Ephraim, and he killed Eglon king of Moab. He used to fight with his left hand and his right hand, so they named him "the man with two right hands." He was the first to forge | two-edged swords; before him swords had backs. In his time al- 1:49

182 Al-Yaʿqūbī (or his source) has combined Numbers 25 (a plague visited on the Israelites because of their sexual relations with Moabite women) and 2 Samuel 24:12 (David, in the wake of displeasing God by taking a census, was offered the choice of three punishments: three years of famine, three months of military defeats, or three days of plague; he chose three days of plague, and 70,000 people died). Cf. also al-Mas'ūdī, *Murūj*, 1:57 (§ 92), for a version of the plague closer to Numbers 25, omitting the motif of the threefold choice, but introducing Joshua (who is absent from Numbers 25).

183 Cushan (M, Dūshān) the Infidel (Arabic, *al-Kufrī*) corresponds to Cushan-rishathaim (Cushan of the Two Evils) of Judges 3:7–11. Cf. al-Ṭabarī, *Taʾrīkh*, 1:545–546; al-Masʿūdī, *Murūj*, 1:57–58 (§ 93–94).

184 Possibly a different person than Cushan the Infidel: M reads Kūshan here, not Dūshān.

185 The MSS read Ahūr, which Houtsma corrected to Ahūd, based on the similarity between *r* and *d* in Arabic script. However, Nöldeke, in his review of Houtsma's edition (ZDMG 38:154) noted that the MSS reading in this case corresponded to the reading of the Syriac Peshitta, which renders Hebrew Ēhūd as Āhūr. This, Nöldeke argued, was evidence that al-Yaʿqūbī's biblical citations go back to a translation made from the Peshitta.

Tabniyya[186] was built in Syria. In the twenty-fifth year of Ehud's rule, the fourth millennium was complete.[187]

After Ehud, the children of Israel relapsed, and God therefore gave Jabin king of Canaan power over them for twenty years. Shamgar son of Anath had ruled the children of Israel before this and had killed six hundred of the Philistines. Then God had mercy on them and sent to them a man named Barak son of Abinoam of the tribe of Naphtali, and he ruled them for forty years.

Then the sons of Israel reverted to unbelief, and God therefore gave the people of Midian power over them for seven years. Then God had mercy on them and sent to them a man named Gideon son of Joash of the tribe of Manasseh, a righteous man.[188] It was he who attacked the Midianites by night and killed two hundred and eighty-five thousand of them. He ruled for forty years. After him, his son Abimelech son of Gideon ruled, but he was evil.[189] It was he who killed seventy of his brothers. He was killed by a woman: she threw a stone at him from atop the city gate and crushed him. He had ruled for three years.

Then Tola son of Puah of the tribe of Issachar ruled. He remained for twenty-three years. Then Gilead[190] of the tribe of Manasseh became ruler. He had thirty
1:50 sons who rode with him on thirty fillies. | His rule was for twenty-two years.

Then the children of Israel reverted to unbelief. God therefore gave the children of Ammon power over them for seventeen years. In his[191] time the city of Tyre in Syria was built. He[192] inflicted a severe punishment on them. Then God, exalted be He, had mercy on them and sent them a man of the people

---

186 Sic M (vocalization uncertain), apparently the name of a city. Ed. Leiden reads *al-baniyya*, with *al-baniyya* apparently to be taken as a proper noun. However, since *al-baniyya* normally refers to the Kaʿba in Mecca, the reading is probably corrupt. Below, at 1:50, al-Yaʿqūbī uses the formula, "In his days the city of … was built." This formula probably occurs here.

187 That is, 4,000 years since the creation of the world; cf. *Schatzhöhle*, 42, 174–175 (trans. Budge, 166). The account of Ehud can be compared to Judges 3:12–30; al-Ṭabarī, *Taʾrīkh*, 1:546; and al-Masʿūdī, *Murūj*, 1:58 (§ 95). Curiously, the RSV of Judges 3:15 calls Ehud "a left-handed man." The Hebrew, as was noted by W. M. Brinner in his translation of al-Ṭabarī, says "who bound up his left hand," but the word used for "bound up" came to mean "withered" in later Hebrew. See William M. Brinner, *The History of al-Ṭabarī, III*, 127n.

188 Cf. Judges 6–8.

189 Cf. Judges 9.

190 He is Jair the Gileadite of Judges 10:3.

191 The antecedent is unclear.

192 Again, the antecedent is unclear—the name of someone who persecuted the children of Israel may have fallen out.

of Gilead named Jephthah.[193] He killed forty-two thousand of the children of Israel of the people of Ephraim—he was of the tribe of Manasseh. His rule was for six years.

Then Ibzan, who was called Nahshon,[194] was over them for seven years. Then Elon, of the tribe of Zebulun, was over them for twenty years. Then for eight years Abdon[195] was over them. Then Alānkashas was over them, and he inflicted a severe punishment on them. He ruled them exceedingly harshly for forty years.[196] Then Samson was over them for twenty years. Then they remained with no one over them for twelve years. Then Eli the High Priest was over them for forty years.

Then Samuel the prophet was over them. He was the one whom God mentioned:[197] *When they said to a prophet of theirs, "Raise up for us a king, and we will fight in God's way."* When they said to the Prophet Samuel, "Ask God to raise up for us a king to fight His enemies," Samuel said, "You have no loyalty or sincere intention." They said, "Not so!" He said, *"Verily, God has raised up Ṭālūt for*

193 Cf. Judges 11–12. Al-Yaʿqūbī's condensation creates the impression that God in His mercy sent the children of Israel someone who killed 42,000 of them. The account in Judges makes it clear that Jephthah first defeated the Ammonites. Only then did the people of Ephraim, chafing under his rule, rebel, whereupon Jephthah and his Gileadites killed 42,000 of them.

194 For Ibzan of Judges 12:8 (Hebrew *Ibṣān*) the original reading of al-Yaʿqūbī seems to have been *Abīṣān*, which is how the Hebrew consonantal text was vocalized by the Septuagint (B: *Abaissan*) and the Syriac (*Abīṣān*). One cannot explain the identification of him with Nahshon (the name occurs in Exodus 6:23 as that of Aaron's brother-in-law); however, the same wording ("Abīṣān who is Naḥshōn") occurs also in *Schatzhöhle*, 42, 176–177 (trans. Budge, 168), and Nahshon is mentioned in al-Masʿūdī, *Murūj*, 1:59 (§ 96).

195 M reads ʿAkrān, which corresponds to the Peshitta reading ʿAkrān in Judges 12:13, where the Hebrew reads ʿAbdōn. Nöldeke, in his review of Houtsma's edition (ZDMG 38:154) adduced this as further evidence that al-Yaʿqūbī's biblical citations go back to a translation made from the Peshitta.

196 No source is known for the name of this foreign ruler (this is the probable reading, but the *n* could be *b, t, th*, or *y*). In Judges, forty years of Philistine rule intervene between Abdon and the coming of Samson, and this is echoed by al-Ṭabarī, *Taʾrīkh*, 1:547 and al-Masʿūdī, *Murūj*, 1:59 (§ 96), without mention of any name.

197 Qurʾān 2:246. The story of Saul (identified with the Qurʾānic Ṭālūt) synthesizes material from 1 Samuel 5–18 and from various passages of the Qurʾān (2:246–251 and 9:91–92). The name Ṭālūt is usually explained as from the Arabic root *ṭ-w-l*, "to be tall," referring to Saul's great height, cf. 1 Samuel 9:2, "He stood head and shoulders above everyone else." For a summary of the material on Saul in Islamic sources, see the article by R. Firestone in EI^2, s.v. Ṭālūt.

you as king,"[198]—his name was Saul. They said: "By God, he is not of the tribe of kingship and prophecy. He is not of the offspring of Levi or of Judah; he is only of the tribe of Benjamin." Samuel said, "It is not for you to choose over God."
1:51 So Samuel summoned | Saul, that is, Ṭālūt, and said to him: "The Lord has commanded me to raise you up as king over the children of Israel. God commands you to take vengeance on Amalek. Therefore, destroy Amalek and everything that is his. Spare him nothing: neither man, nor woman, nor nursling; neither calf, nor sheep, nor camel, nor donkey."

He gave this commission to the whole assembly, whose number was four hundred thousand fighters. So Saul went against Amalek. He killed Amalek's forces and captured Agag, the king of the Amalekites, but he kept him alive and spared him. They refrained from destroying any of the cattle or sheep and kept them for themselves. God therefore sent a revelation to Samuel: "Saul has disobeyed me; he has not destroyed Amalek and everything his kingdom contains." So Samuel said to Saul, "God is angry at what you have done." Saul therefore summoned Agag and said, "What is the bitterest death?" "Having one's throat cut," he said. So Saul cut his throat.[199] Then Saul said to Samuel, "Come with me, so that we can bow down before God, who is exalted." But Samuel refused. So Saul grabbed Samuel's cloak and tore it. Samuel said, "Thus will your kingdom be torn."

Support[200] was taken away from Saul, and an evil spirit entered him. He would become troubled, and his color would change. His companions said to him, "If only a man of good voice, a poet, could be brought to you, to recite for you when this evil spirit enters you." So he sent a message to Jesse: "Send your son David to me." So he sent him to him, and whenever Saul was possessed,[201] David took his harp in hand and recited to its accompaniment, and the evil spirit would leave him.

Then the pagans[202] who were there in the time of Saul gathered together, and he fought them—they were star-worshippers. When Saul went out with

---

198 Qur'ān 2:247.

199 Cf. 1 Samuel 15:32–33, where it is Samuel who summons Agag and kills him.

200 That is, divine support: Arabic, *nuṣrah* (aid, assistance), applied in the Qur'ān mostly to God's assistance. Note that 1 Samuel 16:14 says explicitly that "the spirit of the Lord departed from Saul, and an evil spirit from the Lord tormented him." The Arabic phrase used here for "evil spirit," is strange: instead of the expected *rūḥ sūʾ*, one has *rīḥ sūʾ*, which normally would mean, "an evil wind."

201 Ed. Leiden reads *khuniqa* (was choked), but M reads *kh.b.q*, which is easily corrected to give *khabila*, which is what has been translated.

202 Arabic, *ḥunafāʾ*. In Islamic usage, this term designates monotheists who are not members

his armies to fight them, a man came out from among them whose height was five cubits; his name was Goliath, which is Jālūt.[203] He said, "Let one of your men stand forth for me." David therefore said to Saul, "I will stand forth for him." Saul said to David, | "Go, and may the Lord be with you." So David took a stick 1:52
and five stones and went out to Goliath. When Goliath saw him, he disdained him and said to him, "Have you come out against a dog with sticks and stones?" David said to him, "To one worse[204] than a dog." Then he took a stone from his pouch and hurled it at him, so that the stone sank into the forehead of Jālūt and he fell down. David ran up to him, took his sword, cut off his head, and made good his return. Goliath's army was routed, and the joy of the sons of Judah was great; Saul, however, was grieved. Envious of David, he banished him from his presence and made him chief of a thousand men; he spared him because of the standing of the sons of Judah.[205] David married Saul's daughter Michal.

Intent on killing David, Saul would dispatch him to fight the pagan star-worshippers, but God would grant him victory. So Saul determined to kill him without any subterfuge. David therefore fled to Samuel the prophet and gave him a report about Saul. Saul kept trying to kill David until David finally fled and passed by Achish, king of Gath. When Achish saw him, he recognized him, but David tricked him into releasing him. He went to Sāriʿ[206] and encamped there.

When Saul learned that David had eluded him, he killed the priests who performed the sacred rites. He said, "You knew about him, but you did not inform me." Saul then went out to pursue David, and finally he caught up with him. David had entered a cave. When Saul came to the cave, he dismounted to relieve himself and went into the cave, not knowing that David was in it. David got up and hid. His companions said to him: "David, kill him! God has put him in your power." He said, "I am not one who would do such a thing."

---

of the Jewish or Christian communities; here, however, it is used in the sense of "pagans," the normal meaning of its Syriac cognate *ḥanpē* (gentiles, heathens). Here and subsequently the word refers to the Philistines.

203 Jālūt is the name given to Goliath in Qurʾān 2:249–251. For a discussion of possible sources of the name, see the article by G. Vajda in *EI*², s.v. Djālūt.

204 Reading with M, *asharr*; ed. Leiden has *ashadd* (stronger), a copyist's error that makes little sense.

205 Reading with M, *wa-baqqāhu li-makāni banī yahūdhā*. Ed. Leiden, *wa-nafāhu bi-makāni banī yahūdhā* (he exiled him in the place of the sons of Judah).

206 Cf. 1 Samuel 22:5, "and went into the forest of Hereth." Al-Yaʿqūbī's source followed the reading of the Septuagint, "and he stayed in the city of Sarich."

The prophet Samuel died, and the children of Israel assembled. They grieved and mourned him for thirty days.

Saul went out to fight the pagans. When the battle between them became fierce, they routed the children of Israel, many of whom were killed. Meanwhile, David son of Jesse, with his men from the tribe of Judah, was battling the Amalekites. When all the sons of Israel had been routed, leaving Saul isolated,
1:53 he and his sons set to | fighting by themselves. Then he said to his companion
who was carrying his weapons, "Take your sword and kill me with it, lest these uncircumcised ones kill me and make sport with me." He did not do it; so Saul took his own sword, set it upright, and threw himself on it. He died, and his three sons were killed. Saul's reign was forty years.

David

When Saul, who is Ṭālūt, died, David returned from fighting Amalek and went to Ziglag. He stayed there two days. Then the report of Saul's death reached him, and he was saddened and grieved openly. David became king over the tribe of Judah. David had a number of wives who bore him children.[207] His eldest child was Amnon, whose mother was Ahinoam.[208] The second was Dalūyā son of Abigail. The third was Absalom son of Maacah. The fourth was Ornia son of Daḥāt. The fifth was Shephatiah son of Abital. And the sixth one was Nathan son of Eglah. These six were from six wives. Michal, the daughter of Saul, bore no children. She fled from David to the companions of Saul.

The children of Israel from the tribes assembled to make David king. They made him king after seven years during which he ruled over the tribe of Judah exclusively, until all the tribes of the children of Israel made him king.

David moved his residence[209] to the city of Zion, which is Jerusalem,[210] and there he built a residence and married wives. After he became king, there

207 Cf. the lists in 2 Samuel 3:2–5 and 1 Chronicles 3:1–4. The names in al-Yaʿqūbī's list are closer to the Septuagint than to the Masoretic Hebrew text. The differences can be accounted for—mostly—by miscopying, but some are hard to explain: Shītamūn for Ahinoam, Dalūyā for Chileab, Ornia for Adonijah, Daḥāt for Haggith, and Nathan for Ithream.

208 M, C: Shītamūn. Nöldeke (*ZDMG* 38:154) explained this as derived (by miscopying, perhaps) from an original (A)shīnūm, which, if one assumes "an Egyptian pronunciation of Greek χ as *sh*," corresponds to the Septuagint form of the name: Ἀχινοάμ.

209 Reading with M, *wa-tanazzala*, instead of ed. Leiden, *wa-yanzilu* (and he used to dwell). For this meaning of *tanazzala*, see al-Ṭabarī, *Glossarium*, DX.

210 Arabic, *Bayt al-Maqdis*.

were born to him:[211] Shammua, Shobab, Nathan, | Solomon, Ibhar, Elishua, 1:54
Nepheg, Japhia, Elishama, Eliada, and Eliphelet. David's children were many; his kingdom was strong, and the children of Israel honored him.

When the pagans heard that David had become king over the children of Israel, they assembled to fight him. David fought them and made great slaughter among them, until he had exterminated them. When he finished fighting them, he loaded the Ark of the Shekhina onto a calf[212] to bring it into Jerusalem, and he prepared a meal for the children of Israel, for their men and women.

The prophet Nathan lived at that time. God sent a revelation to Nathan:[213] "Say to my servant David, 'Build me a house; for I have made you king over the children of Israel after you were in the sheepfold, and I have killed your enemies.'" So Nathan the prophet spoke to David, and it was of great importance in David's heart. It is said that Nathan was David's son.[214]

David fought the pagans and defeated them.[215] He fought the people of Moab and defeated them. He fought Hadadezer, king of Zobah, and defeated him. He took for himself a thousand chariots and seven thousand horses.

The people of Syria and Damascus gathered with Hadadezer to fight David. He killed twenty-two thousand of them and gained mastery over the land, so that the Syrians all became servants to him. Then they all assembled to make war on David. He dispatched his sister's son Joab and Abishai his brother[216] against them. David himself went out, crossed the Jordan River, and killed forty thousand of the enemy. He killed Ashan,[217] the enemy leader. Then he dispatched his sister's son Joab to the lowlands of Syria to fight the Ammonites, while he went back to Jerusalem.

---

211 Compare the list in 2 Samuel 5:14.

212 Sic. However, the Arabic word used here, *ʿijl*, can be read as *ʿajal*, a plural of *ʿajala*, (cart). Cf. 2 Samuel 6:3: "They carried the ark of God on a new cart." The reading *ʿajal* could also mean "haste."

213 Cf. 2 Samuel 7. In the biblical account, David initiates the project of building a temple. Nathan at first welcomes it, but receives a revelation overnight that the temple must be built not by David, but by his son.

214 There is no indication of such a relationship in the biblical text. The idea may have arisen from the presence of the name Nathan in the list of David's children.

215 For David's campaigns against the Philistines (the "pagans"), the Moabites, and Hadadezer, see 2 Samuel 8. The numbers (1,000 chariots and 7,000 horse) agree with the Septuagint, rather than with the Massoretic text.

216 Abishai was Joab's brother.

217 2 Samuel 10:18, Shobach. As the Septuagint has a similar name (Sōbak), the reading here is probably due to a copyist.

1:55 David arose to walk on his roof, | and suddenly he caught sight of Bathsheba daughter of Eliam,[218] the wife of Uriah son of Hanan the Hittite. He inquired about her and was told of her situation and that she was the wife of Uriah son of Hanan. He fell in love with her. He sent a message to Uriah son of Hanan and had him come to him. Afterward, he wrote to his sister's son Joab: "Put Uriah at the front of the cavalry to fight." Joab put him forward; he fought and was killed. David then sent for Uriah's wife, married her, and fathered a child by her. God therefore sent the two angels to him, as He has related in His scripture.[219] And He sent to him the prophet Nathan, who said to him, "David, did God not command you to be just in judgment, decide by the truth, and not follow caprice?"[220] He said, "Certainly." So Nathan said: "Now there were two men living in the same city. One was rich, the other poor. The rich man had much cattle and livestock; the poor man had nothing but one little lamb that he had reared. It grew up with him and with his children. It ate of his food, drank from his cup, and slept in his lap. Then a guest descended upon the rich man. But the rich man took none of his own cattle or sheep; he took the poor man's lamb and prepared it for his guest." David became angry and said, "He deserves to die and to pay for that lamb sevenfold."[221] So Nathan the prophet said to David: "You are the man who has done this. The Lord your God says to you, 'I am the one who made you king over the children of Israel after you were a herder of sheep. I rescued you from the hands of Saul, and I gave you the house of Israel and the house of Judah; and yet you have done this. I will assuredly take vengeance on you by means of the worst of your offspring. I will give him power over you and over your wives.'" This was grievous to David, so Nathan said to him, "God has forgiven you; you will not die, but He will take vengeance on you by means
1:56 of the worst of your sons." And God informed him that his child, whom | the woman bore, would die. David grieved, and his grief became intense. The boy fell ill, and when his sickness worsened, David fasted and stood up to pray; he would weep and roll on the ground with his hair disheveled. When the boy died, David's attendants found it hard to inform him of it, but finally he heard their

218 The form of the name used by al-Yaʿqūbī is similar to that of the Septuagint (2 Samuel 11:3): Beersheba (Greek Bērsabee) daughter of Eliab.

219 Cf. Qurʾān 38:20 ff. In the Qurʾānic version of the story, the rich man and the poor man in Nathan's parable are cast as two angels who appear to David in the guise of two brothers, one rich and one poor, one of whom has wronged the other as in Nathan's parable, and David gives his judgment. No context is given for the episode, and Nathan does not appear.

220 Echoing Qurʾān 38:25; the rest of the account of Nathan's words follows 2 Samuel 12.

221 "Sevenfold" follows the Septuagint version of 2 Samuel 12:6; the Massoretic text has "fourfold."

whispering and he knew. He washed his face, put on his garments, sat in his accustomed place, and called for his meal. He said: "I grieved only before he perished. Now, however, my grief will not bring him back to me; rather, I shall go to him." Then he lay with Bathsheba; she bore a male child, and he named him Solomon.

Then David's son Absalom killed his brother Amnon[222] because he suspected Amnon with regard to a full sister of his. So he killed him and rebelled against David. Absalom was large of body and had abundant hair. David sent someone after him to bring him back, with the result that he returned. Then he rebelled a second time. David fled from him, walking on foot, until he ascended the pass of Mount Sinai. He was extremely hungry, until a man who had bread and oil with him caught up with him, and he ate some of it. Meanwhile, Absalom entered his father's city. He went to his house, took his father's concubines, and lay with them. He said, "God has made me king over the children of Israel." He went out with twelve thousand men and pursued David to kill him. David fled across the Jordan River. When he had crossed, a group of his companions rallied to him and a multitude from the villages. He dispatched Joab[223] to do battle with Absalom and said to him, "Take him for me alive and well." So they left and did battle with him. Absalom, who was on a mule, passed under a terebinth[224] tree and became caught in it, and his neck was broken. Joab shot three arrows into him and flung him into a cistern. When the report reached David, he grieved greatly over him. David then returned to his place.

After that Azla[225] came out against David, and with him there were mighty 1:57
warriors. David did battle with them and killed them. When he had killed them and God had saved him from them, he rose to bless God and to praise Him. In his blessing he said:[226]

222 Cf. 2 Samuel 13 for the story of Amnon's rape of his half-sister Tamar, the full sister of Absalom, and Absalom's revenge.

223 Ed. Leiden, "his son Joab," but the word *waladahu* (his son) is absent from M and is apparently a copyist's error. The note in ed. Leiden suggests emending to *walad ukhtihi* (his sister's son).

224 Arabic *buṭm*; the Hebrew (2 Samuel 18:9) *ʾēlā* is also a terebinth, but for some reason AV and RSV both render it as "oak," which is usually *ʾallōn*.

225 Sic. The name here originally may have been Barzillai, based on a confusion with Barzillai the Gileadite who fed David and his army during the revolt of Absalom (2 Samuel 17:27–29, 19:31–40). The leader of the revolt meant here is identified as Sheba son of Bichri in 2 Samuel 20:1.

226 Cf. 2 Samuel 22 = Psalm 18.

You, O Lord, I worship;
to You I make pure my love.
For You are my strength and my readiness,
my refuge and my savior.
After the agonies of death encompassed me,
and the misfortunes of destruction drew near and enclosed me,
I called upon You in my distress,
and asked for Your help, O my God.
You heard my voice and rescued me
from those who struck me by turns and persecuted me.
You became my helper;
You brought me out from distress to relief.
How just You are, O Lord!
How helpful to those who trust You!
Because there is no lord but You,
inspire me with power, and make me to see the right way.
Make my feet firm before You, and strengthen my arm.
Do not empower my enemies against me.
Give me the obedience of the children of Israel;
Make them submissive servants, and inspire me with your thanks.

When David praised God in these words, he raised up a voice so beautiful that no one had heard the like of it. When he recited the Psalms he used to say:[227]

Blessed is the man [...] who has not walked in the path of sinners,
and has not sat in the councils of scoffers.
But his desire is the law of God,
and he studies His law day and night.
He shall be like a tree planted beside water,
that brings forth its fruit in every season,
and its leaves do not fall away.
Not like this are the hypocrites in judgment,
or the sinners in the assembly of the righteous.
For God knows the way of the righteous,
but the way of the wicked will come to naught.

227 Psalm 1.

Then he would say:[228]

Praise God, whoever is in heaven;
let whoever is on high praise Him.
Let all His angels praise Him;
let all His hosts praise Him.
Let the sun and moon praise Him; 1:58
let the stars and the light praise Him.
Let the water above the heavens
give praise to the name of our Lord.
For He said to each thing, "Be," and it was;[229]
He created each thing and originated it.
He made them to last forever;
He set for each thing its measure.
He appointed them a limit and end,
that they should not exceed it.
Therefore let whoever is on earth praise God,
and fire and cold, snow and ice.
For He created the stormy wind by His word.

Praise God with a new song of praise
in the temple of the righteous.[230]
Let Israel rejoice in his Creator;
[sons of] Zion, magnify your Lord.
They praise His name with the tambourine,
the drum, and the harp.
They magnify Him,
because God rejoices in His law.
He gives help to the poor,
that the righteous may celebrate His favor.
They sing praise on their beds:
they magnify God with their throats,
with a two-edged sword in their hands;

228 Psalm 148.

229 The wording is closer to a frequently repeated formula in the Qur'ān (2:117, 3:47, 3:59, 6:73, 16:40, 19:35, 36:82, 40:68) than to Psalm 148:5.

230 Psalm 149. The word translated as "temple," is *masjid*, a mosque, but more generally any place of worship.

To triumph over the peoples,
  that the nations may be warned.
They fasten their kings in fetters,
  and their nobles in chains of iron,
That to them there may be done
  the judgment that was written.

Praise to God by all the righteous![231]
Praise Him in His sanctuary.
Praise Him in the heaven of His might.
Praise Him for His might and strength.
Praise Him for His majesty.
Praise Him with the sound of the stringed instrument.
Praise Him with the lyre and harp.
Praise Him with lutes and horn.
Praise Him with strings and long [sounds of the drum].[232]
Praise Him with resounding cymbals.
1:59 Praise Him with loud voices | and shouts.
Praise our Lord with pure praise, every being with breath.

Then David says at the end of the Psalms:[233]

I was the last of my brothers,
  a servant of my father's house.
I was the shepherd of my father's sheep,
  while my hand made the drum,
  and my fingers cut flutes.
Who is it who has told my Lord of me?
He is my Lord;
  it is He who heard my voice
  and sent His angels to me.
He took me away from my brothers' sheep:
  they were older and comelier than I,
  but my Lord was not pleased with them.
He sent me to meet Goliath's hosts.

---

231 Psalm 150.

232 The text is corrupt, the meaning uncertain.

233 What follows is Psalm 151 in the Septuagint; the RSV includes it in the Apocrypha.

When I saw him worshipping his idols,
He gave me victory over him:
I took his sword and cut off his head.

Then the children of Israel spoke evil of David, and God's anger became great against them.[234] God therefore ordered David to make a census of the children of Israel. He counted them and found them to be eight hundred thousand fighting men; those of the tribe of Judah numbered five hundred thousand men. Then God sent the prophet Hiram[235] to David, to say to him, "Say to David, 'Choose one of three things: a famine for seven years; or that you be given over to your enemies, and they overcome you for three months and deprive you of your authority; or that there be a plague for three days.'" David was distressed by this and said, "Better God than man!" So God gave death power over them, and in a single hour seventy thousand men died. David said: "Lord, it is I who have done wrong. What is the sin of these who are like beasts?" God then sent him a revelation, "Build a temple for me on the threshing floor of the Jebusite." So David went up the mountain and purchased the threshing floor for fifty shekels,[236] and there he built an altar. Then death turned away from the sons of Israel.

David had grown old, and his body had become weak.[237] He had a son named 1:60
Adonijah who won the support of Joab, the master of David's army, and some of David's generals. He said to them, "King David has become old, and I am the person most suited to take his place." When word of this reached David, he sent for Zadok the priest and Nathan the prophet and said to them: "Assemble the people of the kingdom. Mount my son Solomon on my mule, and seat him on my pulpit;[238] for God has appointed him head over the children of Israel, and

234 Cf. 2 Samuel 24. By making the cause of God's anger the evil that the Israelites spoke against David, al-Yaʿqūbī rationalizes a difficult biblical text. In 2 Samuel 24, God, having become angry against Israel for an unspecified reason, incites David to sin by conducting a census. The parallel text in 1 Chronicles 21 makes Satan the inciter of David.

235 In 2 Samuel 24:11, the prophet is named Gad. Unaccountably, the name of Hiram, the king of Tyre who in 1 Kings 5 supplies cedar wood for the construction of the temple, has been substituted here.

236 The Arabic replaces the Hebrew monetary unit, shekel, with something more familiar, but the reading of the MSS is uncertain. M reads *istākhā*, which ed. Leiden emends to *istārā*, a Persian unit of weight borrowed into Greek as *statēr*. The Syriac form is *estayrā* or *estārā*, which corresponds exactly to the Arabic (Sokoloff, *Syriac Lexicon*, 80).

237 Cf. 1 Kings 1.

238 The term in the text is *minbar*, the place of preaching in a mosque. Since both the Hebrew

God will magnify his rule and exalt his rank." So they went with Solomon; he ascended David's pulpit, and the people of the kingdom rallied to him. David said, "Thus did God inform me: that my son Solomon would become king before my very eyes." Solomon was twelve years old at the time.

Then David's illness grew worse, and so he made his testament to Solomon.[239] He said: "I am about to go the way of all the people of the earth. Carry out the commandments of the Lord your God. Keep His statutes, ordinances, and commandments which are in the Torah that was sent down to Moses son of Amram." David died when he was one hundred and twenty years old.[240] His reign was for forty years.

Solomon, the Son of David

When God took David, Solomon arose in his place as prophet and king. God subjected to him jinn and men, winds and clouds, birds and beasts; and, as He has recounted in His mighty Book, He gave him a mighty kingdom.[241]

Joab, the master of David's armies, and some of his companions, along with
1:61 Solomon's brothers, were inclined to undermine Solomon's reign. | Solomon therefore killed them to the last man, and he killed his brother Adonijah;[242] then Solomon's reign prospered, and his authority was established. He married the daughter of Pharaoh, king of Egypt, and brought her into David's house.[243]

Solomon assembled the children of Israel to offer sacrifice, and he offered a thousand victims. One night, Solomon saw as it were the Lord saying to him,

---

and the Greek use the ordinary word for a king's throne (*kissēʾ* and *thronos*, respectively), one is tempted to think that al-Yaʿqūbī or his immediate source had something in mind: perhaps a desire to emphasize that Solomon was a prophet, not merely a king. Muḥammad, for example, had a *minbar*, not a throne.

239 Cf. 1 Kings 2.

240 There is no biblical source for this number. 1 Chronicles 29:28 merely says, "He died in a good old age, full of days, riches, and honor." On the basis of 2 Samuel 5:4 ("David was 30 years old when he began to reign, and he reigned 40 years") one can infer that he was 70 years old at his death. Al-Ṭabarī, *Taʾrīkh*, 1:572, gives his lifespan as 100 years "according to accounts that came from the Messenger of God." He then mentions the figure of 70 according to "one of the People of the Book."

241 An echo of Qurʾān 4:54.

242 Cf. 1 Kings 2:13–25. Al-Yaʿqūbī gives the name of Solomon's half-brother Adonijah in its Greek form, Adonias.

243 Cf. 1 Kings 3:1.

"Ask whatever you like, that I may give it to you."[244] Solomon said: "Lord, you bestowed great favor on David and have made your servant Solomon king after him. Give me therefore a wise heart to judge justly among your servants and to understand good and evil." God said, "Because you have asked this, and have not asked for wealth, or asked for the lives of your enemies, or asked for long life, but have asked for wisdom to judge and decide with understanding, I have granted your request. I have given you an understanding and discerning heart, such as no one before you has had, or anyone after you will have. I have also given you what you did not ask for: wealth, swift horses, and honor. If you walk in my way, and keep my laws and commandments, as David your father kept them, I will lengthen your life and make your undertakings great."

Solomon would take his seat to pass judgment and make rulings among the children of Israel, and they marveled at his wise and just decisions and at his sayings and eloquence. Solomon had officers, ministers, scribes, and deputies.[245] His minister[246] was Zabud son of Nathan. In charge of his wars was Benaiah son of Jehoiada. His treasurer was Ahishar. Adoniram son of Abda was in charge of taxes. He had twelve deputies in charge of his expenditures, each in charge of a month's expenditure. His expenditures were paid by the tribes of the children of Israel. His outlay every day was thirty cors[247] of fine flour, sixty
cors of fine meal, ten | fattened oxen, twenty bulls, and one hundred sheep. He 1:62
had forty thousand tethering posts to which his animals were tethered. He was very fond of horses. God has related something about this.[248]

Solomon started to build the Holy House. He said: "God commanded my father David to build a house, but David was busied with wars. God therefore revealed to him, 'Your son Solomon shall build the house in my name.'" Solomon then sent for a delivery of pine wood and cypress wood. Then he built the Holy House of stone. He fitted it out, dressed it with wood on the inside, and had the wood carved. He made a gilded sanctuary for it, with golden utensils in it. Then he brought the ark of the presence up and put it into the sanctuary. In the ark were the two tablets that Moses had deposited.

---

244 Cf. 1 Kings 3:5–15.

245 Cf. 1 Kings 4.

246 Arabic, *wazīr*, which evokes the powerful figure of the Abbasid court. The Hebrew has *rēʿeh hammelek̲*, which the RSV renders as "king's friend." The Septuagint renders it as ἑταῖρος τοῦ βασιλέως (the king's companion).

247 Cf. 1 Kings 4:22. The cor (Hebrew *kōr*) was a large measure of capacity. The most common estimate is 6 U.S. bushels.

248 Cf. Qurʾān 38:32 ff.

When Solomon had set the ark of the presence in place, he stood before the sanctuary, with the throngs of the children of Israel having assembled.[249] He glorified and blessed God, and he praised Him for His favor in making him king over the children of Israel and in carrying out the building of the Holy House through him. The children of Israel were gathering to him, and he was saying: "Blessed and exalted be the Lord, who has given rest to Israel. His good words have been fulfilled; none of them that He spoke to His servant Moses has fallen away. We ask God our Lord to be with us, as He was with our fathers, and that He not reject us or forsake us. Rather, may He turn our hearts to Him, that we may travel on the way that He approves and that we may keep His laws, His covenants, His commandments, and His statutes, which He commanded our fathers. May He make our words to be close to Him and pleasing in His sight, and make our hearts submissive to Him and mindful of His bidding."

When Solomon finished building the Holy House, he made a feast. He
1:63 offered sacrifices at it and continued doing so for fourteen days, | having assembled the children of Israel to it. When he finished feeding them, he rose to bless and praise God. When he finished, God sent a revelation to him:[250] "I have heard your prayer, and have seen your offering. If you remain obedient to Me, I will confirm your kingdom for you and for your offspring after you, and I will sanctify this house forever. But if you turn aside from My command, or any of you violates My covenants, I will deprive him of his kingdom and destroy this house forever."

Bilqīs, the queen of Sheba, came to Solomon,[251] and the events that God has recounted in His mighty book took place. When she came to him, she brought him camels laden with gold and ambergris. She said to him, "Such word about you reached me that I did not believe it until I saw it." Then she returned to her own country.

Solomon was very fond of women—he is said to have married seven hundred wives. Among them were a daughter of Pharaoh, king of Egypt; several women of the children of Ammon; several women of the people of Moab, the mighty ones of Syria; from Edom; from the Hittites, who are the Sidonians; and from the peoples with whom God had forbidden relations. There were seven

---

249 Cf. 1 Kings 8.

250 Cf. 1 Kings 9.

251 Cf. 1 Kings 10:1–13 and Qur'ān 27:15–45. Neither the Bible nor the Qur'ān gives the Queen of Sheba a name. The name Bilqīs emerged early in Islamic lore. Its origin is unknown, although its similarity to the Greek word for concubine (παλλακίς, borrowed into Hebrew as *pilegesh*) is striking. See the article by E. Ullendorff in *EI*², s.v. Bilḳīs; and the article by Axel Havemann in *EI*³, s.v. Bilqīs.

hundred of them. One of Solomon's wives made a statue after the likeness of her father.[252] When his other wives saw it, they did as she had done. God reproved Solomon, saying: "Idols are being worshipped in your house, and they do not anger you! I will surely deprive you of your rule, divest you of your power, and divide the tribes from your descendants. But mindful for your sake of David your father, I will not divest you of the kingship for the remainder of your life or take away all the tribes. Rather, I will leave two tribes in your control, so that the memory of you will not vanish."

When Solomon was sitting on his throne wrought of gold and crowned with jewels, his signet ring was snatched from him.[253] One of the satans took it, put it on his own hand, and pushed Solomon | off his throne; the satan sat 1:64
on it himself. He stripped off Solomon's clothes and put them on himself. Solomon went wandering aimlessly, wearing a woolen coat, with a reed in his hand, begging for food. He would say: "I am the king of the children of Israel. God has divested me of my kingdom." Whoever heard him scoffed at him and denied his words. He would wait for the fishermen by the sea and ask them for whatever they would give him to eat. However, Solomon's companion Asaph and others found something strange in the satan's behavior, and they did not see him mentioning God. The satan therefore fled and flung the ring into the sea. Solomon remained deprived of kingship for forty days. When his forty days were over, he was walking haplessly along the seashore when a fisherman said to him, "Come, madman, and take this fish." And he gave him a fish whose odor had already turned. Solomon took it to the sea, washed it, and split open its belly, and lo there was another fish within it. He split open the belly of the other fish, and there was his signet ring in its stomach. He put it on and praised God, and God restored his kingdom to him.

Solomon remained king over the children of Israel in the way that God has described regarding his kingship and how He subjected to him the birds, the jinn, and humans to produce marvels of workmanship for him, constructing the building for him, and obeying his every order for forty years. Then he died and was buried beside the tomb of David. Solomon was twelve years old when he became king. He died when he was fifty-two years old.

---

252 For this detail, cf. al-Ṭabarī, *Taʾrīkh*, 1:587.

253 The post-biblical story of how Solomon's ring came into the power of a devil who then impersonated Solomon, while the real Solomon became a beggar, is alluded to in Qurʾān 38:34–35. It is recorded in more detail in al-Ṭabarī, *Taʾrīkh*, 1:589–594. For Jewish versions of the story, see Ginzberg, *The Legends of the Jews*, 4:168 ff.

Rehoboam, the Son of Solomon, and the Kings after Him

When Solomon son of David died, Rehoboam son of Solomon became king.[254]
The tribes of the children of Israel gathered before him and said, "Your father
dealt roughly with us and subjected us to harsh servitude, so lighten our burden
1:65 now." Rehoboam said to them, | "Go away from me today, and come back to
me in three days." So they left him, and he consulted the elders among his
father's companions. "What do you think?" he asked. They said, "We think that
you should reply graciously to the children of Israel and speak softly to them,
so that you may rule them after today." But he abandoned the opinion of the
elders of the children of Israel and consulted some young men who had grown
up with him. They said to him, "We think you should speak harshly to them,
so that things proceed aright for you with them as they did for your father."
When the third day came, they gathered before him to ask him about what
they had mentioned to him. He said to them, "My little finger is heavier than my
father's thumb." When he said this, they left him and dispersed to their villages.
Of all the tribes of the children of Israel, only the tribe of Judah and the tribe
of Benjamin remained with him.

The ten tribes made Jeroboam son of Nebat king over them. He had fled from Solomon into Egypt; however, when the children of Israel parted ways over Rehoboam son of Solomon, he returned. Rehoboam son of Solomon gathered a thousand men from the tribe of Judah and the tribe of Benjamin, intending to make war on Jeroboam son of Nebat and those with him. But God revealed to the prophet Shemaiah:[255] "Say to Rehoboam and those with him, 'Do not make war on the children of Israel.'" They heeded his word and went away. Rehoboam reigned for seventeen years.

Jeroboam, son of Nebat, ruled as king over the ten tribes from the mountains
of Ephraim.[256] Then the children of Israel said, "We wish to make our offerings
to God." Jeroboam was loathe to have them go up to Jerusalem, lest the people
of Judah win them over and they join their kingdom. So he said, "There is no
need for you to go up; I will set up an altar for you." So he set up an altar for them,
procured a golden calf for it, and said, "These are your gods, who brought you
1:66 up from the land of Egypt." He appointed | chief priests for the calf. He made
a feast and offered sacrifices to the calf. The prophet of the children of Israel
came to him and admonished him.[257] Jeroboam stretched out his hand toward

254 Cf. 1 Kings 12.

255 The MSS read "Isaiah," but this seems to be due to the miscopying of an unfamiliar name.

256 The MSS read "the mountains of Farān," but this seems to be due to miscopying.

257 Cf. 1 Kings 13.

him and it dried up. So he said to the prophet, "Pray to God to restore my hand." The prophet prayed for him, and Jeroboam's hand was restored; but Jeroboam persisted in his way and did not turn back from it. God destroyed Jeroboam and all those who were with him. He killed him and brought ruin upon him. His reign was for twenty years.

Then Abijam, son of Rehoboam, became king.[258] He walked in his father's ways, displayed vile behavior, and committed shameful deeds; God therefore cut his life short. His reign lasted for three years.

Then Asa became king.[259] He displayed behavior obedient to God. He forbade fornication and punished people for it and for other immorality. He expelled from his kingdom anyone who worshipped idols, even driving out his mother when word reached him that she was worshipping idols. In his time Zerah became king of Ethiopia, and the king of India advanced toward Jerusalem, but God sent a punishment and destroyed Zerah and the king of India. Asa reigned for forty years. The children of Israel are said to have used the wood of the Indians' weapons as fuel for seven years after Asa killed them.

After him his son Jehoshaphat became king. He walked in his father's ways. He was a devout, truthful man. He ruled the ten tribes and was accepted among all the children of Israel. His rule lasted twenty-five years.

His son Joram reigned after him. He became an infidel, and his people returned to the worship of idols. He married a woman who encouraged his tyranny and led him astray. His reign lasted for forty years.

Ahaziah became king after his father and walked in his ways. The ten tribes had seceded and had made one of their own, a man named Jehu, king. He went
to war with Ahaziah and made great slaughter among his people. | Then God 1:67
gave the king of Syria power over them, and he did the same thing among them. Ahaziah ruled for one year.

Then Athaliah daughter of Omri reigned. She killed David's progeny, so that none of David's descendants remained except a boy named Joash.[260] A woman from the family of his paternal uncle—one named Jehosheba—his paternal aunt, took him; he was still a nursling. Athaliah did evil, worked abominations openly, and corrupted the country. The children of Israel came in assembly to the priest Jehoiada and complained to him about what she was doing to them. They gathered together and killed her. Her rule lasted for seven years.

---

258 Cf. 1 Kings 15:1.

259 Cf. 1 Kings 15:9. Al-Yaʿqūbī supplements the Bible's spare account of Asa's reign with material from other sources. Cf. al-Ṭabarī, *Taʾrīkh*, 1:619–637.

260 Cf. 2 Kings 11.

After Athaliah, the young man who remained of the sons of David, that is, Joash, became king.[261] He was seven years old when he became king. The affairs of the children of Israel improved, and justice prevailed among them; immorality was eliminated, and they abandoned the worship of idols. However, at the end of his life, he became unjust; he made use of murder, even murdering the children of priests. He murdered the child of the priest Jehoiada, who had made him king. Then he died; his reign had lasted forty years. He razed the wall of the Holy House for forty cubits and made off with everything in it.[262]

Amaziah became king after him. At the beginning of his reign, his course of action resembled that of Joash, but then he behaved unjustly and acted oppressively. His reign lasted for twenty-seven years.

Then Uzziah son of Amaziah became king.[263] The prophet Isaiah lived in his time. Uzziah worshipped God aright and did His work obediently, except that he took the censer and entered the sanctuary, which was permitted to no one except the priests. God therefore punished him, and he became a leper. God
1:68 also punished Isaiah the prophet because | he did not forbid him to do it. God divested him of prophecy until Uzziah died. His reign lasted for fifty-two years.

Jotham became king when his father became a leper.[264] His reign lasted for sixteen years.

Then his son Ahaz became king. He became an infidel and worshipped idols. God therefore gave Tiglath-pileser, the king of Babylon, power over him.[265] He took him captive, enslaved him, and imposed a tax[266] on him. He destroyed Sebastea,[267] the city of the ten tribes in Palestine, and brought its people into captivity in the land of Babylon. Then he sent some of his own people to the

261 Cf. 2 Kings 11:21 ff.

262 Cf. 2 Kings 12:18, 14:13. Al-Yaʿqūbī or his source has confused King Joash of Samaria with King Joash of Jerusalem.

263 Cf. 2 Kings 15:1–7 and 2 Chronicles 26. Azariah (2 Kings) and Uzziah (2 Chronicles 26) apparently are variants of the same name.

264 2 Kings 15:32–38; 2 Chronicles 27.

265 Al-Yaʿqūbī or his source has amalgamated the events of 2 Kings 16–17, making it appear that Ahaz ruled from Samaria-Sebastea, rather than Jerusalem, and that he, rather than Hoshea was the king captured and exiled by the Babylonians (Assyrians in 2 Kings 17). The name of the "king of Babylon" in M appears to be Balaʿqīs (the first letter is ambiguous because undotted). Tiglath-pileser is the name that appears in 2 Kings 15–16. The name of the Assyrian ruler who conquered Samaria is given as Shalmaneser in 2 Kings 17:2.

266 Arabic, *jizya*, later used for the poll-tax paid by non-Muslims in Muslim territory. Here the word should be taken in the broader sense of tax or tribute.

267 Anachronism: the capital of the ten tribes was called Samaria; the rebuilt city did not receive the name Sebastea until the reign of Herod the Great.

city, and they restored it and rebuilt it. They are the ones called Samaritans[268] in Palestine and Jordan. When they settled there, God sent lions to attack them. Then he[269] dispatched one of the priests of the children of Israel to them, a descendant of Aaron, to teach them the religion of the children of Israel. When they entered their religion, the lions left them. They became Samaritans. They said, "We believe in no prophet but Moses, and we acknowledge only what is in the Torah." They rejected the prophethood of David and denied the resurrection and the afterlife. They refused to sit or associate with other people, partake of anything from them, or carry the dead. Whoever has carried a dead person goes apart for seven days; he goes apart into the desert, not associating with them, and then he washes himself. It is the same for anyone who has partaken of anything that is not permitted. They do not shelter a menstruating women in their homes. They appointed their leader from the descendants of Aaron, and they name him | the *raʾīs*.[270] They deal with inheritance according 1:69
to the Torah. They are in no other place on earth except the province of Palestine. The reign of Ahaz lasted for sixteen years.

After Ahaz, Hezekiah[271] his son became king. He worshipped God aright. He broke down the idols and destroyed their shrines. In his time, Sennacherib son of Sarāṭum[272] became king of Babylon. He came to Jerusalem and captured the rest of the tribes. Hezekiah bribed him with three hundred talents[273] of silver and thirty talents of gold to leave. He accepted them, but then he acted treacherously. When he did this, Isaiah the prophet and Hezekiah prayed to God against Sennacherib, and God answered their prayer.[274] God subjected Sennacherib's men to slaying: one hundred and eighty-five thousand of them were killed in a single hour. Sennacherib turned back in defeat; and when he

268 On the Samaritans, cf. 2 Kings 17:24–41. See also the article by S. Noja Noseda in *EI*², s.v. al-Sāmira. For Islamic traditions concerning the Samaritans, see the article by B. Heller in *EI*², s.v. al-Sāmirī.

269 The pronoun should refer to the king of Babylon (Assyria) as in 2 Kings 17:27, but in al-Yaʿqūbī's abbreviated version might also refer to God.

270 That is, head, chief, or leader.

271 Given as Ḥizqīl, ordinarily the Arabic form of the name of the prophet Ezekiel; probably a copyist's error.

272 Sic. Sennacherib's father was Sargon II, and Sarāṭum may be a copyist's error for something like the Akkadian form of the name: Sharrukēn. Sennacherib, like Tiglath-pileser and Shalmaneser, was a king of Assyria, not Babylon.

273 Arabic, *qinṭār*, a large unit of weight, c. 100 pounds. The amount of the tribute is given thus in 2 Kings 18:14.

274 Cf. 2 Kings 19; 2 Chronicles 32.

reached Babylon, his own son slew him in a most evil murder. God commanded Isaiah the Prophet to tell Hezekiah that he would die and that he should make his will. When God gave him to understand this, he besought God to prolong his life until He should grant him a son to reign as king after him. God therefore prolonged his life for fifteen years, until a son was born to him. In the days of Hezekiah, the sun went back five signs of the zodiac toward its rising.[275] Hezekiah ruled as king for twenty-seven years.

After Hezekiah, Manasseh son of Hezekiah became king.[276] The children of Israel became infidels during his days. He became an infidel and worshipped idols; he was the worst king among the children of Israel. He built a place of worship for the idols and took an idol of four faces for himself. Isaiah
1:70 forbade him and ordered it | to be sawn from head to foot with a saw. God set against Manasseh Constantine the king of the Romans, who made war on him and took him prisoner, so that Manasseh spent time in captivity.[277] Then he repented to his Lord, and God restored him to his kingdom. He smashed the idol and destroyed the houses of the idols. His reign lasted for fifty-five years; his captivity was for twenty years.

Then Amon son of Manasseh became king. He brought back the idols, so that they became even more numerous. His reign lasted for sixteen years.

After him, Josiah his son became king.[278] He worshipped God aright: he smashed the idols and destroyed their houses, and he killed and burned their custodians. In his justice, right worship of God, and good policy, he resembled David and Solomon. His reign lasted for thirty years.

---

275 Reading with the MSS *khams burūj*. Ed. Leiden emends to *khams darajāt*, five degrees. There are three arguments against the emendation: 1. The text in the MSS is clear and makes sense. 2. A 5-degree retrograde motion, the distance the sun normally travels in 20 minutes, would hardly be perceptible, except to astronomers. 3. The Jewish legendary material, interpreting 2 Kings 20:9–11, says that in this miracle, "the sun shone ten hours longer than its wonted time" (Ginzberg, *The Legends of the Jews*, 4:275), interpreting the Hebrew *maʿalōt* to mean hour marks on a sundial. Since each of the 12 signs of the zodiac covers 360/12 or 30 degrees, the sun, moving across the sky at an apparent 360/24 or 15 degrees an hour, takes 10 hours to cover 5 signs; which is what the text implies—a very apparent miracle.

276 Cf. 2 Kings 21; 2 Chronicles 33.

277 The biblical source for the captivity of Manasseh is 2 Chronicles 33:10–13, where the captor is identified as "the king of Assyria," and Manasseh spends his captivity in Babylon. The source of this anachronistic introduction of Constantine is unknown. It also occurs in al-Masʿūdī, *Murūj*, 1:67 (§ 111).

278 Cf. 2 Kings 22–23; 2 Chronicles 34–35.

Then Jehoahaz his son reigned for three months.[279] Pharaoh the Lame, king of Egypt, took him captive and imposed a tax on his country. Pharaoh made one of his own the king over it and took Jehoahaz away to Egypt, where he died.

After him, Jehoiakim his brother became king; he was the father of the prophet Daniel.[280] In his time, Nebuchadnezzar king of Babylon came to Jerusalem and wrought slaughter among the children of Israel. He took them captive and brought them to the land of Babylon. Then he went into the land of Egypt and killed Pharaoh the Lame, its king. Nebuchadnezzar took the Torah and the books of the prophets that were in the temple; he put them into a well, threw fire onto them, and pressed them down. The prophet Jeremiah lived at that time. When he learned of Nebuchadnezzar's approach, he took the ark of the presence and hid it in a cave where no one knew of it.[281] No one escaped from Nebuchadnezzar except Jeremiah.

The number of those whom Nebuchadnezzar brought to the land of Babylon | was eighteen thousand. Among them were a thousand prophets. Their 1:71
king was Jeconiah son of Jehoiakim.[282] From them are descended the Jews who are in Iraq. It is said that Jeremiah the prophet said: "O God, I know of your justice what no one else knows. Why did you give Nebuchadnezzar power over the children of Israel?" And God revealed to him, "I take vengeance on my servants, when they disobey me, only with the worst of my creatures."

The children of Israel continued in captivity under the power of Nebuchadnezzar until he married one of their women called Sīḥat[283] daughter of Shealtiel. She asked him to restore her people to their land. When the children of Israel returned to their land, they made Zerubbabel son of Shealtiel king over

---

279 Cf. 2 Kings 23:31–35; 2 Chronicles 36:1–4. The name "Pharaoh the Lame" (Arabic, *Firʿawn al-Aʿraj*) derives ultimately from a Jewish folk etymology of the Egyptian name transliterated into Hebrew as Nəḵō (RSV Neco), as if from the adjective *nāḵē* (smitten, stricken), which occurs in 2 Samuel 4:4 and 9:3 in the phrase *nəḵē raḡlayim* (crippled of feet). Cf. al-Ṭabarī, *Taʾrīkh*, 1:643. The same folk etymology is also present in the Syriac Bible, where he is called *Perʿōn Ḥḡīrā*, Pharaoh the Lame.

280 This is deduced from Daniel 1:3–7, where Daniel is said to be "of the royal family."

281 Cf. 2 Maccabees 2:18; Ginzberg, *The Legends of the Jews*, 4:320–321.

282 Cf. Jeremiah 24:1.

283 Sic MSS. The tradition that the exiles' return was furthered by the marriage of the sister of the man who became their leader, Zerubbabel, to the ruler who allowed them to return can also be found in *Schatzhöhle*, 51, and 206, 208 (trans. Budge, 190), although the ruler is correctly named there as Cyrus, not Nebuchadnezzar. The Syriac gives the name of Zerubbabel's sister as Mshīnat (another MS reads Mashḥat) and the Arabic translation reads Masḥat, which in ductus closely resembles the word in M. Thus, although the original form of the name remains obscure, its provenance can be traced.

them. He rebuilt the city of Jerusalem, and he rebuilt the temple, spending forty-six years rebuilding it. In his time, God transformed Nebuchadnezzar into a female beast.[284] He continually wandered among various kinds of beasts for seven years. Then it is said that he turned back to God, who caused him to live as a man again; then he died. Zerubbabel was the one who brought out the Torah and the books of the prophets from the well in which Nebuchadnezzar had buried them. He found them intact, not burnt. He recopied the Torah, the books of the prophets, their traditions,[285] and their laws. He was the first one who copied these books.

The law[286] of the children of Israel was: the declaration of God's oneness;[287] and confessing the prophethood of Moses and Aaron, the sons of Amram son of Kohath son of Levi son of Jacob son of Isaac son of Abraham, God's friend.

Their fasting was six days every year. The first of them is on *Rosh ha-Sha-*
1:72 *nah*.[288] They reckon *Rosh ha-Shanah* to be the first day of Tishrīn. When | ten days of Tishrīn have passed, they fast for one day; it is the day on which the second set of tablets came down to Moses son of Amram.[289] They fast on the tenth of Kānūn II for a single day; it is the day on which God delivered the children of Israel from Haman.[290] They fast on the seventeenth of Tammūz for a single day; it is the day on which Moses came down from the mountain.[291] They fast on the ninth of Āb for a single day; it is the day on which the destruction of Jerusalem took place. They fast on the third of Tishrīn; it is the day on which Gedaliah son of Ahikam was killed.[292]

---

284 Cf. Daniel 4:28–37.

285 Arabic, *sunan*, plural of *sunna*.

286 Arabic, *sharīʿa*, the normal word also for Islamic law.

287 Arabic, *tawḥīd*, literally, "declaring of oneness," the normal word for monotheism in Islam.

288 Given in the Arabic form, *Ra's al-Sana*. The Arabic and Hebrew both mean "Head of the Year," that is, New Year. Curiously, in the next paragraph, the New Year is called a feast-day, which corresponds more closely to its character in Jewish observance.

289 For the Day of Atonement (Yom Kippur) as the day on which Moses received the second set of tablets, see Ginzberg, *The Legends of the Jews*, 3:138–140.

290 The fast of the 10th of Kānūn II (Ṭēḇēṯ in Hebrew) commemorated the beginning of Nebuchadnezzar's siege of Jerusalem (cf. 2 Kings 25:1 and Jeremiah 52:4). Al-Yaʿqūbī or his source has confused it with the fast on 13 Āḏār commemorating Esther's fast, preceding the Feast of Purim, which commemorates the deliverance of the Jews from Haman.

291 That is, when Moses came down from the mountain with the first tablets, which he destroyed when he saw the Israelites worshipping the Golden Calf. The fast commemorates the destruction of the tablets.

292 Cf. 2 Kings 25:22–26. Gedaliah was a Judaean appointed by Nebuchadnezzar to govern his

They have four feasts a year. The feast of unleavened bread is the day on which Moses brought the children of Israel out of Egypt. They carried their dough unfermented and ate it as unleavened bread. It is on the fifteenth of Nīsān and lasts for seven days. Then there is a feast on the sixteenth of Ḥazīrān, the day on which the Torah was sent down to Moses; it is a great feast for them.[293] Then there is a feast of the first of Tishrīn; it is their New Year's Day. Then there is a feast on the fifteenth day of Tishrīn; it is the feast of Tabernacles. Its meaning is that God commanded Moses to command the children of Israel to build a trellis of palm leaves and branches. Therefore they dwell for eight days, making in their synagogues canopies of palm leaves and branches.

Their prayers are three: a prayer in the morning, a prayer at sunset, and a prayer after sunset. When one of them stands for prayer he puts his heels together, puts his right hand on his left shoulder, and his left hand on his right shoulder; with his head lowered, he makes five bows, without making prostration, then he makes a single prostration at the end. He gives praise with the Psalms of | David at the beginning of the prayers; in the sunset prayer he 1:73
recites from the Torah. In their traditions and laws they put their reliance on the books of their scholars. These are the books that are called […][294] in Hebrew, which is the language that became theirs when they crossed the sea.[295] This is a picture of the Hebrew script. It is 27 letters.[296]

Their practice in their marriages is that they marry only with a guardian and two witnesses. The smallest bride-price for a virgin is two hundred dirhams, and for one not a virgin,[297] a hundred dirhams. There is no smaller price than

---

newly conquered province. His assassination put an end to this last semblance of Jewish rule.

293 Hebrew *Shāḇūʿōṯ*, the Feast of Weeks (Pentecost), celebrated fifty days after Passover. The Arabic month name *Ḥazīrān* corresponds to Hebrew *Sīwān*.

294 Lacuna in the text.

295 Al-Yaʿqūbī gives a common etymology of the adjective *ʿibrānī* (Hebrew) from the verb *ʿabara*, to cross. The etymology works in Arabic as well as in Hebrew.

296 What follows in M is curious, and one cannot be sure that it is what al-Yaʿqūbī originally wrote. First, the 27 letters of the Arabic alphabet are written in their customary order. This is followed by what appear to be 11 exotic characters (sometimes one cannot determine whether a complex design is meant as one or two characters); these resemble nothing that one could call Hebrew. As for the figure of 27 for the letters of the Hebrew alphabet, which would make it equal to the Arabic alphabet, one can arrive at that number if one adds to the 22 letters of the Hebrew alphabet the special shapes that 5 letters take in word-final position.

297 Arabic, *thayyib*, includes widows, divorcées, and any other women who are not virgins.

this. Divorce is allowed when they come to abhor one another, and it can only take place in the presence of witnesses.

Their practice in regard to slaughtered animals is not to eat what others slaughter. Whoever is in charge of slaughtering animals must be knowledgeable in the laws. Whenever he wants to slaughter an animal, he brings to the priest the knife he will use. If its edge meets with the priest's approval, he allows him to slaughter with it; if not, he commands him to sharpen it or bring another one. When he slaughters an animal, he does not bring it near a wall, lest it become agitated. When he finishes with it, he inspects its throat, and if he finds the epiglottis not foaming, and the slaughter properly done, it is not to be eaten until he inspects the lung. If he finds any defect in it, any disease, or split, or pustule, or tumor, the slaughtered animal is not to be eaten. If the lung is sound, he inspects the brain. If he finds any disease in it, it is not to be eaten. If the brain is sound, he inspects the heart. If he finds any disease in it, it is not to be eaten. If it is sound, [...].[298] The fat that is in the stomachs and the intestines one does not eat, nor the veins, but everything else one eats.

Their era, according to their reckoning, is from the destruction of Jerusalem; on this basis they reckon. Every day, they must remember the day on which Jerusalem was destroyed and how long it has been since that day.

The Messiah, Jesus, the Son of Mary

1:74 Hannah, the wife of Amram, made a vow that if God gave her a child, she would dedicate it to God.[299] When she gave birth to Mary, she gave her to Zechariah son of Barachiah son of Yashū son of Naḥrā'īl son of Sahlūn son of Arsū son of Shuwayl son of Ya'ūd son of Moses son of Amram, who was a priest at the altar.[300] Mary remained thus until, when she was seventeen years old, God sent the angel to her to give her a blameless child.[301] Of her story there took place

---

298 Lacuna in the text.

299 Cf. Qur'ān 2:35: "The wife of 'Imrān said, 'Lord, I have vowed to Thee, in dedication, what is within my womb.'" The following verses make it clear that "the wife of 'Imrān" is the mother of the Virgin Mary. In Christian tradition, Anne (Ḥannah is the Hebrew and Arabic form of the name), the mother of Mary, was married to a man named Joachim. The identification of her husband as 'Imrān (the same name as Amram, the father of Moses) comes from the Qur'ān.

300 The source of this genealogy for Zechariah is unknown. M omits "son of Barachiah." The vocalization and correct reading of the names is conjectural.

301 Cf. Qur'ān 19:19.

what God has told, until she became pregnant. When her days were complete, the labor pains came upon her, in the way of which God has spoken.[302] He has also described her situation and his, his speaking from beneath her, and his speaking in the cradle. His birth took place in a village called Bethlehem, one of the villages of Palestine, on Tuesday, the twenty-fourth of Kānūn I.

Māshāʾallāh the astrologer said: "The ascendant for the year in which the Messiah was born was in Libra 18°; Jupiter was in Virgo 31′ [2° 30′] retrograde; Saturn was in Capricorn 16° 28′; the Sun was in Aries 1′; Venus was in Taurus 14°; Mars was in Gemini 21° [22′; the Moon was in Gemini 22°] 44′; Mercury was in Aries 4° 17′ [59′]."[303]

As for the authors of the Gospel, they do not say that he spoke in the cradle. They do say that Mary was betrothed to a man named Joseph, a descendant of David. | She conceived, and when the completion of her pregnancy drew 1:75
near, he took her to Bethlehem. When she had given birth, he brought her back to Nazareth, in the hills of Galilee. On the eighth day, according to the law of Moses son of Amram, he circumcised him. The apostles gave accounts describing the Messiah and mentioning his circumstances. We have set down the report of each, one by one, and the description of him that they gave.

The apostles were twelve from the tribes of Jacob. They were: Simon son of Kanʿān, of the tribe of [...; Jacob] son of Zebedee, [...]; John son of Ḥābar son of Fālī, of the tribe of Zebulun; Philip, of the tribe of Asher; Matthew, of the tribe of Issachar son of Jacob; Samʿā, of the tribe of Ephraim son of Jacob; Judah, of the tribe of Judah son of Jacob; Jacob, of the tribe of Joseph the son of Jacob; and Manasseh, of the tribe of Reuben son of Jacob. In addition to these there were seventy men. The four who wrote the Gospel were Matthew, Mark, Luke, and John; two of these were of the twelve; two were not of their number.

As for Matthew, in his Gospel he spoke of the lineage of the Messiah Jesus, the son of David, the son of Abraham, working his way down until he ended with Joseph son of Jacob son of Matthan, after forty-two ancestors. Then he said: Joseph was the husband of Mary. The Messiah was born in Bethlehem, a village of Palestine. The king of Palestine at that time was Herod. Some of the Magi traveled to Bethlehem; | over their heads was a star by which they 1:76
were guided, until they saw him and bowed down to him. Herod the king of Palestine wanted to kill the Messiah, but Joseph took him and his mother away to the land of Egypt. When Herod died, he brought him back and settled him in

302 Cf. Qurʾān 19:23–30.

303 This is the horoscope for the vernal equinox of that year. The figures are somewhat corrupted. See the horoscope as it appears in E. S. Kennedy & David Pingree, *The Astrological History of Māshāʾallāh*, 44–47, 96–97; figures from this source appear in brackets above.

Nazareth, in the hills of Galilee. When the Messiah grew up and reached the age of twenty-nine, he went to John son of Zechariah, to be accepted as a follower, but John son of Zechariah said to him, "I am more in need of you than you are of me." The Messiah said to him, "Desist from this saying, for thus it is fitting that righteousness be fulfilled." So John desisted from it.

Jesus, with the aid of God's Spirit, went out into the desert and fasted for forty days. Satan approached him and said, "If you are now the son of God, command these stones to become bread." Jesus said, "Man does not live by bread alone, but by the word of God." Then he took him and brought him to the pinnacle of the temple. Satan said to him: "Throw yourself to the ground. If you are God's son, His angels will surround you." The Messiah said, "It is written: You shall not put God, your Lord, to the test." Then he said to Satan, "Depart, for I bow down to God and Him do I serve." So Satan left him and departed, and the angels of God came to him and began serving him.

Then his disciples came to him, and he began speaking to them in parables and in revelation without parables. The first part of the Gospel that he spoke, according to what is in the Gospel of Matthew, was: Blessed are the poor whose hearts are content with what is with their Lord; truly theirs is the kingdom of heaven. Blessed are the hungry and thirsty in obedience to God. Blessed are the truthful in their speech, who relinquish lying, who are the salt of the earth and the light of the world. Do not kill. Do not anger anyone; appease whoever is angry at you. Be reconciled with your adversary. Do not commit adultery. Do
1:77 not look at any other than your own wives. If | your right eye summons you to disloyalty, pluck it out in order to save your bodies. Do not divorce your wives except for immorality.[304] Do not swear by God, whether telling the truth or lying, either by His heavens or by His earth. Do not resist evil; rather, whoever strikes you on your right cheek, turn your left cheek to him; whoever wants to take away your shirt, give him your cloak, too; and whoever forces you for a mile, go with him for two miles. Whoever asks of you, give to him. Whoever asks you for a loan, lend to him, and do not deprive him.

You have heard that it is said, love your neighbor[305] and hate your enemy. But I say to you: Love your enemies, be kind to those who mistreat you, and do

---

304 Reading, with M, *rayba*; ed. Leiden *zanya*, adultery.

305 Arabic, *qarīb*, which normally means "near" (as an adjective) and "relative" (as a noun). However, since the Greek of Matthew 5:43 uses for "neighbor" the word πλησίον which etymologically means "someone nearby," and the Syriac Gospels render this as *qarīb*, which means all of "near, neighbor, and relative," one cannot be sure whether "relative" or "neighbor" is intended in the Arabic.

good to those who hate you. If you love those who love you, what reward do you have?

Do not display your alms before men. Let your left hands not know what your right hands are doing. Do not make a show of your prayers before people. When you pray, go into your houses, lock your doors, and let no one hear you. When you pray, say: "Our Father, who art in heaven, hallowed be Thy name. Thy kingdom come. Thy will be done, on earth as in heaven. Give us today our bread that is sufficient for us. Forgive us our debts, as we forgive our debtors. Do not bring us into a trial, O Lord, but deliver us from the Evil One, through Jesus Christ our Lord."[306]

Do not display your fasting to people, when you are fasting for God, your Lord, and do not alter your countenances, so that people will see you, for your Lord knows your situation.

Do not hoard treasures where the worm and devouring termite corrupt and where thieves dig in.[307] Rather, let your treasures be with your Lord, who is in heaven, where no worm goes, and no thief steals.

Do not worry | about your livelihood, or about what you will eat, or about 1:78
what you will drink, or about what you will wear. Consider the birds of the heavens; they do not sow, they do not harvest, and they do not gather into houses, for God sustains them; and you are more precious to God than the birds. Do not worry about your children, for they are like you: as you were created, so were they created; and as you have been sustained, so have they been sustained.

Do not say to your brother, "Remove the speck from your eye," when there is a beam in your own eye. Do not look for people's faults and ignore your own faults. Do not give what is holy or pearls to swine, lest they trample it underfoot. [Ask] your Lord, and He will give to you. Seek Him, for you will find Him compassionate to you. Knock at His door, and He will open to you. As for the door, it is wide and the way is clear, and it brings people to ruin. How small is the door, and how narrow the way that leads people to safety!

Beware of the people of falsehood, who are like ravenous wolves. Just as you cannot pick grapes from thorns, or figs from colocynths, neither can you find a bad tree that bears good herbage, nor a good tree that bears bad fruit.

---

306 The Leiden editor removed the words "through Jesus Christ our Lord" from the text and placed them in a footnote. However, they are present in MSS M and C.

307 Arabic, *yaḥfirūn*, "dig," is evidence for the dependence of al-Yaʿqūbī on Syriac mediation for the text of the Gospel. The Syriac of Matthew 6:19 has *pālshīn*, "break through," but the *paʿʿel* conjugation of the same root means "dig out, excavate." Cf. Sokoloff, *Syriac Lexicon*, 1203.

Everyone who hears my words and understands them is like an intelligent man[308] who built his house on a strong, solid place. The rain came, the rivers flowed abundantly, and winds rose [...][309] and the house fell.

At that time King Herod had arrested John and imprisoned him.[310] This was because Herod used to come to the wife of his brother Philip, and John forbade him to do so. Herod wanted to kill John, but he was fearful, because John was revered. Then his brother's wife told him to kill John. So he dispatched someone
1:79 to the prison, who cut off John's head | and put it on a platter. John's disciples came, took his corpse, and buried it. They went to the Messiah and told him. He therefore went into desert country, and he commanded his companions not to inform anyone.

The Gospel of Mark. As for Mark, he says at the beginning of his Gospel: Jesus the Messiah, the Son of God. As it is written in the prophet Isaiah, "I will send my angel before your face, that I may prepare your way." John, the son of Zechariah, was baptizing with a baptism for repentance. His clothes were of camel's hair, and he bound up his loins with a leather cord. The Messiah came to him from Nazareth of Galilee, that he might baptize him in the Jordan. When he had baptized him, the Holy Spirit came out over the water like a dove, while a voice from heaven cried out, "You are my beloved Son; in you I delight."

Jesus returned to the hills of Galilee. There were some people fishing, among whom were Simon and Andrew. He said to them, "Follow me and I will make you fish for men." So they went with him. He went into a village and cured its sick and its lepers, and he opened the eyes of the blind there. People gathered around him, and he began to speak to them in parables and revelation, saying: "Truly I tell you, the tribe will not pass away until [...]. Heaven and earth will pass away, but my words will not pass away."[311]

The Gospel of Luke. As for Luke, he says at the beginning of the Gospel: Because many people have been pleased to write down the stories and hap-

308 One is tempted to amend the text's *ḥalīm* (forbearing, patient, intelligent) to *ḥakīm* ("wise") to follow the Syriac text of Matthew 7:24. The two words are very similar in Arabic script.

309 A large chunk of text has fallen out by miscopying due to homeoteleuton. Cf. Matthew 7:24–27.

310 Al-Yaʿqūbī jumps suddenly to a summary of Matthew 14.

311 Cf. Mark 13:30–31. The copyist has left out several words. Mark 13:30 reads: "Truly I tell you, this generation will not pass away until *all these things have taken place.*" The choice of the Arabic word *qabīla* (body of men, tribe)—the Greek original is γενεά ("generation")—can be explained through al-Yaʿqūbī's dependence on Syriac mediation. The Peshitta renders γενεά as *sharbtā* (stock, race, family, tribe); hence the choice of *qabīla*.

penings which we have known, I thought it incumbent upon me to write down something that I knew as it truly was.

In the days of King Herod there was a priest named Zechariah, a minister from the family of Abijah, and his wife, a descendant of Aaron named Elizabeth. Both of them were upright before God, carrying out His precepts,
not falling short in obeying Him. They had no child. Elizabeth was | barren; 1:80
Zechariah was sterile; both were elderly. While Zechariah was officiating at the incense offering, he entered the sanctuary, while the assembly of the people was outside of the sanctuary. The angel of the Lord appeared to Zechariah, standing to the right of the altar. Zechariah trembled when he saw him, and fear overwhelmed him. But the angel said to him: "Do not be afraid, Zechariah, for God has heard your prayers and answered your petition. He will give you a son, whom you shall name John.[312] In him you will have good fortune and joy. He will be great with God. He will not drink wine or strong drink. He will be filled with the Holy Spirit, even in his mother's womb. He will turn to God many of the people of Israel. On him will descend the Spirit that descended upon the prophet Elijah, to turn the hearts of the fathers to their sons, that they may become for God a perfect people."

Zechariah said to the angel, "How can I know this, when I am an old man and my wife is elderly?" The angel said to him: "I am Gabriel, who stand in the presence of God. He has sent me to give you this good news. But be silent from this moment, not speaking, until the day on which this comes to pass, because you did not give credence and did not believe in my word, which will be fulfilled in its time."

The people were standing, waiting for Zechariah, astonished at his lingering in the sanctuary. When he came out, he could not speak to them, and they knew and were certain that he had seen a vision in the sanctuary, for he gestured to them, but did not speak.

When the days of his service were complete, he went back to his home. Elizabeth, his wife, conceived. She remained hiding herself for five months, saying "This is what the Lord has done for me in the days of His regarding me, to blot out my disgrace among men."

In the sixth month of the pregnancy of Zechariah's wife, God sent the angel Gabriel to the hills of Galilee, to a city called Nazareth, to a young virgin
betrothed | to a man named Joseph, of the family of David. Her name was Mary. 1:81
The angel came into her presence and said to her, "Peace be with you, O full of

312 Arabic, Yaḥyā, the usual Muslim form of the name. Al-Yaʿqūbī also uses Yuḥannā, the Christian form of the name, as noted below.

grace, O blessed one among women!" When she saw him, she was frightened by his words, and began to think and to say, "What is this greeting?" The angel said: "Do not be afraid, Mary. You have found favor with God.[313] Truly you will conceive[314] and bear a son, and you will name him Jesus. He will be great, and will be called the Son of the Most High, and the Lord his God will give him the throne of David his father. He will rule over the house of Jacob forever, and of his kingdom there will be no end or interruption." Mary said to the angel, "How can this be, when no man has touched me?" The angel said to her: "The Holy Spirit will descend upon you. The one to be born from you is most holy; he will be called Son of God. Behold, your kinswoman Elizabeth is also pregnant with a son in her old age; and this is the sixth month for her who was called barren, for nothing is impossible for God." Mary said, "I am God's maidservant; let it be for me as you have said."

Mary went into Zechariah's house and greeted Elizabeth. When Zechariah's wife heard Mary's words, the babe in her womb became agitated. She was filled with the Holy Spirit and said to Mary: "Blessed are you among women. Truly, when the sound of your greeting came to my ears, the babe in my womb became agitated with a great joy."

Zechariah's wife Elizabeth bore a son. They circumcised him on the eighth day, and named him John.[315] Immediately his mouth was opened; he spoke, and blessed God.[316] Zechariah was filled with the Holy Spirit, and said: "Blessed be the Lord God of Israel, who has bestowed favor upon his people and set them free with salvation. He has raised up for us the horn of salvation from the house of David, as He spoke by the tongues of his holy prophets."

1:82 When Mary's days were complete, | Joseph took her up to the hills of Galilee, and she gave birth to her first-born son.[317] She wrapped him in rags and laid him

313 The manuscripts read *lāqayti wa-wāfayti*, "you have found and you have come into ..." but neither the Greek nor the Syriac has two parallel verbs at this point. It is best to take the doublet as originating in a copyist's uncertainty, faced with an unclear word, about which word was meant.

314 Arabic, *taqbalīna ḥublā*, "you will receive pregnancy," is hardly idiomatic Arabic, but it exactly reproduces the Syriac idiom used in the Peshitta, *tqabblīn baṭnā*.

315 Here al-Yaʿqūbī uses the Christian form of the name, Yuḥannā, rather than the Muslim form Yaḥyā.

316 The translation deliberately leaves the pronoun ambiguous, as it is in the Arabic. Luke 1:64 implies that the mouth of Zechariah, who had been mute, was opened. Al-Yaʿqūbī implies that it was the infant John who spoke. Cf. Qurʾān 19:12, 29, where such a miracle is attributed both to the infant John and to the infant Jesus.

317 This locating of the birth of Jesus in Galilee, as against Luke's narrative of the birth

in a manger, because she had no place where the two were staying. [...][318] The angel of the Lord came to them, and the glory of God shone on them, and they were very afraid of him. But the angel of the Lord said to them: "Do not be afraid or grieve. Truly, I give you good news of a great joy which will encompass the world."

Then Luke traced the genealogy of the Messiah from Joseph back to Adam.[319]

When eight days had passed, they brought him to be circumcised, according to the law of Moses. They named him Jesus and circumcised him. They brought him to the temple, and they brought a sacrifice, a pair of pigeons and two fledgling doves, to offer in his behalf. A man named Simeon was there, one of the prophets. When they approached the altar to make the offering in his behalf, Simeon carried him and said, "My eyes have seen Your mercy, Lord, and so take me now."

Every year his family would take him up to Jerusalem on the feast of Passover. He would serve the great men, and they marveled at him because of what they saw of his wisdom.

When the Messiah was thirty years old, he went into the temple on the Sabbath day.[320] He stood up to read, according to his custom, and the book of the prophet Isaiah was given to him. He opened the book and found written in it:[321] "The Spirit of the Lord is upon me; because of this He has chosen me and anointed me to bring good news to the poor. He has sent me to heal the brokenhearted, to announce salvation to the captives, and sight to the blind; to restore the broken, and announce pardon and forgiveness to the wrongdoer;[322] and to announce the year acceptable to the Lord." Closing the book, he handed it to the attendant, stepped down, and took his seat. People marveled at what he had done, and they said, "Is this not Joseph's son?"

The Gospel of John. As for the apostle John, he speaks at the beginning of his 1:83
Gospel about the genealogy of the Messiah. Before everything was the Word, and that Word was with God, and God was the Word. It was before everything

in Bethlehem, is curious. In M, the word for Galilee (*al-Jalīl*) is undotted and could conceivably be read as al-Khalīl, the Arabic name for Hebron; but Luke says nothing about Hebron; and Hebron, though in Judea, is not Bethlehem.

318 Although the MSS show no gap, one must assume a lacuna involving a reference to the shepherds of Luke 2:8, to whom the angels mentioned in the next sentence speak.

319 Luke 3:23–38.

320 Luke 4:14–22. In Luke the incident is set in a synagogue in Nazareth, not in the temple.

321 Isaiah 61:1–2, 40:7.

322 Following M, *musī*[ʾ]; ed. Leiden, *masbī* (captive, oppressed).

that was. In it was life, and the life is the light of man. That brightness was in the darkness, [but the darkness] did not comprehend it.

[There was a man] whom God had sent whose name was John. He came for witness, to bear witness to the light, so that people might be rightly guided[323] and believe by means of him. He was not the light. The light of truth has never ceased to shine and be visible in the world. [The world] was in his hand,[324] but the world did not recognize him. He came to his own, but his own did not accept him. But to those who accepted him and believed in him, God gave power to be called sons of God, those who believe in his name, he who has been born not of blood, nor of the desire of the flesh, nor of the lust of man, but of God. And the Word became flesh and dwelt among us, and we saw its glory, a glory like the unique one who is of the Father, full of grace and justice.[325]

John bore witness to him and cried out and said: "He I said would come after me, having been before me, because he is more ancient than I. From his fullness is everything we have received: exceeding grace instead of the first grace. For the Torah was sent down through Moses, but truth and grace by Jesus the Messiah [...] the Word that has not ceased to be in the breast of its Father."

This is what the four disciples, the authors of the Gospel, said about the genealogy of the Messiah. After that they gave an account of the reports about him: that he cured the sick and the lepers, made the crippled stand, and opened
1:84 the eyes of the blind. He had a friend named | Lazarus in a village named Bethany in the vicinity of Jerusalem.[326] Lazarus died and was put into a cave, where he remained for four days. Then the Messiah came to the village, and two sisters of Lazarus came out and said to him, "Master, your friend Lazarus has died." The Messiah grieved over him. "Where is his grave?" he asked, and they brought him to the cave. There was a stone over it. "Move the stone aside," he said. They said, "He stinks after four days." He approached the cave and said: "Lord, to You be praise. I know that You give everything, but I will speak for the sake the crowd standing here, that they may have faith and believe that You

323 Arabic, *li-yahtadiya l-nās*, a typically Qurʾānic phrase that al-Yaʿqūbī inserts; it is not in the Greek or Syriac, which merely state, "so that all might believe through him."

324 "[The world] was in his hand" ([...] *kāna fī yadihi*) involves a literal, albeit unidiomatic, rendering of the Syriac: *kul b-ʾīdēh hwā* (all was/came-to-be through Him; literally, "by His hand"), which in turn exactly translates πάντα δι' αὐτοῦ ἐγένετο (John 1:3).

325 This is another example of al-Yaʿqūbī's reliance on Syriac mediation. The Peshitta translates the Greek ἀλήθεια (truth) with the usual Syriac word for truth, *qushtā*. The Arabic translator, seeking to mirror the Syriac as closely as possible, has chosen the Arabic cognate *qisṭ*, although it normally means justice, not truth.

326 Cf. John 11.

have sent me." Then he said to Lazarus, "Arise." And he arose, dragging the cloth that was on him, with his hands and feet bound. Some of the Jews were with them and believed in him, and they came to look at Lazarus and marveled at him. But the leaders of the Jews and their priests assembled and said, "We fear that he will corrupt our religion for us and the people will follow him." Caiaphas, the chief priest, said to them, "That one man should die is better than that the entire nation should perish." So they agreed to kill him.

The Messiah entered Jerusalem on a donkey, and his companions met him with palm fronds. Judas son of Simon was one of the Messiah's companions. The Messiah said to his companions, "One of you who are eating and drinking with me will deliver me up." He meant Judas son of Simon. Then he began to give a testament to his companions. He said to them: "The hour has come for the Son of Man to depart to his Father. I am going where you cannot come with me. Keep my commandment, and the Paraclete will come to you to be with you a prophet.[327] When the Paraclete brings you the Spirit of truth and sincerity, he will be the one who gives testimony about me. I have spoken to you about this
only so that | you will remember it when its time comes. Indeed, I have said it 1:85
to you. As for me, I am going to the one who sent me. When the Spirit of truth comes, he will guide you to all the truth, he will inform you of things far off, and he will praise me. In a little while you will not see me."

Then the Messiah raised his eyes to heaven and said:[328] "The hour has come. I have glorified You on earth. I have accomplished the work that You commanded me to do." Then he said, "O God, if I must drink this cup, make it easy for me; but not as I want it to be, but what You want, O Lord."[329]

Then the Messiah went off with his disciples to the place in which he and his companions used to gather. Judas, one of the apostles, knew the place. When he saw the police looking for the Messiah, he led them on, along with the messengers of the priests who were with them, and showed them the place. The Messiah went out to them and said to them, "Whom do you want?" They said, "Jesus the Nazarene." Jesus said to them, "I am he." They fell back, then

327 The interpretation of the Paraclete as "a prophet," (*nabiyyan*, following the reading of ed. Leiden), specifically the prophet Muḥammad, reflects an Islamic interpretation that goes back to Ibn Isḥāq. However, M apparently should be read as *abadan* (forever), which would make the text an exact reflection of John 14:16: a Paraclete "to be with you forever."

328 Cf. John 17.

329 Cf. Matthew 26:39, Mark 14:36, Luke 22:42. The combination of the Johannine glorification theme with the synoptic saying about the cup shows that al-Yaʿqūbī was working with a source that harmonized the accounts of the passion.

they returned. The Messiah said to them: "I am Jesus the Nazarene. If you want me, take me away, that the word may be fulfilled."

Simon Peter[330] had a sword with him. He unsheathed it and struck the slave of the chief priest, cutting off his right hand.[331] The Messiah said: "Simon, return the sword to its sheath. I will not refuse to drink the cup my Lord has given me." The police arrested the Messiah, bound him, and brought him to Caiaphas, the head of the Jews, who had advised that he should be killed. Simon Peter, who was walking behind him, went in with the servants. Someone said to him, "Are you one of the disciples of this Nazarene?" He said, "No."

When the Messiah was brought before the head of the Jews, the latter began
1:86 to speak to him, but the Messiah gave him answers that he did not understand. | One of the police struck him on his cheeks. Then they took the Messiah away from Caiaphas to the Praetorium.[332] He[333] said to him, "Are you the king of the Jews?" The Messiah said to him, "Do you say this on your own, or have others told you of me?" And he began to speak to him, saying, "My kingdom is not [of] this world."

Then the police took a purple crown[334] and put it on his head, and they began striking him. Then they took him away with that crown on him. The chief priests said to him,[335] "Crucify him." Pilate said to them: "You take him and crucify him. As for me, I have found no cause against him." They said, "He must be crucified and killed because he said that he is the son of God." Then he brought him out and said to them, "You take him and crucify him." So they took the Messiah, brought him out, and made him carry the wooden beam on which they crucified him.

This is in the Gospel of John. As for Matthew, Mark, and Luke, they say that they put the wooden beam on which the Messiah was crucified on the neck of a Cyrenean man. They brought him to a place called the Skull, named *Īmākhālah* in Hebrew,[336] the place where he was crucified. Two others were crucified with him, one on one side and one on the other. Pilate wrote on a tablet: "This is Jesus the Nazarene, the king of the Jews." The chief priests said to him, "Write, 'Who

---

330 For "Peter," here and below, the Arabic has *aṣ-ṣafā*, the rock(s), a translation of the Syriac *kēpā*, reflected in Greek as Kēphas, and translated as Petros (Rock).

331 The language here reflects John 18:10–11; however, in the synoptics and in John, Peter cuts off an ear (Luke and John specify the right ear). Because the Syriac words for ear (*ʾednā*) and hand (*ʾīdā*) are quite similar in script, a copyist's error may be involved.

332 The Leiden editor (1, 86, note a) suggests a lacuna in the text.

333 That is, Pilate.

334 Al-Yaʿqūbī's "purple crown" conflates the *purple* cloak and the *crown* of thorns of John 19:2.

335 That is, to Pilate.

336 The correct reading and the source of this name are a mystery.

said that he was the king of the Jews.'" He said to them, "What I have written I have written."

The police divided the Messiah's garments among themselves. Mary his
mother, and Mary the daughter of | Clopas, and Mary Magdalene were standing 1:87
looking at him. He spoke to his mother from atop the beam of wood. The police took a sponge in which there was vinegar and brought it near his nose, but he loathed it. Then he gave up his spirit. They came to the two who were crucified with him and broke their legs. One of the police took a lance and thrust it into his side, and blood and water came out. Then one of the disciples spoke concerning him to Pilate, so that he took him down. He embalmed him with myrrh and aloes and wrapped him in linen cloths and perfume. There were gardens in that place, and in it was a new tomb. They put the Messiah in it. It was a Friday.

On Sunday, according to what the Christians say, Mary Magdalene came early to the tomb and did not find him. She went to Simon Peter and his companions and told them that he was not in the grave; so they went, but did not find him. Then Mary came a second time to the grave. She saw in the grave two men wearing white garments. They said to her, "Do not weep." Then she turned around and saw the Messiah. He spoke to her and said: "Do not come near me, because I have not ascended to my Father. But go to my brothers, and say to them that I am ascending to my Father and your Father, to my God and your God."

When it was evening on Sunday, he came to them and said to them: "Peace be with you. As my Father has sent me, so I send you. If you forgive the sins of anyone, they are forgiven." They said, "The one speaking to us is a spirit and a ghost." He said to them, "Look at the marks of the nails in my fingers, and at my right side." Then he said to them, "Blessed are those who have not seen me, yet have believed in me."

They brought him a piece of fish and he ate. He said to them: "If you believe
in me, you will do what I do. | Truly, you will not put your hands on someone 1:88
sick without his being cured, and death will not harm him." Then he was taken up from them. He was thirty-three years old.

This is what the authors of the Gospel say, and they differ with one another about all things. God, may He be glorified and exalted, has said: *They did not slay him, neither crucified him, only a likeness of that was shown to them. Those who are at variance concerning him surely are in doubt regarding him; they have no knowledge of him, except the following of surmise; and they slew him not of a certainty—no indeed; God raised him up to Him.*[337]

337 Qur'ān 4:157–158.

When Jesus the Messiah was taken up, the apostles gathered in Jerusalem on the Mount of Olives and made their way to an upper room. There were Peter, James, John, Andrew, Philip, Thomas, Bartholomew, Matthew, and James [...]. Simon stood up on the rock[338] and said, "Company of brothers, it was necessary that the scripture be fulfilled, in which the Holy Spirit foretold [...]." They wanted to appoint a man by whom the twelve would be complete. They put forward Matthias and Barsabbas and said, "O God, show us whom we should choose." It fell on Matthias. A mighty wind struck them, filling the upper room where they were, and they saw something like a tongue of fire and spoke in various tongues. They said to Peter, "What shall we do?" Peter said to them, "Arise, and be baptized, every man of you, in the name of the Messiah, and turn away from this perverse people."[339]

Peter and John persisted. Whenever they entered the assembly,[340] they mentioned the matter of the Messiah, described his deeds, and called the people to worship him. The Jews rebuked them for this. They arrested and imprisoned them, but then they released them. They[341] said, "Let us choose seven men who hallow God and who remember His wisdom and His Messiah." They chose
1:89 Stephen, Philip, Prochorus, Nicanor, | Timon, Parmenas, and Nicolaus of Antioch. They called them forth, prayed over them, and consecrated them. They took up the task of describing the matter of the Messiah and calling the people to their religion.

---

338 Cf. Acts 1:12 ff. However, the origin of this detail is unclear. Perhaps it reflects some early Christian exegesis of Matthew 16:18–19.

339 Cf. Acts 2:38–40. Three points deserve notice. "Arise" (Arabic *qūmū*) could easily be a copyist's error for *tūbū* (repent), exactly reflecting the Syriac translation's *tūbᵘ* and the Greek original lying behind it. The word that has been translated "be baptized," appears to be *iʿmidū*, rather than the expected *iʿtamidū* (be baptized), but this may be a copyist's error or a reflection of the form of Syriac *ʿmadᵘ*. The Arabic word translated "people" (*qabīla*), normally means "tribe," but al-Yaʿqūbī's source has already used it to render Syriac *sharbṯā* (stock, race, family, tribe), the word used by the Syriac translation of Acts 2:40. M apparently reads *qibla*, "turn away from this perverse direction of prayer," which, if it is more than a copyist's error, might reflect a view that this moment in Christian history was analogous to the moment when Muḥammad in Medina ceased facing Jerusalem in prayer and turned instead toward Mecca and the Kaʿba. However, it is more likely that the original reading was *hādhihi l-qabīlati l-muʿwajjati*, exactly reflecting Syriac *sharbṯā hāḏe mʿaqqamtā* and the Greek original behind it (ἀπὸ τῆς γενεᾶς τῆς σκολιᾶς ταύτης).

340 Arabic, *kanīsa*, the usual word for church, but also used for synagogue.

341 In the plural, not dual, in Arabic. Cf. Acts 6:2, where speakers are the twelve.

Paul was the most violent of men against them and most damaging to them.[342] He used to kill any of them whom he could, seeking them out in every place. He set out for Damascus to gather some people who were there. But he heard a voice calling to him, "Paul, how long will you persecute me?" He was so terrified that he could not see. Then Ananias came to him. He blessed him,[343] until he departed and his eyes were healed. He began to stand in the synagogues, making mention of the Messiah and hallowing him. The Jews therefore wanted to kill him. So he fled from them and joined the disciples in summoning the people and in speaking as they spoke. He displayed such renunciation of this world and scorn for it that the apostles all gave him precedence over themselves and made him their head.

He would rise up and speak, recalling the experience of the Israelites and the prophets. He would recall the matter of the Messiah and would say, "Let us turn to the Nations,[344] just as God said to the Messiah, 'I have set you to be a light for the Nations, so that you should become a salvation to the corners of the earth.'"[345] Every one of them spoke in favor of his opinion. They said that a law ought to be kept[346] and that someone should be sent to every land to summon to this religion and to prohibit them from sacrificing to idols, from fornication, and from eating blood.

Paul left for Antioch with two men to establish the religion of baptism. Then Paul returned. He was arrested and taken to the king of Rome. He stood up and

342 Cf. Acts 9.

343 Arabic, *qaddasa ʿalayhi*, "hallowed over him," that is, hallowed God's name over him, recited a blessing over him.

344 That is, the Gentiles. Syriac uses the singular of the word for nation (*ʿammā*) for the Jews, and its plural (*ʿammē*) for the Gentiles (the other nations).

345 Acts 13:46–47, quoting Isaiah 42:6, 49:6.

346 Cf. Acts 15 for the discussion of whether Gentile converts to Christianity were obligated to keep the law of Moses. Paul argued against imposing such an obligation. As a compromise, Gentile converts were obliged to keep a version of what Judaism called the Commandments of the Sons of Noah, usually given as seven commandments, but here summarized as three. Acts leaves the situation of Jewish Christians unclear. The text of al-Yaʿqūbī is unclear and may be corrupt. The first problem is whether the verb "to keep" is active or passive: Does the text say, "that *he* (Paul?) should keep the/a law," or "that the/a law should be kept"? Second, *nāmūs* (law) lacks the definite article, making it unclear whether the intended meaning is "a law" (consisting of the following three commandments) or "the law" (of Moses). It is even possible that a copyist has truncated the phrase *nāmūs Mūsā* ("the law of Moses," as in Acts 15:5).

spoke, mentioning the matter of the Messiah. Some people made a pact to kill him for corrupting their religion and for mentioning the Messiah and hallowing him.

1:90 The Kings of the Syrians

The first of the kings after the flood in the land of Babel were the kings of the Syrians.[347] The first of them who ruled and bound the crown on his head was Shūsān.[348] His reign was sixteen years. After him, his son Barbar[349] ruled twenty years. Then Samāshīr son of Alūl[350] ruled seven years. After him, his son ʿAmraqīm ruled ten years. Then his son Ahrīmūn ruled ten years. Then his son Samādān ruled ten years. Then his son Sabīr ruled eight years. Then Harīmūn ruled eighteen years. His son [Hūriyā][351] ruled twenty-two years. Then Arūd and Ḥalḥābīs ruled, both of them, for twelve years.

347 Arabic, *mulūk al-suryāniyyīn*. What ethnic or political group al-Yaʿqūbī intended by *al-Suryāniyyīn* is unclear. Furthermore, the copyists have badly mangled the names in this and the following lists. Some help can be derived from the fact that the later historian al-Masʿūdī apparently relied on al-Yaʿqūbī's work in writing *Murūj al-dhahab* (see 1:245 ff. [§ 509 ff.] of the latter work), and therefore the spellings found in al-Masʿūdī's work can sometimes help establish the likely original reading of al-Yaʿqūbī—but not always, for the manuscripts of *Murūj al-dhahab* show tremendous variation. Charles Pellat, the editor of *Murūj*, discusses al-Masʿūdī's treatment of the "Syrians" in his notes, *Murūj*, 6:374. He sees a list of the Seleucid rulers of Babylon as lying behind the names, implying that this list is out of place chronologically. For a table setting the lists in al-Yaʿqūbī alongside those in al-Masʿūdī and giving parallels to other lists from antiquity likely to have been available to both historians (particularly relevant are the lists in the *Chronicon* of Eusebius of Caesaria, d. 340), see the notes in al-Masʿūdī, *Murūj*, 7:598–601.

348 The vocalization of this name and of most names in this section is conjectural.

349 M Bārā or possibly Bīrā, corrected by ed. Leiden on the basis of al-Masʿūdī, *Murūj*, 1:245 (§ 509).

350 Thus M; ed. Leiden, Asmāshīr son of Alūl; al-Masʿūdī, ibid., Samāsīr son of Ūṭ.

351 No name appears in ms. M. Ed. Leiden supplied the name Hūriyā on the basis of al-Masʿūdī, *Murūj*, 1:249 (§ 517).

The Kings of Mosul and Nineveh

The first of them to rule was Bālūs, for thirty-two years.[352] Nīnūs son of Bālūs ruled fifty-two years and built the city of Nineveh. Then a woman named Samīram[353] ruled forty years. Then Lāwusnasar ruled forty-five years. Then there ruled fifteen kings who have no chronology or stories.

The Kings of Babel

The first of the kings of Babel after the Syrians was Nimrod the Mighty, who ruled sixty-nine years.[354] Kūdus ruled forty-three years. Arqū ruled ten | years. 1:91
Būlus ruled sixty-two years. Then Samīram ruled forty-two years. Qūsamīs ruled sixty-nine years. Anyūs ruled thirty years. Līlāwus ruled twelve years. Aṭlūs ruled thirty-two years. Safarūs[355] ruled thirty years. Then Ḥāzim-Būs ruled thirty years. Then Saʿālūs ruled thirty years. Sabṭās ruled forty years. Asanṭarus ruled forty years. Damanūṭūs ruled forty-five years. Alʿarūs ruled thirty years. Almaqrandūs ruled fifty-two years. Qāra[b/n?]ūs ruled thirty years. Bābāwus ruled forty-five years. Sharsabā-Adūmūs ruled forty years. Dārāfūs ruled thirty-eight years. Lāwubanas ruled forty-five years. Faṭrīs ruled thirty years. Farṭāwus ruled twenty years. Afraṭā ruled sixty years. Qūlā ruled thirty-five years. Taʿlat-palasar[356] ruled thirty-five years. Asʿalūsarqam ruled fourteen years. Asraʿūn ruled seven years. Qīm-Ḥadūm[357] ruled three years. Fardūḥ ruled forty-seven years. Sanḥārīb ruled thirty-one years. Maʿrasā ruled thirty-three years. Bukht-Naṣṣar ruled forty-five years. Qarmūraj ruled one year. Saṭ-Safar ruled sixty years. Māsūsā ruled eight years. Maʿūsā ruled seven months. Dāryūsh ruled thirty-one years. Kasarjūs[358] ruled twenty years. Qarṭayān ruled seven months.
Manaḥsamt ruled forty-one years. Saʿlas ruled seven | months. Dāryūsh,[359] the 1:92

352 Parallel in al-Masʿūdī, *Murūj*, 1:252–253 (§ 520–521).

353 Sic M and al-Masʿūdī, *Murūj*, 1:252 (§ 520); ed. Leiden, Shamīram. She is better known by the Greek form of her name, Semiramis.

354 Parallel in al-Masʿūdī, *Murūj*, 1:254–259 (§ 522–529).

355 Sic M; ed. Leiden, Safardus (vocalization uncertain).

356 So read by the Leiden editor and connected with Tiglat Pileser.

357 Sic M; ed. Leiden, Qīm-Ḥadūn.

358 Sic M; ed. Leiden, Kasar-Ḥūsh.

359 That is, Darius.

one whom Alexander killed, ruled nineteen years. Arṭaḥshāst[360] ruled twenty-seven years.

These kings were the kings of this world. They were the ones who erected buildings, acquired cities, constructed fortresses, raised palaces, dug [canals], planted trees, drew [water from wells, tilled] the land, extracted minerals, struck coins, fashioned and wore crowns, forged swords, took up weapons, made tools of iron, worked copper and lead, adopted measures and weights, mapped countries, determined climes, captured enemies, enslaved captives, employed prisons, described the seasons, named the months, spoke of the spheres, constellations, and planets, calculated, and made decisions according to what conjunction, separation, trine, quartile, and *mujāsadāt* indicate.[361]

The Kings of India

Scholars have said that the first of the kings of India under whom they became united was Brahman, the king in whose time was the first house.[362] He was the first person who discoursed about the stars. From him was derived knowledge of them and the first book, which the Indians call the *Sindhind*, which means "Eon of Eons."[363] From it were abridged the *Arjamhar*[364] and the *Almagest*.[365]

---

360 That is, Artaxerxes.

361 That is, they established the science of astrology. The Arabic terms used here are *ijtimāʿ* (conjunction of two bodies in the same sign of the zodiac), *iftirāq* (separation of two bodies from each other), *tathlīth* (trine, that is, separation of two bodies by one-third of the zodiac, 120 degrees), *tarbīʿ* (quartile, that is, separation of two bodies by one-fourth of the zodiac, that is, 90 degrees), and *mujāsadāt*, whose meaning is unclear.

362 Following M, *al-bayt al-awwal*. Ed. Leiden, following cod. Schefer, reads *al-badʾ al-awwal* (the first beginning), which is close to the parallel in al-Masʿūdī, *Murūj*, 1:84 (§ 152), where Indian leaders are quoted as saying, "We were the people of the beginning (*al-badʾ*), and ours is the goal, the inception, and the conclusion." Since al-Yaʿqūbī and al-Masʿūdī draw on the some of the same sources for their treatment of India, the text of al-Masʿūdī can elucidate problems in the text of al-Yaʿqūbī. For a study of al-Masʿūdī's treatment of India, see S. Maqbul Ahmad, "Al-Masʿūdī on the Kings of India."

363 *Sindhind* reflects the Sanskrit title of the ancient astronomical treatise *Sūrya Siddhānta*. See Pellat's note in al-Masʿūdī, *Murūj*, 6:397; S. Maqbul Ahmad, "Al-Masʿūdī and the Kings of India," 100.

364 Sic M; ed. Leiden *al-Arjabhar*; al-Masʿūdī, *Murūj*, 1:85 (§ 153), *al-Arjabhad*. This refers to the Sanskrit *Aryabhaṭīya*, composed by Aryabhaṭa (b. 476 CE).

365 Arabic, *al-Majisṭī*, presumably reflecting Greek ἡ Μεγίστη Σύνταξις. Curiously, al-Yaʿqūbī (or his source) viewed Ptolemy's treatise as an abridgement of an Indian treatise.

From the *Arjamhar* they abridged the *Arkand*,[366] and from the *Almagest* the book of Ptolemy. From this they then made abridgements, astronomical tables, and similar things, | such as computation and the invention of the nine Indian 1:93
numerals from which can be derived all computation without limit.[367] They are 1 2 3 4 5 6 7 8 9. The first of them, 1, is also 10 and 100 and 1,000 and 100,000 and 1,000,000 and 10,000,000 and 100,000,000, and so on forever. The second, 2, is also 20 and [200 and 2,000 and 20,]000 and 200,000 and 2,000,000—and one can compute upward similarly for all the nine numerals. However, the place of the unit is distinct from that of the ten, and the place of the ten is distinct from that of the hundred, and so on for each place. Whenever a place is empty of a number, a zero is set in it. Zero is a small circle.

They divided the world into seven climes.[368] *The first clime is India.* Its limit toward the east is the sea and the region of China, to Daybul[369] bordering the land of Iraq, to the gulf of the ocean that borders the land of India, to the land of the Ḥijāz. *The second clime is the Ḥijāz.* Its limit is this gulf, to Aden, to the land of Abyssinia bordering on the land of Egypt, to al-Thaʿlabiyya[370] bordering on the land of Iraq. *The third clime is Egypt.* Its limit is from what borders the land of Abyssinia, to the land of the Ḥijāz, to the Green Sea[371] bordering on the south, to the west, to the gulf that borders (the land of) the Romans,[372] to Naṣībīn[373]

---

366 S. Maqbul Ahmad identifies this as the *Khaṇḍakhādyaka*, composed by Brahmagupta in 665 CE.

367 Arabic *alladhī lā yudraku maʿrifatuhā*, literally, "whose knowledge cannot be overtaken." This seems to be a way of stating that the system of numeration invented by the Indians (known to us as Arabic numerals) is in principle unbounded and capable of representing any number, however large.

368 Arabic *iqlīm*, pl. *aqālīm*, "clime, climate," or more generally, "region," ultimately derived from Greek κλῖμα. Technically, a zone bounded on the north and south by two parallels of latitude. See the article by A. Miquel in *EI*², s.v. Iḳlīm.

369 Daybul was the ancient port of Sind, at the mouth of a creek to the west of the Indus River. It was the first city of Sind conquered by the Muslims. After flourishing for a time, it fell into ruin and its exact location is unknown. See the article by A. S. Bazmee Ansari in *EI*², s.v. Daybul (Dēbal or Dēwal).

370 Al-Thaʿlabiyya was a station on the pilgrimage road from al-Kūfa to Mecca. It lay in Najd, in the northeastern corner of present-day Saudi Arabia, near the Iraqi border. See the article in *EI*², s.v. al-Tha̱ʿlabiyya.

371 Arabic, *al-Baḥr al-Akhḍar*, one of the names for the Atlantic Ocean. See the article by D. M. Dunlop in *EI*², s.v. al-Baḥr al-Muḥīṭ.

372 That is, Anatolia.

373 Classical Nisibis, modern spelling Nusaybin, a town in upper Mesopotamia on the Turkish side of the Turkish-Syrian border.

bordering on the land of Iraq. *The fourth clime is Iraq.* Its limit toward India is Daybul, and toward the Ḥijāz is al-Thaʿlabiyya, and toward Egypt and (the land of) the Romans is Naṣībīn, and toward the land of Khurāsān is the river of Balkh.[374] *The fifth clime is (the land of the) the Romans.* Its limit toward the land of Egypt is the gulf, and toward the West is the sea, and toward the Turks is Yājūj and Mājūj,[375] and toward the land of Iraq is Naṣībīn. *The sixth clime is Yājūj and*
1:94 *Mājūj.* Its limit toward the West is the Turks, and toward | the Khazar[376] is the sea and deserts between it and the extremity of the north, and toward the east is the land of Naṣībīn, and toward Khurāsān is the river of Balkh. *The seventh clime is China.* Its limit toward the west is Yājūj and Mājūj, and toward the east is the sea, and toward India is the land of Kashmir, and toward Khurāsān is the river of Balkh.

They said: Each of these climes is nine hundred *farsakh*s by the same.[377] It has been said that the diameter of the earth is 2,100 *farsakhs* and its diameter is 6,300 *farsakhs*.[378] They fixed this *farsakh* at 16,000 cubits. They mention that the *dhirāʿ* that surrounds the base of the circle of the stars, which is the sphere of the moon, is 125,664 *farsakhs*, and that its diameter from the limit of the beginning of Aries to the limit of the beginning of Libra is 40,000 *farsakh*s, measured by these *farsakh*s by which they measured the earth. The hours of the longest day in the first clime are 13 hours; in the second they are 13½ hours; in the third they are 14 hours; in the fourth they are 14½ hours; in the fifth they are 15 hours; in the sixth they are 15½ hours; and in the seventh they are 16 hours. Each city the measurements of the length of whose day is in this amount is the middle of the clime in which it is. Anything that is between these amounts

---

374 That is, the Oxus (Arabic Jayḥūn, modern Amu Darya).

375 Yājūj and Mājūj (Gog and Magog) are mentioned in the Qurʾān as two peoples against whom Dhū l-Qarnayn (Alexander) built a wall. Later geographers located the wall somewhere in the Caucasus or to the east. See the article by E. van Donzel and Claudia Ott in *EI*², s.v. Yādjūdj wa-Mādjūdj.

376 The Khazar were a nomadic people of the South Russian steppes. See the article by W. Barthold and P. B. Golden in *EI*², s.v. Khazar.

377 Following M: *kullu iqlīmin min hādhihi l-aqālīmi tisʿu miʾati farsakhin fī mithlihā*. Ed. Leiden has in place of *tisʿu miʾati farsakhin* the words *yasaʿu miʾata farsakhin* (encompasses a hundred farsakhs)—which is far too small a number. The *farsakh* originally was the distance that could be covered on foot in one hour, but in Islamic times it was a conventional measure fixed at 3 Arab miles (5.985 km = 3.719 miles). However, al-Yaʿqūbī immediately makes it clear that the Indian unit, consisting of 16,000 cubits (*dhirāʿ*) was different from the Arab *farsakh*, which consisted of 12,000 cubits. See the article by W. Hinz in *EI*², s.v. Farsakh.

378 Literally, "its extension (*madd*) is …" The computation assumes a value of 3 for π.

is of the clime to which it is closest in the amount of hours. Thus it comes about that the middle of the first clime is at a journey of approximately 30 nights from the equator, in the land of Yemen, the city of Saba', and what adjoins it on the east and west, and that is this side of Aden of Abyan[379] by a space of 10 days. The middle of the second clime is Mecca and what adjoins it from the east | to 1:95
the west. The middle of the third clime is Alexandria and what adjoins it from the vicinity of Kufa and Basra on the east to the west. The middle of the fourth clime is Iṣfahān and what adjoins it of that which is on the same latitude from the east to the west. The middle of the fifth clime is in the nearest parts of the land of Marw and whatever adjoins it from east to west that is on the same latitude. The middle of the sixth clime is Bardhaʿa[380] and whatever adjoins it on the same latitude between the east and the west. The middle of the seventh clime is in the mountains of the Turks and whatever adjoins them on the same latitude between the east and the west.

The Indians said that God created the planets[381] in the first minute of Aries, and that was the first day of the world. Then He set them in motion from that position more swiftly than the blinking of an eye and gave each planet a known motion, so that in the number of days of the *sindhind* they all come to the very position where they were created, as they had been, as their first aspect; and then God will decree what He wishes. They said that all the world's days of the *sindhind*, from when the planets first revolved until they all come together in the (first) minute of Aries as they were on the day they were created, are 1,577,716,450,000 days.[382] In months this comes to 60,840,000,000 months.[383] | 1:96
In years it comes to 4,320,000,000 full years, in years according to the circuit of the sun.[384] The year is 365¼ days and 5 and 1/400 hours.[385]

---

379 Abyan is the district (*mikhlāf*) in which the port of Aden is located.

380 Bardhaʿa (Armenian Partav, modern Barda) is a town south of the Caucasus in the central part of modern Azerbaijan. See the article by D. M. Dunlop in *EI*², s.v. Bardhaʿa.

381 Arabic *kawākib* (pl. of *kawkab*) includes, besides the planets of modern astronomy, the sun and the moon.

382 M conveniently writes the number in Indian (Arabic) notation in the margin. Houtsma, the Leiden editor, notes at this point: "I have given the following numbers as they are in the manuscripts, although the numbers of years, months, and days hardly agree with each other."

383 This translates into a month of 25.93 days.

384 This translates into a year of 14.08 months. However, if one divides the number of days by the number of years, one arrives at a year of approximately 365.2121 days, which is remarkably close to the modern figure of approximately 365.2422 days for a solar year.

385 Since the figures given by al-Yaʿqūbī translate into a year of 365.2121 days, one can correct

Then the affairs of the kingdom became disturbed in India for a long time and there were sundry kingdoms in the country, with each group having a kingdom, until kings attacked them and they feared that weakness would overcome them. Being men of wisdom, knowledge, and intellect, exceeding in these things the measure of other nations, they decided to make one man king; and so they made Zāraḥ[386] king. He was a man of great standing and exalted rank, and so his kingdom became great and his authority exalted. He marched to Babel and then beyond it to the kings of Israel. He was the one who attacked the children of Israel twenty years after the death of Solomon son of David. Rehoboam son of [Solomon son of] David was king at the time. The children of Israel cried out to God, and God gave death power over Zāraḥ and his army, so he returned to his country.

Among their kings was Fūr.[387] He it was whose country Alexander attacked, having slain the king of the Persians and conquered the land of Iraq and the adjoining lands that were in the kingdom of Darius. This came to pass because Alexander wrote to Fūr, commanding him to become his obedient subject, but Fūr wrote back that he would march his armies against him. Alexander therefore took the initiative and went to Fūr's land. Fūr marched out against him and made war on him. Fūr brought out elephants, and Alexander was
1:97 overwhelmed: | nothing could stand up to them. Then Alexander made statues of copper. He filled them with naphtha and sulfur, set them on fire inside, put them on wagons, dressed them with weapons, and positioned them in front of the ranks. When the two sides met, the men pushed them toward the elephants. As they drew near, the elephants attacked them with their trunks. They wrapped their trunks around the copper, which was ablaze and scorching hot, and turned back in panic, routing[388] and destroying the Indian troops. Alexander then challenged Fūr, the king of India, to single combat. The latter came forth, and Alexander killed him in single combat with his counterpart and plundered his camp.

[Among their kings was] Kayhan. He was a wise, clever, and cultivated man, and Alexander made him king after Fūr over all the land of India. Kayhan

---

the last figure by assuming that the text should read: "365 days and ¼ day, that is, 5 and 1/400 hours." This works out nicely to approximately 365.2084 days.

386 Sic ed. Leiden, emending the MSS (M apparently reads Zarūḥ or Razūḥ) on the basis of the reading Zāraḥ of ed. Leiden, 1:66. The emendation is uncertain, as the Zāraḥ (Zerah) mentioned there is clearly a different person. The corresponding king in al-Masʿūdī, *Murūj*, 1:88 (§162), is named Zāmān (otherwise unknown).

387 Fūr is the Indian king Porus who was defeated by Alexander in 327 BCE.

388 Sic ed. Leiden (*tafillu*); M has *taqtulu* (killing).

practiced meditation.[389] He was the first to hold the doctrine of imagination[390] and that nature changes into what you imagine. Whatever you imagine will benefit it, will benefit it, though it be harmful. Kayhan would eat aconite, a deadly poison, and imagine that there were loads of ice on his heart, and the aconite would not harm him until its moisture had burned away. He was among the soundest of God's creatures in mind and the most retentive and intelligent of them.

One of their kings was Dabshalim.[391] He it was during whose reign the book *Kalīla and Dimna* was composed.[392] The person who composed it was Baydabā,[393] one of their wise men. He fashioned it | as parables which intelligent 1:98
persons would heed and from which they would gain understanding and be instructed. Its first chapter is the chapter of the ruler to whom wicked men slander his intimate friends and companions, and how he should employ deliberateness and proof and not act hastily upon the word of slander. It is the chapter of the Lion and the Ox. The second chapter is the chapter of investigating matters, how their consequences take place, and the evil results to which envy, rashness, and guile lead. It is the chapter of the Investigation of Dimna's Case. The third chapter is the chapter of enemies: how one should guard against them, devices to deal with them, speech that earns enmity, how one should cozen one's enemies and then seize the opportunity to deal with them when it becomes possible, and how one should humble oneself before them until one can take one's revenge. It is the chapter of the Owls and the Crows. The fourth chapter is the chapter on consulting scholars, on seeking

389 Following M, *istaʿmala l-dhikr*; ed. Leiden reads *istaʿmala l-fikr* (he practiced thinking). This is admittedly a speculative translation, but the following description of Kayhan's doctrine implies that the phrase has some sort of technical sense.

390 Arabic, *tawahhum*, literally, an imagining or supposing a thing to be so. Al-Yaʿqūbī seems to be straining to find an Arabic word for a kind of philosophical idealism.

391 The historical identity of this king and the correct vocalization of the name cannot be established.

392 On the background of the book known in Arabic as *Kalīla wa-Dimna*, see the article by C. Brockelmann in *EI*², s.v. Kalīla wa-Dimna. King Dabshalim and the philosopher Baydabā are mentioned in the introduction to Ibn al-Muqaffaʿ's Arabic translation of *Kalīla wa-Dimna*.

393 Since the time of de Sacy, who published a form of the Arabic translation of the text by Ibn al-Muqaffaʿ, the name is usually transcribed as Bidbā or Bidpai. De Sacy speculated that the name in the Syriac and Arabic may reflect Sanskrit *Veidava* (reader of the Veda) or *vidva* (learned)—cf. Silvestre de Sacy, *Calila et Dimna*, 17, note 1. The oldest Syriac form is probably to be read as Bēdavag or Bīdwāg—see Schulthess, *Kalīla und Dimna*, notes 190 and 191.

help from people of good judgment and trustworthiness, and on disclosing matters to people of intellect. It is the chapter of Bilādh.[394] The fifth chapter is the chapter of favors: to whom they should be done, how ingratitude spoils them when they are misplaced or bestowed on the undeserving,[395] and how one can know how they can be bestowed on those who deserve them and will be grateful for them. It is the chapter of the Turtle, the Panther, the Monkey, and the Carpenter. The sixth chapter is the chapter of obtaining something, but losing it after having acquired it, and the inability to keep it after having gained it. It is the chapter of the Monkey and the Tortoise. The seventh chapter is the chapter of making a show of friendliness and flattering people of importance, being wary of their affection, and gaining the favor of the corrupt until one can rid oneself of the evil. It is the chapter of the Cat and the Rat. The eighth chapter is the chapter of the ruler's knowing his aides, relatives, and intimates; how he
1:99 should render well-affected | those whom his harshness may have harmed and how he should obtain their assistance; how he should seek help in his affairs from people of modesty and affection; how he should examine the state of his aides and entourage and reward those who do good and punish those who do evil for their wickedness. It is the chapter of the Lion and the Jackal. The ninth chapter is the chapter of brothers and those who trust the soundness of their affection, the value of brothers, and the great benefit to be obtained from them and their aid in matters of adversity and in prosperity. It is the chapter of the Ring-Necked Dove. The tenth chapter is the chapter of seeking to benefit people at the price of harm to oneself and on pondering consequences. It is the chapter of the Lioness and the Horseman.

One of the Indian scholars has said that the people of a certain country[396] were being visited constantly by death, until their scholars perished and the kingdom weakened. When Hashrān became king, he sought someone to revive for him the laws of the religion of his ancestors, and so Qaflān, who was exceedingly clever, came to him and said to him: "Men are part of the animal kingdom; the animal kingdom is part of that which grows, and that which grows is composed of the four natures, which are fire, air, earth, and water. That which grows can be divided into three parts: plants, which have only growth; shellfish

394 Bilādh is the name of a wise counselor who foils a plot against his king, along with other examples of his wisdom and prudence.

395 The translation follows the emendation suggested by Landberg, 35: *wa-kayfa yufsiduhu sūʾu l-shukr*. Ed. Leiden reads, *wa-kayfa yufsadu wa-sūʾu l-shukr*, yielding, "and how (favors) are spoiled, and ingratitude when they are …"

396 Ed. Leiden emends to read, "the people of the country [of India]," but M vocalizes as *ahla bilādin*, "people of a (certain) country."

and the like in the sea, which have growth and sense; and land animals, which have growth, sense, and movement. Animals are too small and insignificant for the Creator to govern; they are governed and changed by the celestial sphere." The king said to him, "Show me a picture and proof for what you say." So he invented the backgammon board[397] and said: "Men have agreed that the cycle of seasons is a year, the meaning of which is twelve months, whose meaning is the twelve signs of the zodiac; that the days of the month are thirty, meaning that each sign has thirty degrees; and that the days are seven, meaning the seven planets." He made a representation of that. He devised a board analogous to the year. On it he set | twenty-four points,[398] the number of the hours of 1:100
the night and day, with twelve points on each side, symbolizing the months of the year and the signs of the zodiac. He gave the game thirty counters,[399] to symbolize the days of the month and the degrees of the signs of the zodiac. He made the two dice to symbolize the night and the day. Each die had six sides, because six is a perfect number, having a half, a third, and a sixth. When each die was cast, it had seven points on its top and bottom: under the six was one, under the five was two, under the four was three—to symbolize the number of the days and the seven planets, namely, the sun, the moon, Saturn, Jupiter, Mars, Mercury, and Venus. Then he made it a contest between two players. He gave each a die and said, "Whichever player gets more of the seven points on top than his partner will begin." Then the two dice were joined together for him, and he would throw; the counters would be moved according to whatever came up on the dice. He made this a representation of the good fortune that the deficient person obtains through what the celestial sphere bestows on him and of the deprivation that the prudent man suffers in accordance with what the celestial sphere bestows on him. When this became evident, the king accepted it, and it spread among the people of the kingdom; and so the people of India came to order their affairs in accordance with what the seven planets ordain.[400]

---

397 Arabic, *nard*. Cf. al-Masʿūdī, *Murūj*, 1:88 (§161); see the article by F. Rosenthal in *EI*², s.v. Nard.

398 Arabic *bayt*, "house," the long triangles, twelve on each side and of alternating colors, into which the backgammon board is divided.

399 Arabic, *kalb*, literally "dog," possibly because each counter was originally shaped like a dog, but that is pure speculation and unlikely to be true, as chessmen, none of which took the form of a dog, are also called *kalb* below. Cf. Dozy, *Supplément aux dictionnaires Arabes*, 2:489a.

400 At this point, M adds the following: *Completed with God's praise, help, grace, and beneficence is Part One*. This is followed by a centered title: *Here follows Part Two of the History of Ibn Wāḍiḥ al-Kātib*. Under this, another hand has added the author's full name—*Aḥmad*

Balhīt[401] became king when this religion had become dominant over the people of the kingdom. He had intelligence and knowledge. When he saw the condition of his people, it displeased him and distressed him. He asked whether there remained any man who held the religion of the Brahmins. People pointed to a man of intelligence and religion, and so he sent for him. When the man came to him, he honored him and raised his rank. Then he mentioned what had spread among the people of his kingdom. The man said, "O king, I will invent a compelling demonstration whereby the superiority of the prudent man and the inferiority of the deficient person may be known, and I will make it to be an
1:101 image | of the difference between two men, to illustrate the superiority of the prudent over the deficient, the diligent over the negligent, the cautious over the rash, and the intelligent over the ignorant." He invented chess (*shaṭranj*), which translated into Persian is *hasht ranj*—*hasht* means 'eight' and *ranj* means 'side.'[402] He made it to be eight by eight, so that there were sixty-four squares, and gave it thirty-two pieces divided between two colors, each color having sixteen pieces. He divided the sixteen into six shapes: the king (*shāh*) was a shape, the advisor (*firz*) was a shape, the two elephants (*fīl*) were a shape, the two rooks (*rukh*) were a shape, the two horses (*faras*) were a shape, and the foot soldiers (*bayādiq*) were a shape. This was derived from "the pair of the pair," which is the best that exists in numeration: for if you divide sixty-four, its half is thirty-two, which is the number of all the pieces; if you halve thirty-two, its half is sixteen, which is the number of each player's pieces; if you halve sixteen, its half is eight, which is the number of each player's foot soldiers (pawns); if you halve eight, its half is four, which is the number of each player's rooks and horses; and if you halve four, its half is two. It now has been divided into pairs, and there remains nothing in the division after the pairs except the one, each pair being divisible into units, a unit being neither a number

---

b. Abī Yaʿqūb b. Jaʿfar b. Wahb b. Wāḍiḥ al-ʿAbbāsī—after which yet another hand has added a benediction, *May God have mercy upon him*. The next section begins: *In the name of God, the Merciful, the Compassionate, and His help we seek.*

401 C and M read Bahlīt, which Houtsma emended on the basis of al-Masʿūdī, *Murūj*, 1:89 (§164).

402 The Persian should be read as *rang* (color). Although this derivation is plausible if one begins with the Arabic form of the word and adds one letter at the beginning, converting *sh.ṭ.r.n.g* into *h.sh.ṭ.r.n.g*, it is not the most obvious derivation of *shaṭranj*, which is thought to come from Sanskrit, *catur-aṅga* (having four ranks), referring to the four divisions of an army: infantry (pawns), cavalry (knights), elephants (the modern bishop), and chariots (the modern rook). The king and his vizier (modern queen) stood outside this number. See the article by F. Rosenthal in *EI*^{2}, s.v. Shaṭrandj.

nor counted, neither even nor odd, because the first odd number is three.[403] Then the wise man said: "Nothing is more serious than war, because in it the superiority of good management, judgment, prudence, caution, preparedness, shrewdness, wariness, bravery, fortitude, strength, endurance, and courage is demonstrated. The inferiority of anyone who lacks any of these things will become known, because failing to have them cannot | be excused and lack 1:102
of them destroys lives. Ignorance permits the prohibited; abandonment of prudence leads to destruction of the kingdom; weakness of judgment brings ruin; negligence is the cause of defeat; lack of knowledge of preparedness leads to rout; lack of acquaintance with stratagems casts one into perdition; and abandoning caution is an opportunity for the enemy." He made it after the likeness of war, so that if one hit the mark one would win, and if one missed it one would perish. When the king saw the soundness of the demonstration, and the superiority of the wise man's wisdom became evident, and that he had hit the mark, had represented the matter well, and had clarified what had been obscure, he gathered the people of his kingdom and made known to them how God had removed their distress. He commanded them to set it up and ponder it. He said to them: "We know that there is no living creature in the world that speaks, thinks, laughs, and reasons except man. Man is the point around which everything in the world turns, for the Creator created the firmament and everything in it for man, that thereby he might know what he needs with regard to times and seasons. He likewise made subject to him all that is on the earth and all that God created in the depth of the sea, the air of the sky, and the summits of the mountains. When He made man the king of all He created, man divided it into three parts: one third he ate, one third he subjected to his use, and one third he killed. He ate the birds, the fish, and whatever herd animals and camels he wished; he subjected cattle, asses, and riding animals to his use; and he killed predators, snakes, and vermin. (God) set in him organs by which he might know, reason, perceive, and understand, and made some people superior to others in knowledge, intellect, and understanding."

Some Indian scholars have alleged that when Jūshīr[404] daughter of Balhīt became queen, a rebel rebelled against her. Being an intelligent young woman,

---

403 Modern mathematics defines even numbers as those divisible by two and odd numbers as all the rest. The older tradition, going back to the Greeks, regarded one, the unit, as sui generis, neither even nor odd. This explains the statement that the first odd number is three.

404 Thus apparently in M, although the last two letters of the name are undotted and uncertain. In al-Masʿūdī, *Murūj*, 1:90 (§ 167), Balhīt is succeeded by a man named Kūrush (not to be confused with the Arabic form of the name of Cyrus the Persian), not by his daughter.

she sent one of her sons—she had four children—but the rebel killed her
1:103 son. | This distressed the people of her kingdom. Fearing to tell her the news, they gathered before one of their wise men—he was named Qaflān—a man of wisdom, cleverness, and good judgment—and they told him what had happened. He said, "Give me three days." They did so, and he went apart to think. Then he said to one of his pupils, "Bring me a carpenter and wood of two different colors, white and black." They brought a skilled carpenter and wood of two different colors, white and black. The wise man drew the figure of a chess board and commanded the carpenter, and he made it. Then he said to him, "Bring me a tanned hide." He commanded him to draw sixty-four squares on it; he did so, and it was set aside. Then (the wise man and his pupil) played against each other until they understood the game and became proficient in it. Then he said to his pupil, "This is a war without loss of lives." Then the people of the kingdom came to him, and he brought it out to them. When they saw it, they knew that it was a bit of wisdom that no one could arrive at. He began to play against his pupil, and the latter would suffer checkmate or defeat of his king. The queen was given a report about Qaflān, and she summoned him and commanded him to show her his wisdom. He produced his pupil with the chessboard and set it up between the pupil and himself. The two played, and one defeated the other [and said,] "Checkmate!" Taking notice and realizing what he meant,[405] she said to Qaflān, "Has my son been killed?" "You have said it," he said. She said to her chamberlain, "Let the people in, that they may offer me condolence." When she was finished, she summoned Qaflān and said to him, "Ask for whatever you need." He said, "I ask that I be given wheat according the number of the squares of the chessboard: that I be given one grain in the first square [...][406] and that it be doubled for me in the third square as against the second, and so on according to this formula until the last square." She asked, "And what is the quantity of that?" She commanded the wheat to be brought, but before it was enough, all the wheat of the country was exhausted. Then the wheat was replaced by its value in money, until the money was exhausted. When it had become great, the wise man said: "I have no need of it. A little of this world suffices me." Then she asked him
1:104 about | the number of grains he had asked for. He said to her: "It will come to a number, and this is what is on the chessboard in the way of number:

---

405 Reading with M, *arādahu*; ed. Leiden has *arādāhu* (what the two meant). The implication is clearer in Arabic, where the word for checkmate, *shāhmāt*, can be seen to be composed of two words that mean "the king (*shāh*) has died (*māt*)."

406 The words, "and two grains in the second," have fallen out of the text. See Landberg, 35.

The number of the first row is 255.[407] The second is 32,768.[408] The third is 8,388,608. The fourth is 2,147,483,648. The fifth is 549,755,813,88[8]. The sixth is 140,737,488,355,328. The seventh is 36,028,[797],018,963,968. The eighth is 9,223,372,036,854,775,808. The total of everything on the eight rows of the chess board comes to 18,446,744,073,[7]09,551,615."

Among their kings was Kūsh,[409] who was king during the time of Sindibād the wise. This Kūsh composed the book entitled, *The Cunning of Women*.[410] 1:105

The Indians are masters of wisdom and speculation; they excel mankind in every kind of wisdom. Their doctrine about the stars is the soundest of doctrines. Their book about it is the book of the *Sindhind*,[411] from which each science treated by the Greeks, the Persians, and others was derived. Their doctrine in medicine is the most ancient: theirs is the book on the subject [entitled] *Susrud*.[412] It deals with the symptoms of diseases, knowledge of their treatment, and the drugs for them. There are also the book *Shark*; the book *Nidāna* on the symptoms of 404 diseases and knowledge of them, without treatment; the book *Sindhishān*, whose title means "Image of Attainment"; a

---

407 That is, the *total* number of grains on all the squares of the first row is $1+2+4+8+16+32+64+128=255$.

408 This is the number of grains on square 16 of the chessboard (That is, 128×2^8), and so on for squares 24, 32, 40, 48, 56, and 64, each of which will contain the number of grains on the square at the end of the previous row multiplied by a factor of 2^8 (256).

409 Apparently the same as Kūrush of al-Masʿūdī, *Murūj*, 1:90 (§167), a reading with which Cod. Schefer agrees, according to the note of the Leiden editor.

410 This is the same book as the one that al-Masʿūdī, *Murūj*, 1:90 (§167), refers to as *The Seven Viziers, the Teacher, the Young Man, and the King's Wife*. The book is a collection of tales with a frame story in which a young prince, commanded to keep silence for seven days by his teacher, the sage Sindibād (no relation to Sinbad the Sailor), "is accused by one of his father's wives of having attempted to seduce her; he is condemned to death, but the king's seven viziers take turns in delaying the execution from day to day, each telling a story designed to show the perfidy of women. Each evening, their work is undone by the guilty wife, who tells the king a story presenting the contrary case. After seven days the prince, permitted once more to speak, exculpates himself and then pardons his accuser." (J.-P. Guillaume in EI[2], s.v. Sindbād al-Ḥakīm). The book had apparently been translated into Arabic through Pahlavi by the time of al-Yaʿqūbī, as evidenced his giving it an Arabic title. The work was translated later into Persian, Syriac, Greek, Hebrew, and Spanish.

411 See note 363 above.

412 This refers to the *Suśruta Samhita*, a compendium of texts on Ayurvedic medicine and surgery attributed to the ancient physician Suśruta. See S. Maqbul Ahmad, "Al-Masʿūdī and the Kings of India," 104, n. 3.

book on the disagreements between the Indians and the Greeks concerning the hot, the cold, the virtues of medicines, and division of the year; and a book on the names of drugs, (listing) each drug with ten names. They also have other books on medicine. They have many books of logic and philosophy, which are[413] the first principles of science. Among them is the book *Ṭūfā*[414] on the science of the definitions of logic, and the book *That Wherein the Philosophers of the Indians and Greeks Differ*. They have so many books that it would take too much time to mention them and too much space to list them.

1:106 The religion of the people of India is Brahmanism. | Among them there are idol worshippers. They have various kingdoms and separate kings because of the country's extent in length and width. The first of their kings of the part that borders on the lands that today are within the Abode of Islam is Dāniq.[415] He is a king of great rank, extensive kingdom, and much materiel. After him comes Rahmā,[416] who is greater in rank and more populous[417] in lands. He is located on one of the seas, and in his country there is gold and the like. Then comes the kingdom of Balharā.[418] Then comes al-Kumkam; from them comes teak, and they have extensive lands. Then comes the kingdom of al-Ṭāqā.[419] They are a people of white faces. Then comes the kingdom of Kanbāya.[420] Then come the kingdom of al-Ṭarsūl,[421] the kingdom of al-Mūsha,[422] and the kingdom of al-

413 Reading with M, *hiya*; ed. Leiden, *fī* (on).

414 Otherwise unknown. The reading is uncertain.

415 Otherwise unknown. The reading is uncertain.

416 As emended by the Leiden editor from MS "Wahm" on the basis of al-Masʿūdī, *Murūj*, 1:203 (§ 428). A possible reading would be Dharma, for Dharma-pāla, who ruled Bengal from 769–801 CE or later. See S. Maqbul Ahmad, "Al-Masʿūdī on the Kings of India," 110.

417 Reading with M, *aʿmaru bilādan*; C and ed. Leiden read, *aʿazzu bilādan* (more powerful in lands).

418 Balharā (or Balharay or Ballaharā) is the Arabic transcription of the Prakrit title Ballaharāya (from Sanskrit Vallabha-rāja, "beloved king") of the kings of the Rashṭrakūṭa dynasty of the Deccan (c. 753–975 CE), with its capital at Mānyakheṭa (Arabic Mānkīr). See the article by S. Maqbul Ahmad in *EI*², s.v. Balharā.

419 The MSS read al-Ẓāfir (Arabic for "the victorious"), and the Leiden editor emended on the basis of al-Masʿūdī, *Murūj*, 1:203 (§ 428), to al-Ṭāfin, but a better reading appears to be al-Ṭāqā; see the index to al-Masʿūdī, *Murūj*, 7:439, and S. Maqbul Ahmad, "Al-Masʿūdī and the Kings of India," 110.

420 Kanbāya is modern Cambay in Gujarat. See the article by S. Maqbul Ahmad in *EI*², s.v. Khambāyat.

421 Otherwise unidentified; the reading is uncertain.

422 Otherwise unknown.

Māyid;[423] these kingdoms border China, and they make war on China. Then comes the kingdom of Sarandīb.[424] Then comes the kingdom of Qimār:[425] it is a kingdom of exalted status and great importance, and kings come to their king. Then comes the kingdom of al-Daybul.[426] Then comes al-Fārīṭ, and then the kingdom of al-Ṣaylamān.[427] In some [...] they have kingdoms that women govern.[428]

The Ancient Greeks

The Ancient Greeks had sages who engaged in philosophy, and philosophers who engaged in other sorts of study.[429] Some of them discoursed on medicine; some of them discoursed on the true nature of things; some of them discoursed on calculation and numbers; some of them discoursed on the spheres and the stars; some of them discoursed on calculation and division;[430] some of them discussed geometry[431] and agronomy; some of them discussed alchemy and elixirs;[432] some of them discussed physiognomy; | and some of them discussed 1:107
talismans and devices.[433] It is said that the first wise man to compose a book

423 Possibly to be read as Mābud, for Mahābhota, one of the Sanskrit names for Tibet. See the index to al-Masʿūdī, *Murūj*, 7:622.

424 That is, Ceylon. The Arabic form of the name (*Sarandīb*) comes ultimately from Sanskrit *Siṃhala* (Ceylon) + *dvīpa* (island). See the article by C. E. Bosworth in *EI*², s.v. Sarandīb.

425 Qimār stands for Khmer, the Khmer empire (modern Cambodia). See the article by C. E. Bosworth in *EI*², s.v. Ḳimār.

426 Sic ed. Leiden; M reads something like al-Dabīlā (two undotted letters make the reading uncertain), which points to a different place than Daybul in Sind mentioned above.

427 Neither name can be identified, and the readings are uncertain.

428 Arabic, *wa-lahum fī baʿḍ mamālik yalīhā* [or *talīhā*, the initial letter is ambiguous] *al-nisāʾ*. As it stands, this is ungrammatical. One solution is to assume that a word has fallen out after *baʿḍ*, as indicated in the translation.

429 Arabic, *falāsifa mutakawwir(ūn)*, the apparent reading of M and ed. Leiden. The dictionaries give no help; the translation, "philosophers who engaged in other sorts of study," is a conjecture based on the context. For an overall account of the passage of Greek science and philosophy into Arabic, see the article by Cristina D'Ancona in *EI*³, s.v. Greek into Arabic.

430 Arabic, *qisma*, apparently referring to the division of stellar orbits.

431 Arabic, *handasa*, which includes geometry and surveying.

432 Arabic, *iksīrāt*. On the use of the term in Arabic medicine and alchemy, see the article by M. Ullmann in *EI*², s.v. al-Iksīr.

433 Arabic, *ālāt*, includes a variety of mechanical devices.

and codify a branch of learning was Hippocrates, son of Heraclides, son of Hippocrates.[434] On him the sages rely in medicine,[435] and to him they refer in knowledge. The following books are by him:

(1) the Book of Aphorisms[436]
(2) the Book of Countries, Waters, and Airs[437]
(3) the Book of Barley-water[438]
(4) the Book of Prognostic[439]
(5) the Book of the Embryo[440]
(6) the Book of the Elements[441]
(7) the Book of Nutriment[442]

---

434 Here the MSS give a full form of the name: *ʾbqrʾṭ*, probably to be read as Abuqrāṭ, although the later Arabic form of the name, Buqrāṭ, also occurs in al-Yaʿqūbī. In the MSS, the father's name has been corrupted to *mqlyds*, not preceded by *bnu* (son of). For the biography—mostly fictional—of Hippocrates, see Wesley Smith, *The Hippocratic Tradition*; Jacques Jouanna, *Hippocrates*; Jody Rubin Pinault, *Hippocratic Lives and Legends*. For a comprehensive Hippocratic bibliography see Gerhard Fichtner, *CORPUS HIPPOCRATICUM—Bibliographie der hippokratischen und pseudohippokratischen Werke* [henceforth: Fichtner, *Hippocr.*]. On the reception of the Hippocratic corpus in the Islamic world, see the article by A. Dietrich in *EI*², s.v. Buḳrāṭ. On al-Yaʿqūbī's record of the Hippocratic writings, see Martin Klamroth, "Ueber die Auszüge aus griechischen Schriftstellern bei al-Jaʿqûbî," *ZDMG* 40 (1886): 189–203; cf. Manfred Ullmann, *Die Medizin im Islam*; Fuat Sezgin, *GAS*, III: *Medizin*, 23–30, 32–42.

435 Reading with M *fa-ʿalayhi yuʿawwilu l-ḥukamāʾ fī l-ṭibb*. The first two words have been run together and miscopied in C.

436 Arabic, *Kitāb al-Fuṣūl* (The Book of Sections/Paragraphs/Chapters), corresponds to Greek Ἀφορισμοί.

437 Arabic, *Kitāb al-Buldān wa-l-miyāh wa-l-ahwiya*, corresponds to Greek Περὶ ἀέρων ὑδάτων τόπων, with the order of the three terms reversed.

438 Arabic, *Kitāb Māʾ al-shaʿīr*, corresponds to Greek Περὶ πτισάνης. The prominence of barley gruel is reflected in this alternative title for *Regimen in Acute Diseases* (Περὶ διαίτης ὀξέων).

439 Arabic, *Kitāb Taqdimat al-maʿrifa*, corresponds to Greek Προγνωστικόν.

440 Arabic, *Kitāb al-Janīn* (more common in the plural as *Kitāb al-Ajinna*), corresponds to Greek Περὶ γονῆς and Περὶ φύσιος παιδίου. See Fichtner, *Hippocr.*, nos. 45, 46; edited and translated by M. C. Lyons and J. N. Mattock as *Kitāb al-Ajinna li-Buqrāṭ*.

441 Arabic, *Kitāb al-Arkān*, corresponds to Greek Περὶ φύσιος ἀνθρώπου. The author's title for what is known in Greek as *On the Nature of Man* reflects the prominence given to the four elements in the opening discussion and in Galen's commentary.

442 Arabic *Kitāb al-Ghidhāʾ*, corresponds to Greek Περὶ τροφῆς. See Fichtner, *Hippocr.*, no. 61; edited and translated by J. N. Mattock as *Kitāb Buqrāṭ fīʾl-akhlāṭ* and *Kitāb al-Ghidhāʾ li-Buqrāṭ*.

(8) the Book of Seven Months' Children[443]
(9) the Book of Ailments of Women[444]
(10) the Book of Epidemics.[445]

These are his most famous books, but there are many other books by him.[446] The books of Hippocrates that are indispensable for students of medicine to know are four: the *Book of Aphorisms*, the *Book of Prognostic*, the *Book of Airs and Times*, and the *Book of Barley Water*.[447]

As for the *Book of Aphorisms*,[448] it presents a pithy statement on every aspect of the discipline in fifty-seven chapters, which are called "instructions."[449]

---

443 Arabic, *Kitāb al-Asābīʿ*, corresponds to Greek Περὶ ἑβδομάδων (On Children Born Seven Months After Conception). Arabic *asābiʿ* should be understood as the plural of *subāʿī*, which is used in this sense (see Dozy, *Supplément*, 1:626b). See also Fichtner, *Hippocr.*, no. 58; cf. *idem*, *Corpus Galenicum*—Bibliographie der galenischen und pseudogalenischen Werke [henceforth: Fichtner, *Gal.*]. The Arabic version of Pseudo-Galen's commentary has been published with a German translation: Gotthelf Bergsträßer, *Pseudogaleni in Hippocratis De septimanis commentarium ab Hunaino q. f. Arabice versum.*

444 Arabic, *Kitāb Awjāʿ al-nisāʾ*, corresponds to Greek Γυναικεῖα. See Fichtner, *Hippocr.*, nos. 48, 49.

445 Arabic, *Abīdhīmiyā*, transliterates the Greek Ἐπιδημίαι. See Fichtner, nos. 6, 16, 7, 17–20. Note that the later Arabic equivalent (*al-amrāḍ al-wāfida*) is not used here.

446 A canon of the ten most important titles from the Hippocratic corpus was also cited by Ibn al-Nadīm and Barhebraeus; Ibn Abī Uṣaybiʿa mentions twelve; cf. Ullmann, *Die Medizin im Islam*, 27.

447 Al-Yaʿqūbī may have derived this notion of the ultimate Hippocratic "tetralogy" from Palladius's commentary on *Aphorisms* (fol. 2b; see note 449 below).

448 Fichtner, no. 13.

449 Arabic, *taʿlīmāt*, represents a Greek technical term such as πρᾶξις (discourse, lecture), or possibly διδασκαλία (instruction, elucidation), relating to the Alexandrian system of lecturing on authoritative texts. This would precisely fit Palladius, al-Yaʿqūbī's *Vorlage* in the following, as it does Palladius's Alexandrian fellow commentators (cf. especially, Leendert G. Westerink, *Stephanus of Athens: Commentary on Hippocrates' Aphorisms*). Westerink (II, 11) surmises that Palladius's presumable student Stephanus, who qualified Hippocrates' exposition as κεφαλαιώδη καὶ σύντομον διδασκαλίαν, 'summary and concise in form' (ibid. I, 32:3/33:3), covered the entire work in "sixty to seventy (daily) lectures," which does not seem to differ implausibly from Palladius's fifty-seven. The Arabic translation of Palladius's lost Greek original has not survived complete; a fragmented *unicum*, reaching as far as the eleventh "lecture," is supplemented by the secondary transmission, of which al-Yaʿqūbī is the most substantial witness (see Hinrich Biesterfeldt, "Palladius on the Hippocratic Aphorisms"; Caroline Magdelaine, "Le commentaire de Palladius sur les *Aphorismes* d'Hippocrate et les citations d'al-Yaʿqūbī"; Ullmann, *WGAÜ*, 52–55). Al-Yaʿqūbī preserved Palladius's disposition in fifty-seven chapters, suppressing his reference to and adoption of Galen's division into seven "sections," but for the sake of abridgment he limited himself

The first instruction [I, i]: on the art and its description.[450] Hippocrates says: Life is short, the art long; time is sharp, experiment is a hazard, and judgment difficult.[451]

The second instruction [I, iv]: on the kinds of food for the sick and the determination of its quantity. Hippocrates says: Light foods—very fine—are not (appropriate) either in chronic or in acute diseases. Again, foods that are light to an extreme degree are bad, just as repletion[452] carried to an extreme is bad.

The third instruction [I, viii–xi]: on the height of fever. Hippocrates says: One should (then) exercise restraint in food; an excess of it is harmful. In diseases that occur time after time, restraint should be exercised when they are at their height.

The fourth instruction [I, xii]: on the symptoms of diseases. Hippocrates
1:108 says: The state of the disease is indicated | by any bodily excretion that appears in it. For example, someone with pleurisy: if an immediate expectoration appears from him from the commencement of the disease, his illness will be short; if it appears later, his illness will be long. (The state of the disease appears) also in things such as urine, feces, and sweat—whether in a fashion that can be judged to portend recovery or the contrary, or the shortness or length of diseases.

The fifth instruction [I, xiv]: Hippocrates says: Anything that is growing—that is, inspirited beings—has much innate heat and therefore needs much food; otherwise its body will waste away.[453]

---

to the bare, uncommented initial aphorism of each "lecture." His omission of the subsequent aphorisms may have been facilitated by their dismissive heading as "another aphorism" (*faṣl ākhar*). The translation renders al-Yaʿqūbī's sometimes awkward or erroneous Arabic—even poorer than that of his sometimes infelicitous source al-Biṭrīq—since the stages of corruption cannot be confidently delimited. For the original Greek, one can consult vol. 4 of the Loeb Library edition by W. H. S. Jones, *Hippocrates*. For Ḥunayn's far superior Arabic version of the *Aphorisms*, see Ibn al-Nafīs, *Sharḥ Fuṣūl Buqrāṭ*, edited by Yūsuf Zaydān and Māhir ʿAbd al-Qādir.

450 Reading with M: *wa-ṣifat-hā*; ed. Leiden, *wa-ṣinfuhā* "and its kind."

451 On the history of Arabic commentaries on this aphorism, see Franz Rosenthal, "'Life is Short, the Art is Long': Arabic Commentaries on the First Hippocratic Aphorism." Rosenthal argues that the translation of ὁ δὲ καιρὸς ὀξύς, "time/opportunity is swift/urgent" (that is, in treating diseases, time is critical) may reflect a Syriac translation that rendered ὀξύς as *ḥarrīpā*, which in Syriac means both "sharp" and "swift." Unfortunately, Arabic *ḥadīd* means only "sharp," so the translation cited by al-Yaʿqūbī is misleading. Later Arabic translations have *al-waqt ḍayyiq* (time is narrow/tight), which gives better sense.

452 Reading *al-malʾ*, rendering Greek πληρώσιες, instead of the MSS *al-mā(ʾ)* (water), a copyist's confusion.

453 The Arabic (*kullamā* [possibly to be read *kullu mā*] *nashaʾat* [written without the hamza]

The sixth instruction [I, xvi–xvii]: on what food should be fed to persons with fever. Hippocrates says: Humid diets are most appropriate for all persons with fever, especially for children and for others who are accustomed to that diet—for some once and for some twice, or more or less, or time after time. Give due consideration to the season, the habit, the country, and the age.

The seventh instruction [I, xx]: on knowledge of the proper moment. Hippocrates says: Concerning (an illness) that is turning toward recovery or one that has already turned toward recovery, it should not be moved,[454] neither should anything new be attempted, either by purgatives or by anything else that might exacerbate it.

The eighth instruction [II, i–ii]: on sleep. Hippocrates says: In any illness, if sleep brings pain, the patient will die; but if sleep is beneficial, he is not going to die. If sleep counteracts delirium, that is good.

The ninth instruction [II, ix]: on the administering of purgatives. Hippocrates says: Whoever wants to purge bodies, should cleanse[455] them beforehand, namely by melting the coarse chyme that is in them.

The tenth instruction [II, xv]: on feces. Hippocrates says: If pain occurs in the body[456] or rashes[457] erupt on the body, the feces should thereupon be inspected. If they are bilious, the entire body is diseased; if they are like the feces of the healthy, | ample food (may be given). 1:109

ya'nī dhawāt al-arwāḥ fa-huwa ...) is grammatically problematic, and a gloss seems to have entered the text as an attempt to explain the shift from a verb that implies a plural subject to a singular pronoun. "Inspirited beings" renders the Arabic *dhawāt al-arwāḥ*, which appears to hark back, by way of misunderstanding, to I, xiii. In the Palladius MS, "whatever is growing" is correctly explained with reference to the three kingdoms of life. The aphorism in the original Greek contrasts patients who are still growing, and so require much food, with those who have ceased to grow. One is tempted to translate: "As long as an inspirited being is growing, it has much innate heat and needs much food ..."

454 Arabic, *yanbaghī an lā yuḥarraka*, perhaps, "it should not be agitated," rendering Greek κινεῖν. As Jones, *Hippocrates*, 4:115, notes: "Κινεῖν often means to administer a purge, an enema, or an emetic."

455 Arabic, *yanbaghī li-man arāda tanqiyat al-ajsād an yunaqqiyahā qabla dhālika*. Although the Arabic uses a derivative of the verb *naqqā* twice, the translation—"purge" and "cleanse"—has been varied to avoid awkward repetition.

456 Arabic, *al-jasad*; possibly a corruption for an original reading of *al-ḥalq* (the throat), which would agree with the Greek φάρυνξ.

457 Following the apparent reading of M, *ḥazāzāt*, a term designating a variety of skin rashes. Ed. Leiden emends C *ḥarāzāt* (otherwise unattested) to *khurājāt* (blisters, abscesses).

The eleventh instruction [II, xix]: Hippocrates says: [Prognoses are uncertain][458] in acute diseases because such diseases sometimes rapidly affect the brain, the heart, or the liver, so that the patient succumbs; but sometimes they rapidly subside, so that the patient recovers.

The twelfth instruction [II, xxiii–xxiv]: on judgment concerning recovery. Hippocrates says: Recovery in acute diseases is to be judged in fourteen days, and the eleventh of them is to be observed.[459]

The thirteenth instruction [II, xxix]: Hippocrates says: If at the beginning of diseases you see fit to move something,[460] do it; but if the disease advances, it is better to refrain. That is to say: if you see an occasion for treatment, do it before the disease advances.

The fourteenth instruction [II, xxxiii]: on knowing benign and pernicious diseases. Hippocrates says: In every disease, the soundness of the patient's intellect is good; his acceptance of what is appointed[461] is good and the opposite bad—that is to say, what the patient feels in the brain and the stomach.

The fifteenth instruction [II, xliii]: on those who have been strangled.[462] Hippocrates says: Those who are strangled but released before they die: if foam appears in their mouths, they will not recover.

The sixteenth instruction [II, xlviii]: on exercise to trim the body and exertion. Hippocrates says: In every moving of the body, if it begins to tire and then you let it rest where you are, the tiredness will not hurt it.

The seventeenth instruction [III, i]: on the changing of the seasons. Hippocrates says: The changing of the seasons [generates illness, especially][463] from severe cold and heat and the like—that is to say, the changing of the seasons of time, which are the parts of the year.

---

458 Several words appear to have fallen out of the text, although there is no gap in the MSS. The translation follows the emendation proposed by the Leiden editor.

459 Reading with M, *wa-yutābaʿu l-aḥada ʿashara lahu*, which corresponds exactly to the Greek, θεωρητὴ δὲ ἡ ἑνδεκάτη; ed. Leiden banishes the phrase to a footnote, as C has only the first two words, which Houtsma read as *wa-sābiʿ al-aḥad*, "and the seventh of the one," which makes no sense.

460 "Move" in the sense of administering a purge, enema, or an emetic.

461 "What is appointed" (Arabic, *mā yuqḍā*) corresponds to Greek τὰς προσφοράς (things presented; in medical usage, specifically food).

462 Arabic, *al-makhnūqīn*: perhaps to be translated as "those who have been hanged," as in the Greek.

463 The bracketed words have been added conjecturally by the Leiden editor.

The eighteenth instruction [III, vi]: on sweating. Hippocrates says: When summer is like spring,[464] one should expect copious sweating in any fever that occurs. 1:110

The nineteenth instruction [III, xi]: on the seasons. Hippocrates says: If the winter is dry and lacking humidity and its winds are northerly, (and) the spring is rainy and its winds southerly, in summer there will inevitably be acute fevers, ophthalmia, and dysentery. This will occur mostly in women [and those][465] whose nature is humid.

The twentieth instruction [III, xv–xvi]: on forecasting the years. Hippocrates says: A dry year is more pestilential[466] than a rainy humid one; overall (the latter produces) long fevers, loose bowels, putrescent ulcers,[467] insanity, apoplexy, and quinsy.[468] As for the diseases of dry years, they are ulceration in the lung, eye and joint pain, strangury, and excretion from abscess of the intestines.[469]

The twenty-first instruction [III, xviii]: on the diseases of the seasons and the ages. Hippocrates says: Concerning the seasons, according to the diseases that occur: in spring and early summer, adolescents and those near them in age are healthy and their good condition is better than that of others; in summer and part of autumn, old men are in better condition; in the remainder of autumn and in winter, people of middle age are in better condition.

The twenty-second instruction [III, xxiv]: on the diseases that strike man and begin with children. Hippocrates says: The diseases that strike | young 1:111
children are ulcer, catarrh, insomnia, anxiety, swelling in the navel, and moist discharges of the ear.

The twenty-third instruction [III, xxvi–xxviii]: Hippocrates says: The diseases that strike older children are tonsillitis, asthma, calculi, broad worms, long worms, worms like vinegar worms,[470] warts, induration of the epidermis,

---

464 Emending the MSS *al-zamān* (the time) to *al-qayẓ* (the summer). The Arabic text contains a gloss to explain that the word *ṣayf*, which usually means "summer," here means the same as the more common word for spring, *rabīʿ*.

465 Added by the Leiden editor, who also emends manuscript *fī al-shitā(ʾ)* (in winter) to *fī al-nisāʾ* (in women).

466 So in the Arabic (*awbaʾ*); the Greek says the opposite, ὑγιαινότεροι. One can only speculate about whether the reversal was caused by misunderstanding of a text read aloud or by corruption of the Greek *Vorlage*.

467 Emending the unintelligible MS reading (*qurūḥ maymāsata*?) to *qurūḥ mutamāshiya*.

468 Following the emendation proposed by the Leiden editor: *dhabḥa* for MS *dīna*.

469 MS *ikhtilāf min khurāj al-aʿfāj*, which, without *khurāj* (abscess), would be equivalent to the Greek, which reads "dysentery."

470 Arabic, *dūd al-khall*, "vinegar worms" (*Turbatrix aceti*). The Greek has ἀσκαρίδες, taken

scrofula, and other eruptions. Those who are older and on the point of puberty are affected [by the preceding diseases and] by other diseases.[471] They can be judged to have recovered at the end of forty days; in some diseases at the end of seven months; in some at the end of seventy days;[472] and in some when they are on the verge of puberty. All diseases that [do not] leave boys by the time of puberty and girls by the time they first menstruate are diseases that will last a long time.

The twenty-fourth instruction [IV, i]: on knowing what purgatives can be given to pregnant women. Hippocrates says: Pregnant women can be given such medication at four months; however, their treatment should be avoided before that, due to the smallness of the child, and beyond that, due to its largeness.

The twenty-fifth instruction [IV, iv]: Hippocrates says: What is above should be purged in summer, and what is below in winter—meaning, what is above the lungs[473] and the stomach, and what is lower than the yellow bile and lower than the crude humor[474] and its like.

The twenty-sixth instruction [IV, xiii]: on elaterium.[475] Hippocrates says: When purgatives and hellebore are taken, the bodies of those whose purge from above does not come easily should be humidified with copious food before the purge.

The twenty-seventh instruction [IV, xxi]: on spontaneous evacuation. Hippocrates says: When evacuation comes spontaneously as though it were black
1:112 blood, | whether with fever or without fever, it is an evil evacuation. If it is a multicolored evacuation, changing from wholesome colors to unwholesome ones, that is also an evil evacuation. If the first comes through a purgative, it is better; and (if) a multicolored (evacuation is so caused), there is nothing wrong with it.

---

to refer to a parasitic intestinal roundworm that causes the disease called ascariasis; cf. Ullmann, *WGAÜ*, 140, s.v. ἀσκαρίς.

471 The bracketed addition is based on the Greek. The Arabic, *amr ākhar* (another thing) can be explained as a copyist's omission of two letters. Read, *amr[āḍ u]khar*, (other diseases).

472 Sic, *sabʿīna yawman*. One would expect "seven years," following the Greek.

473 Reading, *al-riʾatayn*, which appears to be indicated by M, rather than ed. Leiden, *al-raʾs* (the head).

474 Arabic, *al-khām* (undotted in M).

475 Arabic, *dhū l-mashī*, translated as "elaterium," a cathartic obtained from the juice of the squirting cucumber (*Ecballium elaterium*), following Klamroth's suggestion ("Auszüge," I, 200). The Greek here refers only to hellebores, which the Arabic mentions specifically as *kharbaq* in the next sentence. See Stephanus in Aphorismos, II, 244:1–11.

The twenty-eighth instruction [IV, xxvii]: on discharge from whatever source. Hippocrates says: Every person with fever is subject to evacuation because abundant discharge of blood relaxes the liver; then coction takes place correctly.[476]

The twenty-ninth instruction [IV, xxxvi]: on sweating. Hippocrates says: Sweating in those with fever is good if it occurs on the third, fifth, [seventh, ninth, eleventh, fourteenth,] seventeenth, twenty-first, [twenty-seventh,] thirty-first, or thirty-fourth day, because it relieves the patient.[477] Sweating on other days portends pain, lengthy illness, and relapse.

The thirtieth instruction [IV, xliii]: on persistent fevers. [Hippocrates says: Persistent fevers] that do not break, but intensify on the third day, are likely to lead to perishing; those that break, in whatever fashion, are less likely to lead to perishing.

The thirty-first instruction [IV, xlviii]: on the signs of death. Hippocrates says: Persistent fevers that do not break—if the outside of the body is cold, while the inside is burning hot, and the patient suffers thirst—are signs of death.

The thirty-second instruction [IV, lvii]: on spasm and tetanus. Hippocrates says: Anyone stricken with spasm or tetanus who subsequently gets fever, his disease will be loosed.

The thirty-third instruction [IV, lxv]: Hippocrates says: Anyone with fever who then is stricken with intense heat in the abdomen and pain in the heart, that is bad.

The thirty-fourth instruction [IV, lxxiii]: Hippocrates says: Anyone who has fever and then his hypochondria swell and rise | and a rumbling appears in his 1:113
abdomen, and, along with this, pain strikes him in his loins and he does not get relief by passing wind or copious urination, or he gets relief by evacuation—such a person will perish.

The thirty-fifth instruction [V, i]: on taking hellebore. Hippocrates says: Anyone stricken with spasm from copious evacuation upon taking hellebore is going to die.

---

476 Coction (Arabic *nadj*, for Greek πέψις) is the body's processing of food in such a way that the humors are in balance. The translation is based on reading, with ed. Leiden, *thumma yastaqīmu l-nadj*, but correcting the printed *tastaqīmu*. M has *lam yastaqīm* (sic) *al-nadj*, which is ungrammatical, but could be corrected to mean "coction has not taken place correctly."

477 The bracketed additions are from the Greek. The MSS show no lacuna. The first omission is a clear case of homeoteleuton.

The thirty-sixth instruction [v, ix]: on ulcerations in the lung and wasting in the lung. [Hippocrates says]: That occurs at ages eighteen to thirty-five.

The thirty-seventh instruction [v, xvi–xvii]: on hot and cold water. Hippocrates says: Hot water taken constantly makes the flesh flabby, destroys the strength of the nerves, numbs the mind,[478] provokes nosebleed, and weakens the soul;[479] if that persists, the person will die. Cold water brings on tetanus and melasma, as well as shivers and fever.

The thirty-eighth instruction [v, xxii]: on the knowledge of waters. Hippocrates says: Hot water furthers the coction of pus, but not in every ulcer. There are many signs of the coction of pus: namely, softness of skin and shrinking of swelling. Whenever hot water acts in this way, it takes away pain, calms shivering, spasm, and tetanus, and relieves headache.

The thirty-ninth instruction [v, xxviii]: on women's matters. Hippocrates says: Aromatic vapors promote menstruation in women and are useful for it and for many other conditions, except that they provoke pain in the head and headache.

The fortieth instruction [v, xxxix]: Hippocrates says: Any woman who is neither pregnant nor nursing, but finds milk in her breasts: that is an indication that her menstrual blood has been obstructed.

The forty-first instruction [v, xlviii]: Hippocrates says: Male children mostly develop on the right side of the womb; females on the left.

The forty-second instruction [v, lv]: Hippocrates says: Pregnant women who
1:114 are stricken with fever and in whom it persists | without a known cause that has become evident: that is a sign of perishing; they will abort and perish.

The forty-third instruction [v, lxiv]: Hippocrates says: Give milk[480] to him who complains of his head and who suffers thirst; also to him who suffers discharge of yellow bile and has acute fever, and to him who discharges copious

478 Reading, *al-ʿaql*, (to agree with Greek γνώμης νάρκωσιν) for MSS and ed. Leiden *al-ʿaḍal* (the muscles).

479 Or, "the breathing." The Arabic can be read either as *al-nafs* (the soul) or as *al-nafas* (the breathing). The Greek, λειποθυμίας (fainting), suggests the former.

480 Following ed. Leiden, *aʿṭi l-laban*. The spelling in M suggests the reading *uʿṭiya* (has been given), which does not fit the context (a present tense would be expected). Furthermore, the Greek gives the opposite advice: "To give milk to sufferers from headache is bad." The Greek contrasts this with the benefit from giving milk to "cases of consumption when there is no very high fever." One is therefore tempted to amend *aʿṭi* (give) to *lā yuʿṭā* (is not given). The strange reading of M gives some support to the assumption of such textual corruption.

blood. It is appropriate to be given to him who suffers wasting and ulceration in his lung, if he is not very feverish. It is also given to him whose fever is mild, lukewarm, and chronic, as long as he does not have any of the symptoms we have mentioned and his body is very lean.

The forty-fourth instruction [VI, i]: on lientery.[481] Hippocrates says: Anyone who is stricken with lientery for a long time and then develops acid belching that he did not have before: that is a good sign. It is an illness which may have three causes: weakness of the stomach, phlegm moistening the stomach, or an ulcer in the stomach.

The forty-fifth instruction [VI, x]: Hippocrates says: If pus or water flows from the nose, ears, or mouth of someone who is stricken with pain in the head and intense throbbing, his pain will be loosened.

The forty-sixth instruction [VI, xviii]: Hippocrates says: Anyone who suffers a deep wound[482] in the bladder, the brain, the heart, the diaphragm, any of the small intestines, the stomach, or the liver: all of this is deadly.

The forty-seventh instruction [VI, xxiii]: Hippocrates says: Anyone stricken with lengthy and persistent anxiety and despondency: it will lead to atrabiliousness.[483]

The forty-eighth instruction [VI, xxxi]: Hippocrates says: Drinking wine neat, a hot poultice, venesection, and taking a purgative make eye pain disappear.

The forty-ninth instruction [VI, xxxviii]: Hippocrates says: It is better to leave every incurable cancerous eruption alone, | for such patients perish quickly if 1:115
treated, but survive for a time if not treated.

The fiftieth instruction [VI, xlv]: Hippocrates says: From an eruption that swells[484] for a year or more, bones will inevitably become detached and their traces will remain like scabs.[485]

---

481 Arabic, *zalaq al-amʿāʾ* (slipperiness of the bowels, pl. *azlāq al-amʿāʾ*, corresponding to Greek λειεντερία): a variety of diarrhea in which food is excreted partially or wholly undigested.

482 Arabic, *inqiṭāʿ*, normally means "blockage," but corresponds here to the Greek διακοπέντι (for someone who has received a gash, a deep wound). The translation mirrors the original sense. For other examples of forms of Arabic *inqaṭaʿ* translating the passive of Greek διακόπτω, see Ullmann, *WGAÜ*, Supplement Band I, 272.

483 Arabic, *al-mirra al-sawdāʾ* (black bile), an excess of which was thought to produce melancholy. Atrabilious is simply the Latin translation of melancholy.

484 Reading with ed. Leiden, *yantū*; M (apparently) *yanbū* (is remote), which does not fit the context.

485 Arabic, *jarab*, scabbiness, mange, scabies.

The fifty-first instruction [VI, liii]: Hippocrates says: Loss of mind[486] that comes together with laughter is preferable; loss of mind together with sadness and frowning is not preferable.

The fifty-second instruction [VII, i]: Hippocrates says: In acute diseases, if the extremities are cold, that is bad.

The fifty-third instruction [VII, xvii]: Hippocrates says: Anyone in whose liver an eruption develops and then it is followed by hiccoughing—that is bad.

The fifty-fourth instruction [VII, xxxi]: Hippocrates says: Anyone with fever in whose urine there is coarse deposit like grainy flour—that is an indication that his disease will be long.

The fifty-fifth instruction [VII, xxxvii]: Hippocrates says: Whoever vomits blood without being stricken with being overcome [by fever],[487] will find deliverance; but if being overcome by fever seizes him, that is noxious, and he should be treated with every kind of styptic—that is, astringent medicines.

The fifty-sixth instruction [VII, xliv–xlv]: Hippocrates says: If a patient vomiting purulent matter is cauterized, and the purulence comes out white and clean, the patient will recover; but if the purulence comes out fetid and dirty, the patient will perish. If he has a suppurating abscess in his liver, is cauterized, and the purulence comes out clean and white, he will recover, because the purulence is in the membrane of the liver; but if the purulence comes out like olive water,[488] such a patient will perish.

The fifty-seventh instruction [VII, xlv]: Hippocrates says: Sneezing occurs from the head when the brain is warm or cold, or when the space between the
1:116 brain and its membrane becomes humid and fills up; | that air is evacuated and makes a noise because its exit is through a narrow passage.

These are the chapters of the *Book of Aphorisms*.

As for his *Book of Prognostic*,[489] it consists of three sections: twenty instructions.[490]

486 Arabic, *dhahāb al-ʿaql*, corresponds to Greek παραφροσύναι (deliriums).

487 Arabic, *ghayra an tuṣībahu ghalaba*. The sense is uncertain. The Greek has ἄνευ πυρετοῦ (without fever). The easiest solution is to assume that the original reading here, as later in the paragraph, was *ghalabat ḥummā* (being overcome by fever).

488 Arabic, *māʾ al-zaytūn*. The Greek has ἀμόργη (dregs of pressed olives), which is how the Arabic phrase probably should be understood.

489 Fichtner, *Hippocrat.*, no. 3.

490 In the following, references (section: page, line) will be to Bengt Alexanderson, *Die Hippokratische Schrift Prognostikon—Überlieferung und Text*. The Alexandrian Stephanus, without regard to the original author's twenty-five topical paragraphs, adhered to Galen's division of the work into three sections (Fichtner, *Gal.*, no. 109) and subdivided these

The first:[491] Hippocrates tells how it behooves the physician to take up prognosis; for he it is who informs the patients of what they have, what they had previously, the outcome of what they have, and what the patients have neglected to mention; also the severity of diseases and their causes,[492] whether they develop out of the distemper of the body or something else, and other such things.

The second instruction:[493] In it he tells how it behooves the physician to examine acute diseases closely, how he should examine patients' faces, whether they resemble the faces of the healthy, the signs on faces that indicate death, and other such things.

The third instruction:[494] In it he says: If the patients have three or four days with their faces in the condition of the faces of the healthy, and so forth, one should think well about the signs and symptoms, according to what has been mentioned previously, and about the signs of the eyes, the eyelashes, and the nose; as well as about the patient's reclining for rest and how it should be handled, and about those of his symptoms that portend death.

The fourth instruction:[495] He describes the patient's legs and their states; how the patient reclines for rest; the gnashing of teeth during fever and what it indicates; whether the patient has a sore that developed during his illness or

---

into, respectively, fourteen, eleven, and five "lectures" (πράξεις), as numbered by the editor (see John M. Duffy, *Stephanus the Philosopher: a Commentary on the Prognosticon of Hippocrates*). Al-Yaʿqūbī gives a rough abstract, omitting to mark the three sections of what originally may have resembled Stephanus's lecture course, even though the pretended division of the course into merely twenty, in places rather illogically divided, installments instead of Stephanus's thirty would seem to point to a superficial redactor of al-Yaʿqūbī's exemplar to begin with. Its text, preserved, according to Klamroth (*ZDMG* 40, p. 201), in MS Gotha 1900, merits closer inspection, because it may antedate Ḥunayn's version (Klamroth, ibid., 203–233). The numbering of Galen's and Stephanus's lemmata, respectively, has been included for comparison (see Hermann Diels, Johannes Mewaldt, Joseph Heeg, edd., *Galeni In Hippocratis Prorrheticum I commentaria III, De comate secundum Hippocratem, In Hippocratis Prognosticum commentaria III*, 195–378).

491 1:193, 1A; Gal. I 2; Steph. I, ii–iii, followed by 1:194, 4A; Gal. I 4; Steph. I, iii–iv.

492 The text is uncertain. The manuscripts insert *wa-an* (and that) before "their strength and their causes." The Leiden editor notes that one could either assume that the word *yaʿrifa* (he should know) has dropped out ("and that [he should know] their strength and their causes") or that something has dropped out after "their strength and their causes."

493 2:194, 10A; Gal. I 5; Steph. I, v.

494 2:195, 9A; Gal. I (8–)9, 10(–12?); Steph. I, vi; followed by 3:197, 4A; Gal. I 13; Steph. I, viii.

495 3:197, 9A; Gal. I 13f.; Steph. I, viii; followed by 3:198, 6A; Gal. I 21; Steph. I, viii; followed by 3:198, 9–4:199, 1A; Gal. I 22f.; Steph. I, ix.

previously, and what it indicates; and he describes the hands, their restlessness, and what they indicate thereby.

The fifth instruction:[496] He mentions frequent fast breathing and what it indicates. He mentions the best kind of perspiration in acute diseases, good
1:117 perspiration, cold perspiration, and noxious perspiration. | He also mentions that perspiration occurs either because of the body's weakness or because of a persistent sore.

The sixth instruction:[497] He mentions the good health of the hypochondrium, and when it is not healthy; the throbbing of its blood vessels, and what is indicated by that; and swellings that are in the side of the hypochondrium. He also gives information about these swellings and what may befall them.

The seventh instruction:[498] In it he mentions abscesses: how they should be examined when they become chronic, how their dimensions should be described, what is discharged from them, and how it should be discharged.

The eighth instruction:[499] In it he mentions dropsy: that which accompanies acute diseases, that which occurs from expectoration,[500] and that which occurs from the liver. (He also mentions) such concomitant symptoms as afflict those with dropsy and the signs that indicate death: blackening of the fingers and the feet and similar signs.

The ninth instruction:[501] He mentions the retraction of the testicles and penis. He also mentions slumber and sleep and how they ought to be, and the feces and how they ought to be.

The tenth instruction:[502] In it he mentions the feces, how they ought to emerge and their causes; how the abdomen should be in every illness; and the colors of the feces that indicate death and other things. He also describes flatulence, stomach rumblings, and the like.

---

496 5:199, 6A; Gal. I 24; Steph. I, x; followed by 6:200, 1A; Gal. I 26; Steph. I, xi; followed by 6:200, 7A, and Gal. I 26 (p. 241:18).

497 7:200, 8A; Gal. I 27–29; Steph. I, xii.

498 7:202, 8A; Gal. I 30 ff.; Steph. I, xiii–xiv.

499 8:203, 8A; Gal. II 1–9; Steph. II, i–ii; followed by 9:204, 14A. In MS Gotha 1900, the second discourse begins here as well.

500 Arabic, *buzāq*. The Greek has ἀπὸ τῶν κενεώνων (from the flanks). Considering the poor quality of the text, the Arabic might echo a later passage where non-productive coughing is mentioned (8:204, 4f. A; Gal. II 3 [p. 262:14 f.]; Steph. II, ii, p. 156:22 ff.).

501 9:205, 8A; Gal. II 10; followed by 10:205, 9A; Gal. II 11 f.; Steph. II, iii; followed by 11:206, 3A; Gal. II 13; Steph. II, iv.

502 11:206, 3A; Gal. II 14–25; Steph. II, iv cont'd.; followed by 11:206, 14A; followed by 11:207, 1A; Steph. II, v.

The eleventh instruction:[503] He gives information about healthy urine, then about urine when it is altered and about the kinds of sediments of the urine coming from the bladder.

The twelfth instruction:[504] In it he mentions vomiting and its reasons; and mucus and how it is coughed up, what its mixture is, and its color. He mentions sneezing in all illnesses that have to do with the lung, such as portends death, and such as foreshadows resolution of the illness.

The thirteenth instruction:[505] In it he describes expectoration in diseases of the lung and its color, together with the colors of expectorations. He also mentions in it the urine, the feces, and the perspiration and what | each one of 1:118
them indicates.

The fourteenth instruction:[506] He mentions suppurating abscesses, the times at which they split open, and how [...].[507] He describes everything that is discharged from them and their occurrence in every human being.

The fifteenth instruction:[508] He mentions the abscesses that grow close to the ears, what produces that in the bodies of those who have lung diseases, and what the indications of that are like; also the abscesses that develop on the legs of those who have an illness, as well as the consequences that they incur.

The sixteenth instruction:[509] He mentions those bad pains that cause a loss of reason.[510] He also mentions fevers and their attendant circumstances on each of their days.

The seventeenth instruction:[511] He mentions prognosis in prolonged, grave, acute diseases. He mentions quartan fevers, the consequences that those afflicted with them incur because of them, and the days on which they occur. He mentions pains that occur in the temples and the forehead, as well as earache and the consequences that patients incur.

---

503 12:208, 4A; Gal. II 26–37; Steph. II, vi–vii.

504 13:210, 4A; Gal. II 38–49; Steph. II, viii; followed by 14:210, 12A; followed by 14:211, 8A.

505 14: 211, 13A; Gal. II 50–52; Steph. II, ix; followed by 15:212, 11A.

506 15:213, 14A; Gal. II 53–63; Steph. II, x.

507 Something apparently has fallen out of the text, although the MSS show no lacuna.

508 18:217, 4A; Gal. II 64–66; followed by 18:218, 5A; Gal. II 67 ff.; Steph. II, xi.

509 19:219, 6A; Gal. III 1 ff.; Steph. III, i; followed by 20:220, 10A. In MS Gotha 1900, this instruction still belongs to the second discourse.

510 Galen rejects this interpretation of ἢν τῶν φρενῶν ἅπτωνται in III 1 (pp. 324:11–325:8), whereas Stephanus does mention mental disorder as a complication in the present context (238:9 f.).

511 20:220, 10A; Gal. III 6–19; Steph. III, i cont'd; followed by 20:220, 11A; followed by 21:222, 11 and 22:223, 6A.

The eighteenth instruction:[512] He mentions suffocating throat aches, redness in the neck and chest, expectoration,[513] and the signs of perishing that come over the patient because of this. He mentions the causes of a rasping throat and sores that occur [...]; and a painful ache in the joints. He mentions abscesses that break out in young people and something on the circumstances that attend on fever.

The nineteenth instruction:[514] In it he mentions fever and heartburn, and he mentioned the days in which the fever extends, together with the pains that occur during the fever.

The twentieth instruction:[515] He tells how anyone who wants to master prognosis should become acquainted with what is brought on by diseases that do not cease causing pain and how it can be known; as well as information
1:119 about the elements,[516] symptoms, the parts | of the year, and the circumstances of countries.

These then are the instructions of the *Book of Prognostic* by Hippocrates.

As for his *Book of Airs, Times, Waters, and Cities*:[517] He gives information

---

512 23:224, 6A; Gal. III (20–)21–25; Steph. III, ii cont'd–iii; followed by 23:226, 3A; Gal. III 26f.; followed by 24:227, 1f. A; Gal. III 28; followed by 24:227, 2f. A; Gal. III 29ff.

513 Reading with M, *al-nafth*; emended in ed. Leiden to *al-thaqb* (lancing), corresponding to Greek ἀποσχάζεσθαι.

514 24:227, 14f. A; Gal. III 35ff.; Steph. III, iv.

515 25:230, 5A; Gal. III 42; Steph. III, v.

516 Arabic, *al-arkān*, lacks basis in the Greek. Stephanus' sole reference to "elements"—remote, intermediate and proximate—as subjects of the Hippocratic work occurs in the introduction to his commentary (32:1–10). If the MS of Galen's commentary on *Airs* is correct (see below for reference), in *Prognostic* Hippocrates speaks of "elements" (*usṭuqussāt*) from which to derive prognosis (5:1f.). Possibly a reader's gloss was incorporated here into the text.

517 Fichtner, no. 2; for the Greek text and German translation, see Hans Diller, *Hippocratis De aere locis aquis* [henceforth: DIL]; for the Arabic, with English translation, see John N. Mattock and Malcolm C. Lyons, eds., *Kitāb Buqrāṭ fī 'l-amrāḍ al-bilādīya* [henceforth: M & L]. Galen's commentary, from which the Hippocratic text could be recovered, served as exemplar of the Arabic translation of *Airs*; see M & L, pp. xi, xxxv, and here below, notes, and especially p. xx (al-Yaʿqūbī's belated reference to Galen's commentary might indicate the defective condition of his exemplar[s]). Galen's work, lost in Greek, is extant in a unique Arabic manuscript (Cairo, Dār al-Kutub, Ṭalʿat, ṭibb 550) and in subsequent—abridged or fragmentary—Hebrew and Latin versions; see Abraham Wasserstein, *Galen's commentary on the Hippocratic treatise* Airs, Waters, Places *in the Hebrew translation of Solomon ha-Me'ati*. A facsimile of the Cairo MS has been published by Fuat Sezgin et al. as *Galen's commentary on the Hippocratic treatise* On airs, waters, places (Περὶ ἀέρων, ὑδάτων, τόπων) *in Arabic translation* [henceforth: Galen]. A critical edition is being prepared

on the diseases, both those that are peculiar (to a region) and those that are universal, those that are uniform and those that are diverse, which their inhabitants contract, with solid definitions and clear indications.[518]

The first chapter:[519] He says that whoever wishes to pursue medicine honestly[520] should first examine the seasons of the year and what occurs in them, as they do not resemble each other, but are contrary to each other, and they may also differ in their changing in themselves.[521]

The second chapter:[522] He says that in years when the seasons maintain their balance and normal states,[523] the illnesses that occur are caused by them[524]

by Gotthard Strohmaier for *Corpus medicorum graecorum*; cf. Strohmaier, "Galen's not uncritical commentary on Hippocrates' *Airs, Waters, Places*," *Bulletin of the Institute of Classical Studies* 47 (2004):1–9.

518 This last qualifying phrase, which also appears in the Arabic of Palladius's commentary on *Aphorisms* (fol. 1b), indicates the derivation of the entire heading from an earlier editor or translator of Hippocratic works.

519 The numbering indicates that the Hippocratic lemmata have been reconstituted from Galen's commentary, where the actual beginning of *Airs* counts as the second chapter, following Galen's introduction. Overall, Galen groups lemmata together in chapters by subject, whereas al-Yaʿqūbī's text counts each Hippocratic lemma as a new chapter. While al-Yaʿqūbī's version is basically identical with M & L's "first," older, version (i), his chapter headings derive from an intermediary reworking; references are given here to both versions.

520 Arabic, *ṣādiqan*, may have originated by permutation from *qāṣidan*, the reading in M & L and Galen, which more accurately renders Greek ὀρθῶς (properly).

521 Arabic, *fī nqilābihā bi-dhātihā* (*bi-dhātihā fī nqilābihā*, Galen, p. 6:6). The likely meaning is that the seasons not only differ from each other, but within each season there may be sudden changes. The Greek is somewhat different, but ultimately means the same thing: "For the seasons are not at all alike, but differ widely both in themselves and at their changes." (Trans. Jones, *Hippocrates*, 1:71.)

522 Here Galen's commentary has intruded on the Hippocratic text; see M & L, pp. xi, 2. Evidently, in al-Yaʿqūbī's exemplar Galen's express attribution of *Aph.* III 8 to Hippocrates (p. 7:8–11) was taken to refer to *Airs* instead. The Arabic version owes much to Galen's periphrastic explanation of this as well as the following aphorism (ed. Kühn, XVII B, pp. 575 f.). Considering the precision of Ḥunayn's wording in *Aph.* III 8 (*apud* Ibn an-Nafīs, p. 223), it seems impossible to attribute al-Yaʿqūbī's rendering to him as well.

523 Arabic, *marājiʿihā* (pl. of *marjiʿ*, the place or state to which something returns); but perhaps a miscopying (by addition of one letter) of *mizājihā* (their temperament); M & L, 3:1/6; Galen, p. 7:9.

524 The text is uncertain. The translation follows the apparent reading of M and C: *takūnu sababahā* (they [viz. the seasons] are their cause). The Leiden editor emended *sababahā* to *shabīhan* (similar), which is grammatically impossible.

and develop regularly, not contrariwise or doubtfully;[525] but in seasons with frequent changes, illnesses occur unequally and irregularly, and their resolution is difficult and intractable.

The third chapter:[526] He says that in hot and cold winds that are general, bodies are subject to alteration.

The fourth chapter: He says that the physician should think about the virtues of waters, as they are different in taste and weight, and differ greatly in virtue.

The fifth chapter:[527] He speaks about waters and what they are like, whether stagnant and soft, hard and flowing from rocky heights, or brackish and slow in coction.[528]

The sixth chapter: He says that the physician should think about the terrain, whether it is bare and arid, wooded and well-watered, depressed and stifling, or elevated and cold.[529]

The seventh chapter:[530] He said that he should keep in mind the diet of the people: in what things they delight, whether in much drink and food and love
1:120 of ease, or in love of work and of food; he should examine | every one of these things in each country.

The eighth chapter:[531] He said that if any part of the season and the year passes, the physician will be expert in every common illness [that occurs to the people of the given city in winter and in summer, and in every particular illness] that occurs to everyone of its people due to changes in their diet.[532]

---

525 Arabic, *mushabbaha* (l. *mushtabiha*?) for *mutabayyina* (distinct); M & L, 3:2.

526 In the Galen MS (p. 8:9 f.), this lemma goes unmarked; al-Yaʿqūbī omits its last qualification, "(general and) peculiar to a country" (M & L, 5:1/9).

527 One lemma has been omitted before this one (DIL, 1,9–13/24:10–15; M & L, 5:5–7:3; Galen, p. 9:8–13).

528 M reads, *māliḥa raṭibat al-nadj* (salty, moist of coction). The translation emends *raṭibat* (moist) to *baṭiyyat* (slow) on the basis of Hippocrates and Galen (M & L, 7:5 ff., and Galen, p. 10:1–5).

529 The translation "depressed and stifling" follows a conjectural restoration (*aw kānat ghāʾira ghamīma*) based on Galen, p. 10:-3f (cf. M & L, 7:7 ff.). The Arabic version in M & L expresses a series of contrasts, expressed as "if it is AB or CD; or if it is EF or GH." In MS C of al-Yaʿqūbī, the pair EF has been corrupted to *aw ʿāmira aw ʿāmira* (or populated/cultivated or populated/cultivated), which gives no sense. MS M apparently reads *ghāʾira* (sunk/depressed). The original reading may have been *ghāʾira ḥārra* (depressed [and] hot).

530 M & L, 7:9/16–9:3/11; Galen, 11:1 ff.

531 M & L, 11:5–8; Galen, 11:-6 ff. Al-Yaʿqūbī skips the lemma preceding this one (DIL, 2,1–7/26:5–10; M & L, 9:4/12–11:4/12; Galen, p. 11:5–11).

532 The bracketed material has been restored on the basis of M & L. Note that al-Yaʿqūbī's exemplar agrees with M & L's version *i* against *ii*.

The ninth chapter:[533] He said that when illnesses do not come from corruption of the air, (illness) will not settle on the inhabitants of a given city altogether but will be sporadic.[534] When the physician thinks about this kind of matter and these things and gains adequate knowledge of how the seasons are going to be, his knowledge will likely be correct, for the science of the stars is no small part of the science of medicine.[535]

As for his *Book of Airs and Countries*, it is a description of the countries, their waters and their properties.[536]

The first discourse[537] is on cities, of which there are four kinds: the first is in the direction of the equator,[538] the second in the direction of the Farqadān,[539] the third faces the sunrise, and the fourth faces the sunset. Concerning the first he said:[540] Every city situated facing the hot winds—those between the winter sunrise and its sunset[541]—they blow towards it constantly, whereas it is [sheltered] as against the Farqadān.[542] The waters of such a city are copious

533 M & L, 13:1/10–15:1/10; Galen, 12:6–13.

534 Again by carelessness, a Hippocratic reference (*De diaeta in morbis acutis*, 2:14) from Galen's commentary has been incorporated into the text of *Airs*.

535 Al-Yaʿqūbī's text only roughly approximates the Greek; cf. DIL, 2,10–15/26:13–17, 26:18f., as well as M & L, 13:9f./17f.

536 This renewed introduction of *Airs* must have derived from a reader's gloss copied into the text; note the variant title, especially *al-buldān* (countries) for *al-amṣār* (cities). The reference to content also points to the opening paragraph of a recension depending on Galen's commentary, which is divided into four discourses (*maqālāt*, see Galen, pp. 2:2, 35:2, 62:10, 95:2).

537 The numbering reflects a different exemplar than in the preceding section.

538 That is, south in the northern hemisphere.

539 That is, the north. Al-Farqadān (The Two Calves) is the Arabic name for the stars that form the end of the bowl of the Little Dipper; their Arabic-derived English names are Pherkad (γ Ursae Minoris) and Kochab (β Ursae Minoris).

540 DIL, 3,2/26:23; M & L, 15:3/11; Galen, p. 13:3.

541 Since in the northern hemisphere the sun rises and sets in winter to the south of due east and due west, this is a way of designating winds that blow from the south. In the Mediterranean, these would be hot winds coming from Africa.

542 The English follows Houtsma's emendation of *al-istiwāʾ* (the equator) to *al-shatwī* (wintry) and addition of *al-shams* (the sun), to agree with the Greek text. However, the text can be translated without emendation: "midway between the rising of the equinox and its setting," i.e., midway between the sun's equinoctial rising and its setting. Unfortunately, this applies equally to due north and to due south, and so Houtsma's emendation is probably justified. On the other hand, both M & L and Galen read *al-istiwāʾ*, which suggests an even earlier corruption; see Diller, 26:24f. + app. For Houtsma's addition of *fī kinn* or *mastūra*, cf. 15:4f./12f., and M & L, app.; Galen, p. 13:2–5.

and hot;[543] they become warm in summer and cool in winter. The heads of the inhabitants of such a city are moist and phlegmatic; their innards evacuate copiously and continually. The women of these people[544] are constantly ill and sickly on account of their copious menstruation, and they do not conceive,[545] not because of their natural disposition, but because of their illnesses; but if they do become pregnant, they miscarry in most cases. [Their children][546] are afflicted with tetanus, asthma, and the [sacred] disease.[547] Their men are subject to diarrhea, bloody dysentery, the illness that is called ague,[548] prolonged fever in winter and at night,[549] and hemorrhoids in the anus. They are also sub-
1:121 ject | to blazing fever, acute illnesses, and prolonged ophthalmia. When they reach fifty, they become subject to fluxes from the brain, and this brings on hemiplegia, which occurs in all countries.

The city that is toward the north wind: He said:[550] Every city situated facing the direction of the cold winds, namely what is near the direction of the summer sunrise and sunset,[551] these winds are its endemic winds, whereas it

543 Sic. The Greek has ὕφαλα (brackish).

544 Reading with M, *wa-nisāʾ hāʾulāʾi l-nās.*

545 Emending MS *lā yusqiṭna* (they do not miscarry), as suggested by Houtsma, to *lā yaḥbalna.* MS *yusqiṭna* may well be a misreading of *yashtamilna*, M & L, 17:6 (*yaslamna*, ibid. 15, and Galen, p. 16:2, obviously also misread).

546 As M stands, the sentence makes grammatical sense: "and tetanus, asthma, and the disease affect them" (viz., the women, with the pronoun "them" being feminine plural). The translation follows the emendation proposed in ed. Leiden on the basis of the Greek (M & L, 17:8f./17f.; Galen, p. 17:-7f; see DIL, 3,16f./28:10ff.), adding the words for "as for their children" and changing the gender of the pronoun.

547 The addition of "sacred" has been made on the same basis; the Hippocratic author's skepticism about such popular notions about epilepsy has been lost in the Arabic. On the Hippocratic monograph *Περὶ Ἱερῆς Νούσου* (On the Sacred Disease), see Fichtner, no. 32.

548 The Arabic transliterates the Greek term ἠπίαλος (M & L, 20, n. 2).

549 The Arabic, *wa-layliyya* (and nocturnal, or, and at night) is due to the translator's misconstruing Greek ἐπινυκτίδας as an attribute of "fevers," rather than as a separate syndrome ("pustules most painful at night").

550 DIL, 4/28:24; M & L, 21:9/17; Galen, p. 20:5. This introductory sentence again confirms the derivation of al-Yaʿqūbī's exemplar from a commentary, rather than from the Hippocratic text directly.

551 Emending MSS *wa-l-quṭbayn* (and the poles) to *al-qayẓiyyayn*, on the basis of the Greek ("between the summer setting and the summer rising of the sun"); cf. M & L, 23:1; Galen, p. 20:6; and DIL, 4:2/28:25f. Since in the northern hemisphere the sun rises and sets in summer to the north of due east and due west, this is a way of designating winds that blow from the north.

is protected from the hot winds. Its waters are hard,[552] slow in coction, and mostly sweet. Most of the inhabitants of this city are strong and powerful; their legs[553] necessarily tend toward thinness; their abdomens are firm;[554] their heads hard, dry, and tough; and they develop hernia. Their ailments are pleurisy, acute diseases, and copious purulence. Their veins are liable to tear. They eat much. They are not quickly subject to ophthalmia, but if they do fall ill with it, their eyes rupture. When they reach the age of thirty, they are much afflicted by nosebleed. They are not subject to the sacred diseases,[555] but if they do occur, they are severe. Their lives are long, and their dispositions wild, neither sedate nor quiet. Their women are liable to be sterile because of the water's coldness and hardness, and that is because menstruation often is not as it should be. When they do conceive, childbirth is difficult for them, but they do not miscarry. Their children's nourishment is meager because of the milk's frigidity, and they[556] are subject to tetanus and lung pain.[557] Boys are subject to dropsy in the testicles, but when they grow up it disappears. They are slow to reach puberty.

The city situated toward the winds from the place of summer and winter sunrise:[558] Hippocrates said: Every city situated toward the rising of the sun is healthier than one situated toward the Farqadān[559] or one situated | toward 1:122 the hot winds; the heat and the cold are less there and easier to bear, and the illnesses of its people are few. Water sources that face the direction of sunrise are bright, luminous, pure, of fragrant odor, and soft, because the air there is not thick, and the sun prevents it from becoming thick.[560] The appearance of the city's inhabitants is of good coloring, luminous, and bright; their men's voices are clear and sharp; and they [do not] become angry quickly.[561] Its plants

552 Arabic, *yābisa*, which normally means "dry," can also mean "hard," which would agree with the Greek σκληρά.

553 An addition from Galen's commentary; see DIL, 4,6/30:4; M & L, 23:7/13 f.; Galen, p. 22:7,9.

554 Another case of abridgment: M & L, 23:8 f./15, and Galen, p. 22:13 f., preserve the differentiation of lower and upper abdomen (DIL, 4,7 f./30:5 f.).

555 Arabic, *al-asqām al-kāhiniyya* (the priestly diseases, i.e., epilepsy) is an attempt to render Greek τὰ ἱερὰ νοσεύματα.

556 That is, the women, as the gender of the Arabic pronoun makes clear.

557 An unspecific translation of φθίσις (consumption).

558 That is, winds that come from the general direction of the east, whether from the northeast, east, or southeast. For the Greek, see DIL, 5/32:6; M & L, 35:2/10; Galen, p. 28:8.

559 That is, the north.

560 This may mean that exposure to the morning sun quickly burns off any mist.

561 Another case of omitted negation, shared with Hippocrates MS D; see M & L, 39:2/11 f.; Galen, p. 30:5.

and grasses are stronger and healthier. In its nature and shape it resembles the season of spring in slightness of heat and cold. Its illnesses are few and mild, and its women conceive often and give birth without difficulty.

The fourth city, which faces the sunset, is sheltered from easterly winds, but hot winds and cold winds blow towards it from the direction of the Farqadān.[562] It therefore has many diseases. Its waters are neither clean nor clear; the reason for this is the air at dawn, because the dawns of this city are very prolonged, the sun not shining there at its first rising, but only when it reaches a certain elevation and height. Cold winds blow there in summer. Its men are sallow and sickly, subject to every manner of disease,[563] and their voices are hoarse. Their daytime in the days of autumn is noxious because of its much changing.[564]

This is the first chapter, on the four (kinds of) cities.

The second discourse is on waters, which are of four kinds.[565] The first of them are stagnant waters like marshes,[566] which do not flow; the second are upwelling springs; the third are waters that come from rain, and the fourth waters that come from snow. Hippocrates said:[567] Exposed bodies of water,
1:123 level with the face of the earth, which | do not flow, while the rains that fall on them remain with them and do not move, and the sun continually shines on them and heats them—such waters therefore are noxious and colorless[568] and generate bile. In winter they are cold, frozen, turbid, phlegmatic; they bestow hoarseness and inflammation of the spleen on those who drink from them. Their innards are coarse and cause their clavicles and faces to become lean and emaciated.[569] Such people eat a great deal, and it raises their thirst and craving for drink. Disease attends on them in winter and spring; in summer

562 DIL, 6/32:25; M & L, 41:4/12; Galen, p. 32:5.

563 Following the apparent, partially vocalized reading of M, *taʿtarīhim al-amrāḍ kulluhā*; ed. Leiden conjectures *taḍīru bihim* (all the diseases harm them), which involves somewhat unidiomatic construction of this Arabic verb with a preposition.

564 The sense of the Greek is that in such cities there is an unhealthy difference between the morning and afternoon weather.

565 The reference to a fourfold division is from Galen's commentary, see p. 35:10 f.

566 Arabic, *al-baṭāʾiḥ*: the word used to designate the marshes of the lower Tigris-Euphrates system.

567 DIL, 34:19; M & L, 47:6/13; Galen, p. 36:4.

568 Arabic, *lā lawna lahā*: a mistranslation of Greek ἄχροα, which here means "ill-colored," not "uncolored."

569 The manuscript *t.n.f.ḥ.hā* gives little sense; the best solution is to assume that two letters have been transposed and read *tuniḥfuhā* (emaciates them).

they are subject to dropsy, dysentery, and prolonged chronic quartan fever. Their young people are subject to lung pains[570] and ailments that addle their minds.[571] The old men are subject to ardent fever, which is called[572] "burning," due to the dryness[573] of their innards. Their women are subject to various kinds of swellings on account of white phlegm; it is hard for them to conceive, and they give birth only with difficulty. Their children are big,[574] but when they are weaned,[575] they lose weight and become thin. The young children are subject to hernia, and the men to sickness and ulcers in their legs.[576] Lifespans are not long in such a city, and old age overcomes them quickly in the course of the seasons.[577] Women sometimes are affected by what they imagine to be pregnancy, but then it comes to naught.

The water of springs that flow from certain rocks is bad because it is hard.[578] Springs that well up from hot ground and from ground with deposits of iron, copper, silver, gold, sulphur, alum, pitch, or natron all well up only because
of the intensity | of the heat; and so there are no beneficial and salubrious 1:124
waters from these soils: most of them are hard, and from them and their consumption come difficulty of urination and constipation. Waters that flow from high places and earthy hills are the best and healthiest waters. They are sweet[579] and do not require much admixture of wine; in winter they are hot, and in summer cold.

570 The Greek has περιπνευμονίαι (pneumonia).

571 Arabic, *asqām tukhaththiru ʿuqūlahum* (ailments that coagulate their minds) renders Greek μανιώδεα νοσεύματα (illnesses attended by delirium).

572 Sic M, *tadullu ʿalā*, but the reading is probably corrupt. The translation follows the reading of M & L, 53:7, *tudʿā* ... (which is called ...).

573 Or, "hardness," Arabic *yubs*.

574 That is, at birth. The Greek has ἔμβρυα, translated more accurately in M & L, 55:2/10, as *ajinnatuhunna*.

575 Arabic, *ʿuzilū*; apparently corrupted from *ghudhū*, "are fed"; cf. M & L, 55:2/11.

576 Arabic, *saqam wa-qurūḥ fī sūqihim*. As the text stands, this looks like a hendiadys for "an ulcerating sickness in their legs," but it may have been corrupted from the reading preserved in M & L, 55:4f./12f.: "the ailment that is called *qirsūs*"—i.e., varicose veins, from Greek κιρσός (cf. DIL, 7,30/36:18).

577 The Arabic *fī ḍimni l-azmān* (in the inside of the seasons) is awkward; *ḍ.m.n* could easily have arisen from a misreading of *mamarr* (passage, cf. M & L 55:7/16), giving better sense, as translated here. The Greek has "they age before the appointed time" (DIL, 7,31f./36:20).

578 DIL, 7,35/36:24; M & L, 57:6/14; Galen, p. 43:-9. Read *ḥāsiya* (M. *ḥāshiya*).

579 Emending MSS *ḥārra* (hot) to *ḥulwa* (sweet) as suggested by ed. Leiden, following the Greek (M & L, 59:14; Galen, p. 45:10).

Such is the condition of the waters that flow from underground springs. The best of them are those that flow from the horizon of the sun,[580] especially the summer sunrise, as they are limpid, bright, and fragrant. Any water that is salty, slow of coction, and hard is not beneficial to those who drink of it without need, although some constitutions and ailments sometimes have benefited from it. Any waters whose taste tends to salinity are bad and noxious. The water of any spring that faces the sunrise is best; next come those springs that come up from between the horizon of the summer sunrise and summer sunset—the most excellent of them are those which are inclined toward the sunrise, then (those) toward (what is) between the winter and summer sunsets. The worst are such springs as are in the direction of the south. As for such springs as descend toward the horizon of winter sunrise and winter sunset: those of them which are in the direction of the south are very bad, but those of them which are in the direction of the north are better. Light, clear waters are beneficial to anyone who has hard viscera, but harmful to anyone who has has soft, supple, and phlegmatic viscera. [… Anyone who maintains] that saline waters loosen the bowels has erred.[581]

1:125 Rainwater is light and sweet. The sun | carries off the finer, lighter parts of the water and causes the water to ascend from rivers, seas, and humid places.[582] Rainwater therefore becomes foul and malodorous because it has been gathered by diverse winds,[583] and so it has become quicker to turn foul and altered. For the moisture that the sun dries up is of sundry kinds; it remains suspended in the air, but when all of it is gathered and rolled together by opposing winds meeting head-on, it then pours down, especially when the

580 Arabic, *min ufuq al-shams*; this might mean "from the direction of the sun," or perhaps one should read *min ufuq* [*sharq*] *al-shams* (from the horizon of the rising of the sun), as M & L, 61:1/10; Galen, p. 46:9.

581 A sentence has apparently been omitted. The Greek points out that because "harsh waters … contract most of these organs and dry them up," they are appropriate for those who have "soft, moist, and phlegmatic digestive organs." Hippocrates notes that this contradicts the common belief about saline waters being "laxative." See M & L, 67:2 f./10 ff.; Galen, p. 50:-3 ff and p. 51:-7 f; and DIL, 7,62–72 /38:22–40:6.

582 DIL, 8,2/40:8; M & L, 69:3/10; Galen, p. 52:-8 f.

583 Arabic, *riyāḥ*. One is tempted to emend the MSS reading to something meaning "places" (e.g., *mawāḍiʿ*, as in the previous sentence). Although this would be logical, the reading "winds" seems to have arisen from al-Yaʿqūbī's abbreviation of his source, which goes on to discuss how a variety of contrary winds differentiate the sublimated mist. Cf. M & L, 71:7/16; Galen, p. 54:-8; and DIL, 8,19/40:24 f.

proportion[584] is as it should be. Most often this happens when a gathering of clouds, having solidified, is met and rent by another wind and when another cloud presses upon the first cloud and cuts it; the moisture then descends because of its weight, the winds rend it,[585] and copious[586] rains result. Such waters are the most excellent of waters, except that[587] they are liable to have a bad odor and that whoever drinks of them is subject to hoarseness, coughing, and heaviness of voice. Moreover, when they are boiled, boiling does not benefit them at all.[588]

As for waters that come from snow and ice:[589] all of them are bad, for once they have been frozen, they do not return to their first nature: whatever in the water is light, sweet, pure, and clean escapes from freezing and flies away,[590] and whatever is murky remains unaffected. This is known by the following: If water be poured into a vessel in the days of winter, measured to a known measure, and set under the sky, it will freeze. If it then be set in the sun until it melts, and that water be measured, it will be found to have diminished noticeably. That is the sign that the fine part of water evaporates and does not undergo freezing and that [the coarse part] does not evaporate and does not depart.[591] Thus the water of snow [and ice][592] is the worst of waters.

When people drink diverse waters,[593] they are subject to strangury, stones in the bladder, pain in the loins, pain | in the haunches, and hernia in the testicles, 1:126
especially when they drink water from rivers that are fed by large rivers or by a

584 Arabic, *muqāyasa* (measurement, proportion). One is tempted to emend to *manāfis* (air passages), as in M & L, 75:1/10, Galen, p. 55:-7, but the Arabic deviates from the Greek: "where it happens to become most compressed" (cf. M & L, 76, n.; DIL, 8,28/42:6 f.).

585 The sentence has been tentatively restored on the basis of the two versions and annotation in M & L, 75:4 ff./13 ff. and 76, n. 6.

586 Arabic, *sābigha*, may be a corruption of *mutatābi'a* (successive), as in M & L, 75:6/15; Galen p. 55:-3; cf. DIL, 8,34/42:12 DIL.

587 Here the loss of a negation and abridgment have again reversed the intended meaning; such waters should not be foul-smelling, but if they exceptionally are, the named disorders ensue; see M & L, 75:8 ff./16 ff.; Galen, p. 56:-7 ff; and cf. DIL, 8,34–37/42:12 ff.

588 This sentence, also in 77:1 f./11 M & L, is a dittography of the first in Galen's following commentary, p. 56:-4 f.; cf. M & L, 78, n. 1; and DIL, 8,36 f./42:14.

589 DIL, 8,37/42:15; M & L, 77:5/12; Galen, p. 57:8.

590 Emending *ṭāba* (is/becomes fragrant) to *ṭāra*, as suggested by the Leiden editor; cf. M & L, 77:8.

591 The lacuna is supplied from M & L, 79:6/14.

592 Restored on the basis of M & L, 79:8/16.

593 DIL, 9,2/44:4; M & L, 81:2/9; Galen, p. 58:9.

lake into which various and sundry streams feed, because some of it is sweet, some saline, some alum-laden,[594] and part is water of a stream from hot places. When it is drunk, ailments occur.[595] Bad milk generates stones in the bladders of nursing infants, whereas women are not afflicted by stones because their urethra is wide.

The third discourse[596] is on the seasons: when they are unwholesome or wholesome. Hippocrates said:[597] If the rising and setting[598] of the stars is as it should be, and there is much water in the autumn and little in winter, with the sunshine not being (too) much or the cold above measure, so that their waters are balanced in the spring and in the summer, they (viz., the seasons) are wholesome and salubrious, and the air is salubrious, too. But when the winter is dry and northerly, and the spring very rainy and southerly, people in summer will be subject to fever,[599] ophthalmia, and, anyone with a humid disposition, dysentery. However, when at the time of the rising of the star called "the Dog," which is Sirius, there is much rain and wintry weather and the winds blow according to their asterisms,[600] they will ward off ailments, and it may be hoped that the autumn will be salubrious. But if that is not the case, there will be death among children and women, but rarely among old men; whoever escapes, will be subject to quartan fever, which sometimes will turn into dropsy. When the winter is southerly and rainy, and the spring dry and northerly, pregnant women will miscarry in the springtime; if they do give birth,
1:127 their children will be sickly, either dying | in short order or living feebly. As for everyone else, some will be subject to dysentery and dry ophthalmia, and some to fluxes from the head to the lung. Phlegmatics and women will be subject to dysentery. The bilious [..., while the elderly][601] will be subject to fluxes because

594 Emending *al-shatwī* (wintry) to *al-shabbī*, following ed. Leiden; cf. M & L, 83:2/9; Galen, p. 58:-8; DIL, 9,8/44:10.

595 Severe cutting has taken place here (cf. M & L, 85:2/11–89:3/11), and the conclusion of the paragraph is similarly abrupt (ibid. 89:4/12–91:5/14).

596 M & L, 91:6; Galen, p. 62.

597 DIL, 10:2/46:18; M & L, 93:1/11; Galen, p. 67:7.

598 Emending *ghayruhā* (other than it/them) to *ghuyūbuhā*, as in M & L, 93:1/11, Galen, p. 68:8.

599 Emending *al-ḥarr* (the heat) to *al-ḥummā*; cf. M & L, 93:9/17.

600 Arabic, *ʿalā anwāʾihā* (according to their *anwāʾ*), that is, seasonably. The Arabs divided the year into twenty-eight periods (*anwāʾ*, pl. of *nawʾ*), each marked by a pair of stars, one of which made its first appearance as a morning star in the east at the beginning of the period, while the other made its last appearance as an evening star at the same time.

601 For the lacuna, see M & L, 101:2ff./9–12, where the missing text reads: "Those that are

of the tenuousness of their skin and the withering of their nerves;[602] sometimes they will die suddenly, and sometimes their right side will become palsied.[603]

Such cities as face the sunrise, whose winds are wholesome and waters sweet,[604] are rarely harmed by alteration of the air; but every city whose people drink warm[605] swamp water, that is not situated toward the east, and whose winds are not wholesome—its people will be harmed by alteration of the air. If the summer is dry generally, diseases will depart quickly; if it is rainy, diseases will last long; if someone gets an ulcer in these ailments, or lientery,[606] or dropsy, he will perish. When summer is rainy and southerly, and the autumn likewise, the winter will be dry and unhealthy; phlegmatics and old men of forty years will come down with a fever called *al-qawsūs*;[607] cholerics will come down with pleurisy and pneumonia. When the summer is dry and southerly and the autumn rainy and northerly, people (in winter) will be subject to [head][608] pain, cough, hoarseness, and colds, and some of them to consumption. When the summer is dry and northerly, and there is no rain at the rise of Sirius, it benefits phlegmatics and those of humid disposition, but it harms the bilious and sometimes brings them to melancholy.

Much change comes about at the turning of the sun: the summer turning brings more change than | the winter one, and the autumnal turning brings 1:128
more change than the spring one.[609]

bilious [will] suffer from dry ophthalmia, because their bodies are overcome by heat and dryness. The elderly …"

602 The Greek refers to veins, rather than sinews. Cf. M & L, 101:4/23; Galen, p. 81:10 ff.; DIL, 10,36/50:2.

603 Literally "dry up"; see M & L, 102, n. 4; DIL, 10,37/50:3.

604 The manuscripts read *ghāʾira* (sinking into the ground), which makes no sense. The Greek speaks of "cities that use good waters." The translation emends to *ʿadhbatan*; cf. M & L, 103:5/13.

605 Arabic, *sākhinan*; perhaps to be emended to *sibākhiyyan* (from salt marshes); cf. M & L, as 103:7/15.

606 Understand [*istirkhāʾ*] *al-baṭn* ([looseness of] the belly), as M & L, 105:6/15; cf. Galen, p. 83: -4 f; DIL, 10:51/50:16.

607 The sentence can be restored on the basis of M & L, 105:9/18–107:3/12 and Galen, p. 84: -6 ff.; cf. DIL, 10,53–56/50:18 ff. The transliterated Greek term καῦσος means "ardent/burning fever."

608 Added by the Leiden editor on the basis of the Greek; cf. M & L, 107:7/15.

609 For this paragraph, cf. DIL, 11,5/52:19; M & L, 113:2/8; Galen, p. 91:6. *Taṣarruf* (turning) appears to comprise both solstice and equinox; the MSS have an otiose second *al-shatawī* (winter) which, if not merely an instance of dittography, may have originally read *al-istiwāʾī* (equinoctial); see DIL, 52:20 + app.

Every country whose seasons change a great deal will not be flat; in it there will be tall, high, towering mountains. But every country whose seasons change only a little will be flat.[610]

Hippocrates then mentions people's differing forms with regard to their states and the equilibrium of their constitution and the reason why some resemble others; it is by agreement with the season and the rising places (of the sun). He mentions the state of men and women with regard to the multitude or fewness of their children, what causes procreation, and what blocks it.[611]

They say that the inhabitants of high, level, well-watered places will have pleasing forms and stout bodies, their dispositions will tend toward mildness and gentleness, and they will not be people of boldness and courage.[612] Whoever inhabits a poor, arid, infertile country where the temperament of the air is not well-balanced will have hard[613] forms, their coloring will tend toward sallowness or to blackness, their dispositions will be bad, their anger intense, and their natures will be at variance with each other; for by difference of seasons comes difference of dispositions, and, after the seasons in the lands, comes sustenance by waters, because man's sustenance, after the lands, comes from them.[614]

After that, Hippocrates discusses the winds and their blowing and those that blow from place to place, dividing them into four divisions. He says that wind is caused by air getting whirled about; its arising comes only from a collision of particles of air.[615]

---

610 Cf. DIL, 13,6/56:19; M & L, 123:13; Galen, p. 103:8. This sentence, probably a marginal correction in the exemplar, was mistakenly entered here instead of in its proper place further on, but in al-Yaʿqūbī's exemplar, the entire fourth discourse of Galen's commentary, covering sections 12–24 of *Airs*, appears to have been severely damaged and disordered.

611 The paragraph summarizes most of Galen's fourth discourse (DIL, 54–78; M & L, 117–157; Galen, pp. 95–143).

612 DIL, 24,21/80:5; M & L, 157:8; Galen, p. 143:3.

613 Arabic, *jāsiya* (hard, dry, solid), the reading of the MSS; ed. Leiden emends unnecessarily to *khāshina* (harsh, rough, coarse).

614 This is the apparent sense of the text in the MSS. On the basis of DIL, 24,27–33/80:11–82:1; M & L, 159:5–10; and Galen, pp. 143:-1 ff, 146:-2 ff, one can restore the text provisionally to read: "For by difference of seasons comes difference of dispositions; then, after the seasons, it comes by (difference of) lands, because man's sustenance comes from them; and, after (difference of lands), it comes by (difference of) waters."

615 Galen's detailed appendix at the end of his commentary, p. 150 ff., is here reduced to a single sentence, corresponding to p. 152:8 f.; its logical place would seem to be at the end of the "second chapter" of the first discourse (p. 9:1), where Galen's commentary is omitted (cf. also p. 29, where a blank has been left for the intended diagram). Al-Yaʿqūbī's next

These are the subjects of Hippocrates' *Book of Airs and Seasons*, on which Galen wrote a commentary; he explicated what Hippocrates meant section by section and point by point.

These then are those of Hippocrates's books that are relied upon and | 1:129 referred to, and these are their subjects.[616] Galen wrote commentaries on them and explicated everything to which he devoted a section and opinion that he held; he clarified his words and interpreted and elucidated his ideas.

As for the *Book of Barley Water*:[617] In it he mentions the acute diseases that are called pain of the side and of the lung,[618] frenzy,[619] and burning fever. He told how barley water was to be taken, the days on which it was to be taken, how it was to be administered, the times at which it should be taken, the times at which it was prohibited, and what diet should go with it. He also mentioned the kinds[620] of acute illnesses and burning diseases and discussed every type of them.

As for his book which he names the *Book of Elements*:[621] The meaning of "elements"—the four natures—is heat, wetness, cold, and dryness, as well as the "elements" of the body,[622] namely nerves, veins, bones, skin, and

---

sentence is more difficult to situate; a single Hippocratic parallel has been found in "On Winds" (*De flatibus*): "Wind is the air's flux and flow" (*Œuvres Complètes d'Hippocrate*, ed. Littré, 3,6/ VI 94:4).

616 This paragraph should follow the next, since *Barley Water* completes the above-mentioned tetralogy of essential Hippocratic treatises.

617 Fichtner, no. 4; for an Arabic version with English translation, see M. C. Lyons, *Kitāb Buqrāṭ fī tadbīr al-amrāḍ al-ḥādda*. The title indicates the prominence of barley gruel in the first section, whereas the following two genuine sections discuss various other treatments of acute diseases. Al-Yaʿqūbī gives a summary of the first section only, although his "types of acute diseases" might reflect subsequent chapters.

618 That is, pleurisy and pneumonia.

619 Arabic, *birsām*, like "frenzy," initially referred to an affection of the diaphragm and then the chest, either of which was thought to entail mental derangement.

620 The original reading of M appears to have been *ḍurūban* (kinds). A later hand (or the same copyist) has corrected the reading by changing the "b" into an "f," apparently to give the reading *ṣunūfan* (types), the plural of the word *ṣinf* that occurs in the next line, but neglected to remove the dot of the "b" or change the beginning of the word, yielding the strange reading *ṣurūfan*, which Houtsma emended to *ṣunūfan*.

621 Arabic, *Kitāb al-Arkān*: Fichtner, no. 25; edited and translated by J. N. Mattock & M. C. Lyons as *Kitāb Buqrāṭ fī ṭabīʿat al-insān*.

622 The title "Elements," as well as the precedence given to the notion of the four elemental qualities (although fundamental to this treatise) would seem to derive, rather than from the Hippocratic text itself, from Galen's commentary (Fichtner, *Gal.*, no. 90; Johannes

blood.[623] By these elements the world subsists. Hippocrates said that if bodies were a single thing, pains would never reach them; however, they consist of diverse things and separate natures some of which are harmful to others.[624] Since the nature of man and the other animals turns out to be of this description, by necessity man cannot be a single thing in himself. Similarly, only by wetness, dryness, heat, and cold do the other natures subsist.[625] He discourses on this in lucid language.

Hippocrates had disciples who interpreted his books; some of them produced books and attributed them to him in acknowledgment of his learning and merit. One of them was Dioscorides, the author of the *Book of Trees and*
1:130 *Herbs*.[626] He composed a book on the benefits of trees, illustrated each | tree with a picture, and mentioned what the tree was good for. Another of them was Archigenes, the author of the *Compendium*, which contains a description of the body.[627]

Mewaldt, ed., *Galeni In Hippocratis De natura hominis commentaria III*). In Galen's introduction, his opening citation of Hippocratic "elements" (p. 3:4) may have been misconstrued as reference to the present text; then, after an historical review of natural philosophy including reference to the four elements air, fire, earth and water (p. 6:1f.), Galen succinctly states the subject of the first part of *On the Nature of Man* to be the four elemental qualities together with the humors composed of them. In the Hippocratic text itself, not only is human "nature" mentioned in the very opening sentence, but air, fire, water, earth figure in the introductory argument against the "monism" of natural philosophers; blood, bile, and phlegm recur frequently after their first mention in rebutting the author's medical opponents (M & L, 1:4, 6f., 15ff., 2:15f.; cf. 1,1, 3f., 11f.; 2,1ff., Jacques Jouanna, *Hippocratis De natura hominis*, 164:3–6, 13, 166:12ff.).

623 One would expect a reference here to the four humors (blood, yellow bile, black bile, and phlegm; cf. M & L, 3:2ff.; Jouanna, 2,4–8/166:15–168:2; Mewaldt, 20:4–19; cf. also M & L, 6:1ff.; Jouanna, 4,1ff./172:13f.; Mewaldt, 32:10ff.). The text as it stands may have resulted from the intrusion of a marginal gloss intended to restore a lacuna (cf. Mewaldt, 30:1–9).

624 Accepting the Leiden editor's correction of *wa-ṭabīʿa musāʿida muḍirr baʿḍuhā bi-baʿḍ*. Because the meaning of the MSS *ṭabīʿa musāʿida* (a helping/accompanying nature) is unclear, the Leiden editor emended to read *ṭabāʾiʿ mutabāʿida* (mutually separate/distinct/antagonistic natures).

625 This appears to paraphrase M & L, 5:13f. (Jouanna, 3,16f./172:9f.), taking into account Galen's commentary, Mewaldt, 30:19ff. (through 31:17).

626 Pedanius Dioscorides (1st century BCE) produced an illustrated catalogue of materia medica that became the basis of Islamic pharmacology. See the article by C. E. Dubler in *EI*[2], s.v. Diyusḳuridīs; Leigh Chipman in *EI*[3], s.v. Dioscorides; M. Klamroth, "Ueber die Auszüge aus griechischen Schriftstellern bei al-Jaʿqūbī, II," *ZDMG* 40 (1886): 613–614.

627 Archigenes of Apamea was a physician who practiced in Rome in the reign of Trajan (late

But the wisest sage after him, the one who took the most interest in medicine and who had the best understanding of the part of Hippocrates's writings on which he commented, was Galen, notwithstanding the distance in years between them, for there was a long time between them.[628] Nevertheless, Galen appears to be, as it were, the immediate successor of Hippocrates in wisdom and his second in knowledge. He wrote commentaries on his books and produced many of the books on medicine that are commonly relied on and referred to: he was a philosopher, logician, and sage.

The first of Galen's books is the book, *On the Sects of Medicine that Differ from Each Other in Kind*[629]—namely, the sect of opinion, reflection, and inference;[630] the second sect, that of experiences;[631] and the third sect, that of methods.[632]

A book, *On Food*.[633]

1st and early 2nd centuries CE). Only fragments of his works have been preserved. See the article by Jerry Stannard in *Complete Dictionary of Scientific Biography*, 1:212–213.

628 Galen (b. c. 129 CE in Pergamum, d. after 200 CE in Rome) lived more than five centuries after Hippocrates. The pioneering study of al-Yaʿqūbī's treatment of Galen and its sources was done by M. Klamroth, "Ueber die Auszüge aus griechischen Schriftstellern bei al-Jaʿqūbī, II," *ZDMG* 40 (1886): 614–638. An overview of the history of Galen's works in Arabic may be found in Fuat Sezgin, *GAS*, 3:68–140. A summary of the latest research on the reception of Galen's works in Arabic, with a discussion of al-Yaʿqūbī's importance and a bibliography of Arabic translations, may be found in the article by Véronique Boudon-Millot in *EI*³, s.v. Galen.

629 Fichtner, *Corpus Galenicum*, no. 4: "De sectis ad eos, qui introducuntur" (Περὶ αἱρέσεων τοῖς εἰσαγομένοις); Klamroth, op. cit., 615–616. For an English translation and introduction to the issues discussed in this treatise, see *Galen: Three Treatises on the Nature of Science*, trans. Richard Walzer and Michael Frede.

630 Arabic, *al-raʾy wa-l-fikr wa-l-qiyās*, a way of referring to the rationalist or theoretical school of medicine (often called dogmatist), which held that only on the basis of a theoretical understanding of the nature and functioning of the body could the physician prescribe proper treatment.

631 Arabic, *tajārib*, a way of referring to the school of empiricism, which held that only on the basis of experience could the physician determine effective treatment, because an adequate theory of disease was either unobtainable or irrelevant.

632 Arabic, *ḥiyal* (pl. of *ḥīla*), a way of referring to the school that came to be called methodist, which subsumed all illnesses under a small number of "generalities," manifest symptoms that could be treated without reference to underlying causes.

633 Arabic, *Fī l-ṭaʿām*. The second word in the title may have resulted from a miscopying of *Fī l-ʿiẓām* (On Bones). The two words differ only in the order of two letters and the presence or absence of a single dot over the Arabic letter. The latter is Fichtner, *Corpus Galenicum*, no. 12: "De ossibus ad tirones" (Περὶ ὀστῶν τοῖς εἰσαγομένοις); Klamroth, op. cit., 618.

A book, *On the Pulse of the Veins*.[634]
A book, *On the Anatomy of the Nerves*.[635]
A book, *On the Anatomy of the Veins and the Arteries*.[636]
Two discourses, *On the Causes of Respiration*.[637]
Four discourses, *On the Voice*.[638]
A book, *On the Uses of the Parts of the Body* (seventeen discourses).[639]
A book, *On the Anatomy of the Womb*.[640]
A book, *On the Signs of [the Diseases of] the Eye*.[641]
A book, *On the Medicine of the Empiricists*.[642]
Three discourses, *On the Motion of the Lungs and the Chest*.[643]

The *Great Book of Anatomy*, in fifteen discourses.[644] The first discourse is on the muscles and ligaments[645] in the arms; the second is on the muscles in the legs; the third is on the nerves, veins, and arteries in the arms and legs;

634 Probably to be identified as "De pulsibus ad tirones" (Περὶ τῶν σφυγμῶν τοῖς εἰσαγομένοις), Fichtner, *Corpus Galenicum*, no. 61; Klamroth, op. cit., 616.

635 Fichtner, *Corpus Galenicum*, no. 14: "De nervorum dissectione" (Περὶ νευρῶν ἀνατομῆς βιβλίον); Klamroth, op. cit., 618.

636 Fichtner, *Corpus Galenicum*, no. 13: "De venarum arteriarumque dissectione" (Περὶ φλεβῶν καὶ ἀρτηριῶν ἀνατομῆς); Klamroth, op. cit., 618.

637 Fichtner, *Corpus Galenicum*, no. 20: "De causis respirationis" (Περὶ τῶν τῆς ἀναπνοῆς αἰτιῶν); Klamroth, op. cit., 622. Note that the Arabic title, *Fī ʿilal al-tanaffus*, could also be translated as "On the Maladies of Respiration."

638 Fichtner, *Corpus Galenicum*, no. 358: "De voce" (Περὶ φωνῆς); Klamroth, op. cit., 622.

639 Fichtner, *Corpus Galenicum*, no. 17, 18: "De usu partium" (Περὶ χρείας τῶν ἐν ἀνθρώπου σώματι μορίων λόγοι); Klamroth, op. cit., 623.

640 Fichtner, *Corpus Galenicum*, no. 16: "De uteri dissectione" (Περὶ μήτρας ἀνατομῆς βιβλίον); Klamroth, op. cit., 623.

641 Arabic, *Fī ʿalāmāt al-ʿayn*, perhaps to be identified with *Fī dalāʾil ʿilal al-ʿayn* (On the Signs of the Diseases of the Eye). Fichtner, *Corpus Galenicum*, no. 275: "De morbis oculorum et eorum curis" (Περὶ τῶν ἐν ὀφθαλμοῖς παθῶν); Klamroth, op. cit., 623.

642 Arabic, *Fī ṭibb aṣḥāb al-tajārib*, is perhaps to be identified with *Kitāb al-Tajriba al-ṭibbiyya* (The Book of Medical Empiricism). Fichtner, *Corpus Galenicum*, no. 235: "De experientia medica," also known as "Sermo contra empiricos medicos" (Περὶ τῆς ἰατρικῆς ἐμπειρίας); Klamroth, op. cit., 623.

643 Fichtner, *Corpus Galenicum*, no. 280: "De motu thoracis et pulmonis" (Περὶ θώρακος καὶ πνεύμονος κινήσεως); Klamroth, op. cit., 623–624.

644 Arabic, *Kitāb al-Tashrīḥ al-kabīr*. Fichtner, *Corpus Galenicum*, no. 11: "De anatomicis administrationibus" (Περὶ ἀνατομικῶν ἐγχειρήσεων); Klamroth, op. cit., 624–625. Translation: Galen's *On Anatomical Procedures*, trans. Charles Singer (London: Oxford University Press, 1956). Note that *Discourses* (Books) 10–15 survive only in Arabic, not in the original Greek.

645 Emending manuscript *ruṭūbāt* (humors) to *ribāṭāt*.

the fourth is on the muscles that move the cheeks and lips and the muscles that move the lower jaw toward the head, toward the neck, and toward the shoulders; the fifth discourse is on the muscles of the chest, the muscles on the sides of the back, and the muscles of the spinal column; | the sixth discourse 1:131
is on the alimentary organs, namely the intestines, the stomach, the liver, the spleen, the kidneys, the bladder, the gall bladder, and the like; the seventh discourse is on the anatomy of the heart; the eighth discourse is on the parts of the chest; the ninth discourse is on the anatomy of the brain;[646] the tenth discourse is on the anatomy of the eyes, the tongue, the esophagus, and what connects to it; the eleventh discourse is on the larynx, the bone connected to it, and the nerves under it; the twelfth discourse is on the anatomy of the organs of procreation, namely the seminal organs, the womb, and the penis; the thirteenth discourse is on the anatomy of the blood vessels that pulsate, namely the arteries, and the blood vessels that do not pulsate; the fourteenth discourse is on the [nerves] that originate from the brain; and the fifteenth discourse is on the nerves that originate in the spine.

There is another *Book of Anatomy* by him in several discourses.[647] In them he mentions the skin; the hair; the nails; the flesh; the fat; the flesh of the face; the membranes that cover some organs, such as the pericardium; the stomach; the kidneys; the liver; the peritonea; the muscle separating the thorax from the abdomen; the ducts; the pulsating blood vessels; phlebotomy;[648] whence the blood vessels begin; the urine ducts between the kidneys and the bladder to the penis; its duct from the bladder to the navel in the embryo; the gall bladder; the pores;[649] the nostrils; the ducts that come out of the ears; the trachea, what originates from it, and what originates in the lung; the milk-containing vessels in the breast; the other secretions in the body that are contained in vessels; any humors and secretions[650] in any vessels; the cranial sutures, adhesion, and so forth; | the sutures in the face; the lower jaw, with its perforations and adhesion; 1:132
the teeth; the bone at the top the trachea and what attaches on either side;

646 The MSS read *al-fuʾād* (the heart), miscopied from *al-dimāgh* (the brain), which corresponds to the content of the ninth discourse.

647 Apparently a reference to a work by Galen that has not survived. Klamroth (op. cit., 625) identifies it as *Epitome of the Anatomical Books of Marinus* (Τῶν Μαρίνου βιβλίων ἀνατομικῶν ἐπιτομή); Fichtner, *Corpus Galenicum*, no. 371.

648 Arabic, *faṣd al-ʿurūq*; emended by the Leiden editor from the manuscript's *faṣl al-ʿurūq* (the division of veins).

649 Reading, with the MSS, *masāmm*; ed. Leiden emends to *mashāmm* (noses).

650 Reading the undotted word as *mufragha*; ed. Leiden, *mufarraʿa* (branched).

the broad bone at the base of the spine;[651] the thigh; the ribs; the shoulder blades; the shoulders; the clavicles; the upper arm; the forearm;[652] the bones of the palm; the fingers; the thigh bone; the base of the neck; that which is on the knee; the shank bone; the bones of the foot; the connection of the skull with the membranes on the brain; all the nerves that originate on the face; the muscles in the temples; the muscles by which chewing takes place; the muscles that move the cheeks and lips; the tongue and the muscles that move it; and the muscles that move the eyes. He mentions the mouth, the lips, the tongue, the gums, the uvula, the epiglottis, the tonsils, the nose, the nostrils, the ears, the neck and its muscles, the muscle over the ribs,[653] [the muscle] under the clavicle, the nature of the neck, and the muscles of the diaphragm and the forearm. He pronounces a discourse about dissection. This is his purpose in it.

Two Discourses on the Causes of Respiration.[654]

A book, *The Natural Faculties*, on the actions of the soul.[655]

A discourse, *On Urination from the Blood.*[656]

A discourse, *On Laxative Medicines.*[657]

A book that he titled, *The Opinions of Hippocrates and Plato.*[658] It is about the faculties of the rational soul, these being imagination, ratiocination, and memory (he says that the brain is the place of origin of the nerves, the heart the place of origin of the pulsating blood vessels, and the liver the place of origin of the nonpulsating blood vessels); and about the faculties by which the body subsists, in ten discourses.

The Uses of the Parts of the Body, in seventeen discourses.[659]

---

651 Reading with M, *al-qaṭan*, (the pelvis); ed. Leiden has *al-baṭn* (the stomach).

652 Emending MSS *sāq* (leg) to *sāʿid*, as suggested by Klamroth, op. cit., 626.

653 Emending MSS *al-aṣābiʿ* (the fingers) to *al-aḍlāʿ*.

654 This appears to be a copyist's mistake, as the book has already been listed above.

655 Fichtner, *Corpus Galenicum*, no. 10: "De facultatibus naturalibus" (Περὶ δυνάμεων φυσικῶν). The words "on the actions of the soul" are not part of the title but come from Galen's introduction to the work, in which he states his intention to compose a further book "on the actions of the soul." See Klamroth, op. cit., 617–618.

656 This title does not correspond to any of Galen's works on urination. See Klamroth, op. cit., 629.

657 Fichtner, *Corpus Galenicum*, no. 75: "De purgantium medicamentorum facultate" (Περὶ τῆς τῶν καθαιρόντων φαρμάκων δυνάμεως); Klamroth, op. cit., 629.

658 Fichtner, *Corpus Galenicum*, no. 33: "De placitis Hippocratis et Platonis libri IX" (Περὶ τῶν Ἱπποκράτους καὶ Πλάτωνος δογμάτων θ'); Klamroth, op. cit., 629–630.

659 Previously listed; see above, 1:130.

The Book of the Elements,[660] in which he says that the hot, the cold, the moist, and the dry are elements common to all bodies that | admit of generation and 1:133
corruption; that the elements are earth, fire, air, and water; that the elements of the human body are blood, phlegm, yellow bile, and black bile; and that an element is the ultimate part of the thing of which it is an element.

The Book of the Temperaments, consisting of three discourses on the classification of the temperaments of men's bodies.[661]

The Excellent Composition of the Body.[662]

Bodily Vigor.[663]

The Bad Temperament That Is Not Balanced.[664]

The Powers of Compounded Medicines.[665]

Medicines That Are Easy to Procure.[666]

A book, *The Preservation of the Healthy*.[667]

A book, *On Foods*.[668]

A book, *On Good and Bad Chyme*.[669]

A book, *On the Thinning Diet*.[670]

---

660 Fichtner, *Corpus Galenicum*, no. 5: "De elementis secundum Hippocratem libri II" (Περὶ τῶν καθ' Ἱπποκράτην στοιχείων β'); Klamroth, op. cit., 617.

661 Fichtner, *Corpus Galenicum*, no. 9: "De temperamentis libri III" (Περὶ κράσεων βιβλία γ'); Klamroth, op. cit., 617.

662 Fichtner, *Corpus Galenicum*, no. 25: "De optima corporis nostri constitutione" (Περὶ ἀρίστης κατασκευῆς τοῦ σώματος ἡμῶν); Klamroth, op. cit., 630.

663 Fichtner, *Corpus Galenicum*, no. 26: "De bono habitu" (Περὶ εὐεξίας); Klamroth, op. cit., 630.

664 Fichtner, *Corpus Galenicum*, no. 58: "De inaequali intemperie" (Περὶ ἀνωμάλου δυσκρασίας βιβλίον); Klamroth, op. cit., 630.

665 Fichtner, *Corpus Galenicum*, nos. 80–82; Klamroth, op. cit., 630–631 This apparently refers to two works combined into one: "De compositione medicamentorum secundum locos" and "De compositione medicamentorum per genera" (Περὶ συνθέσεως φαρμάκων τῶν κατὰ τόπους and Περὶ συνθέσεως φαρμάκων τῶν κατὰ γένη).

666 Fichtner, *Corpus Galenicum*, no. 86: "De remediis parabilibus libri III" (Περὶ εὐπορίστων βιβλίον γ'). The wording in Arabic of the title is merely a way of referring to simple, uncompounded drugs. See Klamroth, op. cit., 631.

667 Fichtner, *Corpus Galenicum*, no. 37: "De sanitate tuenda libri VI" (Ὑγιεινῶν λόγοι στ'); Klamroth, op. cit., 622.

668 Fichtner, *Corpus Galenicum*, no. 38: "De alimentorum facultatibus libri III" (Περὶ τροφῶν δυνάμεως λόγοι γ'); Klamroth, op. cit., 631.

669 That is, which foods produce good chyme (the partially digested food in the stomach) and which produce bad chyme. Fichtner, *Corpus Galenicum*, no. 39: "De probis pravisque alimentarum sucis" (Περὶ εὐχυμίας καὶ κακοχυμίας τροφῶν); Klamroth, op. cit., 632.

670 Fichtner, *Corpus Galenicum*, no. 349: "De victu attenuante" (Περὶ λεπτυνούσης διαίτης); Klamroth, op. cit., 632.

A discourse, *On the Classification of Diseases.*[671]
A discourse, *On the Causes of Diseases.*
A discourse, *On the Classification of Symptoms.*[672]
A discourse, *On Unnatural Thickening.*[673]
A discourse, *On Plethora.*[674]
Two discourses, *On the Classification of Fevers.*[675]
Internal Diseases.[676]
A book, *On the Stages of Diseases.*[677]
A book, *On Shortness of Breath.*[678]
A book, *On Crises.*[679]

A book, *On the Pulse of the Blood Vessels, Recognizing Each of the Types of Pulse, the Efficient Causes of the Types of Pulse, and Prognosis* (in sixteen discourses).[680]

---

671 This and the following two titles refer to a compendium of four originally independent treatises by Galen amalgamated into one work by the Alexandrians. Al-Yaʿqūbī mentions only three titles. Fichtner, *Corpus Galenicum*, nos. 42–47; Klamroth, op. cit., 618–619.

672 Reading with M, *fī taṣnīf al-aʿrāḍ*; in C the last word was miscopied as *al-amrāḍ* (diseases), leading the Leiden editor to bracket the title as a dittography.

673 A treatise on tumors. Fichtner, *Corpus Galenicum*, no. 57: "De tumoribus praeter naturam" (Περὶ τῶν παρὰ φύσιν ὄγκων βιβλίον); Klamroth, op. cit., 632.

674 A treatise on excess of humors. Fichtner, *Corpus Galenicum*, no. 53: "De plenitudine" (Περὶ πλήθους βιβλίον); Klamroth, op. cit., 632.

675 Fichtner, *Corpus Galenicum*, no. 48: "De differentiis febrium libri II" (Περὶ διαφορᾶς πυρετῶν βιβλία β'); Klamroth, op. cit., 620.

676 In the MSS it is not clear whether this is the title of a separate book: the word for "book" or "discourse" does not precede it, but it also is not preceded by the word "and," which would be needed to make it part of the preceding title. The Leiden editor supplied "and," implying that it was part of the title of the previous book, but no such composite title of a work by Galen is known. It is better to follow Klamroth, op. cit., 619–620, who saw this as a reference to a separate book on the diagnosis of diseases of the internal organs. Cf. Fichtner, *Corpus Galenicum*, no. 60: "De locis affectis libri VI" (Περὶ τῶν πεπονθότων τόπων βιβλία).

677 Fichtner, *Corpus Galenicum*, no. 49: "De morborum temporibus" (Περὶ τῶν ἐν ταῖς νόσοις καιρῶν βιβλίον); Klamroth, op. cit., 632.

678 Fichtner, *Corpus Galenicum*, no. 59: "De difficultate respirationis libri III" (Περὶ δυσπνοίας βιβλία γ'); Klamroth, op. cit., 633.

679 That is, of fevers. The Arabic term used here, *buḥrān*, is borrowed from Syriac. Fichtner, *Corpus Galenicum*, no. 67: "De crisibus libri III" (Περὶ κρίσεων βιβλία γ'); Klamroth, op. cit., 621.

680 Al-Yaʿqūbī lumps together the titles of four originally separate books on the subject of the pulse, each in four "discourses" (thus the total of sixteen). In fact, Galen himself prepared

A book, *On the Method of Healing*—a book in which he explained the way of curing all diseases.[681] In this branch, he followed it with:

A discourse, *On Mediating Causes*—that is, the proximate causes that mediate between the remote cause and the disease.[682]

A discourse, *On Urination from the Blood in the Body*.[683]

A book, *On the Sect of the Methodists*.[684]

A discourse, *On Consumption*.[685]

A discourse, *On the Treatment of an Epileptic Child*.[686]

A discourse, *On Hippocrates' Regimen for Acute Diseases*.[687]

A discourse, *On Phlebotomy*.[688]

He commented on Hippocrates' books section by section and point by point, and he explained the import of each.

∴

The leading sage who followed Hippocrates was Socrates, the leader of the sages and the first to express his wisdom as what was memorized from him and 1:134

---

a "synopsis" of the sixteen "discourses," and this may be what al-Yaʿqūbī is referring to. Fichtner, *Corpus Galenicum*, nos. 62–65, 66; Klamroth, op. cit., 616, 620.

681 Fichtner, *Corpus Galenicum*, no. 69: "Methodi medendi libri XIV" (Θεραπευτικῆς μεθόδου βιβλία ιδ'); Klamroth, op. cit., 621–622.

682 A lost work; Klamroth, op. cit., 633, gives the title as Περὶ τῶν συνεκτικῶν (αἰτιῶν). The translation "disease" follows Klamroth's suggested emendation of MSS *al-marīḍ* (the patient) to *al-maraḍ*. In this footnote and the next, no Latin equivalent is given for the Greek title, presumably because the work was lost.

683 This repeats a title listed above (1:132), with the additional words, "From the Body." Again, the book cannot be identified with any of Galen's works on urination.

684 A lost work. Klamroth, op. cit., 633 (Μεθοδικῆς αἱρέσεως στ').

685 Fichtner, *Corpus Galenicum*, no. 56: "De marcore" (Περὶ μαρασμοῦ βιβλίον); Klamroth, op. cit., 633.

686 For *yuṣraʿ* (epileptic) the MSS read *yurḍiʿ* (nursing), clearly a mistake, as it refers to no known work by Galen. The copyist's mistake was the result of the transposition of two letters and the addition of a diacritical dot. Fichtner, *Corpus Galenicum*, no. 77: "Puero epileptico consilium" (Τῷ ἐπιληπτικῷ παιδὶ ὑποθήκη); Klamroth, op. cit., 633.

687 Fichtner, *Corpus Galenicum*, no. 118: "De victus ratione in morbis acutis ex Hippocratis sententia" (Περὶ τῆς κατὰ τὸν Ἱπποκράτην διαίτης ἐπὶ τῶν ὀξέων νοσημάτων); Klamroth, op. cit., 634.

688 Fichtner, *Corpus Galenicum*, no. 125: "De venae sectione" (Περὶ φλεβοτομίας), but cf. no. 71–73 for other works by Galen on the subject; Klamroth, op. cit., 634, notes that Galen himself may have collected three of his works on the subject under one title.

heard from him.[689] It has been related that Timaeus said to him, "Teacher, why do you not record your wisdom for us in books?"[690] Socrates said: "Timaeus, how you trust the skins of dead beasts and how suspicious you are of living, eternal substances! How have you hoped for knowledge from the mine of ignorance and despaired of it from the element of the intellect?"[691] Then his disciple Epictetus[692] said to him, "Why do you not dictate to me a book that shall remain forever after you?" He replied, "Wisdom does not need the skins of sheep." One of his disciples said, "Why do you not provide us with a book of your wisdom by which we may guide[693] our minds?" Socrates said to him, "Do not be so eager to record wisdom on sheepskins that that becomes more persuasive to you than your own knowledge and tongue." When it came time for him to die, his disciples asked him to provide them with wisdom to which they might refer. So he spoke to them about the dispositions of the soul.[694] Then he spoke to them about the firmament, saying that it was spherical; he had already been given poison to drink, and then he died.

After him came Pythagoras. He was the first to speak of numbers, arithmetic, and geometry. He established the musical modes and constructed the lute. He lived at the time of a king named Augustus, from whom he fled but who pursued him. Pythagoras therefore set sail on the sea and reached a temple on an island, but the king set the temple afire while Pythagoras was in it. Pythagoras had a disciple named Archimedes who constructed burning-mirrors, and he burned the enemy's ships at sea.

---

689 That is, who transmitted his teachings orally and, as the next sentence states, wrote no books. Whether Socrates was really the first Greek "sage" to eschew writing is not the issue.

690 Arabic, *maṣāḥif* (pl. of *muṣḥaf*) normally refers to codices rather than rolls. It may be used here instead of the more common *kutub* (books) to suggest a process of collecting texts originally to be found on separate sheets.

691 The translation makes three emendations in the text on the basis of the parallel in the Arabic collection of sayings of the Greek philosophers edited and translated by Dimitri Gutas, *Greek Wisdom Literature in Arabic Translation*, 97, 298: *kayfa rajawta* (MSS *wujūd*) *al-ʿilm* (MSS *al-muʿallim*) *min maʿdin al-jahl wa-ayista* (MSS *wa-l-sabab*) *minhu min ʿunṣur al-ʿaql*. The original text makes some sense: "How can the teacher be found from the source of ignorance, when the means of access to him is from the element of the intellect?"

692 The reading of the name is conjectural. Another suggested reading is "Theaetetus."

693 Emending the MSS *t/n.s.b.r* (possibly to be read *nasburu* or *tasburu*, "that we/you may probe") to *nusayyiru*. The first letter of the Arabic is undotted, so the pronoun may be either "we" or "you."

694 Arabic *akhlāq al-nafs*, the regular way of saying "ethics."

Among them was Apollonius the Carpenter, who is called "the orphan."[695] He was the master of talismans, who made a talisman for everything.

Among them was Diogenes,[696] | the master of geometry, division, and the various sorts of philosophy. He used to be called "Diogenes the Dog."[697] Someone asked him, "Why have you been called 'the dog'?" He said, "Because I growl at knaves, wag my tail at good men, and live in the streets." 1:135

Among them was Philo, the master of mechanics.[698] These are motions that take place because of water: such as the form that is constructed and then the water moves it without any part of it being set in motion, causing it to leave one place and setting it down in another; and devices set in motion by water without being moved, and then it comes out and swallows them, and again it comes out and then swiftly moves away.[699] He has designs of such objects that can be constructed and that work.

Among them was Polemon, the author of the *Physiognomy* and of a book in which he explained what physiognomy indicates with regard to facial features, voices, and constitution and gave proof of that.[700]

---

695 Arabic, Balīnūs al-Najjār (the name is slightly miscopied in the MSS). Al-Yaʿqūbī has lumped together two men who shared the name Apollonius (the confusion almost certainly was present already in his source). The first, the mathematician Apollonius of Perge in Pamphylia (c. 200 BCE), is usually identified in the Arabic sources as al-Najjār ("the Carpenter," although no convincing explanation for the epithet has been found); the second, Apollonius of Tyana in Cappadocia (1st century CE) was famous as a master of talismans. See the article by M. Plessner in *EI*², s.v. Balīnūs; Gotthard Strohmaier in *EI*³, s.v. Apollonius of Tyana.

696 The MSS read *Ūjānis* here, but, because the name is written as *Diyūjānis* in the next sentence, the first name may be a scribal error. However, because Diogenes the Cynic was not known as a geometrician, another name, now unrecoverable, may lie behind *Ūjānis*. On the fame, in Arabic literature, of Diogenes the Cynic (c. 405–320 BCE) see the article by Oliver Overwien in *EI*³, s.v. Diogenes.

697 "The Dog" in Greek is ὁ κύων. The English term "cynic" is derived from its stem (κυν-).

698 The name has been miscopied so that it resembles the next name in the list, that of Polemon; however, the description makes it clear that the person intended is Philo (Arabic, Fīlūn) of Byzantium (3rd century BCE), the author of a book on hydraulic devices. See the article by H. G. Farmer in *EI*², s.v. Urghan.

699 The meaning of the sentence is unclear.

700 Arabic, Aflīmūn: Antonius Polemon (c. 88–144 CE) the author of a book on physiognomy preserved only in Arabic translation. See the article by J. J. Witkam in *EI*², s.v. Aflīmūn. The text of al-Yaʿqūbī, as it stands, implies reference to two books but could easily be emended to read *wa-huwa kitāb*, "which is a book."

Among them was Democritus.[701] He was the one who claimed that the world was composed of motes.[702] He wrote a book on the characteristics of animals and such of them as agree with the characteristics of man.

Among them was Plato, who was a disciple of Socrates.[703] He was the one who spoke of the soul and its attributes, even as Hippocrates spoke of the body and its attributes. He said that the soul has three powers: one of them is in the brain, and by it cognition and deliberation come to pass; the second is in the heart, and by it anger and courage come to pass; and the third is in the liver, and by it desire and love come to pass. Then he went on to discuss the psychic spirit,[704] until he had described all the members, after which he mentioned that which benefits the soul and that which corrupts it. He said: "Every defect is opposed to the deliverance of the soul, so you should not account only life as good but also a good death; you should account life and death as good."

Among them was Euclid, the author of the Book of Euclid on computa-
1:136 tion.[705] The interpretation | of "Euclid," according to Ptolemy, is "key."[706] The book is an introduction to the knowledge of computation and the key to the science of the book *Almagest*[707] on the stars: the knowledge of the chords subtended by the arcs of the segments of the circles that are the orbits of the

---

701 The scribe has distorted the name to Dīmrāṭīs. This is Democritus of Abdera (c. 460–370 BCE), who formulated an atomic theory of the material universe.

702 Arabic, *habāʾ* (motes, particles of dust suspended in air). On the echoes of Democritus' atomism in Islamic theology, see J. van Ess, *Theologie und Gesellschaft*, 3:314 (note 42).

703 For a general discussion of the reception of Plato's writings in Arabic, see the article by R. Walzer in EI^2, s.v. Aflāṭūn. See also Dimitri Gutas, "Platon–Tradition arabe," in *Dictionnaire des philosophes antiques* (Paris, 2012), 5/1: 845–863.

704 Arabic, *al-rūḥ al-nafsāniyya* (the psychic spirit). The meaning of the Arabic phrase is unclear. One would expect it to mean something like "the embodied spirit." The passages in Plato to which al-Yaʿqūbī is referring are Timaeus 42D and following, which discusses how the immortal soul is implanted in a human body, and 69A and following, which discusses the location of various powers of the soul in different parts of the human body.

705 For a discussion of al-Yaʿqūbī's account of Euclid, see M. Klamroth, "Ueber die Auszüge aus griechischen Schriftstellern bei al-Jaʿqūbī, IV," ZDMG 42 (1888): 3–9; to which one should add Klamroth's earlier article, "Ueber den arabischen Euklid," ZDMG 35 (1881): 270–326. On the reception in the Islamic world of Euclid's work generally, see the article by Sonja Brentjes and Greg De Young in EI^3, s.v. Euclid.

706 Ptolemy's fanciful derivation of Euclid's name (Εὐκλείδης) from κλείς, κλειδός (key), emphasizes that knowledge of geometry is the *key* to knowledge of astronomy, the science of the orbits of the planets. In fact, Euclid's name is a patronymic derived from an adjective meaning "of good repute" (εὐκλεής or εὔκλειος).

707 On the derivation of this Arabic title (more properly, *al-Mijisṭī*) for Ptolemy's great work, the Μεγάλη σύνταξις, see the article by M. Plessner in EI^2, s.v. Baṭlamiyūs.

planets—[these the astronomers call *kurdajāt*[708]—in order to determine the path of the stars][709] in latitude and longitude, their speeding up and slowing down, their forward and retrograde motions, their orientality and occidentality, the projections of their rays; as well as knowledge of the hours of the night and the day, the rising places of the signs of the zodiac and how this differs in the climes of the earth, the calculation of conjunction and opposition, eclipses of the sun and the moon, and how the view of all parts of the sky differs from the (different) horizons of the earth.

Euclid's book consists of thirteen discourses, and in these thirteen discourses there are four hundred and fifty-two figures, each with proof and explanation; which, when the student of the science of computation understands, every chapter of computation will become easy and open to him. He begins by mentioning the means by which the science is brought near and by acquaintance with which that which is to be known is comprehended.[710] These are proposition (*khabar*), example (*mithāl*), contradiction (*khulf*), arrangement (*tartīb*), distinction (*faṣl*), demonstration (*burhān*), and completion (*tamām*). The proposition (*khabar*) is the statement prefaced to the whole before the explanation. The example (*mithāl*) is a picture of the figures about which something is proposed and by means of whose description one is guided to the meaning of the proposition. Contradiction (*khulf*) is the contrary of the example and a reduction of the proposition to what is impossible. Arrangement (*tartīb*) is the making of the construction whose stages have been agreed upon in the science. Distinction (*faṣl*) is the distinction between the possible and the impossible proposition. Demonstration (*burhān*) is proof that the proposition has been verified. The completion (*tamām*) is the completion of the knowledge of what was to be known.[711]

The first discourse is about the point, which has no part, and the line, | which 1:137
is a length without breadth. It consists of forty-seven theorems.[712]

---

708 The derivation of the word and its meaning are uncertain. See Klamroth, *ZDMG* 42, 4, for a discussion of the possibilities, the most likely of which are "degrees" and "signs of the zodiac."

709 The bracketed words were supplied by the Leiden editor from MS Leiden 399.

710 The following outline of the methods and stages of a typical Euclidean proof is unclear. The translation is not always certain.

711 As Klamroth has noted, this is simply a reference to the formula closing each proposition or theorem in Euclid, namely "what was to be done (or demonstrated) has been done (or demonstrated)," often abbreviated Q.E.D. (*quod erat demonstrandum*).

712 Literally, "47 figures," but since each proposition or theorem normally contained one figure, "figure" and "theorem" may be used interchangeably. In fact, the Greek text of Book

The second discourse is about any plane figure having parallel sides and right angles, contained by the two lines that contain the right angle. It consists of fourteen[713] theorems.

The third discourse is about equal circles, those whose diameters are equal, the lines that go out from their centers to their circumferences, and the line that touches the circle, passing by it but not cutting it. It consists of thirty-five theorems.[714]

The fourth discourse: When a figure is within a figure and the angles of the inner figure touch the sides of the outer figure.[715] It consists of sixteen theorems.

The fifth discourse is about the part, which is the lesser magnitude in relation to the greater magnitude, when it measures it.[716] It consists of twenty-five theorems.

The sixth discourse is about similar[717] figures, which are figures in which the angles of each figure are equal to the angles of the other figure, while the sides that contain the equal angles [are proportional]; and figures with corresponding sides whose sides are proportional. It consists of thirty-two theorems.

The seventh discourse is about the (number) one; the even number, which can be divided into two equal parts; the odd number, which can[not] be divided into two equal parts and exceeds an even number by one; the number that is called even-times-even, which is that which every even number measures by a number of times whose number is even;[718] the number that is called [even]-times-odd, which is that which every even number measures by a number of times whose number is odd;[719] the number that is called odd-times-odd,

---

One contains 48 theorems. As the last two are closely related, al-Yaʿqūbī's source may have numbered them as one.

713 The MSS read forty-four (*arbaʿa wa-arbaʿūn*), which must be a scribal error for *arbaʿata ʿashara* (fourteen), the actual number of propositions in Book II.

714 The Greek text of Book III contains 37 theorems. Klamroth, "Ueber den arabischen Euklid," 270, 273, found that in some Arabic translations theorems 11 and 12 of the book were combined and one theorem was missing.

715 The text may be corrupt. If one deletes the "and" and supplies one word, the sentence makes more sense: "When a figure is [inscribed] within a figure, the angles of the inner figure touch the sides of the outer figure."

716 Following the emendation suggested by the Leiden editor.

717 Emending MSS *mutasāwiya* (equal) to *mutashābiha*.

718 This is a complicated way of saying "an even multiple of an even number."

719 That is, an odd multiple of an even number.

which is that which every odd number measures by a number of times whose number is odd;[720] the number that is called prime, which is that which | can 1:138
be measured only by (the number) one; numbers each of which is prime to the other, being such as have no common number other than one that can measure them all;[721] the composite number, which can be measured by another number; numbers each of which is composite to the other, being such as can be measured by another number common to them; the number multiplied by another number, which is that which is redoubled[722] as many times as there are units in the number by which it is multiplied and the result is another number; the square number, which is the result of multiplying a number by itself [and is contained by two equal numbers; the cubic number, which is the result of multiplying the number by itself][723] and then by itself and is contained by three equal numbers; the plane number, which is that contained by two numbers; the solid number, which is that contained by three numbers; the perfect number, which is one that is equal to all its parts;[724] proportional numbers, which are numbers such that in the first of them there are as many multiples of the second as in the third there are multiples of the fourth; similar plane and solid numbers are [those] whose sides are proportional. This discourse consists of thirty-nine theorems.

The eighth discourse is about numbers that follow each [other in proportion][725] and the two extremes are prime to each other. It consists of twenty-five theorems.[726]

The ninth discourse is about multiplying similar plane numbers and the square number that results from multiplying the number by the number; the numbers that measure each other; the cubic number times the cubic number; the result of multiplying the cube by a number that is not cubic; the square that results from proportional numbers that follow each other; how | the cube 1:139
results; what results from proportional numbers, from the solid, the square, the plane, and from numbers that measure each other; how even numbers are subtracted from even numbers, odd numbers from odd numbers, even

720 That is, an odd multiple of an odd number.

721 That is, numbers that have no common factor.

722 That is, added to itself.

723 The bracketed text was supplied by the Leiden editor. The omission was the result of the occurrence of similar endings in neighboring words (homoeoteleuton).

724 That is, an integer that is equal to the sum of its factors, excluding itself, such as 6 (1 + 2 + 3 = 6) or 28 (1 + 2 + 4 + 7 + 14 = 28).

725 Supplied on the basis of the Greek text; see Klamroth, op. cit., 8.

726 "27" in the Greek.

numbers from odd numbers, and odd numbers from even numbers. It consists of thirty-eight theorems.

The tenth discourse is about the lines that have a single common measure that measures them all, called commensurable, [and those] that do not [have] a single common measure that measures them all; and the commensurable lines [whose squares have] a single area that is a measure for them that measures them. It consists of one hundred and four theorems.[727]

The eleventh discourse is about the solid, which has length, thickness, and surface.[728] It consists of forty-one theorems.[729]

The twelfth discourse is about the surface of similar polygons, whose value each to the other in circles is as the number of the squares that are from the diameters of the circles.[730] It consists of fifteen theorems.[731]

The thirteenth discourse, the last of Euclid's discourses, is about a line that is divided according to a mean and two extremes.[732] It consists of twenty-one theorems.[733]

By the same Euclid is the book *On Appearances and Their Difference Due to the Points of Emission from the Eyes and the Visual Rays*.[734] In it he says:

---

727 "115" in the Greek.

728 The text may be defective, or the first two definitions of Book 11 have been clumsily stitched together: 1. A solid is that which has length, breadth, and depth. 2. The extremity of a solid is a surface.

729 "39" in the Greek.

730 The Greek of Book 12, Proposition 1 may be translated: "Similar polygons (inscribed) in circles are to one another as the squares (constructed) on the diameters."

731 "18" in the Greek.

732 This is the beginning of Book 13, Proposition 1: If a straight line is cut in extreme and mean ratio, then the square on the greater piece, added to half of the whole, is five times the square on the half.

733 "18" in the Greek.

734 Al-Yaʿqūbī gives the title as *Fī l-manāẓir wa-ikhtilāfihā min makhārij al-ʿuyūn wa-l-shuʿāʿ* (On Appearances/Aspects and Their Difference/Variation Due to the Points of Emission from the Eyes and the Visual Rays). The work is usually known simply as *Optics* (Ὀπτικά). The modern reader should bear in mind that Euclid explained—or was understood by his earliest Arabic translators as having explained—visual phenomena not by the eye's *reception* of light but by the eye's *emission* of bundles of "visual rays" that served as its instrument in vision. On the controversy in Arabic science about the existence of such rays, see the article by A. I. Sabra in *EI*², s.v. Manāẓir. The surviving manuscripts of the several Arabic translations give the title of the work either as *Kitāb al-Manāẓir* (The Book of Aspects) or as *Ikhtilāf al-manāẓir* (The Difference of Aspects). On the problem of al-Yaʿqūbī's long version of the title, see *The Arabic Version of Euclid's Optics* (*Kitāb Uqlīdis*

"The rays[735] issue from the eye in straight lines, and afterward paths of infinite multitude are produced. The objects on which the rays fall are seen, and those on which they do not fall are not seen." He illustrates this with various figures[736] by means of which he explains the point of emission of the view and how it differs. The number of theorems by means of which he explains this is sixty-four.[737]

Among them was Nicomachus, the Pythagorean sage. He was the one who was named "Victor | at the Competition,"[738] and he was Aristotle's father.[739] By 1:140
him is the *Book of Arithmetic*,[740] in which he proposed to elucidate the numbers and mentioned what the philosophers before him had said. Nicomachus said: "The ancients, those who first developed science and become accomplished in it—Pythagoras was the first of them—gave a definition, saying that the meaning of philosophy was 'wisdom' and that its name was derived from it.[741] They said that wisdom was the true knowledge of the things that endure." In the introduction to the book he elaborated on the topic of wisdom, its excellence, and what the sages had said about the value of science. Then he opened his book by saying: "All the things in this world whose order has been well arranged in nature are only by number. Reasoning verifies our doctrine that number serves as the pattern that is followed, it being in its entirety intelligible in its perfection. As for these things to which the category of quantity applies—and they

---

fī ikhtilāf al-manāẓir), ed. and trans. Elaheh Kheirandish, esp. 2:2 ff. Klamroth, "Jaʿqūbī's Auszüge," 9, is a useful older discussion of the passage.

735 Arabic, *shuʿāʿ*, can be interpreted either as a singular (ray) or as a collective (bundle of rays). In Euclid's theory, these rays form a cone with its apex at the eye.

736 Or "theorems," as each theorem normally contains one illustrative diagram.

737 All the Arabic translations of the *Optics* consist of four definitions and 64 propositions; this contrasts with the seven definitions and 58 propositions of the Greek; see Kheirandish, op. cit., 2:xix.

738 "Victor at the Competition" (*al-Qāhir ʿinda l-mufāḍala*) is the literal meaning of the Greek name Νικόμαχος.

739 This confusion of the mathematician Nicomachus of Gerasa (c. 60–120 CE) with Aristotle's father, Nicomachus of Stageira (lived c. 375 BCE), arises from the identity of their names.

740 Arabic, *Kitāb al-Arithmāṭīqī*, transliterates the Greek title rather than translating it into Arabic. Klamroth, "Jaʿqūbī's Auszüge," 9–16, discusses the passage.

741 The Greek reads, "They defined philosophy to be *the love of* wisdom." In fact, the manuscripts of al-Yaʿqūbī seem to be disturbed at this point. They actually read, "they said that philosophy, with it (*maʿahā*) is wisdom." The Leiden editor emended *maʿahā* (with it) to *maʿnāhā* (its meaning), in order to produce a meaningful text, but the text may originally have had something like *maḥabbat al-ḥikma* (love of wisdom), which would exactly translate the Greek.

are different—the number inherent in these things must necessarily be harmoniously composed and quantified in itself, not because of something else; for everything harmoniously composed can be only from things necessarily differing and from things that exist. As for things that do not exist, they cannot be harmoniously composed; neither can things that exist but are incommensurable. Compounded things are composed only of differing, commensurable things; for if it is not different, it is one, not needing to be made harmonious; and if it is incommensurable, it is not related; and if it is not related, it can
1:141 only be mutually contrary, with no harmonious unity occurring. | And number is among these things.[742] For in it there are two different, yet commensurable and related sorts, the even and the odd, and their being brought into an interrelated harmony according their difference has no ending."

The first discourse of the *Arithmetic* is in chapters, one of which is the definitions of number. Number divides into two divisions, one of which is called the odd, the other the even. The odd divides into three divisions: an uncompounded prime, which is that which can be measured by no number,[743] such as seven and eleven; second, a compounded number, one that has a number (that can measure it), such as nine and fifteen;[744] third, a number that is compounded by its nature but upon being related to another compounded number is prime—numbers such that each of them has a number that can measure it, but the two upon comparison have no common number, such as nine to twenty-five. The even divides into three divisions: the even of the even, which is that which can be divided into evens down to the unit, such as sixty-four;[745] the even of the odd, which is that which can be divided a single time into halves but then ceases (to be so divisible), such as fourteen and eighteen; and the even of the even and the odd, which is that which can be divided into halves more than once but does not reach the unit.[746] He discoursed on this extensively.

742 That is, among the things that can be brought together into harmonious relations.

743 In more modern language: a number that can be evenly divided by no other number (treating 1 not as a "number" but as a special category, called "monad"), excluding the trivial case that every number can be divided by itself.

744 That is, 9 can be "measured" by 3, and 15 by 5.

745 That is, 64 can be divided by 32, 16, 8, 4, and 2, all of its factors being even. Again, the unit is exempted as being not a number in the proper sense.

746 The Arabic has an extra negative, which must be deleted to make sense of the passage. It reads literally: "that which can*not* be divided into halves more than once." An example of an "even of the even and the odd" would be 28, which, being even, can be halved to give

The second discourse is about quantity in itself,[747] namely the superabundant number, the balanced number, and the deficient one. The superabundant number is one the total value of whose factors, when they are summed, exceeds the total value of the number, such as twelve and twenty-four; for twelve has a half, a third, a fourth, a sixth, and a twelfth, and if you sum them, the number will exceed.[748] The balanced number is one the total value of whose factors equals the total value of the number, such as six and twenty-eight; for six has a half, a third, and a sixth, and the amount when added comes to six exactly.[749] | 1:142
The deficient number is one the total value of whose factors is less than its total value, such as eight and fourteen;[750] for eight has a half, a fourth, and an eighth, and when they are added it comes to seven, which is one too few.[751] He sets down theorems concerning this.

The most complete discourse is the third discourse, about relative quantity. It is divided into two divisions. One of them is equality to the object of comparison: such as the equality of one hundred to one hundred, or the equality of ten to ten. Another division involves departure from equality, and this can, in turn, be divided into two divisions: one great and the other small. The great divides into five divisions: the double, such as two in relation to four, or four in relation to eight; that which exceeds by one part, such as three in comparison to four, for four is its like and the like of its third;[752] that which exceeds by several parts, such as three, which is the first of the odd numbers, in relation to five, which is the second of the odd numbers, for an excess of two parts has occurred, and in similar manner an excess of ⟨three or more⟩ parts may occur; the double plus one part, which appears between two numbers, one of which is the like of the ⟨double⟩ of the other, plus one part of it, such as five when compared to two, for it is the like of the ⟨double⟩ of two and an addition of one part; and the multiple that exceeds by two parts, such as four with respect to one.

14; which, being even, can in turn be halved to give 7; which, being odd, cannot be divided into halves.

747 Arabic, *al-kammiyya al-mufrada*, that is, the quantity of a given number in relation to the sum of its own factors, rather than in relation to any other number.

748 That is, $6+4+3+2+1=16$, and $16>12$.

749 That is, $3+2+1=6$.

750 The MSS read "twenty-four" (*arbaʿa wa-ʿishrīn*), which must be a scribal error, as its factors ($12+8+6+4+3+2+1$) add up to 36, making 24 a superabundant number. On the other hand, the factors of 14 ($7+2+1$) add up to 10, making it a deficient number. The original reading must have been "fourteen" (*arbaʿata ʿashara*).

751 That is, $4+2+1=7$, and $7<8$.

752 That is, $4=3$ (the like of 3) $+ 1$ (one-third of 3).

The small divides into five parts: the subdouble;[753] the sub-exceeding by one part; the sub-exceeding by several parts; the subdouble [plus one part; and the submultiple plus] several parts.[754]

Then he speaks about three numbers, one of which is great, the other medium, and the third small. If one seeks their equalization, one subtracts from the middle number the value of the smallest number, and from the largest number one subtracts (twice)[755] the value of the remainder of the middle number and the value of the smallest number; then when the numbers are equal, their relation will have become perfect.[756]

Then he speaks about such numbers as exceed and such as are deficient
1:143 among the doubles, making | for this purpose a triangular diagram with two corners and with twenty-one squares.[757] The first (row) is six squares: its beginning is one, after which (he keeps) doubling it until (he reaches) thirty-two. The second (row) is five squares: its beginning is three, after which (he keeps) doubling it until (he reaches) forty-eight. The third (row) is four squares: its beginning is nine, after which (he keeps) doubling it until (he reaches) seventy-two. The fourth (row) is three squares: its beginning is twenty-seven, after which (he keeps) doubling it until (he reaches) one hundred eight. The fifth (row) is two squares: its beginning is eighty-one, and he doubles it so that it becomes one

753 Or the "submultiple": "the number which, when it is compared with a larger, is able to measure it completely more than once" (*Introduction to Arithmetic*, I.18.2, trans., 610).

754 The addition in brackets is based on Klamroth's attempt to restore the text (Klamroth, op. cit., 14).

755 Correcting *mathal* to *mathalā*, as suggested by Klamroth, on the basis of the Greek text.

756 Al-Yaʿqūbī's brief summary of the opening chapters of Book II of the *Arithmetic* leaves the purpose of this operation unclear. Nicomachus is concerned with showing that "equality is the elementary principle of relative number." He demonstrates this by giving an arithmetical procedure by which a sequence of three integers can be reduced to three identical values. This is important because of speculations about the ultimate unity of all numbers and of the cosmos, whose underlying principle is number. To use Klamroth's example: given a sequence such as 5, 20, 80; from 20 one subtracts 5, giving 15 (now the sequence is 5, 15, 80); then from 80 one subtracts 35 (twice the remainder of the middle number plus 5), yielding 45 (now the sequence is 5, 15, 45). Repeating the operation, one obtains 5, 10, 20, and finally 5, 5, 5.

757 The sense of the Arabic is unclear. The text goes on to describe a diagram with successive rows of doubled numbers, each row one square shorter than the preceding, the initial number in each successive row being the sum of the first two numbers in the previous row. Nicomachus then describes the relations between the numbers in the columns of the diagram (*Arithmetic*, II, 3). Klamroth, op. cit., 15, constructed two possible realizations of the diagram, as follows:

hundred sixty-two. The sixth (row) is one square, the last: two hundred forty-three.

Then he speaks about the quadrupled number to which he adds its double.[758]

Then he discourses on planes, lines, and points; he describes triangular, square, and hexagonal planes and the sides of which the planes consist and their areas.[759] Then he speaks about the pentagonal numbers, those with five equal sides, and how their augmentation occurs;[760] then about the hexagonal, heptagonal, and octagonal numbers. He describes how they are derived and

---

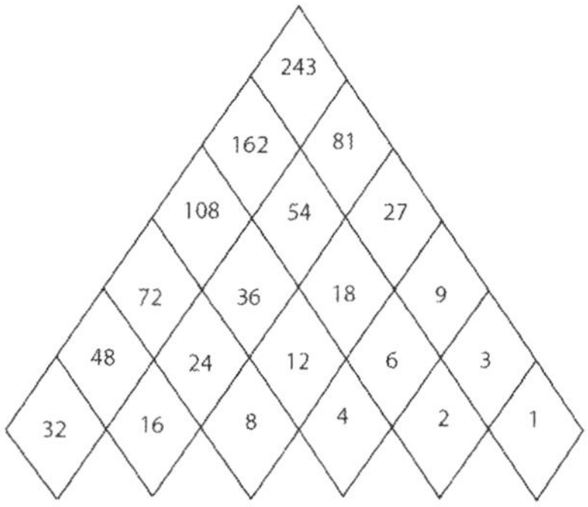

32	16	8	4	2	1
48	24	12	6	3	
72	36	18	9		
108	54	27			
162	81				
243					

758 The sentence as it stands is unintelligible. In the diagram just given, Nicomachus points out that if, in the diagram whose rows are constructed by doubling, one reads the numbers along the hypotenuse of the triangle produced (1, 3, 9, 27, etc.), one finds them to differ by a factor of 3 (i.e., 2+1). This relationship holds true in a diagram whose rows are constructed by tripling (1, 3, 9, 27, 81; 4, 12, 36, 108; 16, 48, 144, etc.): each number along the hypotenuse is the quadruple of the previous; and in a diagram whose rows are constructed by quadrupling (1, 4, 16, 64; 5, 20, 80; 25, 100, etc.) the numbers along the hypotenuse will be quintuples, and so on.

759 To a reader unfamiliar with Nicomachus' work, the Arabic description will suggest, misleadingly, that the *Arithmetic* contains a treatise on geometry. In fact, Nicomachus is concerned with showing which numbers can be represented geometrically as a point, a line, a triangle, a square, a pentagram, a hexagram, and so on. One (the monad) obviously corresponds to a point. Two is a "linear" number because it can be represented as a—a. Three is a "triangular" number because it can be represented as:

a

a a

Four is a "square" number, because it can be represented as:

a a

a a

And so on.

760 That is, he discusses numbers that can be represented as five-sided geometrical figures and how a series of such numbers can be generated.

constructs a five-by-nine table of them.[761] He discusses parts of the triangular, square, pentagonal, and hexagonal numbers—those that have surface without a solid body[762] and those that have a solid body and surface. Then he discusses the composition of the things that are composed of diverse components. Then he speaks about the proportions, which are of three kinds: one arithmetic, the second geometric, and the third harmonic.[763] He says that some of the ancients counted them as ten. He explains arithmetic proportions, geometric proportions, and harmonic proportions, discussing each type in detail and with clear demonstration.

∴

Among them was Aratus, who made a picture of the firmament like the shape of an egg, by which he imitated the firmament and in which he pictured the signs of the zodiac.[764]

∴

761 The table would look like this (Klamroth, op. cit., 16):

Triangle	1	3	6	10	15	21	28	36	45	55
Square	1	4	9	16	25	36	49	64	81	100
Pentagon	1	5	12	22	35	51	70	92	117	145
Hexagon	1	6	15	28	45	66	91	120	153	190
Heptagon	1	7	18	34	55	81	112	148	189	235

762 The Arabic reads, "those that have a solid body without surface," which makes no sense. The easiest solution is to assume that the copyist has inverted the terms for surface (*saṭḥ*) and solid body (*jirm*). Briefly, just as the integers can be displayed schematically as two-dimensional figures, so they can be displayed as a series of (three-dimensional) solids.

763 The translation takes the terminology directly from the source, *Arithmetic*, II, 22. The difficulty of finding Arabic terms to render the Greek is shown by a literal translation of al-Yaʿqūbī's text: "Then he speaks of the means, which are of three sorts: one belonging to arithmetic, the second belonging to surveying, and the third belonging to the harmonization of melodies."

764 Aratus of Soli (c. 315–240 BCE) was not himself an astronomer but a poet, the author of the *Phaenomena*, in which he versified an astronomical treatise by Eudoxus of Cnidus. For a discussion of the book's translation into Arabic and use by Arabic writers, see Fuat Sezgin, GAS, 6:75–77.

Among them was Aristotle, the son of Nicomachus the Gerasene.[765] He was a disciple of Plato. He spoke about the upper world and the lower, about the well-being and corruption of the world, about the dispositions of the soul, and about the truth of logic. He laid down the principles of wisdom, as well as its divisions and branches. 1:144

The first of his books is the *Introduction to the Science of Philosophy*, which is called in Greek *Isagoge*.[766] Its first part is a discussion of definition, whereof it consists, whence the word "definition" is derived, what the virtue of definition is, what makes for a bad definition, and the difference between the definition and the thing defined. The second part is an account of philosophy and of how (the word) was derived. The third part is the book on the faculties of the soul that are in thinking, anger, and desire—whatever departs from this equilibrium is corrupt. The fourth book is about logic, which is the foundation of philosophy. In the fifth book he discusses the division of things into two kinds: that which is indispensable, like food, and that which is dispensable, like the cleaning[767] of a garment. The sixth book is about propositions, which are of three kinds: the necessary, as when you say "Fire is hot"; the possible, as when you say "Zayd is a writer"; and the impossible, as when you say "Fire is cold." The seventh book is about genus, which is of three divisions: the genus of custom, the genus of nature, [and ...].[768] In the eighth book he discusses the indivisible, which falls into four kinds: either because, like a point, it has no parts; or, like a mustard seed, because of its smallness; or, like a stone, because of its solidity; or because it is not (made up) of parts. The ninth book is about relation, which is of four sorts: either by nature, as the relation of father to his son; or by service, as the relation of a disciple to his teacher; or by volition, as the relation of a friend to his friend; or by accident, as the relation of a slave to his master.

---

765 As above (1:140), al-Yaʿqūbī or his source has again confused the later mathematician Nicomachus of Gerasa with the earlier Nicomachus of Stageira, the father of Aristotle. On the reception of Aristotle's works in Arabic and for an extensive bibliography of modern editions of the Arabic translations, see the article by Cristina D'Ancona in *EI*[3], s.v. Aristotle and Aristotelianism.

766 Greek Εἰσαγωγή (Introduction) is the title not of a work in the Aristotelian canon but of a short introduction to logic by the later philosopher Porphyry of Tyre (234–c. 305 CE). Porphyry's work was often taken to be specifically an introduction to the Aristotle's logic, hence the confusion.

767 Following ed. Leiden (*tanẓīf*); M reads *tanṣīf* (division into two parts).

768 As Klamroth noted in his third article (*ZDMG* 41:421), the sentence, as it stands, appears corrupt.

1:145 His books | after that are of four kinds. One kind is about logic; the second is about natural phenomena; the third is about what exists with bodies and is connected to them; and the fourth is about what does not exist with bodies and is not connected to them.

His books on logic are eight in number. The first is titled *Categories*. His aim in it is to speak of the ten simple categories and to describe them by means of that whereby each is distinguished from the other, by what is common to them or is common to a number of them, and what is peculiar to each one of them. He defines the things that precede them in description and similarity, one of which is that a substance as predicate and a substance as subject is not substantial in it, but accidental, and that an accident as subject and an accident to which a predicate is attached, that is, one to which something is annexed [...][769]—in order to explain that perceptible substances and secondary, imperceptible accidents[770] can be predicated of the perceptible and that perceptible accidents and secondary, imperceptible accidents can be predicated of the perceptible. He explains the ten by themselves and by their descriptions, their commonalities, and their specificities. These are the ten: substance, quantity, quality, relation, location, time, acting, being acted on, position,[771] and habitus.[772] The book was titled *Categories* only because these names are genera and can be predicated of species and of the individual—like substance, for it can be predicated of the body. Body can be predicated of the animate and the inanimate; animate can be predicated of animal and plant; animal can be predicated of man, horse, and lion; and man can be predicated of Zayd, ʿAmr, and Khālid, who are individuals. Horse can be predicated of *this* horse by pointing or of *that* horse by similarity. Quantity can be predicated of the continuous and the discrete and of all their parts—and likewise are all the other genera.

1:146 The second is titled *The Book of Interpretation*.[773] His aim | in it is to speak about the interpretation of the propositions that are the premises of meaningful syllogisms, that is, sentences. The latter are positive or negative assertions

---

769 One must assume a lacuna in the text, although the MS shows none.

770 Perhaps to be emended to "substances"; cf. Klamroth, *ZDMG* 41: 423.

771 In the sense of posture (Arabic *waḍʿ*, corresponding to Greek τὸ κεῖσθαι).

772 That is, state: Greek τὸ ἔχειν, explained by Aristotle as referring to such predicates as "shod" or "armed." The Arabic here is problematic. The word in the MSS is undotted and can be read as *ḥadd* (limit) or as *jadd* (newness, good fortune), neither of which clearly renders the Greek.

773 Generally known by its Latin title *De Interpretatione* (Περὶ ἑρμηνείας).

or [...].[774] He explains that from which propositions are composed—noun, particle, verb, inflection, and that which informs about the verb—and about such propositions as are composed of a noun, a particle, a third thing, and a fourth thing: as when we say, "The fire is hot," and what is accidental to that. He examines which propositions are more contrary to each other: the positive to its negative, or the positive to the positive that contradicts it. He titled it *The Book of Interpretation*, having in mind the simple declaration, the utterance wherein there is no equivocal noun, and wanting to distinguish it from the utterance that is not a declaration that can be deemed to be false or true. The latter are of nine kinds: (1) question, as when you say, "From where did you come?" (2) request, as when you say, "O so-and-so, come here!" (3) wish, as when you say concerning something, "I beseech you to do such-and-such"; (4) wonder, as when you say concerning something, "What a thing this is!" (5) ... as when you say, "I swear by God that you shall go"; (6) doubt, as when you say, "Perhaps the matter is as has been said"; (7) determinative, as when you say, "This estate shall be a charitable bequest for the poor"; and (8) promise of reward, as when you say, "If you do such-and-such, I will reward you with such-and-such."[775] A sentence may be called by various bynames, in different respects. If the utterance affirms something of something, it is called affirmative. If it denies something of something, it is called negative. If it is placed ahead, so that something may be inferred from it, it is called a premise. If it has been inferred from prior premises, it is called a conclusion. If premises and their conclusion are together, it is called a figure.[776]

The third is titled *Analytics*, the meaning of which is "contradictions."[777] [His intention in it is] to explain simple | syllogisms, that is, what they are, how they 1:147

774 The text is defective at this point. The MSS read *aw mā fī awwalihi* (or what is in its beginning). As this makes no sense, the Leiden editor assumed a lacuna after *aw* (or). In fact, *De Interpretatione*, 17a, notes that not every sentence is a proposition. Propositions must be either true or false; a prayer is a sentence but, being neither true nor false, is not a proposition.

775 The fact that only eight types of non-propositional sentences are listed can be explained by the fact that the original list was of sentence types, including, as a first type, sentences that are propositions, thus yielding a list of nine items. So Klamroth, *ZDMG* 41:425.

776 Arabic, *ṣīgha*. That is, it can be classified as one of the three types (figures, σχήματα) of the syllogism discussed in Aristotle's *Prior Analytics*. M reads *ṣanīʿa*, which could have the same meaning.

777 Arabic, *naqāʾiḍ* (contradictions, contraries). As this is not a possible meaning for the Greek ἀναλυτικά, the text may be disturbed or may contain a lacuna. One is tempted to

are, and for what they are. His object is the sort that brings together the three notions,[778] what has been said about the simple syllogism, the existence of the syllogism, how syllogisms are constructed, to how many kinds they belong, and, finally, what true conclusions from them become apparent by themselves, and which ones become apparent by conversion.[779]

The fourth book is titled *Apodeictics*, which means "setting right."[780] His aim in it is to explain arguments[781] that are clear and demonstrative, how they are, and what should compose them. This book is called *Demonstration and Proof* because in it he describes the distinction whereby truth is distinguished from falsehood, veracity from lying. He says that premises are of different kinds: There are premises that are agreed upon and known to the general audience, composed of two parts prior in knowledge; as when one says, "Every man is a living being." The second kind of premises, which require discussion for their soundness to be known, while true in themselves, are unknown to the general audience and require mediation for their soundness to be known; as when we say, "Every man is a substance."

His fifth book is titled *Topics*. His purpose in it is to clarify the five terms "genus," "species," "difference," "property," and "accident," [and to clarify] "definition." One must know what genus is and what species is lest, from any (definition), the genus and the species be omitted; and this can be known only by means of the difference that distinguishes the species from the genus and what is the particularity of each or what accidents are in relation to substances.

---

see *al-naqāʾiḍ* as a miscopying of [*taḥlīl*] *al-qiyās*, "[the analysis of] the syllogism," which is an accurate description of the content of the *Prior Analytics*. Note that al-Yaʿqūbī (or his source) gives a separate title, *Apodiktika*, to the work more commonly known as the *Posterior Analytics*.

778 That is, the three terms that are necessary for a valid syllogism (*Prior Analytics*, 25b).

779 Arabic *bi-l-ḥaraka*, literally "by movement." Klamroth (ZDMG 41:426) considered this an attempt to render the Greek term ἀπαγωγή (*Prior Analytics* 29b5, διὰ τῆς εἰς τὸ ἀδύνατον ἀπαγωγῆς, "by a reduction *ad impossibile*").

780 That is, the work usually called *Posterior Analytics*. The Arabic transliterates the alternate Greek title, Ἀποδεικτικά (affording proof, demonstrative). Al-Yaʿqūbī's explanation of the title, if one can trust the reading of the MSS (*iṣlāḥ*) might mean that the subject of the book is the detection and correction of fallacious arguments, but one is tempted to emend the reading to *īḍāḥ* (elucidation), which would be an acceptable equivalent for the Greek. See Klamroth, ZDMG 41:433.

781 Arabic *umūr* (pl. of *amr*), literally means "matters," but here seems to be used like its Syriac cognate *mēmrā* to translate Greek λόγος in the sense of "argument" or "discourse."

In his sixth book, titled *Sophistics*,[782] his aim is to discuss fallacious arguments. He enumerates the types of fallacious argument and tells how one can guard against accepting such fallacies. This is the book in which he replied to | 1:148 the Sophists.

His seventh book is titled *Rhetoric*, which means "eloquence." It is about the three kinds (of eloquence): judicial; deliberative; and laudatory or censuring, both of which are encompassed by [the Arabic] term *taqrīẓ*.[783]

In his eighth book, titled *Poetics*, his purpose is to discuss the art of poetry, what is admissible in it, the meters used in it, and each genre.

These are his purposes in his logical books, the four prior ones and the second four.

As for his physical books: The book *Lecture on Nature*, which is an account of the physical.[784] In it he discussed the physical things, which are five that encompass all physical things and without which no physical thing can exist. They are matter, form, place, motion, and time; for time can have no existence save by motion, motion can have no existence save by place, place can have no existence save by form, and form can have no existence save by matter. Of these five, two are substances—matter and form—and three are substantial accidents.

The second is the one titled *The Book of the Heavens and the World*.[785] His purpose in it is to elucidate the celestial things not subject to corruption. They are of two kinds: One of them is circular in shape, and its movement is rotation: the sphere that surrounds all things; it is a fifth element, not subject to generation or corruption. The other kind is that which is spherical and circular by generation, although it is not circular in motion, namely the four elements: fire, air, earth, and water. These are not circular in motion, but straight in motion, cyclical in generation. Things that are cyclical of generation are such as come into being one from the other by transformation, | 1:149 such as the thing that cycles and transforms: such as fire, which cycles and transforms and comes to be from air, and air from water, and water from earth. Each of these elements cycles by generation, one into the other, fire and air upward, water and earth downward.

---

782 Commonly known by the Latinized version of its Greek title, *Sophistici elenchi* (Sophistical Refutations).

783 In later usage, *taqrīẓ* refers to speeches given in praise, but the older dictionaries note that it could refer to orations in praise or in derision. The Greek term is ἐπιδεικτικόν.

784 Commonly known as the *Physics*. The Arabic (*Kitāb Samʿ al-kiyān*) reflects the longer Greek title, Φυσικὴ ἀκρόασις.

785 Commonly known as *De caelo*. (Περὶ οὐρανοῦ).

His third book is the one titled *The Book of Generation and Corruption*. His purpose [in it] is to explain the nature of coming-to-be and passing-away, as water's becoming air, and air's becoming water, how it comes to be and how it passes away by nature.

The fourth is the *Ordinances*, a book of discourse *On Celestial Phenomena*.[786] His purpose in it is to explain the occurrence of coming-to-be and passing-away, the coming-to-be and passing-away of everything that comes to be between the limit of the sphere of the moon down to the center of the earth, whether in the air, on the earth, or in its interior, as well as such phenomena as occur there: clouds, mist, thunder, lightning, wind, snow, rain, and so forth.

A book *On Minerals*, which is the fifth. His purpose in it is to explain how the bodies that are generated in the interior of the earth come to be, their qualities, their specific and common properties, and their proper places.

The sixth book is an explanation of the causes of plants, their qualities, their specific and common properties, the causes of their organs, the places proper to them, and their movement.

These are his objectives in his physical books.

As for his psychological books, they are two. The first of the two is the *Book of the Soul*.[787] His purpose in it is to explain the nature (*māʾiyya*) of the soul, its substance (*qawām*), its parts, the differentiation of sense perception and the enumeration of its kinds, the soul's virtues and habits, and the things praiseworthy and the things blameworthy in it. The praiseworthy things are logic, justice, wisdom, judgment, forbearance, courage, strength, boldness, magnanim-
1:150 ity, | and restraint; the blameworthy things are injustice, wantonness, hypocrisy, violence, lying, slander, and treachery.

The second book is *On Sense Perception and the Sensible*.[788] It discusses the causes of the perception of perceptibles. His purpose in it is to tell what sense perception is and what a perceptible object is, how the sense receives perceived things, how the sense and the perceived object come to be one thing, while

---

786 The meaning of the Arabic as it stands in the MSS is uncertain. Aristotle's *Meteorology* (Μετεωρολογικά) was translated into Arabic by Yaḥyā b. al-Biṭrīq as *Fī l-āthār al-ʿulwiyya*, and this phrase occurs at the end of al-Yaʿqūbī's sentence, where it has been translated as *On Celestial Phenomena*. The problem is the beginning of the sentence, which designates the book as *Kitāb al-Sharāʾiʿ* (The Book of Ordinances/Paths). The meaning is uncertain.

787 That is, the *De anima* (Περὶ ψυχῆς).

788 Arabic *Fī l-ḥiss wa-l-maḥsūs*, that is, the short treatise (one of the *Parva Naturalia*) entitled Περὶ αἰσθήσεως καὶ αἰσθητῶν.

being different in themselves,[789] and whether things are [perceived] in their natures and in their bodies or in their natures to the exclusion of their bodies.

Next comes his book *On Spiritual Argument*.[790] His purpose in it is to give an account of such form as, being devoid of matter, is in the upper world, and the spiritual faculties, as well as to know how the faculties of those forms join with the natural faculties, whether they are moved or unmoving, how the former faculties govern the latter faculties, and if one[791] of the gross corporeal faculties is part of those exalted things. He explains what the intellect is and what the thing intellected is,[792] what the universal soul is, and what its descent and ascent are.

Next comes his book *On Unity*.[793] He said that the second[794] causality is the cause of causes and that the aeon (*dahr*) is beneath it; the latter is the originator of things and the origination of them.[795] He discourses on this, explaining the doctrine of (divine) unity.

As for his books on ethics (*al-khuluq*) [...] and to elucidate the moral qualities of the soul, happiness in soul and body, the governance of common folk and of people of distinction, a man's governance of his wife, politics, the governance of cities, and stories of the governors of cities.

These are the subjects of the noteworthy and noble books of Aristotle the Wise. The books that came after them depended on them.

789 Emending the text of the manuscripts (*fī l-adawāt*, "in the organs") to *fī l-dhawāt*.

790 Arabic, *Fī l-kalām al-rūḥānī*, perhaps to be rendered "On Theological Argument." This and the following title may refer to Aristotle's *Metaphysics* (divided by al-Yaʿqūbī or his source into two treatises) or to the sections of Plotinus's *Enneads* that came, in Arabic translation, to be known as the "Theology of Aristotle."

791 Retaining the reading of M (*wa-in kāna wāḥid*). Ed. Leiden emends to *wa-anna kulla wāḥid* (and that every one).

792 That is, the object of thought, accepting the emendation proposed by the Leiden editor (*mā l-ʿaql wa-mā l-maʿqūl*). M reads, *mā l-ʿaql wa-mā l-ʿuqūl* (what the intellect is and what the intellects are). The Leiden reading corresponds better with the argument of *Metaphysics* 1074b–1075a.

793 Arabic, *Fī l-tawḥīd*; because *tawḥīd* is the normal Arabic term for "monotheism, the doctrine of God's unity," one might translate the title as "On Monotheism." The Aristotelian work closest to the content described by al-Yaʿqūbī is *Metaphysics* Λ (XII), but al-Yaʿqūbī may well be describing part of the "Theology of Aristotle."

794 Following ed. Leiden in reading the MS as *al-thāniya*. However, as the first letter is undotted, one is tempted to ignore the dot on the *nūn* and read *al-nāʾiya* (the remote [cause]).

795 Alternate translation: "and that origination/being originated belongs to them."

Among the sages of the Greeks was Ptolemy. He was the one who composed
1:151 the book of the | *Almagest*, *The* [*Device of*] *Rings*,[796] *The Device of Plates*, which is the astrolabe, and the *Canon*.[797]

As for the *Almagest*, it is about the science of the stars and motions.[798] The interpretation of "Almagest" is "the greatest book."[799] It consists of thirteen discourses.

He began the first discourse of the *Almagest* with an account of the sun, because it is the foundation: only through it can one arrive at knowledge of any of the motions of the celestial sphere (*al-falak*). He said in the first chapter that the sun has a sphere[800] whose center lies outside the center of the world.[801] On one side of it,[802] the sun becomes elevated, rising toward the part of the sphere of the constellations opposite it, becoming more distant from the center of the earth; on the other side of it, it descends toward the earth, becoming more distant from the part of the sphere of the constellations opposite it. The place of elevation is the place where the sun moves slowly, whereas the place

796 That is, the armillary sphere, a three-dimensional model consisting of a central sphere representing the earth, surrounded by concentric rings to represent the spheres in which the sun, moon, planets, and fixed stars of the Ptolemaic universe moved.

797 As no source from antiquity attributes to Ptolemy independent works on the armillary sphere—*Almagest* v. 1 contains a brief description of a simpler form of such an instrument—the astrolabe, or a work simply entitled *Canon*, al-Yaʿqūbī's attribution of these three books to Ptolemy has been questioned. Klamroth presented evidence that the books in question were by Theon of Alexandria, who also produced an introduction to the *Almagest*, which Klamroth saw as probably the direct source of al-Yaʿqūbī's description of the content of the *Almagest*. See Klamroth, "Ueber die Auszüge aus griechischen Schriftstellern bei al-Jaʿqūbī, IV," *ZDMG* 42 (1888): 18–20. For a summary of the available evidence, see F. Sezgin, *GAS*, 5:180–184.

798 For an annotated English translation of this work, see G. J. Toomer, *Ptolemy's Almagest* (London: Duckworth, 1984). Toomer's introduction also provides a brief history of Arabic translations of the work. Klamroth's article ("Ueber die Auszüge," 17–18) provides an annotated German translation of al-Yaʿqūbī's section on Book I ("the first discourse") but omits any detailed discussion of the section on Books II–IV.

799 In fact, Ptolemy's major work is called simply *Mathematical Treatise* (Μαθηματικὴ σύνταξις) or *Great Compendium* (Μεγάλη σύνθεσις) in Greek, not "the greatest" (μεγίστη), as al-Yaʿqūbī asserts.

800 M reads *anna l-shams*^{a} *falakan* (that the sun, a sphere). This can easily be corrected to read *anna lil-shams*^{i} *falakan*. Ed. Leiden reads simply *anna l-shams*^{a} *falak*^{un} (that the sun is a sphere), which makes no sense.

801 That is, the center of the sphere in which the sun moves is different from the center of the earth, which is, in the Ptolemaic scheme, the center of the universe.

802 That is, of its sphere or orbit.

of lowness is the one where it moves rapidly. He then discussed this in clear words. The second chapter is about the size of the whole of the earth in relation to the whole of the heavens [...][803] and it was placed with the placement of an oblique sphere;[804] the location of the inhabited parts of the earth; the measures of its hours, as between the equator and the North Pole; the difference between these two places; the size of that difference in the directions of the horizon with regard to the different locations of the inhabitants of the earth; and the motion of the sun and moon. The third chapter is about the hypothetical upright sphere in comparison with the arcs of the sphere of the constellations.[805]

The second discourse is thirteen chapters. The first chapter is about the inhabited locations of the earth. The second chapter is about determining the measurement between the upright sphere and the rising point of the inclined sphere from the degrees of arc of the circle of the horizon of the rising and the amounts of daylight in every day with regard to its length and shortness.[806] The third chapter is about determining [the elevation of] | the pole and the 1:152 depression (below the horizon) of the parts that are opposite it, which is the latitude of the clime, from the attribute and the marks vis-à-vis the elevation of the pole—and what remains until the limit of the zenith, which is on the meridian circle.[807] The fourth chapter is about determining the sun's crossing the zenith of a country's inhabitants: where that occurs, when it occurs, and in what place of the divisions of the zodiac the sun is on that day over their heads.[808] The fifth chapter is about the measure of the midday shadow at the equinoctial signs and the solstitial signs.[809] The sixth chapter is about the special characteristics of locations vis-à-vis the path from east to west and

803 A lacuna suspected by the Leiden editor, although the MSS show none.

804 If "it" (feminine in Arabic) refers to the sun (also feminine in Arabic), this could refer to the inclination of the ecliptic (the plane of the sun's apparent path against the background of the fixed stars) relative to the plane of earth's equator.

805 That is, the difference between the arcs traced by the various constellations at differing latitudes and the arcs that these constellations would trace for a hypothetical observer on the earth's equator (the so-called *sphaera recta* or "upright sphere") where all stars would rise and set on arcs perpendicular to the horizon.

806 Cf. Toomer, *Ptolemy's Almagest*, 76: "Given the length of the longest day, how to find the arcs of the horizon cut off between the equator and the ecliptic."

807 Cf. Toomer, *Ptolemy's Almagest*, 77: "If the same quantities be given, how to find the elevation of the pole, and vice versa."

808 Cf. Toomer, *Ptolemy's Almagest*, 80: "How to compute for what regions, when, and how often the sun reaches the zenith."

809 Cf. Toomer, *Ptolemy's Almagest*, 80: "How one can derive the ratios of the gnomon to the equinoctial and solstitial noon shadows from the above-mentioned quantities."

equidistant parallels of latitude.[810] The seventh chapter is about the difference of the risings of the oblique sphere from the rising of the upright sphere.[811] The eighth chapter is a table of rising-times for the parallels of the climes of the earth and the rising-time of its path, parallel by parallel.[812] The ninth chapter is about determining the length of the night and the day, consisting of the seasonal hours of the climes, and determining the risings of the parts of the zodiac and the ascendant and culminating part of the sky.[813] The tenth chapter is about the angles formed between the ecliptic and the meridian circle that is in mid-sky.[814] The eleventh chapter is about the angles formed between the ecliptic and the circle of the horizon of rising toward the south from the quadrants in each clime.[815] The twelfth chapter is about the angles and arcs formed on the horizon circle that circles around the pole of the horizon circle in the locations of the climes.[816] The thirteenth chapter draws up tables of the arcs and angles at the climes of the earth.[817] These are the chapters of the second discourse.

1:153 The third discourse of the *Almagest* consists of ten chapters. The first chapter is about knowing the length of the year and the number of its days. The second chapter draws up tables of the mean motion of the sun. The third chapter is about knowledge of the aspects of uniform circular motion.[818] The fourth

810 Cf. Toomer, *Ptolemy's Almagest*, 82: "Exposition of the special characteristics, parallel by parallel."

811 Cf. Toomer, *Ptolemy's Almagest*, 90: "On simultaneous risings of arcs of the ecliptic and equator at *sphaera obliqua*."

812 Cf. Toomer, *Ptolemy's Almagest*, 100–103: "Table of rising-times at 10° intervals." The table gives rising-times for points located at intervals of 10° along the zodiac for a series of places from the equator to the far north.

813 Cf. Toomer, *Ptolemy's Almagest*, 99: "On the particular features that follow from the rising times."

814 Cf. Toomer, *Ptolemy's Almagest*, 105: "On the angles between the ecliptic and the meridian."

815 Cf. Toomer, *Ptolemy's Almagest*, 110: "On the angles between the ecliptic and the horizon."

816 Cf. Toomer, *Ptolemy's Almagest*, 114: "On the angles and arcs formed with the same circle [that is, the ecliptic] by a circle drawn through the poles of the horizon."

817 Cf. Toomer, *Ptolemy's Almagest*, 114: "Layout of angles and arcs, parallel by parallel." Toomer labels the table, "Table of Zenith Distances and Ecliptic Angles" (123–129).

818 Cf. Toomer, *Ptolemy's Almagest*, 141: "On the hypotheses for uniform circular motion." In Ptolemy's system, the motion of every planet was essentially regular and uniform, in that, "if we imagine the bodies or their circles being carried around by straight lines, in absolutely every case the straight line in question describes equal angles at the center of its revolution in equal times" (trans. Toomer, 141). The apparent irregularity ("anomaly") in the motion of a given planet was explained by hypothesizing that the planet actually

chapter is about knowledge of the apparent anomaly in the motion of the sun according to observation and past records.[819] The fifth chapter is about partial investigations of the anomaly.[820] The sixth chapter is on the construction of the components of tables of the individual subdivisions of the anomaly.[821] The seventh chapter is about establishing tables of the anomaly of the sun's motion. The eighth chapter is about knowledge of the sun's position in its mean motion.[822] The ninth chapter is about the equation of the sun and knowledge of its true position. The tenth chapter is about knowledge of the difference of the days, between one day-and-night and another.[823]

The fourth discourse of the *Almagest* consists of eleven chapters. The first chapter is from which observations (one's) examination of the moon ought to be made.[824] The second chapter is on knowledge of the times of the periods of the moon. The third chapter is on knowledge of the division of the mean motions of the moon. The fourth chapter is on establishing tables containing the mean motions of the moon. The fifth chapter is that the two hypotheses—the eccentric hypothesis and the epicyclic hypothesis—concerning the motions of the moon [indicate one and the same thing].[825] The sixth chapter is about demonstration of the first simple anomaly of the moon's motion. The seventh chapter is on the correction of the moon's course in longitude and anomaly. The eighth chapter is on knowledge of the epoch (*mawḍiʿ*) of the moon's mean courses in longitude | and anomaly. The ninth chapter is on the 1:154

moved on an "epicycle," a smaller circle whose center moved in uniform motion on the main orbit. The motions in both cases were assumed to be regular, but their combined result, seen from the earth, appeared to be irregular ("anomalous").

819 Reading with M: *riwāya*; ed. Leiden emends to *ruʾya* (sight).

820 The text of the MSS is unclear. M seems to read *al-imtiḥānāt al-juzʾiyya* (the partial/individual verifications). Ed. Leiden emends to *al-abḥāth al-juzʾiyya* (the partial/individual investigations) which is closer to what Toomer (p. 157) records as the heading in one of the Arabic translations. Toomer translates, "Investigation of the anomaly for partial stretches [of the sun's apparent orbit]."

821 The text is uncertain.

822 Cf. Toomer, *Ptolemy's Almagest*, 166: "On the epoch of the sun's mean motion."

823 Cf. Toomer, *Ptolemy's Almagest*, 169: "On the inequality of the [solar] days."

824 Cf. Toomer, *Ptolemy's Almagest*, 173: "The kind of observations which one must use to examine lunar phenomena."

825 The phrase in brackets has been supplied by the Leiden editor on the basis of the Greek. The meaning is that one can explain the moon's apparent motions by assuming either that the center of its orbit is "eccentric," that is, not the center of the earth, or that the moon moves on an epicycle, a secondary circle whose center travels around the primary circle of the moon's orbit.

correction of the mean course of the moon in latitude [and][826] in its inception. The tenth chapter concerns the drawing up of tables of the simple anomaly [of the moon].[827] The eleventh chapter is about how much the anomaly of the moon amounts to.

These four discourses provide everything that is needed of the book *Almagest*. Nine discourses after them are about a description of the eccentrics (*al-marākiz*), about preference for (the theory of) epicycles (*al-tadwīr*), and about producing tables of motion and tables of the longitude of the planets.

The book *On the Device of Rings*.[828] It begins with an account of the making of the ring device. It consists of nine rings, one within the other. One of them is provided with a suspensory ring.[829] The second, transverse within it, is from east to west. The third is the ring that turns in these two rings on (an axis) between its lower part and its upper part. The fourth is the one that moves beneath the ring with the suspensory. The fifth carries the band of the zodiacal signs, and the axis is mounted on it. The sixth carries the band of the twelve signs of the zodiac. The seventh is beneath the two rings of the sphere; it is a ring mounted on the axis so that, by means of it, one may take the latitude of the fixed stars that move among the quarters of the celestial sphere. The eighth moves in the two sides of the axis. The ninth ring is mounted in the eighth[830] for the movement of the upright sphere.[831] [...][832] It is set down ...[833] In it he mentions how one begins to make it; how one writes on it; how each ring is mounted in the other; how they are divided into degrees, scored with lines, and fastened so that they do not come apart; and how it is set up. Next he

826 Added by the Leiden editor.

827 Reading, as proposed by the Leiden editor, *ikhtilāf al-qamar al-mufrad*, for MSS *ikhtilāfihim al-mufrad* (their simple anomaly).

828 That is, an armillary sphere. For an annotated German translation of this section, see M. Klamroth, "Ueber die Auszüge aus griechischen Schriftstellern bei al-Jaʿqūbī, IV," ZDMG 42 (1888): 20–23.

829 Arabic, *iḥdāhunna dhāt ʿilāqa*. For evidence for *ʿilāqa* as "suspensory ring," see Dozy, *Supplément*, 2:162. This is the outermost ring, with a suspensory at the top so that it can hang vertically.

830 Emending MSS *al-thāniya* (the second) to *al-thāmina*; the two words are similar in Arabic script.

831 That is, the *sphaera recta*.

832 The Leiden editor inferred a lacuna. The text in the MSS shows no break.

833 The translation of the remainder of the sentence is uncertain. "It is set down in the *south* (?) and the heavens *rise-into-view* (?) according to the *lowering* (?, reading with MSS *isfāl* or *asfāl*, neither of which is attested; ed. Leiden, *isqāla*, scale of) of the upright sphere (*sphaera recta*)."

mentions in thirty-nine chapters how it is used. The first chapter | is about the places of operation[834] in the armillary sphere and the circles in it. The second chapter is about its testing. The third chapter is on determining the shadow of the sun by means of it. The fourth chapter is about when you want to determine by means of it the latitude of a clime, a city, or a place. The fifth chapter is about when you want to determine by means of it what the latitude of each clime is. The sixth chapter is about when you want to know how the daylight decreases and increases in Cancer.[835] The seventh chapter is about when you want to know the length of each of the days of the year. The eighth chapter is about when you want to know about the equal length of night and day in the first clime.[836] The ninth chapter is about when you want to know how the signs of the zodiac rise in the climes by less or more than thirty degrees. The tenth chapter is about why the degrees of the zodiacal constellations can be converted to a degree of the upright sphere.[837] The eleventh chapter is about knowledge of every zodiacal sign and how it sets at the rising of its opposite and rises at the latter's setting in degrees.[838] The twelfth chapter is about when you want to know how the zodiacal signs, according to their difference in degrees, rise to mid-heaven. The thirteenth chapter is about when you want to become 1:155

834 Arabic, *mawāḍiʿ al-ʿamal,* could mean either physical places, that is, the operating parts of the device, or the occasions for using the device.

835 The Arabic is vague and ambiguous: the verbs *yaqṣuru* and *yaṭūlu* mean "to be/become short(er)" and "to be/become long(er)" respectively. They could refer to a static condition: the fact that the sun's crossing the tropic of Cancer marks the shortest day in the southern hemisphere and the longest day in the northern. Or, if one understands the verbs to mean "becomes short(er)/long(er)," the words would refer to the fact that when the sun reaches the tropic of Cancer the daylight hours begin to decrease in the northern hemisphere and begin to increase in the southern hemisphere. Finally, if words have fallen out of the text, one might understand "how the daylight is short ⟨in Capricorn⟩ and long in Cancer [for observers in the northern hemisphere]."

836 Since the first clime comprises lands close to the terrestrial equator, the armillary sphere could be used to demonstrate how little night and day vary seasonally in this clime, being theoretically equal at the equator throughout the year.

837 The text is uncertain. The translation, conjectural at best, retains the word *lima* (for what reason, why) of the manuscript, although it would be easy to emend it to *bima* (by what means, how). Ed. Leiden deletes the word. "Can be converted" translates *rudda ilā* (literally, "have been brought back to"; perhaps to be emended to *turaddu ilā*). "To a degree" (*ilā juzʾ*) is written unambiguously in M.

838 Thus the Arabic. The simplest way to parse the sentence is to take "in degrees" as qualifying "its opposite" (*naẓīrihi fī l-ajzāʾ*), with the phrase designating the sign separated from it by 180°. A more elegant solution would be to see the text as having been truncated and to restore it to *bi-maghībi ⟨naẓīri⟩hi fī l-ajzāʾ*.

acquainted with each sign of them. The fourteenth chapter is about when you want to know the ascendant and the four cardinal signs (*awtād*) during the daytime from the sun.[839] The fifteenth chapter is about when you want to know the ascendant during the night from the moon and the planets. The sixteenth chapter is about when you want to know how many hours of the daytime have passed. The seventeenth chapter is about when you want to know at what hour the moon or one of the fixed stars will become visible. The eighteenth chapter is about when you want to know the hours of the conjunctions. The nineteenth chapter is about when you want to know the amplitude of the summer and winter sunrises and of the summer and winter sunsets in any country.[840] The
1:156 twentieth chapter is about when you want to know for every | zodiacal sign the amplitude of its rising from the east and of its setting from the west. The twenty-first chapter is about when you want to know the stars that are invisible in every country.[841] The twenty-second chapter is about when you want to know the five paths that the sages have mentioned in the sky of every country.[842] The twenty-third chapter is about when you want to know the seven climes. The twenty-fourth chapter is about when you want to become acquainted with each of the climes. The twenty-fifth chapter is when you want to know how (short) the shortest day is, when the sun comes to be in Capricorn, at the location whose latitude is 63°, that being the limit of habitation toward the north: daylight there is approximately four hours, and night twenty hours; the longest day there is twenty hours, and the night four hours; it is the island of Thule, part of the land of Europe, and it is the northernmost part of the land of the Romans. The twenty-sixth chapter is about when you want to know the locations from which the sun becomes invisible for six months, so that there is constant darkness, and over which the sun rises for six months, so that there is constant light: it is the place that is opposite the axis of the north.[843] The twenty-seventh chapter

839 That is, when you want to know, on the basis of the sun's position, what sign of the zodiac is rising on the eastern horizon at that moment and the location of the four cardinal signs of the zodiac (the two solstices and the two equinoxes: Capricorn and Cancer, Libra and Aries).

840 Amplitude (Arabic, *miqdār*) refers to the deviation of sunrise and sunset from due east and due west respectively at any time of the year other than the equinoxes, when the sun rises due east and sets due west for all locations.

841 Because of the ambiguity of Arabic *taghību* (are/become invisible; set) this can refer either to determining which stars can never be seen from a given latitude or which stars, not being circumpolar at that latitude, rise and set.

842 That is, the celestial equator, the Arctic and Antarctic circles, and the tropics of Cancer and Capricorn; see Klamroth, op. cit., 22.

843 That is, the terrestrial location (the north pole) that is directly opposite the celestial pole.

is about when you want to know the degree of the ecliptic for any fixed star that rises in any land you wish. The twenty-eighth chapter is about when you want to know how many longitudinal degrees[844] there are between the beginning of Aries and the ascendant in any country. The twenty-ninth chapter is about when you what to know to which clime any given city or country belongs. The thirtieth chapter is about when you want to know the latitude of the moon or any planet. The thirty-first chapter | is about when you want to establish the 1:157
meridian line in its position relative to the zenith of any country.[845] The thirty-second chapter is about when you want to know the longitude and latitude of the stars after you have become acquainted with the course of the meridian.[846] The thirty-third chapter is about when you want to know the location of the Dragon's Head and the Dragon's Tail and whether it meets with the orbits of the sun and moon.[847] The thirty-fourth chapter is about when you want to know the times of rising by means of the water clock.[848] The thirty-fifth chapter is about when you want to know the course of the sphere in which the fixed stars are. The thirty-sixth chapter is about when you want to know the heliacal risings and settings of the stars.[849] The thirty-seventh chapter is about when you want to know the longitude of a given city. The thirty-eighth chapter is

The MS reading *miḥwarayi l-shamāl* (the *two* axes of the north) may be a rough way of indicating that both poles, north and south, fulfill this condition.

844 The translation is uncertain. Klamroth, op. cit., 23, conjectures that the reference may be to degrees of longitude or to right ascension.

845 The meridian line (Arabic, *khaṭṭ wasaṭ al-samāʾ*) is a great circle passing through the celestial poles and the meridian of any location.

846 Following the emendation proposed by the Leiden editor (*jary wasaṭ al-samāʾ*, instead of MSS *juzʾ wasaṭ al-samāʾ*). The latter would mean, "the degree of the meridian."

847 Dragon's Head and Dragon's Tail designate the ascending and descending nodes: the places where the plane of the moon's orbit crosses the plane of the ecliptic (the plane of the sun's apparent motion against the background of the fixed stars). At the ascending node (Dragon's Head) the moon passes across the ecliptic while traveling north; at the descending node (Dragon's Tail) the moon passes across the ecliptic while traveling south. The significance of the nodes is that lunar and solar eclipses can occur only when the moon and the sun are aligned in the same (or nearly the same) plane at full moon or new moon. Knowledge of the position of the nodes was therefore used to predict eclipses.

848 The translation "water clock" for *sāʿāt al-māʾ* (the hours of water) is conjectural. The text may be corrupt.

849 The heliacal rising of a given star or planet occurs when it first becomes far enough from the sun to be visible in the eastern sky just before sunrise; its heliacal setting occurs when it is last visible in the western sky just before sunset. The heliacal rising and setting of certain stars (pre-eminently Sirius, whose rising heralded the dog days of summer) was used in antiquity to define periods in the calendar.

about knowing the degrees of longitude of cities. The thirty-ninth chapter is about calculating the arc algebraically.[850] These are the chapters of *The Device of Rings*.

The book *On the Device of Plates*,[851] which is the astrolabe, begins with a discussion of its operation and how it is made: its edges[852] and its measurements; the mounting of its rims, its plates, its spider,[853] and its alidade;[854] how it is marked with degrees and divided into parts,[855] and how one maintains the manner of division of its degrees, its circles of altitude,[856] and its inclination. He explains this and describes it: a plate for each clime; the latitude and longitude of each clime; the positions of the stars and the hours in it; the ascendant and the descendant;[857] the inclined, the southern, and the northern;[858] the first point of Capricorn and the first point of Cancer; the first point of Aries and the first point of Libra. Then he mentions its use. The first chapter

850 Arabic, *min ḥisāb al-jabr*; this is a conjectural restoration by the Leiden editor. The MSS read *min ḥisāb al-jaww*, "from calculation of the air," which is meaningless.

851 In addition to the article by Klamroth cited above, al-Yaʿqūbī's discussion of the astrolabe is discussed in O. Neugebauer, "The Early History of the Astrolabe," *ISIS* 40/3 (1949): 240–256, and in the article and bibliography by David A. King in *EI*³, s.v. Astrolabes, quadrants, and calculating devices. The earlier article by W. Hartner in *EI*², s.v. Asṭurlāb, is still useful.

852 Arabic, *ḥudūd* (pl. of *ḥadd*), can have a variety of meanings—"edge, limit, boundary." The exact sense here is uncertain.

853 Arabic, *ʿankabūt*, commonly called "rete" in English, from the Latin *rete* (net). It consists of a movable fretwork fitted over the latitude-specific plate; it carries a circle representing the ecliptic and pointers for any number of fixed stars.

854 Most European languages preserve this technical term in a form derived from Arabic *al-ʿiḍāda* (originally, one of the side-posts of a door). It is a movable ruler, often called a "diopter," affixed, at its center, to the rear of the astrolabe and used to measure the altitude of the sun or other celestial object.

855 Arabic, *kayfa tujazzaʾu wa-tuqsamu*. How specifically this is intended is unclear. Klamroth, op. cit., 24, interprets in a more general sense: "wie man es auseinandernimmt und zerlegt" (how one takes it apart and dismantles it).

856 Arabic, *muqanṭarāt*: a series of circles around the zenith point on the plate representing altitude above the horizon. The Arabic technical term has been preserved in English as "almucantar."

857 Arabic, *al-ṭāliʿ wa-l-ghārib*; normally this would refer to the star or constellation rising (*ṭāliʿ*) or setting (*ghārib*) at a particular moment, but it seems here to mean the line representing the horizon.

858 Arabic, *al-māʾil wa-l-janūbī wa-l-shamālī*. Each astrolabe plate has three circles concentric to its center point, representing the equator, the Tropic of Cancer (the northern limit of the sun's motion) and the Tropic of Capricorn (the southern limit). "The inclined" seems to refer instead to the ecliptic, represented by a circle on the "spider."

is about testing it, so that it will be correct. Chapter two is about testing the two ends of the alidade. The third chapter is about knowing how many hours of daylight have passed and what are the zodiacal sign and the degree of the ascendant. The fourth chapter is about knowing how many hours | of the night 1:158
have passed and what the ascendant is in terms of zodiacal signs and degrees. The fifth chapter is about determining the position of the sun with relation to the signs of the zodiac and degrees. The sixth chapter is about knowing the positions of the moon: in what zodiacal sign and degree it is, and where the seven planets are.[859] The seventh chapter is about knowing the latitude of the moon. The eighth chapter is about knowing the risings of the twelve zodiacal signs in the seven climes and knowing each of these signs. The ninth chapter is about how the risings cross the upright sphere and what (sign) attains each of the equatorial degrees.[860] The tenth chapter is about knowing how many hours of night and day there are at any season in a given clime. The eleventh chapter is about knowing the length of the "day" of a given fixed star[861] and what part of the heavens passes from the time of the rising of (one of) the stars to the time of its setting. The twelfth chapter is about determining the longitude and latitude of the stars. The thirteenth chapter is about determining the shifting of the fixed stars, for they shift one degree in every hundred lunar years.[862] The fourteenth chapter is about determining the declination of the zodiacal signs away from the equator, which is the circle of Aries and Libra.[863] The fifteenth chapter is about determining which cities are closer to the north and

859 That is, the seven "wandering stars" of the visible sky: Sun, Moon, Mercury, Venus, Mars, Jupiter, and Saturn.

860 The translation is uncertain and follows Klamroth, op. cit., 24. Neugebauer, 244, translates: "Rising times for sphaera recta (i.e.) right ascension (of zodiacal signs)."

861 Arabic, *miqdār nahār kull kawkab min al-kawākib*: apparently referring to the diurnal arc of any given star, the length of time that it will be above the horizon.

862 The translation is based on the emendation suggested by Klamroth, op. cit., 25: *fī kull mi'a min sinī l-qamar*. The reference is to the change of the celestial coordinates of stars due to the movement of the rotational axis of the earth, which traces a cone around the pole of the ecliptic in a period of about 26,000 years, or 1° every 72 years. Ptolemy (*Almagest*, VII, 4) gives the value of 1° every 100 years. One degree per lunar century (c. 97 years) is slightly more accurate, but it cannot be determined whether al-Yaʿqūbī's specification of lunar as opposed to solar years represents a correction of Ptolemy or simply reflects the lunar basis of the Islamic calendar.

863 Because the ecliptic and the equator intersect at the vernal equinox (Aries) and the autumnal equinox (Libra), the equator can be called "the circle of Aries and Libra." The angle between the plane of the equator and that of the ecliptic is also called "the obliquity of the ecliptic."

which are closer to the south. The sixteenth chapter is about determining the cities closest to the east and those closest to the west. The seventeenth chapter is about determining the latitude of each clime. The eighteenth chapter is about knowing which clime you are in. The nineteenth chapter is about knowing the latitude of the climes and of whichever cities you wish. The twentieth chapter is about knowing the determination of the five paths and how their paths run.[864] In each of these chapters he offers a long explanation in which he explains whatever is necessary and needs to be known. These, then, are his purposes in *On the Device of Plates*.

1:159 His book, *The Canon: On the Science of the Stars, Their Computation, and the Division and Equation of Their Degrees*, is one of the most complete and clearest books on the stars. Its opening begins with an account of the revolving of the heavens in which these stars revolve.[865] (Then comes) a chapter concerning knowledge of the course of the stars each day. He says that the distance traveled by the sun every day is 59′;[866] the distance traveled by the apogee of the moon is 7′; the distance traveled by the Head of the Dragon,[867] which is the *Jawzahar*,[868] is 3′; the distance traveled by Saturn is 2′; the distance traveled by Jupiter is 5′; the distance traveled by Mars is 31′; the distance traveled by Venus is 1°36′; the distance traveled by Mercury is 4°5′; and the distance traveled by Regulus[869] is 6″.[870] (Then comes) a chapter concerning knowledge of the average movements of the stars and their determination and equation when they can be determined only by their average movements. (Then comes) a chapter about the movement of the quadrants of the sphere, according to the doctrine of the

864 The five paths, mentioned above (at 1:156) are the Arctic Circle, the Tropic of Cancer, the Equator, the Tropic of Capricorn, and the Antarctic Circle.

865 Reading *dawr al-samāʾ* (the revolving of the heavens) and interpreting this to mean that the book began by positing the existence of a heavenly sphere whose motion was perfectly regular and with reference to which the apparently irregular observed motions of the sun, moon, and planets (*al-kawākib*) could be related by various geometrical constructions and mathematical formulas.

866 That is, the apparent eastward motion of the sun against the background of fixed stars. The figure is approximate.

867 That is, the ascending node.

868 More correctly, Gōzihr, a Persian term for an imaginary dragon spanning the sky between the two nodes of the moon, its head located at the ascending note, its tail at the descending node. See the article by D. N. Mackenzie in *Encyclopaedia Iranica*, s.v. Gōzihr.

869 Arabic, *qalb al-asad* (the Lion's heart), the regular term for Regulus (α Leonis).

870 As Klamroth, op. cit., 25, notes 4 and 5, observes: Only for the Sun, Saturn, Jupiter, and Mars are the figures correct. The figure given for Regulus can be corrected by assuming that the original reading was 1″ in 6 days.

astrologers[871] that the quadrants of the sphere move eight "portions" forward and eight "portions" backward—a "portion" being a degree—going forward in every eighty years, and backward over every eighty years, by one degree.[872] (Then comes) a chapter on the inclination of the sun and the latitude of the six planets and their distance from the equator to the north and to the south. He drew up a table for each of these celestial objects: the inclination of the sun is its inclination from the equator; the inclination of the latitude of the planets is their distance from the path of the sun. (Then comes) a chapter on the standing still and retrogression of the seven planets, how one determines it: for Saturn, Jupiter, and Mars, when between each one of them and the sun there are 120 degrees or 240 degrees; and for Venus and Mercury when they are at their maximum distance from the sun—when between Venus and it | there are 1:160
46 degrees, and between Mercury and it there are 23 degrees. (Then comes) a chapter on the coming into view of the seven planets from under the rays of the sun and their disappearance before it and behind it. (Then comes) a chapter on regularizing and adjusting the hours: how one can convert from unequal to equal hours. (Then comes) a chapter on knowing the latitude and longitude of cities. He divided the cities of the world among the seven climes, assigned a longitude and latitude to every city, and put them into a table that he named the Table of Cities. He laid it out in three columns. The first column lists the names of the cities. The second column gives the longitude of each city. The third column gives the latitude of each city, which is its deviation northward from the limit of the first of Aries[873] and of Libra. He also set down the latitude of each clime, which is the deviation of its center northward from the first of Aries and of Libra; he listed it at the head of the table of its points of rising.[874] Thus, when one wants [the clime][875] of any city in the world, and it

871 Arabic, *aṣḥāb al-ṭilasmāt* (the masters of talismans).

872 This refers to the doctrine of "trepidation": that the movement of the equinoxes is not constant but oscillates: it moves forward at the rate of 1° every 80 years, until, having moved 8° forward in 640 years, it reverses direction and moves 8° backward at the same rate. An early version of this theory used it instead of a steady precession; a later version added the motion of trepidation to the steady precession of the equinoxes. See Neugebauer, op. cit., 243.

873 MSS *al-Jady* (Capricorn) must be a copyist's error for *al-Ḥamal* (Aries).

874 Arabic, *wa-athbatahu ʿalā raʾs jadwal maṭāliʿihā*. The meaning is unclear.

875 The translation assumes that the sentence as it stands in the manuscripts is corrupt and that a copyist has substituted the word *ʿarḍ* (latitude) for *iqlīm* (clime). The rest of the sentence describes the procedure for determining the *clime* of a given city; its latitude is presumably already known from the third column of the table.

is one of those set down in the list of cities, and one looks for the latitude of whichever clime is closest, then, to whichever clime the latitude of that city is found to be closest, to that clime that city belongs. (Then comes) a chapter about the latitude of every clime. He says that the first is 16 degrees, [27] minutes.[876] The second is 23 degrees, 11 minutes.[877] The third is 30 degrees, 22 minutes. The fourth is 36 degrees. The fifth is 40 degrees, 56 minutes. The sixth is 45 degrees, 1 minute.[878] The seventh is 48 degrees, 32 minutes. (Then comes) a chapter in which he discusses the deviation of the moon—that which is called parallax. He states that it has to do with the sighting of the moon—namely, that
1:161 the moon has two different positions: | one of them is the position at which it is sighted, the other its corrected place. (Then comes) a chapter on the conjunction and opposition of the sun and moon and how this can be computed correctly. (Then comes) a chapter on the eclipse of the moon and its regions. (Then comes) a chapter on the eclipse of the sun and how it is computed at the time of conjunction. (Then comes) a chapter on correcting what is found in the tables of stars, ascendants, and so forth. (Then comes) a chapter on correction, concerning the computation of the ascendant. It contains 180 tables, and he explains every proposition in an unambiguous way.[879]

And there is a listing of the kings of the Greeks and the Romans and what the reign of each king was, according to our explanation of their names at the end of this section.

The Kings of the Greeks and the Romans

The first of the kings of the Greeks, who are the sons of Yūnān, son of Japheth, son of Noah, and the first of their kings whom Ptolemy named in the *Canon*, was Philip.[880] He was overweening and haughty, and his reign was seven years. Then

---

876 MSS *wa-daqīqa* (and a minute) is a scribal error for *wa-sabʿ wa-ʿishrūna daqīqa* (and 27 minutes). This is the parallel passing through the island of Meroe, defined as where the longest day is 13 hours; see *Almagest* II.6.5 (trans. Toomer, 84).

877 *Almagest* II.6.7 (trans. Toomer, 85) gives the latitude of this parallel (Aswān) as 23 degrees, 51 minutes. A copyist's error is likely.

878 MSS "32 minutes." This must be a scribal error. Cf. *Almagest* II.6.15 (trans. Toomer, 86).

879 Retaining the MSS reading, *bi-mā lā yushkilu*. Ed. Leiden emends to *bi-l-ashkāl* (with figures).

880 Al-Yaʿqūbī is referring to a chronological table of kings' reigns that formed part of Ptolemy's work, the *Canon*, whose contents he has just summarized (ed. Leiden, 1:159–161). For modern editions of this part of the *Canon*, the so-called κανὼν βασιλειῶν, see the article by M. Plessner in *EI*², s.v. Baṭlamyūs. On the various genealogies of the Greeks current

his son Alexander became king. He it is who is called Dhū l-Qarnayn;[881] his mother's name was Olympias, and his teacher was Aristotle the sage. Alexander's might became great, his kingdom became powerful, and his dominion grew strong. Wisdom, intelligence, and learning assisted him. With him were courage, audacity, and high ambition, which led him to write to the kings of lands far and wide, summoning them to obey him; the kings of the Greeks before him had paid tributes to the Persian kings of Babylonia because of the majesty of that kingdom, its great might, and the insignificance of other kingdoms compared to it.[882] When he wrote to the king of Persia, summoning him to obey him, the latter took umbrage, so Alexander marched all the way to Babylonia. The king of the Persians at the time was Darius, son of Darius.[883] Alexander made war on him, killed him, took possession of the treasures of his kingdom, and married his daughter. Then he went | to Persia, killed the 1:162
marzpāns[884] and leaders there, and conquered the country. Then he went to India. Fūr, the king of India, marched out against him, but Alexander fought him and killed him.[885] Alexander then appointed over India a king to rule on his behalf, one of the people of India, someone named Kayhan. Alexander then departed and traveled east and west.[886] Having subdued the earth, he returned to the land of Babylon. When he reached the nearest part of Iraq, the part adjoining the Jazīra, he fell ill, and his illness became severe. Despairing of his life and knowing that death had descended on him, he wrote a letter to his mother to console her for his loss. At its close he said: "Prepare food and gather

among Arabic historians, compare al-Masʿūdī, *Murūj*, 2:242 (§ 664). On Philip, compare al-Masʿūdī, *Murūj*, 2:246–247 (§ 668).

881 That is, "He of the Two Horns," generally identified with the figure of that name mentioned in Qurʾān 18:83. Al-Masʿūdī, *Murūj*, 2:248–249 (§ 671) lists authorities that supported the identification and those who opposed it. Compare the article by W. Montgomery Watt in *EI*², s.v. al-Iskandar.

882 On the nature of this tribute (several golden eggs) and Alexander's contemptuous words of refusal ("I have eaten the chicken that used to lay the eggs"), see al-Masʿūdī, *Murūj*, 2:247 (§ 669).

883 Arabic, Dārā b. Dārā.

884 That is, the military commanders. The title *marzpān* (frontier protector) was used for military governors in the Sasanian empire. Its use here, with reference to the Achaemenid empire conquered by Alexander, is something of an anachronism. See the article by J. H. Kramers and M. Morony in *EI*², s.v. Marzpān.

885 Al-Yaʿqūbī has already mentioned Alexander's campaign against Fūr (Porus) in his account of the kings of India: ed. Leiden, 1:96–97.

886 On Kayhan, see ed. Leiden, 1:97. Cf. al-Masʿūdī, *Murūj*, 2:250 (§ 673) for a detailed account of Alexander's conquests in the East.

whomever you can of the women of the nobility. Let no one eat of your food who has ever been afflicted by misfortune."[887] So she prepared food, gathered the people, and commanded them that no one who had ever been afflicted by misfortune should eat. No one ate, whereupon she understood what Alexander had intended. Alexander died at the place from which he had sent the letter. His companions assembled, shrouded him, embalmed him, and laid him in a coffin of gold. One of the great philosophers stood beside it and said: "This is a momentous day. Kingship has been removed from him. Its evil, which had been in retreat, has come to the fore; and its good, which had been to the fore, has gone into retreat. Whoever would weep over a king, let him weep over this king. Whoever would marvel at an event, let him marvel at an event like this."[888] Then he turned to the philosophers who were present and said: "O sages, let each one of you speak a saying that will console the elite and admonish the common people." One[889] of Aristotle's disciples stood up, struck the coffin with his hand, and said: "O enclosed one, how silent you are! O mighty one, how hum-
1:163 ble you are! O hunter, how have you fallen like prey into the net? | Who is this who is hunting you?" Then another stood up and said: "This is the strong one, who today has become weak; the mighty one, who today has become humble." Another stood up and said: "Your swords were never dry, and no one was safe from your revenge. Your cities could not be attacked, your gifts never ceased, and your light never darkened. Now your light has gone out, your revenge is no longer feared, your gifts are no longer hoped for, your swords are no longer unsheathed, and your cities are not defended." Then another stood up and said:

887 In the more detailed account in al-Masʿūdī, *Murūj*, 2:257–258 (§ 677–678), the letter is taken by Ptolemy to Alexandria, along with Alexander's coffin, and given to Olympias at the time of the announcement of Alexander's death. Alexander's intention in that account is that his funeral banquet should be an occasion of joy, not sadness; the abstention of all from eating—or from attendance, the text being ambiguous—is unexpected, but Olympias derives consolation either from recognizing Alexander's great knowledge of human nature (no man being free of sorrow) or from knowing that everyone shares her grief over this particular misfortune (again, the text is ambiguous). For another Arabic parallel version of the death of Alexander, with two versions of Alexander's letter to his mother, see Albert Loewenthal, "Honein Ibn Ishâk, Sinnsprüche der Philosophen. Nach der hebräischen Übersetzung Charisi's ins Deutsche übertragen und erläutert," in Fuat Sezgin, ed., *Ḥunain ibn Isḥāq (d. 260/873): Texts and Studies*, 25–226, esp. 203 ff.

888 In al-Masʿūdī, *Murūj*, 2:252 ff. (§ 676), thirty funerary speeches follow, which differ from the speeches given by al-Yaʿqūbī; cf. the composite account given by Loewenthal, "Honein Ibn Ishâk, Sinnsprüche der Philosophen," 178 ff.

889 M and ed. Leiden read, "Each one of them." The sense requires deleting "each," which may have originated as a copyist's echoing of "each" from the previous sentence.

"This is he who was for kings a vanquisher; today he has become for the common people a thing vanquished." Another stood up and said: "Your voice was feared and your kingdom victorious; now the voice has been cut off and the kingdom has been brought low." Another stood up and said: "Why were you not immune to death, since you were immune to kings? Why were you not made king over it, since you were made king over them?" Another stood up and said: "By his stillness Alexander has set us in motion, and by his silence he has made us speak." And they continued to speak in this fashion. Then the coffin was closed and carried to Alexandria. His mother received it with the great people of the kingdom. When she saw it, she said: "O you whose wisdom reached the heavens, whose dominion encompassed the ends of the earth, and to whom kings were forced to bow! What has befallen you that you are asleep today, not waking; silent, not speaking? Who will take my message to you, that you admonished me, and I was admonished; you consoled me, and I was consoled? Peace be upon you, living and dying. How excellent you were alive, and how excellent in death!" Then she commanded that he should be buried. Alexander's reign, including his conquests in the world, was twelve years.

After him, Dhū l-Qarnayn Ptolemy, Alexander's successor, became king.[890] He was wise and learned, and his reign lasted twenty years. Then Philadelphus became king.[891] He was | overweening; his power became strong, and 1:164
he behaved with arrogance in his kingdom. In his days the talismans were made.[892] His reign lasted thirty-eight years. Then Euergetes[893] I ruled for twen-

890 Thus in the MSS, implying that Ptolemy inherited the title Dhū l-Qarnayn. The Leiden editor, finding no evidence for such an assertion, suggested emending the text to yield, "After Dhū l-Qarnayn, Ptolemy, the successor of Alexander, became king." This requires two slight changes to the Arabic. An easier solution is to assume that the words "Dhū l-Qarnayn" were written as a marginal gloss to explain "after him" and were mistakenly incorporated into the text by a copyist. In any case, this is Ptolemy I Lagus. The figure of 20 years is correct, if one takes his reign as beginning with his first styling himself king in 305 BCE and ending in 285 BCE.

891 The name has been truncated in the manuscripts to *Fīlifūs* (Philip).

892 The precise meaning of this reference to talismans is unclear, but a slightly longer reference to them in al-Masʿūdī's account of Ptolemy Philadelphus (*Murūj*, 2:281–282 [§ 703]) seems to point toward the practice of making small magical gems carved with various figures and names, to be used as talismans. Why the common source of al-Yaʿqūbī and al-Masʿūdī dated the practice to the reign of Ptolemy II Philadelphus is unclear. The full passage from al-Masʿūdī reads: "In his days the talismans were made, and the worship of statues and idols appeared among them because of sophistries that entered among them, that these things were mediators between them and their Creator, which could bring them closer to Him and cause them to approach Him."

893 The MSS reading *hwrḥyṭwb* can be explained as a corruption of Euergetes.

ty-five years. Then Philopator ruled for seventeen years. Then Epiphanes ruled for twenty-four years. Then Philopator II ruled for twenty-five years. Then Euergetes II ruled for twenty-seven years.[894]

The Kings of the Romans

After the Greeks, the sons of Yūnān, son of Japheth, son of Noah, kingship passed to the Romans, who were descendants of Rūm, the son of Samāḥīr, the son of Hūbā, the son of ʿAlqā, the son of Esau, the son of Isaac, the son of Abraham.[895] They occupied the country, spoke the language of the people, and related themselves to (the city of) Rome. The Greek language disappeared, except for a remnant of their wise sayings that remained in the hands of these people. The first of the Romans to become king after the Greeks was ..., who was ... the Younger, son of Rūm.[896] His reign was twenty-two years. Then Augustus became king. A year into his reign Christ was born. The reign of Augustus continued for forty-three years. Then Tiberius ruled for twenty-two years. Then Gaius ruled for four years.[897] Then Claudius ruled for fourteen years. [...][898]

---

894 The dates for the Ptolemaic rulers of Egypt are: Ptolemy I Soter, 304–285 BCE; Ptolemy II Philadelphus 285–247 BCE, Ptolemy III Euergetes, 247–222 BCE, Ptolemy IV Philopator, 222–205 BCE, Ptolemy V Epiphanes, 205–181 BCE; and Ptolemy VI Philometor (the name has been corrupted to "Philopator" in transmission), 181–146 BCE. The series as given is correct. The 25 years given for the reign of "Philopator II" (i.e., Philometor) should be corrected to 35; the confusion between 25 and 35 is easier to explain on the basis of dates written in numerals rather than spelled out as words. Ptolemy VIII Euergetes II, ruled 146–117 BCE. Al-Yaʿqūbī omits the period of Ptolemaic decline, until Octavian's occupation of Egypt in 30 BCE. A more complete list is found in al-Masʿūdī, *Murūj*, 2:278–291 (§ 699–714).

895 These names have suffered in transmission. One can compare the following variants in al-Masʿūdī, *Murūj*, 2:293–296 (§ 715–717): Samāḥilīq (variant, Samāḥilīn) for Samāḥīr; Haryān for Hūbā; and ʿAyfā (variants, ʿAlqā and Ḥalqā) for ʿAlqā.

896 Because he was succeeded, according to al-Yaʿqūbī, by Augustus, the reference ought to be to Caius Julius Caesar, but the names have been so mangled in transmission that one can hardly conjecture their original forms. Ed. Leiden reads "*F.hāsāt.q*, who was Jāliyūs the Younger." In M, the first name is the same; the second looks like *Jā.b.t.r.s.* The manuscripts of the parallel in al-Masʿūdī, *Murūj*, 2:295 (§ 717) vary between Jāʾiyūs (perhaps for Gaius) and Jālīs (perhaps for Julius).

897 That is, Caligula, whose full name was Gaius Julius Caesar Augustus Germanicus. He ruled from 37 to 41.

898 Although the MSS show no break, one can assume that a lacuna exists. The reigns of Nero

Then Vespasian ruled for ten years, and the people of his kingdom used to call him "the God." He dispatched a son of his named Titus to Jerusalem; the latter besieged the city for four months. A great throng of people | had gathered 1:165
there for one of the festivals of the Jews, and the siege was so severe that they ate their children, and most of them died of hunger. Titus conquered the city, killed and took captives, and set fire to the temple. Then Titus ruled for three years. In his time a mountain called Ubramūr split apart and fire came out of it and burned up many towns.[899] Then Domitian ruled for fifteen years. In his time Apollonius of Tyana, the master of talismans, appeared.[900] The people of his kingdom rose up against Domitian and killed him. Then Nerva ruled for a single year. Then Trajan ruled for nineteen years. Then Hadrian ruled for twenty-one years. The Jews of Jerusalem rose up against him and refused to pay him tribute. He dispatched against them someone who killed them, and he commanded that any of them who remained in Jerusalem should be killed. Then Aelius Antoninus ruled for thirty-three years.[901] [...] Then Severus and Antoninus ruled for twenty-five years.[902] Then Alexander, son of Mamaea,

---

and his three successors have been omitted. Cf. al-Masʿūdī, *Murūj*, 2:299–304 (§ 722–726), which contains an account of the persecution of Christians under Claudius.

899 The reference is clearly to the eruption of Mount Vesuvius in 79 CE, but the reading of the MSS, Ubramūr (the vocalization is conjectural), cannot be explained.

900 Apollonius of Tyana (a town in Cappadocia), usually known in Arabic as Balīnūs, was a philosopher of the first century CE. In *The Life of Apollonius of Tyana*, by the Sophist Philostratus, he appears as a Pythagorean sage with supernatural powers. On the day that Domitian was murdered, Apollonius, according to Philostratus, miraculously witnessed the event in a vision. For a list of works attributed to him known in Arabic, see the article by M. Plessner in *EI*², s.v. Balīnūs, and the article by G. Strohmaier in *EI*³, s.v. Apollonius of Tyana.

901 That is, Antoninus Pius (full name Titus Aelius Hadrianus Antoninus Augustus Pius), ruled from 138 to 161 CE. The length of his reign appears correctly as 23 years in al-Masʿūdī, *Murūj*, 2:305 (§ 728), along with a notice that he rebuilt Jerusalem as a Roman city named Aelia.

902 One must assume a lacuna before "Severus and Antoninus," although neither the MSS nor ed. Leiden indicate one. The Leiden editor emended the manuscript reading "S.w.l.d.y.n" to "Marqus" and deleted *wa-* (and), seeing this as a reference to Marcus Aurelius Antoninus. But the original reading was probably "S.w.ā.r.y.s" (Severus); the references to Marcus Aurelius and his successor Commodus appear to have dropped out of al-Yaʿqūbī, although they appear in al-Masʿūdī, *Murūj*, 2:306 (§ 728). The combined reigns of Severus and his son Antoninus—that is, Marcus Aurelius Severus Antoninus Augustus, known as Caracalla—totaled twenty-five years according to al-Masʿūdī, *Murūj*, 2:306 (§ 728), and to al-Bīrūnī, *al-Āthār al-bāqiya* (trans. Sachau), 94, who lists them as joint rulers for 25 years.

ruled for thirteen years.[903] Then Maximinus ruled for three years.[904] Then Gordian ruled for three years.[905] Then Philip ruled for two years.[906] Then Decius ruled for one year.[907] Then Gallus ruled for three years.[908] Then Valerian ruled for six years.[909] [...] Then Probus ruled for seven years.[910] [...] Then Diocletian ruled for twenty years. Then Constantine and Maxentius ruled for ten years.[911]

1:166 The kings of the Greeks, as well as the Romans who ruled after them, were of differing opinions. One group of them followed the religion of the Ṣābiʾans—they used to be called "the Ḥanīfs."[912] They were those who affirmed and

---

903 That is, Severus Alexander, whose mother was Julia Avita Mamaea. He ruled from 222 to 235 CE.

904 Maximinus (corrupted in the MSS into something like Maxhaminānūs) ruled from 235 to 238 CE.

905 In fact, there were three emperors named Gordian (numbered conventionally I, II, and III) in the period between 238 and 244. Al-Masʿūdī, *Murūj*, 2:306 (§ 729), correctly gives their total reign as six years; similarly al-Bīrūnī, *al-Āthār al-bāqiya* (trans. Sachau), 94, who treats him as one ruler.

906 That is, Philip the Arab, ruled 244–249 CE.

907 One year is the length of reign given also by al-Bīrūnī, *al-Āthār al-bāqiya* (trans. Sachau), 94; al-Masʿūdī, *Murūj*, 2:306 (§ 729) gives a reign of two years, which is more nearly correct historically (249–251 CE).

908 Ruled 251–253 CE.

909 Ruled 253–260 CE.

910 The reign of Probus, 276–282 (the name is badly mangled in the manuscripts into something like Furūs in M), is also given as seven years by al-Bīrūnī, *al-Āthār al-bāqiya* (trans. Sachau), 94.

911 Because al-Yaʿqūbī has an account, below (1:172), of Constantine, the first Christian emperor, and gives his reign as 55 years (much too long), there is a problem here. Possibly, what is intended is the period between the commencement of Constantine's rule (306) until the Edict of Milan (313), which could be seen as the official beginning of Constantine's "Christian" period, but the chronology of ten years cannot be made to fit. Another possibility is that Arabic Qusṭanṭīn is a corruption of some version of the name Constantius, Constantine's father, who was co-emperor with Maximian (not Maxentius) from 293 to 305, but, again, the figure of ten years is a problem.

912 Al-Yaʿqūbī has taken two terms of uncertain meaning from the Qurʾān and used them to describe pre-Islamic religious groups who believed in a Creator and accepted the existence of prophets. On the Ṣābiʾans, see the articles in EI^2 by F. C. de Blois, s.v. Ṣābiʾ, and by T. Fahd, s.v. Ṣābiʾa. On the Ḥanīfs (Arabic, *ḥanīf*, pl. *ḥunafāʾ*), see the article by W. Montgomery Watt in EI^2, s.v. Ḥanīf.

acknowledged a Creator and who claimed to have prophets,[913] such as Ūrānī,[914] Agathodaemon,[915] and Hermes the Threefold-in-Grace—some say that the latter was the prophet Idrīs.[916] He was the first to write with the pen and to teach the science of the stars. Their doctrine about the Creator—powerful and mighty is He—follows that of Hermes: As for grasping God by the intellect, it is difficult, and to discourse about Him is not possible. God is the cause of causes and the creator of the world all at once.

Another group of them were followers of Zeno; they were the Sophists. The interpretation in Arabic of this Greek word is "those who try to induce others into error" or "those who ply contradictions."[917] They held that there is neither knowledge nor anything knowable. They argued on the basis of people's diversity of opinion and the equal claim of some vis-à-vis others.[918] They said: We have examined what people who differ in opinion say and have found their sayings to be divergent, not in agreement. Yet we found that, for all their disagreement, they concurred in holding that truth is self-consistent, not self-contradictory, and that falsehood is self-contradictory, not self-consistent. In

913 Reading with M, *anbiyāʾ*; ed. Leiden reads the singular, *nabiyyan*.

914 Because the Ṣābiʾans of Ḥarrān were worshippers of the heavenly bodies, one can derive Ūrānī from οὐρανός, the Greek word for heaven. See Kevin van Bladel, *The Arabic Hermes*, 188.

915 In M, the ending of the word "daemon" is unambiguous; the first part looks like *ʿ.ā.y.b*, which could be repointed to yield *gh.ā.th.y*. The name often appears in more or less this form in Arabic.

916 On the reception in the Islamic world of the arcane Greek writings attributed to the Egyptian sage Hermes Trismegistos ("the Thrice-Great," also known as "the Thrice-Wise"), see the article by Kevin van Bladel in *EI*³, s.v. Hermes and Hermetica. The prophet Idrīs, who appears in Qurʾān 19:56 and 21:86, is usually identified with the biblical Enoch but occasionally with Hermes. See the article by G. Vajda in *EI*², s.v. Idrīs.

917 Arabic, *al-mughāliṭa* and *al-tanāquḍiyya* (the latter involving a conjectural reading). The former term, in the form of the verbal noun *mughālaṭa*, becomes the standard word in later Arabic for "fallacy." This is, of course, not the original meaning of "sophist," derived as it is from the Greek word for "wise" (σοφός), but it is a fairly accurate description of the method of Zeno of Elea, famous for his ability to argue both sides of a question, with the aim of inducing skepticism, and for his paradoxes, arguments in which a seemingly sound series of inferences yields manifestly irrational results.

918 Arabic *ikhtilāf al-nās wa-ntiṣāf baʿḍihim min baʿḍ*. The first part of the phrase clearly refers to people's holding differing opinions; the second part of the phrase may refer to the skeptical method of showing that both sides of an argument have an equal claim and so no conclusion can be drawn.

their very agreement, there was a witness that they did not know which of them was in the right.[919] They having affirmed this, there remained for truth no place where one could hope to obtain it, except among their elite. But we knew that this could come about only in one of two ways: either by conceding to the claimant [or] by exposing his claim (as false). We therefore examined the claim and found what they had in common, but we did not hold it permissible to assent to them because of two defects: first, that each called the other wrong; second, their agreement that they did not know what was correct. So nothing remained but to expose the claim, and so we did. We found them to be
1:167 people perfectly matched, running neck and neck |, with victory turning against them all equally, now this claim gaining strength, then its opposite. In no group of them did we encounter superiority unshared or argument unrivaled and unchallenged. Because it was impossible to find the truth among their commoners or among their elite by appeal to disputation, there remained for knowledge no place where it might be found, and for truth there remained no method by which it might be attained. So we concluded that there was neither science nor knowledge. For, if something is established indubitably, it must necessarily be comprehended by assent or by disagreement. When, for example, someone mentions (somebody) while the latter is absent and says, "So-and-so is absent," he has hit the mark. Had he or someone else said, "So-and-so is present," when he was not present, thus straying from the truth, and had someone contradicted him, saying, "Nay, he is absent," one of the two must necessarily have been speaking the truth. For, when something is truly established, it must be present or absent; and if it is not a thing, both of them are liars in saying that it is present or absent; for that which is present is a thing, and that which is absent is a thing, whereas, if it is not a thing, it is neither present nor absent. They also argued in a different way and said: If all things are grasped by knowledge, and knowledge (is grasped) by (antecedent) knowledge, (the process) must be either finite or infinite. If it is finite, it must end in something unknown, but whatever is not known is unknown, and how can things be known because of something unknown? If, on the other hand, the process is infinite and has no end, it cannot be comprehended, and what has not been comprehended is also unknown. So both terms of this syllogism are unknown, not known; for how can anything unknown be known unless all

919 The translation is based on a slight emendation of the MSS. The text of ed. Leiden can be translated as: "In their agreement there was witness to them [that they] did not know the right."

the things be known (which is most unlikely)? They took great pains with these two kinds (of argument); they made many efforts and went to great trouble.

A group called Dahriyya[920] held that there is no religion, no Lord, no prophet, no book, no afterlife, no recompense for good or evil, no beginning or ending of anything,[921] no creation or perishing: what is termed creation is merely the composition of something that had been separated, and its perishing is only its separation after having been together. Both aspects in reality are (merely) the becoming present of what was absent and the becoming absent of what was present. They were called Dahriyya only because of their claim that mankind has never ceased to be and will never cease to be and that time (*al-dahr*) revolves without beginning and without end. They argued for their claim by saying: As regards the existence or nonexistence of a thing, only two states, with no third, are known: A state in which the thing exists—and how can what already is and exists come to be? And a state in which there is no thing—and how can a thing come to be in a state that has no likeness?[922]—that is most unlikely. They argued similarly about the claim of perishing: Only two states are known: A state in which the thing subsists—and the statement of anyone who attributes perishing to a thing in the state of its being and subsistence is absurd. And a state in which there is no thing—and how can there be the least perishing?—it is absurd. If our opponents admit that we have spoken the truth, they enter into our argument and refute their own; if they reject our argument, they claim there is a third state, one in which there is neither nonexistence nor existence—and that is the most offensively absurd of the three.[923] 1:168

920 Literally, "believers in time (*dahr*)." The word *dahr* occurs in Qur'ān 45:24, where the pagans are cited as saying, "There is nothing but our present life; we die, and we live, and nothing but Time (*al-dahr*) destroys us." *Dahr* could also be seen as an impersonal fate. *Dahriyya* came to be applied to a variety of materialistic or naturalistic philosophies. See the article by I. Goldziher and A. M. Goichon in *EI*², s.v. Dahriyya, and the article by P. Crone in *EI*³, s.v. Dahrīs; also Hinrich Biesterfeldt, "'Eternalists' and 'Materialists' in Islam: A Note on the *Dahriyya*," 117–123.

921 That is, all things are formed from preexisting matter and dissolve into matter that continues to exist in a different form.

922 The Leiden editor read C as *lā tashbīhᵃ lahā*. (M is more ambiguous, as the first and second latters of *tashbīhᵃ* are undotted). In any case, the sense is unclear. Other possible readings have been suggested: *lā shay'iyyatᵃ lahā* (that has no thingness) or lā *nisbiyyatᵃ lahā* (that has no relationship).

923 The translation follows the apparent reading of M: *fa-dhālika aqbaḥu l-thalāthati iḥālatan*. Ed. Leiden reads the last word as *ḥālatan* ("and that is the most offensive of the three with regard to state").

One group of them held that the origin of things in eternity was a grain that existed and then split open; the world as you see it, with its diversity of colors and sensible qualities, appeared from it. Some of them claimed that it is not diverse [in] its essential qualities (*maʿānī*), but that it differs only with respect to the sense perception of it. Others denied that and asserted of it diversity in essential qualities and reality. Those who rejected the reality of diversity of things held that things differ only through difference of sense perception of them and that none of them has any reality by which it can be distinguished
1:169 from any other of them. | Among the proofs they claimed for this is that, when a person with the disease that originates from yellow bile—someone with jaundice, for example—tastes honey, he finds it bitter, whereas people free of this illness find it sweet. Furthermore, daylight dims the sight of bats, and night sharpens it. Now, if light increases the eyes in light[924] and darkness dims them, it follows that daylight is darkness for bats and for others whose vision is dimmed by light; and this occurs in some people, as well as in some animals and birds. And if, as we have described it, night sharpens some eyes, night must be light for them, just as daylight is light to others and night darkness. If you say that this is due to some defect that has come over these sorts, we say to you, "(Is it) among those who differ from them, or among those who agree with them?" If you say, "Among those who differ from them," we shall say, "Not so; [the defect has come over those who agree with them." And if you say, "Among those who agree with them," we shall say, "Not so;][925] the defect has come over those who differ from them, from their point of view; so neither sort has superiority over the other." They said: "Don't you see the scribe write the document even and straight, and thus he sees it in front of his face; yet if he looks at it from behind, he sees it as other than he knew it.[926] And if he looks at it from one side or the other, he will see it differently. As when you write the letter *alif* with a shape that distinguishes it from all the letters: when you face it you will see it as an *alif*, but if you look at it from behind you will

924 That is, increases their power to see. The expression is based on the Aristotelian notion that vision occurs as the result of a "visual ray" emitted by the eye.

925 The words in brackets have been added by the Leiden editor to make sense of a difficult passage.

926 That is, if you hold the page up to the light and look at the writing from the other side, you will see a mirror image of what you have written. "If you turn aside from it" seems to mean turning the writing 90°. Although this will turn the Arabic letter *alif* (an upright stroke) into a *bāʾ* (a horizontal stroke, minus its distinguishing dot below), it will hardly turn an *alif* into the "earring" shape of *nūn*.

see it as a *bāʾ*, and if you turn aside from it you will see it as a *nūn* or a *bāʾ*." (They said that) what is absent from its place is present in another place; and it is the same for colors, sounds, tastes, individuals, and garments. It is just as when you see a person from nearby as big but from afar as small: the closer one approaches, the bigger the person becomes in size, and the farther away one goes, the smaller the person becomes in one's eyes. | It is the same with a sound: 1:170
from nearby it is heard as loud but soft from afar. Similarly for taste: if you taste a little of something, you find it only slightly sweet, but if you taste more of it, its taste [is very sweet].[927] Similarly for touch: you tap something lightly and find it lukewarm, but then you touch it forcefully and find it hot. You see a shape from nearby as bulging[928] and irregular, but when the beholder gains distance from it, he thinks that it is even and not irregular. They claimed that all things alternate according to balance and equilibrium and came close to adopting the ways of the Sophists.[929]

Another group held that things are derived from four principles that have never ceased and will never cease; they were originated, and the world appeared from them. They are the four simple units: heat, cold, wetness, and dryness. They stand firm[930] in themselves, not by intention, will, or volition.

Another group held that the principles are four. They are the "mothers" of whatever is in the world; but with them there is a fifth, which has never ceased and will never cease organizing and combining them into a whole by will, volition, and wisdom. It combines their pairs into a whole, their products being generated from it and their contraries not abstaining from abiding one with the other; and this is knowledge.[931]

A group, adherents of the doctrine of substance—namely, the Aristotelians—held that things are two things: substance and accident. Substance, in turn, can be divided into two divisions: living and lifeless. Its definition is the self-sufficient, and its differentiation is in the property, not the definition. Accident is of nine kinds. Among them is quantity, which is number, whose forms are four: volume, area, weight, and speech.[932] Next is quality, whose

927 Filling the lacuna as suggested by Landberg, 38.

928 Emending MSS *thābita* (firm, steady) to the graphically similar *nābiʾa*.

929 Adopting the Leiden editor's suggested emendation (*takhallaqū*), rather than the MSS *yaḥlifū* (swear by).

930 Reading with M *tathbutu*; ed. Leiden, *tanbutu* (they grow).

931 Arabic *al-ʿilm* (knowledge), in the sense of Greek λόγος (organizing principle).

932 The inclusion of speech (*qawl*) can be explained by reference to Aristotle, *Categories*, 4b,

forms are eight: generation and corruption, shape and form,[933] strength and weakness, disposition and habit. Next is relation, with its four forms: natural, artificial, preference, and affection. Next is "when," which is that which occurs
1:171 according to the moment; | by moment one means time. The forms of time are three: past, future, and enduring. Next is "where," which is that which occurs according to place—the six directions: before, behind, above, below, right, and left. Next is possession, that is, ownership, and ownership takes (either of) two forms: external or internal. External means something like a slave, a house, furniture, and the like; internal means something like knowledge and wisdom. Next is posture, meaning the aspect of a thing, as when one says that so-and-so is standing, so-and-so is sitting, so-and-so is leaving, and so-and-so is coming. Next is actor, which takes two forms: either the actor acts by choice or acts by nature. That empowered with choice is like whatever is living, enduring, eating, and drinking. The actor by nature is like the movement of the four elements. Fire, for example, rises from the center to the height; [air rises,] though less than fire; earth (moves) from the height to the center, to the position most appropriate for it; and water (moves) from the height, though less than earth. Finally, there is the acted upon, that which receives the effect of what acts upon it, as if it were clay that the actor can render round, square, or of any (other) shape.

These are the doctrines of the Greeks and of the Romans who came after them, the schools of their theologians,[934] philosophers, sages, and speculative thinkers.

---

where the category of quantity is first divided into discrete and continuous, with number and speech (λόγος) being given as examples of discrete quantities. Speech falls into this division, because all utterances can be divided into discrete syllables. Volume, area, and weight are examples of continuous quantities. Al-Yaʿqūbī or his source has simplified Aristotle confusingly.

933 Reading *ḥilya* for M and ed. Leiden *ḥīla* (device, ingenuity). Cf. Aristotle, *Categories* 10a11, where the terms σχῆμα and μορφή refer, respectively, to geometrical figure and to qualities such as straight and crooked.

934 Arabic, *mutakallimīhim*. In an Islamic context, *mutakallim* came to mean a speculative theologian, someone who discussed theological matters on the basis of reason, rather than relying on the text of the Qurʾān or the transmitted traditions of the Prophet. In this context, the term perhaps refers to something more general.

The Roman Kings Who Became Christian

The first of the Romans who became king and departed from the doctrine of Hellenism[935] to Christianity was Constantine. The reason was that, while he was fighting certain enemies, he saw in a dream as if spears had been sent down from heaven with crosses on them. When | he awoke in the morning, 1:172
he mounted crosses on his spears; then he went into battle and was victorious. That was the reason for his becoming Christian. He supported the Christian religion and built churches. He assembled bishops from every town, in order to establish the Christian religion. It was their first assembly.[936] They gathered at Nicaea—three hundred and eighteen bishops and four patriarchs: the Patriarch of Alexandria, the Patriarch of Rome, the Patriarch of Antioch, and the Patriarch of Constantinople. The reason Constantine assembled these men was that, after he had become a Christian and Christianity had settled in his heart, he wanted to acquire profound knowledge of it. He therefore compared[937] the doctrines of its adherents and found that there were thirteen doctrines. Among them was the doctrine of those who held that Christ and his Mother were Gods. Another was the doctrine of those who held that his relation to the Father was like that of a flame of fire split off from another flame of fire without the first being diminished by the splitting off of the second. Another was the doctrine of those who held that he had become divine. Another was the doctrine of those who held that he had been made a servant. Another was the doctrine of those who, like Mānī[938] and his companions, held that his body had been a phantom. Another was the doctrine of those who held that he was the Word. Another was the doctrine of those who held that he was the Son. Another was the doctrine of those who held that he was an eternal spirit. Another was the doctrine of those who held that he was the son of Joseph. Another was the doctrine of those who held that he was one of the prophets. Another was the doctrine of those who held that he was divine and human.

---

935 Arabic, *al-Yūnāniyya*, a literal translation of Greek Ἑλληνισμός in its later sense of paganism.

936 Apparently al-Yaʿqūbī, al-Masʿūdī (*Murūj*, 2:313 ff. [§ 736 ff.]), and al-Bīrūnī, *Āthār*, 295–296, draw on a common source that listed six rather than the seven ecumenical councils that had taken place by the date of composition.

937 Following the reading of M (*aḥḍara*); for this sense, see Dozy, *Supplément*, 1:298. Ed. Leiden has *aḥṣā* (he tallied).

938 The MSS read *Mattā* (Matthew), but the doctrine described is that of Mānī, the founder of Manichaeism. The two names are easily confused in Arabic script.

Constantine assembled three hundred and eighteen bishops and four patriarchs—there were no others at that time. The Patriarch of Alexandria held that Christ had been deified and had been created.[939] Having assembled, they debated the matter with him, and they all reached a consensus that Christ had been born from the Father before creatures had come to be and that he was of the nature of the Father. They did not mention the Holy Spirit or determine whether he was creator or created, but they did agree that the Father was God and the Son was God from him.[940] Then they departed from Nicaea. Constantine reigned for fifty-five years.[941]

1:173 Then Julian ruled for a single year.

Then [...][942] ruled for a single year. In his days, the People of the Cave—they had died previously—reappeared after a long time. They were several persons

939 This nicely represents the position of Arius, who was only a presbyter, not the patriarch of Alexandria.

940 Although the creed approved at the Council of Nicaea in 325 did mention belief in the Holy Spirit, words asserting the divinity of the Holy Spirit were not added to the creed until the Second Ecumenical Council, held at Constantinople in 381, and were further elaborated at the Council of Chalcedon in 451.

941 As Constantine reigned from 306 to 337, this figure is too long, even if one dates his reign from his appointment as tetrarch (assistant to the emperor of the East) in 293. Note that al-Yaʿqūbī, presumably on the basis of another source, has already given the reign of Constantine as co-emperor with Maxentius as ten years (see above, 1:165). The figure given by al-Masʿūdī, *Murūj*, 2:316 (§ 738), is the correct 31 years, although he mentions that others attribute to him a reign of 25 years. The figure of 55 years can be explained as the combined reign of Constantine and of his son and successor Constantius, both of whose names take the form Qusṭanṭīn in Arabic. Al-Yaʿqūbī omits any mention of Constantius, presumably because he assumed the two were the same person. Al-Masʿūdī, *Murūj*, 2:323 (§ 744) gives the reign of Constantius as 24 years; so the two reigns total 55 years. The same chronology can be found in al-Bīrūnī, *Āthār*, 97.

942 Here the MSS read *Dīsūs* or, perhaps, *Dasyūs*. This can hardly have arisen from miscopying of the name of Julian's successor, Jovian, who, in fact, ruled slightly less than a year. In any case, the placement of the incident of the People of the Cave in his reign points to Theodosius, during whose reign the cave of the seven sleepers of Ephesus (the Qurʾānic "People of the Cave") was discovered, and the "sleepers," who had entered the cave to escape persecution during the reign of Decius (mentioned above, 1:165), emerged alive. *Dasyūs* is more likely to have arisen from omission of the first letters of Theodosius' name in Arabic than from the Arabic form of Decius (*Daqiyūs*). (Al-Masʿūdī, *Murūj*, 2:325 [§ 746], however, gives the name of the emperor under whom they emerged as Awālans, that is, Valens.) Note that the form of the story assumed here implies not merely that the youths slept from the reign of Decius to that of Theodosius but that they fell asleep and died, to be

and a shepherd, and the shepherd's dog was with them. Their names were Maxilmīnā, Marāṭūs, Sāh Yūniyūs, Naṭariyūs, Dāwas, Nawālis, Kanīfartū, and Yunūṭur; the name of the shepherd was Malīkhā, and he was the owner of the dog, whose name was Qiṭmīr.[943] They came out after a hundred years—some say three hundred and nine—and sent one of their number with some dirhams to get them food, but the market folk did not recognize the type of his dirhams. They followed him until they arrived at the cave—the people had been in the dark about them. A mosque in which to pray was built by the cave.

Then Valentinian ruled for four years.[944]

Then Theodosius the Elder ruled. In his reign the second assembly of the Christians took place.[945] One hundred fifty bishops and three patriarchs gathered in Constantinople for it; the Patriarch of Rome did not attend. They laid down the document of the creed and affirmed the Holy Spirit.[946] The document of the creed that they laid down was:

I believe in God, the One; the King[947] of everything; the Creator of the heavens and the earth, of what is seen and what is unseen; and in the Lord, the Christ, the Son of God, who was born before the ages; Light from Light; true God

---

resurrected miraculously in the days of the latter ruler. See the article by Roberto Tottoli in *Encyclopaedia of the Qur'ān*, s.v. Men of the Cave.

943 The names must have given the copyist much difficulty; many of the letters are undotted, so the readings given here are conjectural. Another version of the names can be found in al-Ṭabarī, *Ta'rīkh*, 1:777. In the translation by M. Perlmann, *The History of al-Ṭabarī*, IV, 156, they appear as Maksimilinā, Maḥsimilinā, Yamlīkhā, Marṭūs, Kaṣūṭūnaṣ, Bīrūnas, Rasmūnas, Baṭūnas, and Qālūs. The textual notes of the Leiden edition of al-Ṭabarī provide references to possible Syriac sources for these names. In the Syriac tradition closest to al-Ya'qūbī's account, they appear as Maximilianos, Iamlikha (= Iamblichos), Martellos, Dionysios, Ioannis, Serapion, Ex(ak)ostodinos, and Antoninus. See Sebastian Brock, "Jacob of Sarug's Poem on the Sleepers of Ephesus," 324–330.

944 The name has been distorted in the manuscripts to "Albanṭiyānūs," and the name of his successor, Valens, has been omitted. Al-Bīrūnī, *Āthār*, 95, lists Valentinian as ruling one year (probably an error for 11), succeeded by Valens, who ruled for fourteen years.

945 That is, the Second Ecumenical Council, held in Constantinople in 381.

946 That is, added an article to the creed affirming not simply belief in the Holy Spirit, which had been part of the creed affirmed at Nicaea in 325, but that the Holy Spirit was the third person of the Trinity: "the Lord and Giver of life, who proceeds from the Father, who with the Father and the Son together is worshipped and glorified, who spoke through the prophets."

947 Arabic, *malik*; perhaps to be read as *mālik* (possessor), which would correspond more closely to the Greek παντοκράτορα.

[from true God];[948] begotten, not created; of the nature of the Father; by whom everything came to be. For us men and for our salvation he descended from heaven; he became incarnate by the Holy Spirit and from the Virgin Mary, and
1:174 became | man; he was crucified for us in the time of Pontius Pilate; he suffered and was buried; he rose in three days, as in the scriptures; he ascended into heaven, and sat down at the right of the Father; whose kingdom has no end.[949] [And in the Holy Spirit], the Lord, who is derived from the Father; in whom the prophets spoke.[950] In one holy, apostolic Church of the disciples. I believe in one baptism for the forgiveness of sins and in the resurrection of the dead.

Having excommunicated anyone who professed anything else, they departed from Constantinople. The reign of Theodosius was seventeen years.[951]

His brother's son, Theodosius the Younger, and Valentinian ruled after him.[952] The third gathering of the Christians took place. They assembled in Ephesus, and two hundred bishops attended. Nestorius opposed them all. He held that Christ was two substances and two natures: God perfect in his substance and his nature.[953] For the Father begot God; he did not beget a human

948 Added by the Leiden editor; its omission may be due to the copyist's omission of text between two successive occurrences of the same word (homeoteleuton).

949 The text in the MSS becomes defective at this point from the carelessness of a copyist. Having written "of the Father," he skipped ahead to the word *ishtaqqa* ("split off, branched off, was derived from," a free translation of ἐκπορευόμενον, "proceeding from"), leaving out "whose kingdom has no end." He realized his mistake and, without cancelling the misplaced word, wrote "whose kingdom has no end." Then he left out the words, "and in the Holy Spirit," wrote "the Lord," and omitted the phrase "the Giver of life." After writing "who is derived from the Father," he omitted the words "who together with the Father and the Son is worshipped and glorified."

950 Reading, with ed. Leiden, *takallamat*, rather than MSS *tamallakat* (took possession).

951 The same figure is given in al-Masʿūdī, *Murūj*, 2:327 (§ 748), and in al-Bīrūnī, *Āthār*, 95. In fact, his reign fell in parts of 17 calendar years, but he died on 17 January 395, a few days short of the beginning of the 17th year of his rule.

952 Theodosius the Younger (grandson, not nephew of Theodosius the Elder) ruled from 402 to 408 as co-emperor with Arcadius, and from 408 to 450 alone. Al-Yaʿqūbī does not mention the intervening reign of Arcadius. Al-Masʿūdī's figure of 42 years in *Murūj*, 2:329 (§ 750) for the reign of Theodosius II is accurate; al-Yaʿqūbī's figure of 27 years is wrong. Valentinian (if the reading is correct) would refer to the emperor of the West, Valentinian III, who ruled from 425 to 455.

953 The text seems to have been clumsily abbreviated at this point. One would expect something like, "and man perfect in his substance and nature." The next word in the manu-

being; and the mother gave birth to a human being; she did not give birth to God. Cyril said to him: "If it is as you say, whoever worships Christ is an evildoer, because he will have worshipped both an eternal and a temporal; while whoever refrains from worshipping him has become an infidel, for he will have refrained from worshipping the Eternal, even as he has refrained from worshipping the temporal. And whoever worships the God, to the exclusion of the human being, is not worshipping Christ, because Christ is not entitled to be called Christ with regard to one of his aspects to the exclusion of the other." He upheld the necessity of this to those in attendance. [Opposed to him was][954] the Patriarch | of Antioch. Nestorius said, "The Patriarch of Antioch holds what I hold."[955] Nestorius fled to the land of Iraq; and so the Nestorians came to be in Iraq, and, instead of the patriarch, they took as their head a catholicos. Those at the council dispersed on that result. The reign of Theodosius the Younger was twenty-seven years. 1:175

Then Marcian became ruler. In his time the fourth assembly took place.[956] The reason for it was that Eutyches, the leader of the Jacobites, held that Christ was only one substance and only one nature.[957] He was condemned by the Christians. Six hundred and thirty bishops gathered in Constantinople.[958] They disputed with Eutyches and said to him: "If Christ is, as you claim, one single nature, then the eternal nature is (the same as) the temporal nature; and if the eternal is of the temporal, then he who has never ceased to be is (the same as) he who once was not." He did not, however, retract his doctrine, so they anathematized him. He made his way to Egypt and Alexandria—he was a physician—and there he remained. The reign of Marcian was five years.[959]

After him Leo and Anthemius ruled for seventeen years.[960]

---

scripts, *fa-l-ibn* (for the Son) may be a remnant of the original text. The Leiden editor emended it to *fa-l-āb* (for the Father).

954 Added by the Leiden editor.

955 The text has either been corrupted in translation or badly condensed from a more detailed source or, perhaps, both.

956 The Fourth Ecumenical Council, held at Chalcedon, in Asia Minor, in 451.

957 For "Eutyches," the manuscripts read "Alṭarsiyūs," which the Leiden editor suggests reading as Thracius. However, the major historical exponent of what came to be known as the Monophysite position was Eutyches, and the name has been restored here.

958 The council actually took place at Chalcedon.

959 He actually reigned from 25 August 450 to 27 January 457.

960 Leo the Thracian ruled the Eastern empire from 7 February 457 to 18 January 474; Anthemius ruled the Western empire from 12 April 467 to 11 July 472.

Then Zeno ruled for eighteen years.[961]

Then Anastasius ruled.[962] During his reign the fifth assembly of the Christians took place.[963] This was because certain leaders of the Christians held that Christ's body was a phantasm, not real.[964] They assembled because of this and said, "If his body is a phantasm, his[965] action must be a phantasm, not real; but this is more like the doctrine of the Sophists than that of the Christians." Those who held this were cursed, and the Christians disavowed them. The reign of
1:176 Anastasius was | twenty-seven years.

[…][966]

Then Yūsṭūs II ruled for twenty-nine years. Muḥammad, the Messenger of God—may God bless him and grant him peace—was born during his time.[967]

Then Yūsṭūs III ruled for twenty years.[968]

---

961 Al-Yaʿqūbī omits the ten-month reign of Leo II in 474, between the reigns of Leo I and Zeno. Al-Masʿūdī, *Murūj*, 2:330 (§752), mentions it, but al-Bīrūnī omits it. Zeno the Isaurian ruled from 9 February 474 to 9 April 491. The more nearly correct 17 years for the length of his reign is given by al-Masʿūdī, *Murūj*, 2:330 (§752) and by al-Bīrūnī, *Āthār*, 95.

962 Anastasius I, who ruled from 11 April 491 to 9 July 518. Although the name is badly deformed at first (in M it looks like Asṭūs when it first appears), it is clearly written as Asṭasiyūs at the end of the paragraph. The text of al-Yaʿqūbī as preserved in the MSS is clearly defective here: first, the Fifth Ecumenical Council took place in 553, during the reign of Justinian, not that of Anastasius; second, al-Yaʿqūbī follows his account of this reign with accounts of "Yūsṭūs II" and "Yūsṭūs III," with no mention of a "Yūsṭūs I." Historically, the emperors after Anastasius I were Justin I (518–527), Justinian I (527–565), and Justin II (565–578). Apparently, Justin I has been omitted (the Leiden editor marks a presumed lacuna before "Yūsṭūs II"), and the names of both Justinian and Justin have been rendered in Arabic as "Yūsṭūs." Al-Masʿūdī, *Murūj*, 2:331–332 (§752–754) renders the sequence correctly.

963 That is, the Fifth Ecumenical Council (Constantinople II), which took place in 553. Al-Yaʿqūbī's dating is wrong, as the council took place during the reign of Justinian.

964 Arabic, *kāna khayālan ʿalā ghayri ḥaqīqatin*. The reference to "certain leaders of the Christians" (*qawman min ruʾāsāʾ al-naṣārā*) might be a reference to the authors of the so-called Three Chapters condemned by the council (Theodore of Mopsuestia, Theodoret of Cyrrhus, and Ibas of Edessa).

965 Or, "its," as the pronoun could refer either to Christ or to "body," which is masculine in Arabic. It is unclear who these "sophists" were (if the Leiden editor's reading of *al-sūfisṭāʾiyya* is correct; in M the letter *f* is given a second point, which makes it a *q*, so the original word may have been different).

966 Lacuna inferred by the Leiden editor.

967 If Yūsṭūs II is Justinian I, this would place Muḥammad's birth before 565, which is early, as Islamic tradition says that he died in June 632, at the age of 63 (presumably lunar years, equal to 61.12 solar years), which implies a birth year of 570, in the reign of Justin II.

968 That is, Justin II, ruled 565–578.

Then Tiberius ruled for four years.[969]

[…] In his days the sixth assembly of the Christians took place.[970] This was because Cyrus of Alexandria had claimed that Christ was one will and one action. This, they said, was similar to what the Jacobites held.[971] They assembled for this and gave their assent to the patriarch of Rome—he had written a letter, but did not attend.[972] The Christians had no assembly afterward.[973]

[…] The reign of Heraclius and his son Constantine was thirty-two years.[974]

Then Constantine ruled for eighteen years.[975]

Then the Patriarch of Rome ruled for three years.[976]

Then Philippicus ruled for four years.[977]

---

969 That is, Tiberius II, ruled September 578 to August 582.

970 As the Sixth Ecumenical Council did not take place until 680–681, during the reign of Constantine IV, one must assume a lacuna before these words, but the mention of the reign of Heraclius and Constantine (presumably Constantine III) after the account of this council seems to indicate that the account of this council was at first a marginal note and was later copied into the text at the wrong place.

971 "They said," follows the reading of M; ed. Leiden has "he said." At issue was the so-called Monothelete doctrine, declared heretical at the council. It had been accepted and defended by Cyrus of Alexandria (died c. 640) as a way of bridging the gap between those who accepted the Chalcedonian doctrine of two natures (divine and human) united but distinct in Christ and the Monophysites (Jacobites), who held that the incarnate Christ had only one nature (divine and human).

972 That is, Pope Agatho.

973 Al-Yaʿqūbī omits mention of the Seventh Ecumenical Council held at Nicaea in 787, probably because his source for the list of Roman rulers ends with Constantine V (ruled 741 to 775).

974 Although neither the MSS nor ed. Leiden indicate a lacuna before this sentence, stylistic grounds point to one, as the sentence conforms to the formula that al-Yaʿqūbī uses at the end of each reign. Heraclius reigned from 5 October 610 to 11 February 641; his son Constantine III, who had been co-emperor since 614, ruled after his father's death only until May 641.

975 It is not clear whether the reference is to Constans II, whose regnal name was Constantine and who reigned from September 641 to September 668, or to Constantine IV, who ruled from September 668 to September 685. The figure of 18 years suggests the latter. In any event, al-Yaʿqūbī's list of rulers becomes unreliable at this point.

976 A possible reference to the reign of Leontius (695–698), although it is unclear why he should be called "Patriarch of Rome," but for the resemblance of his name to that of Pope Leo I of Rome, whose doctrinal letter played an important role in the Council of Chalcedon in 451.

977 The name has been badly distorted in transmission, but one can restore the reading of M

Then Leo and his son Constantine ruled for twenty-nine years.[978]

The months of the Romans, on the basis of which they make their calculations and fix their dates, are twelve. The first of them is Kānūn II, which they call Yanwāris (Ianuarius) in the Roman language.[979] It is their New Year. These are the names of their months: Yanwāris (Ianuarius), which is Kānūn II; [Fabrāris][980] (Februarius), which is Shubāṭ; [Marṭis][981] (Martius), which is Ādhār; Abrilis (Aprilis), which is Nīsān; Māyus (Maius), which is Ayyār; [Jūnis][982]
1:177 (Iunius), which is Ḥazīrān; [Jūlis][983] (Iulius), which is | Tammūz; Aghusṭus (Augustus), which is Āb; [Sittanbris][984] (Septembris/September), which is Aylūl; [Uktubris][985] (Octobris/October), which is Tishrīn [I]; [Nuwunbris][986] (Novembris/November), which is Tishrīn II; and [Dikimbris][987] (Decembris/December), which is Kānūn I.

Their kingdom stretched from the Euphrates to Alexandria, all of which became part of the land of Islam, besides that part of the land of the Romans that remains in their hands until the present day. The greatest of their cities were al-Ruhā[988] in the Jazīra, in (the area called) Diyār Muḍar; Anṭākiya,[989]

---

to something like *F.l.y.b.gh.r.w.s.* The reference would be to the reign of Philippicus from 711 to 713.

978 This must refer to the reigns of Leo III the Isaurian (March 717 to June 741) and his son Constantine V (June 741 to September 775), although the dates fit neither the individual reigns nor their combined total.

979 It is unclear whether by *al-Rūmiyya* al-Yaʿqūbī means Latin or Greek. In any case, the Greek month names for the Julian calendar were simply an adaptation of the Latin names, with minor adjustments for the phonetics of the Greek language. The translation therefore reproduces the Arabic form found in the manuscripts and adds the Latin form in parentheses. The names are then given in the form current among Syriac-speaking Christians, which became the normal way of referring to the Julian months in Arabic.

980 Garbled by the copyist into something like *Bilyās*. The usual Arabic form, found for example in al-Bīrūnī, *Āthār*, has been substituted in the translation.

981 Garbled into something like *Narlis* in the manuscripts.

982 Written as Jūlis (that is, Julius, July) in the MSS, although the Syriac/Arabic name Ḥazīrān following it clearly refers to June. This miscopying has led to misidentifying the subsequent months and duplication of October in the manuscripts. The translation corrects these mistakes, which are probably the fault of a copyist.

983 Given as Aghusṭus because of the copyist's error.

984 Given as Uktubris because of the copyist's error.

985 Given as N.b.w.s, presumably for something like Nuwunbris.

986 Given as Ukbris, presumably for Uktubris.

987 Truncated into Mūris in the manuscripts.

988 Ancient Edessa.

989 Ancient Antioch.

where, in the Church of al-Qusyān, are the chair of Peter and the hand of John the son of Zacharia.[990] It is the fourth see and great patriarchate.[991] Within the part of the Romans' kingdom that came under Islam is the Jazīra, including Ḥarrān; al-Ruhā and all its dependencies; Bālis;[992] Sumaysāṭ;[993] Malaṭiya; Adana; Ṭarsūs; the military district of Qinnasrīn; al-ʿAwāṣim[994] and all its dependencies; the military district of Ḥimṣ (the city of Ḥimṣ was a noteworthy city in the kingdom of the Romans). Also, al-Lādhiqiyya, which is a dependency of Ḥimṣ; the military district of Damascus (the Roman king's governors there were the Āl Jafna, of the tribe of Ghassān); the military district of the Jordan, which also belonged to them and whose governors on behalf of the Roman king were from the Ghassānid Āl Jafna; and the military district of Palestine, with its dependencies. Also, Tinnīs, Dimyāṭ, and Alexandria. This was the exclusive kingdom of the Romans and became part of the land of Islam.

Also theirs was territory beyond the pass,[995] stretching toward the lands of the Slavs,[996] the Alans,[997] and the Franks.[998]

Among the famous, well-known cities in the land of the Romans are cities such as Rome, Nicaea, Constantinople, Amaseia,[999] Kharshana, Qurra, Amorium, Ṣumālu, al-Qalamiyya, Selinus, Heracleia, Siqilliyya, Falaṭīna, Antioch

---

990 The Church of al-Qusyān is the Church of Cassianus, later known as the Church of St. Peter, which became the main church of Antioch, replacing the older cathedral that was destroyed by an earthquake in 588. It is unclear whether the chair (Arabic *kursī*) is to be interpreted as a physical relic—the parallel with the hand of John the Baptist suggests as much—or simply as a bishop's throne such as would be found in any cathedral church (the next part of the sentence suggests this interpretation). The church was supposedly on the site where the Apostle Peter restored the son of a certain King Qusyān to life. See Hugh Kennedy, "Antioch: from Byzantium to Islam," in *The City in Late Antiquity*, 185–188.

991 That is, following Rome, Constantinople, and Alexandria.

992 A now ruined town in northern Syria on the west bank of the Euphrates. See the article by J. Sourdel-Thomine in *EI*², s.v. Bālis.

993 Ancient Samosata; modern Turkish Samsat; see the article by C. P. Haase in *EI*², s.v. Sumaysāṭ.

994 Al-ʿAwāṣim was the name of a series of frontier fortresses along the border between the caliphate and the Byzantine empire. See the article by M. Canard in *EI*², s.v. al-ʿAwāṣim.

995 Arabic, *al-darb*; apparently referring to the Cilician Gates.

996 Arabic, *Ṣaqāliba* (sg. *Ṣaqlabī*) derives from a Greek form Σκλαβηνός, with an older form Σλάβος derived from the self-designation of the Slavic peoples. See the article by P. B. Golden, P. Guichard, and Mohamed Meouak in *EI*², s.v. al-Ṣaḳāliba.

997 An Iranian people of the northern Caucasus.

998 Arabic, *Ifranj*, a general designation for people of western Europe.

999 Modern Amasya, a provincial capital in north-central Turkey.

1:178 the Burnt, Dahīrnāṭa, | Moloe, Seleucia, Smyrna, Iconium, [...], [...], [...], and Salonica.[1000]

The Kings of Persia

Persia claims for its kings many things of the sort that cannot be accepted. These include physical excrescences, such as one person's having numerous mouths and eyes, another's having a face of copper, and another's having on his shoulders two snakes that devoured men's brains. To certain persons they attribute great longevity or deny their death—and similar things that minds reject and that can be treated as vanities, jest, and unreal. Persians of intellect and knowledge, those of nobility and high family, their princes and their gentry, and people who transmit reliable accounts and possess education have never treated such things as real or true or affirmed them.[1001]

We find that they date the kingdom of Persia only from the time of Ardashīr Bābakān.[1002] According to them, their earliest kings, those of the first kingdom, which existed before Ardashīr, were:[1003] Kayūmarth, who ruled for seventy years; Ūshhanj Fīshdād, who ruled for forty years; Ṭahmūrath, who ruled

1000 The list of cities is badly copied, with most of the place names given in undotted script. Where the forms are too ambiguous to be read even conjecturally, we have inserted [...].

1001 Unfortunately, al-Yaʿqūbī does not list his sources for Persian history, which consisted of Middle Persian works translated into Arabic, most of which do not survive in their original Persian or Arabic forms. The following works deal with the sources used by Arabic historians for reconstructing the history of pre-Islamic Iran: T. Nöldeke, *Geschichte der Perser und Araber zur Zeit der Sasaniden* (especially the "Einleitung," xiii–xxviii); A. Christensen, *L'Iran sous les Sassanides* (especially the "Introduction," 59–74); and C. E. Bosworth, *The History of al-Ṭabarī*, v (not only the introduction, but the extensive footnotes on individual reigns).

1002 That is, from the reign of the founder of the Sasanian dynasty, Ardashīr I (ruled 224–242). The meaning is not that the Persians were ignorant of earlier kings but that the Sasanians dated events from the accession of Ardashīr.

1003 Similar lists of the so-called Pīshdādiān and Kayāniān kings may be found in al-Bīrūnī, *Āthār*, 99ff.; al-Ṭabarī, *Taʾrīkh*, 1:17 (Jayūmart), 147–149 (Jayūmart), 154–155 (Jayūmart, Hōshank/Ōshahanj Pēshdādh), 170–172 (Ōshahanj), 174–176 (Ṭahmūrath), 179–183 (Jamshēd, al-Ḍaḥḥāk), 201–211 (al-Ḍaḥḥāk, Frēdūn/Afrīdūn), 226–230 (Frēdūn/Afrīdūn), 430–440 (Manūshihr, Afrāsiyāb), 528–535 (Afrāsiyāb, Zaw b. Ṭahmāsb, Kayqubādh), 597–604 (Kay Kāwūs), 604–619 (Kaykhusraw, Luhrāsb), 645 (Luhrāsb), 648–649 (Bishtāsb), 675–683 (Bishtāsb), 686–688 (Ardashīr Bahman), 688–690 (Khu-

for thirty years; Jam Shād, who ruled for seven hundred years; al-Ḍaḥḥāk, who ruled for one thousand years; Afrīdūn, who ruled for five hundred years; Mānūjihr, who ruled for one hundred and twenty years; Afrāsiyāb, king of the Turks,[1004] who ruled for one hundred and twenty years; Zaw Ṭahmāsb,[1005] who ruled for five years; Kayqubādh, who ruled for one hundred years; Kay Kāwūs, who ruled for one hundred and twenty years; Kay Khusraw,[1006] who ruled for sixty years; Kay Luhrāsb, who ruled for one hundred and twenty | years; Kay 1:179
Bishtāsb, who ruled for one hundred and twelve years; Kay Ardashīr, who ruled for one hundred and twelve years; Khumānī, daughter of Jihrazād,[1007] who ruled for thirty years; and Dārā, son of Jihrazād, who ruled for twelve years. Alexander, who is called Dhū l-Qarnayn, slew him.[1008] Then the kingdom of Persia became divided and was ruled by kings called the Party Kings.[1009] Their royal residence was located at Balkh. Genealogists assert that they were descendants of Gomer, son of Japheth, son of Noah. They followed the religion of the Ṣābians, venerating the sun, the moon, fire, and the seven stars; they were not Zoroastrians, but followed the ways of the Ṣābians.[1010] Their spoken and writ-

mānī, Dārā/Darius); 692–701 (Dārā/Darius); al-Masʿūdī, *Murūj*, 2:105–132 (§ 530–556); and Ibn Qutayba, *al-Maʿārif* (ed. Cairo), 652–667.

1004 Sic, but cf. al-Masʿūdī, *Murūj*, 2:117–118 (§ 540): "Farāsiyāb's birthplace was in the land of the Turks, and therefore some authors of books and works of history, among others, have mistakenly alleged that he was a Turk."

1005 As emended by the Leiden editor, probably to be interpreted as "Zaw [son of] Ṭahmāsb," as in al-Masʿūdī, *Murūj*, 2:118 (§ 540). M has *w.r.b.h.m.ā.* Al-Bīrūnī, *Āthār*, 104, reads Zāb *and* Garshāsp, marking them as "the two companions," and giving them a joint reign of five years.

1006 As emended by the Leiden editor, in agreement with al-Bīrūnī, who also gives Kay Khusraw a reign of 60 years. M reads Kay Jūbīn, best explained as a copyist's error.

1007 That is, the daughter of Ardashīr Bahman and Jihrazād; however, al-Ṭabarī, *Taʾrīkh*, 1:689, gives Shahrāzād (a variant of Jihrazād/Chihrāzād, "of noble countenance") as the nickname of Khumānī, and al-Yaʿqūbī's naming of Jihrazād as the mother of Dārā seems to agree with this version. Note that Khumānī (the form of her name in al-Yaʿqūbī and al-Ṭabarī) appears as Ḥumāyā in al-Masʿūdī; the two forms can be read from the same (undotted) Arabic ductus.

1008 Al-Yaʿqūbī conflates Dārā, son of Bahman, and Dārā (Darius), son of Dārā; the latter was killed by Alexander. Cf. al-Masʿūdī, *Murūj*, 2:129 (§ 553), and al-Bīrūnī, *Āthār*, 105.

1009 Arabic, *mulūk al-ṭawāʾif*; other possible translations include "regional kings" or "petty princes." Cf. al-Ṭabarī, *Taʾrīkh*, 1:704ff., and al-Masʿūdī, *Murūj*, 2:132–138 (§ 557–562), both of whom devote considerable space to Iranian history in the Parthian/Arsacid period, between the death of Alexander and the rise of the Sasanian dynasty under Ardashīr I, who killed the last of the Arsacids in battle in 224.

1010 That is, they were not Zoroastrians (Arabic, Majūs, "Magians") but followed a form of

ten language was Syriac. Here is an illustration of the Syriac script.[1011] They had historical reports; these were recorded, but, as we have seen, most people reject them and consider them abhorrent; we have omitted them because our policy is to leave out everything abhorrent.

The Second Kingdom: From Ardashīr Bābakān

Ardashīr became king.[1012] He was the first of the Persian kings to profess the Zoroastrian religion.[1013] His royal residence was in Iṣṭakhr.[1014] When one of the districts of Fārs refused him obedience, he fought its people until he conquered it. He made his way to Iṣfahān, then to al-Ahwāz, and then to Maysān,[1015] after which he returned to Fārs. He made war on a king named Ardawān and killed

---

astral religion similar to that of the so-called Ṣābians, later survivors of Hellenistic paganism at Ḥarrān in Syria. On the identity of the Ṣābiʾūn, who are mentioned three times in the Qurʾān, see the article in *EI*², s.v. Ṣābiʾ. The assertion that the Party Kings were not Zoroastrians reflects Sasanian anti-Parthian propaganda branding the Parthians as unorthodox in religion and oversimplifies the historical record.

1011 The surviving MSS omit this.

1012 For an overview of the reign of Ardashīr I, the founder of the Sasanian dynasty, see A. Christensen, *L'Iran sous les Sassanides*, 84–96. Cf. al-Ṭabarī, *Taʾrīkh*, 1:813–822 (trans. Bosworth, *The History of al-Ṭabarī*, V, 2–22). For parallel Arabic accounts of this period of Iranian history, see al-Ṭabarī, *Taʾrīkh*, 1:813–1067 (trans. Bosworth as *The History of al-Ṭabarī*, V); al-Masʿūdī, *Murūj*, 2:151–241 (§ 576–663); al-Dīnawarī, *al-Akhbār al-ṭiwāl*, 44–46; Ibn Qutayba, *al-Maʿārif*, 653–667.

1013 Arabic, *awwalu mulūki l-fursi l-mutamajjisa* (the first of the "Magianizing" kings of the Persians). Historically, Ardashīr was not the first Persian king to profess Zoroastrianism; elements of what later became orthodox Zoroastrianism can be traced to Achaemenid times. It is correct that, under the Sasanians, the Zoroastrian clergy became a state-supported hierarchy; Zoroastrian scriptures and legal texts were codified; orthodoxy was defined in contrast to doctrines branded as heresies; and nonconformists were subjected to varying degrees of persecution. See the chapter on Zoroastrianism as a state religion in A. Christensen, *L'Iran sous les Sassanides*, 141–178, and the article by Joseph Wiesehöfer, in *Encyclopædia Iranica*, s.v. Ardašīr.

1014 A town in Fārs province, now in ruins, north of the ancient capital of Persepolis. According to al-Ṭabarī, *Taʾrīkh*, 1:814, Sāsān, the grandfather of Ardashīr I, was superintendent of the fire temple of the goddess Anāhīd in the town of Iṣṭakhr. See the article by M. Streck and G. C. Miles in *EI*², s.v. Iṣṭakhr.

1015 A region on the lower Tigris, in southeastern Iraq. See the article by M. Streck and M. Morony in *EI*², s.v. Maysān.

him.[1016] Ardashīr received the title King of Kings (Shāhanshāh) and built a fire-temple at Ardashīr Khurrah.[1017] Then he made his way to al-Jazīra,[1018] Armenia, and Azerbaijan, after which he made his way to the Sawād[1019] of Iraq and settled people there. Having made his way to Khurāsān, he conquered some of its districts. After he had consolidated control of the land, he named his son Sābūr heir apparent, crowned him, and styled him king. Ardashīr died after a reign of fourteen years.[1020]

Sābūr[1021] son of Ardashīr became king. He raided the country of the Romans, 1:180
conquered several of its provinces, and took many Romans prisoner. Then he built the city of Jundaysābūr[1022] and settled it with Roman prisoners. The chief of the Romans constructed for him the bridge over Tustar's river, whose width was a thousand cubits.[1023] It was in the days of Sābūr son of Ardashīr that Mānī son of Ḥammād, the *zindīq*, appeared.[1024] He called on Sābūr to profess dualism

1016 At the Battle of Hurmuzjān, in 224, Ardashīr killed the last reigning Arsacid, Ardawān (Artabanus). Cf. al-Ṭabarī, *Taʾrīkh*, 1:818–819; al-Masʿūdī, *Murūj*, 2:135 (§ 559) and 161 (§ 585); al-Dīnawarī, *al-Akhbār al-ṭiwāl*, 44.

1017 The name means "Glory of Ardashīr." The town, originally called Gūr, is located south of Iṣṭakhr, at the location of modern Fīrūzābād. See the article by L. Lockhart in *EI*², s.v. Fīrūzābād.

1018 That is, the northern part of Mesopotamia.

1019 Sawād (literally, the black/dark lands) refers to the southern part of Mesopotamia.

1020 The crowning of Sābūr as heir apparent—indeed, as co-monarch—probably took place in 240, and Ardashīr's death probably took place early in 242; see the article by Joseph Wiesehöfer, in *Encyclopædia Iranica*, s.v. Ardašīr.

1021 Middle Persian, Shāpūr: Shāpūr I, ruled 242–270; cf. al-Ṭabarī, *Taʾrīkh*, 1:822–831 (trans. Bosworth, *The History of al-Ṭabarī*, v, 23–39); al-Masʿūdī, *Murūj*, 2:163–166 (§ 589–593); al-Dīnawarī, *al-Akhbār al-ṭiwāl*, 48.

1022 Middle Persian, Gōndēshāpūr, in Khūzistān. The city later became famous as a center of medical studies; cf. the article by Cl. Huart and Aydin Sayili in *EI*², s.v. Gōndēshāpūr.

1023 Al-Yaʿqūbī's *raʾīs al-Rūm* (the chief of the Romans) is ambiguous, but other accounts attribute the dam's construction explicitly to the Roman emperor Valerian, who was captured by the Persians in 260 and was set to work constructing the dam with Roman laborers; cf. al-Ṭabarī, *Taʾrīkh*, 1:827 (trans. Bosworth, *The History of al-Ṭabarī*, v, 29–31); al-Dīnawarī, *al-Akhbār al-ṭiwāl*, 49.

1024 On the life and doctrines of Mānī, the founder of the Manichaean religion, see the article by Werner Sundermann in *Encyclopædia Iranica*, s.v. Mānī. The designation of Mānī's father as Ḥammād (if one can trust the reading) is unique to al-Yaʿqūbī; other sources give Fāttik/Fātak or some variation on it. The word *zindīq*, used later loosely for a believer in any of various heretical beliefs, here designates any follower of the teachings of Mānī, that is, a Manichaean. See the article by F. C. De Blois in *EI*², s.v. Zindīḳ; and the article by C. E. Bosworth in *EI*², s.v. Mānī b. Fāttik.

and found fault with his religious beliefs. Sābūr was swayed by him.

Mānī taught that the governor of the world is two—two eternal things, light and darkness, two creators: a creator of good and a creator of evil. Darkness and light, each in itself, is a name for five elements: color, taste, odor, touch, and sound. Both of them are all-hearing, all-seeing, and all-knowing. Everything good and beneficial springs from light; everything harmful and painful springs from darkness. They were originally unmixed, but then they became mixed, the proof of that being that form did not exist but then came to be.[1025] It was the darkness that initiated admixture with light; they had been in mutual contact, like shadow and sunlight, the proof of that being the impossibility of the generation of something from nothing. Proof that it was darkness that initiated admixture with light is that, because darkness, by the admixture of obscurity with light, corrupts it, it is inconceivable that light should initiate the admixture, as light has good as its consequence. Proof that they are two eternals, good and evil, is that, because one finds that a single element does not generate two diverse actions—for example, fire, which is hot and burning, does not generate cooling, and that which generates cooling does not generate warming—therefore that which generates good does not generate evil, and that which generates evil does not generate good. Proof that they are two living and active entities is that good can be demonstrated to have an action and evil
1:181 can be demonstrated | to have an action.

Sābūr assented to this doctrine of Mānī's and enjoined the people of his kingdom to adopt it. This was grievous to them, so the sages of his kingdom assembled to turn Sābūr away from it, but he would not do so.

Mānī composed books asserting dualism. Among the works he composed was the book that he titled *The Treasure of the Living*. In it he described the luminous purity and dark corruption in the soul, and he ascribed evil actions to the darkness. In another of his books, which he titled *Shābūraqān*,[1026] he described the pure soul and the soul that has been contaminated by demons and defects. He made the firmament to be a plane, and he said that knowledge was atop a sloping mountain, over which the highest firmament turns. Another work was a book that he titled *The Book of Guidance and Governance*. There were also the twenty-two *Gospels*,[1027] to each of which he gave a letter of the

---

1025 The translation of the second part of the sentence depends on a conjectural emendation by the Leiden editor.

1026 Middle Persian, *Šābuhragān* (The Book of Shāpūr), named for the king to which it was dedicated.

1027 Arabic, *Injīl*; the manuscripts read "twelve," but the reading has been emended here on the basis of what is known about the work, each chapter of which was labeled with

alphabet as a title. He mentioned prayer and the deeds that must be practiced for the salvation of the spirit. There were also *The Book of Time*;[1028] *The Book of Secrets*, in which he inveighed against the signs of the prophets; *The Book of Giants*; and many other books and treatises.

Sābūr continued to adhere to this doctrine for ten years or so. Then the Mōbadh[1029] came to him and said: "This man has corrupted your religion. Arrange a meeting between him and me, so that I can dispute him." Sābūr brought the two together, and the Mōbadh had the better of the argument. Sābūr returned from dualism to the religion of the Magi and sought to kill Mānī, who fled to India, where he remained until Sābūr died.

Hurmuz,[1030] son of Sābūr, became king after Sābūr. He was a courageous man. It was he who built the city of Rāmhurmuz.[1031] He did not live long; his reign was only one year.

Bahrām,[1032] son of Hurmuz, then became king. He was infatuated with 1:182
slaves and entertainments. Mānī's disciples wrote to Mānī, saying that a king tender in years and much preoccupied had come to the throne. So Mānī came to the land of Fārs; his activity became known and his whereabouts apparent. Bahrām summoned him and questioned him about his activity, and Mānī gave him an account. Bahrām arranged a meeting between him and the Mōbadh, and Mānī disputed with him. Then the Mōbadh said to him, "Let some lead be melted for me and for you and let it be poured on my stomach and on yours; whichever of us is unharmed is in possession of the truth." Mānī said, "This is a deed of darkness." At this, Bahrām ordered him to be imprisoned and said to him, "Tomorrow I will summon you and kill you in a way that no one has

one of the twenty-two letters of the Aramaic alphabet.

1028 Arabic, *Kitāb al-Dahr*; this title is omitted in ed. Leiden.

1029 That is, the chief priest of the Zoroastrian religion.

1030 Better known by the Iranian form of his name as Hormizd I, ruled 270–271; cf. al-Ṭabarī, *Taʾrīkh*, 1:831–833 (trans. Bosworth, *The History of al-Ṭabarī*, V, 40–43); al-Masʿūdī, *Murūj*, 2:166 (§ 593).

1031 A town and district in Khūzistān, in southwestern Persia, 55 miles southeast of Ahwāz and 65 miles south-southeast of Shūshtar, at the intersection of the roads from Ahwāz, Shūshtar, Iṣfahān, and Fārs. See the article by V. Minorsky and C. E. Bosworth in *EI*², s.v. Rām-Hurmuz.

1032 That is, Bahrām I, reigned 271–274; cf. al-Ṭabarī, *Taʾrīkh*, 1:833–834 (trans. Bosworth, *The History of al-Ṭabarī*, V, 43–45); al-Masʿūdī, *Murūj*, 2:167 (§ 594), al-Dīnawarī, *al-Akhbār al-ṭiwāl*, 49. As Bosworth notes in his translation of al-Ṭabarī, the Arabic sources, including al-Yaʿqūbī, with the exception of one account in al-Masʿūdī, make Bahrām I the son of Hurmuz (see Bosworth, 45, n. 134, and 48, n. 140), rather than the son of Sābūr, as is the consensus of modern historians.

ever been killed before you." Mānī did not cease being flayed that night until his soul departed. In the morning, Bahrām called for him, but they found that he had already died. Bahrām ordered his head to be cut off and had his body stuffed with straw. He persecuted his adherents and killed a great number of them. Bahrām son of Hurmuz reigned for three years.

Then Bahrām,[1033] son of Bahrām, became king. He reigned for seventeen years.

After him, his son, Bahrām,[1034] son of Bahrām, son of Bahrām, became king; he ruled for four years.

Then his brother, Narsī,[1035] son of Bahrām, reigned for nine years.

Then Hurmuz,[1036] son of Narsī, reigned for nine years. A son was born to him, whom he named Sābūr[1037] and made heir apparent. Hurmuz died while Sābūr was still an infant in the cradle. The people of his kingdom watched over him until he reached adolescence and young manhood. Then he displayed haughtiness and aggressiveness; he raided the country of the Arabs and stopped up their wells with earth. The king of the Romans, Julian, attacked him, aided by Arabs of all the tribes. The Arab tribes turned on Sābūr as fast as they could and attacked him in his capital;[1038] he fled, leaving his kingdom vacant, so that his
1:183 city and treasuries were plundered. | Then, however, a stray arrow killed Julian, king of the Romans. The Romans made Jovian king, and he made peace with Sābūr. Sābūr remained hostile to the Arabs: whenever he got hold of one of

1033 That is, Bahrām II, reigned 274–291; cf. al-Ṭabarī, *Taʾrīkh*, 1:834–835 (trans. Bosworth, *The History of al-Ṭabarī*, V, 46); al-Masʿūdī, *Murūj*, 2:168–174 (§ 595–599).

1034 That is, Bahrām III; his reign was probably much shorter than the four years attributed to him here. Bosworth, *The History of al-Ṭabarī*, V, 47, n. 139, gives evidence that he reigned only four months, in the early part of 292, until he was deposed by his great-uncle Narsī; cf. also al-Masʿūdī, *Murūj*, 2:174 (§ 600).

1035 The pronoun in "his brother" is ambiguous. One might understand the text to mean that Narsī was the son of Bahrām II and brother of Bahrām III, but the wording "son of Bahrām" (without a further "son of Bahrām") might imply that Narsī was the son of Bahrām I and brother of Bahrām II. This is how Bosworth understands the parallel text in al-Ṭabarī, *Taʾrīkh*, 1:835 (trans. 48). The consensus of modern historians is that Narsī was in fact the son of Sābūr I, hence a brother of Bahrām I. This would make him the great-uncle of Bahrām III. He reigned 292–302; see Bosworth, *The History of al-Ṭabarī*, V, 48, n. 140; al-Masʿūdī, *Murūj*, 2:174 (§ 600).

1036 Hormizd II, reigned 302–309; cf. al-Ṭabarī, *Taʾrīkh*, 1:835–836 (trans. Bosworth, *The History of al-Ṭabarī*, V, 49–50); al-Masʿūdī, *Murūj*, 2:174–175 (§ 600).

1037 That is, Shāpūr II, reigned 309–379; cf. al-Ṭabarī, *Taʾrīkh*, 1:836–846 (trans. Bosworth, *The History of al-Ṭabarī*, V, 50–67); al-Masʿūdī, *Murūj*, 2:175–188 (§ 601–611).

1038 That is, Ctesiphon; cf. al-Dīnawarī, *al-Akhbār al-ṭiwāl*, 51–52.

them, he dislocated the man's shoulder.[1039] As a result, Sābūr came to be called Dhū l-Aktāf (The Man of the Shoulders). He reigned for seventy-two years.

Sābūr's brother, Ardashīr,[1040] son of Hurmuz, then became king. He conducted himself badly, killing their nobles and magnates, and he was therefore deposed, after he had reigned for four years.

The Persians made Sābūr, son of Sābūr, king.[1041] The deposed Ardashīr submitted to him and offered him his obedience. A large tent collapsed upon Sābūr and killed him.[1042] He had reigned for five years.

Bahrām,[1043] son of Sābūr, became king after Sābūr. He wrote to the farthest reaches of the kingdom, promising the people justice, equity, and benevolence. He continued to rule for eleven years; then some men rebelled against him and killed him.

Then Yazdajird, son of Sābūr, became king.[1044] He was harsh, coarse, arrogant, and ill-behaved—of little good and much evil—and he subjected people to the worst kind of abuse. Then a horse kicked him and killed him.[1045] He had reigned for twenty-one years.

Then Bahrām Jūr, son of Yazdajird, became king.[1046] He had grown up in the land of the Arabs: his father had sent him off to al-Nuʿmān; the Arab women

---

1039 Arabic, *khalaʿa katifahu*, could mean either "dislocated his shoulder" or "pulled out the shoulder blade." The parallel in al-Ṭabarī, *Taʾrīkh*, 1:844 (*nazaʿa aktāf ruʾasāʾihim*, "tore out the shoulder blades of their leaders") points to the more gruesome interpretation.

1040 Ardashīr II, son of Hormizd II, reigned 379–383; cf. al-Ṭabarī, *Taʾrīkh*, 1:846 (trans. Bosworth, *The History of al-Ṭabarī*, v, 67); al-Masʿūdī, *Murūj*, 2:189 (§ 611).

1041 That is, Shāpūr III, son of Shāpūr II, reigned 383–388; cf. al-Ṭabarī, *Taʾrīkh*, 1:846 (trans. Bosworth, *The History of al-Ṭabarī*, v, 68); al-Masʿūdī, *Murūj*, 2:189 (§ 611).

1042 According to al-Ṭabarī, *Taʾrīkh*, 1:846, this was no accident: "The great men of state and the members of noble houses cut the ropes … and the tent fell down on top of him" (trans. Bosworth, *The History of al-Ṭabarī*, v, 68). Cf. also al-Dīnawarī, *al-Akhbār al-ṭiwāl*, 53, which speaks of "treacherous men."

1043 That is, Bahrām IV, son of Shāpūr II, reigned 388–399; cf. al-Ṭabarī, *Taʾrīkh*, 1:847 (trans. Bosworth, *The History of al-Ṭabarī*, v, 69); al-Masʿūdī, *Murūj*, 2:190 (§ 612).

1044 That is, Yazdajird I (Middle Persian, Yazdgird), son of Shāpūr III, reigned 399–420; cf. al-Ṭabarī, *Taʾrīkh*, 1:847–850; al-Masʿūdī, *Murūj*, 2:190 (§ 612).

1045 In the parallel in al-Ṭabarī, *Taʾrīkh*, 1:850–851 (trans. Bosworth, *The History of al-Ṭabarī*, v, 73), the horse is of supernatural character, sent by God in response to people's complaints, to relieve the Persians of an unjust ruler, and disappears mysteriously after striking Yazdajird.

1046 That is, Bahrām V (reigned 420–438) surnamed Gōr (wild ass), either in reference to his endurance or to his love of hunting. Cf. al-Ṭabarī, *Taʾrīkh*, 1:854–871 (trans. Bosworth, *The History of al-Ṭabarī*, v, 82–106); al-Masʿūdī, *Murūj*, 2:190–193 (§ 612–614). For a discussion of his name, see Bosworth, *The History of al-Ṭabarī*, v, 81, n. 220.

suckled him, and he grew up to have a fine character.[1047] After Yazdajird died, the Persians were loath to appoint any son of Yazdajird because of his bad ways. "As for his son Bahrām," they said, "he has grown up in the land of the Arabs, knowing nothing about kingship," so they decided to make someone else king.[1048] Bahrām then set out accompanied by the Arabs, and when he met the Persians, they were in awe of him. They took the king's crown and the finery that kings wear, set them between two lions, and said to Bahrām and to Kisrā, "Whichever of you takes the crown and finery from between these
1:184 two lions shall be king." They said | to Bahrām, [...].[1049] So he took up a mace, advanced, beat the lions to death, and took the crown and the finery; so they submitted to him and gave him their obedience. He, for his part, promised them benevolence, and he wrote to the farthest reaches of the kingdom promising them the same and informing them of his justice and his intention to bring prosperity to the country. Al-Mundhir b. al-Nuʿmān visited him, and Bahrām raised his rank. Bahrām was a man who loved amusement and neglected his subjects. Once he went in pursuit of animals and amusement and left his brother Narsī as his deputy over the kingdom. When Khāqān, the king of the Turks, learned what sort of man Bahrām was, he became covetous of his kingdom and decided to march against him. When Bahrām learned of this, he marched against Khāqān, killed him, and wrote to his subjects about the victory. Then one day he went out hunting, and while he was intent on pursuing a wild ass, his horse threw him into a place of deep mud and he died. He had ruled for nineteen years.

Then Yazdajird, son of Bahrām, became king; his reign was seventeen years.[1050] This Yazdajird had two sons, one of whom was called Hurmuz and the

---

1047 According to the parallels in al-Ṭabarī, *Taʾrīkh*, 1:855, and al-Dīnawarī, *al-Akhbār al-ṭiwāl*, 53, 57, Bahrām Gōr was educated in the Arabian desert by the Lakhmid ruler of al-Ḥīra, al-Mundhir I (ruled c. 418–462), the son of al-Nuʿmān I (ruled c. 400–418). But al-Yaʿqūbī's narrative, with its later detail of al-Mundhir's journey to Bahrām's court, seems equally plausible.

1048 According to al-Ṭabarī, *Taʾrīkh*, 1:858, and al-Dīnawarī, *al-Akhbār al-ṭiwāl*, 57, the man was named Kisrā/Khusraw and belonged to a collateral branch of the Sasanian family. Al-Yaʿqūbī will mention the name shortly, without explanation. For a discussion of the succession crisis after the death of Yazdajird, see A. Christensen, *L'Iran sous les Sassanides*, 274–276.

1049 Words appear to have been omitted. The parallel in al-Ṭabarī is longer and contains a conversation between the Persians and Bahrām.

1050 That is, Yazdagird II, ruled 438–457; cf. al-Ṭabarī, *Taʾrīkh*, 1:871–872 (trans. Bosworth, *The History of al-Ṭabarī*, V, 106–109); al-Masʿūdī, *Murūj*, 2:193–194 (§ 615–616).

other Fayrūz.[1051] Hurmuz seized the throne after his father's death; Fayrūz fled and reached the country of the Hephthalites.[1052] He told their king his story and informed him of his brother's behavior and his injustice. The king provided him with an army, and Fayrūz advanced with them; he fought his brother, killed him, scattered his forces, and became king. In his days the people suffered severe drought, lack of rain, and famine; the rivers and springs dried up. This continued to be their condition for three years, but then the country revived. Fayrūz marched to the country of the Turks to do battle with their king. There had been peace between the Persians and the Turks; so, when Fayrūz approached the country, the king of the Turks sent him a message asking him to turn back, stressing the gravity of the breach of trust, but Fayrūz would not agree. So the king of the Turks dug a deep trench on account of him and caused it to be covered. When Fayrūz approached it, he deployed his army and rushed blindly toward it; so he, with all | his army, fell into that trench and died. The king of 1:185
the Turks seized his possessions and took a sister of his. Fayrūz had reigned for twenty-seven years.

When the Persians learned of the death of Fayrūz, it distressed them greatly. One of their leaders, a man named Sūkhrā, marched out with a well-equipped host, met the king of the Turks, did battle with him, and bested him. The king of the Turks sued for peace, offering to hand over to him everything he had seized of Fayrūz's treasures and to return his sister and those of his retinue [who were in his hands].[1053] He did this, and Sūkhrā departed.

Balāsh, son of Fayrūz, became king; his period of rule was four years.[1054]

Then his brother Qubādh, son of Fayrūz, became king.[1055] Being young in years, he left the management of the kingdom to Sūkhrā, but, when he came of

---

1051 Respectively, Hurmuz (Hormizd) III, ruled 457–459, and Fayrūz (Pērōz) I, ruled 459–484; cf. al-Ṭabarī, *Taʾrīkh*, 1:872–880 (trans. Bosworth, *The History of al-Ṭabarī*, V, 109–121); al-Masʿūdī, *Murūj*, 2:195 (§ 617).

1052 The Hephthalites (Arabic, al-Hayāṭila) were a steppe people from Mongolia, who settled along the Oxus during the fourth and fifth centuries and formed one, or perhaps several, powerful kingdoms. See the article by A. D. H. Bivar in *EI*², s.v. Hayāṭila. See also the note on the parallel in al-Ṭabarī provided by Bosworth in *The History of al-Ṭabarī*, V, 107, n. 275. Cf. also, al-Dīnawarī, *al-Akhbār al-ṭiwāl*, 60.

1053 Addition by the Leiden editor.

1054 Balāsh (Walāsh) apparently was the brother, not the son, of Fayrūz and ruled 484–488; see Bosworth, *The History of al-Ṭabarī*, V, 126, for the evidence that he was deposed; al-Masʿūdī, *Murūj*, 2:195 (§ 617).

1055 That is, Qubādh (Kawād) I, ruled 488–496, 498 or 499–531. In fact, he was the nephew of Balāsh; cf. al-Ṭabarī, *Taʾrīkh*, 1:883–888 (trans. Bosworth, *The History of al-Ṭabarī*, V, 128–139); al-Masʿūdī, *Murūj*, 2:195 (§ 617).

age and reached manhood, he became dissatisfied with Sūkhrā's management, so he killed him and promoted Mihrān.[1056] Later, the Persians deposed Qubādh, imprisoned him, and made his brother Jāmasb, son of Fayrūz, king.[1057] Qubādh remained in prison, while his brother was king. Then a sister of Qubādh entered the prison; the prison warden confronted her, and she aroused his desire, but she said that she was menstruating. She went inside and stayed with Qubādh for a day. Then she wrapped him in a carpet and had it taken out on the shoulders of a strong young lad. Qubādh fled, intending to reach the king of the Hephthalites. When he reached Abarshahr,[1058] he stopped and stayed with a man there. He asked the man to find him a woman, so the latter brought him a slave girl. He lay with her, pleased with her beauty and grace. Then he made his way to the king of the Hephthalites and stayed with him for a year, and the latter dispatched an army with him. When he returned to Abarshahr, he asked the man with whom he had stayed, "How is that slave girl doing?" He brought her to him: she had given birth to a boy, the most beautiful boy imaginable. He named
1:186 him Kisrā Anūshirwān.[1059] | Qubādh marched to his country, took control of the throne, and became very powerful. He raided the country of the Romans and established new provinces and districts. He made his son Anūshirwān heir apparent: he summoned him, gave him the best of advice, and imparted to him everything he would need to know. The reign of Qubādh was forty-three years.

Then Anūshirwān, son of Qubādh, became king.[1060] He wrote to the people of his kingdom, telling them of the death of Qubādh, promising to treat them benevolently, commanding them to do that which would bring them good for-

---

1056 As corrected by ed. Leiden; the MSS read Bahrām. Cf. al-Ṭabarī, *Taʾrīkh*, 1:885 (trans. Bosworth, *The History of al-Ṭabarī*, V, 131), and al-Dīnawarī, *al-Akhbār al-ṭiwāl*, 66. In al-Ṭabarī, Mihrān is the name of the man's family: "At last, Qubādh became desirous of resuming power ... He wrote to Sābūr of al-Rayy, [a man] from the house called Mihrān, who was Supreme Commander of the Land, to come to him with the troops under his command" (al-Ṭabarī, trans. Bosworth). The arrest and execution of Sūkhrā follow.

1057 The interregnum of Jāmasb (or Jāmāsp) was in 496–498 or 499. According to al-Ṭabarī, *Taʾrīkh*, 1:885–887, and al-Dīnawarī, *al-Akhbār al-ṭiwāl*, 67, Qubādh was deposed for favoring the doctrines of Mazdak, whom al-Yaʿqūbī will mention shortly in connection with the reign of Anūshirwān.

1058 That is, the region around Nīshāpūr, in central Khurāsān.

1059 The future Kisrā (Khusraw) I, surnamed Anūshirwān (Middle Persian, Anōshag-ruwān, "of immortal soul"). The account in al-Dīnawarī, *al-Akhbār al-ṭiwāl*, 67, locates this incident "in a village on the border of al-Ahwāz and Iṣfahān" and identifies the mother of Kisrā Anūshirwān not as a slave girl but as the daughter of a local notable (*dihqān*) with a pedigree going back to the legendary King Farīdūn.

1060 That is, Kisrā I Anūshirwān, reigned 531–579; cf. al-Ṭabarī, *Taʾrīkh*, 1:892–900, 958–

tune and enjoining them to obedience and loyal behavior. He pardoned certain men who had been hostile to him. He killed Mazdaq, who had commanded people to share their property and women equally among themselves,[1061] and he killed Zarādusht[1062] son of Khurrakān, because of the innovations he had introduced into Zoroastrianism;[1063] he killed the followers of both men. He promoted the leading men of the monarchy and the nobility. He raided several countries that not been within the kingdom of the Persians, and he added them to his realm. There took place between him and Justinian, the king of the Romans [...].[1064] So Anūshirwān raided the country of the Romans, killing and taking prisoners, and he captured many cities in the Jazīra and Syria, including Edessa, Manbij, Qinnasrīn, the ʿAwāṣim,[1065] Aleppo, Antioch, Apamea, Emessa (Ḥimṣ), and others. He was so pleased by Antioch that he built a city exactly like it, omitting nothing. Then he took the prisoners from Antioch and sent them to it; there was nothing they did not recognize.[1066]

Anūshirwān surveyed the land and levied taxes on it. He assessed every *jarīb* of cropland according to its yield.[1067] This custom continued to be followed as

---

966 (trans. Bosworth, *The History of al-Ṭabarī*, v, 146–162, 252–267); al-Masʿūdī, *Murūj*, 2:196–211 (§ 618–632); A. Christensen, *L'Iran sous les Sassanides*, 363–440.

1061 On the history of this religious movement, which had arisen during the previous reign and had enjoyed the favor of Qubādh, see the article by M. Guidi and M. Morony in *EI*², s.v. Mazdak̤. Mazdak's life and death formed the basis of a popular narrative in Middle Persian, the *Mazdak-nāmagh*, translated into Arabic; see A. Christensen, *L'Iran sous les Sassanides*, 68–69; 337–362. For a summary of more recent scholarship on Mazdak, see Bosworth, *The History of al-Ṭabarī*, v, 132, n. 342.

1062 According to al-Ṭabarī, *Ta'rīkh*, 1:893 (trans. Bosworth, *The History of al-Ṭabarī*, v, 148), this Zarādusht was the originator of the doctrines propagated by Mazdak.

1063 Arabic, al-Majūsiyya ("the religion of the Magi").

1064 One or more words seem to have dropped out of the MSS, although there is no visible lacuna. The parallel in al-Ṭabarī, *Ta'rīkh*, 1:958–960 (trans. Bosworth, *The History of al-Ṭabarī*, v, 252–255), gives the background: The war began when the Byzantine client al-Ḥārith b. Jabala raided the Persian client al-Mundhir b. Nuʿmān, prompting an ultimatum from Anūshirwān to Justinian, followed by war lasting from 540 to 546.

1065 The term designates what was later to become a frontier area between the caliphate and the Byzantine lands, roughly the area between Antioch and Manbij. Its use here is anachronistic. See the article by M. Canard in *EI*², s.v. al-ʿAwāṣim.

1066 This town, located near the capital, Ctesiphon (al-Madā'in), came to be called al-Rūmiyya because of the Greeks (Rūm) settled there; cf. al-Ṭabarī, *Ta'rīkh*, 1:959 (trans. Bosworth, *The History of al-Ṭabarī*, v, 254–255); al-Dīnawarī, *al-Akhbār al-ṭiwāl*, 70; al-Masʿūdī, *Murūj*, 2:199–200 (§ 621); A. Christensen, *L'Iran sous les Sassanides*, 386–387.

1067 The *jarīb* was a standard measure of agricultural land, originally the area that could

long as the country remained prosperous. He installed as a salaried official over the bureau of soldiers a man whose decisiveness and resolution found favor
1:187 with him, and he required his soldiers | to obtain the arms that were needed. He also set up, in similar fashion, the bureau of payments; the registers of names, equipment, and brands of mounts; and the bureau of army review.[1068]

Anūshirwān was noble, generous, and renowned for justice. No person asked a favor of him without his providing a response to him. Sayf b. Dhī Yazan[1069] journeyed to him and informed him that the Abyssinians had come to the land of Yemen and had conquered it; he himself had gone to Heraclius, the king of the Romans, but had not received from him what he desired. Anūshirwān therefore dispatched prison inmates with him by sea, appointing as their leader one of his senior army commanders, a brave and experienced man named Wahriz. The latter made his way to Yemen and succeeded in killing and destroying the Abyssinians, and he shot and killed their king, Abraha. He stayed in the country and appointed Sayf b. Dhī Yazan king.

Anūshirwān appointed his son Hurmuz heir apparent—Hurmuz's mother was the daughter of Khāqān, the king of the Turks—and wrote for Hurmuz a document in the form of a covenant. In it, he enjoined on him what behooves men of his station and gave him the best of counsels. He tested him and found him to be just as he desired; he responded to his every question with a correct answer and thanked him beautifully and graciously for his appointment.[1070] Anūshirwān died after a reign of forty-eight years.

---

be sown with one *jarīb* (a measure of capacity) of seed. The term is still in use in Iran as a synonym of "hectare." See the articles by C. E. Bosworth in *EI*², s.v. Misāḥa; and by E. Ashtor in *EI*², s.v. Makāyil. According to al-Ṭabarī, *Taʾrīkh*, 1:960–963 (trans. Bosworth, *The History of al-Ṭabarī*, v, 255–262) and al-Dīnawarī, *al-Akhbār al-ṭiwāl*, 72–73, the reform of the land tax was begun by Qubādh and completed by his son Anūshirwān after Qubādh's death. Cf. also al-Masʿūdī, *Murūj*, 2:204–205 (§ 627) for further details.

1068 On these administrative arrangements, see the more elaborate account in al-Ṭabarī, *Taʾrīkh*, 1:963–964 (trans. Bosworth, *The History of al-Ṭabarī*, v, 262–263), and al-Dīnawarī, *al-Akhbār al-ṭiwāl*, 74–75.

1069 Sayf b. Dhī Yazan was a South Arabian leader of a revolt against Abyssinian domination. Despite the fanciful legends and popular romance that developed around him (see the article by J.-P. Guillaume in *EI*², s.v. Sayf Ibn D͟hī Yazan), he seems to have been a real historical figure, as the Yazan family appears in inscriptions and probably dominated all the Ḥaḍramawt and the Ẓufar coastlands. See C. E. Bosworth, *The History of al-Ṭabarī*, v, 236, n. 585. Al-Yaʿqūbī later includes more information about Sayf in his account of the kings of Yemen, ed. Leiden, 1:226–227.

1070 Reading with M: *wa-tashakkara wilāyatahu.*

Then Hurmuz, son of Anūshirwān, became king.[1071] He read out to the people a general letter, promising justice, equity, pardon, and benevolence, and enjoining on them that which would bring benefits. At first he achieved victory and strength, conquering many cities, but then his enemies became emboldened against him and raided his country. His harshest enemy was Shābah,[1072] king of the Turks, who advanced with | a huge army, entered 1:188
Khurāsān, and nearly took possession of it. The king of the Khazars advanced with armies and invaded Azerbaijan. Hurmuz became very distressed, fearing that he might not have the strength to deal with the ruler of the Turks. Then one of his commanders, a man named Bihzād, came and told him that he had with him a knowledgeable man named Mihrān Sitād [...].[1073] [...] And that Khātūn, his wife,[1074] had asked what lay before them. He had told her that her daughter would bear to the king of the Persians a son who would accede to the kingship after his father; that the king of the Turks would advance against him with a great army; that he, in response, would send against him a person not of the nobility,[1075] someone named Bahrām Chūbīn, with an army detachment, and

---

1071 That is, Hormizd IV, ruled 579–590; cf. al-Ṭabarī, *Taʾrīkh*, 1:988–994 (trans. Bosworth, The *History of al-Ṭabarī*, V, 295–305). Al-Dīnawarī, *al-Akhbār al-ṭiwāl*, 77–80, gives what purports to be the full text of Hurmuz's accession speech; cf. also al-Masʿūdī, *Murūj*, 2:211 (§ 232).

1072 As Bosworth notes in his translation of the parallel in al-Ṭabarī (*The History of al-Ṭabarī*, V, 299, n. 701), the name Shābah is "dubious" and corresponds to no known Turkish leader of the time. Al-Dīnawarī, *al-Akhbār al-ṭiwāl*, 82, calls him Shāhānshāh (King of Kings).

1073 The reading "Mihrān Sitād" was conjectured by the Leiden editor on the basis of Ferdowsī and Balʿamī, from what in both MSS looks like *h.m.b/y.r.ʾ.f.s.ʾ.d.* The subsequent lacuna was also inferred by the Leiden editor, although the MSS show no break. The missing text must have included a reference to Khāqān, the king of the Turks, whose daughter, given in marriage to Kisrā Anūshirwān, became the mother of Hurmuz. Bihzād then reports a prophecy current among the Turks about how, in the days of the son (i.e., Hurmuz) born of Kisrā and his Turkish wife, a hero named Bahrām Chūbīn would defeat the Turks.

1074 That is, the wife the king of the Turks.

1075 Arabic, *laysa bi-l-nabīh*. This could also mean simply "not well-known." According to al-Dīnawarī, *al-Akhbār al-ṭiwāl*, 82, however, Bahrām Chūbīn was governor of Azerbaijan and Armenia at the time; and, according to al-Masʿūdī, *Murūj*, 2:213 (§ 653), he was military governor (*marzubān*) of Rayy, so hardly "not well-known." On the varying portrayals of Bahrām Chūbīn, see the note by C. E. Bosworth in *The History of al-Ṭabarī*, V, 301, n. 706. A popular romance about him in Middle Persian, the *Vahrām Chōbēn-nāmagh*, was translated into Arabic and would have been available to al-Yaʿqūbī; see A. Christensen, *L'Iran sous les Sassanides*, 69.

that he would kill that king and uproot his kingdom. When Hurmuz heard this, he was delighted. He inquired about Bahrām Chūbīn and was told, "The only such person we know of is a man from al-Rayy who is now in Azerbaijan." So Hurmuz sent someone to him and had him brought; then he dispatched him against Shābah, king of the Turks, with twelve thousand fighters. But the chief *mōbadh* said to Hurmuz: "How likely it is that he will win a victory! But in the tip of his eyebrow there is a sign of a defeat that he will inflict on your kingdom." An augur he had with him told him the same thing. Hurmuz therefore wrote to Bahrām that he should turn back, but he did not. [Bahrām] came upon Shābah in Herat, catching the latter off guard.[1076] In Shābah's entourage there was a man whom Hurmuz had sent to deceive him, a man named Hurmuz Jarābzīn; finally, Shābah was duped by him,[1077] and he departed from him.
1:189 Shābah then sent out someone who learned | of Bahrām's whereabouts and then returned to Shābah and informed him of Bahrām's situation. Shābah sent Bahrām a message that he should retreat,[1078] but Bahrām replied to him harshly and rudely and confronted him, having mustered his troops. Shābah, for his part, had soothsayers and sorcerers with him, and they were trying to confuse Bahrām's men. Fighting was joined and slaughter raged among Shābah's men, until a great many of them were killed and they turned around in defeat. Bahrām inflicted great carnage on them. He overtook Shābah, hurled a long spear at him, and killed him. He captured a sorcerer who had been with the ruler of the Turks; Bahrām wanted to spare him, so that he might be of use to him in his battles, but then he decided that it would be better to kill him. He wrote of the victory to Hurmuz, and the latter, delighted by it, sent letters far and wide to announce it.

Afterward, [Barmūdhah],[1079] the son of Shābah, came out, and, having encountered Bahrām, fought him and attacked by night. There was heavy fighting

---

1076 The details of the story are unclear from the abbreviated version in al-Yaʿqūbī. The longer version in al-Dīnawarī, *al-Akhbār al-ṭiwāl*, 83, is clearer.

1077 The translation depends on emending the MSS reading (M, C) *farra minhu* (he fled from him) to *ghurra minhu* (he was duped by him). The version in al-Dīnawarī, *al-Akhbār al-ṭiwāl*, 83, states that that the mission of Hurmuz Jarābzīn was intended to gain time by proposing peace terms favorable to the Turks at the very moment Bahrām Chūbīn was advancing toward Herat.

1078 The account in al-Dīnawarī, *al-Akhbār al-ṭiwāl*, 83, has the king of the Turks invite Bahrām to come over to his side and tell Bahrām that he will make him ruler of Iran.

1079 The MSS at this point have only "the son of Shābah" but refer, three sentences later, to "Barmūdhah [unpointed], the son of Shābah." The name seems suspect, although al-Ṭabarī, *Taʾrīkh*, 1:993 (similarly al-Masʿūdī, *Murūj*, 2:213 [§ 633]) has the same name. In al-Dīnawarī, *al-Akhbār al-ṭiwāl*, 84, the name appears as Yaltagīn (variant, Baltagīn),

between them. Then Bahrām attacked him by night, routed him, overtook him, and besieged him in a fortress. Barmūdhah son of Shābah asked for safe-conduct, on condition that it should come from Hurmuz, the king. Bahrām wrote to Hurmuz, who agreed and wrote a letter of safe-conduct for him. He wrote to Bahrām that he should send Barmūdhah on to him, so Barmūdhah, son of Shābah, left the fortress. Hurmuz, meanwhile, had dispatched certain men against[1080] Bahrām Chūbīn. Barmūdhah made his way to Hurmuz; Hurmuz treated him with honor and kindness and seated him on the throne with him. Barmūdhah told him of the great wealth and treasures that had come to Bahrām and that Bahrām had concealed them from the king's agents. Hurmuz's agents told him the same thing and that what Bahrām had sent back was a small part of the whole. Hurmuz therefore wrote to Bahrām, commanding him to send him whatever wealth he had in his possession.[1081] Taking umbrage at this, Bahrām informed his troops; they | spoke of Hurmuz in the ugliest terms, 1:190
and Bahrām, with all his troops, renounced their allegiance to him. When word of this reached Hurmuz, he became worried and wrote to Bahrām, apologizing to him and to his army for such behavior, but neither Bahrām nor his army accepted what Hurmuz said. Bahrām sent Hurmuz a basket containing knives with bent handles; as soon as Hurmuz saw them, he knew that Bahrām had rebelled, and so he cut off the points of the knives and sent them back to him. Bahrām, understanding what Hurmuz meant, sent a message to Khāqān, the king of the Turks, seeking a peace settlement with him and offering to restore to him all the land he had taken from his country. Bahrām set out and made his way to al-Rayy. Then he contrived to sow strife between Hurmuz and his son, Kisrā Abarwīz. Hurmuz was already suspicious of his son, having received word that certain men had incited him to rise against his father. Bahrām therefore struck many dirhams, put the name of Kisrā Abarwīz on them, sent them to the city of Hurmuz, and they became current in the hands of the people.[1082]

---

which looks more Turkish, but, according to Bosworth (*The History of al-Ṭabarī*, v, 302, n. 710), may be the invention of a later writer.

1080 The translation follows the original reading of the manuscripts (*ʿalā*); ed. Leiden emends to *ilā* (to), but the sentence, as it stands, seems to be out of context.

1081 Cf. the more colorful account of Hurmuz's insulting message to Bahrām in al-Dīnawarī, *al-Akhbār al-ṭiwāl*, 85.

1082 Although the pronouns in al-Yaʿqūbī's version are ambiguous, the parallels in al-Dīnawarī, *al-Akhbār al-ṭiwāl*, 86, and al-Masʿūdī, *Murūj*, 2:214 (§ 634) make it clear that the dirhams were struck by Bahrām, with the intention of persuading Hurmuz that his son had already arrogated to himself the royal prerogative of placing his name on the coinage.

When news of them reached Hurmuz, he became very distressed and decided to imprison his son, Kisrā Abarwīz. When Abarwīz learned of this, he fled to Azerbaijan. All the high-ranking military officers[1083] and grandees there joined him; they made an agreement with him and swore allegiance to him. Hurmuz sent an army under a man named Ādhīnjushnas against Bahrām, but when the man had traveled part of the way, he was killed by a certain man from Khūr[1084] whom Ādhīnjushnas had freed from prison and had attached to himself, and his forces dispersed. After Ādhīnjushnas was killed, the position of Hurmuz weakened. His troops became emboldened against him: they were angry with him and hated his regime. They wrote to his son Abarwīz, and the latter advanced with an army from Azerbaijan. They deposed Hurmuz and made Abarwīz king. Hurmuz was seized and imprisoned, and his eyes were
1:191 put out. Hurmuz remained in prison for some days; then | his son came before him and spoke to him. Hurmuz said to him, "Kill whoever did this to me!" The administration of the kingdom had been taken over by Bindī and Bisṭām, the maternal uncles of Abarwīz.[1085] The reign of Hurmuz was twelve years.

When the position of Abarwīz became settled and he received word of Bahrām Chūbīn's march against him, he set out with his army—Bindī and Bisṭām were with him—and confronted Bahrām at al-Nahrawān.[1086] Abarwīz

1083 Arabic, *marāziba* (pl. of *marzubān*), from Middle Persian *marzpān* (frontier protector), used as the title of a military governor of a frontier province. Here it needs to be taken in a broader sense, as there can be no question of several governors of Azerbaijan. See the article by J. H. Kramers and M. Morony in *EI*², s.v. Marzpān.

1084 Arabic, *rajul khūrī*. The reading is uncertain, as the first letter, which is undotted, is ambiguous and could stand for initial *ḥ* (undotted), *j* (dotted below), or *kh* (dotted above). Cf. the more complicated version in al-Dīnawarī, *al-Akhbār al-ṭiwāl*, 87.

1085 The parallel in al-Ṭabarī, *Taʾrīkh*, 1:993 (trans. Bosworth, *The History of al-Ṭabarī*, v, 303) states explicitly that Bindī (perhaps more correctly Bindūya) and Bisṭām had carried out the blinding of Hurmuz. According to the continuation of the account in al-Ṭabarī (1:996 = trans. Bosworth, 307), Abarwīz delayed taking vengeance on the two men with the words (trans. Bosworth), "The rebel Bahrām is threatening us from very near and has on his side courage and bravery; we do not at present have the power to stretch forth our hand against those who perpetrated what they did against you, but if God gives me the upper hand over the false-hearted one, then I shall act as your representative and the willing agent of your hand." Cf. also al-Dīnawarī, *al-Akhbār al-ṭiwāl*, 88, where Abarwīz is portrayed as slyly concealing from his father the fact that Bahrām is advancing to restore Hurmuz.

1086 A town and canal system in the lower Diyālā region of Iraq, east of the Tigris. See the article by M. Morony in *EI*², s.v. al-Nahrawān. According to al-Masʿūdī, *Murūj*, 2:215 (§ 653), the two armies faced off across the canal.

parlayed with him and impressed on him the gravity of his actions. Bahrām replied in strong and coarse terms. Bahrām's brother Kurdūya[1087] was with Kisrā Abarwīz, and Bahrām joined him. Deserted by his troops and abandoned by his companions, Kisrā fled. When he had traveled some distance, Bindī and Bisṭām, his maternal uncles, went back, killed his father Hurmuz, and then rejoined him along the way.[1088] After his flight had continued for some time, his condition deteriorated, and he became very distressed and apprehensive. He sought food but found nothing but barley bread. Bahrām's cavalry overtook him, but his uncle Bindī used trickery and engineered his escape.[1089] Abarwīz made his way to al-Ruhā, while Bindī was taken and brought before Bahrām. Bahrām imprisoned him, but he escaped from prison and made his way to Azerbaijan.[1090] Kisrā reached al-Ruhā, intending to go to Maurice,[1091] the king of the Romans. The governor of al-Ruhā detained him and wrote to Maurice, the king of the Romans, informing him that he had come to him seeking support. The king of the Romans consulted with his companions about the matter: some of them advised that his request should not be granted, while others advised that it should.[1092] The king of the Romans granted it; he gave Abarwīz his daughter in marriage and dispatched a large army with him, imposing certain conditions on him, should his affair finish successfully.[1093] Kisrā sent

---

1087 In the parallel in al-Ṭabarī, *Ta'rīkh*, 1:997, and al-Dīnawarī, *al-Akhbār al-ṭiwāl*, 90, the name appears as Kurdī, perhaps for an original Gurdōy. Al-Dīnawarī makes him Bahrām's nephew.

1088 The motive for their behavior is provided in al-Mas'ūdī, *Murūj*, 2:218 (§ 637): Bindī and Bisṭām tell Abarwīz that they fear that Bahrām Chūbīn might restore Hurmuz to the throne, despite his having been blinded, and might induce Hurmuz to appoint him commander and persuade the Roman king to send Abarwīz back to be punished. Abarwīz, out of piety, is said to have begged Bindī and Bisṭām not to carry out their plan, but they do it nonetheless.

1089 According to al-Ṭabarī, *Ta'rīkh*, 1:998–999 (trans. Bosworth, *The History of al-Ṭabarī*, v, 310), Bindī/Bindūya dressed himself in Abarwīz's armor, showed himself from the roof of a monastery to Bahrām's cavalry commander (confusingly also named Bahrām, but distinguished by al-Dīnawarī, *al-Akhbār al-ṭiwāl*, 91–93, as Bahrām, son of Siyāwush) and offered to surrender the next morning. The commander accepted the offer, and Abarwīz made his escape.

1090 In the more detailed version in al-Dīnawarī, *al-Akhbār al-ṭiwāl*, 94–95, Bindī's jailer, secretly loyal to Kisrā Abarwīz, allows Bindī to escape, for which he pays with his life.

1091 That is, the emperor Maurice, ruled 582–602.

1092 Cf. the vivid portrayal of the scene in al-Dīnawarī, *al-Akhbār al-ṭiwāl*, 96.

1093 Al-Mas'ūdī, *Murūj*, 2:221 (§ 640), notes that these conditions included restoring Syria and Egypt (they had been conquered by Anūshirwān) to Roman rule.

Maurice three of his own companions, and he laid out for them all the conditions that he wished. He dispatched his daughter and the army, commanded
1:192 by a brother of his named Theodosius, with whom there was a man | as valiant as a thousand men.[1094] Having consummated his marriage with the daughter of the king of the Romans, Kisrā marched his army to the region of Azerbaijan, where his uncle Bindī had already arrived. As soon as the latter knew of Kisrā's presence, he joined him with a large army. When Bahrām Chūbīn learned of the forces that had been amassed for Kisrā, he sent letters to the latter's chief companions, telling them of the evil conduct of the Sasanian dynasty, describing its behavior, king by king, and inviting them to go over to him. The letters fell into Kisrā's hand before they reached the intended recipients, and Kisrā wrote an exceedingly harsh reply on behalf of the intended recipients and sent the messenger back to Bahrām. Bahrām advanced against them until he reached Azerbaijan and fought fiercely against him; the fighting took its toll on both sides. The Roman who was as valiant as a thousand men came forward and said to Kisrā, "Where is this slave of yours who has wrested your kingdom from you, that I may kill him?" Kisrā answered, "He is the one with the piebald horse." So he charged him. Bahrām fell back but then turned against him, struck him with his sword, and cut him in two. Kisrā laughed and said "Bravo!" whereupon the brother of the king of the Romans became angry and said, "Are you happy that our man has been killed?" "No," replied Kisrā, "but your companion asked me, 'Where is the slave who has angered you and taken your kingdom?' and I wanted him[1095] to know that the slave strikes several blows just like this, every day." The fighting became so fierce that Kisrā was put to flight and climbed a hill. He almost perished, but then his troops rallied. Bahrām Chūbīn was routed and kept retreating, turning aside for nothing, heading toward the king of the Turks.

When matters had stabilized for Kisrā Abarwīz, he wrote about it to the lord of the Romans, and the king of the Romans presented him with two robes having crosses on them. Kisrā Abarwīz wore them, so the Persians said that he had become a Christian. Furthermore, he wrote concerning the Christians that they should be honored, promoted, and treated generously; he told of what had

---

1094 Arabic *rajulun yajrī majrā alfi rajulin* (a man the equivalent of 1000 men) is a translation of a Persian term for an especially valiant warrior, *hazārmard* (having the strength of 1000 men); the Persian word occurs in the parallel in al-Dīnawarī, *al-Akhbār al-ṭiwāl*, 96, where there are ten such men. See Bosworth's note on the more detailed version of these events in *The History of al-Ṭabarī*, V, 312, n. 731.

1095 Following the apparent reading of M (*an yaʿlama*); ed. Leiden, *an taʿlama* (you to know).

come to pass between himself | and the Roman in the way of defense, marriage alliance, and conciliation, and that no king before him had ever said this.[1096] However, Kisrā's maternal uncle Bindī attacked Theodosius, the brother of the king of the Romans, and beat him, so evil broke out. The brother of the king of the Romans said, "Either you hand over Bindī to me, or evil will return." Kisrā managed to placate him. 1:193

Bahrām Chūbīn arrived in the country of the Turks. Khāqān honored him and was generous to him. Khāqān had a brother named [...],[1097] whom Khāqān used to treat indulgently. Bahrām saw this and said to Khāqān, "How dare this man be so insolent to you?" The brother of Khāqān heard these words and challenged Bahrām to a duel. Bahrām said, "Whenever you wish, come forth!" Khāqān, the king of the Turks, gave his brother an arrow and Bahrām an arrow, and sent them out to the open plain. Khāqān's brother shot at Bahrām, hit him, and pierced his armor, but then Bahrām shot him and killed him. Khāqān was happy that his brother had been killed, because the latter had defied him and because he feared him. Kisrā, on the other hand, was terrified by Bahrām Chūbīn's being with Khāqān and feared that he would stir up evil against him. So he dispatched a Persian notable named Bahrām Jarābzīn, a powerful man among the Persians, with whom he sent presents to Khāqān, asking him to send Bahrām Chūbīn to him. He commanded Jarābzīn to use subtlety in the affair. The latter presented the gifts to Khāqān and mentioned the case of Bahrām to him but did not get from him what he wanted.[1098] So he delicately approached Khāqān's wife Khātūn, gave her jewels and other goods, and made a request to her in the matter of Bahrām. She sent one of her retainers, a man of resolution and boldness, and told him to make his way into Bahrām Chūbīn's presence and kill him. The man set out and asked to be admitted, but it was Bahrām's

---

1096 On the provisions of the peace treaty of autumn 591, see Bosworth, *The History of al-Ṭabarī*, v, 315, n. 738. The phrase "and that no king before him had ever said this" (*wa-lam yaqul hādhā malikun min al-mulūki qablahu*) may possibly be construed as meaning, "and he had never said, 'This is a king,' before him." In any case, it is apparently a reference to the fact that Abarwīz agreed in the treaty to address Maurice in correspondence as king (βασιλεύς) rather than as caesar.

1097 The name, written without dots in the manuscripts, is too ambiguous to read (*b/t/th/n/y, f/q, ā, r, s*). As ed. Leiden notes, Balʿamī reads Bīghū, and Firdousī refers to Maqātūra, either of which could conceivably be traced to readings of the same ductus. Al-Dīnawarī, *al-Akhbār al-ṭiwāl*, 100–102, reads Bughāwīr and gives a more detailed rendition of the scene at the court of Khāqān and the duel.

1098 Al-Dīnawarī, *al-Akhbār al-ṭiwāl*, 103–104, gives a full report of Jarābzīn's speech and Khāqān's angry reply.

1:194 sleeping time, | and he was not admitted. So he said, "King Khāqān has sent me on an important matter," and he was admitted. Having come into Bahrām's presence, he said, "The king has charged me with a message that I am to deliver to you in secret with no one else present." Bahrām rose from his seat. The man approached as if to impart a secret to him and stabbed him with a dagger that he had with him under his arm. The Turk left in haste and mounted his horse. Bahrām's companions entered and, seeing him in such a state, said: "O king, valiant lion, who has felled you? O towering mountain, who has demolished you?" He told them what had happened and wrote to Khāqān, telling him that he had neither loyalty nor gratitude. Bahrām died and was carried to the tomb. As soon as Jarābzīn learned of his death, he journeyed to Kisrā and informed him. Kisrā was delighted; he proclaimed the news in his kingdom and sent letters about it far and wide.

After Bahrām died, the king of the Turks sent a message to Bahrām's wife Kurdīya and to his retainers, telling them of his grief and that he had killed everyone who had been a party to the murder of Bahrām. He dispatched his own brother Naṭrā[1099] to them and wrote to Bahrām Chūbīn's wife Kurdīya, saying that he would espouse her interests[1100] and commanding her to marry Naṭrā. Bahrām's wife Kurdīya, however, took [the troops] of her brother Kurdī[1101] and set out with her retainers and whoever had been with her, heading for the country of the Persians. Naṭrā, the brother of Khāqān, overtook her, but she came out to meet him fully armed and said: "I will marry only someone equal to Bahrām in courage and strength. So come forward to fight me!" Khāqān's brother came forward. She killed him and continued on her way.

Kisrā had become angry with his maternal uncle Bindī and had put out his eyes, cut off his hands and feet, and crucified him alive for what he had

---

1099 The vocalization of the name (*n.ṭ.r.ā*) is unknown.

1100 Arabic, *yarghabu fīhā* (literally, "was desirous of her"). For this meaning, see Dozy, *Supplément*, 1:538.

1101 As the Leiden editor noted, the original account must have made it clear that Kurdīya was both sister and wife to Bahrām Chūbīn, such sibling marriages being permitted under Zoroastrian law. Some transmitter, scandalized by the custom, added the word "Kurdī," thereby attributing the army to Bahrām's brother Kurdī. This is problematic for two reasons. First, the account in al-Ṭabarī, *Taʾrīkh*, 1:998, 1001, identifies Kurdīya as Bahrām's sister-and-wife (similarly in al-Dīnawarī, *al-Akhbār al-ṭiwāl*, 105), and makes it clear that the troops she took were those of her brother-and-husband. Second, in al-Yaʿqūbī's version, there is an apparent inconsistency, in that Kurdīya soon will write a letter to her brother (apparently Kurdī) who is at Kisrā's court. Indeed, in al-Ṭabarī's version, Bahrām's brother Kurdī remains loyal to Kisrā Abarwīz and thus would already be at court, where al-Yaʿqūbī's narrative will soon place him.

done to his father.[1102] When Bindī's brother Bisṭām learned what Kisrā had done to his brother, he threw off his allegiance to Kisrā, went to | al-Rayy, 1:195
and gathered troops. He received word that Bahrām's sister Kurdīya and his wife[1103] had arrived from the country of the Turks; he met with the two them and those who were with them; he denounced Kisrā to them and told them of his treachery and wickedness. He asked the two of them to stay with him, together with their entourage, and that she[1104] should give herself in marriage to him; which she did, and she wrote to her brother Kurdī, informing him of this and asking him to obtain for her and her entourage a safe-conduct from Kisrā. [Meanwhile, Kisrā had learned][1105] of Kurdīya's going to al-Rayy with those of Bahrām's troops and retainers who were with her and of his uncle Bisṭām's marriage to her [and] her residing with him. Kisrā learned of this. He summoned her brother Kurdī and asked him to win her over by subtle means, so that she would kill Bisṭām and come in order that he might marry her. Kurdī therefore sent his wife Abrakha[1106] to his sister Kurdīya to carry out what the king had mentioned to him. He conveyed to her letters of safe-conduct for her and those with her, sworn with the most binding of oaths. And so they killed her companions[1107] and attacked and killed Bisṭām. Kurdīya came to Kisrā, who married her and gave her a high place. Kisrā's affairs stabilized, and his country became submissive.

Then the Romans attacked Maurice, their king, killed him, and made someone else king.[1108] Maurice's son came to Kisrā, who dispatched an army with him. Then Maurice's son was killed, and Heraclius became king.[1109] He attacked Kisrā's forces, killing and dispersing them, and pressed on against them, until he routed Kisrā's companion Shahrbarāz.[1110] When his reign became strong,

1102 For a more detailed account, see al-Dīnawarī, *al-Akhbār al-ṭiwāl*, 105–106.

1103 Here assumed to be two persons, as shown by the dual forms of the verbs and pronouns in the Arabic.

1104 That is, Bahrām's sister Kurdīya; the pronoun reverts to singular.

1105 Conjecturally restored by the Leiden editor.

1106 The vocalization of the name is uncertain. The more detailed parallel in al-Dīnawarī, *al-Akhbār al-ṭiwāl*, 109, calls her only "his wife."

1107 Reading with M: *fa-qatalū aṣḥābahā*. The third letter of first word is ambiguous; ed. Leiden reads *fa-qabilū aṣḥābuhā* (her companions accepted), which is ungrammatical.

1108 Maurice was murdered in 602, the fourteenth year of Kisrā's reign, according to al-Ṭabarī, *Taʾrīkh*, 1:1001–1002 (trans. Bosworth, *The History of al-Ṭabarī*, V, 317). The "someone else" is the Thracian centurion Phocas.

1109 Heraclius became emperor in 610.

1110 As corrected by ed. Leiden from M and C Shahriyār (the two names differ by only one

Kisrā became tyrannical, oppressive, proud, unjust, and despotic; he took people's property and spilled blood. People hated him for the contempt he showed
1:196 for them and his disdain for them. When the Persian grandees considered | the humiliation, affliction, and adversity they suffered at the hands of Kisrā, they renounced their allegiance to him and brought in a son of his, named Shīrūya, whom they made king. They brought him into the capital and proclaimed Shīrūya King of Kings (Shāhanshāh) and released from prison those whom Kisrā had intended to kill. Kisrā fled and entered an orchard belonging to him, but they seized him and imprisoned him. Then they said to Shīrūya: "It is not right for (Kisrā) Abarwīz to be alive. Kill him, or we will renounce our allegiance to you!" Shīrūya therefore sent his father a harsh message, assailing him for his misdeeds and mentioning how badly he had treated the people of his kingdom and what had come to pass because of his evil conduct.[1111] Abarwīz countered with a reply accusing Shīrūya of weak judgment and ignorance. Shīrūya then dispatched to him a man the hand of whose father Kisrā Abarwīz had cut off for no reason or offense, except that he had been told that the man's son would kill him; so he had cut off the hand of the man, who had been a member of his inner circle.[1112] When the son entered Kisrā's presence, the latter asked him what his name was. [...][1113] Kisrā said to him, "Do as you have been commanded!" So he struck him and killed him. Afterward, Shīrūya had his father carried to the tomb and killed his killer. The reign of Kisrā Abarwīz had lasted thirty-eight years.[1114]

When Shīrūya son of Abarwīz became king,[1115] he released whoever was in the prisons, married his father's wives, and wrongfully and unjustly killed seventeen of his brothers; so his reign did not go smoothly and his condition did not prosper. He became very ill and died after eight months.[1116]

---

letter in undotted Arabic script) on the basis of al-Ṭabarī, *Taʾrīkh*, 1:1002, and al-Masʿūdī, *Murūj*, 2:226 (§ 647); al-Dīnawarī, *al-Akhbār al-ṭiwāl*, 111, however, also reads Shahriyār.

1111 For a full text of Shīrūya's letter, with Kisrā's reply, see al-Dīnawarī, *al-Akhbār al-ṭiwāl*, 112–115.

1112 For a longer version of the story, with the names of the father (Mardānshāh) and the son (Mihr Hurmuz), see al-Ṭabarī, *Taʾrīkh*, 1:1058–1060 (trans. Bosworth, *The History of al-Ṭabarī*, v, 395–398).

1113 The MSS show no break, but the son's reply has been omitted.

1114 That is, 590–628; on the chronology, see the article by James Howard-Johnston in *Encyclopædia Iranica*, s.v. Ḵosrow II.

1115 On the eight-month reign in 628 of Shīrūya (Shērōē), whose regnal name was Qubādh (II), see al-Ṭabarī, *Taʾrīkh*, 1:1045–1061 (trans. Bosworth, *The History of al-Ṭabarī*, v, 381–399).

1116 That is, in 628; a plague, mentioned by al-Masʿūdī, *Murūj*, 2:232 (§ 653), is said to have

The Persians made king a son of Shīrūya, a child named Ardashīr, and chose a man named Mih Ādhar Jushnas to care for him and take charge of administering the kingdom.[1117] He administered it well and carried out the task in praiseworthy fashion, and the affairs of the realm ran smoothly. Shahrbarāz, who had been sent to fight the Romans, had, however, become a man of great importance, and he resented the position of | Mih Ādhar Jushnas. He wrote to 1:197
the Persians that they should send to him certain men whom he named, or he would come to do battle with them. When they did not do it, Shahrbarāz advanced on the capital with six thousand men, besieged its inhabitants, and fought them. Then he took thought and used a ruse to enter the city. He seized the Persian grandees, killed them, dishonored their women, and killed the king, Ardashīr. Ardashīr's reign had lasted a year and six months.

Shahrbarāz seated himself on the throne and styled himself king. However, when the Persians considered what Shahbarāz had done, they found it outrageous, and said, "Someone like this shall not rule over us." So they attacked him, killed him, and dragged his corpse by the foot.

Having killed Shahrbarāz, the Persians searched for a man of the royal house, but they found none, so they made Būrān, daughter of Kisrā, queen.[1118] She ruled well and spread justice and benevolence. She wrote to the ends of her kingdom, promising justice and benevolence and enjoining good beliefs, rectitude, and honesty. She made peace with the king of the Romans. Her reign lasted a year and four months.

Then Āzarmīdukht, daughter of Kisrā, became queen.[1119] Things went well for her. Farrukh Hurmuzd, the military governor (*iṣbahbadh*) of Khurāsān, said to her: "Today I am the chief of all men and mainstay of the kingdom of Persia. Give yourself to me in marriage!" She said: "It is not right for a queen to give herself in marriage, but, if you wish to approach me, come to me by night." He

raged in Iraq at the time, and, according to Ibn Qutayba, *al-Maʿārif* (ed. Cairo, 1960), 665, Shīrūya himself died of it.

1117 That is, Ardashīr III, who ruled 628–629. According to al-Ṭabarī, *Taʾrīkh*, 1:1061, and al-Masʿūdī, *Murūj*, 2:233–234 (§ 654), Ardashīr was seven years old at the time of his accession.

1118 Būrān, the daughter of Kisrā II Abarwīz, ruled 630–631. On the chronology, see the article by Marie Louise Chaumont in *Encyclopædia Iranica*, s.v. Bōrān. Note that al-Yaʿqūbī's account of the end of the Sasanian dynasty deliberately passes over details of the Arab conquest of Iraq, which was taking place at this time, postponing the account of it to his treatment of the early caliphate, starting at ed. Leiden, 2:141.

1119 Reigned 631–632; cf. al-Ṭabarī, *Taʾrīkh*, 1:1064–1065 (trans. Bosworth, *The History of al-Ṭabarī*, V, 406–407).

agreed to this. She ordered the commander of her guard to lie in wait for him until he entered and then to kill him. When night fell, he came and entered. Catching sight of him, the commander of the guard asked, "Who are you?" He replied, "I am Farrukh Hurmuzd." "And what," he asked, "are you doing at such
1:198 a time in a place that someone like you must not enter?" | So he struck him, killed him, and threw his body into the courtyard. When the people came in the morning, they found him slain and spread the news about him. His son Rustam—the man who later confronted Saʿd b. Abī Waqqāṣ at (the battle of) al-Qādisiyya—was in Khurāsān, but he came and killed Āzarmīdukht. Her reign had lasted six months.

Then a descendant of Ardashīr, son of Bābak, a man named Kisrā, son of Mihr Jushnas, became king. He had been invited to become king once before but had declined. His residence was in al-Ahwāz. Having been made king, he put on the crown and sat on the throne. They killed him a few days later; he had ruled for not even a month.

The Persian grandees were at a loss for a member of the royal house to make king. Then they found a man named Fīrūz, a descendant of Anūshirwān on his mother's side,[1120] and they made him king, out of necessity. When he was seated to be crowned—he had a large head—he said, "How tight this crown is!" The Persian grandees augured evil from his words, so they killed him.

A son of Kisrā named Farrukhzād Khusraw came forward; he had escaped to Nisibis when Shīrūya went on his killing spree. He was crowned and became king. He was of noble character and reigned for a year.

Then they found Yazdajird, son of Kisrā, whose mother was a cupper with whom Kisrā had lain; she had produced Yazdajird, but they had augured evil and had hidden him. Necessity now made them turn to him, so they brought him out, although their affairs were troubled and the leaders of his realm were inclined to reject him. After four years of his reign, Saʿd b. Abī Waqqāṣ appeared before al-Qādisiyya, and he sent out Rustam against him.[1121] Then the Muslims reached al-Madāʾin, the capital, on the day of Nawrūz,[1122] for which the Persians had prepared with all manner of dishes and beautiful decorations. The Persians were routed. Yazdajird fled, but the Muslims continued to pursue

1120 Cf. al-Ṭabarī, *Taʾrīkh*, 1:1066 (trans. Bosworth, *The History of al-Ṭabarī*, v, 408): "He was the son of Ṣahārbukht, daughter of Yazdāndādh, son of Kisrā (I) Anūshirwān."

1121 Al-Yaʿqūbī defers details of the Muslim conquest of Iraq until his account of the caliphate of ʿUmar; see especially ed. Leiden, 2:161–165.

1122 The Persian New Year festival, falling at the vernal equinox.

him until they reached Marw. He entered a mill, but the owner of the mill killed him.[1123] His reign, until he was killed, had lasted twenty years.

The Persians used to venerate fires. They did not wash with water after relieving themselves, but only with oil.[1124] They did not put doors on their palaces; their only doors were curtains, with guards protecting them from men. They ate only to the accompaniment of *zamzama*, which means "faint speech."[1125] They married their mothers, sisters, and daughters, thinking that this was a gift to them, a way of honoring them, and a way of drawing close to God in them.[1126] They did not have bathhouses or privies. They venerated water, fire, the sun, the moon, and all the (other) luminaries. 1:199

They reckoned the seasons by their months and their feast days. Autumn among them consisted of the months of Shahrīvar, Mihr, and Ābān; winter consisted of Ādhar, Day, and Bahman; spring consisted of Isfandārmudh, Farvardīn, and Ardībihisht; and summer consisted of Khurdādh, Tīr, and Murdādh. In autumn they used to add five days that they called the days of Andargāh; thus the year came to three hundred and sixty-five days, their months being thirty days. Their New Year is the day of Nawrūz, which is the first day of Farvardīn, which falls in Nīsān and Ayyār, when the sun has passed into Aries; it is the day of their greatest festival. The day of Mihrajān falls on the sixteenth day of the month of Mihr. Between Nawrūz and Mihrajān there are one hundred and seventy-five days: five months and twenty-five days. Mihrajān comes in Tishrīn II.

1123 On the reign of Yazdajird III, the last Sasanian ruler of Iran (reigned 632–651), see al-Ṭabarī, *Taʾrīkh*, 1:1067 (trans. Bosworth, *The History of al-Ṭabarī*, V, 409–411); al-Dīnawarī, *al-Akhbār al-ṭiwāl*, 148–149; al-Masʿūdī, *Murūj*, 2:234 (§ 655).

1124 Arabic *tastanjī* refers specifically to washing the anus after defecation. The taboo on using water for this purpose accords with the Zoroastrian prohibition on polluting water.

1125 *Zamzama*, an Arabic word meaning "a confused noise," came to designate the intoning of Zoroastrian prayers and scriptures ("droning"). Zoroastrian priests observed ritual silence during meals, which were accompanied by the recitation of scriptures in a low tone. See the article by M. Morony in EI^2, s.v. Madjūs, and the article in EI^2, s.v. Zamzama. Curiously, the account in al-Masʿūdī, *Murūj*, 2:108–109 (§ 533) explains such mealtime silence medically, as a way of insuring proper digestion, and dates the custom to the days of Kayūmarth.

1126 On the question of such consanguineous marriages (Pahlavi *xwēdōdah*) and to what extent they were practiced outside royal and noble families and perhaps the clergy, see the article by P. O. Skjærvø in *Encyclopædia Iranica*, s.v. Marriage ii. Next-of-Kin Marriage in Zoroastrianism.

The Persians used to give a name to each of the days of their months. These are the *rūzāt*. The first of them is Hurmuz; then Bahman, Ardībihisht, Shahrīvar, Isfandārmudh, Khurdādh, Murdādh, Day-ba-Ādhar, Ādhar, Ābān, Khūr, Māh,
1:200 Tīr, | [Jūsh], Day-ba-Mihr, Mihr, Surūsh, Rashn, Farvardīn, Bahrām, Rām, Bādh, Day-ba-Dīn, [Dīn], Ard, Ashtādh, Āsmān, Zāmyādh, Mārasfand, and Anīrān.[1127]

The doctrine held by the majority of them, as transmitted from Zoroaster, whom they claim was their prophet, is that the existence of Light eternally has never ceased; they give it the name Zurvān. He thought of Evil because of a slip on his part about which he (Zoroaster) taught them.[1128] Because the beautiful can change into the ugly and the fragrant into the malodorous, so the Eternal, according to them, is not immune to alteration and corruption in part, though not in its entirety. When the Eternal thought of Evil, he sighed deeply; that Sorrow emerged from within him and took shape before him. They call that Sorrow that took shape before the Eternal by the name of Ahriman; they also call Zurvān Hurmuz.[1129] They say that Ahriman wanted to fight Hurmuz; Hurmuz, however, was loath to do so, lest he do evil, so he made peace with Ahriman on condition that he would make over to him the creation of everything harmful and corrupt.[1130] They assert that they are two bodies and two spirits and that, between them, there is a gap of rancor, as the two of them can never meet. Hurmuz, they say, is Light, the maker of bodies and their spirits; Ahriman makes only that which is harmful in these substances, such as venom in reptiles, as well as rage, anger, disgust, malevolence, aggression, rancor, and fear in animals. Thus God is the maker of substances and of their permanent accidents.[1131]

1127 The bracketed names, missing from the MSS, are supplied by the Leiden editor on the basis of other sources; see, for example, al-Bīrūnī, *Āthār*, 44. On the significance of these names and logic behind the series, see A. Christensen, *L'Iran sous les Sassanides*, 158–159.

1128 The syntax of the Arabic is strained; the text may be unreliable.

1129 Al-Yaʿqūbī's account here presents an essentially monotheistic version of Iranian religion—Zurvān and Hurmuz are one and the same, eternal and good, while Ahriman, the power of evil, is a lesser emanation—as opposed to a dualistic doctrine that presents Hurmuz/Ahuramazda and Ahriman as coeternal.

1130 Possibly, "that the creation of everything harmful and corrupt be made over to him." The Arabic verb can be read as either active or passive.

1131 That is, Hurmuz/Ahuramazda (here called simply God) is the maker of substances and their permanent accidents, while Ahriman is responsible for the evil affections (passions) that overcome the good nature of these substances.

At the beginning of the reign of Ardashīr Bābakān,[1132] the residences of the Persian kings were in Iṣṭakhr, one of the districts of Fārs. Afterward, the kings moved about until the reign of | Anūshirwān son of Qubādh, who settled at 1:201 al-Madā'in, in the land of Iraq, which became the royal residence. Learned astrologers and physicians agreed that there was no healthier, better, and more temperate place than that site and the part of the region of Babylon near it.

The provinces that the Persians ruled and where their authority held sway included the following:

The districts of Khurāsān: Naysābūr, Herat, Marw, Marw al-Rūd, al-Fāryāb, al-Ṭālaqān, Balkh, Bukhārā, Bādhghīs, Bāward, Gharjīstān, Ṭūs, Sarakhs, and Jurjān. Over these districts was a governor whom they called the Iṣpahbadh of Khurāsān.

The districts of al-Jabal:[1133] Ṭabaristān, al-Rayy, Qazwīn, Zanjān, Qumm, Iṣbahān, Hamadhān, Nihāwand, al-Dīnawar, Ḥulwān, Māsabadhān, Mihrajānqadhaq, Shahrazūr, al-Ṣāmaghān, and Ādharbayjān. These districts had a military commander called the Iṣpahbadh of Ādharbayjān.

Kirmān, and Fārs and its districts:[1134] Iṣṭakhr, Shīrāz, Arrajān, al-Nawbandajān, Jūr, Kāzarūn, Fasā, Dārābjird, Ardashīr Khurra, and Sābūr.

Al-Ahwāz and its districts: Jundaysābūr, al-Sūs, Nahr Tīrā, Manādhir, Tustar, Īdhaj, and Rām Hurmuz. Over them was a military commander called the Iṣpahbadh of Fārs.

The districts of Iraq, which had forty-eight subdivisions on the Euphrates and the Tigris.[1135] The Euphrates watered Bādūrayyā, al-Anbār, Bahrasīr, al-Rūmaqān, Upper al-Zāb, Lower al-Zāb, Middle al-Zāb, Zandaward, Maysān, Kūthā, Nahr Durqīṭ, Nahr Jawbar, Upper al-Fallūja, | Lower al-Fallūja, Bābil, 1:202 Khuṭarniya, al-Jubba, al-Badāt, al-Saylaḥīn, Furāt Bāduqlā, Sūrā, Barbismā,

---

1132 The manuscripts here have Ardashīr ibn ("son of") Bābakān, which may have resulted from a copyist's error, as Bābakān by itself means "son of Bābak." Al-Ya'qūbī's earlier references to him have been correct in form. Curiously, al-Dīnawarī, in *al-Akhbār al-ṭiwāl*, 44, has the same mistake, but immediately follows it with the correct genealogy: "He is Ardashīr b. Bābak b. Sāsān the Younger ..." as in al-Ṭabarī, *Ta'rīkh*, 1:813.

1133 Al-Jabal (the Mountain), occurring more frequently in the plural as al-Jibāl (the Mountains), is a general term for the western part of Persia, corresponding roughly to ancient Media. See the article by C. E. Bosworth in *Encyclopædia Iranica*, s.v. Jebāl.

1134 Because all of the districts in the following list belong to Fārs province, the list of districts for Kirmān has apparently fallen out of the text.

1135 "Subdivisions" translates Arabic *ṭassūj*, from Persian *tasōk* (one-quarter), the regular word for subdivisions of a *kūra* (here translated as "district"). See the article by M. Morony in *EI*², s.v. Ṭassūdj. Note that al-Ya'qūbī's list names only forty-seven subdivisions. For other, more complete, listings see Ibn Qudāma and Ibn Khurdādhbih.

Nahr al-Malik, Bārūsmā, and Nistar. The Tigris watered Nahr Būq, [Nahr Bīn,][1136] Buzurjsābūr, Upper al-Rādhān, Lower al-Rādhān, al-Zābiyayn, al-Daskara, Birāzrūz, Silsil, Mahrūdh, Jalūlāʾ, Upper al-Nahrawān, Middle al-Nahrawān, Lower al-Nahrawān, Jāzir, al-Madāʾin, al-Bandanījīn, Rustuqubādh, Abazqubādh, al-Mubārak, Bādurāyā, and Bākusāyā. They have a fourth military commander called the Iṣpahbadh of the West. The last of the Persian outposts along the Euphrates was al-Anbār; then one reached the outposts of the Romans. Along the Tigris [...];[1137] then one reached the outposts of the Romans. However, the Persians on occasion would enter Roman territory surreptitiously, while the Romans sometimes would enter Persian territory.

The whole name applying to each king of the Persians was Kisrā; and when they named him and mentioned him, they would say "Kisrā Shāhanshāh," meaning "King of Kings."[1138] They called the vizier *buzurj farmadār*, meaning "the one in charge of affairs."[1139] They called the scholar who was in charge of the ordinances of their religion *mōbadh mōbadhān*, meaning "the scholar of scholars."[1140] The first of them to whom the name was applied was Zoroaster. They called the keeper of the fire the *hirbadh*. They called the secretary *dabīrbadh*.[1141] They called the great one among them[1142] the *iṣpahbadh*, meaning "the
1:203 chief," and the one | beneath him was the *fādūsbān*, meaning "the repeller of

1136 Supplied by the Leiden editor.

1137 There is a lacuna in the text, although the MSS show no space.

1138 Kisrā was the Arabicized version of the proper name of two prominent rulers of the later Sasanian dynasty, Khusraw Anūshirwān and Khusraw Aparwīz. The Arabs came to treat the name in its Arabic form as a title held by every ruler of the dynasty, although there is no evidence that it was so used among the Persians. The title *shāhanshāh* (properly, *shāhān shāh*, king of kings) is indeed ancient and can be traced through the Sasanians and Arsacids back to the Achaemenids. See the articles in EI^2, s.v. Kisrā (M. Morony), and s.v. S̲h̲āh "King," and S̲h̲āhans̲h̲āh (F. C. de Blois). The most detailed examination of the Arabic historians' lists of Persian administrative titles may be found in A. Christensen, *L'Iran sous les Sassanides*, 265, 518–526.

1139 Middle Persian *vuzurg-framadhār* (chief giver of commands).

1140 Arabic *ʿālim al-ʿulamāʾ* (chief scholar), the head of the Zoroastrian priesthood. The title *mōbadh* derives from an older form *magupat* (ruler of magi). For the history of the term and the office, see the article by M. Guidi and M. Morony in EI^2, s.v. Mōbad̲h̲.

1141 The title *dabīrbadh* means "chief secretary," an ordinary secretary being simply a *dabīr*. For a history of the term, see the article by Aḥmad Tafażżoli in *Encyclopædia Iranica*, s.v. Dabīr.

1142 The antecedent of the pronoun is unspecified. While it might refer to the subject of the sentence (that is, the Persians called the great one among themselves ...), it makes more sense as "the great one among military ranks."

enemies."[1143] They called the head of a province the *marzbān*. They called the head of districts the *shahrīj*.[1144] They called the masters of warfare and leaders of armies the *asāwira*.[1145] They called the person in charge of the *maẓālim* the *shāhrīsht*.[1146] And they called the head of the chancery the *mardmārghadh*.[1147]

The Kingdoms of the North

[When Peleg, son of Eber, son of Shelah, son of Arpachshad, son of Shem, son of Noah, divided] the earth among the descendants of Noah, the children of Gomer, son of Tubal, [son of Japheth, son of Noah] went out traveling to the east.[1148] A group of them, the children of Nāʿūmā,[1149] crossed toward the north,

---

1143 The *iṣpahbadh* as military chief has already been mentioned. The term *fādūsbān* appears to go back to Pahlavi *pādgōsbān*, of uncertain meaning. See the article by Mansour Shaki in *Encyclopædia Iranica*, s.v. Class System iii. In the Parthian and Sasanian Periods.

1144 Pahlavi *shahrīg*, apparently referring to a rank superior to that of *dihqān*; see A. Christensen, *L'Iran sous les Sassanides*, 140.

1145 Literally, "horsemen," from an Arabic plural of *suwār*, a loanword from Middle Persian *aswār*, pl. *aswārān* (horsemen, cavalry). See the article by P. O. Skjærvø in *Encyclopædia Iranica*, s.v. Aswār.

1146 Literally, "They called the master of the *maẓālim* the *shāhrīsht*." The reference is clearly to a judicial office, but the exact meaning is unclear. The *maẓālim* was an institution that took various shapes at various times in the Islamic world. It essentially was a system of justice outside the regular *qāḍīs*' courts and received petitions against official and unofficial abuses of power; cf. the article by J. S. Nielsen in *EI*², s.v. Maẓālim. The etymology and meaning of *shāhrīsht* are unclear. Christensen, who translated the term as "juges de paix" (*L'Iran sous les Sassanides*, 265, 300) added, "mais nous n'avons pas d'information sur l'activité et la compétence de ces fonctionnaires."

1147 The title for the head of the chancery (*dīwān*) is certainly corrupt. The Leiden editor conjectured an original reading of *al-mardmānbadh*, but this does not correspond to any known title. A. Christensen, *L'Iran sous les Sassanides*, 524–525, referring to this passage, conjectured an original reading of *Ērān-āmārkār*, "préposé comptable de l'empire."

1148 The bracketed words were added by the Leiden editor. Parallel, al-Masʿūdī, *Murūj*, 1:154 (§311). The translation follows the reading of M, *fī sīrat al-mashriq*, instead of the Leiden editor's emendation *fī yusrat al-mashriq* (to the left of the east).

1149 Probably to be restored as Togarmah (cf. Genesis 10:3); in unpointed Arabic script, the two words could easily be confused. The association of Togarmah with peoples of the north goes back at least to Ezekiel 38:6 ("Togarmah of the north quarters"). Al-Masʿūdī, *Murūj*, 1:154 (§311), has *Arʿū*.

bearing left; they spread out in the country and became several kingdoms: the Burjān, the Daylam, the Tatur, the Ṭaylasān, Jīlān, Fīlān, the Alān, the Khazar, the Dūdāniyya, and the Arman. The Khazars, who had taken over most the territory of Armenia, had a king called Khāqān; he had a deputy called Yazīd Balāsh[1150] in charge of al-Rān, Jurzān, al-Basfurrajān, and al-Sīsajān. These districts were called Armenia IV, which Qubādh, the king of the Persians, conquered. It came into the possession of Anūshirwān, up to the Alān Gates, a hundred farsakhs, containing three hundred and sixty cities. The Persians took possession of Bāb al-Abwāb, Ṭabarsarān, and al-Balanjar; they built the city of
1:204 Qālīqalā and many other cities and settled them with people from Fārs. Then | the Khazars retook what the Persians had taken from them, and it remained in their hands for a time. Then the Romans overcame them and installed over Armenia IV a king named al-Mawriyān.[1151] They divided into several fiefdoms, with each leader among them in his own fortress and stronghold. These are well-known kingdoms of theirs.

Some of Gomer's descendants crossed Transoxiana; they spread out in the land and became different kingdoms and many nations.[1152] Belonging to them are al-Khuttal, al-Ruwāsān,[1153] al-Ushrūsana, al-Sughd, al-Farghāna, al-Shāsh, the Karluk Turks,[1154] the Tughuzghuz, the Kīmāk Turks,[1155] and Tibet. Among the Turks there are groups that possess villages, cities, and fortresses. Others live in the high mountains and in the steppes, like the Bedouins; they have long hair, and their dwellings are felt tents. When they go on raids, one tent has twenty fighters. They shoot arrows and never miss. Their homes extend continuously from the first districts of Khurāsān to the mountains of Tibet and the mountains of China.

1150 The reading is conjectural.

1151 This is the conjecture of the Leiden editor; the MSS have "al-Marzbān." Al-Mawriyān would refer to Maurianus, the Byzantine commander of Armenia in 653/654.

1152 More detailed parallel, probably from a common source, in al-Masʿūdī, *Murūj*, 1:154 (§ 312).

1153 Retaining the reading of the manuscripts, rather than the Leiden editor's emendation to al-Qawādiyān. Cf. Marquart, *Ērānšahr*, 304, and Minorsky, *Ḥudūd*, xxxi–xxxiii, 332, 336, which identify the region as Ruwēsān. It may be the same as the region of Rīvshārān mentioned by Ibn Khurdādhbih, 36, 40, and by Yāqūt, 2:171, or as Rāvshār in al-Ṭabarī, *Taʾrīkh*, 3:1875.

1154 The manuscripts read *al-Turk wa-Kharlukhiyya* ("the Turks and the Karluks"), almost certainly a mistake for *al-Turk al-Kharlukhiyya* ("the Karluk Turks"). On this Turkish tribal group in Central Asia, see the article by C. E. Bosworth in EI², s.v. Ḳarluḳ.

1155 On this early Turkish people living in western Siberia, see the article by C. E. Bosworth in EI², s.v. Kimäk.

As for Tibet, it is a large country, greater than China. Their kingdom is mighty; they are people of craftsmanship and wisdom, rivaling the craftsmanship of China. In their country there are gazelles whose navels are musk.[1156] They are idol worshippers and have fire temples. Their prowess is so great that nobody goes to war with them.

The Kings of China[1157]

Experienced transmitters, learned men, and others who have traveled to the land of China and lived there long enough to understand the affairs of the Chinese, to read their books, and to become acquainted with the accounts of their ancient authorities, | having seen (such information) in their books, heard 1:205
it from their (oral) accounts, or (observed it) written over the gates of their cities and on the temples of their idols and inscribed in gold on stone, have stated that the first to rule China was Ṣāyin[1158] son of Bāʿūr son of Yaraj son of ʿĀmūr[1159] son of Japheth son of Noah son of Lamech.[1160] He had built a ship[1161] in imitation of

---

1156 Musk, a secretion from a scent gland located between the genitals and the navel of male musk deer, was exported from Tibet and used in perfumes. See the article by A. Dietrich in *EI*², s.v. Misk.

1157 For another early Arabic description of China, see al-Masʿūdī, *Murūj*, 1:154–173 (§311–355). This section of al-Yaʿqūbī's text has been translated and compared to al-Masʿūdī, without commentary, in G. Ferrand, "Les relations de la Chine avec le golfe Persique avant l'hégire," in *Mélanges Gaudefroy-Demombynes*, 131–140. As Ferrand indicates, al-Yaʿqūbī and al-Masʿūdī had a common source for some of their information. A general introduction to the subject of Islamic writers and China can be found in the article by C. E. Bosworth, M. Hartmann, and R. Israeli in *EI*², s.v. al-Ṣīn.

1158 Al-Yaʿqūbī (or his source) has provided China (*al-Ṣīn* in Arabic) with an eponymous first ruler (*al-Ṣāʾin*). Previous examples of similar etymologies include the derivation of the Arabic name for the Greeks (*al-Yūnāniyyūn*) from their purported ancestor *Yūnān* (ed. Leiden 1:161) and of the name of the Romans (*al-Rūm*) from an ancestor *Rūm* (1:164). Below (1:210), the first ruler of Egypt (*Miṣr* in Arabic) is named *Miṣr*. In fact, the Arabic name for China (*al-Ṣīn*) resembles the name of the Ch'in dynasty, which ruled from 221 to 206 BCE. See Minorsky, *Ḥudūd al-ʿālam*, 237, n. 3.

1159 Perhaps to be read Ghāmūr, for Gomer, as above, ed. Leiden, 1:13.

1160 Here as elsewhere when discussing ethnic origins, al-Yaʿqūbī is concerned to trace their genealogy back to Noah, the point being that as all of humanity apart from the family of Noah was drowned in the flood, all the peoples of the world can be traced back to his dispersed descendants.

1161 Arabic, *fulk*. The choice of this term, rather than the more common term for ship

Noah's ship, and accompanied by many of his children and kinsmen he set sail and crossed the sea. When he came to a certain place of which he approved, he settled there and called it al-Ṣīn, naming it after himself. He had many offspring and his descendants multiplied. They adhered to the religion of his people, and his dynasty continued without interruption for 300 years.[1162]

One of these (kings) was ʿArūn,[1163] who erected buildings and practiced craftsmanship. He initiated the custom of building gilded temples and set within them an image of his father, placing it in the place of honor of the temple. Whenever he entered, he prostrated himself before that image to venerate the image of his father. Ṣāyin had a name whose meaning in Arabic is Son of Heaven.[1164] It was beginning in this time that idols were worshipped in China. The reign of ʿArūn lasted 140 years.[1165]

Another of them was ʿAyīr,[1166] who traveled the length and breadth of China, built great cities, and erected domed temples of bamboo[1167] and gilded copper. He made an image of his father from gold, crowned with a diadem of gems, lead, and inlaid copper. All the people of his kingdom, in the cities and countryside, adopted this image, saying, "The subjects must make an image of a king who ruled them from heaven and dealt justly with them." The reign of ʿAyīr lasted 130 years.

(*safīna*) is significant as being the word used for ship generally in the Qurʾān and specifically for Noah's ark, e.g. Qurʾān 7:64. See Donner, *Narratives of Islamic Origins*, 57–60.

1162 Cf. al-Masʿūdī, *Murūj*, 1:156 (§ 316), where the story of the eponymous founder of China is not given and where the first king to rule in the Chinese capital (Yanṣū in al-Masʿūdī's rendering) is given the otherwise unattested name Nasṭarṭās (vocalization and reading uncertain).

1163 Al-Yaʿqūbī now jumps to the T'ang dynasty (r. 618–907 CE) and several rulers on whom he has found information. Unfortunately, the Arabic transmission of the names is so ambiguous and defective that it is impossible to assign them to particular Chinese rulers.

1164 Arabic, Ibn al-Samāʾ.

1165 The corresponding king in al-Masʿūdī, *Murūj*, 1:156–157 (§ 316), named ʿAwūn or ʿArūn, is given a reign of 250 years.

1166 The reading is uncertain, as the ductus in M is undotted. The corresponding name in al-Masʿūdī, *Murūj*, 1:157 (§ 317), is ʿAythadūn (vocalization uncertain), which Pellat, the editor of al-Masʿūdī (see 7:433 of his edition) conjectured was originally Ghan-thaydūn, standing for Ghwâng Taï T'ong (r. 627–649, modern transliteration Taizong).

1167 Following M: *al-khayzurān*. The Leiden editor conjectured an original reading of *al-jandalāt*, "stones."

Another of them was ʿAynān,[1168] who wronged the people of his kingdom with foul chastisement and expelled them to islands in the sea. They used to go | 1:206
from those islands to places where there were fruits for them to eat, but where they also found wild animals. Eventually they became friendly with the animals and the latter became friendly with them; they would ravish the animals and sometimes the animals would ravish their women, so that misshapen creatures arose among them. The first generation died out, and then one generation after another came and went; knowledge of their original languages faded away, and they began to speak something incomprehensible. In the islands from which one crosses over to the land of China this phenomenon was extremely pronounced, and many peoples (speaking different languages emerged). ʿAynān was given a name whose meaning in Arabic is "He of Evil Constitution." His reign lasted 100 years.

Another of them was Kharābāt,[1169] who came to power when he was of a young age. Then he grew older and more experienced, his authority increased, and he became a good ruler. He sent an embassy representing him to Babylonia and those parts of the land of the Romans adjoining it to familiarize themselves with its traditions of wisdom and craftsmanship. He sent with them samples of the crafts of China, the silken garments and other things made there, and such devices[1170] and other items as had been brought from (adjoining) lands, and ordered them to bring back to him every craft and novelty from Babylonia and the land of the Romans and to familiarize themselves with the laws of the people's religion. This was the first time that the goods of China entered the land of Iraq and adjoining lands and merchants set out across the Sea of China for trade. Much impressed by the elegant Chinese wares brought to them, the kings built ships and used them to engage in trade. That was the first time that merchants entered China. The reign of Kharābāt lasted 60 years.

Another of them was Tūtāl.[1171] The people of China say that on the gates of their cities they found it written that no king like him had ever ruled them.

1168 Sic M. The corresponding name al-Masʿūdī, *Murūj*, 1:157 (§ 318), is given as ʿAythanān (vocalization uncertain), which Pellat identified with Hinen-T'ong (r. 713–756).

1169 Al-Masʿūdī, *Murūj*, 1:157–158 (§ 319), gives the name as Ḥaratān (vocalization uncertain) and describes his expedition to the west—in al-Masʿūdī's account a naval expedition. Pellat identified him with Mou-T'ong (r. 821–825).

1170 Arabic, *al-ālāt*. Sic ed. Leiden, emending on the basis of the parallel in al-Masʿūdī; M reads *al-āfāq*, "the horizons," which is problematical.

1171 According to al-Masʿūdī, *Murūj*, 1:158–160 (§ 320–323), Tūtāl (the reading is uncertain) was the son of the previous ruler and reigned 150 years. Similar events are assigned to his reign.

They regarded him with such affection as they had never bestowed on any
1:207 other king. It was he who established for them every | tradition they follow in their religious rites, social customs, crafts, laws, and precepts. His reign lasted 78 years. When he died, the people continued to weep for him for a long time and to carry him on thrones of gold and carts of silver. Then they prepared aloes, ambergris, sandalwood, and other aromatics for him, set them alight, and cast him into the flames. His retainers even began to throw themselves into the fire because of their grief for him and their loyalty to him. This became a custom among them. They placed his image on their dinars, which they call *al-kawnaḥ*,[1172] and images of him were also placed over the entrances to their homes.

The land of China is an expansive one. One who wishes to travel to China crosses seven seas, each of which has a color, odor, fish, and wind not to be found in the sea that follows it.[1173] The first of these seas is the Sea of Persia,[1174] which one travels beginning at Sīrāf. Its terminal point is Ra's al-Jumjuma,[1175] which is a strait where divers fish for pearls. The second sea, which begins at Ra's al-Jumjuma, is called Lārawī.[1176] It is a great sea; in it lie the islands of the Waqwāq[1177] and other Zanj peoples, and on those islands there are kings. This sea can be navigated only by the stars.[1178] It has enormous fish, and concerning

1172 In M the word is undotted. The reading is uncertain.

1173 On the route described here, see Kennedy, *Historical Atlas*, map 60; also al-Masʿūdī, *Murūj*, 1:156 (§315), where it is stated that it took three months to reach China by sea.

1174 Arabic, *Baḥr Fāris*, here meaning the Persian Gulf, though the term could also refer to the Indian Ocean. The port of Sīrāf lay on the coast of Fārs province, some 200 km south of Būshahr, near the modern village of Ṭāhirī. See the article by C. E. Bosworth in EI^2, s.v. Sīrāf.

1175 Arabic for 'Cape of the Skull.' This appears to be the reading of M (though undotted) and it is the reading of al-Masʿūdī, *Murūj*, 1:177 (§362); ed. Leiden reads Ra's al-Jumḥa. Neither name corresponds to an attested name, although clearly the Strait of Hormuz is meant. The pearl beds lie about 300 to 400 km to the southwest.

1176 That is, the Arabian Sea. Cf. al-Sīrāfī, *Akhbār al-Ṣīn wa-l-Hind*, 29–30; al-Masʿūdī, *Murūj*, 1:177–179 (§362–367); al-Rāmhurmuzī, *ʿAjāʾib al-Hind*, 229 (Excursus A).

1177 Waqwāq was an island or group of islands said to be inhabited by a dark-skinned people (*Zanj* is one of the names for blacks). Many candidates have been proposed off the coast of Africa and in the Indian Ocean. Al-Yaʿqūbī may have the Maldives in mind. See the article by F. Viré in EI^2, s.v. Wāḳwāḳ.

1178 The point is that the direct route across the Arabian Sea to the Malibar coast of southern India crosses the high seas, where there are no landmarks to establish one's bearings. Ships often preferred to "coast," sailing close to shore just at the horizon as

it there are many amazing stories of things beyond description.[1179] Then comes the third sea, which is called Harkand.[1180] In it lies the island of Sarandīb,[1181] which has gemstone,[1182] rubies, and other precious (stones). In this sea lie islands that are ruled by princes, who in turn are ruled by a king. On the islands in this sea there is bamboo and cane.[1183] The fourth sea is called Kalāh Bār,[1184] a shallow sea in which there are enormous serpents. Sometimes even ships sailing with the wind are wrecked in this sea. In it lie islands on which camphor trees grow. The fifth sea is called Salāhiṭ; it is a vast sea | about which many 1:208
amazing stories are told.[1185] The sixth sea is called Kardanj and receives much rain.[1186] The seventh sea is called the Ṣankhay[1187] Sea and also Kanjalā, i.e., the Sea of China.[1188] It can only be traversed on a south wind. Then (mariners)

---

seen from shore to avoid being seen by pirates, and hopping from port to port. See Udovitch, *Time, the Sea and Society*, 541–545; Conrad, "Islam and the Sea," 133.

1179 See, e.g., al-Sīrāfī, *Akhbār al-Ṣīn wa-l-Hind*, 39; al-Rāmhurmuzī, *ʿAjāʾib al-Hind*, *passim*.

1180 That is, the Bay of Bengal. For possible derivations of the Arabic name, see R. Hartmann in *EI*², s.v. Baḥr al-Hind. See also al-Sīrāfī, *Akhbār al-Ṣīn wa-l-Hind*, 30–34.

1181 That is, Ceylon. The Arabic name is derived ultimately from Sanskrit Siṃhaladvīpa (Ceylon Island). See the article by C. E. Bosworth in *EI*², s.v. Sarandīb.

1182 Arabic, *al-jawhar*, here probably ivory.

1183 Arabic, *qanā*, the material used to make long spears, which in Arabic are called *qanāt*, from the material from which they were made.

1184 The Andaman Sea. Cf. al-Sīrāfī, *Akhbār al-Ṣīn wa-l-Hind*, 37; al-Masʿūdī, *Murūj*, 1:181–182 (§ 374); al-Rāmhurmuzī, *ʿAjāʾib al-Hind*, 255–262 (Excursus B). The western coast of the Malay Peninsula was a staging and trading region marking the midpoint on the route between China and the Middle East. Al-Masʿūdī (*Murūj*, 1:166 [§ 336]) explains that traders from Iraq, Iran, and Oman routinely continued on to China; the Chinese, on the other hand, conducted their business on the Malay coast and then returned, though in earlier times they had proceeded to the Persian Gulf, landing at such ports as Sīrāf, al-Ubulla, and Basra. The merchant Sulaymān confirms that Chinese ships were being loaded in Sīrāf in his time (al-Sīrāfī, *Akhbār al-Ṣīn wa-l-Hind*, 35).

1185 The Malacca Strait, between Sumatra and the Malay Peninsula. Al-Yaʿqūbī seems to have confused this body of water with the Andaman Sea, since it is the latter that is quite expansive, and the former that could be said to be shallow (literally, "it has little water").

1186 This toponym often refers to the Gulf of Thailand, but al-Yaʿqūbī seems to have in mind the southern reaches of the South China Sea. Cf. al-Masʿūdī, *Murūj*, 1:182 (§ 375), where this sea is called Baḥr Kanduranj.

1187 Following the reading M (undotted) and al-Masʿūdī, *Murūj*, 1:177 (§ 361). Pellat, in his index (*Murūj*, 6: 430) sees the word as reflecting Chinese Tchang-Khaï. Ed. Leiden, seeing it as a variant of the next name, points it as Ṣanjā or Ṣanjay.

1188 That is, the South China Sea. See al-Sīrāfī, *Akhbār al-Ṣīn wa-l-Hind*, 38.

come to a freshwater sea[1189] that has military garrisons and populated regions, and finally they reach the city of Khānfū.[1190]

One who wishes to travel to China overland proceeds by the Balkh River and crosses the lands of Soghdia, Farghāna, al-Shāsh,[1191] and Tibet until he reaches China.[1192]

The king resides in a palace of his, living in seclusion. His chief of security, the chief of his tax affairs, the chief of his military guard, and the chief of his information office are eunuchs; in fact, most of his retainers are eunuchs and are very trustworthy.[1193] The tax revenue comes from a capitation tax that they levy on every adult male on a per capita basis, because they allow no man not to have a trade: if someone is unable to work because of illness or old age, they maintain him from the king's purse. They revere their dead and grieve for them for long periods. Their punishment for most crimes is death: they execute liars, thieves, and adulterers, except if they belong to a circle of eminent individuals. If someone accuses any tax official[1194] of acting unjustly and the accusation against him is proven to be true, that official is executed; otherwise, the one who accused him, if he has deliberately lied, is executed.[1195]

China has three land frontiers and one by sea. The first frontier is with the Turks and Tughuzghuz,[1196] with whom they were always waging wars; then they

1189 That is, the estuary of the Pearl River, leading from the sites of modern Hong Kong and Macau to the city of Guangzhou (Canton). According to al-Masʿūdī, *Murūj*, 1:163–164 (§ 329), it took six days to sail from the sea up this estuary to Canton. Cf. al-Sīrāfī, *Akhbār al-Ṣīn wa-l-Hind*, 60; and Ibn Baṭṭūṭa, *Travels* (trans. Beckingham), 4:894.

1190 The Arabic name resembles closely the Chinese Guangzhou (Canton). On the Arabs' knowledge of this city see al-Sīrāfī, *Akhbār al-Ṣīn wa-l-Hind*, 36.

1191 Al-Shāsh is the Arabic name for Tashkent and the surrounding area. See the article by W. Barthold et al. in *EI*², s.v. Tas̲h̲kent.

1192 On the overland route to China, see Albert Herrmann, *Die alten Seidenstrassen zwischen China und Syrien*, 77–116; Christoph Baumer, *Southern Silk Road: In the Footsteps of Sir Aurel Stein and Sven Hedin.* As can be seen here, al-Yaʿqūbī seems to have had almost no information about overland travel to China. From Baghdad the usual route would have been the much faster (and less expensive) maritime route down the Tigris to the Persian Gulf, and then by sea to China. But cf. al-Masʿūdī, *Murūj*, 1:186 (§ 385), where he says that in Balkh he met an old man who had visited China many times and had never traveled by sea.

1193 Cf. al-Sīrāfī, *Akhbār al-Ṣīn wa-l-Hind*, 64; al-Masʿūdī, *Murūj*, 1:167 (§ 337).

1194 Emending to read, *ʿāmil min al-ʿummāl*. M reads, *ʿāmil al-ʿummāl*, "the chief of the tax officials." Ed. Leiden has *ʿāmil al-aʿmāl*, perhaps to be rendered "the governor," or more generally any government official.

1195 Cf. al-Sīrāfī, *Akhbār al-Ṣīn wa-l-Hind*, 52–53, 54, 62.

1196 Arabic, *Tughuzghuz*, from Turkish Toḳuz Oghuz (Nine Oghuz), originally a group of

agreed on terms of peace and confirmed the treaty with marriages. The second frontier is Tibet.[1197] Between Tibet and China there is a mountain on which stand military outposts where (Chinese) garrisons stand guard against Tibet and where Tibetan garrisons stand guard against China, all of them in a zone between the frontiers of the two lands.[1198] | The third frontier faces a people 1:209
called the Mānasās, who have an isolated kingdom in a vast land. It is said that their land is so vast in length and breadth that it would take several years to cross it either way. No one is known to live beyond them, and they are on good terms with the people of China. The single seaward frontier, which is the way by which the Muslims come, consists of the various seas that we have mentioned.

Their religion involves the worship of pagan idols, the sun, and the moon, and they have feast days dedicated to their idols. The most important of these feasts, called al-Zārār, comes at [the beginning of] the year.[1199] They go out to a gathering place, prepare food and drink there, and then they bring forth a man who has dedicated himself to that great idol and to all his desires and has been allowed to have whatever he wants. He is brought before the idol, and, having put something highly inflammable on his fingers, he burns his fingers with fire and allows them to serve as a lamp at the feet of the idol, until he himself is consumed in the flames and falls away dead. (His corpse) is then cut up, and whoever is able to gain possession of a splinter of bone or a fragment of his clothing considers it a triumph. Then they bring another man who wishes to dedicate himself to the idol for the new year to come and take the other's place. He dons the (special) clothing, and the people beat cymbals in his honor. Then they disperse, eat and drink and celebrate for a week, and then return home.

The month in which this feast takes place is called Janāḥ and is the first day of June. The Chinese also have a computation,[1200] and the months are called

---

nine clans. Al-Yaʿqūbī's mention of warfare ended by a peace apparently refers to the peace between the ruler of the eastern Turks, Bilgä Ḳaghan, and the T'ang emperor Hiuan-tsang in 721–722 (see the article by Edith Ambrose et al. in *EI*², s.v. Turks; also the article by Cl. Cahen in *EI*², s.v. Ghuzz). See also Minorsky, *Ḥudūd al-ʿĀlam*, 263–277.

1197 Arabic Tubbat, Tibbat, or Tibat. On the source of the name and early Islamic knowledge of and contact with the area, see the article by M. Gaborieau et al. in *EI*², s.v. Tubbat.

1198 See Minorsky, *Ḥudūd al-ʿĀlam*, 254–263.

1199 The MSS read simply *fī l-sana*, "in the year," or perhaps, "annually," which the Leiden editor has emended to read *fī awwal al-sana*.

1200 Arabic, *wa-lil-ṣīn ḥisābun ayḍan*. This could mean, "China also has a computation," or "China has a computation differently." Al-Yaʿqūbī or his source may be referring to the Chinese method for intercalation to keep the calendar of lunar months synchronized with the solar year.

by different names according to a computation that they have understood. The first of them is …[1201]

1:210 ## The Coptic and Other Kings of Egypt

When Bayṣar son of Ham son of Noah left Babylonia with his sons and the people of his family—they were thirty souls: his four sons Miṣr, Fāriq, Māj, and Nāj,[1202] along with their wives and children—he went with them to Manf.[1203] Bayṣar was old and weak, and Miṣr was his eldest son and the one dearest to him, so he appointed him his successor and enjoined him to treat his brothers well. Miṣr took possession for himself and his sons (of a territory) the distance of two months' (journey) in all four directions. The limit of this territory was from al-Shajaratān, between Rafaḥ and al-ʿArīsh, to Aswān in length, and from Barqa to Ayla in breadth. Miṣr remained ruler after his father for a long time and had four sons: Quft, Ashmun, Atrīb, and Ṣā. He divided the shores of the Nile among them and granted each a domain for that son and his offspring to possess. After Miṣr there ruled:[1204] Quft b. Miṣr, then Ashmun b. Miṣr, then Atrīb b. Miṣr, then Tadāris b. Ṣā, then Mālīq b. Tadāris, then Ḥarāyā b. Mālīq, [then …],[1205] then his brother Mālayā b. Ḥarāyā, then Lūṭish b. Mālayā. When Lūṭish died, his daughter Ḥūrayā ruled. When she died, a paternal cousin of hers named Dulayqā bt. Māmūm ruled.

The sons of Bayṣar multiplied and the land was filled with their offspring. When they made women their rulers, the ʿAmāliqa, kings of Syria, became
1:211 covetous of them. | The king of the ʿAmāliqa, who was, at that time, al-Walīd b. Dūmaʿ, invaded them and overran the country. (The people) were willing

---

1201 Twelve names follow in the MSS, written mostly without dots and therefore ambiguous. The Leiden editor notes that the names seem to have nothing to do with the Chinese language.

1202 Thus in M; ed. Leiden emends the last two names to Māḥ and Yāḥ on the basis of the parallel in al-Masʿūdī, *Murūj*, 2:85 (§806).

1203 That is, Memphis.

1204 A similar king list is given in al-Masʿūdī, *Murūj*, 2:86 (§807), with some differences in orthography and order of names. Another version of the list can be found in G. Wiet, *L'Egypte de Murtadi fils du Gaphiphe*, 22. The name Quft, also given as Qibṭ, is the origin of the Arabic and English designation for the Christian inhabitants of Egypt, Qibṭī (Copt). It is also the origin of the Greek name for Egypt (Αἴγυπτος), the ultimate source of English "Egypt."

1205 A name has fallen out of al-Yaʿqūbī's list. It can be restored from al-Masʿūdī, *Murūj*, 2:86 (§808), as Kalkan b. Ḥarāyā (Kharbātā in al-Masʿūdī).

to accept him as their ruler, and he remained in power for a long time. After him there reigned another of the ʿAmāliqa named al-Rayyān b. al-Walīd, who was the pharaoh of Joseph. Then another of the ʿAmāliqa named Dārim b. al-Rayyān ruled. Kāsim b. Maʿdān ruled after him. Then the pharaoh of Moses, al-Walīd b. Muṣʿab, ruled. The authorities have disagreed about his genealogy. Some have said that he was a man of the tribe of Lakhm; others that he was from some other Yemenite tribe, or that he was from the ʿAmāliqa, or that he was from the Copts of Egypt and was named Ẓalmā.[1206] He was the one whose dealings with Moses were related by God (in the Qurʾān).[1207] He [lived] a long time, until he said, *"I am your lord, the Most High."*[1208] God then drowned him and his armies in the Sea of al-Qulzum.[1209]

When God drowned Pharaoh and those with him, there remained in the land only children, slaves, and women; these agreed to designate as their ruler a woman named Dalūka.[1210] Fearful that the kings of the world would encroach on her territory, she built a wall encircling all of the land of Egypt—villages, fields, and cities.[1211] She undertook many public works, and her reign lasted twenty years. Then there reigned:[1212] Darkūn b. Balūṭis, Būdas b. Darkūn, Luqās b. Būdas, and Danayā b. Būdas. Then Namādis b. Marīnā reigned, who was so tyrannical and arrogant that they killed him. Then there reigned Balūṭis b. Manākīl, then Mālīs b. Balūṭis, and then Būla[1213] b. Manākīl, the lame pharaoh who captured the king of Jerusalem and treated the Israelites as no one before had done. He behaved arrogantly, and his excesses reached a level that no one | 1:212
before him, after Pharaoh, had ever reached. Then, however, his mount threw

1206 Unpointed in the MSS and possibly to be read Ṭalmā, as in al-Masʿūdī, *Murūj*, 2:87 (§ 809).

1207 Cf. Qurʾān 7:103–138, 20:9–80, 26:9–68, 28:3–40, 40:23–54, 43:46–56, 79:15–26.

1208 Qurʾān 79:24.

1209 The Red Sea, so named from the town of Qulzum (ancient Clysma) near Suez.

1210 On her, see al-Masʿūdī, *Murūj*, 2:87–93 (§ 809–819).

1211 According to al-Masʿūdī, *Murūj*, 2:87 (§ 809), the ruins of this wall could still be seen in his day (332/943). It was known as Ḥāʾiṭ al-ʿAjūz (The Old Woman's Wall).

1212 A similar king list is given in al-Masʿūdī, *Murūj*, 2:93 (§ 819), with differences in orthography and order of names.

1213 Sic M; ed. Leiden, Nūla; al-Masʿūdī, *Murūj*, 2:93 (§ 819), Balūna. Al-Yaʿqūbī has already narrated the episode above, ed. Leiden, 1:70. The pharaoh was Necho II (RSV Neco, r. 610–595 BCE); the "king of Jerusalem" was Jehoahaz (2 Kings 23:31–35, 2 Chronicles 36:1–4). The name "Pharaoh the Lame" (Arabic, Firʿawn al-Aʿraj) derives ultimately from a Jewish folk etymology of the Egyptian name transliterated into Hebrew as Nəkō (RSV Neco), as if from the Hebrew adjective *nākē* (smitten, stricken).

him and broke his neck. Then there ruled Marīnūs, then Laqās[1214] b. Marīnūs, then Qūmas b. Laqās. Then there reigned the lame Manākīl Ūdāma,[1215] who was L______.[1216] Nebuchadnezzar attacked him and put him to flight, devastated Egypt, and enslaved its people.

Afterward, they continued under Roman rule, and they converted to Christianity at that time. Then Persia conquered Syria in the days of Anūshirwān; they ruled them for ten years, but then the Romans prevailed. The people of Egypt therefore paid a tax to the Romans and a tax to Persia in order to avoid the depredations of both. Then Persia left Syria, and authority over them passed to the Romans, and so they adopted the Christian religion.

The sage of the Copts was Hermes the Copt. The Copts were the masters of the temples, the ones who used to write in the temple script; that script still survives [...],[1217] but in our own time people lack the knowledge to read it.[1218] The reason for this is that none of them could write it except for the elite, and they forbade the common folk (to learn it). It was their sages and priests who used it, for in it lay the secrets of their religion and the principles of their creed, of which no one but their priests could gain knowledge. They did not teach it to anyone, except when the king ordered that they do so. Therefore, when the Romans conquered the Egyptians and exercised absolute power and authority over them, they ceased from the endeavors and tasks that they previously had undertaken and encouraged (the people) to give priority to the religious principles of the Greeks. As a result, their language was corrupted, and their speech mixed with that of the Romans. Then the Romans converted to Christianity and impelled them to do likewise, and so everything that had to do with their religion and customs disappeared. The Romans killed the Egyptians' priests and learned men, so that those who used to be able to understand that writing perished, while those of them who survived were forbidden to teach it

---

1214 Sic M; ed. Leiden, following al-Masʿūdī, *Murūj*, 2:93 (§819), reads Naqās.

1215 Sic M; ed. Leiden, Adadāma (vocalization uncertain). His identity is uncertain, although a resemblance to the Egyptian ruler Urdamane (Egyptian Tantamani, r. 664–653 BCE) mentioned in the Assyrian annals is possible.

1216 The name, approximately ten letters long, is completely undotted in the MSS and cannot be read.

1217 Ed. Leiden indicates a lacuna here, but there is no evidence for it in M, and the text does not seem to be disturbed.

1218 The Arabic word used here for "temple" is *birbā*, pl. *barābī*, from Coptic *perpe*; it remains the word in Egyptian Arabic for pharaonic temples. The "temple script" (*khaṭṭ al-barābī*) is hieroglyphic.

or study it. For this reason no one among them or anyone else can be found | 1:213
who can read it.

Their religion involved the worship of the stars and the belief that they (the stars) direct the course of events according to their own choosing. They held that destinies are a matter of the stars and that the latter bring good and bad fortune; this is because they claimed that the stars were their gods, which brought them life and death and provided them with sustenance and drink. One of their beliefs was that spirits are immortal and were in the highest paradise (before birth) and that once in every 36,000 years everything in the world ceases to exist. This will be caused either by soil, by which they mean the earth with its earthquakes and cave-ins, or by fire, that is by incineration and hot wind, or by wind, that is by a widespread, foul, thick corrupting air that obstructs breathing because it is so thick, causing animals to perish and every green and living thing to wither. Then nature, including every kind of green and living thing, is restored to life,[1219] and the world returns after having fallen to ruin.

They also held that these spirits are divine; they come down and enter into the idols, so that the idols speak, but this was only a deceit that they employed to deceive their common folk, and they concealed the real reason that their idols seemed to speak. By performing a certain technical procedure, using drugs, and resorting to ingenious mechanical devices, their priests were able to make them whistle and utter sounds through a process in which they spoke from the throat of the idol as if it were from the throat of a bird or beast. The voice of that idol thus would be like the sound made by its species of animal.[1220] Then the priests would translate this sound coming from the idol as they wished, depending on the conclusion they had reached from astrology and physiognomy.[1221]

They also have it that when the spirits issue forth,[1222] they proceed to these deities, which are the planets, who cleanse and purify them if they are guilty of any wrongdoing, and then they rise to paradise and to the place where they

1219 Accepting the Leiden editor's emendation, *yaḥyā* (or *taḥyā*), for MSS *tarmī* (casts, shoots).

1220 This apparently refers to the fact that many Egyptian statues combined human bodies with animal heads.

1221 Arabic, *firāsa*, the art of deducing moral character and psychological conditions from the configuration of the human body (e.g., birth marks and lines on the palm) or of finding hidden natural objects. See the article by T. Fahd in *EI*², s.v. Firāsa.

1222 That is, from their bodies at death.

used to be.[1223] They also say that the planets used to speak to their prophets and
1:214 teach them | that the spirits descend to the idols, dwelling within them and giving word of events before they occur. They had an amazing and profound sagacity by which they were able to make the common folk believe that they could speak with the planets and that these would inform them of what was going to happen. But the real reason for (their wisdom) was their excellent knowledge of the secrets of astrology[1224] and their correct understanding of physiognomy. They were rarely wrong, although they claimed to know such things from the planets and that these informed them of what would happen—which is false and absurd.

When the Greeks ruled them, they (the Copts) entered into their religious community. Then the Romans ruled them, and they converted to Christianity.

The kingdom of the Copts was the land of Egypt. Among the districts of Upper Egypt were:[1225] Manf, Wasīm, al-Sharqiyya, al-Qays, al-Bahnasā, Ahnās, Dalāṣ, al-Fayyūm, Ushmūn, Ṭaḥā, Abshāya, Huww, Qifṭ, al-Aqṣur, and Armant. Among the districts of Lower Egypt were: Atrīb, ʿAyn Shams, Tanwā, Tumayy, Banā, Būṣīr, Samannūd, Nawasā, al-Awsiya, al-Bujūm, Basṭa, Ṭarābaya, Qurbayṭ, Ṣān, Iblīl, Sakhā, Tīda, al-Afraḥūn, Naqīza, al-Basharūd, Ṭuwwa, Upper Manūf, Lower Manūf, Damsīs, Ṣā, Shabās, al-Badhāqūn, Ikhnā, Rashīd, Qarṭasā, Kharibtā, Tarnūṭ, Maṣīl, and Malaydash.

1:215 The Copts reckon their year according to a calendar of 365 days. | They have twelve months of thirty days each; their year also has five days which they call intercalation.[1226] The first of the months of the Copts, which they have made the beginning of their year, is [Tūt]; they call the first day of this month Nayrūz, and they say that it was on this day that the populating of the earth began. These are the names of their months: Tūt, Bāba, Hatūr, Kiyahk, Ṭūba, Amshīr, Baramhāt, Barmūda, Bashans, Baʾūna, Abīb, and Misrā. The five days that they intercalate fall between Misrā and Tūt. The script in which the Copts write is something between the Greek and the Roman, and it looks like this ...[1227]

1223 That is, before birth.

1224 Literally, "of the secrets that belong to the ascensions (*ṭawāliʿ*)."

1225 Cf. Kennedy, *Historical Atlas*, Map 29. Many of the following names have been badly transmitted in the MSS and cannot be identified. Cf. al-Yaʿqūbī's detailed description of Egypt in the *Geography*, ed. Leiden, 330–340. In the following list "al-Aqṣur" (modern Luxor) anachronistically reflects the name given by the Arabs to the city—*al-Aqṣur* means "the palaces" in Arabic, referring to the temple complexes at the site.

1226 Arabic, *nasīʾ*.

1227 M at this point gives the letters of the Arabic alphabet in their usual Arabic order with

The Kingdoms of the Berbers and the Africans

The Berbers and the Africans are descendants of Fāriq son of Bayṣar son of Ham son of Noah. When their kinsmen[1228] assumed sovereignty in the land of Egypt, occupying (the territory) from al-ʿArīsh to Aswān in length and from Ayla to Barqa in breadth, (Fāriq and his family) proceeded toward the Maghrib.[1229] When they had traveled through the land of Barqa, they took control of the countries (beyond it), each clan of them subduing a country, until they spread over the land of the Maghrib. The first of them to rule was Luwāta, in a land called Ajdābiya in the mountains of Barqa, and Mazāta ruled in a land called Waddān—these people trace their descent to their (eponymous) forefather.[1230] One of their clans, the Hawwāra, traveled on to a land called Tawargha and ruled there, and others, the Badhraʿa, went to the land of Armīk. Another clan, called the Maṣālīn, | went to Ṭarābulus, and yet another clan, called the Wahīla, 1:216
traveled on to the land west of Ṭarābulus. But the route became too ...[1231] for them, and therefore one group, called the Barqashāna, set out for al-Qayrawān, while others, those called the Kutāma and the ʿAjīsa, turned north and arrived at Tāhart. Another group, who were called the Nafūsa and the Lamāya, set out for Sijilmāsa, and still another group, called the Lamṭa, set out for the mountains of Hakkār;[1232] the latter were named the ʿUbālāt and lived in the desert without houses. One group, called the Maknāsa, set out for Ṭanja, and another, called the Madāsa, set out for al-Sūs al-Aqṣā.

One group of Berbers and Africans have stated that they are descended from Barbar b. ʿAylān b. Nizār; others have said that they are from the Judhām and the Lakhm.[1233] Their homes had been in Palestine, but a certain king drove them

---

an attempt to write their Coptic counterparts under each letter. For the most part, these drawings look nothing like actual Coptic letters.

1228 Arabic, *ikhwatuhum*, literally "their brothers," referring to Fāriq's brother Miṣr and his family, as explained by al-Yaʿqūbī earlier (ed. Leiden, 1:210).

1229 That is, North Africa west of modern Benghazi.

1230 Al-Yaʿqūbī here traces the names of the important Berber tribes of Luwāta and Mazāta to eponymous ancestors.

1231 The reading and the meaning are uncertain. Ed. Leiden reads *istaʿlat* (became [too] high).

1232 Sic M; ed. Leiden, Hakkān.

1233 That is, these Berbers and North Africans claimed Arab descent. Nizār was the common ancestor of the greater part of the Arab tribes of the north; Judhām and Lakhm were Arab tribes of Yemeni descent.

out. When they arrived in Egypt, the kings of Egypt forbade them to settle there; so they crossed the Nile, headed west, and spread over the land. Others have said that they are from Yemen. A certain king banished them from the land of Yemen to the farthest lands of the Maghrib. Each group promotes its own story, and God knows best where the truth in this lies.

The Kingdoms of Ethiopia and the Sudan

When the descendants of Noah dispersed from the land of Babylonia, the descendants of Ham son of Noah set out for the Maghrib and traveled from
1:217 the bank of the Euphrates toward the land of the setting of the sun.[1234] | When they crossed the Nile, the descendants of Kush son of Ham—they were the Ethiopians and the Sudanese[1235]—split into two groups. One group of them, the Nubians, the Buja, the Ethiopians, and the Zanj, traveled due south,[1236] and one group, the Zaghāwa, the Ḥ____,[1237] the Qāqū, the Marawiyyūn, the Maranda, the Kawkaw, and the Ghāna, headed west.[1238] As for the Nubians, when they came to the west bank of the Nile and went beyond[1239] the kingdom of the Copts, who were the descendants of Bayṣar son of Ham son of Noah, they established their sovereignty there.

1234 Parallel in al-Masʿūdī, *Murūj*, 2:110 ff. (§ 844 ff.)

1235 Arabic, *al-Sūdān* (the Blacks), designates the dark-skinned peoples of Africa in general, not only those of present-day Sudan.

1236 Arabic, *al-tayman bayn al-mashriq wa-l-maghrib*, "the south between the east and the west." *Tayman* (south) is borrowed from Syriac.

1237 The reading of the name is uncertain. M reads al-Ḥabash (the Ethiopians) which does not fit the context. C leaves the word undotted. A list of African peoples occurs in al-Masʿūdī, *Murūj*, 2:110 (§ 844) (no name resembling this) and in al-Ṭabarī, *Taʾrīkh*, 3:1428, where the manuscripts vary between al-Khums and al-Ḥamīsh.

1238 Although identification of these peoples or places is risky, *Marwiyyūn* apparently refers to the people of Meroe, which was the capital of the Nubian kingdom. Maranda may be modern Marendet on the banks of the Niger (cf. Pellat in the index to al-Masʿūdī, *Murūj*, 8:675). Kawkaw is modern Gao in Mali, the former capital of the Songhai kingdom (ibid., 8:609). Ghāna was a city of commercial importance located in what is now Mauritania; the modern Republic of Ghana perpetuates the name, though not the location (ibid., 8:543; and R. Cornevin in *EI*^{2}, s.v. Ghāna).

1239 Reading with M, *tajāwazat*; ed. Leiden, *tajāwarat* (became neighbors) is impossible as the context requires a transitive verb such as *tajāwazat* (*tajāwarat* is intransitive).

The Nubians came to comprise two kingdoms.[1240] One of the two was the kingdom of those called the Muqurra;[1241] they were both east and west of the Nile, and their capital was the city of Dunqula.[1242] They were the ones who made peace with the Muslims and paid them the slave tribute.[1243] Their land is a land of date palms, vineyards, and cultivated fields, and the extent of the kingdom is (a journey of) about two months. The second Nubian kingdom comprised those called the ʿAlwa;[1244] they were more powerful than the Muqurra. The capital of their kingdom was a city called Sūba, and they had a land that would take about three months (to cross). It is in their territory that the Nile divides into several channels.

The Kingdom of the Buja

They are between the Nile and the sea and have several kingdoms, with a separate king in each land.[1245]

1240 Parallel in al-Masʿūdī, *Murūj*, 2:126 (§ 873). Cf. al-Yaʿqūbī, *Geography*, ed. Leiden, 335–336.

1241 Makuria, in the northern Sudan.

1242 That is, Dongola.

1243 Arabic, *al-baqṭ*, a borrowing from Greek πάκτον, itself a borrowing from Latin *pactum* (pact). In 31/651–652, an Arab army led by ʿAbdallāh b. Saʿd b. Abī Sarḥ, the governor of Upper Egypt, invaded Nubia and attacked Dongola. The two sides ultimately agreed to an armistice, which provided for annual exchanges of gifts: the Nubians were to hand over a certain number of slaves, and the Muslims were to present the Nubians with agricultural products of equal value. This arrangement was apparently still in effect in al-Yaʿqūbī's time. Although there were mutual exchanges, it was customary for Muslim authorities to regard the *baqṭ*, as al-Yaʿqūbī does here, in terms of the Nubian obligation only. See the article by F. Løkkegaard in *EI*², s.v. Baḳt; Paul Forand, "Early Muslim Relations with Nubia," in *Der Islam* 48 (1972): 111–121; and Martin Hinds and Hamdi Sakkout, "A Letter from the Governor of Egypt Concerning Egyptian-Nubian Relations in 141/758," in Hinds, *Studies in Early Islamic History*, 160–187.

1244 The ʿAlwa kingdom stretched from a little below the confluence of the Nile and the Atbara southward to well beyond the confluence of the White and Blue Niles. Its capital, Soba, was at the site of modern Khartoum, which is where the two main tributaries of the Nile join. See the article by S. M. Stern in *EI*², s.v. ʿAlwa.

1245 The Buja (the usual modern form of the name is Beja) live between the Nile and the Red Sea (so stated by al-Masʿūdī, *Murūj*, 2:127 [§ 875]). See the article by P. M. Holt in *EI*², s.v. Bedja. Cf. al-Yaʿqūbī, *Geography*, ed. Leiden, 336–337.

The beginning of the kingdom of the Buja extends from the frontier at
1:218 Uswān,[1246] which is the last district under the rule of the Muslims, | due south, to the frontier at Barakāt.[1247] These people are the race called the Naqīs, and the capital of their kingdom is called Hajar.[1248] They are organized into tribes and clans as the Bedouin Arabs are; among these are the tribes of al-Ḥadarāt, Ḥajāb, al-ʿAmāʿir, Kawbar, Manāsa, Rasbaʿa, ʿUrayrayʿa, and al-Zanāfij.[1249] In their land there are gold, gem, and emerald mines. They live on peaceful terms with the Muslims, and the Muslims work in their land in the mines.[1250]

The second kingdom of the Buja is a kingdom called Baqlīn, a broad land with many cities. In their religious practices these people resemble the Magians and Dualists; they call God—may He be glorified and exalted—the Supreme Zabjīr, and Satan they call Ṣaḥā Ḥarāqa.[1251] They are the ones who pluck out their facial hair, pull out their incisors, and undergo circumcision. Their land is a rainy one.

The third kingdom is called Bāzīn. These people border on the Nubian kingdom of ʿAlwa and the Bujan kingdom of Baqlīn, and they are at war with the latter. The crops that they eat are …[1252] It is their food, and milk.

The fourth kingdom is called Jārīn. They have a powerful king whose domain extends from the land called Bāḍiʿ on the coast of the Great Sea,[1253] to the Barakāt frontier of the kingdom of Baqlīn, to a place called Ḥall al-Dajāj. They are a people who pull out their upper and lower incisors, saying, "We will not
1:219 have teeth like those of donkeys." | They also pluck out their facial hair.

The fifth kingdom is called that of the Qaṭaʿa, which is the last of the kingdoms of the Buja. The kingdom of these people is extensive, stretching

1246 That is, Aswān.

1247 Roughly, the mountainous and desert regions of eastern Sudan, along the Red Sea coast, from Aswan to the Eritrean frontier. Barakāt is modern Wadi Baraka, about midway between Port Sudan and Asmara, on the frontier between Sudan and Eritrea.

1248 Not to be confused with the town of Hajar in the al-Ḥaṣāʾ region of eastern Arabia.

1249 The reading and vocalization of all these names is uncertain. For Ḥadarāt, one should probably read Ḥadārib; the Zanāfij are also historically attested. The other names are uncertain.

1250 Cf. al-Masʿūdī, *Murūj*, 2:127 (§876), who gives the name of the Muslim overseer of the mines in the year 332/943–944.

1251 The correct reading and derivation of these names is unknown.

1252 The Leiden editor indicated a lacuna in the text, where the names of crops have dropped out, although the MSS show no gap. If one assumes no lacuna, one can translate: "Their produce is what they eat; it is their food, as well as milk."

1253 Bāḍiʿ may be modern Massawa (Maṣawwaʿ) on the Red Sea, although "the Great Sea" suggests a location on the Indian Ocean. M apparently reads, Nāṣiʿ.

from the frontier of a place called Bāḍiʿ to a place called Faykūn. They are fierce-tempered and exceedingly brave. They have a military base called Dār al-Sawā, where there are militia units of battle-hardened young men prepared for war and combat.

The sixth kingdom is that of the Negus.[1254] It is an extensive and important realm whose capital is at Kaʿbar,[1255] to which the Arabs continually come for trade. They have (other) great cities, and their coastal center is Dahlak.[1256] Rulers in the land of Abyssinia are under the authority of the Great King, to whom they give obedience and pay taxes. The Negus adheres to the religion of the Jacobite Christians.[1257]

The frontier of the kingdom of the Abyssinians is the land of the Zanj,[1258] and they have contacts with Sind[1259] and other similar lands. They also have contacts with peoples other than the Zanj in lands bordering Sind and including the Kurk, who are a noble people who live in harmony.

As for the black peoples[1260] who went west and headed toward the Maghrib, passing through various lands, they established several kingdoms.

The first of their kingdoms was that of the Zaghāwa, who settled in a place called Kānim.[1261] They live in cane huts and do not have cities. Their king is called Kākira. One branch of the Zaghāwa is called the Ḥawḍaban,[1262] and these people have a king who is from the Zaghāwa.

There is another kingdom. Its people are called the Mallal; they are hostile[1263] to the ruler of Kānim, and their king is called Mayūsī.

1254 Arabic, *najāshī*, the ruler of Abyssinia (modern Ethiopia). See the article by E. van Donzel in *EI*², s.v. Nadjāshī.

1255 Also given by al-Masʿūdī, *Murūj*, 2:127 (§ 877), with a variant Kaʿban (which apparently is the reading of M). Possibilities for identification are discussed by C. E. Beckingham in *EI*², s.v. Ḥabash (see especially Section iii, "Ḥabash in Muslim Geographical Works").

1256 An archipelago off the Eritrean Red Sea coast east of Massawa.

1257 That is, the Monophysite theology of the Coptic Church, named after one of its early Syrian proponents, Jacob Burdʿānā (Arabic, Bardāʿī, d. 578). See the article by H. G. B. Teule in *EI*², s.v. Yaʿḳūbiyyūn.

1258 Al-Zanj is the general Arabic term for the black peoples of East Africa. See the article by G. S. P. Freeman-Grenville in *EI*², s.v. al-Zandj.

1259 Possibly referring to Sind in modern Pakistan and therefore to trade across the Indian Ocean. However, the reading is far from certain.

1260 Arabic, *al-Sūdān*.

1261 Kānim is a region north of Lake Chad. On the Zaghāwa, see the article by H. T. Norris in *EI*², s.v. Zaghāwa.

1262 The reading and vocalization are uncertain.

1263 Reading *yubādūna*; the same ductus might be read *yubāddūna* (they barter with).

Then there is the kingdom of al-Ḥ_sha.[1264] These people have a capital called _____r,[1265] the king of which is called Maraḥ.[1266] Affiliated with them are
1:220 the Qāqū, but the latter are …[1267] and their king is the king | of _____r.

Then there is the kingdom of the Kawkaw,[1268] which is the greatest, most eminent, and most powerful of the Sudanese kingdoms: all of the (other) kingdoms render obedience (to its king). Al-Kawkaw is also the name of its capital. There are [also] several other kingdoms (whose rulers) render it obedience and acknowledge its leadership, although they are kings over their own lands. These include the kingdom of al-Maraw, an extensive realm whose king resides in a city called al-Ḥayā, as well as the kingdoms of Murdaba, al-Harbar, Ṣanhāja, Badhkarbar, al-Zayānīr, Azūr, and Naqārūt.[1269] All of these trace their descent back to the kingdom of al-Kawkaw.

Then there is the kingdom of Ghāna,[1270] whose king is also very powerful. In his land there are gold mines. Under his authority there are several kings, among them the rulers of the kingdoms of ʿĀm and Sāma, and throughout these lands there is gold.

The Kings of Yemen

The transmitters and those who claim knowledge about the accounts and circumstances of the various peoples and tribes state that the first ruler from the descendants of Qaḥṭān son of the Prophet Hūd[1271] son of Eber son of Shelah

1264 The scribe of M has written *al-Ḥabasha*, the Abyssinians/Ethiopians, which does not fit the context. C and ed. Leiden leave the middle letter undotted.

1265 M gives a four letter word whose first three letters are undotted and therefore ambiguous. Ed. Leiden follows C in reading Thabīr, but this must be rejected as a scribe's attempt to turn an ambiguous reading into something familiar and Arabic: Thabīr is a mountain near Mecca!

1266 Vocalization uncertain.

1267 The word in the text, *m.ʿw.l.y.n*, is unclear in meaning, possibly "dependents," although the grammar is suspicious.

1268 This is the town now known as Gao in Mali on the Niger River. On its history, see the article by R. Cornevin in *EI*², s.v. Gao.

1269 The reading of most of these names is uncertain.

1270 Ghāna was a city of commercial importance located in what is now Mauritania; the modern Republic of Ghana perpetuates the name, though not the location (cf. al-Masʿūdī, *Murūj*, 8:543; and R. Cornevin in *EI*², s.v. Ghāna).

1271 An ancient Arabian prophet mentioned in the Qurʾān and in many legends. See the article by A. J. Wensinck and Charles Pellat in *EI*², s.v. Hūd. The insertion of Hūd

son of Arpachshad son of Shem son of Noah was Saba' b. Ya'rub b. Qaḥṭān. The (real) name of Saba' was 'Abd Shams, (but he came to be known as Saba') because he was the first of the Arab kings who ruled and journeyed in the land and took prisoners.[1272] Ya'rub b. Qaḥṭān was the first person to be greeted with the salutation, "May you have a pleasant morning. May curses be impotent against you."[1273]

Ḥimyar b. Saba' ruled after Saba'. Ḥimyar's (personal) name was Zayd, and he was the first king to wear a crown of gold inlaid with rubies.

After Ḥimyar, his brother Kahlān b. Saba' ruled. He lived for a long time, until he became senile.

After Kahlān, Abū Mālik[1274] | b. 'Ammīkarib b. Saba' ruled. His reign lasted 1:221
300 years.

After Abū Mālik, Ḥanāda[1275] b. Ghālib b. Zayd b. Kahlān ruled. He was the first person to manufacture *mashrafī* swords,[1276] and at night he put out food for the jinn.[1277] He ruled for 120 years.

---

into the genealogy of Genesis 10 is peculiarly Islamic. Genesis 10 ascribes two sons to Eber: "Peleg, for in his days the earth was divided, and his brother's name was Joktan (Yoqṭān)." Arab tradition either identifies Qaḥṭān and Yoqṭān as one and the same person or treats them as brothers, thereby giving the southern Arab tribes a biblical ancestry. See the article by A. Fischer in *EI*², s.v. Ḳaḥṭān.

1272 The Arabic explains the name Saba' by a play on words: He was called Saba' because he took prisoners (*sabā al-sabāyā*). Cf. al-Mas'ūdī, *Murūj*, 2:193 (§ 995).

1273 Arabic, *In'im ṣabāḥan. Abayta l-la'n.* Used together or separately, both were common pre-Islamic greetings.

1274 M: Malik, but this may simply be an orthographic variant; al-Mas'ūdī, *Murūj*, 2:196 (§ 1001), has Mālik.

1275 The reading is uncertain. M has a name written entirely without dots; C points the second letter as *n*; this is the basis of the reading in ed. Leiden. However, from the same ductus, minus the final letter, al-Mas'ūdī, *Murūj*, 2:196 (§ 1001), has derived the name *Jabbār* (*r* and *d* are easily confused in Arabic script). An added complication is that the Andalusian writer Ibn Badrūn, who drew heavily on al-Mas'ūdī, read the name as Ḥayyār (according to the edition of Ibn Badrūn prepared by R. Dozy).

1276 High-quality swords of uncertain type. The name may indicate a "highland" (*mashraf*) origin; see, for example, al-Ṭarsūsī, *Tabṣira*, 51. However, where such an origin is asserted, it is Syria, not Yemen, that is mentioned.

1277 That is, demons of the physical world, who share it with mankind. The point is that Abū Mālik was both generous and clever. The jinn, who favor dark places, come out at night, and when the ruler prepares food for them he demonstrates his hospitality and encourages them to reciprocate by not harming him or his kingdom. Such a tale may suggest a distant memory of evening offerings to demons and gods in pre-Islamic Yemenite religion.

After Ḥanāda, al-Ḥārith b. Mālik b. Ifrīqīs b. Ṣayfī b. Yashjub b. Saba' ruled for 140 years.

After al-Ḥārith b. Mālik, al-Rā'ish ruled. He was al-Ḥārith b. Shaddād b. Milṭāṭ b. ʿAmr b. Dhī Abyan b. Dhī Yaqdam b. al-Ṣawwār b. ʿAbd Shams b. Wā'il b. al-Ghawth b. Ḥaydān b. Qaṭan b. ʿUrayb b. Ayman b. al-Humaysaʿ b. Ḥimyar b. Saba'. He was the first person who raided, seized property, and brought spoils back to Yemen from elsewhere; hence he was called al-Rā'ish,[1278] and the nickname came to prevail. His reign lasted 125 years.

After al-Rā'ish, his son Abraha b. al-Rā'ish ruled. He was called Abraha Dhū Manār, because he traveled toward the west, and whenever he conquered a land, he would light a fire there.[1279] His reign lasted 180 years.

After Abraha, his son Ifrīqīs b. Abraha ruled and followed in his father's ways. His reign lasted 164 years.

After Ifrīqīs, his brother al-ʿAbd b. Abraha ruled. He was called Dhū l-Adhʿār because he terrified[1280] the enemy and used to advance with a force of warriors of awesome physique. His reign lasted 25 years.

After Dhū l-Adhʿār, al-Hadhād b. Shuraḥbīl b. ʿAmr b. al-Rā'ish ruled. His reign
1:222 lasted | one year.

After al-Hadhād, Zayd, who was Tubbaʿ al-Awwal b. Naykaf, ruled.[1281] He lived a long life and ruled oppressively, unjustly, and arrogantly. The transmitters claim that he lived 400 years, and then Bilqīs killed him.

Bilqīs bt. al-Hadhād b. Shuraḥbīl came to the throne, and her reign lasted 120 years.[1282] Then what happened between her and Solomon occurred, and sovereignty over Yemen passed to Solomon son of David for 320 years. Then Rehoboam son of Solomon son of David ruled for ten years. Then power returned to Ḥimyar, and Yāsir Yanʿam b. ʿAmr b. Yaʿfur b. ʿAmr b. Shuraḥbīl came to the throne and his authority became strong. His reign lasted 85 years.

1278 That is, "He who becomes wealthy."

1279 Perhaps as a signal beacon; however, the meaning may simply be that whenever he conquered a town, he set fire to it. The Arabic explains the name *Dhū Manār* ("the possessor of a beacon") as derived from the word for fire (*nār*).

1280 Following ed. Leiden: "he was called *Dhū l-Adhʿār* because he *dhaʿara* (terrified) the enemy." Instead of *dhaʿara*, M reads *ghazā*, "he raided, attacked," which misses the pun.

1281 That is, Tubbaʿ the First, son of Naykaf. Arabic writers used Tubbaʿ as a dynastic title for the Ḥimyarite rulers of southern Arabic between the late 3rd and early 6th centuries CE. Its derivation is unclear. See the article by A. F. L. Beeston in *EI*², s.v. Tubbaʿ.

1282 Bilqīs is usually identified as the biblical Queen of Sheba whose visit to Solomon is mentioned in the Qur'ān (e.g., 27:22–23). Al-Yaʿqūbī has already mentioned her visit to Solomon (ed. Leiden, 1:63). See the translation above and the note there.

Then Shammar[1283] b. Ifrīqīs b. Abraha ruled for 53 years.

Then Tubbaʿ al-Aqran b. Shammar b. ʿUmayd[1284] came to the throne. He raided India and intended to raid China. His reign lasted 163 years.

Then Malkīkarib b. Tubbaʿ came to the throne. He raided lands so far away that he scattered his forces to the ends of the earth, advancing them as far as Sijistān and Khurāsān; but then they united against him and killed him. His reign lasted 320 years.[1285]

Then Ḥassān b. Tubbaʿ came to the throne and remained for some time without raiding. Then there occurred what happened between Ṭasm and Jadīs,[1286] and Tubbaʿ marched out to fight them. As he approached them, a man from the Ṭasm who was with him said to him: "They have a woman with them called al-Yamāma, who can see things and never errs. I fear that she will warn them." So he ordered his companions to cut (branches) from olive trees, and he said, "Let each of you carry a big olive branch behind him." So each man carried a big branch; and when she saw it, she said, "I see trees walking." "And can trees walk?" they replied. | "Yes," she said, "by the Lord of every stone and clod 1:223
of earth! They are behind the men of Ḥimyar." But they disbelieved her, and Ḥassān surprised them at dawn and killed them.

His people wearied of him and his oppressive rule, and so they conspired with his brother, ʿAmr b. Tubbaʿ, to kill him—all except Dhū Ruʿayn, who forbade it—and so he killed him. His reign had lasted 25 years.

After killing his brother, ʿAmr b. Tubbaʿ came to the throne. Unable to sleep and troubled in his mind, he killed all those who had advised him to kill his brother. When he came to Dhū Ruʿayn, the latter said to him, "I advised you not to do it, and I even wrote two lines of verse, which you have." He had indeed given him a scrap bearing these words:

O who would buy insomnia at the price of sleep?
    Happy the man who passes the night in comfort!

1283 The vocalization is uncertain. Arabic tradition favors Shammar, but Shamir or Shimr are equally possible. For a discussion, see the long note by C. E. Bosworth in his translation of *The History of al-Ṭabarī, v: The Sāsānids, the Byzantines, the Lakhmids, and Yemen*, 142.

1284 This should be the son of the previous ruler, Shammar, but his grandfather (ʿUmayd) is not the person named as Shammar's father (Ifrīqīs).

1285 Cf. al-Masʿūdī, *Murūj*, 2:198 (§1005).

1286 This refers to a war famous in Arabian legend. See the article by Wolfhart P. Heinrichs in *EI*², s.v. Ṭasm.

Ḥimyar has committed treachery and betrayal,
but God absolves Dhū Ruʿayn of any part in it.

ʿAmr's reign lasted 64 years.

Then Tubbaʿ b. Ḥassān b. Buḥayla b. Kalīkarib[1287] b. Tubbaʿ al-Aqran came to the throne. He was Asʿad Abū Karib, the one who went from Yemen to (attack) Yathrib. Al-Fiṭyawn had taken power over the Aws and Khazraj, imposing great afflictions on them.[1288] Mālik b. al-ʿAjlān al-Khazrajī set out and complained of this to Tubbaʿ, informing him of how the Qurayẓa and the Naḍīr had gained the upper hand over them. Tubbaʿ thereupon marched against them,[1289] killed some of the Jews, and left a son of his among them as his deputy. When they killed the latter, Tubbaʿ led an army against them and made war on them. Now the leader of the Anṣar[1290] was ʿAmr b. Ṭalḥa al-Khazrajī from the Banū l-Najjār. They would fight him by day and offer him hospitality by night—(ʿAmr) would say, "Our people are indeed noble!"[1291] (Tubbaʿ) called together the leaders of
1:224 the Jews and said, "I am going to lay waste | this town,"—meaning Medina—but the rabbis and leaders of the Jews said, "You will not be able to do it." "Why?" he asked. They answered, "Because it belongs to a prophet from the descendants of Ismāʿīl whose place of emergence will be from beside the Sacred Sanctuary."

1287 Sic ed. Leiden; M has Kīkarib, which may be a scribal error for Malkīkarib (b. Tubbaʿ al-Aqran) mentioned above.

1288 Al-Yaʿqūbī could assume that his readers would be familiar with the history of the city of Yathrib, later known as Medina after Muḥammad's emigration to it. He therefore introduces this story without identifying the principals. More details are added below (ed. Leiden, 1:232). For the benefit of the modern reader: The Aws and the Khazraj were two Arab tribes that had settled in the oasis of Yathrib, which was already occupied by tribes of Jewish agriculturalists, among whom were the Qurayẓa and Naḍīr, mentioned here. The Jews remained dominant over the Arab newcomers until an event in the days of Asʿad Abū Karib, mentioned here, turned the tables. The leader of the Jewish tribes, al-Fiṭyawn, is said to have demanded the *jus primae noctis* of the sister of Mālik b. ʿAjlān of the Khazraj. (Al-Yaʿqūbī's "imposed great afflictions on them" may be a euphamistic allusion to this.) To defend his honor, Mālik killed al-Fiṭyawn and fled to seek help from the Yemeni king, Asʿad Abū Karib. This precipitated the Yemeni expedition described here. See J. Wellhausen, "Medina vor dem Islam," in *Skizzen und Vorarbeiten, IV*, 7 ff.

1289 Accepting Houtsma's emendation, *fa-sāra Tubbaʿ*; the MSS read, *fa-sāqa Tubbaʿan* ("he urged Tubbaʿ" sc. to attack them), and there may be no need to emend.

1290 That is, the Khazraj and the Aws, so called because they later became "helpers" (Anṣār) of the Prophet Muḥammad after his emigration. The term seems anachronistic here, but the anachronism is common.

1291 That is, they combine the virtues of valor and generosity.

So he departed, taking a group of Jewish rabbis with him. When he drew near Mecca, a delegation from the tribe of Hudhayl came to him and said, "This sanctuary in Mecca contains money, treasures, and gems, so why don't you attack it and take what is in it?"—but what they intended was that he should do so and God would slay him. It has been said that some people had in fact advised him to demolish it and transport its stones to Yemen, to use them to build a sanctuary there that the Arabs would venerate. Tubbaʿ summoned the Jewish rabbis and mentioned this to them. They said, "We know of no sanctuary in the world dedicated to God except this one, and no one means it harm but that God slays him." That very night he fell ill, and the rabbis said to him, "If you have harbored any evil intentions against this sanctuary, abandon them and treat it with respect." So he abandoned the plans he had made, and God took away his illness. He killed those who had advised him to demolish it. He circumambulated it and venerated it, slaughtered animals, and shaved his head. In a dream he saw (someone saying), "Cover it!" So he covered it with coarse cloth, but found it repellent. (Again) he dreamt, "Cover it!" So he covered it (this time) with embroidered drapery and recited a poem about it:

We covered the sanctuary that God has declared sacred
    with fine embroidered cloth to drape over it.
And in the ravine we slaughtered six thousand animals,
    toward which you see the people coming.
And we commanded that you should not bring near the Kaʿba
    any dead animal or blood that is fettered.[1292]
Then we circumambulated the sanctuary seven times and seven,
    and we prostrated ourselves at the Maqām.[1293]
We remained there for seven days of the month,
    and we fashioned a key for its door.

Then he returned to Yemen, accompanied by the Jewish rabbis, and he and his 1:225
people converted to Judaism. His reign lasted 78 years.

Then the kings of Qaḥṭān split up, and various different men became kings. One of those (who rose to power in this way) was ʿAmr b. Tubbaʿ, but then they

1292 Arabic *maṣfūdā*. The meaning is unclear.

1293 This apparently refers to the Maqām Ibrāhīm, (Abraham's Standing Place), where Abraham is said to have worshipped. The phrase occurs in Qurʾān 2:125, where Muslims are commanded to take it as a place of prayer. The most common identification is of a stone in the Meccan sanctuary. See the article by M. J. Kister in *EI*², s.v. Maḳām Ibrāhīm.

deposed him and installed as king Marthad b. ʿAbd Kalāl, the brother of Tubbaʿ on his mother's side. He remained for 40 years.

Then Walīʿa b. Marthad ruled for 37 years.[1294]

Then Abraha b. al-Ṣabbāḥ ruled. He was one of the wisest and most learned[1295] of the kings of Yemen. His reign was 73 years.[1296]

Then ʿAmr b. Dhī Qayqān[1297] ruled.

Then Dhū l-Kalāʿ ruled.

Then Lakhīʿa Dhū Shanātir ruled, one of the foulest and most corrupt of the kings of Ḥimyar. He used to do as did the people of Lot.[1298] He would send for a youthful prince, disport himself with him, and then look out expectantly in an upper room of his with a toothstick in his mouth. Things went on like this until he sent for Dhū Nuwās b. Asʿad, to disport himself with him. Dhū Nuwās came in—he had a knife with him—and when the two were alone, Dhū Nuwās jumped on him, killed him, and cut off his head, which he set in the place from which the king liked to look out. When he came out, the soldiers at the gate shouted to him, "Dhū Nuwās, it wasn't so bad, was it?" He said, "It was bad for the owner of the head." So they looked, and there was the head; so they knew that he had killed him, and they made Dhū Nuwās king. The reign of Dhū Shanātir had lasted 27 years.

Then Dhū Nuwās b. Asʿad ruled—his real name was Zurʿa. He was arrogant and was "the Master of the Ditch."[1299] This took place for the following reason:

1294 Ed. Leiden (C) and al-Masʿūdī, *Murūj*, 2:199 (§1006), read 39 years; but M clearly reads 37.

1295 Emending to *aʿlamihim*. The MSS read *aghlaẓihim*, "the coarsest, crudest of them," which does not fit the context. In M the word looks as if a careless scribe wrote *aʿlamihim*, "the most learned of them," and then thoughtlessly added a stroke turning the *m* into a *ẓ* (undotted). This is the most likely reading, given that in al-Masʿūdī, *Murūj*, 2:199 (§1006), Abraha b. al-Ṣabbāḥ is called *ʿallāma* (very learned).

1296 Ed. Leiden emends to 93, apparently on the basis of the parallel in al-Masʿūdī, *Murūj*, 2:199 (§1006). However, the MSS clearly read 73, and al-Masʿūdī reads, "His reign was 93 years, but some have said it was less than that."

1297 The MSS have Qayʿān; al-Masʿūdī, *Murūj*, 2:199 (§1006) has Qayfān. The Leiden editor has emended on the basis of the reading in Ibn Badrūn.

1298 That is, he practiced sodomy. Cf. Qurʾān 7:80.

1299 Arabic, *ṣāḥib al-ukhdūd*. The expression, in the plural (*aṣḥāb al-ukhdūd*, masters/people of the ditch) occurs in Qurʾān 75:4 as part of a narrative usually interpreted to refer to the Christians martyred at Najrān in November 523CE by Dhū Nuwās. Although other interpretations of the phrase are possible (see the article by Christian Julien Robin in *Encylopaedia of the Qurʾān*, s.v. [Al-]Ukhdūd), al-Yaʿqūbī clearly sees the Qurʾānic story as referring to historical events during the reign of Dhū Nuwās.

Dhū Nuwās was an adherent of the Jewish religion, and a man named ʿAbdallāh b. al-Thāmir, a Christian, came to Yemen and openly professed his religion there. Whenever he saw someone sick or infirm, he would say, "I will pray to God for you, that He will cure you and that you will turn from | the religion of 1:226
your people"—and He would do so. Thus the ranks of those who followed him swelled. When word of this reached Dhū Nuwās, he began to search out those who professed this religion, digging the ditch for them in the ground, burning them with fire and slaying them with the sword until he had exterminated them. But one of them made his way to the Negus, who was an adherent of the Christian religion, and the Negus sent an army to Yemen under the command of a man named Aryāṭ—they numbered 70,000, and with Aryāṭ in his army was Abraha al-Ashram.[1300] Dhū Nuwās marched out to confront him, and when they met, Dhū Nuwās was put to flight. When he saw that his forces had been scattered and put to flight, he struck his horse and plunged with it into the sea. This was the last that was ever seen of him. Dhū Nuwās had ruled for 68 years.

Aryāṭ the Ethiopian entered Yemen and remained there for several years. Then Abraha al-Ashram challenged his rule, and the Ethiopians became disunited: one party sided with Aryāṭ and the other with Abraha. They marched forth for war, each side rallying around its leader. When they met, Abraha said to Aryāṭ: "What do we gain, Aryāṭ, by killing the people between us? Come forth in single combat against me, and I against you, and whichever of us strikes down his opponent, to him the latter's army shall return, leaving the latter."[1301] So each one stepped forth to fight his opponent in single combat. Aryāṭ struck Abraha with his short spear and slashed him between the eyes, but then one of Abraha's young men struck Aryāṭ a blow and killed him. The Ethiopians in Yemen agreed to accept Abraha; however, when word of this reached the Negus, he fell into a rage and swore that he would tread his land with his own feet unless he clipped off his forelock.[1302] So Abraha shaved his head and sent (the

1300 The name means "Abraha of the Split Nose," and al-Yaʿqūbī will soon mention the combat that caused this wound. See the article by Uri Rubin in *EI*^{3}, s.v. Abraha.

1301 The Arabic has a tangle of pronouns. Literally: "… whichever of us strikes down his fellow, to him shall his army return from him." The sense, however, is clear.

1302 The most obvious interpretation of al-Yaʿqūbī's wording of the story would be that the Ethiopian ruler vowed to occupy Yemen or else cut off his own forelock as a mark of failure and disgrace. However, the parallel in al-Masʿūdī, *Murūj*, 2:200 (§1008), reads: "He swore by Christ that he would cut off his [viz. Abraha's] forelock, spill his blood, and tread his soil, i.e., the land of Yemen." Moreover, the continuation of the story in al-Yaʿqūbī implies that the forelock to be clipped belonged to Abraha—"He (the Negus)

forelock) to the Negus, along with a sack of earth from his land, saying, "I am only your servant, as was Aryāṭ; we disagreed over who should exercise your authority, but each of us was obedient to you." The Negus was satisfied with his response.

Sayf b. Dhī Yazan went to Qayṣar[1303] to raise an army to fight the Ethiopians; he waited there seven years for a reply. Then Qayṣar replied and said, "They
1:227 are a people | who adhere to the Christian religion: I will not fight them." Then he went to Kisrā,[1304] who sent him some prison inmates, along with a leader named Wahriz. He fought the Ethiopians, killed Abraha the Ethiopian, conquered the country, and made Sayf b. Dhī Yazan b. Dhī Aṣbaḥ king.[1305] Sayf was the one concerning whom Umayya b. Abī l-Ṣalt said:[1306]

No one truly seeks vengeance except Ibn Dhī Yazan:
he remained at sea for years because of his enemies.
He came to Heraclius[1307] when his own might had departed,
but he did not secure from him the matter of which he spoke.
Then he turned to Kisrā after a seventh year—
truly you went far, traveling resolutely—

swore that he (the Negus) would tread his (Abraha's) land, or (else, i.e., unless) he (Abraha) clipped off his forelock (as a sign of disgrace)." In the Arabic, the use of the energetic mode instead of the subjunctive after *aw* in the sense of "unless" is unusual, but this seems to be the sense.

1303 "Caesar," the generic term in Arabic for the Roman (Byzantine) emperor.

1304 That is, the Sasanian ruler of Iran.

1305 Another version of the story can be found in al-Masʿūdī, *Murūj*, 2:202–204 (§1015–1018); also al-Ṭabarī, *Taʾrīkh*, 1:945–958.

1306 Umayya b. Abī l-Ṣalt was a pre-Islamic poet from the tribe of Thaqīf who lived until the lifetime of Muḥammad. He is said to have been familiar with the Jewish and/or Christian scriptures and to have renounced idolatry. See GAS 2:298–300, and the article by J. E. Montgomery in *EI*², s.v. Umayya b. Abī ʾl-Ṣalt. The poem quoted here is more usually ascribed to Umayya's father, Abū l-Ṣalt and can be found with variants and more verses in Ibn Qutayba, *Kitāb al-Shiʿr wa-l-shuʿarāʾ*, 281; Ibn Hishām, *Sīra*, 44; al-Ṭabarī, *Taʾrīkh*, 1:956–957 (translated by C. E. Bosworth, *The History of al-Ṭabarī*, V, 249–250). One verse is given in al-Iṣfahānī, *Kitāb al-Aghānī*, 3:186, in the biography of Umayya, but with the note that the verse is really by Umayya's father, Abū l-Ṣalt, and a full discussion of the circumstances of its composition can be found in the biography of Abū l-Ṣalt in *Kitāb al-Aghānī*, 16:75.

1307 This is an apparent anachronism as Heraclius reigned 610–641 CE.

Until he came bringing the Sons of the Free,[1308] himself at their head.
Hurry on! truly you hastened, much traveled.[1309]

At the beginning of their kingdom the kings of Yemen used to practice the religion of idol worship. Later they professed the religion of the Jews and recited the Torah; this was because some Jewish rabbis came to them and taught them the religion of Judaism. They did not leave Yemen except to raid (other) lands and then would return to the domain of their kingdom.

The districts of the land of Yemen are called *mikhlāf*s,[1310] and they number 84. These are their names: al-Yaḥṣibayn,[1311] Yaklā, Dhimār, Ṭamu', ʿIyān,[1312] Ṭamām, | Hamal, Qudam, Khaywān, [Sinḥān, Rayḥān,][1313] Jurash, Ṣaʿda, al- 1:228
Akhrūj, Mujayyaḥ,[1314] Ḥarāz, Hawzan, Qufāʿa, al-Wazīra, al-Ḥujr, al-Maʿāfir, ʿUnna, al-Shawāfī, Jublān, Waṣāb, al-Sakūn, Sharʿab, al-Janad, Maswar, al-Thujja, al-Muzdaraʿ,[1315] Ḥayrān, Ma'rib, [Ḥaḍūr],[1316] ʿUlqān, Rayshān, Jayshān, al-Nihm, Baysh, Ḍankān, [Qurbā,][1317] Qanawnā, Raniyya,[1318] Zanīf, al-ʿUrsh, al-Khaṣūf, al-Sāʿid, Balja,[1319] al-Mahjam, al-Kadrā', al-Maʿqir, Zabīd, Rimaʿ, al-Rakb, Banī Majīd, Laḥj, Abyan, al-Wādiyayn,[1320] Alhān, Ḥaḍramawt, Muqrā,

1308 Arabic, *Banū l-Aḥrār*, referring to the Persian forces who assisted in the expulsion of the Ethiopians from Yemen and then settled in the country. On the Persian term possibly underlying the Arabic, see Bosworth's note in *The History of al-Ṭabarī*, v, 249–250.

1309 The meaning of the second half of the verse is unclear, and the versions differ wildly, which is usually a sign of faulty transmission.

1310 Arabic *mikhlāf* (pl. *makhālīf*) is a geographic term specific to Yemen. It apparently is related to the Sabaic (Old South Arabian) term *kh.l.f*, meaning "vicinity of a town." See the article by C. E. Bosworth in *EI*², s.v. Mikhlāf. Al-Yaʿqūbī gives a similar list in *Geography*, ed. Leiden, 317–318, where there is a more extensive critical apparatus. Both lists give only 74 districts.

1311 Thus M and Geography, ed. Leiden, 317. Houtsma accepted the variant "al-Yaḥḍibīn" in his edition of the *History*. Yāqūt, *Muʿjam al-buldān*, lists a Mikhlāf al-Yaḥṣibiyyīn.

1312 Thus vocalized by Houtsma, who distinguishes it from the more common ʿAyyān, which he says is a different place, "although al-Yaʿqūbī may have confused the two places" (note to *Geography*, ed. Leiden, 318).

1313 Added from the *Geography*.

1314 *Geography*, 318: Majnaḥ.

1315 *Geography*, 318: al-Mazraʿ.

1316 Added from the *Geography*.

1317 Not in M. Added by Houtsma in ed. Leiden, but on what basis is unclear, as the name is not in the *Geography*.

1318 Conjectural reading. *Geography*: Yaba.

1319 *Geography*, 318: Balḥa, which is Mawr.

1320 *Geography*, 319: Bayn al-Wādiyayn.

1:229 Ḥays, Ḥaraḍ, al-Ḥaqlayn, ʿAns, Banī ʿĀmir, Maʾdhin, Ḥumlān, Dhī | Jura, Khawlān, al-Sarw, al-Dathīna, Kubayba, and Tabāla.

Among the coastal districts are:[1321] ʿAdan, which is the port of Ṣanʿāʾ, al-Mandab, Ghalāfiqa, al-Ḥirda, al-Sharja,[1322] ʿAththar,[1323] al-Ḥamaḍa,[1324] al-Sirrayn, and Judda.

These are the lands and regions of the kingdom of Yemen. Sometimes they invaded other lands, but then they would return to their own territory.

Yemen comprises many tribes, if the Quḍāʿa are included among them. It has been reported that a man asked the Messenger of God, "Messenger of God, which are more numerous, Nizār or Qaḥṭān?"[1325] He replied, "(It depends on) what the Quḍāʿa wish, and at this time the Quḍāʿa assert that they are descendants of Malik [b.] Ḥimyar."[1326]

Here are the main tribes of Yemen, along with those from Nizār—Quḍāʿa, Judhām, Lakhm, Bajīla, and Khathʿam—who entered among them.[1327] The first whose name was memorialized and whose rank was acknowledged was SABAʾ b. Yashjub b. Yaʿrub b. Qaḥṭān. Among his sons were KAHLĀN b. Sabaʾ and ḤIMYAR b. Sabaʾ.

Among the tribes of KAHLĀN are:[1328]

- ṬAYYIʾ b. Udad b. Zayd [b. ʿArīb] b. Kahlān
- AL-ASHʿAR b. Udad b. Zayd

1321 Cf. the similar list in *Geography*, 319.

1322 *Geography*, 319: Sharja, which is Sharjat al-Qarīṣ.

1323 *Geography*, 319: ʿAthr. Yāqūt gives ʿAththar, but mentions the other vocalization.

1324 *Geography*, 319: al-Ḥasaba.

1325 That is, which are more numerous, the northern Arab tribes (descendants of Nizār) or the southern Arab tribes (descendants of Qaḥṭān)?

1326 That is, that they belong to the southern tribes, who outnumber the northern ones. On the differing opinions about the affiliation of the Quḍāʿa, see the article by M. J. Kister in *EI*², s.v. Ḳuḍāʿa.

1327 Uncertainty about northern or southern affiliation could be a product of shifting political alliances. As C. E. Bosworth notes in his article "Dj̲ud̲h̲ām" in *EI*²: "Dj̲ud̲h̲ām: an Arab tribe which in Umayyad times claimed descent from Kahlān b. Sabaʾ of Yemen and relationship with Lak̲h̲m and ʿĀmila; this certainly corresponded with the prevailing political alliances. However, the north Arab tribes claimed that Dj̲ud̲h̲ām, Ḳuḍāʿa and Lak̲h̲m were originally of Nizār but had later assumed Yemenī descent." Bajīla and Khathʿam were also of notoriously uncertain ancestry (see the article by W. Montgomery Watt in *EI*², s.v. Badj̲īla).

1328 Cf. Caskel, *Ǧamharat an-Nasab*, 1:176.

- ʿANS b. Qays b. al-Ḥārith b. Murra b. Udad
- JUDHĀM, LAKHM, and ʿĀMILA, who were sons of ʿAmr b. ʿAdī b. al-Ḥārith b. Murra b. Udad b. Zayd
- [MADHḤIJ b. Udad b. Zayd] b. ʿArīb b. Kahlān

Among the tribes of MADHḤIJ are:[1329]

- SAʿD AL-ʿASHĪRA b. Madhḥij
- MURĀD b. Madhḥij
- AL-NAKHAʿ b. ʿAmr | b. ʿUla b. Jald b. Madhḥij 1:230
- ḤAKAM and JUʿFĪ, sons of Saʿd al-ʿAshīra b. Madhḥij
- KHAWLĀN b. ʿAmr b. Saʿd al-ʿAshīra b. Madhḥij
- ZUBAYD b. al-Ṣaʿb b. Saʿd al-ʿAshīra b. Madhḥij
- HAMDĀN, whose name was Awsala b. Khiyār b. Rabīʿa b. Mālik [b. Zayd] b. Kahlān
- KHATHʿAM and BAJĪLA, sons of Anmār b. Arāsh[1330] b. ʿAmr b. al-Khiyār[1331] b. al-Ghawth b. Nabt b. Mālik b. Zayd b. Kahlān
- [AL-AZD b. al-Ghawth b. Nabt b. Mālik b. Zayd b. Kahlān]

Among the tribes of AL-AZD are:[1332]

- ʿAKK b. ʿUdthān[1333] b. al-Dīth b. ʿAbdallāh b. al-Azd, although ʿAkk is also traced back to ʿAdnān b. Udad
- AL-ʿATĪK b. Asd b. ʿAmr b. al-Azd
- GHASSĀN, who was Māzin b. al-Azd

1329 Cf. Caskel, *Ǧamharat an-Nasab*, 1:258.

1330 The MSS here have Nizār, which is an interesting mistake, as Anmār sometimes is made the son of Nizār b. Maʿadd b. Adnān. However, the rest of the genealogy is the one normally traced from Anmār through Arāsh back to Kahlān.

1331 The MSS read al-Ḥibār, but the name is unknown to the genealogists. Read as al-Khiyār, although this man was the uncle, not the father of ʿAmr.

1332 Caskel, *Ǧamharat an-Nasab*, 1:176.

1333 ʿAkk is another example of a tribe with two genealogies, one northern, one southern. ʿUdthān (the link needed for a southern genealogy) and ʿAdnān (the link needed for the southern genealogy) have the same ductus in Arabic script, and M conveniently neglects to dot the letter that would distinguish them. As the southern genealogy is being asserted here, one should read ʿUdthān. However, al-Dīth (if that is the correct reading) belongs to the northern genealogy; so the genealogy here seems confused. In his article in *EI*^{2}, s.v. ʿAkk, W. Caskel explains how the confusion may have arisen.

Among the tribes of GHASSĀN are:[1334]

- KHUZĀʿA, who was Rabīʿa b. Ḥāritha b. ʿAmr b. ʿĀmir b. Ḥāritha b. Imruʾ al-Qays b. Thaʿlaba b. Ghassān
- [...][1335] b. Wādiʿa b.ʿImrān b. ʿĀmir b. Ḥāritha b. Imruʾ al-Qays
- AL-AWS and AL-KHAZRAJ, sons of Ḥāritha b. Thaʿlaba [b. ʿĀmir b. Ḥāritha b. Imruʾ al-Qays b. Thaʿlaba][1336] b. Ghassān[1337]

Among the tribes of ḤIMYAR are:

- QUḌĀʿA, who, according to what the genealogists claim, was [the son of]
1:231 Nizār b. Maʿadd b. ʿAdnān, and Nizār was given the *kunya* Abū Quḍāʿa.[1338] |

[Among the tribes of QUḌĀʿA are:][1339]

- NAHD b. Zayd b. Layth b. Sūd b. Aslum b. al-Ḥāfi b. Quḍāʿa
- JUHAYNA b. Zayd b. Layth b. Sūd b. Aslum b. al-Ḥāfi b. Quḍāʿa
- ʿUDHRA b. Saʿd b. Zayd b. Layth b. Sūd b. Aslum b. al-Ḥāfi b. Quḍāʿa
- SALĪḤ b. Ḥulwān b. ʿImrān b. al-Ḥāfi b. Quḍāʿa
- KALB b. Wabara b. Taghlib b. Ḥulwān [b.] ʿImrān b. al-Ḥāfi b. Quḍāʿa
- AL-QAYN b. Jasr b. al-Asad b. Wabara b. Taghlib b. Ḥulwān
- TANŪKH, who was Mālik b. Fahm b. Taym Allāh b. al-Asad b. Wabara b. Taghlib b. Ḥulwān

These are the main tribes of QUḌĀʿA.

One of [the tribes descended from of] Ḥimyar b. Sabaʾ[1340] was AL-ṢADIF b. Sahl b. ʿAmr b. Qays b. Muʿāwiya b. Jusham b. Wāʾil b. ʿAbd Shams b. al-Ghawth

---

1334 Caskel, *Ǧamharat an-Nasab*, 1:176.

1335 Although there is no gap in the MSS, one or more names must have fallen out here.

1336 Present in M, but omitted by haplography in C and therefore in ed. Leiden.

1337 At this point, M and C insert in the margin a line of poetry by the Khazrajī poet Ḥassān b. Thābit, praising his tribe: "Ḥassān b. Thābit al-Anṣārī said, 'We are the descendants of al-Ghawth b. Nabt b. Mālik b. Zayd b. Kahlān, and are men of glorious deeds.'" The poem can be found in the *Dīwān* of Ḥassān b. Thābit, 1:482 (no. 320, v. 8).

1338 A *kunya* is a name given to a man or woman on the basis of the person's first child. For a man it takes the form, Abū (Father of) N.; for a woman, Umm (Mother of) N. Of course, if one accepts this genealogy, Quḍāʿa belonged to the northern Arabs, descendents of ʿAdnān, and not to Ḥimyar at all.

1339 Caskel, *Ǧamharat an-Nasab*, 1:279.

1340 Caskel, *Ǧamharat an-Nasab*, 1:274.

b. Qaṭan b. ʿArīb b. Zuhayr b. al-Hamaysaʾ b. Ḥimyar b. Sabaʾ b. Yashjub b. Yaʿrub b. Qaḥṭān. People in Ḥaḍramawt disagree about them. Some have said that they were one of the ancient peoples who became extinct, such as Ṭasm, Jadīs, ʿImlāq, ʿĀd, Thamūd, ʿAbs al-Ūlā, Awbār, and Jurhum.[1341]

The dispersal of the people of Yemen in the various lands and their exodus from their homelands was because of the violent flood.[1342] According to what the transmitters have reported, this began when ʿAmr b. ʿĀmir b. Ḥāritha b. Imruʾ al-Qays b. Thaʿlaba b. Māzin b. al-Azd, who was leader of the tribe and a soothsayer,[1343] saw that the land of Yemen was going to be flooded. He therefore pretended to be angry at one of his sons, sold his dwellings, and departed with his family. | He made his way to the land of the ʿAkk, and then they moved on 1:232 to Najrān, where the Madhḥij fought them. They then left Najrān and passed through Mecca, which was occupied in those days by the Jurhum, who fought them and drove them out of the territory. So they made their way to al-Juḥfa,[1344] and then moved on to Yathrib, where al-Aws and al-Khazraj, the sons of Ḥāritha b. Thaʿlaba b. ʿĀmir, remained behind and were (later) joined by a group of the Azd other than the two sons of Ḥāritha, some of whom settled on the outskirts,[1345] while others entered with them, and so the Azd became dispersed in Yathrib.

1341 In genealogical lore these tribes were the primordial Arabs, the first to speak Arabic after the confusion of tongues at Babel.

1342 Arabic, *al-sayl al-ʿarim*: This refers to the rupture of the great dam at Maʾrib, about 150 km east of Ṣanʿāʾ. The event will be mentioned again at ed. Leiden, 1:234. The dam, which supported a flourishing agriculture, had been breached several times before, but always repaired. The final breach, after which the dam fell into disuse, probably took place in the early 7th century. The syntax of the Arabic shows that by the time of al-Yaʿqūbī, the phrase *al-sayl al-ʿarim* was understood as a noun plus an adjective, something like "the violent flood." The Qurʾān, where the event is mentioned at 34:16, reads, *sayl al-ʿarim*, "the flood of *al-ʿarim*," which led some commentators to treat al-ʿArim as a place-name. However, Yāqūt mentions that the word, according to some, meant "dam," and this is confirmed by the Sabaean inscriptions, where *ʿ.r.m* is the word for dam. See the article by W. W. Müller, in *EI*², s.v. Mārib, Maʾrib.

1343 Arabic, *kāhin*. For a discussion of the development of the term and the functions of the *kāhin* in the Arabian milieu (mostly divining the future) see the article by T. Fahd in *EI*², s.v. Kāhin.

1344 Al-Juḥfa is a town near the Red Sea coast, about 150 km north of Mecca.

1345 Reading with M: *khalfan* (first letter undotted, but *tanwīn*, the suffix *-n*, clearly written). The term normally designates people who have left their tribal encampment to search for water, leaving their possessions behind, but the idea of contrasting those who settled outside the main part of the city and those who mingled with its earlier

Yathrib was the residence of the Jews, who quarreled with (the newcomers) and dominated them by their superior numbers. They overwhelmed them to the point that a Jew would come to the house of an Anṣārī,[1346] and the latter would not be able to protect his family and property from him. Finally, one of them, a man called al-Fiṭyawn, entered the house of Mālik b. al-ʿAjlān,[1347] and the latter attacked him and killed him. He then went to one of the kings of Yemen and complained to him about what they were enduring from the Jews. The king set out against them with his army and slaughtered many of the Jews. Thus the situation of the Aws and the Khazraj was set right. They planted date palms and built houses.

The rest of the people (led by ʿAmr b. ʿĀmir) headed on to Syria and eventually came to the land of al-Sarāt; the Azd Shanūʾa remained in al-Sarāt and the surrounding area, but some tribes of them went on to Oman.[1348] The first of them to arrive in Oman was Mālik b. Fahm b. Ghanm b. Daws b. ʿUdthān b. ʿAbdallāh b. Zahrān b. Kaʿb b. al-Ḥārith b. Kaʿb b. ʿAbdallāh b. Mālik b. Naṣr b. al-Azd. Mālik married a woman of the ʿAbd al-Qays, who bore him several sons. His youngest son is said to have killed him when he was with him among some of his camels: Mālik b. Fahm set out to make his rounds among the camels; his
1:233 son looked up and, taking him for a thief, shot him with an arrow | and killed him. His mother was named Salīma. Mālik b. Fahm is reported to have said:

I taught him to shoot every day,
and when his arm grew strong he shot me.

After the death of Mālik b. Fahm, (those already) in Oman were joined by a group of clans of the Azd, including al-Rabīʿa and ʿImrān, (who were the) Banū

---

inhabitants seems to imply this translation. Ed. Leiden reads, *ḥulafāʾ*, "(they became) allies."

1346 That is, one of the Aws or Khazraj—another example of the apparently anachronistic application of the term Anṣār ("helpers," sc., of the Prophet Muḥammad) to the Aws and Khazraj even before the rise of Islam.

1347 Allusion has already been made to this incident at ed. Leiden, 1:223, above. Al-Yaʿqūbī leaves the reader to deduce from the phrase "and the latter would not be able to protect his family and property" that al-Fiṭyawn's visit was not friendly; in fact, he intended to claim the *jus primae noctis* from Mālik's sister, which explains Mālik's attacking him.

1348 See Caskel, *Ǧamharat an-Nasab*, 1:217a; also the article by G. Strenziok in *EI*², s.v. Azd. Note that al-Yaʿqūbī's condensed narrative makes it seem that al-Sarāt was located in Syria; it was, in fact, located to the north of Yemen, but only as far north as the ʿAsīr highlands of western Arabia.

ʿAmr b. ʿUdayy b. Ḥāritha b. ʿAmr b. ʿĀmir—these were Bāriq and Ghālib; also Yashkur b. Qays b. Ṣaʿb b. Duhmān, and groups from ʿĀmir and Ḥawāla. When they arrived in Oman, they spread as far as al-Baḥrayn and Hajar.

In the land of Tihāma lived the Azd tribe of al-Jadara, who were descendants of ʿAmr b. Khuzayma b. Jiʿthima b. Yashkur b. Mubashshir b. Ṣaʿb b. Duhmān b. Naṣr b. Zahrān b. Kaʿb b. al-Ḥārith b. Kaʿb b. Mālik b. Naṣr b. al-Azd. (They received their name) because ʿAmr built the wall of the Kaʿba, and so was given the name al-Jādir.[1349] One group of them journeyed to Herat[1350] in the land of Khurāsān.

Ghassān set out for Syria and settled in al-Balqāʾ. A group of the Salīḥ was already in Syria; they had become tributaries of the Romans and had converted to Christianity. Ghassān asked them whether they could join them by doing the same; so the Salīḥ wrote to the emperor of the Romans, and he agreed that the Ghassān might do so. Afterward, their relations with the emperor's governor in Damascus deteriorated, and the Roman ruler attacked them with a force of Quḍāʿa Arabs on behalf of the Roman emperor. Ghassān requested a truce, and the emperor of the Romans agreed to this—the leader of Ghassān at that time was Jafna b. ʿAliyya b. ʿAmr b. ʿĀmir. Ghassān converted to Christianity and remained in Syria, confirmed in their sovereignty by the Roman ruler.

Descendants of Ḥawāla | b. al-Hinw b. al-Azd made their way to al-Mawṣil 1:234
and settled there.

Seeing that their land would be flooded by the Dam of Maʾrib (if it burst), the people of Yemen reinforced it and guarded it. But when God sent against them the mighty flood, the water burst through upon them from the burrow of a rat that had been digging in the dam and drowned them.

The Kings of Syria

Syria was the domain of the kingdom of the Israelites. The first to rule in Damascus is said to have been Bālagh b. Baʿūr. Then Yūbāb, who was Job the Righteous, the son of Zāraḥ, ruled, and the events that God has related concerning him took place.[1351] Then Mīnasūs ruled—the Israelites made war

1349 That is, "the Wall-Builder." *Jadara* is a plural of *jādir*. Cf. Caskel, *Ǧamharat an-Nasab*, 1:217, where this figure is named as ʿĀmir b. ʿAmr b. Jaʿthima.

1350 Arabic *Harāt*, in modern Afghanistan.

1351 Al-Yaʿqūbī's insertion of Job into the list of the kings of Syria is based on two biblical passages, both in the Septuagint version, rather than the Masoretic text: Genesis 36:31–39 and Job 42:17a–e. Where the Hebrew text of Genesis 36:32 calls the first king "who

on them. Then Fūsīs,[1352] who was from Ludd, ruled. Then the kingdoms were interrupted, and there were the kings of Israel. Eventually they became extinct, the Romans conquered their kingdom, and the people left their territory.

The Quḍāʿā were the first of the Arabs to arrive in Syria. They went to the kings of the Romans, and the latter made them rulers. Initially the kingship belonged to (the tribe of) Tanūkh b. Mālik b. Fahm b. Taym Allāh b. al-Asad b. Wabara b. Taghlib b. Ḥulwān b. ʿImrān b. al-Ḥāfi b. Quḍāʿa. They adopted the Christian religion, and the king of the Romans made them rulers over the Arabs that were in Syria. The first of them to rule was al-Nuʿmān b. ʿAmr [b. Mālik;
1:235 then] the Banū Salīḥ b. Ḥulwān | b. ʿImrān b. al-Ḥāfi b. Quḍāʿa overwhelmed them and remained in power for a time.

When the Azd dispersed, with elements of them going to Tihāma, Yathrib, Oman, and other lands, the Ghassān made their way to Syria and arrived in the land of al-Balqāʾ. They asked the Salīḥ whether they might join with them in offering their obedience to the king of the Romans and whether they might remain in the land according to the same terms of privileges and obligations as they had. So the head of the Salīḥ, who at the time was Duhmān b. al-ʿAmlaq, wrote to the king of the Romans, who at the time was ______,[1353] with his residence at Antioch. The latter agreed to their request and specified terms to which they had to adhere. They continued thus for a time, but then a dispute broke out between them and the king of the Romans over the tribute that the king of the Romans was collecting. Finally, a man of the Ghassān named Jidhʿ struck an agent of the king of the Romans with his sword and killed

---

reigned in the land of Edom, before any king reigned over the Israelites," Bela son of Beor, the Septuagint reading is Balak son of Beor, who corresponds to al-Yaʿqūbī's Bālagh b. Baʿūr. The identification of his successor (Genesis 36:33), Jobab son of Zerah (al-Yaʿqūbī's Yūbāb b. Zāraḥ) with the biblical Job is based on Job 42:17b–d (Septuagint): "... previously his [viz. Iob's] name was Iobab ... and he in turn had as father Zare, a son of the sons of Esau ... And these are the kings who reigned in Edom, which country he too ruled: first Balak the son of Beor, and the name of his city was Dennaba, and after Balak, Iobab, who is called Iob, and after him Hasom, who was a leader from the Thaimanite country, and after him Hadad son of Barad ..." (NETS Translation). Al-Yaʿqūbī, or his source, apparently identified Dennaba as Damascus. Parallel: al-Masʿūdī, *Murūj*, 2:231 ff. (§ 1076 ff.).

1352 Or, Fawsīs: sic M, although the first letter is undotted and therefore the word might be read Qawsīs/Qūsīs. Ed. Leiden follows C in reading Hawṣīr.

1353 The reading in M is completely undotted and cannot be read. Ed. Leiden has *Nawshar* (vocalization uncertain), with a note suggesting a possible reading of Nasṭūrus on the basis of a reference to Reiske's 1847 *Primae lineae historiae regnorum Arabicorum et rerum ab Arabibus medio inter Christum et Muhammedem tempore gestarum.*

him; whereupon one of the Ghassān said, "Take from Jidhʿ whatever he gives you"—which became a proverb.[1354] The Roman governor thereupon launched a campaign against them. They kept fighting him for a long time in Buṣrā in the territory of Damascus; then they made their way to al-Muḥaffaf.[1355] When the king of the Romans saw how they endured war and resisted his armies, he did not want there to be a breach in their defenses.[1356] So when the tribesmen requested a truce, provided that no king from another people should rule them, the king of the Romans accepted these terms and made Jafna b. ʿAliyya b. ʿAmr b. ʿĀmir king over them. Relations between them and the Romans were good and harmony prevailed in their affairs. The first king from Ghassān to enjoy glory and fame after Jafna b. ʿAliyya was al-Ḥārith b. Mālik b. al-Ḥārith | 1:236
b. Ghaḍab b. Jusham b. al-Khazraj b. Ḥāritha b. Thaʿlaba b. ʿAmr b. ʿĀmir b. Thaʿlaba b. Ḥāritha b. ʿAdī b. Imruʾ al-Qays b. Māzin b. al-Azd. After him there ruled al-Ḥārith al-Akbar[1357] b. Kaʿb b. ʿAliyya b. ʿAmr b. ʿĀmir. This Kaʿb was Jafna; he was the son of Māriya, and his mother Māriya was the daughter of ʿĀdiyā b. ʿĀmir. Then his brother, al-Ḥārith al-Aʿraj,[1358] who settled in the Jawlān, ruled. Then his brother al-Ḥārith al-Aṣghar[1359] ruled. Then Jabala b. al-Mundhir ruled. Then al-Ḥārith b. Jabala ruled. Then al-Ayham b. Jabala ruled, and then Jabala b. al-Ayham. Al-Ḥārith b. Abī Shamir b. al-Ayham was made ruler of al-Urdunn; the residence of Jabala was Damascus. Concerning Jabala b. al-Ayham and his family, Ḥassān b. Thābit says:[1360]

How magnificent the troop with whom I drank
one day in Jilliq[1361] in days of old!

1354 The circumstances behind the proverb are as follows: The Roman tax collector, a member of the Salīḥ named Sabīṭ, refused to accept the sword that Jidhʿ, one of the Ghassān, offered to him as a pawn in lieu of the tax payment, whereupon Jidhʿ unsheathed the sword and killed Sabīṭ. The proverb means something like, "Take whatever is offered to you, and don't press for more." See al-Maydānī, *Majmaʿ al-Amthal*, s.v. *khudh*; also the article by Irfān Shahîd in *EI*^{2}, s.v. Salīḥ.

1355 Sic C and ed. Leiden (vocalization unknown); in M the word is completely undotted. The place is unknown. Houtsma's suggestion of al-Mukhaffiq is impossible, as that is in the eastern part of the Arabian peninsula, far from Damascus.

1356 That is, by alienating such valiant fighters who could be used to defend the Roman borderlands.

1357 That is, al-Ḥārith the Elder.

1358 That is, al-Ḥārith the Lame.

1359 That is, al-Ḥārith the Younger.

1360 The poem may be found in Ḥassān b. Thābit, *Dīwān* 1:74 no. 13 v. 7, 15, 11–13.

1361 Jilliq was a fertile and well-watered site 12 km south of Damascus; the Ghassānids made

Unsullied in honor, noble in reputation,
proud in bearing, men of the first rank.
The descendants of Jafna surrounded the grave of their forefather,
the grave of the noble, most excellent son of Māriya.
They are visited so often that their dogs do not growl,
and they do not bother to ask about the approaching figure.[1362]
To the one who arrives at al-Barīṣ to join them
they serve water of Baradā mixed with smoothest wine.[1363]

The Yemenite Kings of al-Ḥīra

The transmitters and scholars have said that when the people of Yemen dispersed, Mālik b. Fahm b. Ghanm b. Daws pressed on until he settled in Iraq in the days of the factional rulers.[1364] He encountered Arab tribesmen of the
1:237 Maʿadd and other tribes | in al-Jazīra, and they made him king for twenty years.

Then came Jadhīma al-Abrash.[1365] He practiced divination and fashioned two idols called al-Ḍayzanān. He attracted various Arab clans to his ranks and proceeded with them to the land of Iraq, where lay the territory of Iyād b. Nizār, whose domains extended from the land of al-Jazīra to the land of al-Baṣra.[1366]

---

it into a major encampment. The village of Kiswa now occupies the site. See the article by Nikita Elisséeff in *EI*², s.v. Djilliḳ.

1362 The verse praises their generosity. So many guests come to them that their watchdogs no longer growl at the approach of a visitor, and they themselves grant hospitality without asking who the visitor is.

1363 Al-Barīṣ and Baradā are rivers of Damascus.

1364 Arabic, *mulūk al-ṭawāʾif*. The term is more familiar from the history of Muslim Spain, where it designated the regional rulers (*reyes de taifas*) who emerged after the decline of the Córdoba caliphate. The term as used here refers to the regional rulers of the east during the Parthian or Arsacid period. According to the accounts in Arabic historians (see, for example, al-Yaʿqūbī's account, ed. Leiden, 1:179), Alexander the Great, having defeated Darius, appointed local rulers over each district of the dismembered Persian empire, and these local rulers, called *mulūk al-ṭawāʾif*, continued to govern until the rise of the Sasanian dynasty under Ardashīr in 538 CE. See the article by M. Morony in *EI*², s.v. Mulūk al-Ṭawāʾif.

1365 The name means Jadhīma the Speckled (a euphemism for leper). He apparently was a historical figure of the third century CE, although many legends have been attached to his name. According to al-Masʿūdī, *Murūj*, 2:213 (§ 1037), Jadhīma was the son of Mālik b. Fahm. See the article by I. Kawar in *EI*², s.v. Djadhīma al-Abrash or al-Waḍḍāḥ.

1366 That is, all of central and southern Iraq.

The latter fought Jadhīma, but he managed to advance as far as a district called Baqqa on the banks of the Euphrates near al-Anbār. The district was ruled by a woman named al-Zabbāʾ, who had utterly renounced (sexual relations with) men.[1367] When Jadhīma came to the land of al-Anbār and his forces joined him there, he said to his companions, "I have decided to send word to al-Zabbāʾ, so that I might marry her and join her kingdom [to] mine." A retainer of his named Qaṣīr[1368] said to him, "If al-Zabbāʾ were a woman who married men, someone would have gotten to her before you." But Jadhīma wrote to her, and she wrote back to him, saying, "Come to me and I will make you my husband." He therefore set out to go to her. Qaṣīr said to him: "I have never seen a man before you being led in procession to a woman.[1369] Here is your mare al-ʿAṣā; I have readied her, so mount her and save yourself!" But Jadhīma did not do it. When he came into the presence of al-Zabbāʾ, she exposed her thigh and said, "Do you see (here) the behavior of a bride?" He said, "(I see) the behavior of a treacherous, uncircumcised whore." Al-Zabbāʾ then cut him to pieces, and Qaṣīr rode the mare al-ʿAṣā to safety.

When Jadhīma was killed, his sister's son, ʿAmr b. ʿAdī b. Naṣr b. Rabīʿa b. ʿAmr b. al-Ḥārith b. ʿAmam b. Numāra b. Lakhm, took his place as king. Qaṣīr said to ʿAmr, "Don't *you* disobey me!" "Say whatever you think best," replied ʿAmr. | 1:238
Qaṣīr said, "Chop off the end of my nose, cut off my ears, and then leave me (to do as I think best)." So ʿAmr did this. Qaṣīr then went to al-Zabbāʾ and said: "I was a sincere advisor to Jadhīma as I saw best and to ʿAmr, his sister's son, to the point that I made him king—and my reward from him was that he did to me what you see! So I have come to you to be of service to you; hopefully God will cause ʿAmr to be killed by your hand." He kept deceiving her until she sent him on trading journeys, from which he returned time after time with

1367 Al-Zabbāʾ is the Arabic form of the name of Zenobia, the queen of Palmyra whose rule ended with her defeat by the Roman emperor Aurelian in 272 CE. Her story, embellished with novelistic and sensational details, occurs also in al-Masʿūdī, *Murūj*, 2:217–223 (§1046–1057) and al-Ṭabarī, *Taʾrīkh*, 1:756–768. An attempt to extricate fact from fiction was made by Irfan Shahîd in his article in *EI*², s.v. al-Zabbāʾ.

1368 Qaṣīr b. Saʿd b. ʿUmar became famous in Arabic lore as the type of the clever but disregarded advisor, and many proverbs were attributed to him.

1369 The Arabic refers to the ancient custom of leading the bride in a solemn procession (*zaffa*) to the bridegroom. Qaṣīr is drawing attention to the ominous reversal of roles implicit in Jadhīma's traveling to the residence of al-Zabbāʾ, whose reputation as a hater of men must have been known. In the parallel accounts, al-Zabbāʾ initiates matters as part of an elaborate plot by her to take vengeance for her father's battlefield death at the hands of Jadhīma.

great profits. Pleased by this, she began to trust him. When her trust in him was complete, he went to ʿAmr and said, "Seat the men in the chests."[1370] So he loaded four thousand men armed with swords onto two thousand camels and brought them into al-Zabbāʾ's city—ʿAmr was among them. He distributed the chests among the houses of her companions and brought several of them into her residence. When night fell, the men emerged and killed al-Zabbāʾ and many of her courtiers. ʿAmr b. ʿAdī ruled for 55 years.

[Then Imruʾ al-Qays b. ʿAmr ruled for 35 years.][1371]

Then his brother, al-Ḥārith b. ʿAmr, ruled for 87 years.

Then ʿAmr b. Imruʾ al-Qays b. ʿAmr b. ʿAdī ruled for 40 years.

Then al-Mundhir b. Imruʾ al-Qays—he was Muḥarriq[1372]—ruled. He was given this name because he took a group of men who had made war on him and burned them, and so he was called Muḥarriq.

Then al-Nuʿmān ruled. He was the one who built al-Khawarnaq.[1373] One day while he was sitting there gazing out at what lay before him—the Euphrates and the date palms, gardens, and trees beside it—he remembered death and said, "Of what use will this be when death descends and one departs this world?" He therefore became an ascetic and renounced his kingdom. It was
1:239 to him that ʿAdī b. Zayd was referring when he said:[1374] |

Consider the lord of al-Khawarnaq, how he gazed out
  one day—and part of right guidance is taking thought.
His state made him rejoice: all that he ruled,
  and the broad river, and al-Sadīr.[1375]

1370 That is, put the warriors into the chests (*ṣanādīq*) normally used to hold merchandise, so that when al-Zabbāʾ sees the loaded camels she will think that Qaṣīr is returning from another successful trading journey.

1371 Inserted by the Leiden editor.

1372 That is, Burner.

1373 A palace in southern Iraq about 2 km east of Najaf. Built by the Sasanians in the fifth century, it was renowned among the Arab tribes of the region. It was enlarged and used by the early ʿAbbāsids, but was probably already in ruins by al-Yaʿqūbī's time. See G. Le Strange, *The Lands of the Eastern Caliphate*, 75–76; also the article by Louis Massignon in *EI*², s.v. Khawarnaḳ.

1374 ʿAdī b. Zayd (d. c. 600) was a pre-Islamic Christian poet of al-Ḥīra in southern Iraq who was for a time in the service of the Sasanians. The lines are part of a longer poem cited in *Kitāb al-Aghānī*, 2:36, and in al-Ṭabarī, *Taʾrīkh*, 1:853–854. See the articles by F. Gabrieli in *EI*², s.v. ʿAdī b. Zayd, and by Tilman Seidensticker in *EI*³, s.v. ʿAdī b. Zayd.

1375 Another palace near Khawarnaq. See Le Strange, *Lands of the Eastern Caliphate*, 75;

But his heart became troubled, and he said:
"What delight can there be for a living creature fated to die?"

After him, Mundhir b. al-Nuʿmān ruled for 30 years. Then ʿAmr b. al-Mundhir ruled. He was the one in whose presence al-Ḥārith b. Ẓālim killed Khālid b. Jaʿfar b. Kilāb. (ʿAmr) vowed to shed his blood and went in search of him; al-Ḥārith therefore went in search of his son, who was being nursed among the Āl Sinān, and killed him.

Then ʿAmr b. Mundhir the Second ruled. He was the son of Hind and was nicknamed Muḍarriṭ al-Ḥijāra.[1376] He divided time into two kinds of days: a day for hunting and a day for drinking. When he sat down to drink, the people would have to stand waiting at his door until his drinking party broke up. On this subject Ṭarafa b. al-ʿAbd said:[1377]

Would that we had, instead of King ʿAmr,
a little goat bleating around our camp!
You have divided your time into a time for ease—
thus time is (always going back and forth between) being just or unjust.
We have one day and the stone curlew[1378] another:
the wretched ones can fly off, but we cannot fly.[1379]

Creswell, *Early Muslim Architecture*, 2:50–91; and the article by Louis Massignon in *EI*², s.v. Khawarnaḳ.

1376 This ʿAmr was frequently called ʿAmr b. Hind to distinguish him from other members of his ruling house. The nickname Muḍarriṭ al-Ḥijāra (he who makes stones emit [sounds like] farts) was said to have been given to him because of the fear he inspired (so Ibn al-Athīr, *al-Kāmil*, 1:405). See the article by A. J. Wensinck in *EI*², s.v. ʿAmr b. Hind.

1377 Ṭarafa b. al-ʿAbd was a famous pre-Islamic poet. Little is known about his life, beyond the much embroidered story of his premature death. The poem (No. 9 in Seligsohn's edition of the *Dīwān*) is satirical. A later hand has added two verses in the margin of the MSS of al-Yaʿqūbī; they have been omitted here as unlikely to belong to the original text of al-Yaʿqūbī's History. See *GAS* 2:115–118, and the article by J. E. Montgomery in *EI*², s.v. Ṭarafa.

1378 Arabic, *kirwān* or *karwān*. The designation for several members of the family of thick-knees (Burhinidae), birds of arid habitats. Because of the plaintive call of the Egyptian member of the family, the birds are well-known in rural folklore to this day in the Middle East.

1379 This alludes to the fact that on his hunting days ʿAmr b. Hind would kill the first man that he encountered.

As for their day, it is a day of evil:
the falcons pursue them in the lowland.
As for our day, we remain on our mounts
waiting, neither alighting nor departing.

1:240 Ṭarafa kept satirizing ʿAmr and his brother Qābūs, referring to them in vile terms, while composing amorous verses about ʿAmr's sister and defaming her. Among the things he said about ʿAmr was:[1380]

The vilest of kings are all well-known,
and the basest of them in filth are
ʿAmr, and Qābūs, and the son of their mother.
The one who comes to them will be detained for foul abuse.
He who comes is someone who does not fear his own shame:
ʿAmr and Qābūs are two brides' slaves.[1381]
In the morning ʿAmr goes about his business,
having shaken, as a mare, what belongs to a man.[1382]

Al-Mutalammis was an ally of Ṭarafa and used to assist him in composing satires. ʿAmr said to them, "You two have stayed as guests for a long time, and I am out of money here; but I have written on your behalf to my governor in al-Baḥrayn to give each of you 100,000 dirhams." So each of them took a letter. Al-Mutalammis became suspicious of ʿAmr's intentions, and when they reached the canal at al-Ḥīra and met a young Christian lad, al-Mutalammis asked him, "Are you good at reading?" "Yes," he said. Al-Mutalammis said, "Read this letter." Lo and behold it said: "When al-Mutalammis reaches you, cut off his hands and feet." So al-Mutalammis threw away the letter and said to Ṭarafa, "Your letter

1380 The poem does not occur in the *Dīwān* of Ṭarafa. Seligsohn added it in an appendix to his edition and attempted a translation (p. 83), but much, apart from the poem's obscenity and its imputation of homosexuality to ʿAmr and Qābūs, remains unclear. A recent attempt to deal with the poem is a useful commentary by Saʿdī al-Ḍināwī in his *Sharḥ Dīwān Ṭarafa b. al-ʿAbd*, 166–167.

1381 Arabic, *qaynatā ʿurusin*, slave girls who look after the bride's dwelling and wedding outfit—an accusation of weakness and effeminacy.

1382 Arabic, *wa-qad khaḍkhaḍa mā li-l-rijāli ka-l-farasī*. The sense is uncertain. It may mean that ʿAmr has been "mounted" as a mare by a stallion. Al-Ḍināwī, *loc. cit.*, suggests reading *ka-l-farisī*, "like one who desires to be covered," but the particular form he suggests, *faris*, is not given by the dictionaries.

contains the same." But Ṭarafa said, "He would not dare to treat my tribe in such a manner; I am more powerful in that land than ʿAmr." Ṭarafa therefore continued to the governor of al-Baḥrayn, who, when he read the letter, cut off his hands and feet and crucified him.

Then his brother Qābūs b. al-Mundhir ruled, and then al-Mundhir b. al-Mundhir (ruled) for four years.

These kings ruled on behalf of the Persian shahs,[1383] to whom they rendered obedience and submitted tax payments. The tribes of Maʿadd were united against them, and the most obstinate in the opposition were the Ghaṭafān and the Asad b. Khuzayma. A man of the Maʿadd would come to them | as a 1:241 visitor, and they would welcome and honor him; such visits by tribal dignitaries included al-Rabīʿ b. Ziyād al-ʿAbsī, al-Ḥārith b. Ẓālim al-Murrī, Sinān b. Abī Ḥāritha, and the poet al-Nābigha al-Dhubyānī. The kings used to glorify the poets and exalt their rank because of how the latter gave them lasting glory and fame. Al-Nābigha was the foremost of the poets in the eyes of these kings, but then he made an amorous allusion to the wife of al-Mundhir in the ode of his in which he says:[1384]

> The veil fell, though she had not meant to drop it;
> then she reached for it and warded us off with her hand.

Al-Mundhir swore to shed al-Nābigha's blood, and the latter fled to Syria to the kings of the Ghassān. Later he begged forgiveness from al-Mundhir in a poem of his in which he says:[1385]

> You are like the night that will overtake me
> even if I imagine that the place distant from you is spacious.

He also said:[1386]

1383 Arabic, *al-akāsira*, the plural of *kisrā*. Originally a proper name (Persian, Khusraw) in Arabic it was used as a title for all the Persian rulers of the Sasanian dynasty. Since "Kisrās" is awkward in English, the more common "shahs" has been substituted in the translation.

1384 Al-Nābigha al-Dhubyānī, *Dīwān*, 147, v. 1; Arazi and Masalha, *Six Early Arab Poets*, 6, v. 4.

1385 Al-Nābigha al-Dhubyānī, *Dīwān*, 84, v. 2; Arazi and Masalha, *Six Early Arab Poets*, 12, v. 2.

1386 Al-Nābigha al-Dhubyānī, *Dīwān*, 29, v. 3; Arazi and Masalha, *Six Early Arab Poets*, 4, v. 19.

I was told that Abū Qābūs[1387] threatened me—
and who can feel safe when he hears the lion's roar?

Allied with al-Mundhir was a family of the tribe of Imru' al-Qays b. Zayd Manāt b. Tamīm, and one member of this family was ʿAdī b. Zayd al-ʿIbādī, an orator and poet who could write both Arabic and Persian.[1388] Al-Mundhir had placed his son al-Nuʿmān among them; they provided him with a wet-nurse, and he was under their protection. The Persian shah wrote to al-Mundhir to send him a group of Arabs to translate documents for him, and so al-Mundhir sent him ʿAdī b. Zayd and two of his brothers, who joined the ranks of the shah's secretaries and translated for him. When al-Mundhir died, the shah asked ʿAdī b. Zayd,
1:242 "Does anyone remain from this family | who would make a good king?" "Yes," replied ʿAdī, "al-Mundhir had thirteen sons, any of whom would be suitable for what the king intends." So he sent to have them brought, and they proved to be among the handsomest of [al-Mundhir's] family, except al-Nuʿmān, who was ruddy, freckled, and short. He had been raised by the family of ʿAdī b. Zayd, and his mother was a captive named Salmā, who was said to be from the Kalb. ʿAdī b. Zayd gave each of them lodging by himself, but he gave preference in lodging to al-Nuʿmān's brothers over al-Nuʿmān, making it appear to them that he had no hopes for al-Nuʿmān. He would speak privately with each them, saying: "If the king asks you, 'Can you manage the Arabs for me?' say to him, 'No one can manage them for you but al-Nuʿmān.'"[1389] To al-Nuʿmān he said: "If the king

---

1387 Abū Qābūs was the *kunya* of al-Mundhir.

1388 Al-Yaʿqūbī here begins his narrative of the events that led up to the battle of Dhū Qār. Parallels: al-Masʿūdī, *Murūj*, 2:225–227 (§1065–1069); al-Ṭabarī, *Taʾrīkh*, 1:1015–1037; *Kitāb al-Aghānī*, 2:18–43; see also the article by L. Veccia Vaglieri in *EI*², s.v Dhū Ḳār.

1389 Sic M, but there is a textual problem. The reading in M looks like the negative *lan*, followed by a verb whose first letter appears to be *yāʾ*, rather than *nūn* as in ed. Leiden. The sense, which has been followed in this translation, would therefore be, "No one can manage them for you but al-Nuʿman." The parallel in al-Ṭabarī, *Taʾrīkh*, 1:1017–1018, lacks the negative and reads the verb in the 1st person plural (initial *nūn*), yielding, "We can manage them, except al-Nuʿmān." And in fact these are the very words that the brothers say in al-Yaʿqūbī's account to the king when they come before him. But even if one deletes the offending *lan* in the first occurrence, the meaning is ambiguous. To what does the exception refer? Is it, "We, except al-Nuʿmān, can manage them?" or, "We can manage them, except al-Nuʿman, whom we cannot manage?" Nöldeke in his 1879 translation of this section of al-Ṭabarī opted for the latter and put al-Nuʿmān into the accusative case (Nöldeke, *Geschichte der Perser und Araber zur Zeit der Sasaniden*, 315). The clearest explanation of what is going on can be found in the parallel in *Kitāb al-*

asks you about your brothers, say to him, 'If I am incapable of managing them, I am even less capable of managing the Arabs.'"

Now among the sons of al-Mundhir there was a man named al-Aswad. His mother was from the Banū l-Ribāb, and he was an impressive man. He had been raised by a family from al-Ḥīra called the Banū Marīnā, who were notables. One of them was a man named ʿAdī b. Aws b. Marīnā, who was a troublemaker and a poet. He would say to al-Aswad b. al-Mundhir, al-Nuʿmān's brother: "You know that I want the best for you. What I want and desire is that you do the opposite of whatever ʿAdī b. Zayd says, for, by God, he never gives you sincere advice." But al-Aswad paid no heed to what he said.

When the shah ordered ʿAdī to admit them into his presence, he did so one by one, and the shah saw men whose like he had never seen before. When he asked them, "Can you manage for me what you used to manage?" they said, "We will manage the Arabs for you, except al-Nuʿmān." When al-Nuʿmān came into his presence, he saw an ill-favored[1390] man, and he spoke to him, saying, "Can you manage the Arabs for me?" "Yes," he replied. "And how will you | deal with your brothers?" asked the shah. He replied, "If I am incapable of managing them, I am even less capable of dealing with anyone else." So the shah made him king, gave him a robe of honor, and dressed him in pearls. When al-Nuʿmān emerged, having been made king, ʿAdī b. Aws b. Marīnā said to al-Aswad, "Here is the result of your acting against good advice!" 1:243

Al-Nuʿmān went forth having been made king despite ʿAdī b. Marīnā. The latter commanded certain of al-Nuʿmān's courtiers and companions to make references before him to ʿAdī b. Zayd. They were to say that ʿAdī b. Zayd was claiming that the king was his underling, that he himself had brought him to power, that but for him he would never have come to power, and such things.

Aghānī, 2:22–23, which makes it clear that ʿAdī from the beginning favored al-Nuʿmān and arranged an elaborate deception, beginning with the better lodging he gave to the other brothers. In the *Aghānī* account, ʿAdī sends word to al-Nuʿmān, saying, "I intend to make no one else but you king; do not be put off by the preference I am going to give your brothers over you in accommodation, for I am going to deceive them by it." ʿAdī instructed the brothers to dress in their finest clothing and display their best table manners in the king's presence. When he asked whether they could take care of the Arabs, they were to say yes; and when he asked them what they would do if one of them became disobedient, they were to show their prowess by saying that none of them would be strong enough to deal with another. Al-Nuʿmān, on the contrary, was instructed to wear dusty traveling clothes, wolf his food, and boast of his ability to deal with his brothers. The ruse paid off, and the king chose the rough-looking al-Nuʿmān.

1390 Ed. Leiden follows the MSS in reading *wasīman*, "handsome," but surely this is a copyist's error for the reading in al-Ṭabarī and the Aghānī, *damīman*, "ugly, ill-favored."

They spoke incessantly in the presence of al-Nuʿmān, provoking his irritation and anger against ʿAdī b. Zayd. Al-Nuʿmān therefore wrote to ʿAdī, "I enjoin you to come and visit me." So ʿAdī took leave of the shah and came to him. When he reached al-Nuʿmān, the latter ordered him to be cast into a prison where no one could have access to him. Now ʿAdī had two brothers at the shah's court, one named Ubayy, the other Sumayy. Both were at the shah's court—one rejoicing over his destruction, the other desiring his welfare. ʿAdī began to compose poetry in his place of confinement, appealing to al-Nuʿmān's compassion, reminding him of inviolability (as a guest), and admonishing him with the example of kings of the past. But none of this did him any good. His enemies from the Marīnā family took to provoking al-Nuʿmān against him by saying to him, "If he gets away, he will kill you and be the cause of your destruction."

Having despaired of meeting with any good at the hands of al-Nuʿmān, ʿAdī wrote to his brother:

Carry this word to Ubayy, however far he may be—
for sometimes what a man has learned can kill him[1391]—
That your brother, the dear one of your heart,
about whom you were so solicitous while he was safe,
Is in the hands of a king, bound with iron,
whether justly or unjustly.
1:244 May you not be found to be like a woman with a child
who when she finds no one to suck (her breast) sucks it herself.[1392]
Stay where you are! Stay where you are! If you come to us
you will sleep a sleep in which there is no dream.[1393]

He also wrote to his son, ʿAmr b. ʿAdī, who enjoyed the shah's favor:

For whom does a night become long on account of a prisoner,
distressful because he is riven with penetrating grief?
What is the iniquity of a man with fetters on his neck,
and on his legs long links of chains?

1391 Thus in M. The more common reading of the second part of the line (al-Ṭabarī and the *Aghānī*) is: "and is what a man has come to know of any use to him?"

1392 The simile is proverbial for someone who undertakes a task incumbent on someone else. The point is that Ubayy should not come himself to al-Nuʿmān's court to seek his brother's release. The line is discussed in al-Ṭabarī, *Glossarium*, ccclix.

1393 That is, you will die.

May your mother, O ʿAmr, be bereaved of you after me!
Will you sit while I am bound, and not go on the attack?
Does it not grieve you that your father is a miserable captive
and you are all on your own? May a ghoul make off with you!
A daughter of al-Qayn b. Jasr[1394] sings to you in madness,
and wine is your companion.
Were you the prisoner—may you not be so!—
Then all of Maʿadd would know what I have to say.
If I perish, I have conferred great benefit upon my people,
all of it good and fine.
I have not fallen short in the quest for achievements,
whether the fate of death cuts me short or grants long life.

So his brother and his son and those on their side went to the shah and spoke to him about ʿAdī, and the shah wrote a letter to al-Nuʿmān, commanding him to release ʿAdī, and dispatched a messenger with it. Ubayy b. Zayd asked the messenger to begin by (visiting) ʿAdī. So the messenger began by (visiting) ʿAdī, who said to him, "If you leave me, I shall be killed." "Certainly not," replied the messenger, "al-Nuʿmān will not dare to defy the king." Meanwhile, al-Nuʿmān received word that the shah's messenger had gotten to ʿAdī; so when the messenger left ʿAdī, al-Nuʿmān sent someone to kill ʿAdī, pressing a pillow over ʿAdī's face until he died. Then al-Nuʿmān told the messenger that ʿAdī had already died; he gave him gifts and rewards and gained assurances from him that all he would tell the shah was that he had found ʿAdī dead. Then al-Nuʿmān wrote to the shah to inform him that ʿAdī had died.

ʿAmr b. ʿAdī used to translate documents for the shah. | Now the shah sought 1:245
a slave girl; he gave a description of the kind of girl he wanted, but none could be found for him. So ʿAmr b. ʿAdī b. Zayd said to him, "O King, your servant al-Nuʿmān has more daughters and female relations of [this description] than the king could ever desire, but he holds himself superior to the king and claims to be better than he." So the shah sent to al-Nuʿmān, commanding him to send him his daughter, so that he might marry her. Al-Nuʿmān said, "Are there not among the wide-eyed ones[1395] of the Sawād and Persia enough to meet the needs of the king?" When the messenger returned, he told the shah what al-Nuʿmān had said. The shah asked, "What does he mean by 'wide-eyed ones'?" ʿAmr b. ʿAdī

1394 That is, a singing girl.

1395 Arabic, *ʿīn*, a poetic epithet for the largest of the antelopes, the *mahāh*, considered as a type of feminine gracefulness and beauty.

b. Zayd replied, "He means cows,[1396] so as to avoid sending his daughter to the king." Furious at this, the shah said, "Many a servant has risen to greater heights than he, but has come to ruin in the end."

When word of this reached al-Nuʿmān, he prepared himself. The shah held back from him for a month, and then he wrote to him to come to him. Knowing what the shah had in mind, al-Nuʿmān took up his weapons and whatever else he could carry and made his way to the two mountains of the Ṭayyiʾ—he was married to Suʿdā bt. Ḥāritha[1397]—and asked the Ṭayyiʾ for protection from the shah, but they said, "We have no power against him." So he departed. All the Arab tribes refused to receive him; so in the end he encamped in the valley of Dhū Qār in the territory of the Banū Shaybān. There he met Hāniʾ b. Masʿūd b. ʿĀmir b. ʿAmr b. Abī Rabīʿa b. Dhuhl b. Shaybān. He gave him his weapons, entrusted him with his daughter and the other women of his family, and then he made his way to the shah and presented himself at his gate. The shah ordered that he be bound in chains and sent to Khāniqīn.[1398] ʿAmr b. ʿAdī b. Zayd met
1:246 him and said, belittling him, "Nuʿaym,[1399] | I have fastened for you tethering stakes that only a wild young stallion could uproot."[1400] Al-Nuʿmān replied, "I hope …"[1401] When he was brought to Khāniqīn, he was cast under the feet of elephants and trampled to death and then given to the lions to eat.

1396 Arabic, *baqar*. This is the ordinary word for domestic cattle. In a way, this is correct, as the *mahāh* is also called "wild cow," but by leaving out "wild" ʿAmr cleverly turns a poetic way of referring to graceful women into an insult.

1397 She was from the tribe of Ṭayyiʾ and therefore al-Nuʿmān could claim protection. Cf. Nöldeke, *Geschichte der Perser und Araber zur Zeit der Sasaniden*, 329, n. 2.

1398 A town about 160 km northeast of present-day Baghdad, on the border between modern Iraq and Iran. The point was to take him far from his former sphere of influence in southern Iraq.

1399 Nuʿaym is the diminutive of al-Nuʿmān, and its use here is meant as an insult.

1400 There is a play on words here. Arabic *ākhiyya* (pl. *awākhin*) is a stake with a tether firmly sunk into the ground so that an animal tied to it cannot escape, but metaphorically it is a sacred right that cannot be escaped, i.e., the son's right and duty to avenge his father's murder. The parallel in al-Masʿūdī, *Murūj*, 2:227 (§1068), reads, "I have fastened for you a tethering stake that a wild young stallion could not uproot."

1401 There is no lacuna, but the text and the meaning are so opaque that one can only conjecture the meaning. A rough stab at a translation and interpretation, accepting the emendation of the Leiden editor, is, "I hope that you have yoked to it a camel that is pregnant." This would be a kind of prophetic reference made by al-Nuʿmān at the point of death to the coming battle of Dhū Qār, in which the Arabs, by defeating the Persians, will symbolically avenge the death of al-Nuʿmān. Unfortunately, none of the parallels includes this riposte by al-Nuʿmān.

The shah sent word to Hāniʾ b. Masʿūd, saying, "Send me the property of my servant that you have, as well as his weapons and daughters." When Hāniʾ did not do it, the shah sent an army against him. The Rabīʿa assembled and the battle of Dhū Qār took place. The Arabs tore the Persians to pieces, and this was the first time that the Arabs triumphed over the Persians. It has been transmitted from the Messenger of God that he said, "This was the first day[1402] on which the Arabs obtained their just due from the Persians, and it was because of me that they were given victory."

The War of Kinda

There were wars between the Kinda and Ḥaḍramawt that wiped out most of them. Kinda rallied around two men, one of whom was Saʿīd b. ʿAmr b. al-Nuʿmān b. Wahb. Leading the Banū l-Ḥārith b. Muʿāwiya was ʿAmr b. Zayd, and Shuraḥbīl b. al-Ḥārith led the Sakūn. The Ḥaḍramawt rallied around several leaders, including Masʿar b. Mustaʿir, Salāma b. Ḥujr, Sharāḥīl b. Murra, and others after these. All these leaders passed away, but the war among (their followers) persisted, and their men perished.[1403] It lasted so long that it ground them down—the killing was especially great among the Kinda. The Ḥaḍramawt took as their king ʿAlqama b. Thaʿlab, who was only a boy at the time, so the Kinda | relented somewhat and were loathe to fight the Ḥaḍramawt. The 1:247
people of Yemen[1404] passed into a state of dispersal and fragmentation, and when they scattered and spread through the lands, each group made its leader their king.

When the Kinda reached the territory of the Maʿadd, they allied with them. Then they took as their ruler—the first of their kings—a man called Murtiʿ b. Muʿāwiya b. Thawr. He ruled for twenty years.

Then his son Thawr b. Murtiʿ became king, but he lasted only a short time before he died.

After him, Muʿāwiya b. Thawr became king.

Then al-Ḥārith b. Muʿāwiya became king; his reign lasted forty years.

Then Wahb b. al-Ḥārith ruled for twenty years.

1402 That is, battle-day.

1403 Reading with M: *wa-faniyat rijāluhum*; ed. Leiden emends unnecessarily to *wa-fattanat rijālahum* (and it [sc. the war] tested their men).

1404 That is, the tribes claiming "southern" descent.

Then Ḥujr b. ʿAmr Ākil al-Murār[1405] ruled for twenty-three years. He was the one who created the alliance between the Kinda and the Rabīʿa. Their alliance took place at al-Dhanāʾib.

Then ʿAmr b. Ḥujr ruled after him for forty years. He, along with the Rabīʿa, raided Syria. Al-Ḥārith b. [Abī] Shamir[1406] encountered him [in battle] and killed him.

Then al-Ḥārith b. ʿAmr ruled after him—his mother was the daughter of ʿAwf b. Mulḥam[1407] al-Shaybānī.[1408] He settled in al-Ḥīra and divided his kingdom among his sons, who were four in number: Ḥujr, Shuraḥbīl, Salama al-Ghalfāʾ, and Maʿdīkarib. He made Ḥujr king of the Asad and Kināna; Shuraḥbīl king of the Ghanm, Ṭayyiʾ, and al-Ribāb; Salama al-Ghalfāʾ king [of the Taghlib and al-Namir b. Qāsiṭ; and Maʿdīkarib king][1409] of the Qays b. ʿAylān. They used to compete for superiority with the kings of al-Ḥīra. When al-Ḥārith was killed, his sons arose with whatever forces they could muster and determined to fight al-Mundhir until they had taken their due from him.[1410] When al-Mundhir saw that they were gaining mastery over the land of the Arab tribes, he became jealous of them on this account and provoked conflict among them. He sent
1:248 presents to Salama al-Ghalfāʾ, and then guilefully sent someone | to Shuraḥbīl who told him, "Salama is more important than you; look at these presents that are coming to him from al-Mundhir!" So he waylaid (the caravan bringing) the presents and seized them. (Al-Mundhir) then provoked conflict between the two of them until they went to war. Shuraḥbīl was killed, and the Tamīm and Ḍabba were defeated[1411] with him. When this happened, the people were afraid to say to his brother Salama, "Your brother has been killed." He, however, began to hear things they were saying. Grieving at the killing of his brother and regretting the fact that al-Mundhir had only wanted them to kill each other, he said:[1412]

1405 Ākil al-Murār (Eater of Bitter Herbs) is a nickname that he received on account of his behavior in his rage at his wife's infidelity. See *Aghānī*, 8:63, for two versions of the story.

1406 Cf. *Aghānī*, 8:65: full name al-Ḥārith b. Abī Shamir al-Ghassānī.

1407 *Aghānī*, 8:65: Muḥallim.

1408 Parallels with many variations: *Aghānī*, 8:63 ff. and 11:63 ff.

1409 The text in brackets was added by the Leiden editor on the basis of *Aghānī*, 11:64.

1410 For the circumstances of al-Ḥārith's death in 528 CE and the role in it of his rival al-Mundhir, the Lakhmid ruler of al-Ḥīra whom the Persians once had deposed in favor of al-Ḥārith, but later reinstated, see *Aghānī*, 8:63–64; also the article by I. Shahîd and A. F. L. Beeston in *EI*², s.v. Kinda.

1411 Reading with M: *fa-kubita*. Ed. Leiden, *wa-kānat* (were).

1412 Longer version with variants in *Aghānī*, 11:63.

My flank draws away from my bed,
as a galled camel shrinks from stony ground.
Because of word that has reached me, my tears
do not cease to flow, and I cannot swallow my drink.

The Banū Asad became estranged from Ḥujr b. ʿAmr, and his manner of dealing with them became offensive. Ḥujr was married to Fāṭima bt. Rabīʿa, the sister of Kulayb and Muhalhil; she bore him (his daughter) Hind, and when he began to fear for his life he mounted her (on a camel).[1413] The Banū Asad then came together to kill him, and they did kill him. Various tribes of the Banū Asad claimed [to have killed Ḥujr]—the person who took charge of the affair for the Banū Asad was ʿIlbāʾ b. al-Ḥārith, a member of the Banū Thaʿlaba. Imruʾ al-Qays b. Ḥujr was away at the time, and when word of his father's murder reached him, he gathered a band of warriors and set out for the Banū Asad.[1414] On the night before the morning on which he planned to attack them, he encamped with his band and startled a flock of sandgrouse, which flew up from their resting places and passed by the Banū Asad. The daughter of ʿIlbāʾ said, "Never have I seen so many sandgrouse as tonight!" ʿIlbāʾ replied, "Had the sandgrouse been undisturbed, they would have become drowsy and fallen asleep," a saying that became proverbial. Realizing that a hostile force had drawn close to him, ʿIlbāʾ departed. The next morning, Imruʾ al-Qays fell upon the Kināna and attacked them, crying: "Vengeance!" (His victims) replied, "By God, we are only some men of the Kināna." Imruʾ al-Qays therefore said:[1415] | 1:249

Alas my soul's sorrow, after (the escape) of foemen
who (by their death) would have sated my soul, but were not slain!
Their luck protected them by means of their father's sons,[1416]
and the punishment descended on the more unfortunate ones.

1413 Cf. *Aghānī*, 8:66: "When Ḥujr became afraid of the Banū Asad, he asked ʿUwayr b. Shajna, one of the Banū ʿUṭārid b. Kaʿb b. Saʿd b. Zayd Manāt b. Tamīm, to give refuge to his daughter Hind bt. Ḥujr and his children."

1414 The story of how Imruʾ al-Qays avenged his father's death (a father who for his part had almost killed Imruʾ al-Qays) became the stuff of legend. See the article by S. Boustany in *EI*^{2}, s.v. Imruʾ al-Ḳays b. Ḥudjr.

1415 Imruʾ al-Qays, *Dīwān*, 138–139; *Aghānī*, 8:69.

1416 That is, the Banū Asad were protected from their fate by Imruʾ al-Qays's mistaken slaying of the Banū Kināna, to whom the Banū Asad were related.

'Ilbā', choking on his own spittle, eluded the horses;
had they overtaken him, the milk skin would have become empty.[1417]

It was at this time that 'Abīd b. al-Abraṣ al-Asadī said, referring to Imru' al-Qays b. Ḥujr, in a long ode:[1418]

O you who threaten us with abasement
and death for the killing of your father:
Do you claim, falsely and lyingly,
that you have killed our chieftains?
It were better for you to shed tears for Ḥujr,
the son of Umm Qaṭām, rather than for us.
When the straightening-clip bites into
the head of our lance, we leap back.[1419]
We defend what we ought to defend, while some of
the foemen fall one after another.[1420]

About this subject 'Abīd also says, in a long ode of his:[1421]

O you who ask about our glory,
you are weak in judgment, ignorant of us!
If reports about us have not reached you,
then[1422] ask about us, O you who ask.
Ask Ḥujr about us, on the morning of the fray,
the day his fleeing[1423] band turned back,[1424]

1417 A metaphorical way of saying that he would have become a corpse, as empty of breath as an empty milk skin is empty of milk.

1418 Cf. *Aghānī*, 19:85; 'Abīd b. al-Abraṣ, *Dīwān* (ed. Lyall), p. 27, no. 7, v. 1–5.

1419 The straightening clip (*thiqāf*) was a device to hold a spear shaft or bow during the shaping process. The line means that when someone tries to parry our lance-thrust, the deflected shaft springs back and kills him.

1420 Arabic: *bayna bayna*, variously glossed. Lane, *Lexicon*, 1:288a: "fall, one after another, in a state of weakness, not regarded as of any account."

1421 'Abīd b. al-Abraṣ, *Dīwān*, p. 72, no. 26, v. 9–13.

1422 Reading with M *fa-s'al*; ed. Leiden has *wa-s'al* (and ask).

1423 Reading with M and the Dīwān, *al-jāfilu*, as opposed to ed. Leiden, *al-ḥāfilu* (numerous).

1424 Reading with M *tawallā*; ed. Leiden has *ta'attā* (prepared itself).

The day they encountered Saʿd in the thick of the fighting,
and Kāhil galloped in pursuit of him.[1425]
They brought his throng to drink from hard dry lances,
(bloodied) until they looked like burning flames.

When Imruʾ al-Qays found he had no strength against the Banū Asad and their allies from the Qays, he made his way to Yemen and stayed there for a time, drinking constantly with his boon companions. One day he looked out from his vantage point and noticed a rider approaching. He asked him, "From where have you come?" "From Najd," he said. So Imruʾ al-Qays gave the man some of what he was drinking. When the wine took effect, the man raised his voice and said:[1426] | 1:250

We gave Imruʾ al-Qays b. Ḥujr cups of grief to drink,
until he became accustomed to subjection.
Drinking sweet wine and sweet-voiced singers diverted him;
the vengeance he sought for Ḥujr was too difficult for him.
That, by my life, was an easier way for him
than (facing) trenchant swords and dusky spears.

Startled at hearing this, Imruʾ al-Qays said, "O brother of the people of the Ḥijāz, who is the author of this poem?" "ʿAbīd b. al-Abraṣ," was the reply. "You have spoken the truth," said Imruʾ al-Qays. Then he took to horse. He sought help from his kinsmen, and they reinforced him with five hundred men from the Madhḥij. Then he set out for the land of the Maʿadd. He fell upon certain tribes from the Maʿadd, killed al-Ashqar b. ʿAmr, who was the chief of the Banū Asad, and drank from his skull. As Imruʾ al-Qays said in a poem of his:[1427]

Say to the Dūdān, the slaves of the rod:
"What beguiled you about the intrepid lion?"[1428]

1425 For *wa-ḥāwalat* read *wa-jāwalat*, with the *Dīwān*.

1426 ʿAbīd b. al-Abraṣ, *Dīwān*, p. 83 no. 8.

1427 Imruʾ al-Qays, *Dīwān*, pp. 119–122, no. 16 v. 3, 9.

1428 The verse is addressed to the Banū Dūdān, a clan of the Banū Asad, from whom Imruʾ al-Qays exacted vengeance for his father's death. Contemptuously, he calls them "slaves of the rod" because, according to a well-known proverb, slaves could be disciplined only by being beaten. "The intrepid lion" is either the poet himself or a reference to his father. The fact that the tribal name, Banū Asad, meant "Sons of the Lion" introduces yet another level of wordplay.

O you who would inquire about our nature,
the one who knows is not like the one who is ignorant.
Wine has become permissible for me, who previously was a man
whose mission kept him from drinking it.[1429]

The tribes of Maʿadd pursued Imruʾ al-Qays, and the men who had been on his side went away. Word reached him that al-Mundhir, the king of al-Ḥīra, had sworn to shed his blood, so he decided to return to Yemen; but he feared the Ḥaḍramawt. The Banū Asad and the tribes of Maʿadd pursued him. When he realized that he had no way to escape al-Mundhir's reach, that the tribes of the Maʿadd were all agreed on hunting him down, and that it would not be possible for him to return (to Yemen), he made his way to Saʿd b. al-Ḍibāb al-Iyādī, who was Kisrā's[1430] governor over certain districts of Iraq, and hid with him for a time, until Saʿd b. al-Ḍibāb died. When Saʿd died, Imruʾ al-Qays left for the Two Mountains of the Ṭayyiʾ, where he met Ṭarīf b. [...] al-Ṭayyiʾ and asked him for protection. "By God," Ṭarīf replied, "I have nothing in the Two Mountains but the place of my campfire." Imruʾ al-Qays stayed with a clan of
1:251 the Ṭayyiʾ. He kept moving about, | spending time with the Ṭayyiʾ, then with the Jadīla, then with the Nabhān. Finally he made his way to Taymāʾ and stayed with al-Samawʾal b. ʿĀdiyā,[1431] whom he asked for protection. But al-Samawʾal said to him, "I do not give protection against kings, nor am I able to fight them." So Imruʾ al-Qays deposited some armor with him and departed to seek out the king of the Romans. Ultimately he reached Caesar,[1432] the king of the Romans, and asked for his assistance, and the latter sent him back with seven hundred sons of patricians.[1433] Imruʾ al-Qays had praised Caesar (in his verse), but then

1429 This refers to the poet's vow not to drink wine until he had exacted vengeance for his father's death.

1430 Kisrā (a generic name in Arabic for all the shahs of Sasanian Iran) is probably Khusraw Anūshirwān (r. 531–579).

1431 On al-Samawʾal b. ʿĀdiyā, a famous pre-Islamic Jewish-Arab poet who lived in the castle of Ablaq in Taymāʾ, see the article by Th. Bauer in *EI*², s.v. al-Samawʾal b. ʿĀdiyā.

1432 Arabic, *Qayṣar*, a generic title for all the Roman emperors.

1433 Arabic, *abnāʾ al-baṭāriqa*, literally, "sons of the *baṭrīq*s." *Baṭrīq* is an Arabicized form of the Roman title *patricius*. Originally a dignity conferred by the emperors for exceptional service to the state, it was used in Arabic as the regular term for a Byzantine commander. In other words, Imruʾ al-Qays came back from his visit to the "king of the Romans" accompanied by a force of seven hundred (ed. Leiden, nine hundred) military officers. On the term, see the article by Irfan Kawar in *EI*², s.v. Baṭrīḳ.

al-Ṭammāḥ al-Asadī went to Caesar and said to him, "Imruʾ al-Qays has reviled you in his poetry and called you an uncircumcised peasant." Caesar therefore sent Imruʾ al-Qays a suit of clothes that had been sprinkled with poison. When he donned the clothing, his skin broke out in sores. Knowing that his death was nigh, he said:[1434]

My old sickness has returned to me at night, coming in the darkness;
 I fear that my sickness will increase and that I shall suffer a relapse.
Al-Ṭammāḥ from the remoteness of his land set his sights
 to clothe me with his stealthy illness.
Would that it were a soul that could die all at once!
 But it is a soul that falls away in gasps.

These verses are part of a long ode by him. He also said about his condition:[1435]

Send word to the children of Ḥujr b. ʿAmr,
 and to that clan who live apart:
That I have remained as long as a soul may remain,
 and have not been worn down by stones or by iron.
If I were perishing in the land of my people,
 I would say, "Death comes by right; no one lives forever."
But I have perished in the land of a foe,
 Far away, remote from your dwellings:
In the land of Syria,[1436] with no close kin,
 And without a patron to lend assistance or be generous.

Imruʾ al-Qays died in Anqira,[1437] in the land of the Romans.

The Descendants of Ismāʿīl b. Ibrāhīm

The only reason we have postponed an account of Ismāʿīl and his descendants 1:252
and brought our accounts of the nations to a close with them is that God

1434 Imruʾ al-Qays, *Dīwān*, 105–108, no. 13, v. 5, 13, 11; *Aghānī*, 8:73.

1435 Imruʾ al-Qays, *Dīwān*, 212–214, no. 46, v. 1–4, 6.

1436 *Dīwān*: "In the land of the Romans," which is accurate historically but may be a later correction.

1437 This is Greek Ancyra, modern Ankara.

brought prophecy and kingship to a close with them, and their history is continuous with that of the Apostle of God and the caliphs.[1438]

The transmitters and scholars have stated that Ismāʿīl b. Ibrāhīm was the first to speak Arabic, rebuild the Sacred Sanctuary of God[1439] after his father Ibrāhīm, and perform the rites (of the pilgrimage). He was the first to ride thoroughbred horses, which previously ran wild and were not ridden. Some of them have said that Ismāʿīl was the first one to whom God granted the ability to speak Arabic. When he reached boyhood, God gave him the Arab bow, with which he shot and struck every target at which he aimed. When he attained maturity, God brought a hundred mares out of the sea; these remained grazing in Mecca for as long as God willed, then God drove them to Ismāʿīl, who awoke one morning to find them at his door. People's mounts had previously been common hacks, but now Ismāʿīl reined, rode, and bred the (thoroughbreds), and he and his sons and descendants rode them. Concerning Ismāʿīl one of the poets of the Maʿadd says:

> Our forefather, before whom no horses were ridden,
> and before whom no elder knew how they should be ridden.

It is said that the these horses were called the "thoroughbreds of Mecca" (*ajyād Makka*) for the following reason. The horses were there, and then God revealed to Ismāʿīl that he should go to the horses, which he did, and there remained not a single mare that did not allow him to take hold of her forelock. He rode them, as also did his descendants; Ismāʿīl was the first man to ride horses and the first to make use of them.[1440]

He was also the first to banish transgressors from the Sanctuary. He said, "I declare it to be evil (*uʿarribuhū*)." Because of this they were called the Arabs (*al-ʿAraba*).[1441]

1438 Like all Muslim historians of the medieval Middle East, al-Yaʿqūbī sees history as culminating with the rise of Islam. The Prophet Muḥammad was regarded as a descendant of Ismāʿīl, so it was appropriate that al-Yaʿqūbī's history of the ancient nations should conclude with Ismāʿīl and his progeny, leading directly to an account of Muḥammad and the rise of Islam. Parallel: al-Ṭabarī, *Taʾrīkh*, 1:352 ff.

1439 The Kaʿba in Mecca, considered to have been built by Ibrāhīm and his son Ismāʿīl.

1440 These legends concerning the role of the ancient Arabs in the domestication of the horse were common and played an important part in asserting the nobility of Ismāʿīl and his family.

1441 There is a play on words here, involving the root *ʿ.r.b.*

When the Banū Qaḥṭān b. ʿĀmir, who were kinsmen of the Jurhum b. ʿĀmir, arrived in Yemen and established their authority there, the Jurhum themselves went to the land of Tihāma.[1442] There they became neighbors of Ismāʿīl b. Ibrāhīm, who married al-Ḥanfāʾ bt. al-Ḥārith b. Muḍāḍ al-Jurhumī, who bore him twelve sons: Qaydār, Nābit, Adbīl, Mibsām, Mishmaʿ, Dūmā, Massā, Ḥadād, Taymā, Yaṭūr, Nāfis, and Qaydmā.[1443] These names vary in spelling and pronunciation because they are translated from Hebrew. When Ismāʿīl had completed one hundred and thirty [years], he died and was buried in the Ḥijr.[1444] 1:253

When Ismāʿīl died, authority over the Sanctuary after him passed to Nābit b. Ismāʿīl; it is also said that Qaydār assumed authority, and after Qaydār Nābit b. Ismāʿīl. The descendants of Ismāʿīl then dispersed, seeking more room in other lands, but one group devoted themselves entirely to the Sanctuary, saying, "We will not depart from the Sanctuary of God." The descendants of Ismāʿīl had already dispersed when Nābit died, so authority over the Sanctuary was assumed by al-Muḍāḍ b. ʿAmr al-Jurhumī, the (maternal great-) grandfather of the descendants of Ismāʿīl. This was because those of Ismāʿīl's descendants who remained in the Sanctuary were only children. When al-Muḍāḍ assumed authority, al-Samaydaʿ ibn Hawbar challenged him, but al-Muḍāḍ triumphed over him, so al-Samaydaʿ went to Syria—he was one of the kings of the ʿAmāliqa. Authority remained in the hands of al-Muḍāḍ until he died.

Al-Ḥārith b. Muḍāḍ ruled after him. Then ʿAmr b. al-Ḥārith b. Muḍāḍ ruled. Then al-Muʿtashim[1445] b. al-Ẓalīm ruled. Then al-Ḥawās b. Jaḥsh b. Muḍāḍ ruled. Then ʿIdād b. Ṣadād b. Jandal b. Muḍāḍ ruled. Then Finḥaṣ b. ʿIdād b. Ṣadād ruled. Then | al-Ḥārith b. Muḍāḍ b. ʿAmr ruled—he was the last of the 1:254
Jurhum to rule. The Jurhum became tyrannical, oppressive, and unjust, and they behaved wantonly in the Sanctuary, so God sent a plague of tiny ants[1446] against them, and every last one of them was destroyed by it.

The descendants of Ismāʿīl spread through the lands, subduing all who opposed them, but they granted the kingship to the Jurhum as they were

1442 Tihāma is the Red Sea coastal region of the Arabian peninsula, loosely including Mecca.

1443 Cf. Genesis 25:12–16; similar lists in al-Masʿūdī, *Murūj*, 1:69 (§ 116) and 2:164 (§ 944); al-Ṭabarī, *Taʾrīkh*, 1:351–352.

1444 The Ḥijr is the area immediately around the Kaʿba.

1445 Sic M; C and ed. Leiden: al-Muʿtasim.

1446 Arabic: *al-dharr*; the same word occurs in al-Ṭabarī, *Taʾrīkh*, 1:1121, which is more graphic: "Tiny ants followed in the tracks of those of them who survived, penetrated into their ears, and destroyed them." Cf. the longer account of the history of the Kaʿba in al-Ṭabarī, *Taʾrīkh*, 1:1130 ff.

related through a maternal uncle; the Jurhum remained obedient to them in their days. In the days of the Jurhum, only descendants of Ismāʿīl were in charge of the affairs of the Kaʿba, which was Jurhum's way of glorifying them and acknowledging their status. Those who were in charge of the Kaʿba after Nābit were Amīn, then Yashjub b. Amīn, then al-Hamaysaʿ, and then Udad.[1447] The latter's reputation increased among his tribe and he rose to high standing; he took the Jurhum to task for their actions, and it was in his time that the Jurhum perished. Then there was ʿAdnān b. Udad, followed by Maʿadd b. ʿAdnān. The descendants of ʿAdnān then scattered through the lands. Some of them made their way to Yemen: these included the ʿAkk, al-Dīth, and al-Nuʿmān. ʿAkk had a son by a daughter of Argham b. Jumāhir al-Ashʿarī; then he died. His descendants survived him, and they traced their descent through their maternal uncles and their family.

ʿAdnān was the first to set up sacred stones[1448] and cover the Kaʿba. Maʿadd b. ʿAdnān was the noblest of the descendants of Ismāʿīl in his time. His mother was from the Jurhum, and he never left the territory of the Sanctuary. He had ten sons: Nizār, Quḍāʿa, ʿUbayd al-Rammāḥ, Qanaṣ, Qunāṣa, Junāda, ʿAwf, Awd, Salham, and Janb. Maʿadd bore the *kunya* of Abū Quḍāʿa. Most of his descendants, who were very numerous, traced their ancestry to Yemen.[1449]

1:255 The Quḍāʿa traced their ancestry to the king of Ḥimyar. Quḍāʿa | himself is said to have been born on the bed of Maʿadd. Maʿadd was the first to place a saddle on male and female camels and the first to provide them with a nose-rein.

Nizār b. Maʿadd was the elder and leader of his father's tribe. His residence was in Mecca. His mother was Nāʿima bt. Jawsham b. ʿAdī b. Dubb al-Jurhumīya, and he had four sons: Muḍar, Iyād, Rabīʿa, and Anmār. Their mother was Sawda bt. ʿAkk b. ʿAdnān, although it is said that the mother of Muḍar and Iyād was Ḥayiyya[1450] bt. ʿAkk b. ʿAdnān and that the mother of Rabīʿa and Anmār was

1447 The translation follows the somewhat conjectural emendations of ed. Leiden. In M the list is badly garbled to read something like: "Those who were in charge of the Kaʿba after Nābit were Balyāmīn b. Yashjub, Binyāmīn b. al-Hamaysaʿ, and Ibn Udad."

1448 Arabic *anṣāb*, plural of *nuṣub*: a block of stone over which the blood of sacrifices was poured. Unlike idols, for which Arabic has a separate word (*ṣanam*, plural *aṣnām*), these stones were not carved to represent a god.

1449 Al-Yaʿqūbī has already mentioned the uncertainty about whether certain tribes belonged, through ʿAdnān, to the descendants of Ismāʿīl (the northern Arabs) or were descended from Qaḥṭān, the progenitor of the southern Arabs; see above, ed. Leiden, 1:229–231.

1450 Sic ed. Leiden and, apparently, M. Perhaps to be read Khabiyya, as in al-Zubayrī, *Nasab Quraysh*, 6. The reading is uncertain.

Jadāla bt. Waʿlān b. Jawsham al-Jurhumī. When Nizār was on his deathbed, he divided his estate among his four sons and gave his property to Muḍar, Iyād, Rabīʿa, and Anmār. Muḍar and Rabīʿa were the two of pure descent from Ismāʿīl. He gave Muḍar his russet she-camel (*al-ḥamrāʾ*) and other like-colored camels, so he was called al-Ḥamrāʾ; to Rabīʿa he gave his mare (*al-faras*) and other similar horses, so Rabīʿa was called al-Faras. He gave Iyād his sheep and goats and his shepherd's crook; as the animals had coats of black and white (*barqāʾ*), Iyād was called Iyād al-Barqāʾ—he was also called Iyād of the Staff. He gave Anmār a slave girl of his named Bajīla, and so Anmār was named after her. He ordered them that if they disagreed they should refer the dispute to al-Afʿā b. al-Afʿā al-Jurhumī, whose home was in Najrān, and they did so.

As for ANMĀR B. NIZĀR, he married in Yemen, and his children traced their descent through their maternal uncle. Among them were the Bajīla and Khathʿam. Apart from them, none of the descendants of Nizār departed.[1451]

As for RABĪʿA B. NIZĀR, he left his brothers and went to the lands extending from the Baṭn ʿIrq to Baṭn al-Furāt. He had several sons, among them Asad, Ḍubayʿa, Aklub, | and nine others. Their descent is not traced through the 1:256
Yemenite tribes. The sons of Rabīʿa b. Nizār spread out and had so many sons of their own that their ranks multiplied and the lands were filled with them. The major tribes descended from Rabīʿa are as follows:

- BUHTHA b. Wahb b. Julayy b. Aḥmas b. Ḍubayʿa b. Rabīʿa,
- ʿANAZA b. Asad b. Rabīʿa,
- ʿABD AL-QAYS b. Afṣā [b. Duʿmī] b. Jadīla b. Asad b. Rabīʿa,
- YASHKUR b. Bakr b. Wāʾil b. Qāsiṭ b. Hinb b. Afṣā,
- ḤANĪFA b. Lujaym b. Ṣaʿb b. ʿAlī b. Bakr b. Wāʾil b. Qāsiṭ,
- ʿIJL b. Lujaym b. Ṣaʿb b. ʿAlī b. Bakr,
- QAYS b. Thaʿlaba b. ʿUkāba b. ʿAlī b. Bakr,
- TAYM AL-LĀT b. Thaʿlaba b. ʿUkāba.

Adjudication and leadership among the Rabīʿa was exercised by the Banū Ḍubayʿa, the descendants of Buhtha b. Wahb b. Julayy b. Aḥmas b. Ḍubayʿa b. Rabīʿa; then these functions passed to the descendants of ʿAnaza b. Asad b. Rabīʿa, and then to the ʿAbd al-Qays b. Afṣā b. Duʿmī b. Jadīla b. Asad b. Rabīʿa. The ʿAbd al-Qays then moved and settled in al-Yamāma because of war that broke out between them and the Banū l-Namir b. Qāsiṭ. The Iyād were in

1451 Probably in the sense of leaving their ancestral descent and tracing their descent through the female line, as implied in the next paragraph.

al-Yamāma, and so they drove them out.[1452] Leadership [of the Rabīʿa] then passed to the al-Namir b. Qāsiṭ, and then it passed from the al-Namir b. Qāsiṭ
1:257 and came to the Banū Yashkur b. Ṣaʿb b. ʿAlī b. Bakr. Then | the leadership passed from the Yashkur b. Ṣaʿb and came to the Banū Taghlib and then to the Banū Shaybān.

The Rabīʿa were involved in famous battle days and well-known wars. One of their famous battle days was the Day of al-Sullān. The Madhḥij approached with the intention of raiding the people of the Tihāma and the descendants of Maʿadd who lived there. The descendants of Maʿadd therefore gathered to fight the Madhḥij. The majority [of them] were from the Rabīʿa, so they entrusted their leadership to Rabīʿa b. al-Ḥārith b. Murra b. Zuhayr b. Jusham b. Bakr. They encountered the Madhḥij at al-Sullān and put the Madhḥij to flight, and so they emerged victorious.

As for the Day of Khazāz, that was an occasion when the Yemeni tribes approached under the leadership of Salama b. al-Ḥārith b. ʿAmr al-Kindī. The descendants of Maʿadd made Kulayb b. Rabīʿa [b. al-Ḥārith] b. Murra their leader, and when Salama saw how numerous his enemy was he sought the assistance of one of the kings. This ruler reinforced him, and the two sides met at Khazāz, with the descendants of Maʿadd led by Kulayb. The Yemeni forces were routed.

As for the Day of al-Kulāb, Salama and Shuraḥbīl, two sons of al-Ḥārith b. ʿAmr al-Kindī, went to war with each other. Supporting Salama were the Rabīʿa, and supporting Shuraḥbīl were the Qays, who were outnumbered by the Rabīʿa. The Rabīʿa killed Shuraḥbīl [b. al-Ḥārith] b. ʿAmr and gained the ascendancy.

As for the Days of al-Basūs, they were between the tribes of Shaybān and Taghlib over the killing of Kulayb b. Rabīʿa b. al-Ḥārith b. Murra b. Zuhayr b. Jusham al-Taghlibī by Jassās b. Murra b. Dhuhl b. Shaybān. The conflict became confused[1453] and continued unabated until it wiped them out; it lasted forty years.

As for the Day of Dhū Qār:[1454] when Kisrā Aparwīz killed al-Nuʿmān b. al-Mundhir, he sent word to Hāniʾ b. Masʿūd al-Shaybānī, telling him, "Send me

1452 The pronouns in the Arabic text leave the outcome of this conflict unclear.

1453 Reading with M: *fa-rtabakat*; ed. Leiden, *fa-shtabakat*, "it became intricate."

1454 Al-Yaʿqūbī has already given some of the background for this battle that took place at the watering place of Dhū Qār, near Kufa, sometime between 604 and 611 CE. See the narrative above, beginning at ed. Leiden 1:241. The death of the Lakhmid ruler of al-Ḥīra, al-Nuʿmān b. al-Mundhir, at the hands of Kisrā Aparwīz has already been mentioned by al-Yaʿqūbī at ed. Leiden 1:245–246. For the parallel accounts, see the note above to ed. Leiden 1:241; see also the article by L. Veccia Vaglieri in *EI*^{2}, s.v Dhū Ḳār.

the kinfolk of my servant al-Nuʿmān that he left in your custody, | as well as his property and weapons!"—al-Nuʿmān had left his daughter and four thousand sets of armor in trust with him. Hāniʾ and his tribesmen refused to do it, and so Kisrā dispatched armies of Arabs and Persians (against them), and they met at Dhū Qār. Ḥanẓala b. Thaʿlaba al-ʿIjlī came to them, and they invested him with command over them. Then they said to Hāniʾ, "Your promise of protection is our promise of protection, and we will not break our promise." Then they fought the Persians and put them to flight, along with the Arab tribes allied with them, including Iyās b. Qabīṣa al-Ṭāʾī and others who were tribesmen of Maʿadd and Qaḥṭān. ʿAmr b. ʿAdī b. Zayd came to Kisrā and told him the news, and he heaved his shoulders and died. This was the first battle in which the Arabs triumphed over the Persians.[1455] 1:258

As for IYĀD B. NIZĀR, he settled in al-Yamāma and had sons who claimed descent among the tribes. The genealogists say that Thaqīf was Qasī[1456] b. al-Nabt b. Munabbih b. Manṣūr b. Yaqdum b. Afṣā b. Duʿmī b. Iyād and that they themselves claimed descent from the Qays.[1457] The territories of Iyād, after al-Yamāma, included al-Ḥīra, where their dwelling places were al-Khawarnaq, al-Sadīr, and Bāriq.[1458] Then Kisrā expelled them from their dwelling places and settled them in Takrīt, an ancient city on the bank of the Tigris, and then he expelled them from Takrīt to the lands of the Romans—they settled at Anqira in Roman territory. Their leader in those days was Kaʿb b. Māma. Afterward they left (Roman territory). The major tribes of Iyād are four: Mālik, Ḥudhāqa, Yaqdum, and Nizār.[1459] These are the clans of Iyād, and concerning them al-Aswad b. Yaʿfur al-Tamīmī says:[1460] | 1:259

1455 This sentence paraphrases a well-known tradition from the Prophet, as is noted in the margin of C and M. The tradition has already been quoted by al-Yaʿqūbī above, ed. Leiden 1:246.

1456 Ed. Leiden, M: Qays.

1457 That is, the genealogists placed the tribe of Thaqīf among the descendants of Iyād b. Nizār, but noted that the Thaqīf themselves traced their descent to Qays ʿAylan, the son of Muḍar b. Nizār, a brother of Iyād. Al-Yaʿqūbī will give this alternate genealogy below, ed. Leiden 1:260.

1458 Two of these places are famous for their palaces. Al-Khawarnaq, about one mile east of Najaf in Iraq, was the site of a famous palace built by the Lakhmid ruler al-Nuʿmān. Al-Sadīr was nearby. See the article by L. Massignon in *EI*², s.v. Khawarnaḳ.

1459 Sic M and ed. Leiden. The identity of this Nizār (if that is the original reading) is unknown.

1460 Biography, with three verses of the poem cited in *Aghānī*, 11:134–139.

[They were] the people of al-Khawarnaq, al-Sadīr, and Bāriq,
and of the battlement-embellished castle at Sindād,
People who trod on the tips of their sandals,
walking about in striped cloth and flowing garments.
The winds have obliterated the place where they had their dwelling,
as if they had a rendezvous with time.
They settled at Anqira, with the waters of the Euphrates
flowing past them, coming down from the mountains:
A land favored for its far-extending tenting grounds
by Kaʿb b. Māma and Ibn Umm Du'ād.

Abū Du'ād al-Iyādī recited part of this poem. He was their best poet, followed by Laqīṭ in Iraq. When word reached (Laqīṭ) that Kisrā had sworn to himself that he would expel the Iyād from Takrīt, which was in the territory of al-Mawṣil, he wrote a letter that he sent to them. In this letter he said:[1461]

Greetings in the letter from Laqīṭ
to those of the Iyād who live in al-Jazīra:[1462]
The lion is coming to attack you suddenly,
so let not herding vile sheep restrain you.[1463]
Seventy thousand men have come to attack you,
driving their squadrons forward like locusts.

As for MUḌAR B. NIZĀR, he was the lord of his father's progeny, a noble man and a wise adjudicator. It is reported of him that he said to his sons: "He who sows evil will reap regret. The best good is what comes fastest. Make your soul bear what it loathes when it will benefit you, and turn your soul away from its desire when it will harm you. Only patience for as much time as separates two milkings of a camel stands between benefit and harm." The Messenger of God is reported to have said, "Do not revile Muḍar and Rabīʿa, for they were Muslims." According to another *ḥadīth* [he said], "They were followers of the religion of

1461 For a parallel account of the attempt by the Persians in the reign of Shāpūr to expel the Iyād and of the poem composed as a warning by Laqīṭ, see al-Masʿūdī, *Murūj*, 1:295–296 (§601–603).

1462 Al-Jazīra is the northern part of the territory between the Tigris and Euphrates.

1463 Reading: *fa-lā yaḥbiskumū sawqu l-niqādī*. In M, the last two lines of the poem are added in a different hand in the margin. The word *yaḥbiskumū* (restrain you) is not clearly written, but is attested in other witnesses to the poem (see the note to the parallel in al-Masʿūdī). Ed. Leiden emends to *yashghalkumū* (busy you).

Ibrāhīm." Muḍar b. Nizār begot | al-Yās[1464] b. Muḍar and ʿAylān b. Muḍar (their 1:260
mother was al-Ḥanfāʾ bt. Iyād b. Maʿadd). ʿAylān b. Muḍar begot Qays b. ʿAylān, whose progeny spread far and wide, proliferated, and became numerous and powerful. The major tribes descended from Qays b. ʿAylān are:

- ʿADWĀN b. ʿAmr b. Qays,
- FAHM b. ʿAmr b. Qays,
- MUḤĀRIB b. Khaṣafa b. Qays,
- BĀHILA b. Aʿṣar b. Saʿd b. Qays
- FAZĀRA b. Dhubyān b. Baghīḍ [b. Rayth b. Ghaṭafān b. Saʿd b. Qays],
- SULAYM b. Manṣūr b. ʿIkrima [b. Khaṣafa] b. Qays,
- ʿĀMIR b. Ṣaʿṣaʿa b. Muʿāwiya b. Bakr b. Hawāzin,
- MĀZIN b. Ṣaʿṣaʿa b. Muʿāwiya b. Bakr b. Hawāzin b. Manṣūr b. ʿIkrima b. Khaṣafa b. Qays,
- SALŪL b. Ṣaʿṣaʿa b. Muʿāwiya b. Bakr b. Hawāzin,
- THAQĪF, who was Qasī b. Munabbih b. Bakr b. Hawāzin (although the lineage of Thaqīf is also traced back to Iyād b. Nizār),
- KILĀB b. Rabīʿa b. ʿĀmir b. Ṣaʿṣaʿa,
- ʿAQĪL b. Kaʿb b. Rabīʿa b. ʿĀmir b. Ṣaʿṣaʿa,
- QUSHAYR b. Kaʿb b. Rabīʿa,
- AL-ḤARĪSH b. Kaʿb b. Rabīʿa b. ʿĀmir,
- ʿAWF b. ʿĀmir b. Rabīʿa b. ʿĀmir,
- AL-BAKKĀʾ b. ʿĀmir b. Rabīʿa.

Leadership and adjudication were exercised by the Qays and then passed to the ʿAdwān, the first of whom to adjudicate and lead was ʿĀmir b. al-Ḍarib.
Then these prerogatives passed to the Fazāra, then to the ʿAbs, and then | to 1:261
the Banū ʿĀmir b. Ṣaʿṣaʿa, among whom they remained. The Qays were involved in famous battle days and continuous wars, including the Day of al-Baydāʾ, the Day of Shiʿb Jabala, the Day of al-Habāʾa, the Day of al-Raqm, the Day of Fayf al-Rīḥ, the Day of al-Milbaṭ, the Day of Raḥraḥān, the Day of al-ʿUrrā, and the War of Dāḥis and al-Ghabrāʾ between the ʿAbs and Fazāra.

1464 The name is vocalized as Ilyās in al-Zubaydī, *Nasab Quraysh*, 7, and al-Ṭabarī, *Taʾrīkh*, 1:1108, but the evidence points to al-Yaʿqūbī's having read the name as al-Yās, treating the first two letters as the definite article. This is confirmed a few lines later by the phrase *li-l-Yās* ("belonging to al-Yās"), and by the treatment of the name in the following poem (*ʿalā l-Yāsi*, "for al-Yās"). Al-Yās (el-Jâs) is the form in which the name appears in Wüstenfeld, *Genealogische Tabellen*, 2:254. Another argument for the reading al-Yās is that he is said to have had brother named al-Nās—al-Yās and al-Nās.

Al-Yās b. Muḍar was a most noble man whose excellence became evident. He was the first to rebuke the children of Ismāʿīl for the changes they had made in the traditions of their forefathers. The virtuous deeds he performed led them to view him with a degree of approval that they had not bestowed upon any of the descendants of Ismāʿīl since Udad. He brought them back to the ways of their forefathers until their tradition was completely restored to its original form. He was the first to offer camels as sacrifices to the House, and the first to lay the cornerstone[1465] after the death of Ibrāhīm. The Arabs revered al-Yās as a person of wisdom. Among the sons of al-Yās were Mudrika, whose name was ʿĀmir, Ṭābikha, whose name was ʿAmr, and Qamaʿa, whose name was ʿUmayr—the mother of all of them was Khindif, whose name was Laylā bt. Ḥulwān b. ʿImrān b. al-Ḥāfi b. Quḍāʿa. Al-Yās suffered from consumption, and so his wife Khindif said, "If he perishes, may I never live in a land in which he died." [She swore] that no tent should cast a shadow over her and that she would roam the earth. When he died, she set out wandering through the land until she died of grief. His death took place on a Thursday. She would weep for him; and when the sun rose on that day of the week, she would weep until it set. For this she became the subject of a proverb. Once someone said to a man of the Iyād whose wife had died, "Aren't you going to weep for her?" He replied:

> Had it availed, I would have wept as Khindif wept
> for al-Yās, wailing until her heart was weary.
> When the first shafts of sunlight of the (day called) Intimate appeared,
> she wept through the morning and until she saw the sun set.

1:262 When he says "Intimate," he means Thursday, because the Arabs used to call the days of the week by other names than at this time: they called Sunday *al-Awwal* (the First), Monday *Ahwan* (Easy), Tuesday *Jubār* (Great), Wednesday *Dubār* (Lapsing), Thursday *Muʾnis* (Intimate), Friday *ʿArūba* (Manifest),[1466] and Saturday *Shiyār*. They also used to have ten names for the days of the month, one name for each three-night period. The first three days after the sighting of the moon were called al-Ghurar, then al-Nufal, al-Tusaʿ, al-ʿUshar, al-Bīḍ, al-Ẓulam, al-Khunnas, al-Ḥanādis, al-Muḥāq, and finally Laylat al-Sarār, when the moon was hidden from view. Their names for the lunar months were:

1465 Arabic *al-rukn* (the corner) is ambiguous. It can refer to any corner or cornerstone of the Kaʿba, but often refers to the corner near which the Black Stone is affixed.

1466 The Arabic lexicographers tried to give an Arabic etymology for the word as "manifest," but some recognized that it was simply the Aramaic word for Friday; cf. Syriac *ʿrūbtā*. See Lane, *Lexicon*, s.v.

Muḥarram	Mu'tamir
Ṣafar	Nājir
Rabīʿ al-Awwal	Khawwān
Rabīʿ al-Ākhir	Wabṣān
Jumādā al-Ulā	Ḥanīn
Jumādā al-Ākhira	[Rubbā
Rajab	al-Aṣamm
Shaʿbān	ʿĀdhil
Ramaḍān]	Nātiq
Shawwāl	Waʿl
Dhū l-Qaʿda	Warna
Dhū l-Ḥijja	Burak

Others of the tribal Arabs called the three nights at the beginning of the month Halāl; the next three Qamar, when the moon brightens (*yuqmiru*); the next thee Buhr, when it gives light and its color becomes overpowering (*yabharu*); the next three Nuqal; the next three Bīḍ, the next three Duraʿ; the next three Ẓulam; the next three Ḥanādis; then next three Da'ādī; then the two nights called Muḥāq and Laylat Sarār.

Ṭābikha b. al-Yās begot Udd b. Ṭābikha, and from the descendants of the latter there emerged four tribes: Tamīm b. Murr b. Udd; al-Ribāb, who was ʿAbd Manāt b. Udd; Ḍabba b. Udd; and Muzayna b. Udd. The Tamīm b. Murr b. Udd grew so numerous that the lands became filled with them and tribes [of Tamīm] dispersed. | Among the major tribes of Tamīm are: Kaʿb b. Saʿd b. 1:263
Zayd Manāt; Ḥanẓala b. Mālik b. Zayd Manāt, who were called the Barājim; the Banū Dārim; the Banū Zurāra b. ʿUdas; the Banū Asad; and ʿAmr b. Tamīm. These were the descendants of Udd b. Ṭābikha b. al-Yās b. Muḍar. They were numerous, powerful, courageous, and intrepid; they produced many poets and were elegant speakers. Leadership was exercised by the Tamīm. The first leader among them was Saʿd b. Zayd Manāt b. Tamīm, followed by Ḥanẓala b. Mālik b. Zayd Manāt. They were involved in famous battle days and well-known wars, including the Day of al-Kulāb, the Day of al-Murrūt, the Day of Jadūd, and the Day of al-Nisār.

Mudrika b. al-Yās was the lord of the descendants of Nizār, and a man well-known for his virtues and distinction.[1467] His brother Qamaʿa went out to the Khuzāʿa and married among them, and so his descendants came to trace their lineage with them and were among them. Among his sons was ʿAmr b. Luḥayy b.

1467 Reading with M *majd*, for ed. Leiden *maḥd*.

Qamaʿa, who was the first to alter the religion of Ibrāhīm.[1468] Mudrika b. al-Yās begot Khuzayma, Hudhayl, Ḥāritha and Ghālib—their mother was Salmā bt. (al-Aswad b.)[1469] Aslam b. al-Ḥāfi b. Quḍāʿa, though some say that she was the daughter of Asad b. Rabīʿa b. Nizār. As for Ḥāritha, he passed away as a child. The descendants of Ghālib traced their lineage through the Banū Khuzayma. The largest number of the descendants of Hudhayl b. Mudrika was to be found in the Banū Saʿd b. Hudhayl, followed by the Tamīm b. Saʿd, and then the Muʿāwiya b. Tamīm and the al-Ḥārith b. Tamīm. The Hudhayl were brave men who fought in many wars and raids, men of courage, eloquence, and poetry.

1:264 Khuzayma was one of the Arab tribal arbitrators and a man esteemed for his virtue and chieftainship. Khuzayma b. Mudrika begot Kināna (his mother was ʿUwāna bt. Qays b. ʿAylān), as well as Asad, Asada,[1470] and al-Hūn (their mother was Barra bt. Murr b. Udd b. Ṭābikha, the sister of Tamīm b. Murr). As for Asada b. Khuzayma, his descendants spread out in Yemen: they were the Judhām, Lakhm, and ʿĀmila, the sons of ʿAmr b. Asad. The Muḍar used to lay claim to Judhām particularly, and the Banū Asad maintain that they are descended from them; they keep up good relations with them for that reason and count the Judhām as one of their own clans. Imruʾ al-Qays b. Ḥujr al-Kindī said:[1471]

We endured with patience the loss of our kin, and they departed,
just as Khuzayma endured with patience the loss of Judhām.

ʿAbd al-Muṭṭalib b. Hāshim said in a poem of his:

Say to Judhām, if you come to their lands,
and in particular to the Banū Saʿd there and the Wāʾil:
"Gather up and hold close the relations of your people,
so that they incline to you, before you sever relations."

1468 Al-Yaʿqūbī gives details below of how ʿAmr b. Luḥayy introduced the worship of the idol Hubal into the cult at the Kaʿba, which until then had been dedicated to the monotheistic religion of Abraham (Ibrāhīm); see ed. Leiden, 1:295.

1469 The words in parentheses occur in ed. Leiden and M, but, according to the Leiden editor, should be deleted on the basis of Wüstenfeld, *Genealogische Tabellen*, 1:14.

1470 Sic M. Ed. Leiden omits Asada, but the name is found in parallel texts; cf. al-Zubayrī, *Nasab Quraysh*, 8, and al-Ṭabarī, *Taʾrīkh*, 1:1106. Both of these sources make Asada (not Asad) the father of Judhām, and this is also the reading of M.

1471 Imruʾ al-Qays, *Dīwān*, p. 278, no. 65 v. 2.

ʿAbīd b. al-Abraṣ said in a long poem of his:[1472]

Inform Judhām and Lakhm, if you meet them—
and knowledge is useful to people, when they have it:
"In God's book[1473] you were our brothers,
when the ties of kinship and lives were portioned out."

Some say that this poem is by Shamʿān b. Hubayra al-Asadī.

As for the Judhām b. ʿAdī b. al-Ḥārith, they maintain that their lineage is among the Yemeni tribes; they say that it is Judhām b. ʿAdī b. al-Ḥārith b. Murra b. Udad b. Yashjub b. ʿArīb b. Mālik b. Kahlān.

Among the sons of Asad b. Khuzayma were Dūdān, Kāhil, ʿAmr, Hind, al-Ṣaʿb, and Taʿlab.[1474] The largest number were of the Dūdān, and it was from him that the Banū Asad divided. The tribes of the Banū Asad are Quʿayn, | Faqʿas, 1:265
Munqidh, Dubān,[1475] Wāliba, Lāḥiq, Ḥurthān, Riʾāb, and the Banū l-Ṣaydāʾ. The Asad were spread out from near the palaces of al-Ḥīra to Tihāma. [The Ṭayyiʾ] had an alliance concluded with them, and the territory of the two was almost the same. They were at war with Kinda, until they killed Ḥujr b. al-Ḥārith b. ʿAmr al-Kindī. Imruʾ al-Qays[1476] fled, and Kinda became submissive. Then they made war on the Banū Fazāra, until they killed Badr b. ʿAmr. Then they fell out with the Ṭayyiʾ and the two tribes, Asad and Ṭayyiʾ, made war on each other, until they killed Lām b. ʿAmr al-Ṭāʾī, captured Zayd ibn Muhalhil, who is Zayd al-Khayl,[1477] and took female prisoners. Zayd al-Khayl said:

1472 ʿAbīd ibn al-Abraṣ, *Dīwān*, p. 87, fragment no. 16.

1473 Here in the general sense, not referring specifically to the Qurʾān, as ʿAbīd b. al-Abraṣ died before the coming of Islam. See the article by Reinhard Weipert in *EI*[3], s.v. ʿAbīd b. al-Abraṣ.

1474 Sic M (undotted) and ed. Leiden, but no such name is known, and the most likely readings (Thaʿlab or Taghlib) do not fit the context.

1475 Thus in the MSS, otherwise unidentified; vocalization uncertain.

1476 Ḥujr's son, the famous poet. Al-Yaʿqūbī has already related the story of Ḥujr's death and the vengeance of his son; see above, ed. Leiden, 1:248–251. See also the article by S. Boustany in *EI*[2], s.v. Imruʾ al-Ḳays b. Ḥudjr.

1477 The poet Zayd al-Khayl (Zayd of the Horses) of the tribe of Ṭayyiʾ received his name because of the many horses he kept. Born in late pre-Islamic times, he is said to have met Muḥammad and to have accepted Islam. The second of the two poems is quoted in two versions with additional verses in *Kitāb al-Aghānī*, 16:47 and 16:48 (ed. Cairo, 18:6544 and 18:6550).

Tell the Qayses—Qays b. Nawfal,
 Qays b. Uhbān, and Qays b. Jābir:
"Banū Asad, return to us our women
 and our children. Enjoy the camels
And the property, for property is of little value and perishable,
 when one of the passing nights comes.
Do not make it a custom to be followed
 by the Banū Asad, but remit with powerful hands."

So they released him and returned their women, when they heard these verses. However, a horse belonging to Zayd, who loved horses, remained behind. Zayd therefore said:

"Banū al-Ṣaydā', give back my horse:
 this is done only to one who is submissive.
Accustom my colt to what I accustomed it:
 to travel by night and to make it trample the slain."

So they returned his horse to him. The Banū Asad therefore used to say, "We killed four men, all of whom were sons of 'Amr and each of whom was the chief of his people: we killed Ḥujr b. 'Amr, the king of Kinda; Lām ibn 'Amr al-Ṭā'ī; Ṣakhr b. 'Amr al-Sulamī, and Badr b. 'Amr al-Fazārī."

1:266 As for al-Hūn[1478] b. Khuzayma, he is al-Qāra. (His descendants) received the name *al-Qāra*[1479] because the Banū Kināna, when the Banū Asad b. Khuzayma left Tihāma and (the Banū l-Hūn) allied themselves[1480] with Kināna, joining the few (sc. the Banū l-Hūn) to the many (sc. the Kināna), made the Banū l-Hūn a *qāra*, i.e. a small mountain, in their midst, not one individual (or family) separated from another.[1481] Others say that the Banū l-Hūn settled on depressed ground and that the Arabs call depressed ground *qāra*,[1482] and so

---

1478 Sometimes vocalized as al-Hawn.

1479 Al-Qāra means "an isolated small mountain among other mountains" (*Lisān al-Arab*, under root q-w-r).

1480 Following the original reading of both manuscripts: *ḥālafū*, rather than Houtsma's emendation *khālafū* (fell out with). This interpretation is confirmed by al-Maydānī, *Majma' al-Amthāl*, no. 2867, s.v. *qad anṣafa*.

1481 The translation follows M: *lā aḥada dūna aḥadin*.

1482 The normal word for such depressed ground is *qarāra*, not *qāra*, so the explanation seems unlikely; however, *qāra* is also used for rough ground covered with black stones.

they were called "the inhabitants of *al-qāra*." The Qāra were archers. One of them once said, "Whoever competes with the Qāra at shooting has given them their due." Fighting is said [to have taken place] between al-Hūn b. Khuzayma and Bakr b. Kināna. One of the Banū Bakr asked, "Which would you rather do: shoot arrows or race?" One of them said:

Salm and those allied with them know
 that we turn horses away from their desire.
Whoever competes with the Qāra at shooting has given them their due.
 Whenever we encounter a party of men,
 We turn them back, their kidneys bleeding.

The tribes of the Banū l-Hūn b. Khuzayma are ʿAḍal and Dīsh, the sons of Yaythaʿ b. al-Hūn b. Khuzayma. As for al-Ḥakam b. Hūn b. Khuzayma, he went to Yemen and settled in the territory of Madhḥij. Sons were born to him there. He died, and his sons traced their ancestry to Ḥakam b. Saʿd al-ʿAshīra.

Virtues whose excellence cannot be enumerated became apparent in Kināna b. Khuzayma. The Arabs extolled him. It has been related that Kināna was visited while he was sleeping in the Ḥijr.[1483] It was said to him, "Choose, Father of al-Naḍr, between the neighing of horses, the braying (of camels),[1484] the building of walls, or lasting might." He said, "All of this, Lord!"—and it was given to him.

Kināna b. Khuzayma begot al-Naḍr,[1485] | Ḥudāl, Saʿd, Malk,[1486] ʿAwf, and 1:267
Makhrama[1487] (their mother was Hāla bt. Suwayd b. al-Ghiṭrīf, who was Ḥāritha b. Imruʾ al-Qays b. Thaʿlaba b. Māzin b. al-Ghawth), ʿAlī and Ghazwān (their mother was Barra bt. Murr), Jarwal and al-Ḥārith (their mother was from the Azd Shanūʾa), and ʿAbd Manāt (his mother was al-Dhafrāʾ, whose name was

1483 The Ḥijr is the area northwest of the Kaʿba.

1484 Reading with M, *al-hadr*, which can mean either "the braying of camels" or "sonorous and fluent speech," that is, eloquence. See Lane, *Arabic-English Lexicon*, s.v.

1485 Margin M and C adds: "He is Quraysh, and anyone not of his children is no Qurashī." The margin of M also has at the bottom of the previous page: "He is the one named Quraysh, and to him is traced the genealogy of the tribes of Quraysh."

1486 Sic M; so vocalized in al-Zubayrī, *Nasab Quraysh*, 10. Ed. Leiden: Mālik.

1487 Thus in ed. Leiden. The reading is uncertain. C and M appear to read Maḥraba, and the name later appears as Maḥzama (or Makhzama). The corresponding name in al-Zubayrī, *Nasab Quraysh*, 10, is Mujarraba. The parallel in Ibn al-Athir, *al-Kāmil*, 2:19, reads Makhzama.

Fukayha[1488] bt. Hanī [b. Balī] b. ʿAmr b. al-Ḥāfi b. Quḍāʿa). As for Makhrama, it is said that they were the Banū Sāʿida, the clan (*rahṭ*) of Saʿd b. ʿUbāda.[1489]

Belonging to the Banū ʿAbd Manāt b. Kināna—they are the most numerous of Kināna—are the Banū Layth b. Bakr b. ʿAbd Manāt; the Banū l-Duʾil b. Bakr; the Banū Ḍamra b. Bakr (to whom belong the Banū Ghifār b. Mulayk b. Ḍamra); and the Banū Jadhīma b. ʿĀmir b. ʿAbd Manāt, whom Khālid b. al-Walīd smote at al-Ghumayṣāʾ;[1490] and the Banū Mudlij b. Murra b. ʿAbd Manāt.

Belonging to the Banū Malk[1491] b. Kināna b. Khuzayma are the Banū Fuqaym b. ʿAdī b. ʿĀmir b. Thaʿlaba b. al-Ḥārith b. Mālik[1492] b. Kināna. Belonging to the Banū Fuqaym were those with the office of regulating the calendar, and they were those named al-Qalammas.[1493] They used to postpone months and declare them profane or sacred. The first of them was Ḥudhayfa b. ʿAbd Fuqaym, who was named al-Qalammas; then this devolved on his children. After him arose ʿAbbād b. Ḥudhayfa, his son. After ʿAbbād came Qalaʿ b. ʿAbbād, Umayya b. Qalaʿ, ʿAwf b. Umayya, and Junāda b. ʿAwf, who was Abū Thumāma.

1488 Sic ed. Leiden and in al-Zubayrī, *Nasab Quraysh*, 10; M: Fakha.

1489 Saʿd b. ʿUbāda was the leader of the Medinan clan of Banū Sāʿida of the tribe of Khazraj in the days of the Prophet. He was one of the Medinans who pledged loyalty to Muḥammad at the Second Pledge of al-ʿAqaba before the *hijra* and became one of the leaders of the Muslims of Medina.

1490 For an account of this raid, which took place soon after Muḥammad's conquest of Mecca in 8 A.H. (early in 630 CE), see al-Ṭabarī, *Taʾrīkh*, 1:1649–1653; al-Wāqidī, *Kitāb al-Maghāzī*, 3:875–884; and Ibn Hishām, *Sīra*, 4:428–436 (tr. Guillaume, 561–565).

1491 Sic M; ed. Leiden: Mālik.

1492 Sic M and ed. Leiden. This may simply be a copyist's error for the less common 'Malk.'

1493 Literally, "Belonging to the Banū Fuqaym were the *nasaʾa* and the *qalāmis*." The word *nasaʾa* derives from a verb meaning "to postpone"; *al-qalāmis* is the plural of the proper name *al-Qalammas*. The word is glossed by the *Lisān al-ʿArab* as "overflowing," applied to a great chieftain or a well full of water. It adds that "al-Qalammas al-Kinānī was one of the postponers (*nasaʾa*) of months for the Arabs in the Time of Ignorance." The pre-Islamic Arabs observed a lunar calendar, beginning each month at the sighting of the new moon, and counting twelve months to a normal year. However, like the Jews and unlike later Muslims, they interpolated a leap month at intervals in order to synchronize the lunar year with the solar year and the seasons, a practice prohibited by Qurʾān 9:36–37. The office of proclaiming such a leap month (*nasīʾ*) was at one time vested in the Banū Fuqaym. Because interpolating such a month would also disturb the sequence of sacred and profane months, the practice came to be known as "delaying" or "postponing."

Also belonging to them[1494] is Firās b. | Ghanm b. Mālik[1495] b. Kināna. These are the most numerous of the tribes of Kināna. 1:268

As for AL-NAḌR b. Kināna, he was the first who was called al-Qurashī.[1496] He is said to have received the name because of his "providing for his family" (*taqarrush*) and lofty ambition. Others have said that it was on account of his trading and affluence. It is also said to have been on account of a sea creature called *qarsh* (shark)—his mother named him Quraysh, which is the diminutive of *qarsh*.[1497] Therefore, anyone not of the descendants of al-Naḍr b. Kināna is not a Qurashī.

Al-Naḍr b. Kināna begot Mālik, Yakhlud, and al-Ṣalt. Al-Naḍr was (called) Abū al-Ṣalt. The mother of al-Naḍr's children was ʿIkrisha bt. ʿAdwān b. ʿAmr b. Qays b. ʿAylān. As for the descendants of Yakhlud, no one belonging to them is known to have survived. As for the descendants of al-Ṣalt, they went among the Khuzāʿa. Among his descendants was the poet Kuthayyir b. ʿAbd al-Raḥmān, who said concerning his genealogy:[1498]

> Isn't my father al-Ṣalt? Aren't my brothers
> every noble, most illustrious man of the Banū l-Naḍr?

Mālik b. al-Naḍr was a man of great standing. Among his children were Fihr, al-Ḥārith, and Shaybān (their mother was Jandala bt. al-Ḥārith b. Muḍāḍ b. ʿAmr b. al-Ḥārith al-Jurhumī). Some say that the real name of Fihr b. Mālik was Quraysh—Fihr was only a nickname (*laqab*) and Quraysh was his name. Signs of excellence appeared in Fihr b. Mālik during his father's lifetime. When his father died, he took his place.

Among the children of Fihr b. Mālik were Ghālib, al-Ḥārith, Muḥārib, and Jandala—their mother was Laylā bt. al-Ḥārith b. Tamīm | b. Saʿd b. Hudhayl. 1:269

1494 That is, to the Banū Malk/Mālik b. Kināna.

1495 Sic M and ed. Leiden. This may be a copyist's error for the less common 'Malk.'

1496 That is, the one of Quraysh. The relative adjective from Quraysh is Qurashī, with omission of the *y*.

1497 The derivation of the name of the Prophet's tribe, Quraysh, fascinated Arab genealogists and lexicographers, who cited many possible explanations, none backed by much evidence. See W. Montgomery Watt's article in *EI*², s.v. Ḳuraysh; al-Ṭabarī, *Taʾrīkh*, 1:1103–1104.

1498 See *Kitāb al-Aghānī*, 8:28 (ed. Cairo, 9:3126); and *Dīwān Kuthayyir ʿAzza* (ed. Iḥsān ʿAbbās), 233–235, for variants and an account of the circumstances of composition.

Among the children of al-Ḥārith b. Fihr was Ḍabba b. al-Ḥārith, the clan (*raht*) of Abū ʿUbayda b. al-Jarrāḥ.[1499]

Among the children of Muḥārib b. Fihr was Shaybān b. Muḥārib, the clan (*raht*) of al-Ḍaḥḥāk b. Qays.[1500]

Ghālib b. Fihr was the most excellent of them and the one whose nobility was most apparent. It is related that when Fihr b. Mālik was about to die, he said to his son Ghālib: "My son, in fearful anticipation there is distress for the soul. Agitation is only before misfortunes; when a misfortune does occur, its heat cools.[1501] Anxiety is only in the (misfortune's) boiling; when it does arise, cool the heat of your misfortune by means of your seeing the befalling of fate before you, behind you, at your right, and at your left, and by means of what you see in its wake in the way of effacement of life; then content yourself with your little, even though its benefit be small; for a little that is in your hand will profit you more than much that will disgrace you[1502] if it comes to you." When Fihr died, Ghālib b. Fihr became eminent and his fortunes rose. Among his children were Luʾayy and Taym al-Adram (their mother was ʿĀtika bt. Yakhlud b. al-Naḍr b. Kināna), as well as Yaʿlub, Wahb, Kathīr, and Ḥarrāq—of the latter there is no remnant, but Taym al-Adram had offspring.

Luʾayy b. Ghālib was an eminent *sayyid* of clear merit. It is related that while he was yet a young lad, he said to his father, Ghālib b. Fihr: "Father, many a favor receives small recompense. [...][1503] When something is rendered obscure, it is not remembered. A client (*mawlā*) must magnify and publicize what is small, and a patron (*mawlā*) must minimize and cover over what is large." His father said to him: "Son, I find proof of your merit in what I hear of your words, and I pray that you may have abundance among your people in return for them. If
1:270 you obtain abundance, bestow favor | on your people, and protect against the vehemence of their hotheadedness (*jahl*) by means of your levelheadedness

1499 Abū ʿUbayda b. al-Jarrāḥ was an early Meccan convert to Islam. He emigrated to Medina, led several military expeditions, and was active in the conquest of Mecca. See the article by H. A. R. Gibb in *EI*², s.v. Abū ʿUbayda ʿĀmir b. ʿAbd Allāh b. al-Djarrāḥ.

1500 Al-Ḍaḥḥāk b. Qays al-Fihrī became a partisan of Muʿāwiya, but later supported the caliphal claims of Ibn al-Zubayr. He was killed in 64/684. See the article by A. Dietrich in *EI*², s.v. al-Ḍaḥḥāk b. Ḳays al-Fihrī.

1501 Reading with M: *barada ḥarruhā* (carefully pointed). The ductus in C is undotted, which led the Leiden editor to read, *tazdajirhā* (you should restrain it), which is grammatically problematic and makes less sense.

1502 Literally, "what will wear out your face."

1503 Five or six words follow whose reading and translation are unintelligible.

(*ḥilm*).[1504] Bring them together by your gentleness (*rifq*). For men are superior to (other) men on account of their deeds; so associate with them[1505] according to their weights. And cause merit to fall ...[1506] Anyone whose rank is not higher than another person's will have no merit. The higher will always have merit over the lower." When Ghālib b. Fihr died, Luʾayy b. Ghālib took his place.

Among the children of Luʾayy were Kaʿb, ʿĀmir, Sāma, and Khuzayma (their mother was ʿĀʾidha); ʿAwf, al-Ḥārith, and Jusham (their mother was Māwiyya bt. Kaʿb b. al-Qayn); and Saʿd b. Luʾayy (his mother was Yasra[1507] bt. Ghālib b. al-Hūn b. Khuzayma).

As for Sāma b. Luʾayy, he fled from his brother ʿĀmir b. Luʾayy.[1508] This is because there was a quarrel between them and Sāma assaulted ʿĀmir and put out his eye. ʿĀmir then put him in fear, and so he fled from him and went to Oman. It is said that as he passed on a camel of his one day, the camel put its lip to the ground and an adder clung to it. The camel shook it off, and it fell on Sāma. The adder bit his leg and killed him. People allege that when he felt death coming, he said:

My eye, weep for Sāma b. Luʾayy!
  The Clinger-Fast[1509] has clung to his leg.
Never did they see the like of Sāma b. Luʾayy,
  when they came upon him slain by a camel.
Send a messenger to tell ʿĀmir and Kaʿb
  that my soul yearns for the two of them.
If my abode is in Oman, verily I
  am a man of glory; I went forth without need.
To ward off death, O son of Luʾayy,
  your poured out many a cup that was not (truly) poured out.[1510]
You wished to repel the death-decrees, O son of Luʾayy,
  but no one who wishes to do that has any power over death.

1504 The antithetical characteristics of *ḥilm* and *jahl* are frequently contrasted in Arabic. The concepts are discussed in the article by Ch. Pellat in *EI*², s.v. Ḥilm.

1505 Following the apparent reading of M: *fa-ānishā*. Ed. Leiden: *fa-innahā* (and they are).

1506 The text is uncertain. Several words appear to have fallen out.

1507 Vowels uncertain. Al-Zubayrī, *Nasab Quraysh*, 13, reads 'Busra.'

1508 Parallels: Ibn Hishām, *Sīra*, 63 (which quotes the entire poem, with variants); *Kitāb al-Aghānī*, 9:104 (ed. Cairo, 10:3667), which quotes two lines of the poem and identifies them as part of an elegy composed by Sāma's brother.

1509 *Al-ʿAllāqa*, an epithet for Death, or the Decree of Death.

1510 That is, that was ineffective in repelling death.

1:271 As for Khuzayma b. Lu'ayy, who is ʿĀ'idha, he settled among Shaybān, and his children traced their descent to Rabīʿa. As for al-Ḥārith, Jusham,[1511] and Saʿd, they settled among the Hizzān and traced their descent to them. Jarīr b. al-Khaṭafī says about them:

Banū Jusham, you are not of the Hizzān; trace your descent
to the highest of the hills: Lu'ayy b. Ghālib.

As for ʿAwf b. Lu'ayy, he went out—so they say—in a caravan from the Quraysh, and when he was in the territory of Ghaṭafān, his camel slowed down, and those of his people who were with him went on ahead. Thaʿlaba b. Saʿd b. Dhubyān came to him, took him in, and made him his brother; and so his genealogy came to be among ʿAwf b. Saʿd b. Dhubyān. Al-Ḥārith b. Ẓālim, who was one of the Banū Murra b. ʿAwf, said:[1512]

My people are not Thaʿlaba b. Saʿd,
nor Fazāra, who have long hair on their necks.[1513]
My people—if you ask the Banū Lu'ayy
in Mecca—taught Muḍar how to fight.
We were foolish to follow the Banū Baghīḍ
and to leave those who were most closely related to us.

Al-Ḥārith b. Ẓālim also said regarding this:[1514]

When you separate yourselves from Thaʿlaba b. Saʿd
and their brothers, you are ascribed to Lu'ayy:
To a genealogy noble and not ...,[1515]
a tribe who are the most noble of each tribe.

1511 Deleting MS "and he is" before Jusham, which makes no sense. In M, the word is written above "al-Ḥārith," apparently to correct the copyist's omission of "and." Also, the pronoun afterward is in the plural, not the dual, indicating that at least three persons are meant.

1512 Parallels, with more verses and an account of the circumstances of the poem, in Ibn Hishām, *Sīra*, 64; *Mufaḍḍaliyyāt*, No. 90; *Kitāb al-Aghānī*, 10:28 (the account of al-Ḥārith b. Ẓālim begins at 10:17).

1513 According to the dictionaries, this is a compliment, implying comparison to the lion with its mane, a symbol of fortitude. See Lane, *Lexicon*, s.v. *ashʿar*.

1514 This sentence and the following poem are written in the margin of M and C and may not be part of the original text.

1515 A word has fallen out.

> Though my kindred among them are far away, of them
> are God's favorites, the Banū Quṣayy.

There is much poetry by al-Ḥārith b. Ẓālim about this. ʿUmar b. al-Khaṭṭāb summoned the Banū ʿAwf, so that he might restore them to their genealogy in Quraysh. They consulted ʿAlī b. Abī Ṭālib, who said to them: "You are exalted among your people; do not be | adjuncts in Quraysh." 1:272

As for ʿĀmir b. Luʾayy, among his children were Ḥisl b. ʿĀmir, Maʿīṣ b. ʿĀmir, and ʿUwayṣ b. ʿĀmir (their mother was a woman from Qaran). ʿUwayṣ b. ʿĀmir had no surviving descendants; the surviving descendants are from Ḥisl and Maʿīṣ.

As for KAʿB b. Luʾayy, he was the greatest of his father's children in rank and nobility. He was the first to call Friday "the Day of Congregation"[1516]—the Arabs used to call it "[the Day of] ʿArūba."[1517] He gathered them together on it, and he would address them, saying: "Hear and learn! Understand and know. Verily the nighttime is silent, and the daytime shadeless.[1518] The earth is a cradle, the heaven a tent-pole, the mountains pegs, and the stars signposts.[1519] The earliest (men) are as the latest.[1520] Sons are a memorial; therefore, tie close your ties of kinship, and maintain your ties by marriage. Make your wealth abundant. Have you ever seen a mortal who has returned or a dead man who was revived? The abode[1521] is before you, and the (likely) opinion[1522] is other than what you say.

1516 Arabic, *yawm al-jumuʿa*.

1517 The meaning of ʿArūba was unclear to the Arabic lexicographers. Some thought the word had been borrowed from "Nabatean" (that is, Aramaic), and indeed Syriac *ʿrubtā* means Friday, so this seems the most likely derivation. Others derived it from the Arabic verb *aʿraba*, "to make clear, plain," and said that it meant "manifest and magnified." See Lane, *Lexicon*, s.v.

1518 Arabic, *inna al-layla sājin wa-l-nahāra ḍāḥin*. This clearly anticipates Qurʾān 93:3, "*wa-l-ḍuḥā wa-l-layli idhā sajā*," "By white forenoon and the brooding night!" (Arberry translation).

1519 Arabic, *wa-l-arḍa mihādun wa-l-jibāla awtādun*. This clearly anticipates Qurʾān 78:6–7: "*a-lam najʿali l-arḍa mihādan wa-l-jibāla awtādan*," "Have We not made the earth as a cradle and the mountains as pegs?"

1520 This is somewhat cryptic. The form of the Arabic plural (*al-awwalūn ka-l-ākhirīn*) normally refers to people.

1521 Arabic *dār*, again cryptic. It sometimes means simply a house, or the territory in which a tribe dwells, but it can also refer to the grave, or (in Islamic usage) the *dār al-ākhira*, the hereafter.

1522 Arabic *al-ẓann*.

As for your sanctuary, adorn it, glorify it, and hold to it; for a mighty tiding shall come to you,[1523] and from it shall emerge a noble prophet." Then he would say:

> Day and night—each will return bringing an event:
> equal to us its night and its day.
> Both will return bringing events, when they return,
> and bringing blessings whose coverings are pure over us:
> Vicissitudes and tidings that will overcome their people:
> they shall have knots, whose rope cannot be undone.
> Suddenly shall come the Prophet Muḥammad,
> and he shall bring messages whose knower is truthful.

He also would say: "Would that I might witness the secret discourse of his summoning. If I were possessed of hearing, sight, a hand, and a foot, I would
1:273 stand up for him like a calf, and go swiftly like a camel, glad | at his summons, joyful at his call."

When Kaʿb died, Quraysh dated events from the death of Kaʿb. Among the children of Kaʿb were Murra and Huṣayṣ (their mother was Waḥshiyya bt. Shaybān b. Muḥārib b. Fihr, b. Mālik), also ʿAdī b. Kaʿb (his mother was Ḥabība bt. Bajāla b. Saʿd b. Fahm b. ʿAmr b. Qays b. ʿAylān). ʿAdī b. Kaʿb was the clan (*rahṭ*) of ʿUmar b. al-Khaṭṭāb. The children of Huṣayṣ b. Kaʿb were Sahm and Jumaḥ.

Murra b. Kaʿb was an ambitious *sayyid*. He married Hind bt. Surayr[1524] b. Thaʿlaba b. al-Ḥārith b. Mālik b. Kināna—Surayr was the first to postpone months. Hind bore to Murra Kilāb. Then Murra married the daughter of Saʿd b. Bāriq, and she bore him Taym and Yaqaẓa. Taym b. Murra was the clan (*rahṭ*) of Abū Bakr, and Makhzūm b. Yaqaẓa b. Murra was his clan also.[1525]

Kilāb b. Murra was an eminent man and his standing was high. He united the eminence of his father and of his grandfather on his mother's side, because they used to give the pilgrimage permission to proceed and would declare months

---

1523 Cf. Qurʾān 78:1–2: "Of what do they question one another? Of the mighty tiding whereon they are at variance."

1524 MSS Shurayq, corrected by ed. Leiden on basis of Wüstenfeld, *Genealogische Tabellen*, N14. The same name occurs in al-Zubayrī, *Nasab Quraysh*, 13, vocalized as Sarīr. Note that on p. 1:267 above, the office of correcting the calendar by postponing months is traced to the descendants of Surayr's brother ʿĀmir, specifically to the children of Fuqaym b. ʿAdī b. ʿĀmir b. Thaʿlaba.

1525 This seems to mean that Makhzūm b. Yaqaẓa b. Murra was also a clan descended from Murra, not that Abū Bakr was somehow descended also from Makhzūm.

holy or profane. They used to be called "the postponers" and "the people named al-Qalammas."[1526]

Among the children of Kilāb b. Murra were Quṣayy, Zuhra, and Nuʿm.[1527] The Messenger of God said, "The purest of Quraysh are the two sons of Kilāb." Their mother was Fāṭima bt. Saʿd b. Sayal al-Azdī. Saʿd b. Sayal was the first for whom swords were adorned with gold and silver. The poet says concerning him:[1528]

> I think that among men there is no person—
> know this!—like Saʿd b. Sayal.

When Kilāb died, Fāṭima bt. Saʿd b. Sayal married Rabīʿa b. Ḥarām al-ʿUdhrī. He took her away to his people's territory, and she carried Quṣayy with her. | His name had been Zayd, but when he became far from the territory of his people, she named him Quṣayy.[1529] When Quṣayy, who was still under the guardianship of Rabīʿa, became a young man, one of the Banū ʿUdhra said to him, "Go join your own people, for you are not one of us." "To whom do I belong?" he asked. "Ask your mother!" he said. So he asked her. She said, "You are more noble than he in soul, father, and descent. You are the son of Kilāb b. Murra. Your people are God's folk and in His sanctuary." Now the Quraysh never left Mecca; however, when they became many, water became scarce for them, and so they dispersed into the side-valleys. Quṣayy disliked being a stranger and wanted to depart to his people. His mother, however, said to him: "Do not be in a hurry. Wait until the sacred month comes, and then go out with the pilgrims of Quḍāʿa,[1530] for I fear for you." When the sacred month came, he went out with them and reached Mecca. Quṣayy stayed in Mecca until he became a prominent and powerful man and children were born to him.

1:274

Now the office of doorkeeper (*ḥijāba*) of the Kaʿba had come into the possession of the Khuzāʿa. This was because it had gone to the Iyād, and when

1526 See note 1493 to 1:267, above.

1527 The name of Nuʿm, a daughter, is present in the manuscripts (vocalized in M); the Leiden editor emended *wa-nuʿm* unnecessarily to *wa-fīhimā*, "and concerning the two."

1528 Parallel, with more verses, in Ibn Hishām, *Sīra*, 68. Biographies of Quṣayy can be found in Ibn Saʿd, *Ṭabaqāt*, 1/1, 36–42; al-Ṭabarī, *Taʾrīkh*, 1:1092–1100; Ibn Athīr, *al-Kāmil*, 2:12–17. See also the article by G. Levi Della Vida in *EI*², s.v. Ḳuṣayy.

1529 The name is a diminutive of the adjective *qaṣiyy* (remote).

1530 The Banū ʿUdhra belonged to the larger group of Quḍāʿa, the tribal genealogy being ʿUdhra b. Saʿd Hudhaym b. Zayd b. Layth b. Sūd b. Aslum b. al-Ḥāfi b. Quḍāʿa. See article by M. Lecker in *EI*², s.v. ʿUdhra.

the latter decided to depart from Mecca, they loaded the Black Stone[1531] onto a camel, but the camel would not get up; so they buried the stone and departed. A woman of the Khuzāʿa saw them when they buried it. When the Iyād departed, it grieved the Muḍar, and the Quraysh and the others of Muḍar found it distressing. The woman of the Khuzāʿa said to her people, "Stipulate to the Quraysh and the rest of Muḍar that they transfer the office of doorkeeper of the Kaʿba to you, and I will show you where the Black Stone is." They did this, and when they uncovered the Black Stone, they transferred the office of doorkeeper to them. Thus, when Quṣayy b. Kilāb arrived in Mecca, the office of doorkeeper had come into the possession of the Khuzāʿa. The office of giving the signal for the pilgrims to set forth had gone to Ṣūfa[1532] (he was al-Ghawth b. Murr, the brother of Tamīm)—the pilgrimage and the office of giving the pilgrims the signal to depart from ʿArafāt had gone to him. Then it went to his descendants after him. The Banū l-Qays b. Kināna used to postpone the months, declaring them profane or sacred. When Quṣayy saw this, he gathered his kinsmen from
1:275 the Banū Fihr b. Mālik and drew them to himself. When the pilgrimage arrived, | he prevented Ṣūfa from giving the signal to set forth. The Khuzāʿa and the Banū Bakr stood with him. Then, however, realizing that Quṣayy would do to them as he had done to Ṣūfa and that he would deprive them of the command of Mecca and the office of doorkeeper of the Kaʿba, they withdrew from him and turned against him. When he saw that, he decided to fight them. He sent word to his half-brother on his mother's side, Darrāj[1533] b. Rabīʿa al-ʿUdhrī, and his brother came to him, bringing those of the Quḍāʿa whom he could muster. Some have said that Darrāj arrived when Quṣayy had already declared war on the men; Darrāj, who intended to go to the Kaʿba, aided his brother by means of himself and his people. The two sides fought fiercely in the valley of Mecca, until there were many slain on both sides. Then they called each other to a truce and that a man from the Arabs should mediate between them concerning their dispute. They chose Yaʿmur b. ʿAwf b. Kaʿb b. Layth b. Bakr b. Kināna as mediator. He ruled that Quṣayy was more entitled than the Khuzāʿa to the Kaʿba and the command of Mecca; that all the blood that Quṣayy had spilt of the Khuzāʿa and the Banū Bakr was remitted and trampled under his feet,[1534] but that whatever injuries the Khuzāʿa and the Banū Bakr had inflicted on Quraysh were subject to bloodwite (they paid 25 camels fattened for slaughter and 30 lean camels as

1531 Arabic, *al-rukn*, the Black Stone affixed to the east corner of the Kaʿba.

1532 Ṣūfa, here treated by al-Yaʿqūbī as the name of an individual, is to be understood as the progenitor of a tribe. Cf. Ibn Saʿd, *Ṭabaqāt*, 1/1, p. 38: "Ṣūfa, and they were al-Ghawth ..."

1533 Called Rizāḥ in Ibn Saʿd and al-Ṭabarī; the two words are very similar in Arabic script.

1534 That is, not subject to retaliation or the payment of bloodwite.

bloodwit); and that they should give Quṣayy control of the Kaʿba and Mecca. Yaʿmur accordingly was called "al-Shaddākh."[1535]

In Mecca there was no house in the Sanctuary (Ḥaram). The people would be there only by day, and when evening came they would depart. When Quṣayy gathered the Quraysh together—he was the most sagacious person ever seen among the Arabs—he settled the Quraysh in the Sanctuary: he gathered them together at night and stayed with them until morning around the Kaʿba. So the nobles of the Banū Kināna went to him and said: "This is something terrible in the eyes of the Arabs. Even if we left you alone (to do it), the Arabs would not leave you alone." He said, "By God, I will not depart from it." So he stood firm. When the pilgrimage arrived, he said to the Quraysh: "The pilgrimage has arrived. The Arabs have heard what | you have done, and they are upset at you. 1:276
However, I know of no deed more noble in the eyes of the Arabs than providing food; so let each man among you bring out an expenditure from his wealth." They did this, and he gathered up a large quantity from it. When the first of the pilgrims arrived, he slaughtered a camel on each of the roads to Mecca and slaughtered also in Mecca. He set up an enclosure and put into it food consisting of bread and meat, and he provided water and milk to drink. He then turned his attention to the Kaʿba, appointed a key for it and doorkeepers, and prevented the Khuzāʿa from having access to it; and so the Kaʿba came into the hands of Quṣayy. Then he built his house in Mecca—it was the first dwelling built in Mecca—and it is the Dār al-Nadwa.[1536]

Some have related that—when Quṣayy allied himself to Ḥulayl b. Ḥubshiyya al-Khuzāʿī, by marrying his daughter Ḥubbā and she bore him children—Ḥulayl at his death bequeathed the custodianship of the House[1537] to Quṣayy. He said: "Your children are my children. You are most entitled to the House." Ḥubbā bt. [Ḥulayl b.] Ḥubshiyya had borne to Quṣayy b. Kilāb: ʿAbd Manāf, ʿAbd al-Dār, ʿAbd al-ʿUzzā, and ʿAbd Quṣayy.

Others have said that Ḥulayl b. Ḥubshiyya gave the key to Abū Ghubshān (he was Sulaymān b. ʿAmr b. Buwayy b. Malakān[1538] b. Afṣā b. Ḥāritha b. ʿAmr b. ʿĀmir) and that Quṣayy bought it and the custodianship of the House from him

---

1535 That is, the one who allows claims for retaliation and bloodwite to be "trampled under foot."

1536 The House of Gathering, which later served as a kind of town hall where important matters were decided. See the article by R. Paret in *EI*², s.v. Dār al-Nadwa.

1537 That is, the Kaʿba.

1538 Ed. Leiden vocalizes 'Malakān,' as in Wüstenfeld, *Genealogische Tabellen*, 2:581, and Table 12. The editors of the Leiden Ṭabarī preferred 'Milkān,' as recommended by the *Lisān al-ʿArab*, s.v.

for a skin of wine and a young camel.[1539] So it was said, "More contemptible than Abū Ghubshān's bargain."[1540] The Khuzāʿa jumped up and said, "We do not accept what Abū Ghubshān has done," and so fighting broke out between them. Someone said:

Abū Ghubshān is more unjust than Quṣayy,
and the Khuzāʿa are more unjust than the sons of Fihr.
So do not revile Quṣayy for his purchase;
blame your shaykh, since he sold it.

Quṣayy took control of the Kaʿba, the command of Mecca, and rule. He gath-
1:277 ered the tribes of Quraysh together and commanded | them (to dwell) in the valley of Mecca. Some of them had been in the side-valleys and on the hilltops. He divided their dwelling places among them, and therefore he received the name Mujammiʿ.[1541] The poet says concerning them:

Your father Quṣayy was called Mujammiʿ:
by him God gathered together the tribes of Fihr.

Their men made him king over themselves. Quṣayy was the first of the descendants of Kaʿb b. Luʾayy who attained to kingship. When he divided the valley of Mecca into quarters among the Quraysh, they were afraid to cut the trees of the sacred precinct to build their houses; so Quṣayy cut them with his own hand, and then they continued doing so. Quṣayy was the first who rendered the Quraysh mighty; their honor, glory, splendor, and cohesion[1542] became apparent through him. He gathered them together and settled them in Mecca. They had previously been dispersed in abode, small in might, and lowly in lands, until God brought them together in union, honored their abode, and strengthened their habitation. All of Quraysh was in the valley, except the

1539 Arabic, *qaʿūd*. The parallels in al-Ṭabarī, *Taʾrīkh*, 1:1094, and Ibn al-Athīr, *al-Kāmil*, 2:13, read *ʿawd* (an old camel).

1540 M reads "More unprofitable (*akhsar*) than ..." This is also the reading of Ibn al-Athīr, *al-Kāmil*, 2:13. But the proverb is usually quoted in the form given by the Leiden editor (*akhass*). The two words are easily confused in Arabic script.

1541 That is, Gatherer.

1542 Arabic, "their *taqarrush*," playing on the name Quraysh. The dictionaries (cf. *Lisān al-ʿArab*, s.v.) gloss *taqarrush* as "gather together, adhere, cohere," and explain that they were called *Quraysh* "because of their gathering together in Mecca from around it after having been scattered in the lands." Cf. also Ibn Saʿd, *Ṭabaqāt*, 1/1, p. 38.

Banū Muḥārib and (Banū) l-Ḥārith, the sons of Fihr; some of the Banū Taym b. Ghālib, i.e., (Taym) al-Adram; and the Banū ʿĀmir b. Luʾayy—these settled in the outskirts (*ẓawāhir*).

Having obtained preeminence over all Mecca, having divided it among the Quraysh, having become secure in his authority, and having expelled the Khuzāʿa, Quṣayy tore down the Kaʿba and rebuilt it as no one had ever built it. The length of its walls had been nine cubits, but he made it eighteen cubits. He roofed it with wood of the doum palm (Arabic, *dawm*) and fronds of the date palm. He built the House of Assembly (Dār al-Nadwa)—no man of Quraysh would marry, neither would they take counsel on any matter, or appoint anyone to a military command, or circumcise a boy, except in the House of Assembly. During his life and after his death, the Quraysh regarded his command as a religion to be followed. He was the first to dig in Mecca, after Ismāʿīl b. Ibrāhīm: he dug (the well) al-ʿAjūl, and it was completed[1543] during his lifetime and after his death. It is said to be in the house of Umm Hāniʾ bt. Abī Ṭālib. | Quṣayy was 1:278
the first to give a name to a horse: he had a mount called 'the Eagle' that was black.

Among the children of Quṣayy were ʿAbd Manāf, who was called al-Qamar[1544]—he was the *sayyid* who was (as generous as) a river,[1545] and his name was al-Mughīra; ʿAbd al-Dār; ʿAbd al-ʿUzzā; and ʿAbd Quṣayy. Quṣayy is said to have said, "I named two after my two gods, another after my dwelling place, and another after myself." Quṣayy made division among his children: he gave the office of providing the pilgrims with water (*siqāya*) and the leadership (*riʾāsa*) to ʿAbd Manāf; the House (of Assembly)[1546] to ʿAbd al-Dār; the office of providing the pilgrims with food (*rifāda*)[1547] to ʿAbd al-ʿUzzā; and the two sides of the valley to ʿAbd Quṣayy. Quṣayy said to his children: "Whoever esteems a villain, shares in his villainy. Whoever regards as fair one who should

1543 Reading with M: *fa-tamma*, instead of ed. Leiden *fī*.

1544 That is, "Moon"—al-Ṭabarī, *Taʾrīkh*, 1:1091, adds "on account of his beauty."

1545 The reading and meaning are uncertain. M reads either *al-sayyid al-fahir* or *al-sayyid al-nahir/al-nahr*, and ed. Leiden follows the second of these readings. It might mean, "the sayyid (chief) who was (as generous as) a river (*nahr*)," or "the sayyid who traveled by day (*nahir*)." The meaning of *al-sayyid al-fahir* is obscure.

1546 Al-Yaʿqūbī has simply, "*Wa-l-dār li-ʿAbd al-Dār*." Al-Ṭabarī, *Taʾrīkh*, 1:1099, is more specific: "Then he gave him his own house, the House of Assembly."

1547 On the *rifāda*, cf. Ibn Hishām, *Sīra*, 83: "The *rifāda* was a tax which Quraysh used to pay from their property to Quṣayy at every festival. With it he used to provide food for the pilgrims who were unable to afford their own provisions." (Trans. Guillaume, 55).

be regarded as foul, becomes his partner. Whomever your generosity cannot correct, guide him by contempt for him,[1548] for the remedy stops the disease."

Quṣayy died and was buried at al-Ḥajūn,[1549] and ʿAbd Manāf b. Quṣayy became the leader. His standing became high and his esteem great. When the authority of ʿAbd Manāf became great, the Khuzāʿa and the Banū l-Ḥārith b. ʿAbd Manāt b. Kināna came to him to ask him to institute an alliance, so that they might become powerful through it; and so he made an alliance between them (and the Quraysh) called the Alliance of the Aḥābīsh.[1550] The chief[1551] of the Banū Kināna who asked ʿAbd Manāf to institute the alliance was ʿAmr b. Halal b. Maʿīṣ b. ʿĀmir.[1552] The alliance of the Aḥābīsh was sworn at the corner of the Kaʿba.[1553] A man from Quraysh and another from the Aḥābīsh would stand there. They would place their hands on the corner and swear by Allāh the Slayer and by the sanctity of this house, the standing place (*maqām*), the corner, and the sacred month, for help against all men, until Allāh shall inherit the earth and whoever is on it; a mutual compact and cooperation against anyone from
1:279 among all men who would conspire against them, | as long as sea shall wet seaweed, as long as Ḥirā and Thabīr[1554] shall stand, and as long as the sun shall rise from its rising place, until the day of resurrection. It was called [the Alliance of] the Aḥābīsh.

ʿAbd Manāf b. Quṣayy begot Hāshim[1555] (his name was ʿAmr, and he was called ʿAmr al-ʿUlā; he received the name Hāshim because he used to crum-

1548 Arabic: *fa-dullūhu bi-hawānihi*. The meaning is not clear.

1549 Al-Ḥajūn was a cemetery outside Mecca at the foot of a hill of the same name.

1550 The meaning of *aḥābīsh* is unclear. Superficially, it seems connected with the word for Abyssinians (Ḥabash), but nothing in the context indicates any connection between these Arab tribes and people of Abyssinian origin. Other possible explanations are that the word is the plural of *uḥbūsh* or *uḥbūsha* and means "companies or bodies of men, not all of one tribe" (Lane), or that the confederacy took its name from a mountain called al-Ḥubshī or a wadi called Aḥbash (Ibn Hishām's explanation, v. *Sīra*, 246). See the article by W. Montgomery Watt in *EI*², s.v. Ḥabas̲h̲.

1551 Reading with M: *mudrih* (as vocalized in the manuscript; the more common form is *midrah*); emended unnecessarily in ed. Leiden to *mudabbir* ("manager").

1552 At this point, the manuscripts insert a sentence, apparently misplaced (M precedes it with a curious x-shaped mark), which the Leiden editor moved below: "She bore him all of these, and she it was [at whose hands] the Alliance of the Aḥābīsh took place."

1553 That is, by the Black Stone.

1554 Ḥirā and Thabīr are two mountains to the north-east of Mecca.

1555 Parallels in Ibn Hishām, *Sīra*, 87–89; al-Ṭabarī, *Taʾrīkh*, 1:1088–1091; Ibn al-Athīr, *al-Kāmil*, 2:11–12. See the article by W. Montgomery Watt in *EI*², s.v. Hās̲h̲im b. ʿAbd Manāf.

ble[1556] bread and pour broth and meat on it in a year of dearth that struck the Quraysh), ʿAbd Shams, al-Muṭṭalib, Nawfal, Abū ʿAmr, Ḥanna,[1557] Tumāḍir, Umm al-Akhtham, Umm Sufyān,[1558] Hāla, and Qilāba. The mother of all of them, except Nawfal and Abū ʿAmr, was ʿĀtika bt. Murra b. Hilāl b. Fālij b. Dhakwān b. Thaʿlaba b. Buhtha b. Sulaym. She bore him all of these, and she it was [at whose hands] the Alliance of the Aḥābīsh took place.[1559] The mother of Nawfal and Abū ʿAmr was Wāqida bt. Abī ʿAdī (he was ʿĀmir b. ʿAbd Nuhm) of the Banū ʿĀmir b. Ṣaṣaʿa. Hāshim and ʿAbd Shams are said to have been twins.[1560] Hāshim came out, and ʿAbd Shams followed him, his heel adhering to his heel, and so they were cut apart with a razor. People said, "There will surely emerge between the children of these two such severance as has never taken place between any."

Hāshim rose to eminence after his father and became powerful. The Quraysh agreed to bestow on Hāshim b. ʿAbd Manāf the primacy (*riʾāsa*) and the offices of providing the pilgrims with water (*siqāya*) and food (*rifāda*). When the pilgrimage arrived, he would stand up among the Quraysh as an orator, saying: "People of Quraysh, you | are God's neighbors, the people of His sacred house. 1:280
God's visitors come to you at this season to magnify the sanctity of His house. They are God's guests, and the guests most entitled to generosity are His guests. God has chosen you for this and honored you by it, and He has preserved with regard to you the most excellent part of what one neighbor has ever preserved with regard to another. Therefore be generous to His guests and visitors, for they come from every land, disheveled and dusty, on camels as thin as arrows. They have become weak and weary,[1561] infested with lice, and covered with sand. Receive them and relieve their need!" The Quraysh would thereupon bring gifts. Hāshim would bring out much wealth and order leather basins to be placed at the site of Zamzam. Water would be poured into them from the wells that were in Mecca, and the pilgrims would drink from them. He used to feed them at Mecca, Minā, ʿArafa, and Jamʿ.[1562] He would make gruel for them consisting of

---

1556 Arabic *yahshimu*, explaining the name *Hāshim* (the active participle of the same verb).

1557 MSS Ḥasana, corrected by ed. Leiden; cf. Ibn Saʿd, *Ṭabaqāt*, 1/1, 43. Ibn Hishām, *Sīra*, 67. and al-Zubayrī, *Nasab Quraysh*, 14, read "Ḥayya."

1558 MSS: Umm Shaybān.

1559 This sentence has been moved by the Leiden editor. See note 1552 above.

1560 The margin of the MSS adds a verse, apparently to illustrate that the two were regarded as twins: "You (plural) have inherited robes of glory, not from remote kin / [but] from the two sons of ʿAbd Manāf: ʿAbd Shams and Hāshim."

1561 Following M (*wa-qad wahanū wa-thaqilū*). Ed. Leiden: *wa-qad aʿyaw wa-tafilū* (they have become weary and malodorous).

1562 Jamʿ (gathering) is usually taken as another name for Muzdalifa, a station on the

bread, meat, butter, and barley-meal, and carry water to them, until the people dispersed to their countries, and so he came to be called Hāshim.[1563]

Hāshim was the first to establish the two caravans: a caravan to Syria and a summer caravan to Abyssinia, to the Negus.[1564] This was because the commerce of the Quraysh did not extend beyond Mecca, and so they were in distress, until Hāshim rode to Syria and stayed in the territory of the Byzantine emperor.[1565] He would slaughter a sheep every day, set a bowl before him, and invite those around him. He was one of the best-featured and handsomest of men. This was mentioned to the emperor, who sent for him. When the emperor saw him and heard him speak, he was pleased, and so he kept summoning him back repeatedly. Hāshim said: "King, I have kinsmen. They are the merchants of the Arabs. Do you therefore write a document for them, granting safe passage to them and their merchandise, so that they may bring rarities such as leather and garments[1566] of the Ḥijāz." The emperor did this. Hāshim departed, and whenever he passed through one of the tribes of the Arabs, he secured from their chiefs a pact[1567] that they would be safe among them and in their territory,
1:281 and so they secured a pact regarding Mecca | and Syria.

Al-Aswad b. Siʿr[1568] al-Kalbī said: "I was the hired man of one of the women of the tribe. I would ride over rough ground and level. I would leave no place where I could hope for any gain without ...[1569] to it with household items and furniture from Syria, trying to ... the Arabs. When I came back, the (pilgrimage) season had come. I reached (Mecca) in the dark. I tied up my camel until the cloak of night lifted from me. Lo and behold, there were pitched lofty round tents made of leather from al-Ṭāʾif; there were camels being slaughtered, and

---

pilgrimage route about halfway between Minā and ʿArafah. See F. Buhl in *EI*², s.v. Muzdalifa.

1563 Meaning "the crumbler," sc. of bread.

1564 Cf. Qurʾān, 106:1–2.

1565 Reading with the correction in the margin of M: *fa-nazala bi-arḍ Qayṣar*, with the word *arḍ* (land, territory) added in the margin. The copyist of C (and hence ed. Leiden) omitted the marginal addition, yielding "and stayed with Caesar" (that is, the Byzantine emperor). The omission disturbs the flow of the narrative.

1566 Arabic *thiyāb*, as corrected by ed. Leiden; MSS *nabāt* (plants).

1567 Arabic, *īlāf*, which is the word used in Qurʾān, 106:1–2. The meaning of the word was discussed by commentators, who gave a variety of interpretations. See the article in *EI*², s.v. Īlāf.

1568 Sic M; ed. Leiden Shiʿr. The person is otherwise unknown, although the name Siʿr is attested.

1569 The MSS and ed. Leiden read *yarghabu* (desires), but the text must be disturbed.

others being driven …[1570] 'Make haste!' What I saw dazzled me. I went forward, seeking their chief. 'Straight ahead!' said someone, realizing my intention. So I approached. There was a man on a high throne, with a cushion under him. He had wound a black turban on his head, and allowed beautiful long hair to flow out from its folds. It seemed as if the star Sirius were rising from his brow. In his hand was a staff. Around him were many old men with their heads inclined,[1571] not one of them uttering a word, and before them were servants with their garments tucked halfway up their legs. Lo and behold, there was a man with a loud voice on a high piece of ground, calling out: 'Ambassadors of God,[1572] come to the early meal!' And there were two men on the path of those who had eaten, calling out, 'Ambassadors of God, let whoever has had his early meal come back for his evening meal.' Now it had been related to me by a certain rabbi of the Jews that this was the time to expect the Gentile prophet.[1573] So I said, in order to know what he thought, 'O prophet of God!' 'Stop!' he said, as if my […] were […] to him.[1574] So I said to a man who was at my side, 'Who is this?' He said, 'Abū Naḍla Hāshim b. 'Abd Manāf.' So I departed, saying, 'This, by God, is true glory, not that of the Āl Jafna.'"[1575]

Maṭrūd b. Kaʿb al-Khuzāʿī once passed by a man who lived as a neighbor[1576] among the Banū Hāshim, along with daughters of his and a wife, in a year | of 1:282
dearth. The man had gone out carrying his belongings and furnishings, he and his children and his wife, but no one would shelter him. So Maṭrūd al-Khuzāʿī said:[1577]

1570 The next four words seem to mean, "and eaters and [?] in a state of purity." Additional words seem to have fallen out, as the next words need to be introduced by a phrase such as "Someone said."

1571 That is, in respect. The Arabic, *munakkisū l-adhqān*, means literally, "lowering their beards, or chins."

1572 Arabic, *yā wafd Allāh*: perhaps better understood as "ambassadors to God," on the analogy of people who come to the court of a king to seek his favor.

1573 Arabic, *al-nabī al-ummī*, often translated "the illiterate prophet," referring to Muḥammad's supposed inability to read and write. The debate over the interpretations of the phrase is summarized in the article by E. Geoffroy in *EI*², s.v. Ummī.

1574 The text and its meaning are unclear. Ed. Leiden: *wa-ka'an waqada lahu*, "as if it kindled for him," makes little sense. M inserts a word: *wa-ka'an* (or *wa-kāna*) *qad* [illegible word] *lahu*.

1575 That is, the Ghassānid rulers of Syria who served as allies of the Byzantines, so called after their ancestor Jafna b. 'Amr Muzayqiyā'.

1576 Arabic: *mujāwir*, which implies both living as a neighbor and living under the protection of a family.

1577 Version with additional verses in Ibn Hishām, *Sīra*, 113–114, identified as part of an elegy

O man, you who are moving your dwelling,
why do you not settle with the family of ʿAbd Manāf?
Fool![1578] Had you settled in their abode,
they would have safeguarded you from hunger and loathsome deeds.[1579]
ʿAmr al-ʿUlā crumbled (bread to make) gruel for his people,
when the people of Mecca were drought-stricken and lean.
They ascribed to him the caravans, both of them:
the one in winter and the summer caravan.
They are the ones who obtained a covenant on their borders,
who travel for the caravan guaranteed by pact.[1580]

Hāshim set out for Syria with much merchandise. He would stop by the dignitaries of the Arab tribes, carry merchandise for them, and not impose on them any provisioning for it, until he arrived at Gaza. He died there.

When Hāshim b. ʿAbd Manāf perished, the Quraysh grieved and became afraid that the Arab tribes would overpower them. ʿAbd Shams therefore set out to the Negus, the king of Abyssinia, and renewed the compact between himself and him. Then he returned. He died in Mecca shortly thereafter and was buried in al-Ḥajūn. Nawfal set out for Iraq and obtained a treaty from Kisrā. He returned and died at a place called Salmān. Al-Muṭṭalib b. ʿAbd Manāf took charge of the affairs of Mecca.

Hāshim had the following children: ʿAbd al-Muṭṭalib and al-Shifāʾ (their mother was Salmā bt. ʿAmr b. Zayd b. Khidāsh b. ʿĀmir b. Ghanm b. ʿAdī b. al-Najjār, and the name of al-Najjār was Taym Allāh b. Thaʿlaba b. ʿAmr b. al-Khazraj), Naḍla b. Hāshim [(his mother was Umayma bt. ʿAdī b. ʿAbd Allāh), Asad] (the father of Fāṭima bt. Asad, who was the mother of ʿAlī b. Abī Ṭālib, and
1:283 whose mother was Qayla bt. | ʿĀmir b. Mālik b. al-Muṭṭalib), Abū Ṣayfī (his line died out except for those descended from Raqīqa bt. Abī Ṣayfī) and Ṣayfī who died young (their mother was Hind bt. ʿAmr b. Thaʿlaba b. al-Khazraj), Ḍaʿīfa and Khālida (their mother was Wāqida bt. Abī ʿAdī), and Ḥanna bt. Hāshim (her mother was Umm ʿUdayy bt. Ḥubayb b. al-Ḥārith al-Thaqafiyya).

---

for ʿAbd al-Muṭṭalib and the sons of ʿAbd Manāf. Two verses are cited by al-Masʿūdī, *Murūj*, 2:178 (§ 971).

1578 Literally, "May your mother be bereaved of you!" The idiom, despite its literal sense, is really a mild imprecation.

1579 The commentary on Ibn Hishām explains this as meaning that the man might be forced by his poverty to marry off his daughters to base or unworthy persons.

1580 Literally, for the caravan or journey of *īlāf*. See the discussion above.

When Hāshim decided to set out for Syria, he moved his wife Salmā bt. ʿAmr to Medina, so that she might be with her father and family. With Hāshim was his son ʿAbd al-Muṭṭalib. When Hāshim died, she stayed in Medina.

Al-Muṭṭalib b. ʿAbd Manāf had taken charge of the affairs of Mecca after the death of his brother Hāshim. When ʿAbd al-Muṭṭalib grew up,[1581] word reached al-Muṭṭalib about where he was and the boy's condition was described to him. A man from the Tihāma passed through Medina and saw some boys competing with each other. Suddenly one of the boys among them, when he hit the target, said, "I am the son of Hāshim. I am the son of the lord of Mecca's valley."[1582] So the man asked him, "Who are you, boy?" The boy replied, "I am Shayba b. Hāshim b. ʿAbd Manāf." The man then left and reached Mecca. He found al-Muṭṭalib sitting in the area near the Kaʿba,[1583] and said: "Abū al-Ḥārith, do you know that I have come from Yathrib? I found some boys competing with each other." He told him what he had seen concerning ʿAbd al-Muṭṭalib, and added, "Lo, he was the finest lad I have ever seen." Al-Muṭṭalib said: "I have neglected him. By God, I will not return to my family until I bring him (back)." So al-Muṭṭalib set out and reached Medina in the evening. Then he set out on his camel until he came to the Banū ʿAdī b. al-Najjār. When he looked at his brother's son, he asked, "Is this is the son of Hāshim?" "Yes," said the people—they recognized al-Muṭṭalib—"this is your brother's son. If you want to take him right now, his mother will not know.[1584] If she finds out, we will keep you from him." | So he made his camel kneel and called to the boy: "Nephew, I 1:284
am your uncle. I want to take you to your people. Mount!" ʿAbd al-Muṭṭalib did not delay to seat himself on the rump of the camel; al-Muṭṭalib sat on the saddle and made the camel get up, and off it went. When the mother of ʿAbd al-Muṭṭalib found out, she did not cease crying out her grief. She was told that his uncle had taken him away. Al-Muṭṭalib entered Mecca with the boy behind him. People were in their markets and gathering places, and they stood up to welcome him and greet him. "Who is this with you?" they would ask. He would say, "My slave, whom I bought in Yathrib." Then he set out for al-Ḥazwara[1585]

1581 As the parallel versions make explicit, ʿAbd al-Muṭṭalib lived his first seven or eight years with his mother in Yathrib (Medina). See al-Ṭabarī, *Taʾrīkh*, 1:1082.

1582 Arabic: "I am the son of the lord of al-Baṭḥāʾ," referring to the flat basin making up the central part of Mecca.

1583 Arabic: al-Ḥijr.

1584 Following ed. Leiden: *lā taʿlamu ummuhū* (his mother will not know). M leaves the first letter of the verb undotted, which makes it possible to read, *lā nuʿlimu ummahū*, "we shall not inform his mother."

1585 Al-Ḥazwara was the marketplace of Mecca. See Yāqūt, *Muʿjam al-Buldān*, s.v.

and bought him a suit of clothing. He brought him in to his wife, Khadīja bt. Saʿīd b. Sahm. When evening came, he dressed him up and took a seat in the assembly of the Banū ʿAbd Manāf and told them his story. Afterward, the boy took to going out in that suit of clothes and strolling the streets of Mecca. He was the most handsome of people. The Quraysh would say, "This is ʿAbd al-Muṭṭalib."[1586] So the name ʿAbd al-Muṭṭalib persisted, and Shayba fell into disuse. When it came time for al-Muṭṭalib to set out for Yemen, he said to ʿAbd al-Muṭṭalib, "You, my nephew, are most entitled to your father's place, so take charge of Mecca." And thus he took the place of al-Muṭṭalib. Al-Muṭṭalib died while he was on his journey at Radmān. ʿAbd al-Muṭṭalib took charge of Mecca, became eminent, ruled, gave out food to eat and milk and honey to drink, until his name rose high and his merit became apparent. The Quraysh accorded him honor, and thus he continued.

Muḥammad b. al-Ḥasan[1587] said: When the glory of ʿAbd al-Muṭṭalib was complete and the Quraysh acknowledged his excellence, while he was sleeping in the area by the Kaʿba, he saw[1588] someone come to him and say: "Arise, father of Mecca's valley. Dig Zamzam, the excavation of the Great Shaykh!" When he woke up, he said, "God, make it clear to me in a dream again." So again
1:285 he saw the person say, "Arise! Dig Barra!" "What," he asked, "is Barra?" | The person said, "A thing in high esteem withheld from mankind but which you have been given."[1589] Then ʿAbd al-Muṭṭalib saw someone saying to him: "Arise, Abū l-Ḥārith, and dig Zamzam. It will not be exhausted or dispraised. It will water the great pilgrimage." Then he dreamt a third time: "Arise and dig!" He asked, "What shall I dig?" The person said: "Dig between dung and blood, at the scraping place of the white-legged crow and the ant colony, and when you see water, say, 'Come to abundant water, which I have been given in despite of foes.'"

When ʿAbd al-Muṭṭalib became certain that he had been told the truth, he sat down by the Kaʿba to consider the matter. A cow had been slaughtered at al-Ḥazwara, but it escaped and came walking, until it threw itself down at the site of Zamzam. It was skinned there and its meat distributed; the dung and blood

---

1586 That is, "the slave of al-Muṭṭalib."

1587 The identity of this source is uncertain. Al-Yaʿqūbī (ed. Leiden, 2:524) lists a Muḥammad b. al-Ḥasan as a jurist (*faqīh*) of the time of Hārūn al-Rashīd, and this would be the famous Ḥanafī jurist Muḥammad b. al-Ḥasan al-Shaybānī (d. c. 187)—the index of the Leiden edition identifies this Muḥammad b. al-Ḥasan as the same person, but the identification must remain tentative.

1588 That is, in a dream.

1589 The Arabic is laconic: *"Maḍannatun ḍunna bihā ʿalā l-ʿālamīna wa-uʿṭītahā."*

remained. ʿAbd al-Muṭṭalib said, "God is great!" Then he went forward to look. Lo and behold, there was an ant colony that had come together in the ground. He went and brought a mattock and his only son al-Ḥārith. The Quraysh gathered around him, saying, "What is this?" He said, "My Lord has commanded me to dig up water that will quench the thirst of the great company of pilgrims." They said to him: "Your Lord has commanded foolishness. Why are you digging in our mosque?" He said, "That is what my Lord commanded me." He had only dug a little when the well casing appeared. "God is great!" he shouted. The Quraysh gathered, and they realized when they saw the well casing that he had told the truth. Now he had no son but al-Ḥārith at that time; so when he considered his solitude, he said, "O God, I vow to you that if you give me ten male children I will sacrifice one of them to you." He dug until he found swords, weapons, and a golden gazelle, adorned[1590] and inlaid with gold and silver. When the Quraysh saw this, they said: "Abū al-Ḥārith [...] from above the ground and from beneath it. Therefore give us this wealth that God has given to you, for it is the well of our father Ismāʿīl; give us a share with you." He said, "I was given no command about the wealth; I was commanded only concerning the water; so allow me some time." | He continued to dig until the water became 1:286
apparent and abundant. Then he said, "Enlarge it and it will not dry up." He built a basin by it, filled it with water, and cried out, "Come to abundant water, which I have been given in despite of foes." The Quraysh kept sullying that basin and breaking it. So he saw in a dream, "Arise and say, 'O God, I do not permit it for a bather, but it is permitted for a drinker.'" ʿAbd al-Muṭṭalib arose and said this. As a result, anyone who sullied that basin was immediately afflicted with sickness, and so they left it. When the water was in order for him, he called for six divining arrows. He set two black arrows aside for God, two white arrows for the Kaʿba, and two red arrows for the Quraysh. He took them in his hand, faced the Kaʿba, and shuffled them, saying:

> Lord, you are the one, the sole, the eternal.
> If you wish, you inspire the truth and right course.
> You increase wealth and multiply children.
> I am your client, in despite of Maʿadd.

Then he cast them, and the two black arrows for God came out; so he said, "Your Lord has said, 'It is my wealth.'" Then he shuffled, saying:

1590 Arabic, *muqarraṭ*. Normally this means "adorned with earrings." The exact sense is uncertain.

O God, you are the King, the one who is praised.
You are my Lord, who originates and restores.
From you come inherited wealth and wealth newly acquired.
If you wish, You inspire what You will.

The two white arrows for the Kaʿba came out; so he said, "My Lord has told me that all the wealth is His." Therefore he adorned the Kaʿba with it and turned it into plates on the door of the Kaʿba. He was the first person who adorned the Kaʿba. When the Quraysh saw what had been given to him, they became envious of him and said, "We are partners with you, because it is the well of our father Ismāʿīl." He said, "This is something for which I have been singled
1:287 out apart from you." | They therefore competed with him before the female soothsayer[1591] of the Banū Saʿd, and she decided in his favor against them.

Someone has related that while they were on the way, ʿAbd al-Muṭṭalib's water, as well as that of the people, ran out, and they feared that they would perish. ʿAbd al-Muṭṭalib therefore said, "Let each of us dig a hole for himself and squat in it until death comes to him." They did it. Then he said: "Our casting ourselves (to destruction) by our own hands is weakness. Why don't we mount and seek water?" As soon as he was seated on his camel, a fountain of water sprang up under its chest. "Go to the water," he said. They said: "God has decided in your favor against us. There is no need for us to oppose you." So they returned.

When the Quraysh saw the glory that ʿAbd al-Muṭṭalib had obtained, they sought to ally themselves with each other so as to become strong. The first who sought this were the Banū ʿAbd al-Dār, when they saw the position of ʿAbd al-Muṭṭalib. The Banū ʿAbd al-Dār went to the Banū Sahm and said, "Protect us from the Banū ʿAbd Manāf." When the Banū ʿAbd Manāf saw this, they met together, except for the Banū ʿAbd Shams. According to al-Zubayrī, the children of ʿAbd Shams were not in the confederacy of the scented ones,[1592] nor were the children of ʿAbd Manāf; among them were only Hāshim, the Banū l-Muṭṭalib, and the Banū Nawfal.[1593] Others say that the Banū ʿAbd Shams were among

1591 Arabic, *kāhina*.

1592 Arabic, *ḥilf al-muṭayyabīn*. The manuscripts consistently write *al-mutaṭayyibūn*, which has the same meaning. Al-Yaʿqūbī's abridged account of the formation of two factions within the Quraysh telescopes what was a more complex process. For a summary of what can be reconstructed about these alliances, see the article by Ch. Pellat in *EI*^{2}, s.v. Laʿaḳat al-Dam.

1593 "nor were the children of ʿAbd Manāf; among them were only Hāshim, the Banū al-them. | Umm Ḥakīm al-Bayḍāʾ, the daughter of ʿAbd al-Muṭṭalib, brought out a bowl of perfume for them and set it near the Kaʿba. The Banū ʿAbd Manāf, the Asad, the Zuhra, the Banū Taym, and the Banū l-Ḥārith b. Fihr perfumed themselves, and so they were called the Pact of the Perfumed Ones. When the Banū Sahm heard of this, they slaughtered a cow and said, "Whoever puts his hand into the blood and licks some of it is one of us." The Banū Sahm, the Banū ʿAbd al-Dār, the Banū Jumaḥ, the Banū ʿAdī, and the Banū Makhzūm put their hands in, and so they were called the Lickers [of Blood]. The alliance of the Perfumed Ones was that they would not abandon each other and would not betray one another. The Lickers [of Blood] said, "We have readied for every tribe a tribe." 1:288

When ʿAbd al-Muṭṭalib had dug Zamzam, he went to al-Ṭāʾif. There he dug himself a well called Dhū l-Haram.[1594] He would sometimes go there and stay at that watering place. On one occasion he came and found two groups of the Qays ʿAylān there: the Banū Kilāb and the Banū l-Ribāb. ʿAbd al-Muṭṭalib said: "The water is mine. I have the greatest right to it." The Qaysīs said: "The water is ours. We have the greatest right to it." So he said, "I will dispute with you before whomever you wish to arbitrate between me and you." They disputed with him before Saṭīḥ al-Ghassānī, who was the Arabs' soothsayer[1595] to whom they would bring their disputes. The men promised each other and made a compact that if Saṭīḥ awarded the water to ʿAbd al-Muṭṭalib, the Kilāb and Banū l-Ribāb would owe a hundred camels to ʿAbd al-Muṭṭalib and ten to Saṭīḥ; if Saṭīḥ awarded the water to the two tribes, ʿAbd al-Muṭṭalib would owe [the men] a hundred camels and twenty to Saṭīḥ. They set out, and ʿAbd al-Muṭṭalib set out with ten men of the Quraysh, among whom was Ḥarb b. Umayya. ʿAbd al-Muṭṭalib halted at no camping place without slaughtering a

---

Muṭṭalib, and the Banū Nawfal": These words are given an initial and final mark in M, as if to set them in parentheses, and a marginal comment referring to them has been added. In C the comment has been copied with the prefatory words: "These words are not by the author of the book; they were in the margin." The marginal note in both MSS reads: "And who might the children of ʿAbd Manāf be other than these four? God break your mouth! The Banū ʿAbd Shams were indeed part of the Pact of the Perfumed Ones. Certainly! Indisputably! No doubt about it! As the poet has said: We have been named the most fragrant of Quraysh / for generosity; he anointed us and perfumed us. / What good is there that we have not reached first / and not opened a door to it for men?"

1594 Vocalization uncertain; also given as Dhū l-Harm or Dhū l-Harim.

1595 Arabic, *kāhin*.

camel and feeding the people. The Qaysīs therefore said: "This man is of great importance, of high standing, and noble in his actions. We fear that our judge
1:289 will hope to obtain some of this[1596] and will award | the water to him. Consider, therefore. Do not accept Saṭīḥ's decision until you conceal something hidden from him. If he tells us what it is, we will agree to his decision; otherwise, we will not agree to it." While ʿAbd al-Muṭṭalib was on the way, his water and the water of his companions ran out. He asked the Qaysīs for something to drink from their excess water. They refused to give them anything to drink, saying: "You are the ones who brought suit against us and contended with us over our water. By God, we will not give you anything to drink!" ʿAbd al-Muṭṭalib said: "Shall ten of the Quraysh perish while I am alive? I will seek water for them until the cord of my neck is severed and I absolve myself from blame." So he mounted his camel and turned into the desert. While he was there, his camel knelt down. The men[1597] saw him and said, "ʿAbd al-Muṭṭalib has perished!" The Qurayshīs said: "No, by God! He is too dear to God for Him to allow him to perish. He has only gone in order to affirm the bonds of kinship." When they reached him, his camel had hollowed out with the callus on its breast a large pool of sweet water that flowed over the surface of the ground. When the Qaysīs saw it, they poured out their water skins and came toward the Qurayshīs to take some of the water. "No, by God!" said the Qurayshīs. "Aren't you the ones who withheld your surplus water from us?" ʿAbd al-Muṭṭalib said: "Leave the men. The water shall not be withheld." "This," said the Qaysīs, "is a noble man, a lord! We fear that Saṭīḥ will decide in his favor against us." When they reached Saṭīḥ, they said, "We have hidden something from you." One of them took a date in his hand [and said, "Tell us what it is."] Saṭīḥ said: "You have hidden from me something that lengthened and thickened; then it ripened and did not perish.[1598] Throw the date from your hand." They said to the man, "Damn him! Hide from him something more obscure." So one of them took a locust. They said to him: "We have hidden something from you. Tell us what it is." He said, "You have hidden from me something whose leg
1:290 is like a saw and whose eye is like a dinar." "Explain!"[1599] they said. | He said: "Something that flew and rose glistening; then it darted forth and fell, and

1596 The Arabic can also be taken to mean, "We fear that he may cause our judge to hope to obtain some of this."

1597 Arabic, *al-qawm*, that is, the Qaysīs.

1598 Arabic, *halaka*, a conjectural reading by the Leiden editor; M is illegible.

1599 Reading with the MSS, *abin*, rather than with ed. Leiden's emendation, *ī* (yes).

it left the upland[1600] with barren patches."[1601] They said, "What's with him! Damn him! Hide from him something even more obscure than it." So they took the head of a locust, put it into the seam of a water bag, and hung it on the neck of a dog of theirs called Sawwār. They hit the dog, so that it went away and then came back on the road. They said: "We have hidden something from you. Tell us what it is." He said, "You have hidden from me the head of a locust in the seam of a water bag between Sawwār's neck and collar." So they said, "Judge between us!" He said: "I have judged. You and ʿAbd al-Muṭṭalib have disputed over a watering place in al-Ṭāʾif called Dhū l-Haram. The water belongs to ʿAbd al-Muṭṭalib. You have no right to it. So pay ʿAbd al-Muṭṭalib a hundred camels and twenty to Saṭīḥ." They did so. ʿAbd al-Muṭṭalib set out, slaughtering and feeding, until he entered Mecca. Then his crier called out, "People of Mecca, ʿAbd al-Muṭṭalib asks you only for kinship's sake that each of you who sees fit should relieve me of this loss and take up whatever he sees fit." So they stood up and took one camel, or two, or three, as each of them saw fit. Afterward, when some butchered camels were left over, ʿAbd al-Muṭṭalib said to his son Abū Ṭālib, "My son, I have fed the people; now take these camels and slaughter them on Abū Qubays,[1602] so that the birds and beasts can eat them." Abū Ṭālib did this, and the birds and beasts ate them. Abū Ṭālib said:

We provide food until the birds eat from our surplus,
  when the hands of the pilgrims rushing back[1603] begin to quiver.

According to Abū Isḥāq[1604] and other men of learning: ʿAbd al-Muṭṭalib married women, and children were born to him. When there were ten in all, he 1:291

1600 Reading with M *al-ṣaʿīd*, rather than ed. Leiden *al-ṣayd* (the hunt).

1601 Reading on the basis of M: *fa-taraka l-ṣaʿīd abqaʿ*. The last word has been miscopied as *anfaʿ* (more profitable), but the emendation on the basis of al-Maydānī is probably correct.

1602 A mountain on the eastern edge of Mecca. See the article by G. Rentz in *EI*², s.v. Abū Ḳubays; and by Uri Rubin in *EI*³, s.v. Abū Qubays.

1603 Arabic, the *mufīḍīn*, that is, the pilgrims rushing back toward Muzdalifa after having stood at ʿArafāt.

1604 Of uncertain identity; he may be the jurist Abū Isḥāq al-Sabīʿī, whom al-Yaʿqūbī mentions as active during the reigns of al-Walīd, Sulaymān, Yazīd II, and Hishām. See ed. Leiden, 2:195, 350, 371, 378, 396. For other accounts of the vow of ʿAbd al-Muṭṭalib and the substitution of the sacrifice of 100 camels for the sacrifice of ʿAbdallāh, the future

said: "O God, I vowed to You to sacrifice one of them. I will cast lots among them; take the one You wish." So he cast lots, and the lot fell on ʿAbdallāh b. ʿAbd al-Muṭṭalib, his most beloved son. His ten[1605] sons were al-Ḥārith (after whom he received the name[1606] of Abū l-Ḥārith) and Qutham (their mother was Ṣafiyya bt. Jundub, of the ʿĀmir b. Ṣaʿṣaʿa); al-Zubayr, Abū Ṭālib, ʿAbdallāh, and al-Muqawwam, who was ʿAbd al-Kaʿba (the mother of the four was Fāṭima bt. ʿAmr b. ʿĀʾidh b. ʿImrān b. Makhzūm); Ḥamza (his mother was Hāla bt. Uhayb b. ʿAbd Manāf b. Zuhra); al-ʿAbbās and Ḍirār (their mother was Nutayla bt. Jannāb b. Kulayb b. al-Nimr b. Qāsiṭ); Abū Lahab, who was ʿAbd al-ʿUzzā (his mother was Lubnā bt. Hājir b. ʿAbd Manāf b. Ḍāṭir al-Khuzāʿī); and al-Ghaydāq, who is Ḥajl[1607] (his mother was Mumannaʿa bt. ʿAmr b. Mālik b. Nawfal al-Khuzāʿī). His daughters were six: Umm Ḥakīm al-Bayḍāʾ, ʿĀtika, Barra, Arwā, and Umayma (the mother of all of them was Fāṭima bt. ʿAmr b. ʿĀʾidh b. ʿImrān b. Makhzūm); and Ṣafiyya (her mother was Hāla bt. Uhayb). ʿAbd al-Muṭṭalib set out with ʿAbdallāh, to sacrifice him. He took the knife, and his son al-Ḥārith followed him. When the Quraysh got word of this, they overtook him and said, "Abū l-Ḥārith, if you do this, it will become a custom among your people, and a man will not cease to bring his child here to sacrifice him." He said, "I have promised my Lord, and I will fulfill to him what I have promised." One of them
1:292 said to him, "Ransom him!" So he stood up, saying: |

I have promised my Lord, and will fulfill his covenant.
 I fear my Lord, if I abandon his promise.
Nothing is praised as God is praised.

He then had a hundred camels brought and cast divining arrows over them and over ʿAbdallāh. The lot fell upon the camels, and the people shouted, "God is great!" They said, "Your Lord is satisfied." ʿAbd al-Muṭṭalib said:

O God, Lord of the most sacred city,
 the goodly, blessed, and exalted:
You are the one who assisted me with Zamzam.

---

father of Muḥammad, see Ibn Hishām, *Sīra*, 97–100; al-Ṭabarī, *Taʾrīkh*, 1:1073–1079; Ibn Saʿd, *Ṭabaqāt*, 1/1, 53–54.

1605 The list contains eleven names, which may be explained by the fact that Qutham is said to have died young and is indeed omitted in the list of ten sons given by Ibn Saʿd, *Ṭabaqāt*, 1/1, 53. Cf. al-Zubayrī, *Nasab Quraysh*, 17.

1606 Arabic, *kunya*.

1607 As in M; cf. Wüstenfeld, *Register*, 196. Ed. Leiden reads Jaḥl.

Then he said, "I will repeat the divining arrows." He repeated them, and they fell on the camels. He said:

> O God, you have given me my request;
> you have multiplied my children after they were few:
> Make his ransom today the bulk of my wealth.

Then he shook the arrows a third time, and lot came out on the camels, and so he slaughtered them. His crier called out, "Come, take their meat." He went away from it, and the people jumped up to take it. Therefore Murra b. Khalaf al-Fahmī says:

> As the ransom payments of Hāshim's son were divided by despoiling,
> in the sacred valley where the camels collect.

The wergild of camels came to be paid according to what ʿAbd al-Muṭṭalib had established.[1608]

When Abraha the king of Abyssinia, the master of the elephant, came to Mecca to destroy the Kaʿba, and the Quraysh fled to the mountain tops, ʿAbd al-Muṭṭalib said, "If we only came together and drove this army from the House of God!" The Quraysh said, "It is inevitable for us." ʿAbd al-Muṭṭalib then stayed in the sacred precinct and said, "I will not leave God's sanctuary or take refuge in anyone but God." | Abraha's men took some camels belonging to ʿAbd al- 1:293
Muṭṭalib. ʿAbd al-Muṭṭalib went to Abraha. When he asked permission to come before him, Abraha was told, "The lord of the Arabs, the ruler of Quraysh, and most noble of men has come to you." When ʿAbd al-Muṭṭalib came into his presence, Abraha honored him and had an exalted impression of him because of his visible beauty, perfection, and nobility. He said to his translator, "Say to him, 'Ask whatever seems best to you!'" ʿAbd al-Muṭṭalib said, "Some of my camels, which your men took." Abraha said: "I saw you, esteemed you, and honored you. You see that I have come to destroy the thing that brings you esteem and honor, yet you did not ask me to depart, and you speak to me about your camels." ʿAbd al-Muṭṭalib said: "I am the lord of these camels. This house, which you have said you intend to destroy, has a Lord to defend it; so return the camels!" Abraha became frightened because of what ʿAbd al-Muṭṭalib said.

1608 That is, on the basis of this precedent, the *diya* (ransom payment due in cases of homicide or severe injury) was fixed at 100 camels to be paid by the tribe of the offender to the tribe of the victim. See the article by E. Tyan in *EI*², s.v. Diya.

When ʿAbd al-Muṭṭalib returned, he gathered his children and those who sided with him and went to the door of the Kaʿba. He clung to it and said:

> O God, if You forgive, they will be Your dependents;
> if not, then whatever seems best to You.[1609]

Then he left, saying:

> O God, a man protects his dwelling; so protect Your neighbors!
> Let not their cross and their craft prevail tomorrow over Your craft.
> If You do it, it will be an affair whereby You complete your plan of action.

He stayed in his place. The next day, he sent his son ʿAbdallāh to bring him news. He drew near. A group of the Quraysh had gathered together to fight beside him if they could. ʿAbdallāh came galloping on a sorrel mare with his knee bared. ʿAbd al-Muṭṭalib said, "ʿAbdallāh has come to you as a bearer of good news and warner. By God, I have never seen his knee before today!" So he told them what
1:294 God had done to the people | of the elephant. When what happened to the people of the elephant took place, ʿAbd al-Muṭṭalib said:

> O caller, you have caused me to hear.
> Now call (others) from deafness to your cry.
> Is the hand of God tightly bound? or does He have
> a way of dealing with the foe other than (how He deals) with the nations?
> I said, while the horses of al-Ashram were beating the ground,[1610]
> "This man with the mutilated nose has been beguiled by the sanctuary."
> Verily the House has a protecting Lord;
> whoever attempts it will be extirpated as punishment for sin.

1609 As Houtsma observes, the text of the verse in al-Yaʿqūbī is problematic. It is also quoted below, at 2:9. Longer versions of this poem and the following can be found in Ibn Saʿd, *Ṭabaqāt*, 1/1, 56; al-Ṭabarī, *Taʾrīkh*, 1:940–941.

1610 Vocalizing *tardī*, as in M; if one vocalizes *tardā*, the meaning would be "were perishing." *Al-Ashram*, which means "having the tip of his nose cut off," was a nickname for Abraha. The incident in which he was thus mutilated is related at al-Ṭabarī, *Taʾrīkh*, 1:931.

Tubbaʿ tried to take it in the past;
likewise Ḥimyar, and the people were bold.
He turned back from it, with a constriction in his veins
that caused his windpipe to tighten.
Jurhum perished for acting wrongfully toward it
after Ṭasm, Jadīs, and Jusham.[1611]
Such is the affair of anyone who plots war against it:
for God's command disposes the affair.[1612]
We are acquainted with God. Among us it is custom
to maintain the bond of kinship and fulfill compacts.
God has not ceased to have among us a conclusive claim,
because of which God repels punishments from us.[1613]
We are God's people in His town—
that did not cease to be in the time of Abraha.[1614]

The Religions of the Arabs[1615]

The religions of the Arabs differed according to their proximity to people belonging to religious communities,[1616] their movement into countries, and their wanderings in search of pasture. Quraysh and the majority of descendants

1611 Ṭasm and Jadīs were two tribes said to have inhabited the area of Mecca in early times, but to have died out. They were sometimes said to belong to ʿĀd. Cf. *Lisān al-ʿArab*, s.v. Ṭasm. The reading Jusham is conjectural; the word is indistinct in the manuscripts, and ed. Leiden gives the otherwise unknown 'Jamam.' The context implies that it is the name of another extinct tribe.

1612 The line puns on two senses of the word *amr*: affair and command.

1613 The sense is that because of their maintenance of the bond of kinship and fulfillment of their promises, God judges them to be worthy of protection. Their righteousness is a claim (*ḥujja*) that wins them God's protection.

1614 *Abraha* has been changed to *Abraham* for the sake of the rhyme. The verse is written in the margin of M and introduced by the word, *wa-minhā* ("and from it," i.e., also part of the poem). The verse may be an addition to al-Yaʿqūbī's text.

1615 For a thorough, if sometimes speculative and controversial, account of what can be deduced about the religion of the Arabs before Islam, see Toufic Fahd, *Le Panthéon de l'Arabie centrale à la veille de l'hégire*, and the articles on individual deities in *EI*².

1616 Arabic: their proximities to *ahl al-milal*, people belonging to a *milla* (organized religious community).

of Ma'add b. 'Adnān followed part of the religion of Ibrāhīm:[1617] they made pilgrimage to the House,[1618] performed the rites (of the pilgrimage), were hospitable to guests, venerated the sacred months, disapproved of immoral
1:295 acts, severance of kinship bonds, | and mutual wrongdoing, and punished crimes. They continued in this way as long as they were in charge of the House. The last of the descendants of Ma'add to be in charge of the Sacred House was Tha'laba b. Iyād b. Nizār b. Ma'add. When Iyād departed, the Khuzā'a assumed custodianship of the House and changed the way the rites were performed. They would even rush from 'Arafāt[1619] before sunset and from Jam'[1620] after the sun rose. 'Amr b. Luḥayy[1621] (Luḥayy's name was Rabī'a b. Ḥāritha b. 'Amr b. 'Āmir) went out to the land of Syria, where there was a tribe of Amalekites[1622] worshipping idols.[1623] He asked them, "What are these idols that I see you worshipping?" They said: "These are idols that we worship. We ask them for aid and we are aided. We ask them for rain and we are rained on." He said, "Won't you give me one of them to take to the land of the Arabs, to be beside the House of God to which the Arabs come?" They gave him an idol called Hubal.[1624] He brought it to Mecca and placed it by the Ka'ba. It was the first idol placed in Mecca. Then they put beside it[1625] Isāf and Nā'ila,[1626] each of them at a corner of the House. When a person circumambulated, he would

1617 Reading *'alā ba'ḍ dīn Ibrāhīm*, following ed. Leiden. The MSS read *'alā bu'd diyār Ibrāhīm*, "despite the distance of the dwellings of Ibrāhīm."

1618 That is, the Ka'ba.

1619 Arabic *kānū yufīḍūna min 'Arafāt*, they would perform the *ifāḍa*, the ceremonial departure from the plain of 'Arafāt after the *waqfa*, the standing, that formed the climax of the pilgrimage.

1620 That is, Muzdalifa; see note 1564 to p. 280 above.

1621 See the article by Uri Rubin in *EI*[3], s.v. 'Amr b. Luḥayy.

1622 Arabic *'Amāliqa*, the Amalekites of the Bible, although the Arabic legends about them have little to do with the Biblical traditions. See the article by G. Vajda in *EI*[2], s.v. 'Amālīḳ.

1623 Arabic *aṣnām*, pl. of *ṣanam*, an image (cognate to Aramaic *ṣalmā*, Hebrew *ṣelem*, and Akkadian *ṣalmu*). In the next sentence, the word used for "idols" is the synonym *awthān* (pl. of *wathan*). See the article by T. Fahd in *EI*[2], s.v. Ṣanam.

1624 On Hubal, see T. Fahd, *Le Panthéon*, 95–103, and the article by Fahd in *EI*[2], s.v. Hubal. The god was represented by a statue made of cornelian with a truncated right arm which the Quraysh are said to have replaced by a golden arm. It was before this statue that sacred lots were drawn.

1625 That is, at or by the House.

1626 On Isāf and Nā'ila, see T. Fahd, *Le Panthéon*, 103–109, and the article by Fahd in *EI*[2], s.v. Isāf wa-Nā'ila. They were stones of vaguely human form over which the blood of

begin at Isāf and kiss it, and he would conclude by it. They set up on (the hill of) al-Ṣafā an idol called *Mujāwir al-Rīḥ*, and on (the hill of) Marwa an idol called *Muṭʿim al-Ṭayr*.[1627] When the Arabs made the pilgrimage to the House and saw those idols, they questioned the Quraysh and the Khuzāʿa, who would say, "We worship them that they may bring us nigh in nearness to God."[1628] When the Arabs saw this, they took idols for themselves. Each tribe set up its own idol to which they would pray in order "to draw near to God," as they used to say. Kalb b. Wabara and the tribes of Quḍāʿa had Wadd,[1629] which was set up in Dūmat al-Jandal.[1630] Ḥimyar and Hamdān had Nasr,[1631] which was set up in Ṣanʿāʾ. Kināna had Suwāʿ.[1632] Ghaṭafān had | al-ʿUzzā.[1633] Hind, Bajīla, and 1:296
Khathʿam had Dhū l-Khalaṣa.[1634] Ṭayyiʾ had al-Fuls,[1635] which was set up in al-Ḥibs. Rabīʿa and Iyād had Dhū l-Kaʿabāt[1636] in Sindād in the land of Irāq. Thaqīf had al-Lāt,[1637] which was set up in al-Ṭāʾif. Al-Aws and al-Khazraj had

---

sacrifices was poured. A later legend identified them as a human couple who were changed into stones for having had intercourse inside the Kaʿba.

1627 *Mujāwir al-Rīḥ* would mean "Neighbor of the Wind," but is probably to be corrected to *Mujāwid al-Rīḥ* (He who Makes the Wind Bring Abundant Rain). *Muṭʿim al-Ṭayr* would mean "He who Provides Food to the Birds." See Fahd, *Le Panthéon*, 106–108, and the article by T. Fahd in *EI*², s.v. Isāf wa-Nāʾila.

1628 Echoing Qurʾān 39:4, where these words are put into the mouths of idolaters.

1629 On Wadd, see Fahd, *Le Panthéon*, 182–191, and the article by Ch. Robin in *EI*², s.v. Wadd.

1630 Dūmat al-Jandal is an oasis at the head of Wādī Sirḥān, close to the modern border of Jordan and Saudi Arabia. The text here adds "in Ḥ (or J)—R—Sh," which the Leiden editor conjectured might stand for Jurash. If that is the case, one must assume that a sentence referring to the idol of another tribe has fallen out, as Jurash is in Yemen.

1631 The name of the deity *Nasr* means vulture. See Fahd, *Le Panthéon*, 132–134, and the article by T. Fahd in *EI*², s.v. Nasr.

1632 On Suwāʿ, see Fahd, *Le Panthéon*, 154–156, and the article by T. Fahd in *EI*², s.v. Suwāʿ.

1633 Al-ʿUzzā (the Most Powerful), the most important of the pre-Islamic Arabian goddesses, was associated in Qurʾān 53:19–20 with Manāt and al-Lāt, on the basis of which later commentators saw her as part of a triad of pagan goddesses, the "daughters of Allāh." See Fahd, *Le Panthéon*, 163–182, and the article by M. C. A. Macdonald and Laila Nehmé in *EI*², s.v. al-ʿUzzā.

1634 On Dhū l-Khalaṣa, see Fahd, *Le Panthéon*, 61–68, and the article by T. Fahd in *EI*², s.v. Dhū al-Khalaṣa.

1635 So ed. Leiden; M *al-Qays*. The vocalization of the reading of ed. Leiden is uncertain: al-Fals, al-Fulus, and al-Fils are given by various authorities. See Fahd, *Le Panthéon*, 75–77.

1636 On Dhū l-Kaʿabāt, see Fahd, *Le Panthéon*, 68–69.

1637 On the goddess al-Lāt, see Fahd, *Le Panthéon*, 111–120, and the article by T. Fahd in *EI*², s.v. al-Lāt.

Manāt,[1638] which was set up at Fadak near the seashore. Daws had an idol called Dhū l-Kaffayn.[1639] The Banū Bakr b. Kināna had an idol called Saʿd.[1640] A group of the ʿUdhra had an idol called Shams.[1641] The Azd had an idol called Riʾām.[1642]

When the Arabs desired to go on pilgrimage to the Sacred House, each tribe would stand beside its idol and pray beside it. Then they would recite an invocation[1643] until they reached Mecca. Their invocations were various. The invocation of the Quraysh was: "Here we are, O God! Here we are! Here we are! You have no partner, unless it be a partner whom you dominate and whatever he has dominated."[1644] The invocation of Kināna was: "Here we are, O God! Here we are! Today is the [day of] going to ʿArafāt, the day of prayer and standing." The invocation of the Banū Asad was: "Here we are, O God! Here we

1638 On Manāt, usually identified as the goddess of fortune or destiny on the basis of the etymology (Syriac *mnātā*, part, portion; Arabic *maniyya*, death, destiny), see Fahd, *Le Panthéon*, 123–126, and the article by T. Fahd in *EI*², s.v. Manāt.

1639 On Dhū l-Kaffayn (the One with the Two Palms), see Fahd, *Le Panthéon*, 69–70.

1640 On Saʿd, see Fahd, *Le Panthéon*, 147–150.

1641 On Shams (the name means "Sun," grammatically feminine in Arabic, but the gender of the divinity is unclear), see Fahd, *Le Panthéon*, 150–153, and the article by T. Fahd in *EI*², s.v. Shams.

1642 On Riʾām, an idol said to have been worshipped by the Ḥimyarites in Yemen before their conversion to Judaism, see Fahd, *Le Panthéon*, 141–143.

1643 Arabic *talabbaw*, "they recited a *talbiya*," a formula beginning with the word *labbayka* ("we have set foot in your place"). The *talbiya* is an invocation that a pilgrim makes upon entering the state of ritual consecration (*iḥrām*) to perform the pilgrimage to Mecca; in Islamic usage it is addressed to Allāh and is strictly monotheistic. Al-Yaʿqūbī's point is that before Islam each tribe began to recite its *talbiya* in the presence of its idol. However, his examples make it clear that these formulas were addressed to Allāh (I have translated simply "God"), the overlord of the pilgrimage and of any subordinate gods. Many such pagan invocations are recorded in the sources. For a discussion of the pre-Islamic *talbiya* formulas preserved in the Arabic sources, see M. J. Kister, "Labbayka, Allāhumma, Labbayka," in M. J. Kister, *Society and Religion from Jāhiliyya to Islam*, 33–57 (which gives the full text of a section of a Qurʾān commentary by Muqātil b. Sulaymān, d. 150/767, providing fuller versions of many formulas that al-Yaʿqūbī has abbreviated), and the article by T. Fahd in *EI*², s.v. Talbiya.

1644 Following M: *lā sharīk^{a} laka illā sharīk^{un} tamlikuhū wa mā malak*. In C, the manuscript used for ed. Leiden, the formula was abbreviated by homeoteleuton, causing omission of the words *laka illā sharīk^{un}*. This is how Kister understands the formula and probably the most likely meaning; Fahd prefers to take *mā* as negative and translates: "unless it is a partner whom you dominate and who has no power."

are! O Lord, the Banū Asad have come to you, people of high deeds,[1645] loyalty, and endurance." The invocation of the Banū Tamīm was: "Here we are, O God! Here we are! Here we are! Here we are on behalf of Tamīm! You see them, that their garments and the garments of those behind them have worn out, and that they have made their prayer sincere toward their Lord." The invocation of Qays ʿAylān was: "Here we are, O God! Here we are! Here we are! You are the Merciful One. Qays ʿAylān has come to you, walking and riding." The invocation of Thaqīf was: "Here we are, O God! Thaqīf have come to you. They have left their wealth behind them,[1646] hoping in you." The invocation of Hudhayl was: "Here we are on behalf of Hudhayl! They have traveled at night with camels and horses." The invocation of Rabīʿa was: "Here we are, O our Lord! Here we are! Here we are! Our course is toward you." Others (of Rabīʿa) would say: "Here we are on behalf of Rabīʿa, obedient and submissive!" | Ḥimyar and Hamdān used to say: "Here 1:297
we are on behalf of Ḥimyar and Hamdān and the two confederates, Ḥāshid and Alhān."[1647] The invocation of the Azd was: "Here we are, Lord of lords! You know that the passing of judgment belongs to the ruler of every place of assembly." The invocation of Madhḥij was: "He we are, O Lord of Sirius and Lord of al-Lāt and al-ʿUzzā!" The invocation of Kinda and Ḥaḍramawt was: "Here we are! You have no partner. You dominate him or you destroy him. You are the wise one; therefore leave him."[1648] The invocation of Ghassān was: "Here we are, O Lord of Ghassān, of those who come on foot and those who ride!" The invocation of Bajīla was: "Here we are on behalf of Bajīla, amid shining clouds promising rain!" The invocation of Quḍāʿa was: "Here we are on behalf of Quḍāʿa, who rush toward their Lord in obedience to him and submission!" The invocation of Judhām was: "Here we are on behalf of Judhām, the possessors of understanding and judgment!" The invocation of ʿAkk and the Ashʿarīs was: "We come in pilgrimage to a house belonging to the Merciful One—wondrous, safeguarded, barred, protected!"

1645 Correcting ed. Leiden and M: *ahl al-tawānī* (people of weakness, languor, negligence), to *ahl al-ʿawāli*, the reading of Muqātil's *Tafsīr*, cited by Kister, op. cit., 54.

1646 Arabic: *akhlafū al-māl*. This could refer to the humility of the pilgrims or to a prohibition on trading during the pilgrimage, a prohibition lifted under Islam. A *talbiya* ascribed by Muqātil to the Rabīʿa stated that they did not come "from love of gain." See Kister, op. cit., 50, and note that al-Yaʿqūbī below (1:298) says that some of the tribes "did not buy and sell during the pilgrimage."

1647 Two tribes.

1648 Sic ed. Leiden, M. A better reading is provided by Muqātil's *Tafsīr*, cited by Kister, op. cit. 56: "You have no partner, except a partner whom you dominate, to destroy him or leave him. You are the forbearing one; therefore leave him."

The Arabs were of two sorts in their religions: the *Ḥums* and the *Ḥilla*.[1649] As for the Ḥums, they were Quraysh in its entirety, and then[1650] Khuzāʿa due to their inhabiting Mecca and being neighbors of the Quraysh. They were strict with themselves in their religion. When they performed the rites, they did not clarify butter, store milk, or separate a nursing woman from her suckling until he disliked nursing. They did not cut their hair or fingernails or anoint themselves. They did not touch women or perfume. They did not eat meat. In their pilgrimage they did not wear camel's hair, sheep's wool, or any kind of hair. They wore new clothes. They circumambulated the House in their shoes and did not tread on the ground of the mosque out of reverence for it. They did not enter houses through their doors[1651] or go out to ʿArafāt. They stayed
1:298 at Muzdalifa. While performing their rites, they dwelt in | tents of leather. The Ḥilla—they were Tamīm, Ḍabba, Muzayna, al-Ribāb, ʿUkl, Thawr, all of Qays ʿAylān except for ʿAdwān, Thaqīf, ʿĀmir b. Ṣaṣaʿa, all of the Rabīʿa b. Nizār, Quḍāʿa, Ḥaḍramawt, ʿAkk, and some tribes of al-Azd—did not forbid hunting while performing the rites. They wore all garments. They clarified butter. They did not enter through the door of a house or building, neither would one shelter them, as long as they were in a state of consecration. They anointed and perfumed themselves and ate meat. When they entered Mecca after finishing, they took off the clothes they were wearing. If they could don the garments of the Ḥums by renting or borrowing, they did so; otherwise they

---

1649 *Ḥums* comes from the plural of an adjective *aḥmas* (hard, strong [in fighting or in religion]). It alludes to the more rigorous religious taboos that these tribes observed. *Ḥilla* is a collective noun from the verb *ḥalla*, meaning, among other things, "to be free of obligation," alluding to the fact that these tribes did not practice the taboos of the Ḥums and were in a sense "profane." See the article by W. Montgomery Watt in *EI*[2], s.v. Ḥums. Curiously, M apparently points the word in all three of its occurrences as *Jilla*, and the dictionaries do mention a phrase *qawm jilla*, "a great people; lords, chiefs, or people of rank or quality" (Lane, *Lexicon*, 2:437, s.v. *jalīl*). However, on the basis of the description of the group as not observing certain taboos during the pilgrimage, the term *Ḥilla* is more likely because of its meaning.

1650 The MSS and ed. Leiden at this point introduce the words *wa-ammā l-ḥilla* ("and as for the Ḥilla [they were …]," which must be a copyist's mistake or a corruption of the original text. This is clear on internal grounds—proximity to the Quraysh can logically only be a reason for the Khuzāʿa to adopt the position of their neighbors, that of the Ḥums)—as well as on the evidence of all the other sources, which reckon the Khuzāʿa among the Ḥums.

1651 This taboo on entering houses through their doors at certain seasons is mentioned in Qurʾān 3:189, where it is lifted from Muslims.

circumambulated the House naked. They did not buy and sell during their pilgrimage. These are the two religious laws that the Arabs followed.

Then some of the Arabs entered the religion of the Jews and left this religion, and others entered Christianity. Some of them became *Zindīq*s and followed dualism.[1652] As for those of them who became Jewish, they were Yemen in its entirety. Tubbaʿ[1653] brought two Jewish rabbis to Yemen and abolished idols, and the inhabitants of Yemen became Jewish. After their departure from Yemen, some of the Aws and Khazraj also became Jewish due to their living as neighbors of the Jews of Khaybar, the Qurayẓa, and al-Naḍīr. Some of the Banū l-Ḥārith b. Kaʿb, some of the Ghassān, and some of the Judhām also became Jewish.

The Arab tribes that became Christian included some of the Quraysh, from the Banū Asad b. ʿAbd al-ʿUzzā, one of whom was ʿUthmān b. al-Ḥuwayrith b. Asad b. ʿAbd al-ʿUzzā and another of whom was Waraqa b. Nawfal b. Asad. From the Banū Tamīm there were the Banū Imruʾ al-Qays b. Zayd Manāt. From the Rabīʿa there were the Banū Taghlib. From the Yemen there were the Ṭayyiʾ, Madhḥij, Bahrāʾ, Salīḥ, | Tanūkh, Ghassān, and Lakhm. Ḥujr b. ʿAmr al-Kindī 1:299
became a Zindīq.

The Arbitrators of the Arabs

The Arabs had arbitrators[1654] to whom they referred their affairs. These would adjudicate concerning disagreements, inheritance, access to water, and the

---

1652 *Zindīq*, borrowed from Middle Persian *zandīk*, itself probably borrowed from Aramaic *zaddīq* "righteous," originally referred to the followers of Mānī (b. c. 216, d. 274 or 277 CE) and his dualistic religion. It was later extended to include other sorts of "heretical" religion. See the article by F. C. de Blois in *EI*², s.v. Zindīḳ.

1653 On Tubbaʿ as a dynastic title for the Ḥimyarite rulers of Southwest Arabia, see note 1281 [to 1:222] above. The legend of how Tubbaʿ Abūkarib Asʿad (ruled toward the end of the fourth century CE) attacked Medina, was deterred from destroying it by two Jewish rabbis, subsequently embraced Judaism, and induced his people to adopt it is narrated by al-Ṭabarī, *Taʾrīkh*, 1:901–908.

1654 Arabic, *ḥukkām*, formally the plural of *ḥākim* (ruler), but also serving as the plural of *ḥakam* (arbitrator). "In pre-Islamic Arabia, given the lack of any public authority responsible for the settling of disputes, *taḥkīm* [the appointment of an arbitrator] was the sole judicial procedure available to individuals who did not wish to exercise their right of private justice or who were unable to settle their differences by means of a direct friendly agreement. This procedure was of a purely private character, depending

shedding of blood, because there was no religion to whose sacred law one could turn. They therefore appointed as arbitrators men known for their nobility, truthfulness, trustworthiness, leadership, age, renown, and experience. The first one whose judgment was sought and who arbitrated was al-Afʿā b. al-Afʿā al-Jurhumī, who was the one who arbitrated among the Banū Nizār over inheritance matters. After him came:

Sulaymān b. Nawfal,
Muʿāwiya b. ʿUrwa,
Sakhr b. Yaʿmur b. Nufātha b. ʿAdī b. al-Duʾil,
al-Shaddākh, who was Yaʿmur b. ʿAwf b. Kaʿb b. ʿĀmir b. Layth b. Bakr b. ʿAbd Manāt b. Kināna,
Suwayd b. Rabīʿa b. Ḥudhār b. Murra b. al-Ḥārith b. Saʿd,
Mukhāshin b. Muʿāwiya b. Shurayf b. Jurwa b. Usayyid b. ʿAmr b. Tamīm, who used to sit on a wooden throne and was called Dhū l-Aʿwād,[1655]
Aktham b. Ṣayfī b. Rabāḥ b. [al-Ḥārith b.] Mukhāshin,
ʿĀmir b. al-Ḍarib b. ʿAmr b. ʿIyādh b. Yashkur b. ʿAdwān b. ʿAmr b. Qays,
Harim b. Quṭba b. Sayyār al-Fazārī,
Ghaylān b. Salima b. Muʿattib al-Thaqafī,
Sinān b. Abī Ḥāritha al-Murrī,
al-Ḥārith b. ʿUbād b. Ḍubayʿa b. Qays b. Thaʿlaba,
1:300 ʿĀmir [al-Ḍaḥyān] b. al-Ḍaḥḥāk b. al-Namir b. Qāsiṭ,
al-Jaʿd b. Ṣabra al-Shaybānī,
Wakīʿ [b. Salama] b. Zuhayr al-Iyādī, the master of the castle in al-Ḥazwara,
Quss b. Sāʿida al-Iyādī,
Ḥanẓala b. Nahd al-Quḍāʿī, and
ʿAmr b. Ḥumama al-Dawsī.

There were also arbitrators among the Quraysh. Among them were:

---

throughout solely on the goodwill of the parties involved … Nevertheless arbitration acquired a certain systematization and an institutional character amounting to public justice in the fairs held periodically in various localities, such as ʿUkāẓ: a *ḥakam* was appointed there, to whom, by force of custom, recourse was made for the settlement of disputes arising from the transactions being carried out there." (E. Tyan, in *EI*², s.v. Ḥakam).

1655 "He of the Timbers."

ʿAbd al-Muṭṭalib,
Ḥarb b. Umayya,
al-Zubayr b. ʿAbd al-Muṭṭalib,
ʿAbdallāh b. Judʿān, and
al-Walīd b. al-Mughīra al-Makhzūmī.

Arab Divination

The Arabs used to resort to divination with arrows (*azlām*) in all their affairs; these were also called *qidāḥ*.[1656] They resorted to divining arrows in every case of moving or staying put, of marriage, or of any kind of information. The arrows were seven. On one was (written), "God, may He be praised and exalted" (*Allāh ʿazza wa-jalla*); on another, "For you" (*lakum*); on another, "Against you" (*ʿalaykum*); on another, "Yes" (*naʿam*); on another, "Of you" (*minkum*); on another "Of others" (*min ghayrikum*); and on another, "The promise" (*al-waʿd*). Whenever they wished to do something, they would resort to the arrows, cast them, and then act as the arrows came out, neither going beyond it nor falling short of it. They had people who were responsible for the arrows, and they would trust no one else with them.

If the Arabs found themselves stricken by drought in winter and their camels gave little milk, they engaged in *maysir*.[1657] This consisted of arrows with which they gambled with each other. They cast these arrows. The *maysir* arrows were ten: seven of them stood for | shares and three did not. Of the seven that 1:301
stood for shares, one was called *al-Fadhdh* ("the Single") and stood for one share; *al-Taw'am* ("the Twin") stood for two shares; *al-Raqīb* ("the Supervisor") stood for three shares; *al-Ḥils* ("the Saddlecloth") stood for four shares; *al-Nāfis* ("the Precious") stood for five shares; *al-Musbil* ("the Elongated") stood for six shares; and *al-Muʿallā* ("the Superior") stood for seven shares. The three that

1656 The general term for such divination is *istiqsām*. As al-Yaʿqūbī will explain, the arrows used (*zalam*, plural *azlām*) were a set of seven headless and featherless arrows, each bearing an inscription that was expected to resolve the problem for which the arrows were being cast. See the article by T. Fahd in *EI*², s.v. Istiḳsām.

1657 As opposed to the preceding procedure, *maysir* was not a process of divination associated with shrines or idols, but a game of chance in which one or more slaughtered camels were divided by lot among the participants. See the article by T. Fahd in *EI*², s.v. Maysir. The most detailed discussion of the game, including a commentary on this section of al-Yaʿqūbī, can be found in Anton Huber, *Über das 'Meisir' genannte Spiel der heidnischen Araber*.

did not stand for shares were unmarked, having no names on them. They were called *al-Manīḥ* ("the Generous"), *al-Safīḥ* ("the Profitless"), and *al-Waghd* ("the Scoundrel").[1658] A camel for slaughter would be purchased for its price, but the money would not be paid. The butcher would be summoned, and he would divide the camel into ten portions. When the portions had been divided equally, the butcher would take his portion, consisting of the head and the feet. The ten arrows would be brought out, and the young men[1659] of the tribe would gather. Each team would take (an arrow) according to its condition, its affluence, and what it could afford. The first would take *al-Fadhdh*, which stood for one share out of the ten: if it came out for him,[1660] he would take one portion of the slaughtered camel;[1661] if it did not come out, he would have to pay for one portion of the camel. The second would take *al-Taw'am*, which stood for two shares of the slaughtered camel: if it came out, he would take two portions of the camel; if it did not, he would have to pay for two portions. And the rest of the arrows were similar to those we have just named: when one came out, its owner would take what it stood for; when it did not come out, he would have to pay for the number of portions it stood for. When each man had put a mark on his arrow, they gave the arrows to another man, more lowly than they, someone who would not look at them and who was known never to eat meat for a price—he was called *al-Ḥurḍa* ("the Useless"). Then the *mijwal*—a very white cloth—was brought out and put on his hand. Then someone would
1:302 take | the *sulfa*—this was a piece of skin with which his hand was bound so that he could not find by touch an arrow for whose owner he had a liking and then take it out. A man would come and sit behind the *Ḥurḍa*—he was called the *Raqīb* ("the Observer"). The *Ḥurḍa* then shook the arrows. When one of them protruded, the *Ḥurḍa* would pull it out and, without looking at it, give it to the *Raqīb*, who would look to see whose it was and hand it to its owner. The latter would take of the portions of the slaughtered camel according to his share of

---

1658 Probable English equivalents have been given for the names of the arrows, but the reader should be aware that the Arabic sources give various and conflicting explanations for the names.

1659 Arabic *fityān*, which carries overtones of nobility, generosity, and chivalry—that is, young men willing to gamble for potential gain or loss, as opposed to the overseer of the game, who will be characterized as "more lowly" (*akhass*) in the sense of being less willing (or able) to put his wealth at risk.

1660 The singular pronoun is inconsistent. Apparently, each team had one leader who "owned" its arrow.

1661 Correcting the text according to Huber, 40–41. Reading: *fa-idhā kharaja lahu akhadha juz'an wāḥidan min al-jazūr*.

them. If any of the three arrows that did not stand for shares emerged, it would be put back immediately. If *al-Fadhdh* emerged as the first of the arrows,[1662] its owner would take his share, and they would play, using the remaining arrows, for the nine other portions. If *al-Taw'am* [came out next], its owner would take two portions, and they would play, using the remaining arrows, for the seven[1663] other portions. If *al-Mu'allā* came out (next), its owner would take his share—the seven remaining portions—and they would depart immediately; the price of the camel would be paid by the four whose arrows had not come out: the owners of *al-Raqīb*, *al-Ḥils*, *al-Nāfis*, and *al-Musbil*. Because these arrows stood for eighteen shares,[1664] the price would be divided into eighteen parts, and each individual would pay of the price the like of what his share of meat would have been if his arrow had come out.[1665] If al-Mu'allā came out as the first of the arrows, its owner would take seven portions of the camel; the owners of the arrows that had not come out had to pay, and they would need to slaughter another camel. This was because among their arrows was *al-Musbil*, which stood for six portions, while only three portions of meat remained. It was unfitting for anyone whose arrow had not come out in the play for the first camel to eat any of it; it would be disgraceful for him. If they slaughtered the second camel and cast | arrows for it and *al-Musbil* came out, its owner 1:303 would take six portions of the camel: the three remaining portions[1666] of the first camel and three portions of the second camel. He had to pay for the first camel,[1667] but he did not have to pay anything for the second, because his arrow had won. Seven portions of the second camel remained; they would be played for with the arrows of the remaining players. If *al-Nāfis* came out, its owner would take five portions, and he would not have to pay anything toward the price of the second camel, because his arrow had won, though he would have to pay toward the first camel. Two portions of meat remained; however, inasmuch as one of the remaining arrows was *al-Ḥils*, which stood for four portions, they needed to slaughter another camel in order to complete the four. It was unfitting for anyone whose arrow had not come out in the play for the second camel to eat any of it;[1668] it would be disgraceful for him. If they slaughtered the

1662 Reading, *wa-in kharaja l-fadhdhu awwala l-qidāhi*, as suggested by Huber, 51.

1663 Ed. Leiden, M: eight; corrected by Huber, 51.

1664 That is, *al-Raqīb* (3) + *al-Ḥils* (4) + *al-Nāfis* (5) + *al-Musbil* (6) = 18.

1665 That is, the owner of *al-Raqīb* would pay 3/18 of the total price; the owner of *al-Ḥils* 4/18; the owner of *al-Nāfis* 5/18; and the owner of *al-Musbil* 6/18.

1666 Reading with Huber, 52: *al-ajzā'* for ed. Leiden, M. *al-ukhrā*.

1667 That is, $6/(1+2+3+4+5+6) = 6/21$ of the total price.

1668 "If no one else had entered the game, which was allowed, these would be the owners

third camel and it (i.e., *al-Ḥils*) came out, its owner would take four portions: two portions from the second camel and two portions from the third camel. He did not have to pay for any of the third camel, because his arrow had won. Eight portions of the third camel remained, and they would play, using the remaining arrows, for them, until their arrows came out in agreement with the portions of the camel. Their payment toward the price was computed as I have described. Sometimes the portions of meat coincided with the portions for which the arrows stood, and so they did not need to slaughter anything else. Another camel was slaughtered only when the portions of meat were too few for some of the arrows. If someone who had won returned his arrow to be played again and lost, he had to pay toward the price of the camel for which his arrow had lost, according to this computation. If any portions of the meat were left over when all the arrows had come out, those portions were for the poor of the tribe.
1:304 This is the explanation of *maysir*. The Arabs used to boast of it and regarded it | as an act of generosity and honor. They composed many poems boasting of it.

The Poets of the Arabs

The Arabs used to attribute the same value to poetry as they did to wisdom and much knowledge. If a tribe had a skilled poet who could express his themes with well-chosen words, they would bring him to the fairs that took place for them during the year and to their festivals when they came on pilgrimage to the Kaʿba, so that the tribes and clans would stop and gather and listen to his poetry. This they made into a point of their pride and honor. When an issue arose in tribal adjudication or deciding a course of action, the only source to which they referred was poetry. By means of it they quarreled among themselves, cited proverbs, vied with each other for eminence, bound each other by oaths, competed with each other, and were glorified or reviled.

Some, according to the consensus of transmitters and men learned in poetry and in the literary works and historical reports handed down from the Arab poets, were poets whose poetry was deemed superior in pre-Islamic times.[1669] Along with them were others who survived into Islamic times and were called

---

of *al-Ḥils, al-Raqīb, al-Tawʾam, and al-Fadhdh*, who would have to pay for the second camel (4+3+2+1)/10, as well as (4+3+2+1)/21 for the first camel." Huber, 54 (my translation).

1669 Arabic, *fī jāhiliyyat al-ʿArab* (in the Arabs' Age of Ignorance).

mukhaḍram.[1670] The latter came to be classified together with those who came earlier, and (all) were called "Stallions"[1671] in accordance with the superior quality of their poems, although some were more ancient than others. They were as we have clarified their names and ranks in order:

- [al-Nābigha al-Dhubyānī, who was] Ziyād b. Muʿāwiya b. Ḍibāb b. Jābir b. Yarbūʿ b. Ghayẓ b. Murra b. ʿAwf b. Saʿd b. Dhubyān,
- Zuhayr b. Abī Sulmā (Abū Sulmā's name was Rabīʿa) b. Riyāḥ b. | Qurṭ b. al-Ḥārith b. Māzin b. Thaʿlaba b. Thawr b. Hudhma b. Lāṭim b. ʿUthmān b. ʿAmr b. Udd, 1:305
- al-Aʿshā (i.e., al-Aʿshā of the Wāʾil), who was Maymūn b. Qays b. Jandal b. Sharāḥīl b. ʿAwf b. Saʿd b. Ḍubayʿa b. Qays b. Thaʿlaba,
- ʿAbīd b. al-Abraṣ b. Jusham[1672] b. ʿĀmir b. Mālik [b. Zuhayr b. Mālik] b. al-Ḥārith b. Saʿd b. Thaʿlaba b. Dūdān b. Asad,
- Muhalhil, who was Imruʾ al-Qays b. Rabīʿa b. al-Ḥārith b. Zuhayr b. Jusham b. Bakr b. Ḥubayb b. ʿAmr b. Ghanm b. Taghlib b. Wāʾil,
- ʿAlqama b. al-ʿAbada b. Nāshira b. Qays b. ʿAbd b. Rabīʿa b. Mālik b. Zayd Manāt [b.] Tamīm,
- al-Ḥārith b. Ḥilliza [b. Makrūh] b. Yazīd b. ʿAbdallāh b. Mālik b. [ʿAbd b.] Saʿd b. Jusham b. ʿĀmir b. Dhubyān b. Kināna b. Yashkur b. Bakr b. Wāʾil,
- ʿAmr b. Kulthūm b. Mālik b. ʿAttāb b. Saʿd b. Zuhayr b. Jusham b. Bakr b. Ḥubayb b. ʿAmr b. Ghanm b. Taghlib b. Wāʾil,
- Saʿd b. Mālik b. Ḍubayʿa b. Qays b. Thaʿlaba b. ʿUkāba b. ʿAlī b. Bakr b. Wāʾil
- al-Aswad b. Yaʿfur b. ʿAbd al-Aswad b. Jandal b. Nahshal b. Dārim b. Mālik b. Ḥanẓala b. Mālik b. Zayd Manāt b. Tamīm,
- Suwayd | b. [Abī] Kāhil b. Ḥāritha b. Ḥisl b. Mālik b. ʿAbd b. Saʿd b. Jusham b. Dhubyān b. Kināna b. Yashkur b. [Bakr b.] Wāʾil, 1:306
- Aws b. Ḥajar b. Mālik b. Ḥazn b. ʿAmr b. Khalaf b. Numayr b. Usayyid b. ʿAmr b. Tamīm b. Murr,
- Dhū l-Iṣbaʿ al-ʿAdwānī, who was Ḥurthān b. Ḥārith b. Muḥarrith [b. Thaʿlaba b. Sayyār] b. Rabīʿa b. Hubayra b. Thaʿlaba b. Ẓarib b. ʿAmr b. ʿAbbād b. Bakr b. Yashkur b. ʿAdwān ([ʿAdwān] being [a byname for] al-Ḥārith b. ʿAmr b. Qays b. ʿAylān),

---

1670 The term *mukhaḍram* refers to poets whose lifetimes spanned both the pre-Islamic era and early Islamic times.

1671 Arabic *fuḥūl*.

1672 As in M; ed. Leiden: *Ḥantam*. Both forms occur in his genealogy. See Lyall, *The Dīwāns of ʿAbīd ibn al-Abraṣ* …, 1 (Arabic).

- Bishr b. Abī Khāzim, who was ʿAmr b. ʿAwf b. Ḥanash b. Nāshira b. Usāma b. Wāliba,
- ʿAntara b. Shaddād b. Muʿāwiya b. Nizār b. Makhzūm b. Mālik b. Ghālib b. Quṭayʿa b. ʿAbs b. Baghīḍ,
- ʿAbda b. al-Ṭabīb al-Tamīmī,
- al-Mutalammis, who was Jarīr b. ʿAbd al-Masīḥ b. ʿAbdallāh b. Zayd b. Dawfān b. Ḥarb b. Wahb b. Aḥmas b. Ḍubayʿa b. Rabīʿa b. Nizār,
- Abū Duʾād al-Iyādī, who was Ḥawthara b. al-Ḥārith b. al-Ḥajjāj,
- al-Muraqqish the Elder, [who was …[1673]
- al-Muraqqish the Younger,] who was Rabīʿa b. Muʿāwiya b. Saʿd b. Mālik b. Ḍubayʿa b. Qays b. Thaʿlaba,
- 1:307 al-Musayyab b. ʿAlas b. ʿAmr b. | Quḍāʿa b. ʿAmr b. Zayd b. Thaʿlaba b. Daʿdī b. Mālik b. Jusham b. Mālik b. Jumāʿa b. Julayy,
- ʿAdī b. Zayd b. Ḥammād [b. Zayd] b. Ayyūb b. Maḥrūf b. ʿĀmir [b.] ʿUṣayya b. Imruʾ al-Qays b. Zayd Manāt b. Tamīm,
- Salāma b. Jandal b. ʿAbd ʿAmr b. ʿAbd al-Ḥārith, who was Muqāʿis b. ʿAmr b. Kaʿb b. Saʿd b. Zayd Manāt b. Tamīm,
- Suḥaym b. Wathīl b. ʿAmr b. Kurz b. Wuhayb b. Ḥimyarī b. Riyāḥ b. Yarbūʿ b. Ḥanẓala b. Mālik b. Zayd Manāt b. Tamīm,
- al-Jumayḥ al-Asadī, who was Munqidh b. [al-Ṭammāḥ b. Qays b.] Ṭarīf b. ʿAmr b. Quʿayn,
- Ḥātim al-Ṭāʾī, [who was] Ḥātim b. ʿAbdallāh b. Saʿd b. al-Ḥashraj b. Imruʾ al-Qays b. ʿAdī b. Akhzam b. Rabīʿa b. Jarwal b. Thuʿal b. ʿAmr b. al-Ghawth,
- Ṭufayl al-Khayl, who was Ṭufayl b. ʿAwf b. Khulayf b. Ḍabīs b. Mālik b. Saʿd b. ʿAwf b. Hillān b. Ghanm b. Ghanī,
- al-Saffāḥ, who was Salama b. Khālid b. Kaʿb b. Zuhayr b. Taym b. Usāma b. Mālik b. Bakr b. Ḥubayb b. Ghanm b. Taghlib,
- 1:308 Taʾabbaṭa | Sharran, who was Thābit b. Jābir b. Sufyān b. ʿAdī b. Kaʿb b. Fahm b. ʿAmr b. Qays ʿAylān,
- Ibn al-Muḍallal al-Asadī, who was Jald b. Qays [b. Mālik] b. Munqidh b. Ṭarīf [b.] ʿAmr b. Quʿayn,
- Kaʿb al-Amthāl al-Ghanawī, who was Kaʿb b. Saʿd b. ʿAlqama b. Rabīʿa b. Zayd b. Abī Malīl b. Rifāʿa b. Muslim b. Saʿd,
- al-Ḥakam b. […],[1674]
- Marwān al-Qaraẓ b. Zinbāʿ b. Jadhīma b. Rawāḥa b. Quṭayʿa b. ʿAbs,

1673 The copyist has skipped the remaining part of the poet's name by homeoteleuton.

1674 The copyist has again skipped part of a poet's name.

- Durayd b. al-Ṣimma b. al-Ḥārith b. Bakr b. ʿAlaqa b. Judāʿa b. ʿAwf b. Jusham b. Muʿāwiya b. Bakr b. Hawāzin,
- Umayya b. Abī l-Ṣalt, who was ʿAbdallāh b. Rabīʿa b. ʿUqda b. Ghiyara b. ʿAwf b. Qasī (i.e., Thaqīf),
- al-Afwah al-Awdī, who was Ṣalāʾa[1675] b. ʿAmr b. Mālik [b. ʿAwf] b. al-Ḥārith b. ʿAwf [b. Munabbih] b. Awd b. Ṣaʿb b. Saʿd al-ʿAshīra b. Madhḥij,
- ʿAmr b. Qamīʾa[1676] b. Dharīḥ b. Saʿd b. Mālik b. Ḍubayʿa b. Qays b. Thaʿlaba,
- Ḍābiʾ b. al-Ḥārith b. Arṭāt b. Shihāb b. ʿUbayd b. Ḥalūl | b. Qays b. Ḥanẓala b. 1:309 Mālik,
- Khufāf b. Nadba—Nadba was his mother—whose father was ʿUmayr b. al-Ḥārith b. ʿAmr b. al-Sharīd b. Riyāḥ b. Yaqaẓa b. ʿUṣayya b. Khufāf b. Imruʾ al-Qays b. Buhtha b. Sulaym,
- al-Mutanakhkhil al-Hudhalī, who was Mālik b. Ghanm b. Suwayd b. Ḥubshī[1677] b. Khunāʿa b. al-Dīl b. ʿĀdiya b. Ṣaʿṣaʿa b. Kaʿb b. Ṭābikha b. Liḥyān b. Hudhayl,
- al-Dhihāb al-Faḥl, who was Mālik b. Jandal b. Maslama b. Mujammaʿ b. Ḍubayʿa b. ʿIjl,
- ʿUrwa b. al-Ward b. Zayd b. ʿAbdallāh b. Nāshib b. Sufyān b. ʿAwdh b. Ghālib b. Quṭayʿa b. ʿAbs b. Baghīḍ,
- al-Ḥārith b. ʿUbād b. Ḍubayʿa b. Qays b. Thaʿlaba, who was Fāris al-Naʿāma,
- Anas b. Mudrik b. ʿAmr b. Saʿd b. ʿAwf b. al-ʿAtīk b. Ḥāritha b. ʿĀmir b. Taym Allāh b. Mubashshir b. Aklub b. Rabīʿa b. ʿIfris b. Ḥalf b. Khathʿam,
- al-Munakhkhal b. Masʿūd b. Aflat b. Qaṭan b. Sūʾa[1678] b. Mālik b. Thaʿlaba b. Ghanm b. Ḥubayyib b. Kaʿb b. Yashkur,
- Ashyam b. Sharāḥīl b. ʿAbd Ruḍā b. ʿAbd ʿAwf | b. Mālik b. Ḍubayʿa b. Qays b. 1:310 Thaʿlaba,
- al-Ḥārith b. Ẓālim b. Ḥadhīma b. Yarbūʿ b. Ghayḍ[1679] b. Murra b. ʿAwf b. Saʿd b. Dhubyān,
- Ṣafwān b. Ḥuṣayn b. Mālik b. Rifāʿa b. Sālim b. ʿUbayd b. Saʿd al-ʿAnazī,
- al-Samawʾal b. ʿĀdiyā—his lineage is traced back to Ghassān, but some say that he was a Jew of the tribe of Judah,

---

1675 Vocalizing as in *Aghānī*, 11:44. Ed. Leiden and M have *Ṣalāh*, but omission of *hamza* is normal in manuscripts.

1676 Restored as *Qamiʾa* by the Leiden editor from MSS *Qamīd*, but the preferable reading is *Qamīʾa*; cf. *Aghānī*, 16:163.

1677 Mss *Ḥ-l-s*; thus restored by the Leiden editor; *Aghānī*, 20:145, reads *Khunays*, but notes many variants.

1678 Cf. *Aghānī*, 18:152; ed. Leiden *Sawāda*, M *Sawād*.

1679 Sic ed. Leiden; MSS *ʿUbayd*. Probably to be read *Ghayẓ*; cf. *Aghānī*, 10:17.

- ʿAmr b. al-Ahtam b. Sumayy b. Sinān b. Khālid b. Minqar b. ʿUbayd b. ʿAmr b. Kaʿb b. Saʿd b. Zayd Manāt b. Tamīm,
- Maṭrūd b. Kaʿb b. ʿUrfuṭa b. al-Nāfidh b. Murra b. Taym b. Saʿd b. Kaʿb b. ʿAmr b. Rabīʿa al-Khuzāʿī,
- Aws b. Ghalfāʾ b. Faqīṭ[1680] b. Maʿbad b. ʿĀmir b. Yamāma,
- Ḥuṣayn b. al-Ḥumām b. Rabīʿa b. Ḥarām b. Wāʾila b. Sahm b. [...] ʿĀmir b. Ṣaʿṣaʿa,
- al-Rakkāḍ al-Asadī, who was Rakkāḍ b. Abbāq b. Budayl, one of the Banū Dubayr,
- Suwayd b. Kurāʿ al-ʿUklī,
- al-Ḥuwaydara,[1681] whose name was Quṭba b. [Aws b.] Miḥṣan b. Jarwal b. Ḥabīb al-Aʿẓam b. ʿAbd al-ʿUzzā b. Khuzayma b. Rizām b. Māzin b. Thaʿlaba b. Saʿd b. Dhubyān,
- 1:311 Aʿshā Banī Asad, who was Qays b. Bujara b. Munqidh b. Ṭarīf | b. ʿAmr b. Quʿayn,
- Ibn al-Zibaʿrā al-Sahmī, who was ʿAbdallāh b. Qays b. ʿAdī [b. Saʿd] b. Sahm, one of the Quraysh,
- [...][1682] Qaṭan b. Nahshal b. Dārim b. Mālik b. Ḥanẓala,
- Ibn Dajāja al-Fuqaym,[1683] who was Bukayr b. Yazīd b. Anas b. Imruʾ al-Qays,
- Suwayd b. Salāma b. Ḥudayj b. Qays b. ʿAmr b. Qaṭan b. Nahshal b. Dārim [b. Mālik] b. Ḥanẓala,
- Qays b. Zuhayr b. Jadhīma b. Rawāḥa b. Rabīʿa b. al-Ḥārith b. Māzin b. Quṭayʿa b. ʿAbs b. Baghīḍ,
- Miqyas b. Ṣubāba, a member of the Banū Kalb b. ʿAwf b. Kaʿb b. ʿĀmir b. Layth b. Kināna. He survived into Islamic times and converted to Islam, but then he apostatized. He was killed as an infidel on the day of the conquest of Mecca.
- al-Musayyab b. al-Rifall[1684] b. Ḥāritha b. Janāb[1685] b. Qays b. Abī Jābir b. Zuhayr b. Janāb b. Hubal al-Kalbī,

1680 Known as Aws b. Ghalfāʾ al-Hujaymī, but the sources, other than al-Yaʿqūbī, give no further genealogy. The text is defective. What is given here as *Faqīṭ*, is completely unpointed in M, and the first letter of what is given here as *Yamāma* is also unpointed and could be *b, t, th*, or *n*.

1681 Also known as *al-Ḥādira* (having heavy-set shoulders), of which *al-Ḥuwaydira* is a diminutive. See *Aghānī*, 3:82–84.

1682 Lacuna, several names seem to have been omitted.

1683 The identity of the poet and the vocalization of his name are unknown.

1684 Reading with *Aghānī*, 21:69. MSS. *al-Raqīl* or *al-Ruqayl*, an unknown name, for which the Leiden editor conjectured *al-Rafīl*.

1685 Reading with M and *Aghānī*, 21:69; ed. Leiden *Ḥayyān*.

- al-Barrāḍ b. Qays b. Rāfiʿ b. Qays b. Judayy b. Ḍamra al-Kinānī,
- Sabra b. ʿAmr b. Ahnān b. Dithār b. Faqʿas,
- Shāfiʿ b. ʿAbd al-ʿUzzā al-Ḍamrī,
- Surāqa b. Mālik b. Juʿshum al-Mudlijī,
- Maṣrūf, whose name was ʿAmr b. Qays b. Masʿūd b. ʿĀmir b. ʿAmr | b. Abī Rabīʿa b. Dhuhl, 1:312
- Ibn Rumayla al-Ḍabbī,
- Qays b. Masʿūd b. ʿĀmir b. ʿAmr b. Abī Rabīʿa b. Dhuhl,
- Mirdās b. Abī ʿĀmir b. Jāriya b. ʿAbd b. ʿAbs b. Rifāʿa b. al-Ḥārith b. Buhtha b. Sulaym b. Manṣūr.

Among the early "Stallion" poets[1686] of the Jāhiliyya who survived into Islamic times were:

- al-Nābigha al-Jaʿdī, who was similar in age to al-Nābigha al-Dhubyānī and whose name was Qays b. [ʿAbdallāh b. ʿUdas b. Rabīʿa b. Jaʿda b. Kaʿb b. Rabīʿa b. ʿĀmir b. Ṣaʿṣaʿa],[1687]
- Labīd[1688] b. Rabīʿa b. Mālik b. Jaʿfar b. Kilāb b. ʿĀmir b. Ṣaʿṣaʿa,
- Tamīm b. Ubayy [b.] Muqbil b. ʿAwf b. Ḥunayf [b. Qutayba] b. al-ʿAjlān b. ʿAbdallāh b. Kaʿb b. Rabīʿa b. ʿĀmir b. Ṣaʿṣaʿa,
- Kaʿb b. Zuhayr, who was Rabīʿa b. Riyāḥ b. Qurṭ b. al-Ḥārith b. Māzin b. Thaʿlaba b. Thawr b. Hudhma b. Lāṭim b. ʿUthmān b. ʿAmr b. Udd,
- ʿAbdallāh b. ʿĀmir b. Karib al-Kindī,
- Abū Sammāl al-Asadī, whose name was Shimʿān[1689] b. Hubayra b. Masāḥiq,
- Zayd b. Muhalhil, who was Zayd al-Khayl b. Yazīd b. Munhib b. ʿAbd Ruḍā b. al-Muḥlas b. Thawr [b. ʿAdī b. Kināna] b. Mālik b. Nabhān b. ʿAmr b. | al-Ghawth, 1:313
- al-Ḥuṭayʾa, whose name was Jarwal b. Aws b. Mālik b. Juwayya[1690] b. Makhzūm b. Mālik b. Ghālib b. Quṭayʿa b. ʿAbs,
- Ḍirār b. al-Khaṭṭāb b. Mirdās b. Kabīr b. ʿAmr al-Muḥāribī,

1686 Arabic, *fuḥūl*, plural of *faḥl*.

1687 The material in brackets was restored by the Leiden editor on the basis of other authorities; cf. *Aghānī*, 4:128, where the genealogy begins, "Ḥibbān b. Qays b. ʿAbdallāh b. Waḥwaḥ (or ʿAmr) b. ʿUdas …"

1688 Ed. Leiden, M: *al-Walīd*.

1689 Sic ed. Leiden, M; more often given as Simʿān; see Sezgin, *GAS*, 2:228–229.

1690 Variant, *Juʿayya*; *Aghānī*, 2:43.

- al-Shammākh b. Ḍirār b. Sinān b. Umayya b. ʿAmr b. Jiḥāsh b. Bajāla b. Māzin b. Thaʿlaba b. Saʿd b. Dhubyān,
- Abū Dhuʾayb al-Hudhalī, who was Khuwaylid [b. Khālid] b. Muḥarrith b. Zubayd[1691] b. Makhzūm b. Ṣāhila b. Kāhil b. Tamīm b. Saʿd b. Hudhayl,
- Abū Kabīr al-Hudhalī, who was ʿĀmir b. al-Ḥulays,
- al-Ḥārith b. ʿAmr b. Jurja b. Yarbūʿ b. Fazāra,
- Suḥaym, a slave of the Banī l-Ḥasḥās b. Hind b. Sufyān[1692] b. Thaʿlaba b. Dūdān[1693] b. Asad b. Khuzayma.[1694]

The Fairs of the Arabs

The fairs[1695] of the Arabs were ten in number. They gathered at them for their trade, and the rest of the people would gather there as well, knowing that their lives and property would be safe. These fairs were:

DŪMAT AL-JANDAL,[1696] which was held in the month of Rabīʿ al-Awwal. Those in charge of it were the Ghassān and the Kalb—whichever of the two tribes was ascendant (in a given year) took control.

1691 Following M and *Aghānī*, 6:58; ed. Leiden, *Rabīd* (or *Rubayd*).

1692 Unpointed in ed. Leiden, M; reading uncertain.

1693 Sic ed. Leiden and *Aghānī*, 22:2 (ed. Cairo, 26:9041); M: *Dhūdān*.

1694 The apparent meaning of the text as it stands in M and C is, "The slave of the Banū l-Ḥasḥās, who is Suḥaym b. Hind ..." Nöldeke, in a footnote to his review of Houtsma's edition (ZDMG 38:160), noted the incongruity of attributing an Arab genealogy to a poet who, according to *Aghānī*, 22:2 (ed. Cairo, 26:9041) was "a black Nubian slave, a non-Arab (*aʿjamī*) with a natural gift for poetry, whom the Banū l-Ḥasḥās, a clan of the Banū Asad, purchased." Nöldeke explained the text as having arisen from omission of the words "and al-Ḥasḥās is ..." after "who is Suḥaym." Another possibility is that the text originally did not mention Suḥaym's name at all (according to the *Aghānī* there was disagreement over whether it was Suḥaym or Ḥayya) and read simply, "A slave of the Banū l-Ḥasḥās b. Hind ..." A copyist then inserted a marginal gloss, "who is Suḥaym," which subsequently was copied into the main text, interrupting the flow of the genealogy of the Banū l-Ḥasḥās. On Suḥaym, see Sezgin, GAS, 2:288–289.

1695 Arabic, *aswāq*, pl. of *sūq*, the general term for market; here applied to seasonal gatherings for trade.

1696 Dūmat al-Jandal (modern al-Jawf in northwestern Saudi Arabia) is an oasis at the head of Wādī Sirḥān on the trade route between Medina and Damascus. See the article by L. Veccia Vaglieri in EI^2, s.v. Dūmat al-Djandal.

AL-MUSHAQQAR in Hajar,[1697] whose fair was held in Jumādā al-Ūlā under the supervision of the Banū Taym,[1698] the clan of al-Mundhir b. Sāwā.

ṢUḤĀR,[1699] which was held in | Rajab on the first day of the month. During this fair one did not need to pay protection money.[1700] [Traders] would depart from Ṣuḥār for RAYYĀ, where al-Julandā and his clan collected a tenth [of their proceeds]. 1:314

The fair of AL-SHIḤR[1701]—al-Shiḥr of the Mahra—which was held in the shadow of the mountain where lies the grave of the prophet Hūd.[1702] No protection money had to be paid at it, and the Mahra were in charge of it.

The fair of ʿADAN,[1703] which was held on the first day of the month of Ramaḍān, with the Abnāʾ[1704] collecting ten percent of the traders' proceeds. It was from the fair at ʿAdan that incense used to be carried far and wide.

The fair of ṢANʿĀʾ, which was held in the middle of the month of Ramaḍān, with the Abnāʾ collecting ten percent of the traders' proceeds.

The fair of AL-RĀBIYA in Ḥaḍramawt. One could reach this fair only by paying protection money, since it was not a land controlled by a ruler.[1705]

1697 Al-Mushaqqar was a port on the eastern coast of Arabia in the region of Hajar and Baḥrayn. Its exact location is unknown. See the article by C. E. Bosworth in EI^2, s.v. al-Mushaḳḳar.

1698 Sic ed. Leiden and M. Probably to be corrected to *Tamīm*, as al-Mundhir b. Sāwā belonged to the tribal division Dārim of Tamīm. He controlled the area of Hajar for the Persians, but converted to Islam and continued to control the area in the days of the Prophet. See the article by M. J. Kister in EI^2, s.v. al-Mundhir b. Sāwā.

1699 Ṣuḥār (modern Sohar) is on the coast of Oman, about halfway between modern Moscat and Fujairah. It was the emporium for products of the fertile coastal plain and for copper and stone from the mountains of the Jebel Akhdar. See the article by Monique Kervran in EI^2, s.v. Ṣuḥār.

1700 Arabic *khifāra* (or *khafāra*): payment by a merchant or other traveler to the Arab tribe, tribes, or rulers controlling an area in return for protected passage. See the article by Cl. Cahen in EI^2, s.v Khafāra.

1701 Al-Shiḥr was the main port of Ḥaḍramawt on the southern coast of the Arabian peninsula. Mahra is the name of the tribe that controlled it. The area was famous for the production of frankincense and fine camels. See the article by G. R. Smith in EI^2, s.v. al-Shiḥr.

1702 For an interesting modern account of this tomb, see al-Sabban, *Visits and Customs: The Visit to the Tomb of the Prophet Hud*.

1703 ʿAdan is the modern Aden.

1704 Al-Abnāʾ (the Sons) was a term applied to the descendants born in Yemen of Persian immigrants sent by the Sasanians. See the article in EI^2 by K. V. Zettersteen, s.v. al-Abnāʾ.

1705 Arabic, *arḍ mumallaka*, a land having a *malik*, a king, prince, or ruler.

Anyone who was strong enough engaged in robbery. It was the Kinda who collected protection money during this fair.

The fair of ʿUKĀẒ[1706] in the Najd highland, which was held in the month of Dhū l-Qaʿda. The Quraysh and the rest of the Arabs camped there, but mainly the Muḍar. It was here that the Arabs held their poetical boasting matches[1707] and their negotiations over matters of bloodwit[1708] and truces.

The fair of DHŪ L-MAJĀZ.[1709] After the fairs at ʿUkāẓ and Dhū l-Majāz, traders would depart for Mecca for their pilgrimage.

Among the Arabs there was a group who held certain wrongful actions to be licit when they attended these fairs; they came to be called *al-Muḥillūn*.[1710] Among the Arabs there were some who rejected this and would take it upon themselves to assist the wronged party and prevent bloodshed and the commission of reprehensible acts; these were called the Consecrated Protectors (*al-Dhāda al-Muḥrimūn*). The *Muḥillūn* were certain tribes from the Asad, Ṭayyiʾ, and Banū Bakr b. ʿAbd Manāt b. Kināna, and a group from the Banū ʿĀmir b. Ṣaʿṣaʿa. The Consecrated Protectors were from the Banū ʿAmr b. Tamīm, Banū Ḥanẓala b. Zayd Manāt, a group from the Hudhayl, a group from the
1:315 Banū Shaybān, and a group from the Banū | Kalb b. Wabara. The latter used to carry weapons to repel the former from the people; however, during the sacred months all of the Arabs among these groups would lay down their arms ...[1711] The Arabs used to attend the fair of ʿUkāẓ wearing veils over their faces. It is said that the first Arab to remove his mask was Ẓarīf b. Ghanm al-ʿAnbarī. The other Arabs then followed his example.

1706 ʿUkaẓ was located southeast of Mecca. See the article in *EI*[2] by Irfan Shahîd, s.v. ʿUkāẓ.

1707 Arabic, *mufākhara*. These were contests in which tribal poets or orators boasted of the exploits of their tribe. The *mufākhara* could be a ritualized prelude to battle, but also could take place at fairs. The fair at ʿUkaẓ was particularly famous as such an occasion. See the article by E. Wagner and Bichr Farès in *EI*[2], s.v. Mufākhara.

1708 Arabic, *ḥamāla*, the payment of compensation (*diya*) for the death of a person caused by oneself or by one's relatives.

1709 Dhū l-Majāz was another fair held near Mecca—Yāqūt locates the site one league (*farsakh*) from ʿArafāt, gives the duration of the fair as eight days, but does not give its month. See Yāqūt, *Muʿjam al-Buldān*, s.v. Majāz.

1710 The Arabic expression for "held wrongful actions to be licit" is *yastaḥillūna l-maẓālim*. It may refer to defrauding, as the word *maẓālim* can refer to wrongful actions in general, but specifically to wrongful gains. The term *muḥillūn*, is derived from the same root as *yastaḥillūna*. It means "those who account licit" or "those not in a state of ritual consecration" to abstain from certain actions. Its opposite is *muḥrimūn*, "those in a state of ritual consecration" to abstain from certain actions.

1711 Because of the sudden change in sense after this passage, Houtsma, the Leiden editor, inferred that the scribe had again skipped something in the text.

Printed in the United States
By Bookmasters